FILM ART

AN INTRODUCTION

NINTH EDITION

David Bordwell   **Kristin Thompson**

University of Wisconsin

McGraw Hill

*Connect
Learn
Succeed*™

Film Art: An Introduction

Published by McGraw-Hill, an imprint of The McGraw-Hill Companies, Inc., 1221 Avenue of the Americas, New York, NY 10020. Copyright © 2010 by Hamilton Gregory. All rights reserved. No part of this publication may be reproduced or distributed in any form or by any means, or stored in a database or retrieval system, without the prior written consent of The McGraw-Hill Companies, Inc., including, but not limited to, in any network or other electronic storage or transmission, or broadcast for distance learning.

2 3 4 5 6 7 8 9 0 DOW/DOW 0

ISBN: 978-0-07-338616-4
MHID: 0-0-7338616-2

Vice President, Editorial: *Michael J. Ryan*
Director, Editorial: *William R. Glass*
Publisher: *Christopher Freitag*
Director of Development: *Nancy Crochiere*
Associate Sponsoring Editor: *Betty Chen*
Editorial Coordinator: *Sarah Remington*
Executive Marketing Manager: *Pamela Cooper*
Development Editor: *Nadia Bidwell, Barking Dog Editorial*
Senior Production Editor: *Mel Valentín*
Manuscript Editor: *Thomas Briggs*
Design Manager: *Laurie Entringer*
Cover and Interior Design: *Jesi Lazar, BrainWorx Studio*
Visual Coordinator: *Sonia Brown*
Media Project Manager: *Thomas Brierly*
Senior Production Supervisor: *Tandra Jorgensen*
Composition: *10.5/12 Times by Thompson Type*
Printing: *45# Pub Matte, R. R. Donnelley & Sons*

Cover Image: DreamWorks/Paramount/The Kobal Collection/Conner, Frank

Credits: The credits section for this book begins on page 496 and is considered an extension of the copyright page.

Library of Congress Cataloging-in-Publication Data
Bordwell, David.
    Film art : an introduction / David Bordwell, Kristin Thompson.
        p. cm.
    Includes bibliographical references and index.
    ISBN-13: 978-0-07-338616-4 (alk. paper)
    ISBN-10: 0-07-338616-2 (alk. paper)
    1. Motion pictures—Aesthetics. I. Thompson, Kristin, 1950– II. Title.
 PN1995.B617 2009
 791.4301—dc22

                                    2009042923

The Internet addresses listed in the text were accurate at the time of publication. The inclusion of a Web site does not indicate an endorsement by the authors or McGraw-Hill, and McGraw-Hill does not guarantee the accuracy of the information presented at these sites.

www.mhhe.com

To our parents
Marjorie and Jay Bordwell
and Jean and Roger Thompson

ABOUT THE AUTHORS

David Bordwell is Jacques Ledoux Professor Emeritus of Film Studies at the University of Wisconsin–Madison. He holds a master's degree and a doctorate in film from the University of Iowa. His books include *The Films of Carl-Theodor Dreyer* (University of California Press, 1981), *Narration in the Fiction Film* (University of Wisconsin Press, 1985), *Ozu and the Poetics of Cinema* (Princeton University Press, 1988), *Making Meaning: Inference and Rhetoric in the Interpretation of Cinema* (Harvard University Press, 1989), *The Cinema of Eisenstein* (Harvard University Press, 1993), *On the History of Film Style* (Harvard University Press, 1997), *Planet Hong Kong: Popular Cinema and the Art of Entertainment* (Harvard University Press, 2000), *Figures Traced in Light: On Cinematic Staging* (University of California Press, 2005), *The Way Hollywood Tells It: Story and Style in Modern Movies* (University of California Press, 2006), and *Poetics of Cinema* (Routledge, 2008). He has won a University Distinguished Teaching Award and was awarded an honorary degree by the University of Copenhagen. His website is www.davidbordwell.net.

Kristin Thompson is an Honorary Fellow at the University of Wisconsin–Madison. She holds a master's degree in film from the University of Iowa and a doctorate in film from the University of Wisconsin–Madison. She has published *Eisenstein's Ivan the Terrible: A Neoformalist Analysis* (Princeton University Press, 1981), *Exporting Entertainment: America in the World Film Market 1907–1934* (British Film Institute, 1985), *Breaking the Glass Armor: Neoformalist Film Analysis* (Princeton University Press, 1988), *Wooster Proposes, Jeeves Disposes, or, Le Mot Juste* (James H. Heineman, 1992), *Storytelling in the New Hollywood: Understanding Classical Narrative Technique* (Harvard University Press, 1999), *Storytelling in Film and Television* (Harvard University Press, 2003), *Herr Lubitsch Goes To Hollywood: German and American Film After World War I* (Amsterdam University Press, 2005), and *The Frodo Franchise: The Lord of the Rings and Modern Hollywood* (University of California Press, 2007). She blogs with David at www.davidbordwell.net/blog. She maintains her own blog, "The Frodo Franchise," at www.kristinthompson.net/blog. In her spare time, she studies Egyptology.

The authors have also collaborated on *Film History: An Introduction* (McGraw-Hill, 3rd. ed., 2010) and, with Janet Staiger, on *The Classical Hollywood Cinema: Film Style and Mode of Production to 1960* (Columbia University Press, 1985).

BRIEF CONTENTS

CONTENTS

CHAPTER 3   Narrative as a Formal System   78

PART THREE • Film Style

CHAPTER 4   The Shot: Mise-en-Scene   118

CHAPTER 5   The Shot: Cinematography   *167*

CHAPTER 6   The Relation of Shot to Shot: Editing   *223*

PART FOUR • Types of Films

PART FIVE • Critical Analysis of Films

PART SIX • Film History

W e started to write *Film Art: An Introduction* in 1977, when film had just become a regular subject of study in colleges and universities. There were a few introductory film textbooks available, but they seemed to us oversimplified and lacking a clear sense of organization. After studying film since the 1960s and after teaching an introductory course at the University of Wisconsin–Madison, we tried to pull together what we'd learned.

We had two purposes. First, we wanted to describe the basic techniques of cinema—mise-en-scene, cinematography, editing, and sound—clearly and thoroughly. Beyond that, we wanted to do something that earlier books hadn't tried to do. We wanted to show students how to understand the overall form, or structure, of a film. The goal was to analyze whole films, not just isolated scenes. We wanted to show how the separate techniques of the film medium functioned in the film's larger context.

To achieve these aims, we tried to go beyond summarizing what critics and theorists before us had said. Of course we couldn't neglect important thinkers. But the more we studied films, the more we realized that there were many crucial aspects of film that had long gone unnoticed. We had to do more than synthesize; we had to innovate.

Sometimes the survey books that appear early in the history of a discipline produce original work, and *Film Art* wound up doing that. For instance, we found that film editing harbored a range of possibilities that had never been systematically presented. Similarly, no one had tried to survey the various sorts of overall form that a film can utilize. At almost every turn, we tried to fill gaps in understanding and come up with fresh insights into the creative choices that filmmakers had made.

In the thirty-plus years since we began the project, *Film Art* has undergone several revisions. We've adjusted it to the needs of the educators who have found it useful, and we've tried to accommodate changes in the ways in which films are made and seen. When the first edition came out in 1979, Betamax videotape was just emerging as a consumer item. Today, people are watching films on their iPods. Over all these years, though, the art of cinema hasn't fundamentally changed. Internet and digital films use the same basic techniques and formal strategies that filmmakers have always employed. Likewise, the goal of *Film Art* has remained the same: to introduce the reader to the fundamental features of cinema as an art form.

We envision readers of three sorts. First is the interested general reader who likes movies and wants to know more about them. Second is the student in an introductory film course, for whom *Film Art* functions as a textbook. Third is the more advanced student of film, who can find here a convenient outline on film aesthetics and suggestions for more specialized work.

Since *Film Art* first appeared, a number of other introductory texts have been published. We believe that our book still offers the most comprehensive and systematic layout of the art of film. It also offers discussions of creative possibilities that aren't considered elsewhere. It's gratifying to us that scholarly works on cinema often cite *Film Art* as an authoritative and original source on film aesthetics.

Organization of *Film Art*

One way to organize a book like this would be to survey all contemporary approaches to film studies, and there's no shortage of books following that approach.

But we believe that the student wants to know the core features of the film medium before he or she is introduced to different academic approaches. So *Film Art* pioneered an approach that leads the reader in logical steps through the techniques and structures that make up the whole film.

Moviegoers become absorbed by films as complete experiences, not fragments. The approach we've chosen emphasizes the film as a whole—made in particular ways, displaying overall coherence, using concrete techniques of expression, and existing in history. Our approach breaks down into a series of questions.

How does a film get from the planning stages to the screen? To understand film as an art, it helps to know how people create a film and get it to audiences. This question leads to a study in Part One, "Film Art and Filmmaking," of film production, distribution, and exhibition. We can then see how these activities shape the final product. Decisions at every stage affect what we see and hear on the screen.

How does an entire film function? We assume that like all artworks, a film has a *form*. It's made up of parts that relate to one another in specific and deliberate ways, in order to have an effect on an audience. In Part Two, "Film Form," we examine the idea of film form and how it affects us. We also introduce the most familiar type of form, the narrative.

How do film techniques contribute to film form? Film is a distinct medium, and every film integrates various techniques into its overall form. In Part Three, "Film Style," we examine the artistic possibilities of the primary film techniques: mise-en-scene, cinematography, editing, and sound. A chapter is devoted to each one, and each chapter ends with an analysis of how these techniques contribute to a film's overall form.

How do we classify films? We seldom go to the movies without having some idea of the kind of film we'll be seeing. Part Four, "Types of Films," examines two principal ways of grouping films. One way is by *genre*. When we label a film a science-fiction movie, a horror film, or a musical, we're using genre categories. We also usually classify films by some conception of the film's relation to reality or to its manner of production. So, besides live-action fiction films, we recognize *documentaries, animated films,* and *experimental films.* These types also exemplify non-narrative approaches to overall form.

How may we analyze a film critically? Once we have some conception of the possibilities of the medium, we can go on to analyze specific films. We try to show techniques of analysis by studying several important films in Part Five, "Critical Analysis of Films."

How does film art change through history? We conclude our book by suggesting how formal aspects of film have changed in historical contexts. In Part Six, "Film Art and Film History," we survey some noteworthy periods and movements in film history to show how understanding form helps us define films's larger context.

Our Approach: Analyzing the Whole Film

Our holistic approach to film resulted from several years of teaching. We wanted students to see and hear more in the films we studied, but simply providing the lecturer's view wouldn't help students understand cinema on their own. Ideally, we decided, students should master a toolkit of principles that would help them examine films. We became convinced that the best way to introduce film's artistic potential is to highlight general principles of form and style and to show those principles at work in particular movies. That is, we emphasized skills. By studying basic concepts of technique and form, students can sharpen their appreciation of any film that comes their way.

The stress on skills has another consequence. We refer to a great many films, largely to show the range and variety of cinema. But we know that most readers won't recognize all of them. Because *Film Art* stresses the importance of conceptual skills, readers don't have to have seen the films we mention in order to grasp the general principles. Many other films could be used to make similar points.

For example, many possibilities of camera movement could be illustrated as easily with *La Ronde* or *Elephant* as with *Grand Illusion*. To exemplify classical Hollywood filmmaking, *My Darling Clementine* could serve as well as *North by Northwest*. Although a course syllabus could adhere closely to the series of major examples used in *Film Art,* teachers might decide to use a wholly different set of films. Our book rests not on titles but on concepts.

That said, we do believe that an introduction to any art should balance familiar examples with unfamiliar ones. If we want to suggest the range of creative possibilities in cinema, we can't limit ourselves just to recent Hollywood releases. One of an educator's tasks is to broaden the horizons and tastes of students, to take them beyond what they're accustomed to. Films can change the ways we think and feel, and we benefit from opening ourselves up to them as widely as possible. So we haven't hesitated to mention films that lie off the beaten track, coming from the silent era, from other countries, and from experimental traditions. Many of these films have changed our own lives, and maybe they can change others' lives as well.

Features of *Film Art*

Frame Enlargements and Captions

A book on film must be heavily illustrated, and most are. Many film books, however, use production stills—photographs taken during filming. These are shot with a still camera, almost never placed in the same position as the motion picture camera. The result is a picture that doesn't correspond to any image in the finished film. Nearly all of our images from films are frame enlargements—magnified photographs taken from images on 16mm and 35mm film copies. *Film Art* contains more illustrations than any other book of its type, and all stills from color films appear in full color. (For more on frame enlargements, see the "Where to Go from Here" section in Chapter 1.)

"Where to Go from Here" Sections

In the first edition of *Film Art,* we thought it was important to include a section at the end of each chapter that would steer readers to other sources, but without the simple listing of ordinary bibliographies. So our chapter supplements, called "Where to Go from Here," raise issues, provoke discussion, and suggest further reading and viewing. They also indicate websites and DVD supplements that illustrate or develop ideas in the chapter.

"A Closer Look" Boxes

These boxes relate ideas in the main text to issues in current filmmaking. For example, computer-generated imagery (CGI) is addressed in a discussion of *The Lord of the Rings*.

"If you wander unbidden onto a set, you'll always know the AD because he or she is the one who'll probably throw you off. That's the AD yelling, 'Places!' 'Quiet on the set!' 'Lunch— one-half hour!' and 'That's a wrap, people!' It's all very ritualistic, like reveille and taps on a military base, at once grating and oddly comforting."

— Christine Vachon, independent producer, on assistant directors

Marginal Quotes

Throughout the book, quotes from authors, screenwriters, producers, directors, cinematographers, and actors appear in the margin. Whether amusing or insightful, informative or opinionated, these marginal quotes seek to engage students from a filmmaker's point of view.

Glossary

Like all art forms, film has specialized terminology, and so we've included a glossary. The initial mention of a term in the text is signaled in boldface, which indicates that the glossary provides further information.

New to the Ninth Edition

Revised Chapter 1

Chapter 1 has been completely recast to take account of the increasing merger of photochemically based cinema and digital cinema. Along with information on how digital technologies are inserted into production, distribution, and exhibition, the chapter takes as a case study the making of Michael Mann's film *Collateral*. The material on *Shadow of a Doubt*, which was highlighted in the first chapter of the eighth edition and which many instructors found useful, has been moved to Chapter 8. There it serves as a summary example of the functions of film style.

Chapter 7: A New Case Study

Since the first edition, our chapter on sound has included an analysis of Robert Bresson's *A Man Escaped*. The fact that the film is in French rather than English poses a problem for some instructors; their students found that reading the subtitles distracted them from concentrating on the sound track. We have therefore replaced *A Man Escaped* with Christopher Nolan's *The Prestige*, another film that makes wide-ranging uses of noise, music, and voice-over commentary. The original *Man Escaped* analysis is available at www.davidbordwell.net/filmart/index.php.

Revised "Where to Go from Here" Sections

Appearing at the end of each chapter, these sections raise issues that provoke class discussions. They also suggest further reading for research, acting as a bibliographic source for specific issues in the chapter.

David Bordwell and Kristin Thompson's Blog at www.davidbordwell.net

David and Kristin share their ideas and experiences with teachers and students on their blog. Updated frequently, the blog features film and book reviews, reports from festivals, and essays that connect ideas in *Film Art* to the current film scene.

To make the blog entries more accessible, this ninth edition has listed relevant URLs in the margins of chapters. These will take instructors and students to entries keyed to specific ideas, terms, and film examples.

Supplementary Instructional Materials

For the Student

A **text-specific tutorial CD-ROM** will help clarify and reinforce specific concepts addressed in the text with the use of film clips (1–2 per chapter), a corresponding commentary for each film clip, and a quiz for students to take to test their understanding of the materials. This CD-ROM is packaged free with all new copies of *Film Art, Ninth Edition*.

The **student website** to accompany *Film Art* is www.mhhe.com/filmart9. Students will find numerous opportunities here to reinforce what they've learned from the text, as well as extend their knowledge. Sample Multiple Choice Quizzes, Essay Questions, Internet Exercises, and links tied to each chapter are included.

For the Instructor

All instructor resources can be found at www.mhhe.com/filmart9. For lecture preparations, the **Instructor's Manual** contains chapter outlines, goals for the chapter, and suggestions for guest lectures, case studies, bibliography, and suggestions for essay assignments and DVD supplements.

For quizzes and tests, you can also find a **Password Protected Test Bank** at the book website. This contains sample multiple-choice, true/false, and essay questions.

Acknowledgments

Over three decades, many people have aided us in the writing and revision of this book. We are grateful to Ernest R. Acevedo-Muñoz, David Allen, Rick Altman, Tino Balio, Lucius Barre, John Belton, Joe Beres, Ralph Berets, Jake Black, Robin Blaetz, Les Blank, Vince Bohlinger, Eileen Bowser, Edward Branigan, Martin Bresnick, Ben Brewster, Michael Budd, Peter Bukalski, Colin Burnett, Elaine Burrows, Richard B. Byrne, Mary Carbine, Jerome Carolfi, Corbin Carnell, Jerry Carlson, Kent Carroll, Noël Carroll, Paolo Cherchi Usai, Jeffrey Chown, Gary Christenson, Anne Ciecko, Gabrielle Claes and the staff of the Cinémathèque Royale de Belgique, Bruce Conner, Kelley Conway, Mary Corliss of the Museum of Modern Art Film Stills Department, Susan Dalton, Robert E. Davis, Ethan De Seife, Dorothy Desmond, Marshall Deutelbaum, Kathleen Domenig, Suzanne Fedak, Susan Felleman, Maxine Fleckner-Ducey of the Wisconsin Center for Film and Theater Research, Don Fredericksen, Jon Gartenberg, Ernie Gehr, Kristi Gehring, Kathe Geist, Rocky Gersbach, Douglas Gomery, Claudia Gorbman, Ron Gottesman, Eric Gunneson, Debbie Hanson, Howard Harper, Dorinda Hartman, Denise Hartsough, Kevin Heffernan, Paul Helford, Linda Henzl, Rodney Hill, Michele Hilmes, Richard Hincha, Jan-Christopher Horak of the UCLA Film Archive, Lea Jacobs, Bruce Jenkins, Derek Johnson, Kathryn Kalinak, Charlie Keil, Vance Kepley, Laura Kipnis, Barbara Klinger, Jim Kreul, Don Larsson, Jenny Lau, Thomas M. Leitch, Gary London, José Lopez, Patrick Loughney of the Library of Congress Motion Picture Division, Moya Luckett, Mike Maggiore of the Film Forum, Charles Maland, Mark McClelland, Roger L. Mayer, Norman McLaren, Donald Meckiffe, Jackie Morris of the National Film Archive, Charles Musser, Kazuto Ohira of Toho Films, David Popowski, Badia Rahman, Hema Ramachandran, Paul Rayton, Matt Rockwell, Cynthia S. Runions, Leo Salzman, James Schamus of Focus Features, Ethan de Seife, Rob Silberman, Charles Silver of the Museum of Modern Art Film Study Center, John Simons, Ben Singer, Scott Sklenar, Joseph Evans Slate, Harry

W. Smith, Jeff Smith, Michael Snow, Katerina Soukup, Katherine Spring, John C. Stubbs, Dan Talbot of New Yorker Films, Richard Terrill, Jim Udden, Edyth von Slyck, Susan White, Tona Williams, Beth Wintour, Chuck Wolfe, James Yates, and Andrew Yonda.

In preparing this edition, we are grateful to many of the above, as well as to George Angell, Michael Barker of Sony Pictures Classics, Christina King, James Naremore, Daniel Reynolds, and Jonathan Rosenbaum. We also appreciate the suggestions for revision offered by Kevin Joel Berland (Pennsylvania State–Shenango), María Elena de las Carreras (California State University–Northridge, University of California–Los Angeles), Anna Froula (East Carolina University), Gregory Leon Miller (University of Lodz), Randall Moon (Hazard Community and Tech College), Brian Price (Oklahoma State University), Lynn Ramey (Vanderbilt University), Todd Rendleman (Seattle Pacific University), Laura E. Ruberto (Berkeley City College), Ann Sorenson (Northwestern College), Nicholas Tanis (New York University), Theresa Villeneuve (Citrus College), Diane Waldman (University of Denver), and Ken Windrum (Los Angeles Pierce College).

As ever, we're indebted to the McGraw-Hill publishing team, particularly Nadia Bidwell, Betty Chen, Chris Freitag, and Mel Valentin.

1

Film is a young medium, at least compared to most other media. Painting, literature, dance, and theater have existed for thousands of years, but film came into existence only a little more than a century ago. Yet in this fairly short span, the newcomer has established itself as an energetic and powerful art form.

It's this aspect of film that we explore in this book. The chapters that follow show how creative people have used film to give us experiences that we value. We'll examine the principles and techniques that give film its power to tell stories, express emotions, and trigger ideas.

But this art has some unusual features we should note up front. More than most arts, film depends on complex technology. Without machines, movies wouldn't move, and filmmakers would have no tools. In addition, film art usually requires collaboration among many participants, people who follow well-proven work routines. Films are not only created but produced. Just as important, they are firmly tied to their social and economic context. Films are distributed and exhibited for audiences, and money matters at every step.

Film Art and Filmmaking

Chapter 1 surveys all these aspects of the filmmaking process. We start by considering film art in general, and we look at one film that illustrates how skillful and effective that art can be. The chapter goes on to examine the technology, the work practices, and the business side of cinema. All these components shape and sustain film as an art.

CHAPTER

Film as Art: Creativity, Technology, and Business

Motion pictures are so much a part of our lives that it's hard to imagine a world without them. We enjoy them in theaters, at home, in offices, in cars and buses, and on airplanes. We carry films with us in our laptops and iPods. We press the button, and our machines conjure up movies for our pleasure.

For over a hundred years, people have been trying to understand why this medium has so captivated us. Films communicate information and ideas, and they show us places and ways of life we might not otherwise know. Important as these benefits are, though, something more is at stake. Films offer us ways of seeing and feeling that we find deeply gratifying. They take us through experiences. The experiences are often driven by stories, with characters we come to care about, but a film might also develop an idea or explore visual qualities or sound textures. A film takes us on a journey, offering a patterned experience that engages our minds and emotions.

It doesn't happen by accident. Films are *designed* to have effects on viewers. Late in the 19th century, moving pictures emerged as a public amusement. They succeeded because they spoke to the imaginative needs of a broad-based audience. All the traditions that emerged—telling fictional stories, recording actual events, animating objects or pictures, experimenting with pure form—aimed to give viewers experiences they couldn't get from other media. The men and women who made films discovered that they could control aspects of cinema to give their audience richer, more engaging experiences. Learning from one another, expanding and refining the options available, filmmakers developed skills that became the basis of film as an art form.

The popular origins of cinema suggest that some common ways of talking won't help us much in understanding film. Take the distinction between *art* and *entertainment*. Some people would say that blockbusters playing at the multiplex are merely "entertainment," whereas films for a narrower public—perhaps independent films, or festival fare, or specialized experimental works—are true art. Usually the art/entertainment split carries a not-so-hidden value judgment: art is high-brow, whereas entertainment is superficial. Yet things aren't that simple. As we just indicated, many of the artistic resources of cinema were discovered by filmmakers working for the general public. During the 1910s and 1920s, for instance, many films that aimed only to be entertaining opened up new possibilities for film editing. As for the matter of value, it's clear that popular traditions can foster art of high quality. Just as Shakespeare and Dickens wrote for a broad audience, much of the greatest 20th-century music, including jazz and the blues, was rooted in popular traditions. Cinema is an art because it offers filmmakers ways to design experiences for viewers, and those experiences can be valuable regardless of their pedigree. Films for audiences both small and large belong to that very inclusive art we call *cinema*.

Sometimes, too, people treat film *art* as opposed to film as a *business*. This split is related to the issue of entertainment, since entertainment generally is sold to a mass audience. Again, however, in most modern societies, no art floats free from economic ties. Novels good, bad, or indifferent are published because publishers expect to sell them. Painters hope that collectors and museums will acquire their work. True, some artworks are subsidized through taxes or private donations, but that process, too, involves the artist in a financial transaction. Films are no different. Some movies are made in the hope that consumers will pay to see them. Others are funded by patronage (an investor or organization wants to see the film made) or public monies (France, for instance, generously subsidizes film projects). Even if you decide to make your own digital movie, you face the problem of paying for it—and you may hope to earn a little extra for all your time and effort.

The crucial point is that considerations of money don't necessarily make the artist any less creative or the project any less worthwhile. Money can corrupt any line of business (consider politics), but it doesn't have to. In Renaissance Italy, painters were commissioned by the Catholic church to illustrate events from the Bible. Michelangelo and Leonardo da Vinci worked for hire, but it would be hard to argue that it hurt their artistry.

Here we won't assume that film art precludes entertainment. We won't take the opposite position either—claiming that only Hollywood mass-market movies are worth our attention. Similarly, we don't think that film art rises above commercial demands, but we also won't assume that money rules everything. Any art form offers a vast range of creative possibilities. Our basic assumption is that as an art, film offers experiences that viewers find worthwhile—diverting, provocative, puzzling, or rapturous. But how do films do that?

To answer that question, we'll go back a step and ask, Where do movies come from? Most basically, they come from three places. They come from the imagination and hard work of the filmmakers who create them. They come from an extraordinarily complex set of machines that capture and replay images. And they come from companies or individuals that pay for the filmmakers and the technology. This chapter examines the artistic, technological, and business sides of how films come into being.

CONNECT TO THE BLOG
Film art comes from many places and eras. For a personal take on why it's important not to watch only recent English-language color movies, see "Subtitles 101," at
www.davidbordwell.net/blog/?p=361.

Artistic Decisions In Filmmaking

In *Day for Night,* French filmmaker François Truffaut plays a director making a movie called *Meet Pamela*. Crew members bring set designs, wigs, cars, and prop pistols to him, and we hear his voice telling us his thoughts: "What is a director? A director is someone who is asked questions about everything."

Making a film can be seen as a long process of decision making, not just by the director but by all the specialists who work on his or her team. Early decisions come as the script is written and the various elements are designed. More decisions come daily during the actual filming, especially as unexpected problems or opportunities arise. Decisions continue up to the point where the director okays the last shot to be completed. These decisions could be as important as who plays the lead or as trivial as which buttons look best on a costume.

A great many decisions, however, do affect what we see and hear on the screen. There are the artistic choices made by the filmmakers. What lights will enhance the atmosphere of a love scene? Given the kind of story being told, would it be better to let the audience know what the central character is thinking or to keep him enigmatic? When a scene opens, what is the most economical, understandable way of letting the audience know the time and place? Which is more dramatic, to show an explosion or just have it heard from offscreen? The sum total of all such decisions culminates in a finished film.

Sometimes the decisions have to do with the business side of the production. What are some ways to save money? Which of the planned special effects being done on a tight budget are more important and necessary? These decisions, too, affect what we see and hear in the finished film. Other times the decisions are practical ones that won't affect the look or sound of the final film, as when a source of electricity has to be found to power the lights when a movie is shooting on location.

In this book, we'll be looking at two basic aspects of film art: form and style. **Form** is the sum of all the parts of the film, unified and given shape by patterns such as repetition and variation, story lines, and character traits (Chapters 2 and 3). **Style** is the way a film uses the techniques of filmmaking. Those techniques fall into four categories: (1) mise-en-scene, or the arrangement of people, places, and objects to be filmed (Chapter 4); (2) cinematography, the use of cameras and other machines to record images and sounds (Chapter 5); (3) editing, the piecing together of individual shots (Chapter 6); and (4) sound, the voices, effects, and music that blend on a film's audio track (Chapter 7). Throughout the book, we'll discuss how they can be patterned and combined to create movies that entertain us, inform us, and engage our imaginations.

The first time we watch a film, we usually don't know or think about the artistic decisions that were made during its production. For much of film history, most spectators never got a chance to learn much about the making of a specific movie. Today, however, DVD supplements offer "making of" documentaries and voice-over commentaries by the filmmakers. The Internet offers a vast array of clips, articles, and interviews about specific movies' creation. Let's examine how choices made by filmmakers lead to artistic results by looking at the production of a single movie.

To See into the Night: Artistic Decisions in the Making of *Collateral*

Michael Mann's *Collateral* was released in 2004. It's a visually beautiful psychological crime thriller. Set in Los Angeles, it introduces Vincent (Tom Cruise), a mysterious man who hires a cab driver, Max (Jamie Foxx), to drive him to a series of appointments in the course of one night. When Max learns that those appointments are a series of killings, he struggles to break their bargain and escape. But Vincent forces him to carry on as an unwilling getaway driver. In the course of the evening, the two men spar verbally and gradually force each other to confront his flaws.

Mann and his crew made thousands of decisions during the making of *Collateral*. Here we'll look at five important choices: one that impacted the film's form and one apiece for our four categories of mise-en-scene, cinematography, editing, and sound.

Scriptwriter Stuart Beattie originally set *Collateral* in New York City. Max was to be portrayed as a loser, hiding from the world in his cab and getting little out of life. Vincent was to goad him about his failures until Max had finally had enough and stood up to him. Once Mann came on board as director, he made numerous changes. The setting was changed to Los Angeles. Max became less a loser and more a laid-back, intelligent man content to observe the world from behind a steering wheel and to interact with his passengers, endlessly delaying his plans to start his own limousine service. The story largely consists of this pair interacting, so Mann's decision to change Max's traits altered the nature of the conflict between them. Moments of reluctant mutual respect and even hints of friendship complicate their relationship. This more appealing Max becomes our point-of-view figure for most of the film. Unusually for a film about a professional killer, we don't see the first murder but stay with Max in the cab until the shocking moment when the body falls onto his cab roof.

The switch to Los Angeles profoundly affected many aspects of the film's style. For Mann, one of the attractions was that this tale of a random crossing of destinies took place almost entirely at night, from 6:04 p.m. to 4:20 a.m. He wanted to portray the atmospheric Los Angeles night, where haze and cloud cover reflect the artificial lights of the city back to the huge, flat grid of streets. According to one of the cinematographers, Paul Cameron, "The goal was to make the L.A. night as much of a character in the story as Vincent and Max were."

This was a major decision that created much of the film's look. Mann was determined not to use any more artificial light than was absolutely necessary. He relied to a considerable degree on the existing street lights, neon signs, vehicle headlights, and other sources in the locations where filming took place. To achieve an eerie glow, his team came up with a cutting-edge combination of technologies.

High-Definition Cinematography   Although Part Three will deal with mise-en-scene first, here we're beginning with cinematography. That's because certain choices about photographing *Collateral* were absolutely central to its final look and also dictated many other decisions.

For many decades, traditional Hollywood productions employed cameras loaded with rolls of photographic film. For exterior scenes shot at night, large banks of specialized spot- and floodlights would pump enough illumination into the scene to register on the film stock. If not enough light was used, objects in dark areas would tend to go a uniform black.

Mann and his cinematographers decided to shoot extensive portions of *Collateral* on recently developed high-definition digital cameras. Those cameras could shoot on location with little or no light added to the scene (**1.1**). They could also capture and convey the distinctive night glow of Los Angeles. As Mann put it, "Film doesn't record what our eyes can see at night. That's why I moved into shooting digital video in high definition—to see into the night, to see everything the naked eye can see and more. You see this moody landscape with hills and trees and strange light patterns. I wanted that to be the world that Vincent and Max are moving through." Cinematographer Dion Beebe enthused, "The format's strong point is its incredible sensitivity to light. We were able to shoot Los Angeles at night and actually see silhouettes of palm trees against the night sky, which was very exciting" (**1.2**).

The filmmaking team pushed the digital cameras' capabilities in one particularly dark scene, when Vincent stalks one of his victims in a law library with huge windows overlooking the cityscape. In several shots, the characters become visible only as black shapes outlined by the myriad lights behind them (**1.3**). As we strain to see who is where in each shot, the suspense is heightened.

1.2   An eerily beautiful cityscape, with a row of palm trees against a dark sky visible in a way that could only be achieved with digital cameras.

1.1   A digital camera filming in a dimly lit alley in *Collateral*. Here and in many other shots, the skyline of downtown Los Angeles figures prominently.

1.3   Digital filming in extremely low lighting conditions. This technique creates suspense in this scene where Vincent tries to find his next victim. On regular photographic film, the background would go uniformly dark.

Custom-Made Lights   Though digital cameras could pick up a great deal in dark situations, the audience needed to see the faces of the actors clearly. Much of the action takes place inside the cab as Max and Vincent drive around and talk. The filmmakers had to light the actors' faces, but they wanted the added illumination to be so low and diffuse that there would not seem to be any artificial light within the cab.

To create that effect, the filmmakers tried an innovative approach: electroluminescent display (ELD) panels. It's the same technology used to make the light-up backings of digital watches and cell phones, but it had never been employed in lighting units for filming. Flexible plastic panels of various sizes and shapes were custom-made for the production, all with Velcro backings that would attach to the seats and ceiling of the cab (**1.4, 1.5**). These ELD panels could then be turned on in various combinations. Although they look bright in Figure 1.5, the effect on the screen was a soft glow on the actors. In a shot like Figure **1.6**, we might simply take it for granted that the light coming through the windows and the glow of the dashboard panel are all that shines on the characters. Such dim illumination on their faces allows the lights visible through the windows to be brighter than they are, helping to keeping the city "as much of a character in the story as Vincent and Max were."

Here's a case where an artistic decision led to new technology. The filmmakers could have said, "We have various types of lights available. Which one would work best in the cab?" Instead, they realized that the type of dim illumination they wanted could not be achieved by existing lighting units. It was a problem, and one that the team went to considerable lengths to solve by ordering a new type of light made.

Seamless Editing   As a thriller, *Collateral* contains several dynamic action scenes, including a spectacular car crash. The plan was for a cab going nearly 60 miles per hour to flip and then bounce and roll several times before coming to rest on its top. At that speed, the vehicle would have traveled hundreds of feet. The filmmakers had options about how to portray the crash onscreen. They could have put

1.4   One of the ELD panels specially made for illuminating the cab interior.

1.5   Several such panels attached to the back of a seat to shine on Tom Cruise as Vincent.

1.6   The dim glow created by such lighting on the two main characters.

the camera in a single spot and had it swivel as the car rolled past, keeping it in the frame from the beginning of the accident to the end. That would have been a good idea if the scene showed us the crash through the eyes of an onlooker whose head turns to watch it. But there is no character looking on.

The filmmakers wanted to generate excitement by showing several shots of the car rolling, each taken from a different point along the trajectory of the crash. One possible approach would have been to have multiple cabs and execute numerous similar crashes, each time filmed by a single camera that would be moved between crashes from place to place to record the action from a new vantage. Such a procedure would have been very expensive, however, and no two crashes would have taken place in exactly the same way. Splicing together shots from each crash might have created discrepancies in the car's position, resulting in poor "matches on action," as we'll term this technique in Chapter 5.

Instead, the team settled on a technique commonly used for big action scenes. Multiple cameras were placed along the route of the crash, all filming at once **(1.7)**. The economic benefits were that only one car had to be crashed and the high expense of keeping many crew members working on retakes was reduced. Artistically, the resulting shots allowed the editing team considerable flexibility to choose portions of any of the shots and splice them together to match the action of the car precisely **(1.8, 1.9)**. The result is an exciting series of shots, each taken from farther along the path of the crash and keeping the cab in clear view.

Music in Movements   Composers are fond of saying that their music for a film should serve the story so well that the audience doesn't notice it. For *Collateral*, Mann needed help from James Newton Howard to score the climax so as to not build too quickly to a high pitch of excitement. According to Howard, "Michael was very clear about the climax taking place in three movements." "Movements" as an artistic term is usually applied to the parts of a symphony, a concerto, or a sonata.

1.7   On location after the execution of the car crash in *Collateral*, director Michael Mann surveys digital monitors displaying shots taken by multiple cameras covering the action.

1.8   A seamless continuation of the cab's movement results as a shot taken from one camera shows the car flipping over, its hood flapping wildly, followed by a cut to . . .

1.9   . . . another shot, taken from a camera placed on the ground and continuing the same movement, now with the vehicle hurtling directly toward the viewer. This particular camera was placed in a very thick metal case.

Thus the idea was that the score for this last part of the film should play a major role in shaping the progression and rhythm of the action.

The climax involves Vincent trying to kill a character who is important to Max and Max trying frantically to save both himself and this other character. Howard and Mann called the first movement "The Race to Warn," since Vincent gets ahead of Max in running to the building where the potential victim is located. Despite the fact that both men are running and the situation is suspenseful, Howard avoids very fast rhythms. He begins with long-held string chords over a deep, rumbling sound, then adds sustained brass chords with a strong beat accompanying them. The accompaniment is dynamic but doesn't reach a high pitch of excitement.

The second movement, "The Cat and Mouse," involves Vincent getting into the building, turning off the electricity, and stalking his victim in near darkness (1.3). Again, the chords are slow, with ominous undertones, dissonant glides, and, at a few points, fast, eerie high-string figures as Vincent nears his goal. During the most suspenseful moments in the scene, when Vincent and his prey are in the darkened room, strings and soft, clicking percussion accompany their cautious, hesitant movements.

Finally, there is a rapid chase sequence, and here Howard finally makes the music louder and faster, with driving tympani beats that ratchet up to a very quick rhythm as the danger grows. Once the final climactic events occur, the percussion ends, and slow, low strings create a sort of coda to accompany the final quiet shots.

As the making of *Collateral* demonstrates, the technological basis of filmmaking plays a crucial role in bringing the artistic plans of its makers into reality. With the recent proliferation of digital tools for production, filming teams have more choices than ever to make.

These decisions and many others that Mann and his team made during their work on *Collateral* affect our experience of the film. The unfamiliar look that the digital cameras and innovative lighting give Los Angeles may draw our attention to the settings and give us a more vivid sense of the world through which the characters move. The music accompanying the fast-chase/slow-stalking/fast-chase progression of the climax helps heighten the suspense and build the excitement.

Mechanics of the Movies

Films are everywhere now, almost as widely available as print or music. But how do they get made in the first place? "Making a movie" means two very different things. First, people make films with machines. Anyone with a pen and paper can write a novel, and a talented kid with a guitar can become a musician. Movies require much more. Even the simplest home video camera is based on fiendishly complex technology. A major film involves elaborate cameras, lighting equipment, multi-track sound-mixing studios, sophisticated laboratories, and computer-generated special effects. Making a movie also involves businesses. Companies manufacture the equipment, other companies provide funding for the film, still others distribute it, and finally theaters or other venues present the result to an audience. In the rest of this chapter, we'll consider how these two sides of making movies—technology and business—shape film as an art.

Illusion Machines

Moving-image media such as film and video couldn't exist if human vision were perfect. Our eyes are very sensitive, but they can be tricked. As anyone who has paused a DVD knows, a film consists of a series of *frames,* or still pictures. Yet we don't perceive the separate frames. Instead, we see continuous light and movement. What creates this impression?

No one knows the full answer. Many people have speculated that the effect results from "persistence of vision," the tendency of an image to linger briefly on our retina. Yet if this were the cause, we'd see a bewildering blur of superimposed stills instead of smooth action. At present, researchers believe that two psychological processes are involved in cinematic motion: critical flicker fusion and apparent motion.

If you flash a light faster and faster, at a certain point (around 50 flashes per second), you see not a pulsating light but a continuous beam. A film is usually shot and projected at 24 still frames per second. The projector shutter breaks the light beam once as a new image is slid into place and once while it is held in place. Thus each frame is actually projected on the screen twice. This raises the number of flashes to the threshold of what is called *critical flicker fusion*. Early silent films were shot at a lower rate (often 16 or 20 images per second), and projectors broke the beam only once per image. The picture had a pronounced flicker—hence an early slang term for movies, "flickers," which survives today when people call a film a "flick."

Apparent motion is a second factor in creating cinema's illusion. If a visual display is changed rapidly enough, our eye can be fooled into seeing movement. Neon advertising signs often seem to show a thrusting arrow, but that illusion is created simply by static lights flashing on and off at a particular rate. Certain cells in our eyes and brain are devoted to analyzing motion, and any stimulus resembling movement apparently tricks those cells into sending the wrong message.

Apparent motion and critical flicker fusion are quirks in our visual system, and technology can exploit those quirks to produce illusions. Some moving-image machines predate the invention of film (**1.10, 1.11**). Film as we know it came into being when photographic images were first imprinted on strips of flexible celluloid.

1.10 The Zoetrope, which dates back to 1834, spun its images on a strip of paper in a rotating drum.

Machines That Use Film

At all stages of a film's life, machines move the film strip one frame at a time past a light source. First, there is the *camera* (**1.12**). In a light-tight chamber, a drive mechanism feeds the unexposed motion picture film from a reel (a) past a lens (b) and aperture (c) to a take-up reel (d). The lens focuses light reflected from a scene onto each frame of film (e). The mechanism moves the film intermittently, with a brief pause while each frame is held in the aperture. A shutter (f) admits light through the lens only when each frame is unmoving and ready for exposure. The standard shooting rate for sound film is 24 frames per second (fps).

The projector is basically an inverted camera, with the light source inside the machine rather than in the world outside (**1.13**). A drive mechanism feeds the film from a reel (a) past a lens (b) and aperture (c) to a take-up reel (d). Light is beamed through the images (e) and magnified by the lens for projection on a screen. Again, a mechanism moves the film intermittently past the aperture, while a shutter (f) admits light only when each frame is pausing. As we've seen, the standard projection rate for sound film is 24 fps, and the shutter blocks and reveals each frame twice in order to reduce the flicker effect on the screen.

A feature-length film is a very long ribbon of images, about two miles for a two-hour movie. In most theaters, the projector carries the film at the rate of 90 feet per minute. In the typical theater, the film is mounted on one big platter, with another platter underneath to take it up after it has passed through the projector (**1.14**). In digital theatrical projection, the film is stored on discs.

The film strip that emerges from the camera is usually a *negative*. That is, its colors and light values are the opposite of those in the original scene. For the images to be projected, a *positive* print must be made. This is done on another machine, the *printer*, which duplicates or modifies the footage from the camera. Like a projector, the printer controls the passage of light through film—in this case, a negative. Like a camera, it focuses light to form an image—in this case, on the unexposed roll of film. All printers are light-tight chambers that drive a negative or positive roll of film from a reel (a) past an aperture (b) to a take-up reel (c). At the same time, a roll of unexposed film (a′, c′) moves through the aperture (b), either

1.11 The Mutoscope, an early-20th-century entertainment, displayed images by flipping a row of cards in front of a peephole.

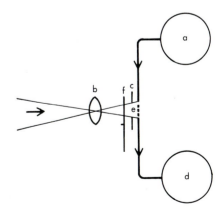

1.12 The camera.

1.13   The projector.

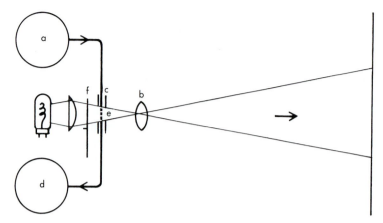

1.14   Most multiscreen theaters use platter projection, which winds the film in long strips and feeds it to a projector (seen in the left rear). The film on the platters is an Imax 70mm print.

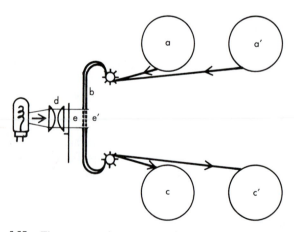

1.15   The contact printer.

intermittently or continuously. By means of a lens (d), light beamed through the aperture prints the image (e) on the unexposed film (e′). The two rolls of film may pass through the aperture simultaneously. A printer of this sort is called a *contact printer* **(1.15)**. Contact printers are used for making work prints and release prints, as well as for various special effects.

Although the filmmaker can create nonphotographic images on the filmstrip by drawing, painting, or scratching, most filmmakers have relied on the camera, the printer, and other photographic technology.

If you were to handle the film that runs through these machines, you'd notice several things. One side is much shinier than the other. Motion picture film consists of a transparent acetate *base* (the shiny side), which supports an *emulsion,* layers of gelatin containing light-sensitive materials. On a black-and-white filmstrip, the emulsion contains grains of silver halide. When light reflecting from a scene strikes them, it triggers a chemical reaction that makes the crystals cluster into tiny specks. Billions of these specks are formed on each frame of exposed film. Taken together, these specks form a latent image that corresponds to the areas of light and dark in the scene filmed. Chemical processing makes the latent image visible as a configuration of black grains on a white ground. The resulting strip of images is the negative, from which positive prints can be struck.

Color film emulsion has more layers. Three of these contain chemical dyes, each one sensitive to a primary color (red, yellow, or blue). Extra layers filter out the light from other colors. During exposure and development, the silver halide crystals create an image by reacting with the dyes and other organic chemicals in the emulsion layers. With color negative film, the developing process yields an image that is opposite, or complementary, to the original color values: for example, blue shows up on the negative as yellow.

What enables film to run through a camera, a printer, and a projector? The strip is perforated along both edges, so that small teeth (called *sprockets*) in the machines can seize the perforations (sprocket holes) and pull the film at a uniform rate and smoothness. The strip also reserves space for a sound track.

The size and placement of the perforations and the area occupied by the sound track have been standardized around the world. So, too, has the width of the film strip, which is called the *gauge* and is measured in millimeters. Commercial theaters use 35mm film, but other gauges also have been standardized internationally: Super 8mm, 16mm, and 70mm (**1.16–1.20**).

Usually image quality increases with the width of the film because the greater picture area gives the images better definition and detail. All other things being equal, 35mm provides significantly better picture quality than does 16mm, and 70mm is superior to both. The finest image quality currently available for public screenings is that offered by the Imax system (**1.21**).

The sound track runs down along the side of the filmstrip. The sound track may be either *magnetic* or *optical.* In the magnetic type (1.20), one or more strips of magnetic recording tape run along the film's edges. During projection, the film's track is "read" by a sound head similar to that on a tape recorder. Magnetic tracks are nearly obsolete in theaters today.

Most filmstrips have an optical sound track, which encodes sonic information in the form of patches of light and dark running down along the frames. During production, electrical impulses from a microphone are translated into pulsations of light, which are photographically inscribed on the moving filmstrip. When the film is projected, the optical track produces varying intensities of light that are translated back into electrical impulses and then into sound waves. The optical sound track of 16mm film is on the right side (1.17), whereas 35mm puts an optical track on the left (1.18, 1.19). In each, the sound is encoded as *variable-area,* a wavy contour of black and white along the picture strip.

A film's sound track may be *monophonic* or *stereophonic.* The 16mm filmstrip (1.17) and the first 35mm film strip (1.18) have monophonic optical tracks. Stereophonic optical sound is registered as a pair of squiggles running down the left side (1.19). For digital sound, a string of dots and dashes running along the film's perforations, or between the perforations, or close to the very left edge of the frames provides the sound-track information. The projector scans these marks as if reading a bar code.

1.17   16mm film is used for both amateur and professional film work. A variable-area optical sound track (p. 11) runs down the right side.

1.16   Super 8mm has been a popular gauge for amateurs and experimental filmmakers. *Year of the Horse,* a concert film featuring Neil Young, was shot partly on Super 8.

1.18   35mm is the standard theatrical film gauge. The sound track, a variable-area one (p. 11), runs down the left alongside the images.

1.19   In this 35mm strip from *Jurassic Park,* note the optical stereophonic sound track (p. 11), encoded as two parallel squiggles. The stripe along the left edge, the Morse code–like dots between the stereophonic track and the picture area, and the speckled areas around the sprocket holds indicate that the print can also be run on various digital sound systems.

1.20   70mm film, another theatrical gauge, was used for historical spectacles and epic action films into the 1990s. In this strip from *The Hunt for Red October,* a stereophonic magnetic sound track runs along both edges of the filmstrip.

1.21 The Imax image is printed on 70mm film but runs horizontally along the strip, allowing each image to be 10 times larger than 35mm and triple the size of 70mm. The Imax film can be projected on a very large screen with no loss of detail.

It's odd to think that our memories of the films we love have their origins in something as inert-looking as a strip of perforated celluloid. With all their appeals to our emotions and imagination, movies depend on some very tangible materials and machines. Without them, the filmmaker would be as lost as a painter without paint. Much of the artistry we'll be examining in the chapters to come depends on how filmmakers choose to use the palette provided by technology.

Machines That Use Digital Media

Digital cinema cameras gradually came into common use in the 1990s and early 2000s, about a hundred years after the initial spread of filmmaking. Some predicted that the digital revolution would soon make 35mm film obsolete. That didn't happen, because 35mm has many advantages that even high-end, high-definition (HD) video cannot duplicate.

Instead, a few filmmakers enthusiastically embraced HD, finding it cheaper, easier, and more flexible to use at every stage of production. Yet within the movie industry, most filmmakers have continued shooting on film, then taking advantage of digital tools for editing, special effects, and sound mixing.

In some ways, digital motion picture cameras are not that different from 35mm ones. They record scenes by using a lens to gather light. They have a viewer for the operator to frame the scene and controls to manipulate factors like the amount of light entering through the lens and the speed of recording. A casual observer probably couldn't tell the difference between a 35mm camera and a digital one. Indeed, manufacturers have tried to make digital cameras as familiar as possible to cinematographers reluctant to embrace the new technology. Some of these cameras can even use lenses made for traditional 35mm cameras.

The most important difference in a digital camera is the medium it records on. As the light passes through the lens, it hits a computer chip functioning as a sensor to convey visual information digitally, encoded as a complex series of 0's and 1's, onto digital tape, discs, memory cards, or hard drives. The material on these storage media can be loaded into computers after shooting ends, leaving the media free to be used again—thus eliminating the considerable cost of film stock. Even here, the recording unit that holds the tape and attaches to the camera looks something like a traditional film magazine that attaches to a 35mm camera (**l.22**).

As with film, there are different image formats of digital video (DV), and they are shot on different types of cameras. *Consumer* cameras are more or less the equivalent of Super 8mm. They give relatively low-resolution images and are mainly used by amateurs. These are the little cameras the fit in the palm of a hand

1.22 The Panavision Genesis, which has been used on such films as *Superman Returns*. A recorder containing a digital tape cassette attaches to the rear or top. The tape can run for 50 minutes.

and are used to record a birthday party or a baseball game. Using consumer cameras, children can shoot and edit their own films with simple computer programs.

The next step up is the *prosumer* camera, comparable to 16mm. As the name implies, this type of camera appeals to both professionals and those amateurs enthusiastic enough to pay for a camera yielding better image quality. Independent filmmakers also use such cameras, which are cheaper than high-end ones but yield good enough results to show in festivals or sell on DVD.

Finally there are the professional HD digital cameras (1.22). These cameras have two big advantages over prosumer and consumer models: (1) they primarily use files with low or no compression, and (2) they shoot at 24 fps. (Non-professional DV is shot at higher rates per second.) These factors make for higher image quality and ease of transfer onto 35mm film stock for release to theaters. Such cameras also have larger sensors behind the lenses, capturing higher-resolution images. Often these sensors are about the same size as a frame of 35mm film.

As with all digital technology, the storage capacity for digital files is constantly increasing. Digital recording capacities are measured in *pixels* (short for "picture elements"), the tiny dots that make up the electronic image on TVs and monitors. There are now four commonly used levels of resolution in professional digital recording: 720p, 1080p, 2K, and 4K. Since the information carried on each image increases both vertically and horizontally, each step up multiplies the resolution: 4K carries not twice, but four times the amount of information as 2K.

The 720p formula is used mainly in broadcast television and Internet distribution of HD video. George Lucas commissioned Sony to make a high-quality digital camera for *Star Wars: Episode II—Attack of the Clones.* It used the 1080p format, which has remained the most widely used standard in Hollywood. The digital camera Michael Mann used in making *Collateral* delivered 1080p images. (See 1.1.)

The company that introduced the first 4K camera, Red One, commissioned Peter Jackson to make a short, *Crossing the Line,* which was used in 2008 as a demonstration film at industry conventions. Steven Soderbergh used the same cameras for *Che* (2008), and the technology was quickly adopted. Many have claimed that 4K images are the equal in visual quality to those of 35mm.

Although research on and development of 6K systems is ongoing, it seems unlikely that film production will move beyond 4K in the near future. For one thing, digital exhibition has not spread widely, and most digital projectors are 2K or less. For another thing, beyond about the sixth row of a theater, the difference in detail between 2K and 4K is not visible to the human eye. Moreover, filming and project-

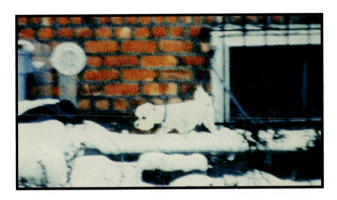

1.23   In *julien donkey-boy,* pixels and grain yield a unique texture, and the high contrast exaggerates pure colors and shapes to create a hallucinatory image.

ing at high resolution produces staggering quantities of data that need to be transferred, manipulated, and stored.

During the 1990s, low-budget filmmakers were drawn to the low costs and flexibility of DV. Lit by an experienced cinematographer, even consumer format video can look attractive, as in Spike Lee's *Bamboozled,* shot by Ellen Kuras. Perhaps most important, audiences don't notice shortcomings in image quality if the story is engrossing. Strong plots and performances helped carry *Chuck and Buck, Pieces of April, Personal Velocity: Three Portraits,* and other independent films shot on DV.

Some filmmakers have also seized upon DV's distinctive pictorial qualities. Lars von Trier's *Dancer in the Dark* uses saturated DV imagery to suggest the fantasy world of a young mother going blind. Harmony Korine shot *julien donkey-boy* with mini-DV consumer cameras, transferred the footage to film, and reprinted it several times **(1.23).**

Some directors making big-budget films have embraced HD digital formats wholeheartedly. Lucas claimed that apart from creating spectacular special effects, using HD for *Attack of the Clones* and *Revenge of the Sith* saved millions of dollars. A comparable system was used for *Sin City,* which combined HD footage of the actors with graphic landscapes created in postproduction. Basing the entire project on digital technology allowed director Robert Rodriguez to edit, mix sound, and create special effects in his home studio in Austin, Texas. These two prominent directors thoroughly embraced the new format and vowed never to shoot on film again. Rodriguez declared, "I've abandoned film forever. You can't go back. It's like trying to go back to vinyl after you've got recordable DVD."

Within mainstream Hollywood filmmaking, however, these directors remain in the minority. The complexity of digital filming technology, the incompatibility among various makes of camera, and innovations in equipment have led many cinematographers and directors to stick with tried-and-true 35mm systems. They may also use both 35mm cameras and digital ones for the same film, exploiting the best capabilities of each. Despite shooting most of *Collateral* with digital cameras, for instance, Michael Mann chose 35mm for some interiors and for slow motion shots.

Some cinematographers dispute the notion that digital filmmaking saves money, citing extra time spent on the set solving glitches. Christian Berger, who shot Michael Haneke's *Caché,* complained, "We ended up using six cameras because they kept breaking, and we *still* had focus problems two or three times a day. . . . It all worked out in the end, but shooting digitally was definitely *not* cheaper for the producer."

The debate will no doubt continue, but for now, most directors and cinematographers are relying chiefly on film and turning to HD only for occasional scenes.

Most professional filmmaking, both 35mm and digital, is done on rented cameras. Older models continue to be available. The Viper model used for *Collateral* is still available, and 2K and 4K are not likely to make these obsolete. All yield an image of high enough quality to be acceptable to audiences when projected in theaters.

Making the Movie: Film Production

Important as technology is, films are part of social institutions as well. Sometimes the social context is very intimate, as when a family records their lives on film to show friends and relations. But films that aim at the public enter a wider range of institutions. A movie typically goes through three phases: *production, distribution,* and *exhibition.* A group or company makes the film, a distribution company rents copies to theater chains, and local theaters exhibit the film. Later, the DVD version is distributed to chain stores or rental shops, and it's exhibited on TV monitors, computer screens, or portable displays. For video on demand and many amateur videos, the Internet serves as a distribution medium.

The whole system depends on having movies to circulate, so let's start by considering the process of production. Most films go through four distinct phases:

1. *Scriptwriting and funding.* The idea for the film is developed and a screenplay is written. The filmmakers also acquire financial support for the project.

2. *Preparation for filming.* Once a script is more or less complete and at least some funding is assured, the filmmakers plan the physical production.

3. *Shooting.* The filmmakers create the film's images and sounds.

4. *Assembly.* The images and sounds are combined in their final form. This involves cutting picture and sound, executing special effects, inserting music or extra dialogue, and adding titles.

CONNECT TO THE BLOG
In "Do filmmakers deserve the last word?" we suggest why we should always be cautious in accepting claims filmmakers offer.
See www.davidbordwell.net/blog/?p=1174.

The phases can overlap. Filmmakers may be scrambling for funding while shooting and assembling the film, and some assembly is usually taking place during filming. In addition, each stage modifies what went before. The idea for the film may be radically altered when the script is hammered out; the script's presentation of the action may be drastically changed in shooting; and the material that is shot takes on new significance in the process of assembly. As the French director Robert Bresson puts it, "A film is born in my head and I kill it on paper. It is brought back to life by the actors and then killed in the camera. It is then resurrected into a third and final life in the editing room where the dismembered pieces are assembled into their finished form."

These four phases include many particular jobs. Most films that we see in theaters result from dozens of specialized tasks carried out by hundreds of experts. This fine-grained division of labor has proved to be a reliable way to prepare, shoot, and assemble large-budget movies. On smaller productions, individuals perform several roles. A director might also edit the film, or the principal sound recordist on the set might also oversee the sound mixing. For *Tarnation,* a memoir of growing up in a troubled family, Jonathan Caouette assembled 19 years worth of photographs, audiotape, home movies, and videotape. Some of the footage was filmed by his parents, and some by himself as a boy. Caouette shot new scenes, edited everything on iMovie, mixed the sound, and transferred the result to digital video. In making this personal documentary, Caouette executed virtually all the phases of film production himself.

CONNECT TO THE BLOG
Aspiring filmmakers might want to check out our entry "The magic number 30, give or take 4."
See www.davidbordwell.net/blog/?p=1300.

The Scriptwriting and Funding Phase

Two roles are central in this phase: producer and screenwriter. The tasks of the *producer* are chiefly financial and organizational. She or he may be an "independent" producer, unearthing film projects and trying to convince production companies or distributors to finance the film. Or the producer may work for a distribution company and generate ideas for films. A studio may also hire a producer to put together a particular package.

The producer nurses the project through the scriptwriting process, obtains financial support, and arranges to hire the personnel who will work on the film. During shooting and assembly, the producer usually acts as the liaison between the writer or director and the company that is financing the film. After the film is completed, the producer will often have the task of arranging the distribution, promotion, and marketing of the film and of monitoring the paying back of the money invested in the production.

A single producer may take on all these tasks, but in the contemporary American film industry, the producer's work is further subdivided. The *executive producer* is often the person who arranged the financing for the project or obtained the literary property (although many filmmakers complain that the credit of executive producer is sometimes given to people who did little work). Once the production is under way, the *line producer* oversees the day-to-day activities of director, cast, and crew. The line producer is assisted by an *associate producer,* who acts as a liaison with laboratories or technical personnel.

The chief task of the *screenwriter* is to prepare the *screenplay* (or script). Sometimes the writer will send a screenplay to an agent, who submits it to a production company. Or an experienced screenwriter meets with a producer in a "pitch session," where the writer can propose ideas for scripts. The first scene of Robert Altman's *The Player* satirizes pitch sessions by showing celebrity screenwriters proposing strained ideas like "*Pretty Woman* meets *Out of Africa.*" Alternatively, sometimes the producer has an idea for a film and hires a screenwriter to develop it. This approach is common if the producer has bought the rights to a novel or play and wants to adapt it for the screen.

The screenplay goes through several stages. These include a *treatment,* a synopsis of the action; then one or more full-length scripts; and a final version, the *shooting script.* Extensive rewriting is common, and writers often must resign themselves to seeing their work recast over and over.

Shooting scripts are constantly altered, too. Some directors allow actors to modify the dialogue, and problems on location or on a set may necessitate changes in the scene. In the assembly stage, script scenes that have been shot are often condensed, rearranged, or dropped entirely.

If the producer or director finds one writer's screenplay unsatisfactory, other writers may be hired to revise it. Most Hollywood screenwriters earn their living by rewriting other writers' scripts. As you can imagine, this often leads to conflicts about which writer or writers deserve onscreen credit for the film. In the American film industry, these disputes are adjudicated by the Screen Writers' Guild.

As the screenplay is being written or rewritten, the producer is planning the film's finances. He or she has sought out a director and stars to make the package seem a promising investment. The producer must prepare a budget spelling out *above-the-line costs* (the costs of literary property, scriptwriter, director, and major cast) and *below-the-line costs* (the expenses allotted to the crew, secondary cast, the shooting and assembly phases, insurance, and publicity). The sum of above- and below-the-line costs is called the *negative cost* (that is, the total cost of producing the film's master negative). In 2005, the average Hollywood negative cost ran to about $60 million.

Some films don't follow a full-blown screenplay. Documentaries, for instance, are difficult to script fully in advance. In order to get funding, however, the projects typically require a summary or an outline, and some documentarists prefer to have a written plan even if they recognize that the film will evolve in the course of filming. When making a **compilation documentary** from existing footage, the filmmakers often prepare an outline of the main points to be covered in the voice-over commentary before writing a final version of the text keyed to the image track.

"A screenplay bears somewhat the same relationship to a movie as the musical score does to a symphonic performance. There are people who can read a musical score and 'hear' the symphony—but no two directors will see the same images when they read a movie script. The two-dimensional patterns of colored light involved are far more complex than the one-dimensional thread of sound."

— Arthur C. Clarke, co-screenwriter, *2001: A Space Odyssey*

1.24   A page from the storyboard for Hitchcock's *The Birds*.

The Preparation Phase

When funding is more or less secure and the script is solid enough to start filming, the filmmakers can prepare for the physical production. In commercial filmmaking, this stage of activity is called **pre-production.** The *director,* who may have come on board the project at an earlier point, plays a central role in this and later phases. The director coordinates the staff to create the film. Although the director's authority isn't absolute, he or she is usually considered the person most responsible for the final look and sound of the film.

At this point, the producer and the director set up a production office, hire crew and cast the roles, and scout locations for filming. They also prepare a daily schedule for shooting. This is done with an eye on the budget. The producer assumes that the separate shots will be made out of continuity—that is, in the most convenient order for production—and put in proper order in the editing room. Since transporting equipment and personnel to a location is a major expense, producers usually prefer to shoot all the scenes taking place in one location at one time. For *Jurassic Park,* the main characters' arrival on the island and their departure at the end of the film were both shot at the start of production, during the three weeks on location in Hawaii. A producer must also plan to shoot around actors who can't be on the set every day. Many producers try to schedule the most difficult scenes early, before cast and crew begin to tire. For *Raging Bull,* the complex prizefight sequences were filmed first, with the dialogue scenes shot later. Keeping all such contingencies in mind, the producer comes up with a schedule that juggles cast, crew, locations, and even seasons most efficiently.

During pre-production, several things are happening at the same time under the supervision of the director and producer. A writer may be revising the screenplay while a casting supervisor is searching out actors. Because of the specialized division of labor in large-scale production, the director orchestrates the contributions of several units. He or she works with the *set unit,* or *production design unit,* headed by a *production designer.* The production designer is in charge of visualizing the film's settings. This unit creates drawings and plans that determine the architecture and the color schemes of the sets. Under the production designer's supervision, an *art director* oversees the construction and painting of the sets. The *set decorator,* often someone with experience in interior decoration, modifies the sets for specific filming purposes, supervising workers who find props and a *set dresser* who arranges things on the set during shooting. The *costume designer* is in charge of planning and executing the wardrobe for the production.

Working with the production designer, a *graphic artist* may be assigned to produce a **storyboard,** a series of comic strip–like sketches of the shots in each scene, including notations about costume, lighting, and camera work **(1.24).** Most directors do not demand a storyboard for every scene, but action sequences and shots using special effects or complicated camera work tend to be storyboarded in detail. The storyboard gives the cinematography unit and the special-effects unit a preliminary sense of what the finished shots should look like. The storyboard images may be filmed, cut together, and played with sound to help visualize the scene. This is one form of *animatics.*

Computer graphics can take planning further. The process of **previsualization,** or "previz," reworks the storyboards into three-dimensional animation, complete with moving figures, dialogue, sound effects, and music. Contemporary software can create settings and characters reasonably close to what will be filmed, and textures and shading can be added. Previsualization animatics are most often used to plan complicated action scenes or special effects **(1.25).** For *Star Wars: Episode III—Revenge of the Sith,* George Lucas's previsualization team created 6500 detailed shots, a third of which formed the basis for shots in the finished film. In addition, previsualization helps the director test options for staging scenes, moving cameras, and timing sequences.

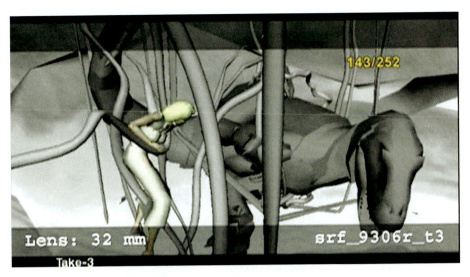

1.25   Animated previsualization from *King Kong*.

The Shooting Phase

Although the term *production* refers to the entire process of making a film, Hollywood filmmakers also use it to refer to the *shooting phase*. Shooting is also known as *principal photography*.

During shooting, the director supervises what is called the *director's crew*, consisting of these personnel:

- The *script supervisor,* known in the classic studio era as a "script girl." (Today one-fifth of Hollywood script supervisors are male.) The script supervisor is in charge of all details of **continuity** from shot to shot. The supervisor checks details of performers' appearances (in the last scene, was the carnation in the left or right buttonhole?), props, lighting, movement, camera position, and the running time of each shot.

- The *first assistant director (AD),* a jack-of-all-trades who, with the director, plans each day's shooting schedule. The AD sets up each shot for the director's approval while keeping track of the actors, monitoring safety conditions, and keeping the energy level high.

- The *second assistant director,* who is the liaison among the first AD, the camera crew, and the electricians' crew.

- The *third assistant director,* who serves as messenger for director and staff.

- The *dialogue coach,* who feeds performers their lines and speaks the lines of offscreen characters during shots of other performers.

- The *second unit director,* who films stunts, location footage, action scenes, and the like, at a distance from where principal shooting is taking place.

The most visible group of workers is the *cast.* The cast may include *stars*—well-known players assigned to major roles and likely to attract audiences. The cast also includes *supporting players,* or performers in secondary roles; *minor players;* and *extras,* those anonymous persons who pass by in the street, come together for crowd scenes, and occupy distant desks in large office sets. One of the director's major jobs is to shape the performances of the cast. Most directors spend a good deal of time explaining how a line or gesture should be rendered, reminding the actor of the place of this scene in the overall film, and helping the actor create a coherent performance. The first AD usually works with the extras and takes charge of arranging crowd scenes.

"If you wander unbidden onto a set, you'll always know the AD because he or she is the one who'll probably throw you off. That's the AD yelling, 'Places!' 'Quiet on the set!' 'Lunch— one-half hour!' and 'That's a wrap, people!' It's all very ritualistic, like reveille and taps on a military base, at once grating and oddly comforting."

— Christine Vachon, independent producer, on assistant directors

On some productions, there are still more specialized roles. *Stunt artists* will be supervised by a *stunt coordinator;* professional dancers will work with a *choreographer.* If animals join the cast, they will be handled by a *wrangler.* There have been pig wranglers (*Mad Max Beyond Thunder Dome*), snake wranglers (*Raiders of the Lost Ark*), and spider wranglers (*Arachnophobia*).

Another unit of specialized labor is the *photography unit.* The leader is the *cinematographer,* also known as the *director of photography* (or *DP*). The cinematographer is an expert on photographic processes, lighting, and camera technique. We have already seen how important Michael Mann's two DPs, Dion Beebe and Paul Cameron, were in achieving the desired look for *Collateral* (pp. 4–5). The cinematographer consults with the director on how each scene will be lit and filmed **(1.26).** The cinematographer supervises the following:

- The *camera operator,* who runs the machine and who may also have assistants to load the camera, adjust and follow focus, push a dolly, and so on.

- The *key grip,* who supervises the *grips.* These workers carry and arrange equipment, props, and elements of the setting and lighting.

- The *gaffer,* the head electrician who supervises the placement and rigging of the lights.

Parallel to the photography unit is the *sound unit.* This is headed by the *production recordist* (also called the *sound mixer*). The recordist's principal responsibility is to record dialogue during shooting. Typically, the recordist uses a tape or digital recorder, several sorts of microphones, and a console to balance and combine the inputs. The recordist also tries to capture some ambient sound when no actors are speaking. These bits of room tone are later inserted to fill pauses in the dialogue. The recordist's staff includes the following:

- The *boom operator,* who manipulates the boom microphone and conceals radio microphones on the actors.

- The *third man,* who places other microphones, lays sound cables, and is in charge of controlling ambient sound.

1.26   On the set of *Citizen Kane,* Orson Welles directs from his wheelchair on the far right, cinematographer Gregg Toland crouches below the camera, and actress Dorothy Comingore kneels at the left. The script supervisor is seated in the left background.

1.27 Sculpting a model dinosaur for *Jurassic Park: The Lost World*. The model was scanned into a computer for digital manipulation.

Some productions also have a *sound designer,* who enters the process during the preparation phase and who plans a sonic style appropriate for the entire film.

A *visual-effects unit,* overseen by the *visual-effects supervisor,* is charged with preparing and executing process shots, miniatures, matte work, computer-generated graphics, and other technical shots **(1.27).** During the planning phase, the director and the production designer will have determined what effects are needed, and the supervisor consults with the director and the cinematographer on an ongoing basis. The visual-effects unit can number hundreds of workers, from puppet- and model-makers to specialists in digital compositing.

A miscellaneous unit includes a *makeup staff,* a *costume staff, hairdressers,* and *drivers* who transport cast and crew. During shooting, the producer is represented by a unit called the *producer's crew.* Central here is the *line producer,* who manages daily organizational business, such as arranging for meals and accommodations. A *production accountant* (or *production auditor*) monitors expenditures, a *production secretary* coordinates telephone communications among units and with the producer, and *production assistants* (or *PAs*) run errands. Newcomers to the film industry often start out working as production assistants.

All this coordinated effort, involving perhaps hundreds of workers, results in many thousands of feet of exposed film and recorded sound-on-tape. For every shot called for in the script or storyboard, the director usually does several takes, or versions. For instance, if the finished film requires one shot of an actor saying a line, the director may do several takes of that speech, each time asking the actor to vary the delivery. Not all takes are printed, and only one of those becomes the shot included in the finished film. Extra footage can be used in coming-attractions trailers and electronic press kits.

Because scenes seldom are filmed in story order, the director and crew must have some way of labeling each take. As soon as the camera starts, one of the cinematographer's staff holds up a *slate* before the lens. On the slate is written the production, scene, shot, and take. A hinged arm at the top, the clapboard, makes a sharp smack that allows the recordist to synchronize the sound track with the footage in the assembly phase **(1.28).** Thus every take is identified for future reference. There are also electronic slates that keep track of each take automatically and provide digital readouts.

In filming a scene, most directors and technicians follow an organized procedure. While crews set up the lighting and test the sound recording, the director rehearses the actors and instructs the cinematographer. The director then supervises the filming of a *master shot.* The master shot typically records the entire action and

1.28 A slate shown at the beginning of a shot in Jean-Luc Godard's *La Chinoise.*

1.29   For the climax of *Jurassic Park,* the actors were shot in the set of the visitor's center, but the velociraptors and the *Tyrannosaurus rex* were computer-generated images added later.

dialogue of the scene. There may be several takes of the master shot. Then portions of the scene are restaged and shot in closer views or from different angles. These shots are called *coverage,* and each one may require many takes. Today most directors shoot a great deal of coverage, often by using two or more cameras filming at the same time. The script supervisor checks to ensure that details are consistent within all these shots.

For most of film history, scenes were filmed with a single camera, which was moved to different points for different setups. More recently, under pressure to finish principal photography as quickly as possible, the director and the camera unit might use two or more cameras. Action scenes are often shot from several angles simultaneously because chases, crashes, and explosions are difficult to repeat for retakes. The battle scenes in *Gladiator* were filmed by 7 cameras, whereas 13 cameras were used for stunts in *XXX.* For dialogue scenes, a common tactic is to film with an A camera and a B camera, an arrangement that can capture two actors in alternating shots. The lower cost of digital video cameras has allowed some directors to experiment with shooting conversations from many angles at once, hoping to capture unexpected spontaneity in the performance. Some scenes in Lars von Trier's *Dancer in the Dark* employed a hundred digital cameras.

When special effects are to be included, the shooting phase must carefully plan for them. In many cases, actors will be filmed against blue or green backgrounds so that their figures can be inserted into computer-created settings. Or the director may film performers with the understanding that other material will be composited into the frame **(1.29).** If a moving person or animal needs to be created by computer, a specialized unit will use *motion capture.* Here small sensors are attached all over the body of the subject, and as that subject moves against a blank background or a set, a special camera records the movement **(1.30, 1.31).** Each sensor provides a point in a wire-frame figure on a computer. That image can then be animated and built up to a completely rendered person or animal to be inserted digitally into the film.

The Assembly Phase

Filmmakers call the assembly phase **post-production.** (If something goes wrong, someone may promise to "fix it in post.") Yet this phase does not begin after the shooting is finished. Rather, post-production staff members work behind the scenes throughout shooting.

Before the shooting begins, the director or producer probably hires an *editor* (also known as the *supervising editor).* This person catalogues and assembles the takes produced during shooting. The editor also works with the director to make creative decisions about how the footage can best be cut together.

1.30 For *Iron Man,* Robert Downey Jr. performed in a motion-capture suit covered with sensors.

1.31 The same scene with computer animation partially added over his figure.

Because each shot usually exists in several takes, because the film is shot out of story order, and because the master-shot/coverage approach yields so much footage, the editor's job can be a huge one. A 100-minute feature, which amounts to about 9000 feet of 35mm film, may have been carved out of 500,000 feet of film. For this reason, postproduction on major Hollywood pictures often takes up to seven months. Sometimes several editors and assistants are brought in.

Typically, the editor receives the processed footage from the laboratory as quickly as possible. This footage is known as the *dailies* or the *rushes*. The editor inspects the dailies, leaving it to the *assistant editor* to synchronize image and sound and to sort the takes by scene. The editor meets with the director to examine the dailies, or if the production is filming far away, the editor informs the director of how the footage looks. Since retaking shots is costly and troublesome, constant checking of the dailies is important for spotting any problems with focus, exposure, framing, or other visual factors. From the dailies, the director selects the best takes, and the editor records the choices. To save money, "digital dailies" are often shown

"A couple of guys in a coffee shop set out to write a gag; a couple of guys with a camera set out to film a gag; a couple of guys in an editing room set out to make sense of the trash that's been dumped on their desks."

— David Mamet, director, *The Spanish Prisoner* and *Redbelt*

SOME TERMS AND ROLES IN FILM PRODUCTION

The rise of packaged productions, pressures from unionized workers, and other factors have led producers to credit everyone who worked on a film. Meanwhile, the specialization of large-scale filmmaking has created its own jargon. Some of the most colorful terms are explained in the text. Here are some other terms that you may see in a film's credits.

ACE: After the name of the editor; abbreviation for the American Cinema Editors, a professional association.

ASC: After the name of the director of photography; abbreviation for the American Society of Cinematographers, a professional association. The British equivalent is the BSC.

Additional photography: Crew shooting footage apart from the *principal photography,* supervised by the director of photography.

Best boy: Term from the classic studio years, originally applied to the gaffer's assistant. Today film credits may list both a *best boy electric* and a *best boy grip,* the assistant to the key grip.

Casting director: Member who searches for and auditions performers for the film, and suggests actors for *leading roles* (principal characters) and *character parts* (fairly standardized or stereotyped roles). She or he may also cast *extras* (background or nonspeaking roles).

Clapper boy: Crew member who operates the clapboard (slate) that identifies each take.

Concept artist: Designer who creates illustrations of the settings and costumes that the director has in mind for the film.

Dialogue editor: Sound editor specializing in making sure recorded speech is audible.

Dolly grip: Crew member who pushes the dolly that carries the camera, either from one setup to another or during a take for moving camera shots.

Foley artist: Sound-effects specialist who creates sounds of body movement by walking or by moving materials across large trays of different substances (sand, earth, glass, and so on). Named for Jack Foley, a pioneer in postproduction sound.

---

to the producer and director, but since video can conceal defects in the original footage, editors check the original shots before cutting the film.

As the footage accumulates, the editor assembles it into a *rough cut*—the shots loosely strung in sequence, without sound effects or music. Rough cuts tend to run long—the rough cut for *Apocalypse Now* ran 7½ hours. From the rough cut, the editor, in consultation with the director, builds toward a *fine cut* or *final cut.* The unused shots constitute the *outtakes.* While the final cut is being prepared, a *second unit* may be shooting *inserts,* footage to fill in at certain places. These are typically long shots of cities or airports or close-ups of objects. At this point, titles are prepared, and further laboratory work or special-effects work may be done.

Until the mid-1980s, editors cut and spliced the *work print,* footage printed from the camera negative. In trying out their options, editors were obliged to rearrange the shots physically. Now virtually all commercial films are edited digitally. The dailies are transferred first to tape or disc, then to a hard drive. The editor enters notes on each take directly into a computer database. Such digital editing systems, usually known as *nonlinear* systems, permit random access to the entire store of footage. The editor can call up any shot, paste it alongside any other shots, trim it, or junk it. Some systems allow special effects and music to be tried out as well. Although nonlinear systems have greatly speeded up the process of cutting, the editor usually asks for a 35mm projection print of key scenes in order to check for color, details, and pacing.

As the editing team puts the footage in order, other members of the team work to manipulate the look of the shots via computer. If the footage has been shot on film, it is scanned frame by frame into computer files to create a *digital intermediate* (DI). The DI is manipulated in many ways, including changing its look through *digital color grading.* The color grader may work alone on a low-budget film or, on a larger one, supervise a group of assistants.

Greenery man: Crew member who chooses and maintains trees, shrubs, and grass in settings.

Lead man: Member of set crew responsible for tracking down various props and items of decor for the set.

Loader: Member of photography unit who loads and unloads camera magazines, as well as logging the shots taken and sending the film to the laboratory.

Matte artist: Member of special-effects unit who paints backdrops that are then photographically or digitally incorporated into a shot in order to suggest a particular setting.

Model maker: (1) Member of production design unit who prepares architectural models for sets to be built. (2) Member of the special-effects unit who fabricates scale models of locales, vehicles, or characters to be filmed as substitutes for full-size ones.

Property master: Member of set crew who supervises the use of all *props,* or movable objects in the film.

Publicist, unit publicist: Member of producer's crew who creates promotional material regarding the production. The publicist may arrange for press and television interviews with the director and stars and for coverage of the production in the mass media.

Scenic artist: Member of set crew responsible for painting surfaces of set.

Still photographer: Member of crew who takes photographs of scenes and behind-the-scenes shots of cast members and others. These photographs may be used to check lighting or set design or color, and many will be used in promoting and publicizing the film.

Timer, color timer: Laboratory worker who inspects the negative film and adjusts the printer light to achieve consistency of color across the finished product.

Video assist: The use of a video camera mounted alongside the motion picture camera to check lighting, framing, or performances. In this way, the director and the cinematographer can try out a shot or scene on tape before committing it to film.

For special effects, filmmakers turn to computer-generated imagery (CGI). Their tasks may be as simple as deleting distracting background elements or building a crowd out of a few spectators. George Lucas has claimed that if an actor blinked at the wrong time, he would digitally erase the blink. CGI can also create imagery that would be virtually impossible with photographic film (**1.32**). Computers can conjure up photorealistic characters such as Gollum in *The Lord of the Rings.* (See p. 184–185.) Fantasy and science fiction have fostered the development of CGI, but all genres have benefited, from the comic multiplication of a single actor in *Charlie and the Chocolate Factory* to the grisly realism of the digitally enhanced Omaha Beach assault in *Saving Private Ryan.* In *The Curious Case of Benjamin*

1.32 In the chase through the airways of Coruscant in *Attack of the Clones,* the actor was shot against a blue or green screen, and the backgrounds and moving vehicles were created through CGI.

Button, CGI substituted for make-up, allowing Brad Pitt and Cate Blanchett to plausibly portray their characters through youth to old age.

Once the shots are arranged in something approaching final form, the *sound editor* takes charge of building up the sound track. The director, the composer, the picture editor, and the sound editor view the film and agree on where music and effects will be placed, a process known as *spotting.* The sound editor may have a staff whose members specialize in mixing dialogue, music, or sound effects.

Surprisingly little of the sound recorded during filming winds up in the finished movie. Often half or more of the dialogue is rerecorded in postproduction, using a process known as *automated dialogue replacement (ADR).* ADR usually yields better quality than location sound does. With the on-set recording serving as a *guide track,* the sound editor records actors in the studio speaking their lines (called *dubbing* or *looping*). Nonsynchronized dialogue such as the babble of a crowd (known in Hollywood as "walla") is added by ADR as well.

Similarly, very few of the noises we hear in a film were recorded during filming. A sound editor adds sound effects, drawing on the library of stock sounds or creating particular effects for the film. Sound editors routinely manufacture footsteps, car crashes, pistol shots, and fists thudding into flesh (often produced by whacking a watermelon with an axe). In *Terminator 2,* the sound of the T-1000 cyborg passing through jail cell bars is that of dog food sliding slowly out of a can. Sound-effects technicians have sensitive hearing. One veteran noted the differences among doors: "The bathroom door has a little air as opposed to the closet door. The front door has to sound solid; you have to hear the latch sound. . . . Don't just put in any door, make sure it's right."

Like picture editing, modern sound editing relies on computer technology. The editor can store recorded sounds in a database, classifying and rearranging them in any way desired. A sound's qualities can be modified digitally—clipping off high or low frequencies and changing pitch, reverberation, equalization, or speed. The boom and throb of underwater action in *The Hunt for Red October* were slowed down and reprocessed from such mundane sources as a diver plunging into a swimming pool, water bubbling from a garden hose, and the hum of Disneyland's air-conditioning plant. One technician on the film called digital sound editing "sound sculpting."

During the spotting of the sound track, the film's *composer* enters the assembly phase as well. The composer compiles cue sheets that list exactly where the music will go and how long it should run. The composer writes the score, although she or he will probably not orchestrate it personally. While the composer is working, the rough cut is synchronized with a *temp dub*—accompaniment pulled from recorded songs or classical pieces. Musicians record the score with the aid of a *click track,* a taped series of metronome beats synchronized with the final cut.

Dialogue, effects, and music are recorded on separate tracks, and each type of sound, however minor, will occupy a separate track. During the mixing, for each scene, the image track is run over, once for each sound, to ensure proper synchronization. The specialist who performs the task is the *rerecording mixer,* usually supervising a team of mixers. Each scene may involve dozens of tracks of individual sounds, which are all mixed together. Equalization, filtering, and other adjustment take place at this stage. The director typically oversees the final mixing session, where final adjustments to the sound result in the final mix. So many tracks are involved that the director often has the ability to change even the musical orchestration, eliminating instruments or raising the volume of certain sections of the orchestra. Once fully mixed, the master track is transferred onto 35mm sound-recording film, which encodes it as optical or digital information.

The film's *camera negative,* which was the source of the dailies and the work print, is too precious to serve as the source for final prints. Traditionally, from the negative footage, the laboratory draws an *interpositive,* which in turn provides an *internegative.* The internegative is then assembled in accordance with the final cut, and it serves as the primary source of future prints. An alternative is to create a *digital intermediate.* Here the negative is scanned digitally, frame by frame, at high resolution. The result is then recorded back to film as an internegative. The digital intermediate allows the cinematographer to correct color, remove scratches and dust, and add special effects easily.

Once the internegative has been created, the master sound track is synchronized with it. The first positive print, complete with picture and sound, is called the *answer print.* After the director, producer, and cinematographer have approved an answer print, *release prints* are made for distribution. Using a digital intermediate makes it possible to generate additional internegatives as old ones wear out, all without any wear on the original negative or interpositive.

The work of production does not end when the final theatrical version has been assembled. In consultation with the producer and director, the postproduction staff prepares airline and broadcast television versions. For a successful film, a director's cut or an extended edition may be released on DVD. In some cases, different versions may be prepared for different countries. Scenes in Sergio Leone's *Once upon a Time in America* were completely rearranged for its American release. European prints of Stanley Kubrick's *Eyes Wide Shut* featured more nudity than did American ones, in which some naked couples were blocked by digital figures added to the foreground. Once the various versions are decided upon, each is copied to a master videotape or hard drive, the source of future versions. This video transfer process often demands new judgments about color quality and sound balance.

Many fictional films have been made about the process of film production. Federico Fellini's *8½* concerns itself with the preproduction stage of a film that is abandoned before shooting starts. François Truffaut's *Day for Night,* David Mamet's *State and Main,* Christopher Guest's *For Your Consideration,* and Tom DiCillo's *Living in Oblivion* all center on the shooting phase. The action of Brian De Palma's *Blow Out* occurs while a low-budget thriller is in sound editing. *Singin' in the Rain* follows a single film through the entire process, with a gigantic publicity billboard filling the final shot.

Artistic Implications of the Production Process

Every artist works within constraints of time, money, and opportunity. Of all the arts, filmmaking is one of the most constraining. Budgets must be maintained, deadlines must be met, weather and locations are unpredictable, and the coordination of any group of people involves unforeseeable twists and turns. Even a Hollywood blockbuster, which might seem to offer unlimited freedom, is actually confining on many levels. Big-budget filmmakers sometimes get tired of coordinating hundreds of staff and wrestling with million-dollar decisions, and they start to long for smaller projects that offer more time to reflect on what might work best.

We appreciate films more when we realize that in production, every film is a compromise made within constraints. When Mark and Michael Polish conceived their independent film *Twin Falls Idaho,* they had planned for the story to unfold in several countries. But the cost of travel and location shooting forced them to rethink the film's plot: "We had to decide whether the film was about twins or travel." Similarly, the involvement of a powerful director can reshape the film at the screenplay stage. In the original screenplay of *Witness,* the protagonist was Rachel, the Amish widow with whom John Book falls in love. The romance and Rachel's confused feelings about Book formed the central plot line. But the director, Peter Weir, wanted to emphasize the clash between pacifism and violence. So William Kelley and Earl Wallace revised their screenplay to stress the mystery plot line and to center the action on Book and the introduction of urban crime into the peaceful Amish community. Given the new constraints, the screenwriters found a new form for *Witness.*

Some filmmakers struggle against their constraints, pushing the limits of what's considered doable. The production of a film we'll study in upcoming chapters,

Citizen Kane, was highly innovative on many fronts. Yet even this project had to accept studio routines and the limits of current technology. More commonly, a filmmaker works with the same menu of choices available to others. In directing *Collateral,* Michael Mann made creative choices about how to use digital cameras, low lighting levels, and script structure that other filmmakers working in 2004 could have made—except that Mann saw new ways of employing such techniques. His choices even led to experimentation with a new type of lighting device, the ELD panels for the cab interior. The overall result was a visual style that no other film had ever achieved, though others soon imitated it.

Everything we notice on the screen in the finished movie springs from decisions made by filmmakers during the production process. Starting our study of film art with a survey of production allows us to understand some of the possibilities offered by images and sounds. Later chapters will discuss the artistic consequences of decisions made in production—everything from storytelling strategies to techniques of staging, shooting, editing, and sound work. By choosing within production constraints, filmmakers create film form and style.

Modes of Production

Large-Scale Production

The fine-grained division of labor we've been describing is characteristic of *studio* filmmaking. A studio is a company in the business of manufacturing films. The most famous studios flourished in Hollywood from the 1920s to the 1960s—Paramount, Warner Bros., Columbia, and so on. These companies owned equipment and extensive physical plants, and they retained most of their workers on long-term contracts. Each studio's central management planned all projects, then delegated authority to individual supervisors, who in turn assembled casts and crews from the studio's pool of workers.

Organized as efficient businesses, the studios created a tradition of carefully tracking the entire process through paper records. At the start, there were versions of the script; during shooting, reports were written about camera footage, sound recording, special-effects work, and laboratory results; in the assembly phase, there were logs of shots catalogued in editing and a variety of cue sheets for music, mixing, looping, and title layout. This sort of record keeping has remained a part of large-scale filmmaking, though now it is done mostly on computer.

Although studio production might seem to resemble a factory's assembly line, it was always more creative, collaborative, and chaotic than turning out cars or TV sets is. Each film is a unique product, not a replica of a prototype. In studio filmmaking, skilled specialists collaborated to create such a product while still adhering to a "blueprint" prepared by management **(1.33).**

The centralized studio production system has virtually disappeared. The giants of Hollywood's golden age have become distribution companies, although they often initiate, fund, and oversee the making of films they distribute. The old studios had stars and staff under contract, so the same group of people might work together on film after film. Now each film is planned as a distinct package, with director, actors, staff, and technicians brought together for this project alone. The studio may provide its own soundstages, sets, and offices for the project, but in most cases, the producer arranges with outside firms to supply cameras, catering, locations, special effects, and anything else required.

Still, the detailed production stages remain similar to what they were in the heyday of studio production. In fact, filmmaking has become vastly more complicated in recent years, largely because of the expansion of production budgets and the growth of computer-based special effects. *Titanic* listed over 1400 names in its final credits.

1.33 Studio production was characterized by a large number of highly specialized production roles. Here several units prepare a moving-camera shot for *Wells Fargo* (1937).

Exploitation, Independent Production, and DIY

Not all films using the division of labor we have outlined are big-budget projects financed by major companies. There are also low-budget *exploitation* products tailored to a particular market—in earlier decades, fringe theaters and drive-ins; now, video rentals and sales. Troma Films, maker of *The Toxic Avenger*, is probably the most famous exploitation company, turning out horror movies and teen sex comedies for $100,000 or less. Nonetheless, exploitation filmmakers usually divide the labor along studio lines. There is the producer's role, the director's role, and so on, and the production tasks are parceled out in ways that roughly conform to mass-production practices.

Exploitation production often forces people to double up on jobs. Robert Rodriguez made *El Mariachi* as an exploitation film for the Spanish-language video market. The 21-year-old director also functioned as producer, scriptwriter,

> *"Deep down inside, everybody in the United States has a desperate need to believe that some day, if the breaks fall their way, they can quit their jobs as claims adjusters, legal secretaries, certified public accountants, or mobsters, and go out and make their own low-budget movie. Otherwise, the future is just too bleak."*
>
> — Joe Queenan, critic and independent filmmaker

cinematographer, camera operator, still photographer, and sound recordist and mixer. Rodriguez's friend Carlos Gallardo starred, coproduced, and coscripted; he also served as unit production manager and grip. Gallardo's mother fed the cast and crew. *El Mariachi* wound up costing only about $7000.

Unlike *El Mariachi,* most exploitation films don't enter the theatrical market, but other low-budget productions, loosely known as *independent* films, may. Independent films are made for the theatrical market but without major distributor financing. Sometimes the independent filmmaker is a well-known director, such as Spike Lee, David Cronenberg, or Joel and Ethan Cohen, who prefer to work with budgets significantly below the industry norm. The lower scale of investment allows the filmmaker more freedom in choosing stories and performers. The director usually initiates the project and partners with a producer to get it realized. Financing often comes from European television firms, with major U.S. distributors buying the rights if the project seems to have good prospects. For example, David Lynch's low-budget *The Straight Story* was financed by French and British television before it was bought for distribution by Disney. Danny Boyle's *Slumdog Millionaire* was made for about $15 million and nearly went straight to DVD when Warner Bros. declined to release it. Art film distributor Fox Searchlight picked it up, and it became an unexpected critical and financial success. Roughly half of *Slumdog Millionaire* was shot on 35mm. The rest was done on 2K digital cameras, which are smaller and facilitated shooting in the crowded streets of Mumbai.

As we would expect, these industry-based independents organize production in ways very close to the full-fledged studio mode. Nonetheless, because these projects require less financing, the directors can demand more control over the production process. Woody Allen, for instance, is allowed by his contract to rewrite and reshoot extensive portions of his film after he has assembled an initial cut.

The category of independent production is a roomy one, and it also includes more modest projects by less well-known filmmakers. Examples are Victor Nuñez's *Ulee's Gold,* Phil Morrison's *Junebug,* and Miranda July's *Me and You and Everyone We Know.* Even though their budgets are much smaller than for most commercial films, independent productions face many obstacles **(1.34)**. Filmmakers may have to finance the project themselves, with the help of relatives and friendly investors; they must also find a distributor specializing in independent and low-budget films. Still, many filmmakers believe the advantages of independence outweigh the drawbacks. Independent production can treat subjects that large-scale studio production ignores. No film studios would have supported Jim Jarmusch's *Stranger Than Paradise* or Kevin Smith's *Clerks.* Because the independent film does not need as large an audience to repay its costs, it can be more personal and controversial. And the production process, no matter how low-budget, still relies on the basic roles and phases established by the studio tradition.

Small-Scale Production

In large-scale and independent production, many people work on the film, each one a specialist in a particular task. But it is also possible for one person to do everything: plan the film, finance it, perform in it, run the camera, record the sound, and put it all together. Such films are seldom seen in commercial theatres, but they are central to experimental and documentary traditions.

Consider Stan Brakhage, whose films are among the most directly personal ever made. Some, such as *Window Water Baby Moving,* are lyrical studies of his home and family **(1.35)**. Others, such as *Dog Star Man,* are mythic treatments of nature; still others, such as *23rd Psalm Branch,* are quasi-documentary studies of war and death. Funded by grants and his personal finances, Brakhage prepared, shot, and edited his films virtually unaided. While he was working in a film laboratory, he also developed and printed his footage. With over 150 films to his credit,

CONNECT TO THE BLOG
Studio films and independent ones aren't always that far apart, as we suggest in "Independent film: How different?"

See www.davidbordwell.net/blog/?p=22.

1.34   In making *Just Another Girl on the IRT,* independent director Leslie Harris used locations and available lighting in order to shoot quickly; she finished filming in just 17 days.

1.35   In *The Riddle of Lumen,* Stan Brakhage turned shadows and everyday objects into vivid distant patterns.

Brakhage proved that the individual filmmaker can become an artisan, executing all the basic production tasks.

The 16mm and digital video formats are customary for small-scale production. Financial backing often comes from the filmmaker, from grants, and perhaps from obliging friends and relatives. There is very little division of labor: the filmmaker oversees every production task and performs many of them. Although technicians or performers may help out, the creative decisions rest with the filmmaker. Experimentalist Maya Deren's *Meshes of the Afternoon* was shot by her husband, Alexander Hammid, but she scripted, directed, and edited it and performed in the central role **(1.36)**. Amos Poe made his lengthy, evocative experimental film *Empire II* by placing a small digital camera in a window of his Manhattan apartment and exposing single frames in bursts at intervals over an entire year **(1.37)**. Poe edited the film himself, manipulated the images digitally, and assembled the sound track from existing songs and original music by Mader.

Such small-scale production is also common in documentary filmmaking. Jean Rouch, a French anthropologist, has made several films alone or with a small crew in his efforts to record the lives of marginal people living in alien cultures. Rouch wrote, directed, and photographed *Les Maîtres fous* (1955), his first widely seen film. Here he examined the ceremonies of a Ghanaian cult whose members lived a double life: most of the time they worked as low-paid laborers, but in their rituals, they passed into a frenzied trance and assumed the identities of their colonial rulers.

Similarly, Barbara Koppel devoted four years to making *Harlan County, U.S.A.*, a record of Kentucky coal miners' struggles for union representation. After eventually obtaining funding from several foundations, she and a small crew spent 13 months living with miners during the workers' strike. During filming, Koppel acted as sound recordist, working with cameraman Hart Perry and sometimes also a lighting person. A large crew was ruled out not only by Koppel's budget but also by the need to fit naturally into the community. Like the miners, the filmmakers were constantly threatened with violence from strikebreakers **(1.38)**.

Sometimes small-scale production becomes *collective* production. Here, instead of a single filmmaker shaping the project, several film workers participate equally. The group shares common goals and makes production decisions democratically. Roles may also be rotated: the sound recordist on one day may serve as cinematographer on the next. A recent instance is the Canadian film *Atanarjuat: The Fast Runner*. Three Inuits (Zacharias Kunuk, Paul Apak Angilirq, and Paul Qulitalik) and one New Yorker (Norman Cohn) formed Igloolik Isuma Productions in 1990. After making several video shorts and a television series, the group composed a screenplay based on an oral tale about love, murder, and revenge. With funding from television and the National Film Board, cast and crew spent six months shooting in the Arctic, camping in tents and eating seal meat. "We don't have a hierarchy," Cohn explained. "There's no director, second, third or fourth assistant director. We have a team of people trying to figure out how to make this work." Because of the communal nature of Inuit life, the Igloolik team expanded the collective effort by bringing local people into the project. Some had to relearn traditional skills for making tools and clothes from bone, stone, and animal skins. "The Inuit process is very horizontal," Cohn explained. "We made our film in an Inuit way, through consensus and collaboration." Showcasing the strengths of digital Beta video **(1.39)**, *Atanarjuat: The Fast Runner* won the prize for best first film at the 2002 Cannes Film Festival. That, said Cohn, convinced people "that a bunch of Eskimos from the end of the world could be sophisticated enough to make a movie."

Small-scale production allows the filmmakers to retain tight control of the project. The rise of digital video formats has made small-scale production more visible. *The Gleaners and I* (see 5.42), *The Yes Men, Encounters at the End of the World,*

1.36   In *Meshes of the Afternoon,* multiple versions of the protagonist were played by the filmmaker, Maya Deren.

1.37   For *Empire II,* Amos Poe digitally manipulated this tantalizing glimpse of the Manhattan skyline, making it lyrical.

1.38   In *Harlan County, U.S.A.,* the driver of a passing truck fires at the crew.

CONNECT TO THE BLOG
For more on Poe's *Empire II,* plus a link to his website.

See www.davidbordwell.net/blog/?p=1709.

1.39   The hero of *Atanarjuat: The Fast Runner* pauses in his flight across the ice.

and other recent releases indicate that the theatrical market and festival circuit have room for works made by single filmmakers or tiny production units.

The introduction of consumer and prosumer digital cameras and affordable software for computer post-production has led to the rise of "do it yourself" (DIY) filmmaking. Individuals or small groups of amateurs can make their own films and share them over the Internet via YouTube and other websites. Perhaps the most prominent DIY film is Arin Crumley and Susan Buice's *Four Eyed Monsters,* a filmed reenactment of the couple's unconventional romance. Although it was shown in a few theaters and at some festivals, the film's main distribution was via a self-published DVD. The filmmakers promoted it in Second Life, on YouTube, and on their own website. *Four Eyed Monsters* ultimately receiving screenings on the Independent Film Channel, which also published a new edition of the DVD.

Artistic Implications of Different Modes of Production

We categorize films on the basis of how they were made. We can distinguish a *documentary* film from a *fiction* film on the basis of production phases. Usually, the documentary filmmaker controls only certain variables of preparation, shooting, and assembly. Some variables (such as script and rehearsal) may be omitted, whereas others (such as setting, lighting, and behavior of the figures) are present but often uncontrolled. In interviewing an eyewitness to an event, the filmmaker typically controls camera work and editing but does not tell the witness what to say or how to act. For example, there was no script for the documentary *Manufacturing Consent: Noam Chomsky and the Media.* Filmmakers Mark Achbar and Peter Wintonick instead shot long interviews in which Chomsky explained his ideas. The fiction film, in contrast, is characterized by much more control over the preparation and shooting phases.

Similarly, a *compilation* film assembles existing images and sounds that provide historical evidence on a topic. The compilation filmmaker may minimize the shooting stage and create a story from archival footage. For *The Power of Nightmares,* Adam Curtis gathered newsreel and television footage, television commercials, and clips from fiction films to track the rise of fundamentalist politics and religion after World War II.

One more kind of film is distinguished by the way it's produced. The *animated* film is created frame by frame. Images may be drawn directly on the film strip, or the camera may photograph drawings or three-dimensional models, as in the *Wallace and Grommit* movies. *Corpse Bride* was created without using motion picture cameras; instead, each frame was registered by a digital still camera and transferred to film. Today most animated films, both on theater screens and on the Internet, are created directly on computer with imaging software.

Production and Authorship   Production practices have another implication for film as an art form. Who, it is often asked, is the "author," the person responsible for the film? In individual production, the author must be the solitary filmmaker—Stan Brakhage, Louis Lumière, you. Collective film production creates collective authorship: the author is the entire group. The question of authorship becomes difficult to answer only when asked about large-scale production, particularly in the studio mode.

Studio film production assigns tasks to so many individuals that it is often difficult to determine who controls or decides what. Is the producer the author? In the prime years of the Hollywood system, the producer might have had nothing to do with shooting. The writer? The writer's script might be completely transformed in shooting and editing. So is this situation like collective production, with group authorship? No, because there is a hierarchy in which a few main players make the key decisions.

Moreover, if we consider not only control and decision making but also individual style, it seems certain that some studio workers leave recognizable and unique traces on the films they make. Cinematographers such as Gregg Toland, set designers such as Hermann Warm, costumers such as Edith Head, choreographers such as Gene Kelly—the contributions of these people stand out within the films they made. So where does the studio-produced film leave the idea of authorship?

Most people who study cinema regard the director as the film's primary "author." Although the writer prepares a screenplay, later phases of production can modify it beyond recognition. And although the producer monitors the entire process, he or she seldom controls moment-by-moment activity on the set. It is the director who makes the crucial decisions about performance, staging, lighting, framing, cutting, and sound. On the whole, the director usually has most control over how a movie looks and sounds.

This doesn't mean that the director is an expert at every job or dictates every detail. The director can delegate tasks to trusted personnel, and directors often work habitually with certain actors, cinematographers, composers, and editors. In the days of studio filmmaking, directors learned how to blend the distinctive talents of cast and crew into the overall movie. Humphrey Bogart's unique talents were used very differently by Michael Curtiz in *Casablanca,* John Huston in *The Maltese Falcon,* and Howard Hawks in *The Big Sleep.* Gregg Toland's cinematography was pushed in different directions by Orson Welles (*Citizen Kane*) and William Wyler (*The Best Years of Our Lives*).

During the 1950s, young French critics applied the word *auteur* (author) to Hollywood directors whom they felt had created a distinctive approach to filmmaking while working within the Hollywood studio system. Soon American critics picked up the "auteur theory," which remained a central idea for film academics and students. Now you will occasionally read reviews or see spots on television that use the term, which has become a common term for a well-respected director.

Today well-established directors can control large-scale production to a remarkable degree. Steven Spielberg and Ethan and Joel Coen can insist on editing manually, not digitally. The late Robert Altman disliked ADR and used much of the on-set dialogue in the finished film (Martin Scorsese does as well). In the days of Hollywood's studio system, some directors exercised power more indirectly. Most studios did not permit the director to supervise editing, but John Ford often did only one take of each shot. Precutting the film "in his head," Ford virtually forced the editor to put the shots together as he had planned.

Around the world, the director is generally recognized as the key player. In Europe, Asia, and South America, directors frequently initiate the film and work closely with scriptwriters. In Hollywood, directors usually operate on a freelance basis, and the top ones select their own projects. For the most part, it is the director who shapes the film's unique form and style, and these two components are central to cinema as an art.

"The thing that makes me sad is that there's tons of kids that I meet all the time . . . who don't know anything about film history. . . . The number who couldn't say that Orson Welles directed Citizen Kane *was staggering. . . . They were infatuated with the business and the glamour of the business, and not filmmaking."*

— Stacy Sher, producer, *Pulp Fiction* and *Erin Brockovich*

CONNECT TO THE BLOG
Screenwriters often take issue with this idea, but we defend it in "Who the devil wrote it? (Apologies to Peter Bogdanovich)."
See www.davidbordwell.net/blog/?p=41.

Bringing the Film to the Audience: Distribution and Exhibition

We've spent some time considering film production because that is where film art begins. What of the other two phases of filmmaking? As in production, money plays a significant role in both distribution and exhibition. We'll see as well that these phases have effects on film art and viewers' experiences of particular films.

Distribution: The Center of Power

Distribution companies form the core of economic power in the commercial film industry. Filmmakers need them to circulate their work; exhibitors need them to supply their screens. Europe and Asia are home to some significant media companies, but six Hollywood firms remain the world's major distributors. The names are familiar: Warner Bros., Paramount, Walt Disney/Buena Vista, Sony/Columbia, Twentieth Century Fox, and Universal.

These firms provide mainstream entertainment to theaters around the world. The films they release account for 95 percent of ticket sales in the United States and Canada, and about half of the international market. In world capitals, the majors maintain branch offices that advertise films, schedule releases, and arrange for prints to be made in local languages (either dubbing in the dialogue or adding subtitling). With vigorous marketing units in every region, the majors can distribute non-U.S. films as well as Hollywood titles. For example, Hayao Miyazaki's popular animated films (*Spirited Away, Howl's Moving Castle*) are distributed on video by Disney's Buena Vista arm—even in Miyazaki's homeland of Japan.

The major distributors have won such power because large companies can best endure the risks of theatrical moviemaking. Filmmaking is costly, and most films don't earn profits in theatrical release. Worldwide, the top 10 percent of all films released garner 50 percent of all box office receipts. The most popular 30 percent of films account for 80 percent of receipts. Typically, a film breaks even or shows a profit only after it has been released on cable, satellite, and home video.

In the United States, theater owners bid for each film a distributor releases, and in most states, they must be allowed to see the film before bidding. Elsewhere in the world, distributors may force exhibitors to rent a film without seeing it (called *blind booking*), perhaps even before it has been completed. Exhibitors may also be pressured to rent a package of films in order to get a few desirable items (*block booking*).

Once the exhibitor has contracted to screen the film, the distributor can demand stiff terms. The theater keeps a surprisingly small percentage of total box office receipts (known as the *gross* or *grosses*). One standard arrangement guarantees the distributor a minimum of 90 percent of the first week's gross, dropping gradually to 30 percent after several weeks. These terms aren't favorable to the exhibitor. A failure that closes quickly will yield almost nothing to the theater, and even a successful film will make most of its money in the first two or three weeks of release, when the exhibitor gets less of the revenue. Averaged out, a long-running success will yield no more than 50 percent of the gross to the theater. To make up for this drawback, the distributor allows the exhibitor to deduct from the gross the expenses of running the theater (a negotiated figure called the *house nut*). In addition, the exhibitor gets all the cash from the concession stand, which may deliver up to 70 percent of the theater's profits. Without high-priced snacks, movie houses couldn't survive.

Once the grosses are split with the exhibitor, the distributor receives its share (the *rentals*) and divides it further. A major U.S. distributor typically takes 35 percent of the rentals as its distribution fee. If the distributor helped finance the film, it takes another percentage off the top. The costs of prints and advertising are deducted as well. What remains comes back to the filmmakers. Out of the proceeds,

"Selling food is my job. I just happen to work in a theater."

— Theater manager in upstate New York

CONNECT TO THE BLOG
Every Monday, the weekend box-office figures are news, but what do they mean? We add some nuance in "What won the weekend? or how to understand box-office figures."
See www.davidbordwell.net/blog/?p=21.

the producer must pay all *profit participants*—the directors, actors, executives, and investors who have negotiated a share of the rental returns.

For most films, the amount returned to the production company is relatively small. Once the salaried workers have been paid, the producer and other major players usually must wait to receive their share from video and other ancillary markets. Because of this delay, and the suspicion that the major distributors practice misleading accounting, powerful actors and directors may demand "first-dollar" participation, meaning that their share will derive from the earliest money the picture returns to the distributor.

Majors and Minors   The major distributors all belong to multinational corporations devoted to leisure activities. For example, Time Warner owns Warner Bros., which produces and distributes films while also controlling subsidiary companies New Line Cinema, Picturehouse, and Warner Independent Pictures. In addition, Time Warner owns the Internet provider America On Line. The conglomerate owns broadcast and cable services such as CNN, HBO, and the Cartoon Network; publishing houses and magazines (*Time, Life, Sports Illustrated, People,* and DC Comics); music companies (Atlantic, Elektra); theme parks (Six Flags); and sports teams (the Atlanta Braves and the Atlanta Hawks). Since distribution firms are constantly acquiring and spinning off companies, the overall picture can change unexpectedly. In late 2005, for instance, DreamWorks SKG, a production company that was strongly aligned with Universal, was purchased by Paramount. In 2008, DreamWorks announced that it was leaving Paramount to become an independent company distributing through Universal, before abruptly revealing in early 2009 that its distribution partner would instead be Disney.

Independent and overseas filmmakers usually don't have access to direct funding from major distribution companies, so they try to presell distribution rights in order to finance production. Once the film is finished, they try to attract distributors' attention at film festivals. In 2005, after strong reviews at the Cannes Film Festival, Woody Allen's *Match Point* was picked up for U.S. distribution by DreamWorks SKG. In the same year, the South African production *Tsotsi* won the People's Choice Award at the Toronto International Film Festival, and its North American rights were bought by Buena Vista.

Specialized distributors, such as the New York firms Kino and Milestone, acquire rights to foreign and independent films for rental to art cinemas, colleges, and museums. As the audience for these films grew during the 1990s, major distributors sought to enter this market. The independent firm Miramax generated enough low-budget hits to be purchased by the Disney corporation. With the benefit of Disney's funding and wider distribution reach, Miramax movies such as *Pulp Fiction, Scream, Shakespeare in Love,* and *Hero* earned even bigger box-office receipts. Sony Pictures Classics funded art house fare that sometimes crossed over to the multiplexes, as *Crouching Tiger, Hidden Dragon* did. More recently, Fox Searchlight released a film that Warner Bros. had turned down, and it achieved popular and critical success with *Slumdog Millionaire*.

By belonging to multinational conglomerates, film distributors gain access to bank financing, stock issues, and other sources of funding. Branch offices in major countries can carry a film into worldwide markets. Sony's global reach allowed it to release 11 different sound track CDs for *Spider-Man 2,* each one featuring artists familiar in local territories. Just as important, media conglomerates can build *synergy*—the coordination of sectors within the company around a single piece of content, usually one that is "branded." *Batman* and *The X-Files* are famous instances of how the film, television, publishing, and music wings of a firm can reinforce one another. Every product promotes the others, and each wing of the parent company gets a bit of the business. One film can even advertise another within its story **(1.40)**. Although synergy sometimes fails, multimedia giants are in the best position to take advantage of it.

CONNECT TO THE BLOG
One example of how such a change affects the rest of the industry is discussed in our entry on the absorption of New Line Cinema into Warner Bros. in 2008—"Filling the New Line gap."
See www.davidbordwell.net/blog/?p=2983.

"Our underlying philosophy is that all media are one."
— Rupert Murdoch, owner of News Corp. and Twentieth Century Fox

1.40   In *Lethal Weapon,* as Murtaugh and Riggs leave a hot-dog stand, they pass in front of a movie theater advertising *The Lost Boys,* another Warner Bros. film (released four months after *Lethal Weapon*). The prominence of Pepsi-Cola in this shot is an example of *product placement*—featuring well-known brands in a film in exchange for payment or cross-promotional services.

Distributors arrange release dates, make prints, and launch advertising campaigns. For big companies, distribution can be efficient because the costs can be spread out over many units. One poster design can be used in several markets, and a distributor who orders a thousand prints from a laboratory will pay less per print than the filmmaker who orders one. Large companies are also in the best position to cope with the rise of distribution costs. Today, the average Hollywood film is estimated to cost around $70.8 million to make and an additional $35.9 million to distribute.

The risky nature of mass-market filmmaking has led the majors to two distribution strategies: *platforming* and *wide release.* With platforming, the film opens first in a few big cities. It's then gradually expanded to theaters around the country, though it may never play in every community. If the strategy is successful, anticipation for the film builds, and it remains a point of discussion for months. The major distributors tend to use platforming for unusual films, such as *Munich* and *Brokeback Mountain,* which need time to accumulate critical support and generate positive word-of-mouth. Smaller distributors use platforming out of necessity, since they can't afford to make enough prints to open wide, but the gradual accumulation of buzz can work in their favor, too.

In wide release, a film opens at the same time in many cities and towns. In the United States, this requires that thousands of prints be made, so wide release is available only to the deep-pocketed major distributors. Wide release is the typical strategy for mainstream films, with two or three new titles opening each weekend on 2000–4000 screens. A film in wide release may be a midbudget one—a comedy, an action picture, a horror or science fiction film, or a children's animated movie. It may also be a very big-budget item, a *tentpole* picture such as *War of the Worlds* or the latest Harry Potter installment.

CONNECT TO THE BLOG
With help from some colleagues, we examine the recent phenomenon of movie franchises and defend the idea in "Live with it! There'll always be movie sequels. Good thing, too."

See www.davidbordwell.net/blog/?p=836.

Distributors hope that a wide opening signals a "must-see" film, the latest big thing. Just as important, opening wide helps recoup costs faster, since the distributor gets a larger portion of box office receipts early in the run. But it's a gamble. If a film fails in its first weekend, it almost never recovers momentum and can lose money very quickly. Even successful films usually lose revenues by 40 percent or more every week they run. So when two high-budget films open wide the same weekend, the competition is harmful to all. Companies tend to plan their tentpole release dates to avoid head-to-head conflict. On the weekend in May 2005 when the final installment of Fox's *Star Wars* saga opened on nearly 3700 U.S. screens, other distributors offered no wide releases at all. *Episode III—Revenge of the Sith* grossed nearly $160 million in four days.

Wide releasing has extended across the world. As video piracy spread, distribution companies realized the risks of opening wide in the United States and then waiting weeks or months before opening overseas. By then, illegal DVDs and Internet downloads would be available. As a result, U.S. companies have begun experimenting with *day-and-date* releasing for their biggest tentpole pictures. *Matrix: Revolutions* opened simultaneously on 8000 screens in the United States and 10,000 screens in 107 other countries. In a stroke of showmanship, the first screening was synchronized to start at the same minute across all time zones.

Selling the Film   The distributor provides not only the movie but a publicity campaign. The theater is supplied with a *trailer,* a short preview of the upcoming film. Many executives believe that a trailer is the single most effective piece of advertising. Shown in theaters, it gets the attention of confirmed moviegoers. Posted on an official movie website, YouTube, and many fan sites, a trailer gains mass viewership.

Publicists run press junkets, flying entertainment reporters to interview the stars and principal filmmakers on-set or in hotels. "Infotainment" coverage in print and broadcast media or online build audience awareness. A "making of" documentary, commissioned by the studio, may be shown on cable channels. A prominent film's premiere creates an occasion for further press coverage (**1.41**). For journalists, the distributor provides electronic press kits (EPKs), complete with photos, background information, star interviews, and clips of key scenes. Even a modestly budgeted production such as *Waiting to Exhale* had heavy promotion: five separate music videos, star visits to Oprah Winfrey, and displays in thousands of bookstores and beauty salons. *My Big Fat Greek Wedding* cost $5 million to produce, but the distributors spent over $10 million publicizing it.

In 1999, two young directors found their target audience by creating a website purporting to investigate sightings of the Blair Witch. "The movie was an extension of the website," noted a studio executive. When *The Blair Witch Project* earned over $130 million in the United States, distributors woke up to the power of the Internet. Now every film has a web page, enticing viewers with plot information,

CONNECT TO THE BLOG
Recently, fan events like Comic-Con have provided a new way for Hollywood distributors to publicize popular films directly to moviegoers, as we discuss in "Comic-Con 2008, Part 2."
See www.davidbordwell.net/blog/?p=2710.

CONNECT TO THE BLOG
Even Oscar races become the subject of considerable publicity. For one gimmick a studio used to promote the award chances of *There Will Be Blood,* check out "I drink your Oscar promo."
See www.davidbordwell.net/blog/?p=1959.

1.41   A press conference held at Te Papa Museum in Wellington, New Zealand, as part of the December 1, 2003, world premiere of *The Lord of the Rings: The Return of the King.*

CONNECT TO THE BLOG
Internet sites are no guarantee of success. We speculate on why in "Snakes, no, Borat, yes. Not all Internet publicity is the same."
See www.davidbordwell.net/blog/?p=269.

star biographies, games, screen savers, and links to merchandise. Distributors have realized that web surfers will eagerly create "viral marketing" if they're allowed to participate in getting the word out. Fan sites such as Harry Knowles's Ain't It Cool News can publicize upcoming films through steady leaks and exclusive access. On-line contests can harvest email addresses for promotion of products and other films. Building on the thriving *Lord of the Rings* web culture, Peter Jackson sent nearly 90 Production Diaries of *King Kong* to a fan site, and they were later released as an elaborate boxed set of DVDs. Wireless communication became the next logical step, with trailers downloaded to cell phones and text-messaging campaigns such as that for *Cry Wolf.*

Merchandising is a form of promotion that pays back its investment directly. Manufacturing companies buy the rights to use the film's characters, title, or images on products. These licensing fees defray production and distribution costs, and if the merchandise catches on, it can provide the distributor with long-term income from an audience that might never have seen the film. Although *Tron* did poorly in theatrical release in 1982, the *Discs of Tron* video game became a popular arcade attraction. Today nearly all major motion pictures rely on merchandising, if only of a novelization or a sound track CD, but children's films tend to exploit the gamut of possibilities: toys, games, clothing, lunch boxes, and schoolbags. There were *Shrek* ring tones, bowling balls, and hospital scrubs. The basis for George Lucas's entertainment empire came from his retention of the licensing rights for *Star Wars* merchandise.

A similar tactic is *cross-promotion,* or *brand partnering,* which allows a film and a product line to be advertised simultaneously. The partner companies agree to spend a certain amount on ads, a practice that can shift tens of millions of dollars in publicity costs away from the studios. MGM arranged for the stars of the James Bond film *Tomorrow Never Dies* to appear in advertisements for Heineken, Smirnoff, BMW, Visa, and Ericsson. The five partner companies spent nearly $100 million on the campaign, which publicized the film around the world. As payback, the film included scenes prominently featuring the products. For *Shrek 2,* several companies committed to cobranded ads, including Burger King, Pepsi-Cola, General Mills, Hewlett-Packard, and Activision. Baskin-Robbins stores featured cardboard stand-up figures of Shrek, Donkey, and Puss-in-Boots grouped around a giant "Shrek's Hot Sludge Sundae." The U.S. Postal Service was drawn into the act, stamping billions of letters with a postmark featuring Shrek and Donkey. Less mainstream fare has relied on cross-promotion, too. Starbucks filled its stores with posters, coffee cup sleeves, and other promotional material for *Akeelah and the Bee.* The documentary *Hoop Dreams* was promoted by Nike and the National Basketball Association.

Exhibition: Theatrical and Nontheatrical

We're most familiar with the exhibition phase of the business, the moment when we pay for a movie ticket or drop in a DVD or download a movie. *Theatrical* exhibition involves screening to a public that pays admission, as in commercial movie houses. Other theatrical sites are city arts centers, museums, film festivals, and cinema clubs. *Nontheatrical* exhibition includes all other presentations, such as home video, cable and satellite transmissions, and screenings in schools and colleges.

Public movie exhibition, however, centers on the commercial theater. Most theaters screen wide releases from the major distributors, while others specialize in foreign-language or independent films. In all, the theatrical moviegoing audience is not a colossal one. In the United States, admissions average around 30 million per week, which sounds like a huge number until we realize that the weekly television audience numbers about 200 million. Only about a fifth of the population visits movie theaters regularly.

The most heavily patronized theaters belong to chains or circuits, and in most countries, these circuits are controlled by a few companies. Until the 1980s, most theaters housed only one screen, but exhibitors began to realize that several

GUS VAN SANT: *Your films have dominated the museum circuit in America—Minneapolis, Columbus . . .*

DEREK JARMAN: *Yes, Minneapolis in particular. That's where the films have actually had their life. They've crept into the student curriculum—which is a life. And now they go on through video. I never really feel shut out.*

— Gus Van Sant, director, interviewing Derek Jarman, independent filmmaker

Movies on Screens: A 2007 Profile of International Theatrical Exhibition

Worldwide production of theatrical motion pictures: **5039 features**
Worldwide attendance: **7.1 billion admissions**
Worldwide number of screens: **147,207**
Worldwide box-office gross receipts: **$26 billion**

USA box-office receipts: **$8.84 billion**
Western Europe box-office receipts: **$7.5 billion**
Japan box-office receipts: **$1.69 billion**

Countries and Numbers of Screens

Highest: USA 38,974; China 36,112; India 10,189; France 5398; German 4832; Spain 4296; Italy 4071; Mexico 3936; UK 3596; Japan 3221

Lowest: Luxembourg 24; Oman 19; Azerbaijan 17; Algeria 10

Screens per Million People

Highest: Iceland 156

Lowest: India 9.2

Others: USA 129; Sweden 115; Spain 95; Australia 95; Canada 91; UK 59; China 27; Japan 25; Russia 19

Average Ticket Prices

Highest: Norway $12.80; Denmark $12.47; Switzerland $12.17; Sweden $11.71

Lowest: Peru $1.79; Bolivia $1.67; Philippines $1.61; India $0.53

Others: UK $10.12; Australia $8.87; France $8.16; Canada $7.70; USA $6.82

Domestic Films' Share of Box-Office Revenues Abroad

Highest: China, 54.5%; Japan, 47.7%; South Korea, 44.6%

Lowest: Austria, 1.9%; Lithuania, 2.6%; Portugal, 2.7%

Others: Italy, 31.7%; Mexico, 13.2%; Latvia, 5.4%

Source: *Screen Digest*

screens under one roof could reduce costs. The multiplex theater, containing 3 or more screens, and the megaplex, with 16 or more, lured far bigger crowds than a single-screen cinema could. Centralized projection booths and concession stands also cut costs. The boom in building multiplexes allowed exhibitors to upgrade the presentation, offering stadium seating, digital sound, and in some cases Imax and 3D. Multiplexes can also devote occasional screenings to niche markets, as when live opera broadcasts are shown digitally or a weekly morning matinee is aimed at women with babies. Multiplexes are now the norm in North America, Europe, and parts of Asia, with snacks adjusted to local tastes—popcorn and candy nearly everywhere, but also beer (in Europe) and dried squid (in Hong Kong).

The United States is the most lucrative theatrical market, contributing 32 percent of global box office receipts. (See chart.) By nation, Japan comes in second, chiefly because ticket prices are very high. Western European and Asian-Pacific countries follow. Providing about 25 percent of the global box office, western Europe (including the United Kingdom and the Nordic countries) is the most important regional

CONNECT TO THE BLOG
Why cater to mothers and babies? We investigate in "Women and children first."

See www.davidbordwell.net/blog/?p=2917.

market outside North America. For these reasons, filmmakers around the world aim for distribution in these prosperous countries.

The less significant markets are Latin America, eastern Europe, mainland China, India, the Middle East, and Africa. The multiplex strategy has been the wedge opening up these territories. They have few screens per head of population, and entrepreneurs have launched ambitious multiplex projects in Russia, China, and Latin America. Hollywood distributors see overseas multiplexes as a golden opportunity. By investing in theaters overseas, they are guaranteed an outlet for their product. (U.S. antitrust law blocks them from owning theaters at home.) Historically, Hollywood distributors have withheld films from many countries when the local ticket prices were too low to yield much profit. In 2000, the average ticket price in the Philippines hovered around 70¢; in India, 20¢. As underdeveloped countries expanded their middle class, comfortable multiplexes began to attract upscale viewers who wouldn't visit aging single-screen cinemas. By 2007, thanks largely to multiplex expansion, the global average ticket price was $3.73, an all-time high.

In 1999, four of the 3126 theaters in which *Star Wars: Episode I—The Phantom Menace* played had digital projectors. Those four made headlines, though, and many people predicted that theaters would steadily convert to digital. The advantages were obvious. The thousands of 35mm prints needed for such a wide release cost an enormous amount, and the shipping costs were a burden to distributor and theater alike. Films delivered to theaters on compact hard drives would be far cheaper. With no film to thread, high-paid projectionists would be eliminated; a theater manager could press buttons to start showings, no matter how many screens a theater had. No scratches or dust would accumulate on the print.

The obstacle was that outfitting a single screen with digital projection would cost $150,000 or more, while 35mm projectors cost only around $30,000—and many theaters already had projectors that would last for years. The rate of conversion to digital was slower than expected, and the Hollywood studios pressed reluctant exhibitors hard, offering rental discounts. Producers like Jeffrey Katzenberg of DreamWorks Animation and directors like James Cameron wanted to work exclusively in 3D, which required digital projectors. In mid-2008, when the scope of the world financial crisis was beginning to become apparent, only 4847 screens of the total 38,159 in the United States had converted to digital projection. The severe economic downturn slowed the changeover even further. In 2009, Katzenberg had to abandon his plan to release *Monsters vs. Aliens* on over 5000 3D screens. He had to settle for about 2000.

Although films are shown in venues like museums, archives, and film clubs, the most important theatrical alternative to commercial movie houses has become the *film festival*.

The first major annual film festival was held in Venice in 1938, and although it had to be suspended during World War II, it was revived afterwards and endures today. Festivals were mounted in Cannes, Berlin, Karlovy Vary, Moscow, Edinburgh, and many other cities. Today there are thousands of festivals all over the world—some large and influential, such as the Toronto Film Festival, and others aimed primarily at bringing unusual films to local audiences, such as the Wisconsin Film Festival in Madison. Some festivals promote specific genres, such as the Brussels International Festival of Fantastic Film, or specific subject matter, such as the New York Gay and Lesbian Film Festival.

Occasionally, such festivals show major Hollywood films. In 2006, *The Da Vinci Code* was the opening-night presentation at the Cannes International Film Festival. Usually, however, the focus is on less mainstream cinema. Some festivals, like those in Cannes and Pusan, South Korea, include markets where such films can find distributors. The International Film Festival Rotterdam even helps finance films made in developing countries. Not all festivals award prizes, but the bigger ones that do—most notably Cannes, Venice, and Berlin—can draw attention to films that might otherwise get lost among the hundreds of movies circulating among festivals.

CONNECT TO THE BLOG
The Cannes Film Festival is the biggest of them all. We review an excellent history of it in "Cannes: Behind the art, hype, and politics."
See www.davidbordwell.net/blog/?p=931.

Festivals offer a distribution and exhibition outlet for films that might never be picked up for release beyond their country of origin. For example, during the mid-1980s, festival programmers were drawn to new and exciting work coming from Iran. Even without much exhibition in theaters, the films of Abbas Kiarostami, Mohsen Makhmalbaf, and their compatriots became major attractions at festivals. Their high profiles led to occasional films being given commercial distribution in Europe and North America. Although festival screenings didn't make films profitable, the Iranian government sponsored such works as a way for the country and its culture to gain a higher profile internationally.

Passing from festival to festival becomes a mode of distribution for many films, which are sometimes promoted by the stars or directors in question-and-answer sessions. If a film fails to find a theatrical distributor, it may go straight to DVD and to screenings on specialized cable channels, such as the Sundance Channel and the Independent Film Channel in the United States.

Film festivals offer "theatrical" exhibition, since most of them show films in local theaters and sell tickets. At the two-week Palm Springs International Film Festival, for example, one nine-screen multiplex, a three-screen one, an auditorium in a local museum, and one in a community arts center all participate in the festival.

"I've come to realize that my festival run is my theatrical run."

— Joe Swanberg, independent film director, *Hannah Takes the Stairs*

Ancillary Markets: Taking Movies Beyond the Theater

When a film leaves theatrical distribution, it lives on. Since the late 1970s, video has created a vast array of ancillary markets, and these typically return more money than the theatrical release. Distributors carefully plan the timing of their video release, putting the film first on airline flights and hotel television systems, then on pay-per-view TV, then on DVD release, and eventually on network broadcast, satellite and cable stations, and cable reruns. Video has proved a boon to smaller distributors, too. Foreign and independent films yield slim theatrical returns, but video markets can make these items profitable.

With only a fifth of Americans being regular moviegoers, television, in one form or another, has kept the theatrical market going. During the 1960s, the U.S. television networks began supporting Hollywood production by purchasing broadcast rights to the studios' output. Lower-budget filmmakers depended on sales to European television and U.S. cable outlets. Television created an important nontheatrical market for films, one that film studios have exploited ever since.

When videocassette rentals became popular in the 1980s, studios were initially convinced that their business would suffer. It didn't. During the 1990s, worldwide film attendance increased significantly. In 1997, when the DVD format was introduced, consumers embraced it eagerly. The disc was portable, took up less storage space than a VHS tape, and offered superior picture and sound quality. It could be played on tabletop players, portable players, game consoles, and computers. It encouraged families to install home theaters with big-screen TVs and multiple speakers. And it was widely available. In the United States, the Wal-Mart chain became the main purveyor of DVDs, accounting for over a third of all sales. Again, despite studio fears, even the arrival of the DVD failed to draw people away from theaters.

The major U.S. studios started their own home entertainment divisions to sell DVDs. Because the discs cost less than VHS tapes to create, the studios reaped huge rewards. In 2007, the major U.S. studios earned about $9.6 billion worldwide in theaters, whereas home video sales and rentals yielded $24 billion. Most of the video income came from DVD sales, which yield much higher profits to studios than rentals do.

Today the DVD market sustains most of the world's theatrical filmmaking. Yet movie theaters remain central to the exhibition system. A theatrical screening focuses public interest. Critics review the film, television and the press publicize it, and people talk about it. The theatrical run is the film's launching pad, usually determining how successful it will be in ancillary markets. Theatrical hits may account for as much as 80 percent of a video store's or an Internet service's rentals.

CONNECT TO THE BLOG
Have DVDs changed the way movies tell their stories? Not much, we argue in "New media and old storytelling."
See www.davidbordwell.net/blog/?p=827.

Even though the worldwide audience grew during the 1990s, most of the growth was in new markets. U.S. and European attendance showed signs of dwindling slowly. Commercial theaters were competing with home theaters, video games, and Internet entertainment. Since the early 2000s, exhibitors have worried especially about shrinking windows—the time between a film's theatrical release and its release on DVD and other platforms. The concern is that if the DVD comes out too soon after the theatrical run, people will simply wait for the DVD. Some small distribution firms are experimenting with simultaneously releasing a film to theaters, on DVD, and on cable television, a practice that would eliminate the window that protects the exhibitors.

One lure that exhibitors are using to keep audiences loyal is building Imax screens in multiplexes and showing studio tentpole pictures in that immersive format. *The Polar Express, Chicken Little,* and other releases earned a large portion of their returns in Imax and in Imax 3-D. Entries in the Harry Potter and Batman series also play in both Imax and regular theaters. Higher ticket prices benefit exhibitor and film studio alike.

Apart from using the Internet to promote films, Hollywood sells DVDs through online merchants like Amazon.com. These offer a far wider choice of titles than a bricks-and-mortar store, and courier delivery reaches remote parts of the United States and other countries where such stores did not exist. DVD rentals could also be profitable if handled online through Netflix, which offers unlimited rentals for a subscription fee. The big rental chains like Blockbuster have established similar programs in addition to walk-in stores.

The next step for the studios has been to eliminate the cost of physical copies by selling movies as downloads or renting them as streaming video. As broadband access increases in capacity and more people acquire high-speed connections, films of any length can be made available online. Video on demand promises huge profits, and digital encryption can be used to prevent consumers from copying films. The distributors' aim is to create a system depending less on buying or renting an object than on purchasing a service.

To further this goal, Netflix has expanded its service, added its "Watch Instantly" feature. As part of customers' monthly fee, they gain access to streaming-video copies of movies at near-DVD quality. Instead of the lengthy wait necessary in downloading a feature film to own, viewers can begin watching the video within a minute but are not able to save or burn a copy. Apple also has a service through its iTunes store, renting access to streaming video of films on PCs, Macs, iPhones, and iPods. Recent movies are available a month after their DVD release, with older titles available for a lower fee.

Despite the swift success of the format, DVDs caused distributors some worries as well. The discs were easy to copy and manufacture in bulk, so piracy took off worldwide. A bootleg DVD of a Hollywood movie could sell for as little as 80¢ in China. Moreover, with nearly 60,000 titles available at the end of 2005, shelf space was at a premium, so discount chains dumped slow-moving titles into bargain bins. DVD retail prices began to drop. The distributors hoped that a new format, the high-definition DVD, would block piracy and recharge the market, coaxing viewers into buying their favorite titles yet again. In the long run, they hoped, consumers would start to bypass packaged media. Far better to purchase films online and, using a convergence device such as XBox 360 or PlayStation, watch them on the family television monitor. But then the movie theater would be even more jeopardized.

Home video in all its varieties brings commercial films into the home. A major additional type of nontheatrical exhibition arises from movies made by amateurs and by aspiring filmmakers. Most of these are shared over the Internet on YouTube and other sites. Some filmmakers, however, want to show their work before a live audience.

To meet that desire, festivals of DIY films have arisen, including the DIY Film Festival, based in Los Angeles and traveling to other cities. Another started in 2001, when 10 small teams of filmmakers in Washington, DC, accepted a challenge to make a short film in 48 hours. All the completed shorts would be screened as a

CONNECT TO THE BLOG

Many movies are available on the Internet, for legal or illegal downloading. That doesn't mean every movie ever made will someday be online. We talk about why with two restoration experts in "The celestial multiplex."

See www.davidbordwell.net/blog/?p=595.

CONNECT TO THE BLOG

For thoughts on watching movies on iPods, see "Area man lives in fear that attractive woman will ask what's on his iPod."

See www.davidbordwell.net/blog/?p=40.

CONNECT TO THE BLOG

We talk about bootleg DVD covers in "Our first anniversary, with a note on the unexpected fruits of film piracy."

See www.davidbordwell.net/blog/?p=1351.

program immediately after the deadline. The result was the 48 Hours Film Project, which has offered similar challenges annually in an increasing number of cities, totaling over 70 by 2009. More informally, the Kino movement began in 1999 in Montréal with the slogan "Do well with nothing, do better with little, and do it right now!" The movement consists of local chapters in about 50 cities internationally. These typically meet once a month to screen their members' latest films.

With the spread of small-format video capacity to cell phones and the availability of cheap post-production software, more people can shoot moving images with no training. Much of what they shoot remains raw footage. It may be shown to friends or family and then erased. Handheld personal music devices have added video screens, so that movies can be viewed on the go. Digital technology has made nontheatrical film viewing more casual and omnipresent than ever.

Artistic Implications of Distribution and Exhibition

Grosses, synergy, ticket prices, and movies on video game consoles might seem very remote from issues of film as an art. Yet film is a technological medium usually aimed at a broad public, so the ways in which movies are circulated and shown can affect viewers' experiences. Home video turns viewing into a small-group or individual activity, but seeing a film in a packed theater yields a different response. Comedies, most people feel, seem funnier in a theater, where infectious laughter can ripple through a crowd. Filmmakers are aware of this difference, and they try to pace comedies slowly enough that crowd laughter doesn't drown out a key line.

Video distribution and exhibition have created new choices in the realm of storytelling. Until the 1980s, people couldn't rewatch a movie whenever they wished. With videotape and, especially DVDs, viewers can pore over a film. Bonus materials encourage them to rerun the movie to spot things they missed. Some filmmakers have taken advantage of this opportunity by creating *puzzle films* like *Memento* and *Donnie Darko,* which fans scrutinize for clues to plot enigmas **(1.42, 1.43).** Video versions can complicate the theatrical release version, as the extra ending of *The Butterfly Effect* does. Some interactive DVD movies permit the viewers to choose how the plot develops. The DVD of Greg Marks's *11:14* allows you to enter parallel story lines at various points, in effect recasting the film's overall form.

As the Internet becomes a more common platform for distribution, we should expect variations in narrative form. Short-form storytelling is already at home online, in cartoons and comedy. Events like the festivals run by the 48 Hour Film Project also encourage the making of short films, especially given the assumption that most of the films will later be posted on the Internet. We're likely to find movies designed specifically for mobile phones; television series like *24* are already creating "mobisodes" branching off the broadcast story line. The web is the logical place for interactive films that use hyperlinks to amplify or detour a line of action.

Marketing and merchandising can extend a theatrical film's story in intriguing ways. The *Star Wars* novels and video games give the characters more adventures and expand spectators' engagement with the movies. The *Memento* website hinted at ways to interpret the film. The *Matrix* video games supplied key information for the films' plots, while the second movie in the trilogy sneaked in hints for winning the games. As a story world shifts from platform to platform, a multimedia saga is created, and viewers' experiences will shift accordingly. *Matrix* viewers who've never played the games understand the story somewhat differently from those who have.

Style can be affected by distribution and exhibition, as is evident in image size. From the 1920s through the 1950s, films were designed to be shown in large venues **(1.44).** A typical urban movie house seated 1500 viewers and boasted a screen 50 feet wide. This scale gave the image great presence, and it allowed details to be seen easily. Directors could stage dialogue scenes showing several characters in the frame, all of whom would be prominent **(1.45).** In a theater of that time, a tight close-up would have had a powerful impact.

CONNECT TO THE BLOG
In this age of new media, have movies lost their importance to audiences? Some would say yes, but we argue against that idea in "Movies still matter."
See www.davidbordwell.net/blog/?p=475.

Have Hollywood films declined in popularity internationally? Again, we don't believe it, as we explain in "World rejects Hollywood blockbusters!?"
See www.davidbordwell.net/blog/?p=458.

"The Matrix is entertainment for the age of media convergence, integrating multiple texts to create a narrative so large that it cannot be contained within a single medium."
— Henry Jenkins, media analyst

CONNECT TO THE BLOG
For some pictures of a spectacularly restored movie palace, see "A tale of 2—make that 1 and 1/3 screens," at
www.davidbordwell.net/blog/?p=3941.

1.42   In *Magnolia,* the extraordinary meterological event at the climax is predicted by the recurring numerals 82, referring to chapter and verse in the biblical book of Exodus.

1.43   In *Magnolia,* the figure 82 appears as coils in the rooftop hose.

1.44   The interior of the Paramount Theater in Portland, Oregon, built in 1928. Capacity was 3000 seats, at a time when the city population was about 300,000. Note the elaborate decoration on the walls and ceilings, typical of the "picture palaces" of the era.

When television became popular in the 1950s, its image was rather unclear and very small, in some cases only 10 inches diagonally. Early TV shows tended to rely on close shots (**1.46**), which could be read easily on the small monitor. In the 1960s and 1970s, movie attendance dropped and theaters became smaller. As screens shrank, filmmakers began to rely more on close-ups in the TV manner. This tendency has continued until today. Although modern multiplex screens can be fairly large, audiences have become accustomed to scenes that consist chiefly of big faces (**1.47**). Now that most films are viewed on video, and many will be watched on handheld devices, it seems likely that commercial films will continue to treat conversation scenes in tight close-ups. In this respect, technology and exhibition circumstances have created stylistic constraints. Yet some contemporary filmmakers have stuck to the older technique (**1.48**), in effect demanding that audiences view their films on a large theater screen.

There's also the matter of image proportions, and here again, television exhibition exercised some influence. Since the mid-1950s, virtually all theaters have shown films on screens that were wider than the traditional TV monitor. For decades, when movies were shown on television, they were cropped, with certain areas simply left out (**1.49–1.51**). In response, some filmmakers composed their shots to include a "safe area," placing the key action in a spot that could fit snugly on the television screen. This created subtle differences in a shot's visual effects

1.45   On the large screen of a picture palace, all the figures and faces in this shot from *The Thin Man* (1934) would have been quite visible.

1.46   *Dragnet* (1953): Early television relied heavily on close-ups because of the small screen size.

1.47   *Red Eye:* Extreme close-ups of actors' faces are common in modern cinema, due partly to the fact that most viewing takes place on video formats.

"Not until seeing [North by Northwest] *again on the big screen did I realize conclusively what a gigantic difference screen size does make. . . . This may be yet another reason why younger people have a hard time with older pictures: they've only seen them on the tube, and that reduces films' mystery and mythic impact."*

— Peter Bogdanovich, director, *The Last Picture Show* and *Mask*

CONNECT TO THE BLOG
We explore another peril of watching films on video—logos superimposed on films—in "Bugs: the secret history."
See www.davidbordwell.net/blog/?p=3296.

1.48   In *Flowers of Shanghai,* director Hou Hsiao-hsien builds every scene out of full shots of several characters. The result loses information on a small display and is best seen on a theater screen.

1.49   In Otto Preminger's *Advise and Consent,* a single shot in the original . . .

1.50   . . . becomes a pair of shots in the television version . . .

1.51   . . . thus losing the sense of actors simultaneously reacting to each other.

1.52   As Rose, the heroine of *Titanic,* feels the exhilaration of "flying" on the ship's prow, the strongly horizontal composition emphasizes her outstretched arms as wings against a wide horizon.

1.53   In the video version, nearly all sense of the horizontal composition has disappeared.

(1.52, 1.53). Relying on the safe area often encouraged filmmakers to employ more *singles,* shots showing only one player. In a wide-screen frame, a single can compensate for the cropping that TV would demand **(1.54).**

Today most cable and DVD versions of films are *letterboxed*. Dark bands at the top and bottom of the screen approximate the film's theatrical proportions. The great majority of filmmakers approve of this, but Stanley Kubrick preferred that video versions of some of his films be shown "full frame." This is why we've reproduced the shots from *The Shining* (2.7, 2.8) full-frame, even though nobody who watched the movie in a theater saw so much headroom. Almost no commercial theaters can show films full-frame today, but Jean-Luc Godard usually composes his shots for that format; you couldn't letterbox **1.55** without undermining the composi-

> *"What about a mobile version of every film? Maybe in the future there will be four versions—film, TV, DVD, and mobile. No one knows yet."*
>
> — Arvind Ethan David, managing director of multimedia company Slingshot

1.54 *Catch Me If You Can:* As with many modern wide-screen films, the essential information on screen left would fit within a traditional television frame. Still, cropping this image would lose a secondary piece of information—the pile of take-out food cartons that implies that Agent Hanratty has been at his desk for days.

1.55 A very dense shot from the climax of Godard's *Detective*. Although Godard's films are sometimes cropped for theater screenings and DVD versions, the compositions show to best advantage in the older, squarer format.

1.56 *Angel Face* as rendered on an incorrectly set widescreen television monitor.

tion. In these instances, distribution and theatrical exhibition initially constrained the filmmakers' choices, but video versions expanded them.

The introduction of widescreen TV sets has created a new problem for film images. The screens of traditional sets had a 4:3 ratio, partly because a lot of programming either consisted of old films or was shot on film. Widescreen TVs may be fine for recent films, but older material can suffer—including TV shows originally made to fit standard sets. A widescreen TV image has an aspect ratio of 16:9. If we multiply a 4:3 ratio by three, we get 12:9. So the widescreen image is a third wider than the standard one. Some sets have controls to adjust the ratio and allow black bands on the sides to provide "windowboxing," the vertical equivalent of letterboxing. But if there's no windowboxing, the picture is stretched horizontally, so that people and objects look squashed **(1.56).** Many viewers do not know how to change the ratio, and some video monitors make it difficult to correct the problem.

Even product placement offers some artistic opportunities. We're usually distracted when a Toyota truck or a box of Frosted Flakes pops up on the screen, but *Back to the Future* cleverly integrates brands into its story. Marty McFly is catapulted from 1985 to 1955. Trapped in a period when diet soda didn't exist, he asks for a Pepsi Free at a soda fountain, but the counterman says that it's not free—he'll have to pay for it. Later, buying a bottle of Pepsi from a vending machine, Marty tries frantically to twist off the cap, but his father-to-be George McFly casually pops it off at the machine's built-in opener. Pepsi soft drinks weave through the movie, reasserting Marty's comic inability to adjust to his parents' era—and perhaps stirring some nostalgia in viewers who remember how bits of everyday life have changed since their youth.

CONNECT TO THE BLOG
Jean-Luc Godard's films present special challenges to the projectionist and DVD producer, as we show in "Godard comes in many shapes and sizes."
See www.davidbordwell.net/blog/?p=1592.

SUMMARY

The art of film depends on technology, from the earliest experiments in apparent motion to the most recent computer programs. It also depends on people who use that technology, who come together to make films, distribute them, and show them. As long as a film is aimed at a public, however small, it enters into the social dynamic of production, distribution, and exhibition. Out of technology and work processes, filmmakers create an experience for audiences. Along the way, they inevitably make choices about form and style. What options are available to them? How might filmmakers organize the film as a whole? How might they draw on the techniques of the medium? The next two parts of this book survey the possibilities.

WHERE TO GO FROM HERE

The Making of *Collateral*

Our case study of *Collateral*'s production derives in part from the making-of supplement, "City of Night: The Making of *Collateral*." This 39-minute documentary covers the decisions about filming on HD-video, about lighting the interior of the taxi, and about the three-movement musical track that accompanies the climax. This and some short films on the actors rehearsing and on the special effects of the final sequence appear in the two-disc DVD set (Dream-Works Home Entertainment #91734; this DVD was issued only in a letterboxed version).

Jay Holben's *American Cinematographer* article "Hell on Wheels" (pp. 40–51 in the August 2004 issue) deals in greater detail with the cameras used in the production and with the lighting. David Goldsmith describes the original version of the script, set in New York City, in "*Collateral*: Stuart Beattie's Character-Driven Thriller," *Creative Screenwriting*, 11, 4 (2004): 50–53. Two online articles that deal with the film's filmmaking choices and style are Bryant Frazer's "How DP Dion Beebe Adapted to HD for Michael Mann's *Collateral*," on the website of the International Cinematographers Guild (n.d.), www.cameraguild.com/interviews/chat_beebe/beebe_collateral.html, and Daniel Restuccio's "Seeing in the Dark for *Collateral*: Director Michael Mann Re-invents Digital Filmmaking" (August 2004), findarticles.com/p/articles/mi_m0HNN/is_8_19/ai_n6171215/pg_1.

The Illusion of Cinematic Motion

For about 80 years, writers on film have maintained that the reason we see movement in movies is due to "persistence of vision." Today, no researcher into perception is likely to accept this explanation. Several optical processes are involved, but as we indicate on p. 000, the two most prominent are flicker fusion and apparent motion. More specifically, the stimuli in a film instantiate "short-range" apparent motion, in which small-scale changes in the display trigger activity in different parts of the visual cortex. Filmic motion takes place in our brain, not on our retina. For an explanation of these ideas, and a thorough critique of the traditional explanation, see Joseph and Barbara Anderson, "The Myth of Persistence of Vision Revisited," *Journal of Film and Video*, 45, 1 (Spring 1993): 3–12. It is available online at www.uca.edu/org/ccsmi/ccsmi/classicwork/myth%20revisited.htm.

Film's Roots in Technology

André Bazin suggests that humankind dreamed of cinema long before it actually appeared: "The concept men had of it existed so to speak fully armed in their minds, as if in some platonic heaven" (*What Is Cinema?* vol. 1 [Berkeley: University of California Press, 1967], p. 17). Still, whatever its antecedents in ancient Greece and the Renaissance, the cinema became technically feasible only in the 19th century.

Motion pictures depended on many discoveries in various scientific and industrial fields: optics and lens making, the control of light (especially by means of arc lamps), chemistry (involving particularly the production of cellulose), steel production, precision machining, and other areas. The cinema machine is closely related to other machines of the period. For example, engineers in the 19th century designed machines that could intermittently unwind, advance, perforate, advance again, and wind up a strip of material at a constant rate. The drive apparatus on cameras and projectors is a late development of a technology that had already made feasible the sewing machine, the telegraph tape, and the machine gun. The 19-century origins of film, based on mechanical and chemical processes, are particularly evident today, since we've become accustomed to electronic and digital media.

On the history of film technology, see Barry Salt's *Film Style and Technology: History and Analysis* (London: Starword, 1983); and Leo Enticknap, *Moving Image Technology: From Zoetrope to Digital* (London: Wallflower, 2005). Douglas Gomery has pioneered the economic history of film technology: For a survey, see Robert C. Allen and Douglas Gomery, *Film History: Theory and Practice* (New York: Knopf, 1985). The most comprehensive reference book on the subject is Ira Konigsberg, *The Complete Film Dictionary* (New York: Penguin, 1997). An entertaining appreciation of film technology is Nicholson Baker's "The Projector," in his *The Size of Thoughts* (New York: Vintage, 1994), pp. 36–50. Brian McKernan provides an overview of the introduction and development of digital technology in *Digital Cinema: The Revolution in Cinematography, Post-production, and Distribution* (New York: McGraw-Hill, 2005).

Film Distribution and Exhibition

For comprehensive surveys of the major "content providers" today, see Benjamin M. Compaine and Douglas Gomery, *Who Owns the Media? Competition and Concentration in the Mass Media Industry* (Mahwah, NJ: Erlbaum, 2000); Barry R. Litman, *The Motion Picture Mega-Industry* (Boston: Allyn & Bacon, 1998); and Edward S. Herman and Robert W. McChesney, *The Global Media: The New Missionaries of Global Capitalism* (London: Cassell, 1997).

Edward J. Epstein offers an excellent overview of the major distributors' activities in *The Big Picture: The New Logic of Money and Power in Hollywood* (New York: Random House, 2005). Douglas Gomery's *The Hollywood Studio System: A History* (London: British Film Institute, 2005) traces the history of the distributors, showing their roots in vertically integrated studios, which controlled production and exhibition as well.

On moviegoing, see Bruce A. Austin, *Immediate Seating: A Look at Movie Audiences* (Belmont, CA: Wadsworth, 1988); Gregory A. Waller, ed., *Moviegoing in America: A Sourcebook in the History of Film Exhibition* (Oxford: Blackwell, 2002); and Richard Maltby, Melvyn Stokes, and Robert C. Allen, eds., *Going to the Movies: Hollywood and the Social Experience of Cinema* (Exeter: University of Exeter Press, 2007). Douglas Gomery's *Shared Pleasures: A History of Moviegoing in America* (Madison: University of Wisconsin Press, 1992) offers a history of U.S. exhibition.

Stages of Film Production

A very good survey of production is Stephen Asch and Edward Pincus's *The Filmmaker's Handbook* (New York: Plume, 1999). For the producer, see Paul N. Lazarus III, *The Film Producer* (New York: St. Martin's Press, 1991) and Lynda Obst's acerbic memoir, *Hello, He Lied* (New York: Broadway, 1996). Art Linson, producer of *The Untouchables* and *Fight Club,* has written two entertaining books about his role: *A Pound of Flesh: Perilous Tales of How to Produce Movies in Hollywood* (New York: Grove Press, 1993) and *What Just Happened? Bitter Hollywood Tales from the Front Line* (New York: Bloomsbury, 2002). The details of organizing preparation and shooting are explained in Alain Silver and Elizabeth Ward's *The Film Director's Team: A Practical Guide for Production Managers, Assistant Directors, and All Filmmakers* (Los Angeles: Silman-James, 1992). For a survey of directing, see Tom Kingdon, *Total Directing: Integrating Camera and Performance in*

Film and Television (Beverly Hills, CA: Silman-James, 2004). Many "making-of" books include examples of storyboards; see also Steven D. Katz, *Film Directing Shot by Shot* (Studio City, CA: Wiese, 1991). On setting and production design, see Ward Preston, *What an Art Director Does* (Los Angeles: Silman-James, 1994). Norman Hollyn's *The Film Editing Room Handbook* (Los Angeles: Lone Eagle, 1999) offers a detailed account of image and sound editing procedures. Computer-based methods are discussed in Gael Chandler, *Cut by Cut: Editing Your Film or Video* (Studio City, CA: Michael Wiese, 2004). A wide range of job titles, from Assistant Director to Mouth/Beak Replacement Coordinator, is explained by the workers themselves in Barbara Baker, *Let the Credits Roll: Interviews with Film Crew* (Jefferson, NC: McFarland, 2003).

Several books explain how independent films are financed, produced, and sold. The most wide-ranging are David Rosen and Peter Hamilton, *Off-Hollywood: The Making and Marketing of Independent Films* (New York: Grove Weidenfeld, 1990), and Gregory Goodell, *Independent Feature Film Production: A Complete Guide from Concept Through Distribution,* 2d ed. (New York: St. Martin's Press, 1998). Billy Frolick's *What I Really Want to Do Is Direct* (New York: Plume, 1997) follows seven film-school graduates trying to make low-budget features. Christine Vachon, producer of *Boys Don't Cry* and *Far from Heaven,* shares her insights in *Shooting to Kill* (New York: Avon, 1998). See also Mark Polish, Michael Polish, and Jonathan Sheldon, *The Declaration of Independent Filmmaking: An Insider's Guide to Making Movies Outside of Hollywood* (Orlando, FL: Harcourt, 2005).

In *How I Made a Hundred Movies in Hollywood and Never Lost a Dime* (New York: Random House, 1990), Roger Corman reviews his career in exploitation cinema. A sample passage: "In the first half of 1957 I capitalized on the sensational headlines following the Russians' launch of their Sputnik satellite. . . . I shot *War of the Satellites* in a little under ten days. No one even knew what the satellite was supposed to look like. It was whatever I said it should look like" (pp. 44–45). Corman also supplies the introduction to Lloyd Kaufman's *All I Needed to Know about Filmmaking I Learned from the Toxic Avenger: The Shocking True Story of Troma Studios* (New York: Berkeley, 1998), which details the making of such Troma classics as *The Class of Nuke 'Em High* and *Chopper Chicks in Zombietown.* See as well the interviews collected in Philip Gaines and David J. Rhodes, *Micro-Budget Hollywood: Budgeting (and Making) Feature Films for $50,000 to $500,000* (Los Angeles: Silman-James, 1995).

John Pierson, a producer, distributor, and festival scout, traces how *Clerks; She's Gotta Have It; sex, lies, and videotape;* and other low-budget films found success in *Spike, Mike, Slackers, and Dykes* (New York: Hyperion Press, 1995). Emanuel Levy's *Cinema of Outsiders: The Rise of American Independent Film* (New York: New York University Press, 1999) provides a historical survey. The early history of an important distributor of independent films, Miramax, is examined in Alissa Perren, "sex, lies and marketing: Miramax and the Development of the Quality Indie Blockbuster," *Film Quarterly* 55, 2 (Winter 2001–2002): 30–39.

We can learn a great deal about production from careful case studies. See Rudy Behlmer, *America's Favorite Movies: Behind the Scenes* (New York: Ungar, 1982); Aljean Harmetz, *The Making of "The Wizard of Oz"* (New York: Limelight, 1984); John Sayles, *Thinking in Pictures: The Making of the Movie "Matewan"* (Boston: Houghton Mifflin, 1987); Ronald Haver, *"A Star Is Born": The Making of the 1954 Movie and Its 1985 Restoration* (New York: Knopf, 1988); Stephen Rebello, *Alfred Hitchcock and the Making of "Psycho"* (New York: Dembuer, 1990); Paul M. Sammon, *Future Noir: The Making of "Blade Runner"* (New York: HarperPrism, 1996); and Dan Auiler, *"Vertigo": The Making of a Hitchcock Classic* (New York: St. Martin's, 1998). John Gregory Dunne's *Monster: Living off the Big Screen* (New York: Vintage, 1997) is a memoir of eight years spent rewriting the script that became *Up Close and Personal*. Many of Spike Lee's productions have been documented with published journals and production notes; see, for example, *"Do The Right Thing": A Spike Lee Joint* (New York: Simon & Schuster, 1989). For the independent scene, Vachon's *Shooting to Kill,* mentioned above, documents the making of Todd Haynes's *Velvet Goldmine.*

Moviemakers Speak

Collections of interviews with filmmakers have become common in recent decades. We will mention interviews with designers, cinematographers, editors, sound technicians, and others in the chapters on individual film techniques. The director, however, supervises the entire process of filmmaking, so we list here some of the best interview books: Peter Bogdanovich, *Who the Devil Made It* (New York: Knopf, 1997); Mike Goodrich, *Directing* (Crans-Prés-Céligny, 2002); Jeremy Kagan, *Directors Close Up* (Boston: Focal Press, 2000); Andrew Sarris, ed., *Interviews with Film Directors* (Indianapolis: Bobbs-Merrill, 1967); and Gerald Duchovnay, *Film Voices: Interviews from Post Script* (Albany: SUNY Press, 2004). Paul Cronin has collected the writings of Alexander Mackendrick in *On Filmmaking* (London: Faber & Faber, 2004). Mackendrick was a fine director and a superb teacher, and the book offers incisive advice on all phases of production, from screenwriting ("Use coincidence to get characters into trouble, not out of trouble") to editing ("The geography of the scene must be immediately apparent to the audience"). See also Laurent Tirard, *Moviemakers' Master Class: Private Lessons from the World's Foremost Directors* (New York: Faber & Faber, 2002). Some important directors have written books on their craft, including Edward Dmytryk, *On Screen Directing* (Boston: Focal Press, 1984); David Mamet, *On Directing Film* (New York: Penguin, 1992); Sidney Lumet,

Making Movies (New York, Knopf, 1995); and Mike Figgis, *Digital Filmmaking* (New York: Faber & Faber, 2007).

Rick Lyman had the intriguing idea of asking a director or performer to choose a film and comment on it as it was screening. The results are in *Watching Movies: The Biggest Names in Cinema Talk About the Films That Matter Most* (New York: Henry Holt, 2003). See also Mark Cousins's *Scene by Scene: Film Actors and Directors Discuss Their Work* (London: Laurence King, 2002).

Screenwriting and Rules

In mass-production filmmaking, the screenwriter is expected to follow traditional storytelling patterns. For several decades, Hollywood has called for scripts about strong central characters who struggle to achieve well-defined goals. According to most experts, a script ought to have a three-act structure, with the first-act climax coming about a quarter of the way into the film, the second-act climax appearing about three-quarters of the way through, and the climax of the final act resolving the protagonist's problem. Writers will also be expected to include *plot points,* twists that turn the action in new directions.

These formulas are discussed in Syd Field, *Screenplay: The Foundations of Screenwriting* (New York: Delta, 1979); Linda Seger, *Making a Good Script Great* (New York: Dodd, Mead, 1987); and Michael Hauge, *Writing Screenplays That Sell* (New York: HarperCollins, 1988). Kristin Thompson has argued that many finished films have not three but four major parts, depending on how the protagonist defines and changes important goals. See her *Storytelling in the New Hollywood: Understanding Classical Narrative Technique* (Cambridge, MA: Harvard University Press, 1999). See also David Bordwell, *The Way Hollywood Tells It: Story and Style in Modern Movies* (Berkeley: University of California Press, 2006). Older but still useful books on screenwriting are Eugene Vale, *The Technique of Screenplay Writing* (New York: Grosset & Dunlap, 1972), and Lewis Herman, *A Practical Manual of Screen Playwriting for Theater and Television Films* (New York: New American Library, 1974).

Filmmaker J. J. Murphy identifies and examines the distinctive conventions of independent screenplay writing in *Me and You and Memento and Fargo: How Independent Screenplays Work* (New York: Continuum, 2007).

Roger Ebert provides an entertaining collection of overworked storytelling conventions in *Ebert's Little Movie Glossary* (Kansas City: Andrews & McMeel, 1994). Learn about "The Fallacy of the Talking Killer "and "The Moe Rule of Bomb Disposal."

Small-Scale Production

There are few studies of artisanal and collective film production, but here are some informative works. On Jean Rouch, see Mick Eaton, ed., *Anthropology—Reality—*

Cinema: The Films of Jean Rouch (London: British Film Institute, 1979). The makers of *Harlan County, U.S.A.* and other independent documentaries discuss their production methods in Alan Rosenthal, *The Documentary Conscience: A Casebook in Film Making* (Berkeley: University of California Press, 1980). Maya Deren's work is analyzed in P. Adams Sitney, *Visionary Film: The American Avant-Garde, 1943–2000,* 3rd ed. (New York: Oxford University Press, 2002). Stan Brakhage ruminates on his approach to filmmaking in *Brakhage Scrapbook: Collected Writings* (New Paltz, NY: Documentext, 1982). For information on other experimentalists, see Scott MacDonald, *A Critical Cinema: Interviews with Independent Filmmakers* (Berkeley: University of California Press, 1988), and David E. James, *Allegories of Cinema: American Film in the Sixties* (Princeton, NJ: Princeton University Press, 1989).

Collective film production is the subject of Bill Nichols, *Newsreel: Documentary Filmmaking on the American Left* (New York: Arno, 1980), and Michael Renov, "Newsreel: Old and New—Towards an Historical Profile," *Film Quarterly* 41, 1 (Fall 1987): 20–33. Collective production in film and other media is discussed in John Downing, *Radical Media: The Political Experience of Alternative Communication* (Boston: South End Press, 1984).

The DIY movement has largely been fostered on the Internet. For the DIY Film Festival, see its homepage, www .diyconvention.com/. The 48 Hour Film Project is here: www.48hourfilm.com/. Many of the films can be found on the website or on YouTube, where a search on either "DIY film" or "48 Hour Film Project" yields thousands of results. For a list of the cities that hold screenings of locally made 48 Hour films, see en.wikipedia.org/wiki/48_Hour_Film_Project. New Zealand has created its own version, 48Hours; see www.48hours.co.nz. Films from this festival can be found at YouTube by searching "48 Hour New Zealand."

Production Stills Versus Frame Enlargements

A film may live in our memory as much through photographs as through our experiences of the movie. The photograph may be a copy of a single frame taken from the finished film; this is usually called a *frame enlargement.* Most movie photographs we see in books and magazines, however, are *production stills,* images shot by a still photographer on the set.

Production stills are usually photographically clearer than frame enlargements, and they can be useful for studying details of setting or costume. But they differ from the image on the filmstrip. Usually, the still photographer rearranges and relights the actors and takes the shot from an angle and distance not comparable to that shown in the finished film. Frame enlargements therefore offer a much more faithful record of the finished film.

For example, both **1.57** and **1.58** have been used to illustrate discussion of Jean Renoir's *Rules of the Game.* In

1.57, a production still, the actors have been posed for the most balanced composition and the clearest view of all three. It is not, however, faithful to the finished film. The actual shot from the film is shown in 1.58. The frame enlargement shows that the composition is looser than that of the production still. The frame enlargement also reveals that Renoir uses the central doorway to suggest action taking place in depth. Here, as often happens, a production still does not capture important features of the director's visual style.

Virtually all of the photographs in this book are frame enlargements.

1.57 A production still from Renoir's *The Rules of the Game.*

1.58 A frame from *The Rules of the Game.*

Websites

General Reference

www.imdb.com/ A basic reference for films, people, and companies worldwide. The Power Search is particularly helpful. Not infallible, so double-check on other sites.

www.afi.chadwyck.com/ The American Film Institute catalogue of U.S. motion pictures. Offers detailed film-by-film information, including extensive plot synopses. Proprietary site accessed through libraries.

www.fii.chadwyck.com/ A Film Index International site containing bibliographical information about films and people. Accessed through libraries.

For a description of two useful podcasts on filmmaking and the movie industry, see "Movies on the radio," at www.davidbordwell.net/blog/?p=902.

On the Film Industry

www.cjr.org/tools/owners/ The *Columbia Journalism Review* site on media conglomerates, with up-to-date lists of holdings.

www.boxofficemojo.com/ Lists U.S. and international gross receipts for current films, as well as records of films released in previous decades.

www.indiewire.com/ Provides current information on U.S. independent cinema.

www.wis-kino.com/kino.htm/ Offers links to the worldwide Kino movement.

www.aintitcoolnews.com/ A popular film fansite hosted by Harry Knowles.

www.mpaa.org/ The official site of the major distribution companies, with heavy emphasis on antipiracy activities.

www.natoonline.org/ The official site of the National Association of Theatre Owners, with some statistics.

For a description of two useful podcasts on filmmaking and the movie industry, see "Movies on the radio," at www.davidbordwell.net/blog/?p=902.

Recommended DVDs

Sunday Morning Shootout: Best of Season 1. Peter Bart, editor of *Variety,* and Peter Guber of Mandalay Pictures discuss current industry trends. Our marginal quotation from Stacy Sher comes from the third disc in this set.

Recommended DVD Supplements

Before laser discs and DVDs, making-of documentaries weren't common, but some documentaries on older films have been put together using modern cast and crew interviews, finished footage, still photography, and other material. Excellent examples of these include "The Making of *American Graffiti,*" "The Making of *Jaws,*" "The Making of *Amadeus,*" "Guns for Hire: The Making of *The Magnificent Seven,*" and "Destination Hitchcock: The Making

of *North by Northwest.*" The supplements for *Alien* are grouped in "preproduction," "production," and "postproduction" sections, and a particularly good example of a screen test (Sigourney Weaver) is included. "The Making of *20,000 Leagues Under the Sea*" is one of several supplements on the DVD for that film, making it an unusually thorough treatment of an older film (1954).

Once the laser disc and especially the DVD age began, supplements came to be a part of the filmmaking process, with on-set footage and interviews planned in advance. A good early example is "The Making of *Jurassic Park,*" with its accompanying supplements. As the popularity of DVD supplements became apparent, longer and more systematic supplements were concocted. An outstanding example is "The Hundred Days" documentary for *Master and Commander.* The extended-edition DVDs for *The Lord of the Rings* raised the bar for in-depth coverage, with two supplemental discs for each entry in the trilogy.

Supplements often include storyboard images as galleries. Director Ridley Scott trained in painting and design, and some of the impressive storyboard images that he created for *Alien* are covered in its supplements. The "Story" section of *Toy Story*'s documentaries shows scenes of a storyboard artist explaining the action to the main filmmakers, with the sketches shown side-by-side with his presentation. Later the storyboard images are compared with the final images.

Many making-ofs stick to the most prominent parts of filmmaking: design, musical composition, casting. Occasionally, however, unusual aspects of the process receive coverage. Take animal wrangling. Horses are the obvious topic, and the "Home of the Horse Lords" track of the *Lord of the Rings: The Return of the King* deals with them. "Inside the Labyrinth," a making-of for *The Silence of the Lambs,* includes a moth wrangler. One of the funniest of such segments must be "Attack of the Squirrels" on the *Charlie and the Chocolate Factory* DVD.

Some unusual supplements include an unconventional production diary for the independent film *Magnolia* and an evocative 8-minute compilation, "T2: On the Set," of footage from the shooting of *Terminator 2: Judgment Day.* "The Making of *My Own Private Idaho*" demonstrates well how cost-cutting can be done on a low-budget indie.

As previsualization becomes more common, DVD supplements are beginning to include selections: "Previsualization" on the *War of the Worlds* disc (where the animatics run in split screen, beside finished footage), animatics for each part of *The Lord of the Rings,* and the "Day 27: Previsualization" entry in *King Kong: Peter Jackson's Production Diaries,* as well as a featurette on previz, "The Making of a Shot: The T-Rex Fight" (including the scene in 1.26).

The marketing of a film seldom gets described on DVD, apart from the fact that trailers and posters come with most discs. There are rare cases of coverage of the still photographer making publicity shots on-set: "Taking Testimonial Pictures" (*A Hard Day's Night*) and "Day 127: Unit Photography" (*King Kong: Peter Jackson's Production Diaries*). The same two DVDs include "Dealing with 'The Men from the Press,'" an interview with the Beatles' publicist, and "Day 53: International Press Junket," where *King Kong*'s unit publicist squires a group of reporters around a working set.

In general, the *King Kong: Peter Jackson's Production Diaries* discs deal with many specifics of filmmaking and distribution that we mention in this chapter: "Day 25: Clapperboards," "Day 62: Cameras" (where camera operators working on-set open their machines to show how they work), "Day 113: Second Unit," and "Day 110: Global Partner Summit," on a distributors' junket.

Agnès Varda includes a superb film-essay on the making of *Vagabond* in the French DVD, which bears the original title *Sans toit ni loi*. (Both the film and the supplements have English subtitles.) Director Varda's charmingly personal making-of covers the production, marketing, and showcasing of *Vagabond* at international film festivals. Varda also prepared an affectionate making-of featurette about her husband Jacques Demy's 1967 *Young Girls of Rochefort*, which is available on the British Film Institute's DVD release.

Hellboy II: The Golden Army has a lengthy making-of documentary, "*Hellboy*: In Service of the Demon," that touches on most phases of production. *Pirates of the Caribbean: Dead Man's Chest* has two detailed, surprisingly candid supplements: "Charting the Return," on preproduction, and "According to Plan," on principal photography. *The Golden Compass* has a series of short documentaries that are more interesting than their bland titles suggest. "Finding Lyra Belacqua" traces the casting process rather than simply showing audition tapes; "The Launch" deals briefly with press junkets and even interviews a junket producer. Other useful making-ofs are "Deciphering Zodiac" (*Zodiac*) and "I Am Iron Man" (*Iron Man*).

For more details on some of the supplements we have recommended in *Film Art*, see "Beyond praise: DVD supplements that really tell you something," at www.davidbordwell.net/blog/?p=1339, and "Beyond praise 2: More DVD supplements that really tell you something," at www.davidbordwell.net/blog/?p=4004. On the DVD of *The Da Vinci Code*, discussed in that entry, see "Another little *Da Vinci Code* mystery," at www.davidbordwell.net/blog/?p=224. Further entries in this series will be added occasionally.

2

Chapter 1 outlined some ways in which people, working with technology, make films. Now we can get a little more abstract and ask other questions. By what principles is a film put together? How do the various parts relate to one another to create a whole? Answering these questions will help us understand how we respond to individual movies and how cinema works as an artistic medium.

In the next two chapters, we will start to answer such questions. We assume that a film is not a random collection of elements. If it were, viewers would not care if they missed the beginnings or endings of films or if films were projected out of sequence. But viewers do care. When you describe a book as "hard to put down" or a piece of music as "compelling," you are implying that a pattern exists there, that some overall logic governs the relations among parts and engages your interest. This system of relationships among parts we shall call *form*. Chapter 2 examines form in film to see what makes that concept so important to the understanding of cinema as an art.

Film Form

Although there are several ways of organizing films into unified formal wholes, the one that we most commonly encounter in films involves telling a story. Chapter 3 examines how *narrative form* can arouse our interest and coax us to follow a series of events from start to finish. Narrative form holds out the expectation that these events are headed toward dramatic changes and a satisfying outcome.

CHAPTER

The Significance of Film Form

The experience that art offers us can be intensely involving. We say that movies *draw us in* or *immerse us*. We get absorbed in a book or lost in a song. When we can't finish a novel, we say, "I couldn't get into it," and we say that music we don't like "doesn't speak to me," as if it were a sluggish conversational partner.

All these ways of talking suggest that artworks involve us by engaging our senses, feelings, and mind in a process. That process sharpens our interest, tightens our involvement, urges us forward. How does this happen? Because the artist has created a pattern. Artworks arouse and gratify our human craving for form. Artists design their works—they give them form—so that we can have a structured experience.

For this reason, form is of central importance in any artwork, regardless of its medium. The idea of artistic form has occupied the thinking of philosophers, artists, and critics for centuries. We can't do justice to it here, but some well-established ideas about form are very helpful for understanding films. This chapter reviews them.

The Concept of Form in Film

Form as System

Artistic form is best thought of in relation to the human being who watches the play, reads the novel, listens to the piece of music, or views the film. Perception in all phases of life is an *activity*. As you walk down the street, you scan your surroundings for salient aspects—a friend's face, a familiar landmark, a sign of rain. The mind is never at rest. It is constantly seeking order and significance, testing the world for breaks in the habitual pattern.

Artworks rely on this dynamic, unifying quality of the human mind. They provide organized occasions in which we exercise and develop our ability to pay attention, to anticipate upcoming events, to construct a whole out of parts, and to feel an emotional response to that whole. Every novel leaves something to the imagination. A song asks us to expect certain developments in the melody. A film coaxes us to connect sequences into a larger whole. But how does this process work? How does an inert object—the poem on a piece of paper or the sculpture in the park—draw us into such activities?

Some answers are clearly inadequate. Our activity cannot be *in* the artwork itself. A poem is only words on paper; a song, just acoustic vibrations; a film, merely

patterns of light and dark on a screen. Objects do nothing. Evidently, then, the artwork and the person experiencing it depend on each other.

The best answer to our question would seem to be that the artwork *cues* us to perform a specific activity. Without the artwork's prompting, we couldn't start the process or keep it going. Without our playing along and picking up the cues, the artwork remains only an artifact. A painting uses color, lines, and other techniques to invite us to imagine the space portrayed or to run our eye over the composition in a certain direction. A poem's words may guide us to imagine a scene, to notice a break in rhythm, or to expect a rhyme.

Like a painting or a poem, a film employs cues in order to involve us. At the start of *Collateral,* the taxi driver Max is shown wiping down his cab's dashboard and steering wheel before setting out on his night shift. He then carefully attaches a snapshot to his sun visor. For a moment, he simply gazes at the postcard view of a tropical island. These gestures prompt us to see Max's personality as neat and orderly. They also suggest that in the city's turmoil, he clears a quiet mental space for himself. The next scene's cues reinforce our judgment of Max's character. While a couple quarrel in the back seat, he tips down the visor and stares at the island vista, as if to shut out the unpleasantness behind him.

We can go further in describing how an artwork cues us to perform activities. These cues are not simply random; they are organized into *systems.* In any system, a group of elements affects one another. The human body is one such system; if one component, the heart, ceases to function, all of the other parts will be in danger. Within the body, there are individual, smaller systems, such as the nervous system or the optical system. One small malfunction in a car's workings may bring the whole machine to a standstill; the other parts may not need repair, but the whole system depends on the operation of each part. More abstract sets of relationships also constitute systems, such as a body of laws governing a country or the ecological balance of the wildlife in a lake.

As with each of these instances, a film is not simply a random batch of elements. Like all artworks, a film has **form.** By film form, in its broadest sense, we mean the overall system of relations that we can perceive among the elements in the whole film. In this part of the book and in Part Three (on film style), we survey the elements that interact with one another. Since the viewer makes sense of the film by recognizing these elements and reacting to them in various ways, we'll also be considering how form and style participate in the spectator's experience.

This description of form is still very abstract, so let's draw some examples from one movie that many people have seen. In *The Wizard of Oz,* the viewer can notice many particular elements. There is, most obviously, a set of *narrative* elements; these constitute the film's story. Dorothy dreams that a tornado blows her to Oz, where she has adventures. The narrative continues to the point where Dorothy awakens from her dream to find herself home in Kansas. We can also pick out a set of *stylistic* elements: the way the camera moves, the patterns of color in the frame, the use of music, and other devices. Stylistic elements utilize the various film techniques we'll be considering in later chapters.

Because *The Wizard of Oz* is a system and not just a hodgepodge, we actively relate the elements within each set to one another. We link and compare narrative elements. We see the tornado as causing Dorothy's trip to Oz; we identify the characters in Oz as similar to characters in Dorothy's Kansas life. Various stylistic elements can also be connected. For instance, we recognize the "We're Off to See the Wizard" tune whenever Dorothy picks up a new companion. We attribute unity to the film by positing two organizing principles—a narrative one and a stylistic one—within the larger system of the total film.

Moreover, our minds seek to tie these systems to one another. In *The Wizard of Oz,* the narrative development can be linked to the stylistic patterning. Colors identify prominent landmarks, such as Kansas (in black and white) and the Yellow Brick

"Screenplays are structure."

— William Goldman, scriptwriter, *Butch Cassidy and the Sundance Kid*

"Because of my character, I have always been interested in the engineering of direction. I loved hearing about how [director] Mark Sandrich would draw charts of Fred Astaire's musicals to work out where to put the dance numbers. What do you want the audience to understand? How do you make things clear? How do you structure sequences within a film? Afterwards—what have you got away with?"

— Stephen Frears, director, *The Grifters*

Road. Movements of the camera call our attention to story action. And the music serves to describe certain characters and situations. It is the overall pattern of relationships among the various elements that makes up the form of *The Wizard of Oz*.

"Form" Versus "Content"

Very often people think of "form" as the opposite of something called "content." This implies that a poem or a musical piece or a film is like a jug. An external shape, the jug, *contains* something that could just as easily be held in a cup or a pail. Under this assumption, form becomes less important than whatever it's presumed to contain.

We don't accept this assumption. If form is the total system that the viewer attributes to the film, there is no inside or outside. Every component *functions as part of the overall pattern* that engages the viewer. So we'll treat as formal elements many things that some people consider content. From our standpoint, subject matter and abstract ideas all enter into the total system of the artwork. They may cue us to frame certain expectations or draw certain inferences. The viewer relates such elements to one another dynamically. Consequently, subject matter and ideas become somewhat different from what they might be outside the work.

Consider a historical subject, such as the American Civil War. The real Civil War may be studied, its causes and consequences disputed. But in a film such as D. W. Griffith's *The Birth of a Nation*, the Civil War is not neutral content. It enters into relationships with other elements: a story about two families, political ideas about the Reconstruction, and the epic film style of the battle scenes. Griffith's film depicts the Civil War in a way that is coordinated with other elements in the film. A different film by another filmmaker might draw on the same subject matter, the Civil War, but there the subject would play a different role in a different formal system. In *Gone with the Wind*, the Civil War functions as a backdrop for the heroine's romance, but in *The Good, the Bad, and the Ugly*, the war aids three cynical men in their search for gold. Thus subject matter is shaped by the film's formal context and our perceptions of it.

Formal Expectations

We're now in a better position to see how film form guides the audience's activity. Why does an interrupted song or an uncompleted story frustrate us? Because of our urge for form. We realize that the system of relationships within the work has not yet been completed. Something more is needed to make the form whole and satisfying. We have been caught up in the interrelations among elements, and we want to develop and complete the patterns.

One way in which form affects our experience, then, is to create the sense that "everything is there." Why is it satisfying when a character glimpsed early in a film reappears an hour later, or when a shape in the frame is balanced by another shape? Because such relations among parts suggest that the film has its own organizing laws or rules—its own system.

Moreover, an artwork's form creates a special sort of involvement on the part of the spectator. In everyday life, we perceive things around us in a practical way. But in a film, the things that happen on the screen serve no such practical end for us. We can see them differently. In life, if someone fell down on the street, we would probably hurry to help the person up. But in a film, when Buster Keaton or Charlie Chaplin falls, we laugh. We shall see in Chapter 5 how even as basic an act of filmmaking as framing a shot creates a particular way of seeing. We watch a pattern that is no longer just "out there" in the everyday world; it has become a calculated part within a self-contained whole. Film form can even make us perceive things anew, shaking us out of our accustomed habits and suggesting fresh ways of hearing, seeing, feeling, and thinking.

"Now, if you're going to do action films, a certain amount of repetition, which certainly is a kind of straitjacket, is inevitable. You are going to have to deal with gunfights and chases. . . . So it becomes a kind of game. The audience knows what the conclusion will be, but you still have to entertain them. So you are always walking on the edge of a precipice—trying to juggle the genre expectations. . . ."

— Walter Hill, director, *The Driver* and *The Warriors*

To get a sense of the ways in which purely formal features can involve the audience, try the following experiment. Assume that "A" is the first letter of a series. What follows?

AB

"A" was a cue, and on this basis, you made a formal hypothesis, probably that the letters would run in alphabetical order. Your expectation was confirmed. What follows AB? Most people would say "C." But form does not always follow our initial expectation:

ABA

Here form takes us a little by surprise. If we are puzzled by a formal development, we readjust our expectations and try again. What follows ABA?

ABAC

Here the main possibilities were either ABAB or ABAC. (Note that your expectations *limit* possibilities as well as select them.) If you expected ABAC, your expectation was gratified, and you can confidently predict the next letter. If you expected ABAB, you still should be able to make a strong hypothesis about the next letter:

ABACA

Simple as this game is, it illustrates the involving power of form. You as a viewer or listener don't simply let the parts parade past you. You enter into an active participation with them, creating and readjusting expectations as the pattern develops.

Now consider a story in a film. *The Wizard of Oz* begins with Dorothy running down a road with her dog **(2.1)**. Immediately, we form *expectations*. Perhaps she will meet another character or arrive at her destination. Even such a simple action asks the audience to participate actively in the ongoing process by wondering about what will happen next and readjusting expectations accordingly. Much later in the film, we come to expect that Dorothy will get her wish to return to Kansas. Indeed, the settings of the film give *The Wizard of Oz* a large-scale ABA form: Kansas-Oz-Kansas.

Expectation pervades our experience of art. In reading a mystery, we expect that a solution will be offered at some point, usually the end. In listening to a piece of music, we expect repetition of a melody or a motif. (Songs that alternate verses and refrains follow the ABACA pattern we have just outlined.) In looking at a painting, we search for what we expect to be the most significant features, then scan the less prominent portions. From beginning to end, our involvement with a work of art depends largely on expectations.

This does not mean that the expectations must be immediately satisfied. The satisfaction of our expectations may be delayed. In our alphabet exercise, instead of presenting ABA, we might have presented this:

AB . . .

The ellipsis puts off the revelation of the next letter, and you must wait to find it out. What we normally call *suspense* involves a delay in fulfilling an established expectation. As the term implies, suspense leaves something suspended—not only the next element in a pattern but also our urge for completion.

Expectations may also be cheated, as when we expect ABC but get ABA. In general, *surprise* is a result of an expectation that is revealed to be incorrect. We do not expect that a gangster in 1930s Chicago will find a rocket ship in his garage; if he does, our reaction may require us to readjust our assumptions about what can happen in this story. (This example suggests that comedy often depends on cheating expectations.)

One more pattern of our expectations needs tracing. Sometimes an artwork will cue us to hazard guesses about what has come *before* this point in the work. When Dorothy runs down the road at the beginning of *The Wizard of Oz*, we wonder

"The idea of suspense is closely bound up with the idea of fiction. This is as it should be: to tell a story is to create suspense, and the art of the story-teller resides in this ability to make dull subjects sound entertaining and plots whose solution everyone knows in advance, exciting."

— Thomas Mann

2.1 Dorothy pauses while fleeing with Toto at the beginning of *The Wizard of Oz.*

CONNECT TO THE BLOG
Why is it that we feel suspense even if we're rewatching a film and know the outcome? We talk about why that happens in "This is your brain on movies, maybe."

See www.davidbordwell.net/blog/?p=300.

not only where she is going but where she's been and what she's fleeing from. Similarly, a painting or photograph may depict a scene that asks the viewer to speculate on some earlier event. Let's call this ability of the spectator to wonder about prior events *curiosity*. As Chapter 3 will show, curiosity is an important factor in narrative form.

Already we have several possible ways in which the artwork can actively engage us. Artistic form may cue us to make expectations and then gratify them. They may be gratified quickly or after a delay. Or form may work to disturb our expectations. We often associate art with peace and serenity, but many artworks offer us conflict, tension, and shock. An artwork's form may even strike us as unpleasant because of its imbalances or contradictions. For example, experimental films may jar rather than soothe us. Viewers frequently feel puzzled or shocked by *Eat, Scorpio Rising,* and other avant-garde works (pp. 366–367). And we'll encounter similar problems when we examine the editing of Sergei Eisenstein's *October* (Chapter 6) and the style of Jean-Loc Godard's *Breathless* (Chapter 11).

Yet even in disturbing us, such films still arouse and shape formal expectations. For example, on the basis of our experience of most movie stories, we expect that the main characters introduced in the first half of a film will be present in the second half. Yet this does not happen in Wong Kar-wai's *Chungking Express* (pp. 445–446). When our expectations are thwarted, we may feel disoriented, but then we adjust them to look for other, more appropriate, ways of engaging with the film's form.

If we can adjust our expectations to a disorienting work, it may involve us deeply. Our uneasiness may lessen as we get accustomed to a work's unusual formal system. Hollis Frampton's *Zorns Lemma,* for example, slowly trains the viewer to associate a series of images with the letters of the alphabet. Viewers often become quite absorbed in watching the series take shape as a cinematic picture puzzle. As *Chungking Express* and *Zorns Lemma* also suggest, a disturbing work can reveal to us our normal expectations about form. Such films are valuable because they coax us to reflect on our taken-for-granted assumptions about how a movie must behave.

There is no limit to the number of ways in which a film can be organized. Some films will ask us to recast our expectations in drastic ways. Still, our enjoyment of the cinema can increase if we welcome the unfamiliar experiences offered by formally challenging films.

Conventions and Experience

Our ABAC example illustrates still another point. One guide to your expectations is your *prior experience.* Your knowledge of the English alphabet makes ABA an unlikely sequence. This fact suggests that aesthetic form is not a pure activity isolated from other experiences.

Because artworks are human creations and because the artist lives in history and society, he or she cannot avoid relating the work, in some way, to other works and to aspects of the world in general. A tradition, a dominant style, a popular form—some such elements will be common to several different artworks. These common traits are usually called *conventions.* For example, the first few scenes of a film often explain background information about the characters and the action; this sort of exposition is a narrative convention. *Genres,* as we will see in Chapter 9, depend heavily on conventions. Urban crime thrillers tend to feature spectacular car crashes, so Michael Mann's use of the device in *Collateral* (p. 28) accords with that genre convention. It's a convention of the musical film that characters sing and dance, as in *The Wixard of Oz.* It's one convention of narrative form that the conclusion solves the problems that the characters confront, and *Wizard* likewise accepts this convention by letting Dorothy return to Kansas.

If the filmmaker can't avoid connecting to both art and the larger world, neither can the audience. When we respond to cues in the film, we call on our prior experiences of everyday life and of other artworks. You were able to play the ABAC

CONNECT TO THE BLOG
Slumdog Millionaire uses many conventions in novel ways, as we show in "Slumdogged by the past."
See www.davidbordwell.net/blog/?p=3592.

game because you had learned the alphabet. You may have learned it in everyday life (in a classroom or from your parents) or from an artwork (as some children now learn the alphabet from television cartoons). Similarly, we are able to recognize the journey pattern in *The Wizard of Oz*. We've taken trips and we've seen other films organized around this pattern (such as *Stagecoach* or *North by Northwest*), and the convention is to be found in other artworks, such as Homer's *Odyssey* and J.R.R. Tolkien's *The Lord of the Rings*.

In recognizing film form, then, the audience must be prepared to understand formal cues through knowledge of life and of other artworks. But what if the two principles come into conflict? In ordinary life, people don't simply start to sing and dance, as they do in *The Wizard of Oz*. Very often conventions demarcate art from life, saying implicitly, "In artworks of this sort, the laws of everyday reality don't operate. By the rules of *this* game, something 'unreal' *can* happen." All stylized art, from opera, ballet, and pantomime to slapstick comedy, depends on the audience's willingness to suspend the laws of ordinary experience and to accept particular conventions. It is simply beside the point to insist that such conventions are unreal or to ask why Tristan sings to Isolde or why Buster Keaton doesn't smile. Very often the most relevant prior experience for perceiving form is not everyday experience but previous encounters with works having similar conventions.

Further, artworks can create new conventions. A highly innovative work can at first seem odd because it refuses to conform to the norms we expect. Cubist painting, the French "New Novel" of the 1950s, and ambient music seemed bizarre initially because of their refusal to adhere to conventions. But a closer look may show that an unusual artwork has its own rules, creating an unorthodox formal system that we can learn to recognize and respond to. Eventually, the new systems offered by such unusual works may themselves furnish conventions and thus create new expectations.

> "To a story-teller a journey is a marvelous device. It provides a strong thread on which a multitude of things that he has in mind may be strung to make a new thing, various, unpredictable, and yet coherent. My chief reason for using this form was technical."
>
> — J.R.R. Tolkien

Form and Feeling

Certainly, emotion plays a large role in our experience of form. To understand this role, let's distinguish between *emotions represented* in the artwork and an *emotional response* felt by the spectator. If an actor grimaces in agony, the emotion of pain is represented within the film. If, however, the viewer who sees the painful expression laughs (as the viewer of a comedy might), the emotion of amusement is felt by the spectator. Both types of emotion have formal implications.

Emotions represented within the film interact as parts of the film's total system. For example, that grimace of pain might be consistent with the character's response to bad news. A character's sly expression may prepare us for the later revelation of his or her villainous side. Or a cheerful scene might stand in contrast to a mournful one. A tragic event might be undercut by light-hearted music. All emotions present in a film may be seen as systematically related to one another through that film's form.

The spectator's emotional response to the film is related to form as well. We have just seen how cues in the artwork interact with our prior experience, especially our experience of artistic conventions. Often form in artworks appeals to ready-made reactions to certain images (for example, involving sexuality, race, or social class). But form can create new responses instead of harping on old ones. Just as formal conventions often lead us to suspend our normal sense of real-life experience, so form may lead us to override our everyday emotional responses. People whom we would despise in life may become spellbinding as characters in a film. We can be enthralled by a film about a subject that normally bores us. One cause of these experiences lies in the systematic way we become involved in form. In *The Wizard of Oz,* we might, for example, find the land of Oz far more attractive than Kansas. But because the film's form leads us to sympathize with Dorothy in her desire to go home, we feel great satisfaction when she finally returns to Kansas.

It is first and foremost the dynamic aspect of form that engages our feelings. Expectation, for instance, spurs emotion. To have an expectation about "what happens next" is to invest some emotion in the situation. Delayed fulfillment of an expectation—suspense—may produce anxiety or sympathy. (Will the detective find the criminal? Will boy get girl? Will the melody return?) Gratified expectations may produce a feeling of satisfaction or relief. (The detective solves the mystery; boy does get girl; the melody returns one more time.) Cheated expectations and curiosity about past material may produce puzzlement or keener interest. (So he isn't the detective? This isn't a romance story? Has a second melody replaced the first one?)

Note that all of these possibilities *may* occur. There is no general recipe for concocting a novel or film to produce the "correct" emotional response. It is all a matter of context—that is, of the particular system that is each artwork's overall form. All we can say for certain is that the emotion felt by the spectator will emerge from the totality of formal relationships she or he perceives in the work. This is one reason why we should try to notice as many formal relations as possible in a film; the richer our perception, the deeper and more complex our response may become.

Taken in context, the relations between the feelings represented in the film and those felt by the spectator can be quite complicated. Let's take an example. Many people believe that no more sorrowful event can occur than the death of a child. In most films, this event would be represented so as to summon up the sadness we would also feel in life. But the power of artistic form can alter the emotional tenor of even this event. In Jean Renoir's *The Crime of M. Lange,* the cynical publisher Batala rapes and abandons Estelle, a young laundress. After Batala disappears, Estelle becomes integrated into the neighborhood and returns to her former fiancé. But Estelle is pregnant by Batala and bears his child.

The scene when Estelle's employer, Valentine, announces that the child was born dead is one of the most emotionally complex in cinema. The first reactions represented are solemnity and sorrow **(2.2)**. Suddenly, Batala's cousin remarks, "Too bad. It was a relative." In the film's context, this is taken as a joke **(2.3)**. The shift in the emotion represented in the film catches us off guard. Since these characters are not heartless, we must readjust our reaction to the death and respond as they do—with relief. Estelle's survival is far more important than the death of Batala's child. The film's formal development has rendered appropriate a reaction that might be perverse in ordinary life. This is a daring, extreme example, but it dramatically illustrates how both emotions onscreen and our responses depend on the context created by form.

2.2   In *The Crime of M. Lange,* the neighbors initially display grief at the news of Batala and Estelle's baby.

2.3   The same characters soon break out in smiles and laughter in reaction to Batala's cousin's remark.

Form and Meaning

Like emotion, **meaning** is important to our experience of artworks. As an alert perceiver, the spectator is constantly testing the work for larger significance, for what it says or suggests. The sorts of meanings that the spectator attributes to a film may vary considerably. Let's look at four things we might say about the meaning of *The Wizard of Oz.*

1. *Referential meaning. During the Depression, a tornado takes a girl from her family's Kansas farm to the mythical land of Oz. After a series of adventures, she returns home.*

This is very concrete, close to a bare-bones plot summary. Here the meaning depends on the spectator's ability to identify specific items: the hard times of America in the 1930s and features of midwestern climate. A viewer unacquainted with such information would miss some of the meanings cued by the film. We can call such tangible meanings *referential,* since the film refers to things or places already invested with significance.

A film's subject matter—in *The Wizard of Oz,* American farm life in the 1930s—is often established through referential meaning. And, as you might expect, referential meaning functions within the film's overall form, in the way that we have argued that the subject of the Civil War functions within *The Birth of a Nation*. Suppose that instead of having Dorothy live in flat, spare, rural Kansas, the film made Dorothy a child living in Beverly Hills. When she got to Oz (transported there, perhaps, by a hillside flash flood), the contrast between the crowded opulence of Oz and her home would not have been nearly as sharp. Here the referential meanings of Kansas play a definite role in the overall contrast of settings that the film's form creates.

2. Explicit meaning. *A girl dreams of leaving home to escape her troubles. Only after she leaves does she realize how much she loves her family and friends.*

This assertion is still fairly concrete in the meaning it attributes to the film. If someone were to ask you the *point* of the film—what it seems to be trying to get across—you might answer with something like this. Perhaps you would also mention Dorothy's closing line, "There's no place like home," as a summary of what she has learned. Let us call this sort of openly asserted meaning an *explicit meaning*.

Like referential meanings, explicit meanings function within the film's overall form. They are defined by context. For instance, we might want to take "There's no place like home" as a statement of the meaning of the entire film. But, first, *why* do we take that as a strongly meaningful line? In ordinary conversation, it's a cliché. In context, however, the line gains great force. It's uttered in close-up, it comes at the end of the film (a formally privileged moment), and it refers back to all of Dorothy's desires and ordeals, recalling the film's narrative movement toward her goal. It is the *form* of the film that gives the homily an unfamiliar weight.

This example suggests that we must examine how explicit meanings in a film interact with other elements of the overall system. If "There's no place like home" adequately and exhaustively summarizes the meaning of *The Wizard of Oz,* no one need ever see the film; the summary would suffice. But like feelings, meanings are born from the dynamics of form. They play a part along with other elements to make up the total system.

Usually, we can't isolate a particularly significant moment and declare it to be *the* meaning of the whole film. Dorothy's "There's no place like home," however strong as a summary of *one* meaningful element in *The Wizard of Oz,* must be placed in the context of the film's entire beguiling Oz fantasy. If "There's no place like home" were the whole point of the film, why is there so much that is pleasant in Oz? The explicit meanings of a film arise from the *whole* film and are set in dynamic formal relation to one another.

In trying to see the meaningful moments of a film as parts of a larger whole, it's useful to set individually significant moments against one another. Thus Dorothy's final line could be juxtaposed to the scene of the characters getting spruced up after their arrival at the Emerald City. We can try to see the film as about not one or the other, but rather the relation of the two—the delight and risk of a fantasy world versus the comfort and stability of home. Thus the film's total system is larger than any one explicit meaning we can find in it. Instead of asking, "What is this film's meaning?" we can ask, "How do *all* the film's meanings relate to one another?"

3. Implicit meaning. *An adolescent who must soon face the adult world yearns for a return to the simple world of childhood, but she eventually accepts the demands of growing up.*

This is more abstract than the first two statements. It goes beyond what is explicitly stated in the film, suggesting that *The Wizard of Oz* is in some sense about the passage from childhood to adulthood. In this view, the film suggests or implies that, in adolescence, people may desire to return to the apparently uncomplicated world of childhood. Dorothy's frustration with her aunt and uncle and her urge to flee to a place "over the rainbow" become examples of a general conception of adolescence. Unlike the "no place like home" line, this meaning isn't stated directly. We can call this suggestion an *implicit meaning.* When perceivers ascribe implicit meanings to an artwork, they're usually said to be *interpreting* it.

Clearly, **interpretations** vary. One viewer might propose that *The Wizard of Oz* is really about adolescence. Another might suggest that it is really about courage and persistence, or that it is a satire on the adult world. One of the appeals of artworks is that they ask us to interpret them, often in several ways at once. Again, the artwork invites us to perform certain activities—here, building up implicit meanings. But once again, the artwork's overall form shapes our sense of implicit meanings.

Some viewers approach a film expecting to learn lessons about life. They may admire a film because it conveys a profound or relevant message. But once we identify a film's meaning, we're often tempted to split up the film into the content portion (the meaning) and the form (the vehicle for the content). The abstract quality of implicit meanings can lead to very broad concepts, often called *themes.* A film may have as its theme courage or the power of faithful love. Such descriptions have some value, but they are very general; hundreds of films fit them. To summarize *The Wizard of Oz* as being simply about the problems of adolescence does not do justice to the specific qualities of the film as an experience. We suggest that the search for implicit meanings should not leave behind the *particular* and *concrete* features of a film.

This is not to say that we should not interpret films. But we should strive to make our interpretations precise by seeing how each film's thematic meanings are suggested by the film's total system. In a film, both explicit and implicit meanings depend closely on the relations between narrative and style. In *The Wizard of Oz,* the Yellow Brick Road has no meaning in and of itself. But if we examine the function it fulfills in relation to the narrative, the music, the colors, and so on, we can argue that the Yellow Brick Road does indeed function meaningfully. Dorothy's strong desire to go home makes the road represent that desire. We want Dorothy to be successful in getting to the end of the road, as well as in getting back to Kansas; thus the road participates in the theme of the desirability of home.

Interpretation need not be an end in itself. It also helps in understanding the overall form of the film. Nor does interpretation exhaust the possibilities of a device. We can say many things about the Yellow Brick Road other than how its meaning relates to the film's thematic material. We could note that the road marks Oz as a fantastical land, since real-world bricks are a brownish-red color. We could analyze how the road becomes the stage for dances and songs along the way. We could see how it is narratively important because Dorothy's indecision at a crossroads allows her to meet the Scarecrow. We could work out a color scheme for the film, contrasting the yellow road, the red slippers, the green Emerald City, and so forth. From this standpoint, interpretation may be seen as one kind of formal analysis, one that seeks to reveal a film's implicit meanings. Those meanings should be constantly tested by placing them within the concrete texture of the whole film.

4. *Symptomatic meaning. In a society in which human worth is measured by money, the home and the family may seem to be the last refuge of human values. This belief is especially strong in times of economic crisis, such as that in the United States in the 1930s.*

Like statement 3, this is abstract and general. It situates the film within a trend of thought that is assumed to be characteristic of American society during the 1930s. The claim could apply equally well to many other films, as well as to many novels, plays, poems, paintings, advertisements, radio shows, political speeches, and a host of cultural products of the period.

But there is something else worth noticing about the statement. It treats an explicit meaning in *The Wizard of Oz* ("There's no place like home") as a manifestation of a wider set of values characteristic of a whole society. We could treat implicit meanings the same way. If we say the film implies something about adoles-

"Critics enable us to see how parts of an artwork serve larger designs. Often this requires that the critics offer interpretations or explications of the larger aims of the work, but these overviews are often introduced, in large measure, in order to explain why the works have the parts they do."

— Noël Carroll, philosopher of art

cence as a crucial time of transition, we could suggest that emphasis on adolescence as a special period of life is also a recurrent concern of American society. So, it's possible to understand a film's explicit or implicit meanings as bearing traces of a particular set of social values. We can call this *symptomatic meaning,* and the set of values that get revealed can be considered a social **ideology.**

The possibility of noticing symptomatic meanings reminds us that meaning, whether referential, explicit, or implicit, is largely a social phenomenon. Many meanings of films are ultimately ideological; that is, they spring from systems of culturally specific beliefs about the world. Religious beliefs, political opinions, conceptions of race or sex or social class, even our most deeply seated notions of life's values—all these constitute our ideological frame of reference. Although we may live as if our beliefs were the only true and real explanations of how the world is, we need only compare our own ideology with that of another group or culture or era to see how historically and socially shaped many of those views are. In other times and places, *home* and *adolescence* don't carry the meanings they carried in 1930s America.

Films, like other artworks, can be examined for their symptomatic meanings. Again, however, the abstract and general quality of such meanings can lead us away from the concrete form of the film. As when we analyze implicit meanings, we should ground symptomatic meanings in the film's specific aspects. A film *enacts* ideological meanings through its particular and unique formal system. We'll see in Chapter 11 how the narrative and stylistic system of *Meet Me in St. Louis* can be analyzed for ideological implications.

To sum up: Films have meaning because we attribute meanings to them. We cannot therefore regard meaning as a simple content to be extracted from the film. Sometimes the filmmaker guides us toward certain meanings; sometimes we find meanings the filmmaker didn't intend. Our minds will probe an artwork for significance at several levels. One mark of our engagement with the film as an experience is our search for referential, explicit, implicit, and symptomatic meanings. The more abstract and general our attributions of meaning, the more we risk loosening our grasp on the film's specific formal system. In analyzing films, we should balance our concern for that concrete system with our urge to assign it wider significance.

Evaluation

In talking about an artwork, people often *evaluate* it; that is, they make claims about its goodness or badness. Reviews in newspapers and magazines and on the Internet exist almost solely to tell us whether a film is worth seeing; our friends often urge us to go to their latest favorite. But all too often we discover that the film that someone else esteemed appears only mediocre to us. At that point, we may complain that most people evaluate films only on the basis of their own, highly personal, tastes.

How, then, are we to evaluate films with any degree of objectivity? We can start by realizing that there is a difference between *personal taste* and *evaluative judgment.* To say "I liked this film" or "I hated it" is not equal to saying "It's a good film" or "It's wretched." Very few of us limit our enjoyment to the greatest works. Most people can enjoy a film they know is not particularly good. This is perfectly reasonable—unless they start trying to convince people that these pleasant films actually rank among the undying masterpieces. At that point, others will probably stop listening to their judgments at all.

So personal preference need not be the sole basis for judging a film's quality. Instead, the critic who wishes to make a relatively objective evaluation will use specific *criteria.* A criterion is a standard that can be applied in the judgment of many works. By using a criterion, the critic gains a basis for comparing films for relative quality.

There are many different criteria. Some people evaluate films on *realistic* criteria. Aficionados of military history might judge a film entirely on whether the battle scenes use historically accurate weaponry; the narrative, editing, characterization, sound, and visual style might be of little interest to them.

Other people condemn films because they don't find the action plausible. They dismiss a scene by saying, "Who'd really believe that X would meet Y just at the right moment?" We have already seen, though, that artworks often violate laws of reality and operate by their own conventions and internal rules. Coincidental encounters, usually at embarrassing moments, are a convention of comedy.

Viewers can also use *moral* criteria to evaluate films. Most narrowly, aspects of the film can be judged outside their context in the film's formal system. Some viewers might feel that any film with nudity or profanity or violence is bad, while other viewers might find just these aspects praiseworthy. So some viewers might condemn the death of the newborn baby in *The Crime of M. Lange,* regardless of the scene's context. More broadly, viewers and critics may employ moral criteria to evaluate a film's overall significance, and here the film's complete formal system becomes pertinent. A film might be judged good because of its overall view of life, its willingness to show opposing points of view, or its emotional range.

While realistic and moral criteria are well suited to particular purposes, this book suggests criteria that assess films as artistic wholes. Such criteria should allow us to take each film's form into account as much as possible. *Coherence* is one such criterion. This quality, often referred to as *unity,* has traditionally been held to be a positive feature of artworks. So, too, has *intensity of effect.* If an artwork is vivid, striking, and emotionally engaging, it may be considered more valuable.

Another criterion is *complexity.* We can argue that, all other things being equal, complex films are good. A complex film engages our interest on many levels, creates a multiplicity of relations among many separate formal elements, and tends to create intriguing patterns of feelings and meanings.

Yet another formal criterion is *originality.* Originality for its own sake is pointless, of course. Just because something is different does not mean that it is good. But if an artist takes a familiar convention and uses it in a way that makes it a fresh experience, then (all other things being equal) the resulting work may be considered good from an aesthetic standpoint.

Note that all these criteria are matters of degree. One film may be more complex than another, but the simpler film may be more complex than a third one. Moreover, there is often a give-and-take among the criteria. A film might be complex but lack coherence or intensity. Ninety minutes of a black screen would make for an original film but not a very complex one. A slasher movie may create great intensity in certain scenes but may be wholly unoriginal, as well as disorganized and simplistic. In applying the criteria, the analyst often must weigh one against another.

Evaluation can serve many useful ends. It can call attention to neglected artworks or make us rethink our attitudes toward accepted classics. But just as the discovery of meanings is not the only purpose of formal analysis, we suggest that evaluation is most fruitful when it is backed up by a close examination of the film. General statements ("*The Wizard of Oz* is a masterpiece") seldom enlighten us very much. Usually, an evaluation is helpful insofar as it points to aspects of the film and shows us relations and qualities we have missed: "*The Wizard of Oz* subtly compares characters in Kansas and Oz, as when Miss Gulch's written order to take Toto is echoed by the Wicked Witch's fiery skywriting addressed to the citizens of the Emerald City, 'Surrender Dorothy.'" Like interpretation, evaluation is most useful when it drives us back to the film itself as a formal system, helping us to understand that system better.

In reading this book, you'll find that we have generally minimized evaluation. We think that most of the films and sequences we analyze are more or less good based on the artistic criteria we mentioned, but the purpose of this book is not to persuade you to accept a list of masterpieces. Rather, we believe that if we show in detail how films may be understood as artistic systems, you will have an informed basis for whatever evaluations you wish to make.

Principles of Film Form

Because film form is a system—that is, a unified set of related, interdependent elements—there must be some principles that help create the relationships among the parts. In the sciences, principles may take the form of physical laws or mathematical propositions. For researchers and inventors, such principles provide firm guidelines as to what is possible. For example, engineers designing an airplane must obey fundamental laws of aerodynamics.

In the arts, however, there are no absolute principles of form that all artists must follow. Artworks are products of culture. Thus many of the principles of artistic form are matters of convention. In Chapter 9, we shall examine how various genres can have very different conventions. A Western is not violating a law of nature if it does not follow the conventions of classic Westerns. The artist follows (or disobeys) *norms*—bodies of conventions, not laws.

But within these conventions, each artwork tends to set up its own specific formal principles. The forms of different films can vary enormously. We can distinguish, however, five general principles that we notice in experiencing a film's formal system: function, similarity and repetition, difference and variation, development, and unity/disunity.

Function

If form in cinema is the overall interrelation among various systems of elements, we can assume that every element has one or more **functions.** That is, every element will be seen as fulfilling roles within the whole system.

Of any element within a film we can ask, What are its functions? In *The Wizard of Oz,* every major character fulfills one or more roles. For instance, Miss Gulch, the woman who wants to take Toto from Dorothy, reappears in the Oz section as the Wicked Witch. In the opening portion of the film, Miss Gulch frightens Dorothy into running away from home. In Oz, the Witch prevents Dorothy from returning home by keeping her away from the Emerald City and by trying to seize the ruby slippers.

Even an element as apparently minor as the dog Toto serves many functions. The dispute over Toto causes Dorothy to run away from home and to get back too late to take shelter from the tornado. Later, when Dorothy is about to leave Oz, Toto's pursuit of a cat makes her jump out of the ascending balloon. Toto's gray color, set off against the brightness of Oz, creates a link to the black and white of the Kansas episodes at the film's beginning. Functions, then, are almost always multiple. Both narrative and stylistic elements have functions.

One useful way to grasp the function of an element is to ask what other elements demand that it be present. For instance, the narrative requires that Dorothy run away from home, so Toto functions to trigger this action. Or, to take another example, Dorothy must seem completely different from the Wicked Witch, so costume, age, voice, and other characteristics function to contrast the two. Additionally, the switch from black-and-white to color film functions to signal the arrival in the bright fantasy land of Oz.

Note that the concept of function does not always depend on the filmmaker's intention. Often discussions of films get bogged down in the question of whether the filmmaker really knew what he or she was doing by including a certain element. In asking about function, we do not ask for a production history. From the standpoint of intention, Dorothy may sing "Over the Rainbow" because MGM wanted Judy Garland to launch a hit song. From the standpoint of function, however, we can say that Dorothy's singing that song fulfills certain narrative and stylistic functions. It establishes her desire to leave home, its reference to the rainbow foreshadows her trip through the air to the colorful land of Oz, and so forth. In asking about formal function, therefore, we ask not, "How did this element get there?" but rather, "What is this element *doing* there?" and "How does it cue us to respond?"

One way to notice the functions of an element is to consider the element's **motivation.** Because films are human constructs, we can expect that any one element in a film will have some justification for being there. This justification is the motivation for that element. For example, when Miss Gulch appears as the Witch in Oz, we justify her new incarnation by appealing to the fact that early scenes in Kansas have established her as a threat to Dorothy. When Toto jumps from the balloon to chase a cat, we motivate his action by appealing to notions of how dogs are likely to act when cats are around.

Sometimes people use the word "motivation" to apply only to reasons for characters' actions, as when a murderer acts from certain motives. Here, however, we'll use "motivation" to apply to any element in the film that the viewer justifies on some grounds. A costume, for example, needs motivation. If we see a man in beggar's clothes in the middle of an elegant society ball, we will ask why he is dressed in this way. He could be the victim of practical jokers who have deluded him into believing that this is a masquerade. He could be an eccentric millionaire out to shock his friends. Such a scene does occur in *My Man Godfrey*. The motivation for the beggar's presence at the ball is a scavenger hunt; the young society people have been assigned to bring back, among other things, a homeless man **(2.4).** An event, the hunt, *motivates* the presence of an inappropriately dressed character.

Motivation is so common in films that spectators take it for granted. Shadowy, flickering light on a character may be motivated by the presence of a candle in the room. (In production the light is provided by offscreen lamps, but the candle purports to be the source and thus motivates the pattern of light.) A character wandering across a room may motivate the moving of the camera to follow the action and keep the character within the frame. When we study principles of narrative form (Chapter 3) and various types of films (Chapters 9 and 10), we will look more closely at how motivation works to give elements specific functions.

Similarity and Repetition

In our example of the ABACA pattern, we saw how we were able to predict the next steps in the series. One reason for this was a regular pattern of repeated elements. Like beats in music or meter in poetry, the repetition of the A's in our pattern established and satisfied formal expectations. Similarity and repetition, then, constitute an important principle of film form.

Repetition is basic to our understanding any film. For instance, we must be able to recall and identify characters and settings each time they reappear. More subtly, throughout any film, we can observe repetitions of everything from lines of dialogue and bits of music to camera positions, characters' behavior, and story action.

It's useful to have a term to describe formal repetitions, and the most common term is **motif.** We shall call *any significant repeated element in a film* a motif. A motif may be an object, a color, a place, a person, a sound, or even a character trait. We may call a pattern of lighting or camera position a motif if it is repeated through the course of a film. (See "A Closer Look," pp. 69–70.) The form of *The Wizard of Oz* uses all these kinds of motifs. Even in such a relatively simple film, we can see the pervasive presence of similarity and repetition as formal principles.

Film form uses general similarities as well as exact duplication. To understand *The Wizard of Oz,* we must see the similarities between the three Kansas farmhands and the Scarecrow, the Tin Man, and the Cowardly Lion. We must notice additional echoes between characters in the frame story and in the fantasy **(2.9–2.12).** The duplication isn't perfect, but the similarity is very strong. Such similarities are called *parallelism,* the process whereby the film cues the spectator to compare two or more distinct elements by highlighting some similarity. For example, at one point, Dorothy says she feels that she has known the Scarecrow, the Tin Man, and

2.4   The heroine of *My Man Godfrey* studies her prize while the society crowd urges the unemployed Godfrey to make a speech.

"You can take a movie, for example, like Angels with Dirty Faces, *where James Cagney is a child and says to his pal Pat O'Brien, 'What do you hear, what do you say?'—cocky kid—and then as a young rough on the way up when things are going great for him he says, 'What do you hear, what do you say?' Then when he is about to be executed in the electric chair and Pat O'Brien is there to hear his confession, he says, 'What do you hear, what do you say?' and the simple repetition of the last line of dialogue in three different places with the same characters brings home the dramatically changed circumstances much more than any extensive diatribe would."*

— Robert Towne, screenwriter, *Chinatown*

PICKING OUT PATTERNS

In studying film as an art, you might sometimes wonder: Are all the patterns of form and style we notice really in the film? Do filmmakers actually put them there, or are we just reading them in?

When asked, filmmakers often say that their formal and stylistic choices aim to create specific effects. Hitchcock, a director who had an engineering bent, planned his stories carefully and chose techniques in full awareness of their possibilities. His film *Rope* confines the action to a single apartment and presents it in only 11 shots. *Rear Window* limits the action to what the hero can see from his apartment. In these and other films, Hitchcock deliberately created formal and stylistic challenges for himself, inviting his audience to come along. Most directors aren't so adventurous, but throughout this book, we'll include comments from filmmakers that show how the ideas we present are part of their working craft.

Sometimes filmmakers work in a more intuitive way, but they still must choose one story development or another, one technique or another. The finished film can have an overall unity because the momentary choices tend to mesh. Joel and Ethan Coen, the brothers who created *Blood Simple, Raising Arizona,* and *Fargo,* say they don't set out with a particular style in mind. As Ethan puts it, "At the point of making the movie, it's just about making individual choices." Joel picks up the thread:

> . . . about the best way to tell the story, scene by scene. You make specific choices that you think are appropriate or compelling or interesting for that particular

CONNECT TO THE BLOG
In "Do filmmakers deserve the last word?" we suggest why we should always be cautious in accepting claims filmmakers offer.

See www.davidbordwell.net/blog/?p=1174.

scene. Then, at the end of the day, you put it all together and somebody looks at it and, if there's some consistency to it, they say, "Well, that's their style."

Even if the Coens don't map out every option in advance, the finished films display distinctive patterns of form and style **(2.5, 2.6).**

Professionals pay attention to other filmmakers' formal and stylistic choices. While watching Stanley Kubrick's *The Shining,* Nicole Kidman pointed out how the composition of one shot had both an immediate point and a long-range story purpose **(2.7):**

> Here, in this scene, look at how there is this rack of knives hanging in the background over the boy's head. . . . It's important because it not only shows that the boy is in danger, but one of those very knives is used later in the story when Wendy takes it to protect herself from her husband **[2.8].**

Kubrick told Kidman that a director had to repeat story information so that the audience could keep up. In other words, the pattern helped organize the film and in doing so shaped the viewer's experience, if only unconsciously.

2.5 In the *Hudsucker Proxy,* the boss dangles above the street in a very steep, centered-perspective composition.

2.6 The same sort of composition is used to show the impersonal layout of desks in the Hudsucker company.

Kubrick's comment points up another reason we can have some confidence when we pick out patterns. A filmmaker doesn't create a movie from scratch. All films borrow ideas and storytelling strategies from other movies and other art forms. A lot that happens in films is governed by traditional rules, usually called *conventions*. When Kubrick shows us the knives behind Danny, he's following a very old storytelling convention: prepare the audience for action that will come

later. In contrast, *The Hudsucker Proxy* is a satirical comedy, and the perspective in 2.5 and 2.6 follows a convention of using exaggeration to create humor.

Very often, patterns in one film resemble patterns we've seen in other films. Even when filmmakers don't explain what they're doing, as experienced viewers, we can notice how they treat familiar conventions of form and technique.

2.7 In *The Shining,* an early scene in the Hotel Overlook kitchen displays the telepathic rapport between Halloran and Danny, whose parents are caretaking the hotel for the winter. The knives are a natural part of the kitchen set but are aligned above Danny.

2.8 Later Danny's mother, Wendy, goes to the same knife rack, seen from a different angle, to grab a weapon.

the Cowardly Lion before. At another point, the staging of a shot reinforces this familiarity **(2.13, 2.14).**

Motifs can assist in creating parallelism. The viewer will notice, and even come to expect, that every time Dorothy meets a character in Oz, the scene will end with the song "We're Off to See the Wizard." Our recognition of parallelism provides part of our pleasure in watching a film, much as the echo of rhymes contributes to the power of poetry.

Difference and Variation

A film couldn't rely only on repetitions. AAAAAA is rather boring. There must also be some changes, or *variations,* however small. Thus difference is another fundamental principle of film form.

We readily understand the need for variety, contrast, and change in films. Characters must be differentiated, environments delineated, and different times or activities established. Even within the image, we must distinguish differences in tonality, texture, direction and speed of movement, and so on. Form needs its stable background of similarity and repetition, but it also demands that differences be created.

This means that although motifs (scenes, settings, actions, objects, stylistic devices) may be repeated, those motifs will seldom be repeated *exactly.* Variation will

2.9   The itinerant Kansas fortune-teller, Professor Marvell, bears a striking resemblance to . . .

2.10   . . . the old charlatan known as the Wizard of Oz.

2.11   Miss Gulch's bicycle in the opening section becomes . . .

2.12   . . . the Witch's broom in Oz.

2.13   As the Lion describes his timidity, the characters are lined up to form a mirror reversal of . . .

2.14   . . . the earlier scene in which the others teased Zeke for being afraid of pigs.

appear. In *The Wizard of Oz,* the three Kansas hired hands aren't exactly the same as their "twins" in Oz. Parallelism thus requires a degree of difference as well as striking similarity. When Professor Marvel pretends to read Dorothy's future in a small crystal ball, we see no images in it (2.9). Dorothy's dream transforms the crystal into a large globe in the Witch's castle, where it displays frightening scenes **(2.15).** Similarly, the repeated motif of Toto's disruption of a situation changes its function. In Kansas, it disturbs Miss Gulch and induces Dorothy to take Toto away from home, but in Oz, his disruption prevents Dorothy from returning home.

Differences among the elements may often sharpen into downright opposition among them. We're most familiar with formal oppositions as clashes among characters. In *The Wizard of Oz,* Dorothy's desires are opposed, at various points, by the differing desires of Aunt Em, Miss Gulch, the Wicked Witch, and the Wizard, so that our experience of the film is engaged through dramatic conflict. But character conflict isn't the only way the formal principle of difference may manifest itself. Settings, actions, and other elements may be opposed. *The Wizard of Oz* presents color oppositions: black-and-white Kansas versus colorful Oz; Dorothy in red, white, and blue versus the Witch in black. Settings are opposed as well—not only Oz versus Kansas but also the various locales within Oz **(2.16, 2.17).** Voice quality, musical tunes, and a host of other elements play off against one another, demonstrating that any motif may be opposed by any other motif.

Not all differences are simple oppositions, of course. Dorothy's three Oz friends—the Scarecrow, the Tin Woodman, and the Lion—are distinguished not only by external features but also by means of a three-term comparison of what they lack (a brain, a heart, courage). Other films may rely on less sharp differences, suggesting a scale of gradations among the characters, as in Jean Renoir's

2.15   Through her crystal ball, the Wicked Witch mocks Dorothy.

2.16   Centered in the upper half of the frame, the Emerald City creates a striking contrast to . . .

2.17   . . . the similar composition showing the castle of the Wicked Witch of the West.

2.18   Dorothy puts her feet on the literal beginning of the Yellow Brick Road, as it widens out from a thin line.

The Rules of the Game. At the extreme, an abstract film may create minimal variations among its parts, such as in the slight changes that accompany each return of the same footage in J. J. Murphy's *Print Generation* (p. 000).

Repetition and variation are two sides of the same coin. To notice one is to notice the other. In thinking about films, we ought to look for similarities *and* differences. Shuttling between the two, we can point out motifs and contrast the changes they undergo, recognize parallelisms as repetition, and still spot crucial variations.

Development

One way to keep ourselves aware of how similarity and difference operate in film form is to look for principles of development from part to part. Development constitutes some patterning of similar and differing elements. Our pattern ABACA is based not only on repetition (the recurring motif of A) and difference (the insertion of B and C) but also on a principle of *progression* that we could state as a rule: alternate A with successive letters in alphabetical order. Though simple, this is a principle of *development,* governing the form of the whole series.

Think of formal development as *a progression moving from beginning through middle to end.* The story of *The Wizard of Oz* shows development in many ways. It is, for one thing, a *journey:* from Kansas through Oz to Kansas. The good witch Glinda emphasizes this formal pattern by telling Dorothy that "It's always best to start at the beginning" **(2.18).** Many films possess such a journey plot. *The Wizard of Oz* is also a *search,* beginning with an initial separation from home, tracing a series of efforts to find a way home, and ending with home being found. Within the film, there is also a pattern of *mystery,* which usually has the same beginning-middle-end pattern. We begin with a question (Who is the Wizard of Oz?), pass through attempts to answer it, and conclude with the question answered. (The Wizard is a fraud.) Most feature-length films are composed of several developmental patterns.

In order to analyze a film's pattern of development, it is usually a good idea to make a *segmentation.* A segmentation is simply a written outline of the film that breaks it into its major and minor parts, with the parts marked by consecutive numbers or letters. If a narrative film has 40 *scenes,* then we can label each scene with a number running from 1 to 40. It may be useful to divide some parts further (for example, scenes 6a and 6b). Segmenting a film enables us not only to notice similarities and differences among parts but also to plot the overall formal progression. Following is a segmentation for *The Wizard of Oz.* (In segmenting films, we'll label the opening credits with a "C," the end title with an "E," and all other segments with numbers.)

THE WIZARD OF OZ: PLOT SEGMENTATION

C. Credits
1. Kansas
    a. Dorothy is at home, worried about Miss Gulch's threat to Toto.
    b. Running away, Dorothy meets Professor Marvel, who induces her to return home.
    c. A tornado lifts the house, with Dorothy and Toto, into the sky.
2. Munchkin City
    a. Dorothy meets Glinda, and the Munchkins celebrate the death of the Wicked Witch of the East.
    b. The Wicked Witch of the West threatens Dorothy over the Ruby Slippers.
    c. Glinda sends Dorothy to seek the Wizard's help.
3. The Yellow Brick Road
    a. Dorothy meets the Scarecrow.
    b. Dorothy meets the Tin Man.
    c. Dorothy meets the Cowardly Lion.

4. **The Emerald City**
   a. The Witch creates a poppy field near the city, but Glinda rescues the travelers.
   b. The group is welcomed by the city's citizens.
   c. As they wait to see the Wizard, the Lion sings of being king.
   d. The terrifying Wizard agrees to help the group if they obtain the Wicked Witch's broomstick.
5. **The Witch's castle and nearby woods**
   a. In the woods, flying monkeys carry off Dorothy and Toto.
   b. The Witch realizes that she must kill Dorothy to get the ruby slippers.
   c. The Scarecrow, Tin Man, and Lion sneak into the Castle; in the ensuing chase, Dorothy kills the Witch.
6. **The Emerald City**
   a. Although revealed as a humbug, the Wizard grants the wishes of the Scarecrow, Tin Man, and Lion.
   b. Dorothy fails to leave in the Wizard's hot-air balloon but is transported home by the ruby slippers.
7. **Kansas—Dorothy describes Oz to her family and friends**
E. **End credits**

Preparing a segmentation may look a little fussy, but in the course of this book, we'll try to convince you that it sheds a lot of light on films. For now, just consider this comparison.

As you walk into a building, your experience develops over time. In many cathedrals, for example, the entryway is fairly narrow. But as you emerge into the open area inside (the nave), space expands outward and upward, your sense of your body seems to shrink, and your attention is directed toward the altar, centrally located in the distance. The somewhat cramped entryway makes you feel a contrast when you enter the broad and soaring space. Your experience has been as carefully planned as any theme park ride. Only by thinking back on it can you realize that the planned progression of the building's different parts shaped your experience. If you could study the builder's blueprints, you'd see the whole layout at a glance. It would be very different from your moment-by-moment experience of it, but it would shed light on how your experience was shaped.

A film isn't that different. As we watch the film, we're in the thick of it. We follow the formal development moment by moment, and we may get more and more involved. If we want to study the overall shape of things, though, we need to stand back a bit. Films don't come with blueprints, but by creating a plot segmentation, we can get a comparable sense of the film's overall design. In a way, we're recovering the basic architecture of the movie. A segmentation lets us see the patterning that we felt intuitively in watching the film. In Chapters 3 and 10, we'll consider how to segment different types of films, and several of our sample analyses in Chapter 11 will use segmentations to show how the films work.

Another way to size up how a film develops formally is to *compare the beginning with the ending.* By looking at the similarities and the differences between the beginning and the ending, we can start to understand the overall pattern of the film. We can test this advice on *The Wizard of Oz.* A comparison of the beginning and the ending reveals that Dorothy's journey ends with her return home; the journey, a search for an ideal place "over the rainbow," has turned into a search for a way back to Kansas. The final scene repeats and develops the narrative elements of the opening. Stylistically, the beginning and ending are the only parts that use black-and-white film stock. This repetition supports the contrast the narrative creates between the dreamland of Oz and the bleak landscape of Kansas.

At the film's end, Professor Marvel comes to visit Dorothy **(2.19)**, reversing the situation of her visit to him when she had tried to run away. At the beginning, he had convinced her to return home; then, as the Wizard in the Oz section, he had

CONNECT TO THE BLOG
If beginnings are important, then the very beginning is even more important, as "First shots" demonstrates.
See www.davidbordwell.net/blog/?p=139.

2.19 The visits of the final scene.

also represented her hopes of returning home. Finally, when she recognizes Professor Marvel and the farmhands as the basis of the characters in her dream, she remembers how much she had wanted to come home from Oz.

Earlier, we suggested that film form engages our emotions and expectations in a dynamic way. Now we are in a better position to see why. The constant interplay between similarity and difference, and repetition and variation, leads the viewer to an active engagement with the film's developing system. It may be handy to visualize a movie's development in static terms by segmenting it, but we ought not to forget that formal development is a *process*. Form shapes our experience of the film.

Unity and Disunity

All of the relationships among elements in a film create the total filmic system. Even if an element seems utterly out of place in relation to the rest of the film, we cannot really say that it isn't part of the film. At most, the unrelated element is enigmatic or incoherent. It may be a flaw in the otherwise integrated system of the film—but it does affect the whole film.

When all the relationships we perceive within a film are clear and economically interwoven, we say that the film has *unity*. We call a unified film tight, because there seem to be no gaps in the formal relationships. Every element present has a specific set of functions, similarities and differences are determinable, the form develops logically, and no element is superfluous. In turn, the film's overall unity gives our experience a sense of completeness and fulfillment.

Unity is, however, a matter of degree. Almost no film is so tight as to leave no ends dangling. For example, at one point in *The Wizard of Oz,* the Witch refers to her having attacked Dorothy and her friends with insects, yet we have never seen them, and the mention becomes puzzling. In fact, a sequence of a bee attack was originally shot but then cut from the finished film. The Witch's line about the insect attack now lacks motivation. More striking is a dangling element at the film's end: we never find out what happens to Miss Gulch. Presumably, she still has her legal order to take Toto away, but no one refers to this in the last scene. The viewer may be inclined to overlook this disunity, however, because Miss Gulch's parallel character, the Witch, has been killed off in the Oz fantasy, and we don't expect to see her alive again. Since perfect unity is scarcely ever achieved, we ought to expect that even a unified film may still contain a few unintegrated elements or unanswered questions.

CONNECT TO THE BLOG
One distinctive type of film form comes in the anthology film, combining short segments by several directors. It's a theme-and-variations approach that we discuss in "Can you spot all the auteurs in this picture?"

See www.davidbordwell.net/blog/?p=932.

If we look at unity as a criterion of evaluation, we may judge a film containing several unmotivated elements as a failure. But unity and disunity may be looked at nonevaluatively as well, as the results of particular formal conventions. For example, *Pulp Fiction* lacks a bit of closure in that it never reveals what is inside a briefcase that is at the center of the gangster plot. The contents, however, give off a golden glow, suggesting that they are of very great value (as well as evoking the "whatsit" in *Kiss Me Deadly,* a classic film noir). By not specifying the goods, the film invites us to compare characters' reactions to them—most notably, in the last scene in the diner, when Pumpkin gazes at it lustfully and the newly spiritual hitman Jules calmly insists that he will deliver it to his boss. In such ways, momentary disunities contribute to broader patterns and thematic meanings.

SUMMARY

If one issue has governed our treatment of aesthetic form, it might be said to be *concreteness*. Form is a specific system of patterned relationships that we perceive in an artwork. Such a concept helps us understand how even elements of what is normally considered content—subject matter, or abstract ideas—take on particular functions within any work.

Our experience of an artwork is also a concrete one. Picking up cues in the work, we frame specific expectations that are aroused, guided, delayed, cheated, satisfied, or disturbed. We undergo curiosity, suspense, and surprise. We compare the particular aspects of the artwork with things that we know from life and with conventions found in art.

The concrete context of the artwork expresses and stimulates emotions. It enables us to construct many types of meanings. And even when we apply general criteria in evaluating artworks, we ought to use those criteria to help us discriminate more, to penetrate more deeply into the particular aspects of the artwork. The rest of this book is devoted to studying these properties of artistic form in cinema.

We can summarize the principles of film form as a set of questions that you can ask about any film:

1. For any element in the film, what are its functions in the overall form? How is it motivated?

2. Are elements or patterns repeated throughout the film? If so, how and at what points? Are motifs and parallelisms asking us to compare elements?

3. How are elements contrasted and differentiated from one another? How are different elements opposed to one another?

4. What principles of progression or development are at work throughout the form of the film? More specifically, how does a comparison of the beginning and ending reveal the overall form of a film?

5. What degree of unity is present in the film's overall form? Is disunity subordinate to the overall unity, or does disunity dominate?

In this chapter, we examined some major ways in which films as artworks can engage us as spectators. We also reviewed some broad principles of film form. Armed with these general principles, we can press on to distinguish more specific *types* of form that are central to understanding film art.

WHERE TO GO FROM HERE

Form in Film and the Other Arts

Many of the ideas in this chapter are based on ideas of form to be found in other arts. All of the following constitute helpful further reading: Monroe Beardsley, *Aesthetics* (New York: Harcourt Brace & World, 1958), especially chaps. 4 and 5; Rudolf Arnheim, *Art and Visual Perception* (Berkeley: University of California Press, 1974), especially chaps. 2, 3, and 9; Leonard Meyer, *Emotion and Meaning in Music* (Chicago: University of Chicago Press, 1956); and E. H. Gombrich, *Art and Illusion* (Princeton, NJ: Princeton University Press, 1961).

On the relation of form to the audience, see the book by Meyer mentioned above. The ABACA example is borrowed from Barbara Herrnstein Smith's excellent study of literary form, *Poetic Closure* (Chicago: University of Chicago Press, 1968). Compare Kenneth Burke's claim: "Form is the creation of an appetite in the mind of the auditor and the adequate satisfying of that appetite." (See Kenneth Burke, "Psychology and Form," in *Counter-Statement* [Chicago: University of Chicago Press, 1957], pp. 29–44.)

This chapter presupposes that any filmmaker uses basic formal principles. But is the filmmaker fully aware of doing so? Many filmmakers use formal principles intuitively, but others apply them quite deliberately. Spike Lee's cinematographer Ernest Dickerson remarks, "A motif we used throughout *[School Daze]* was two people in profile, 'up in each other's face.' That was a conscious decision" (*Uplift the Race: The Construction of "School Daze"* [New York: Simon & Schuster, 1988], p. 110). Sidney Lumet decided to give *Twelve Angry Men* a strict progression by shooting from different camera positions as the story developed. "As the picture unfolded I wanted the room to seem smaller and smaller. . . . I shot the first third of the movie above eye level, the second third at eye level, and the last third from below eye level. In that way, toward the end, the ceiling began to appear" (Sidney Lumet, *Making Movies* [New York: Knopf, 1995], p. 81). Our quotation from Nicole Kidman on the knife motif in *The Shining* comes from *Watching Movies: The Biggest Names in Cinema Talk About the Films That Matter Most* (New York: Henry Holt, 2003).

Maya Deren, the American experimentalist who made *Meshes of the Afternoon* (p. 000), was quite self-conscious about formal principles. She argued that a film should exploit the features that differentiate cinema from other arts—chiefly, its unique handling of space and time.

Deren believed that a film's organization emerges from the ways in which all the images subtly affect one another. "The elements, or parts, lose their original value and assume those conferred upon them by their function in this specific whole." For more thoughts on this, see her 1946 essay "An Anagram of Ideas on Art, Form and Film," in *Essential Deren: Collected Writings on Film by Maya Deren*, ed. Bruce R. McPherson (Kingston, N.Y.: Documentext, 2005).

Form, Meaning, and Feeling

How does cinema evoke emotion? It's actually a bit of a puzzle. If a giant ape were lumbering toward us on the street, we'd run away in fright. But if King Kong is lumbering toward us on the screen, we feel frightened, but we don't flee the theater. Do we feel real fear but somehow block our impulse to run? Or do we feel something that isn't real fear but is a kind of pretend-fear? Similarly, when we say that we *identify* with a character, what does that mean? That we feel exactly the same emotions that the character does? Sometimes, though, we feel some emotions that the character isn't feeling, as when sympathy for her or him is mixed with pity or anxiety. Can we identify with a character and not have the same feelings she has?

In the 1990s, philosophers and film theorists tried to shed light on these issues. For a sampling, see Carl Plantinga and Greg M. Smith, eds., *Passionate Views: Film, Cognition, and Emotion* (Baltimore: Johns Hopkins University Press, 1999). The essays in this collection grew out of debates around some influential books: Noël Carroll, *The Philosophy of Horror; or, Paradoxes of the Heart* (London: Routledge, 1990); Murray Smith, *Engaging Characters: Fiction, Emotion and the Cinema* (Oxford: Oxford University Press, 1995); Joseph Anderson, *The Reality of Illusion: An Ecological Approach to Cognitive Film Theory* (Carbondale: University of Southern Illinois Press, 1996); and Torben Grodal, *Moving Pictures: A New Theory of Film Genres, Feelings, and Cognition* (Oxford: Oxford University Press, 1997). See also Greg M. Smith, *Film Structure and the Emotion System* (Cambridge: Cambridge University Press, 2003).

Most of these authors draw upon an approach called *cognitive studies*. We reflect on similar topics on our blog. In "Minding movies," at www.davidbordwell.net/blog/?p=2004, we give a sketch of how cognitive studies can help understand how we perceive and understand films. For a related approach, see "Simplicity, clarity, balance: A tribute to Rudolf Arnheim," at www.davidbordwell.net/blog/?p=956.

An alternative approach to understanding spectators' response to films has been called *reception studies*. For an overview, see Janet Staiger, *Media Reception Studies* (New York: New York University Press, 2005). Often scholars working in this tradition seek to understand how specific social groups, such as ethnic groups or historically located audiences, respond to the films offered to them. Influential examples are Kate Brooks and Martin Barker's *Judge Dredd: Its Friends, Fans, and Foes* (Luton: University of Luton Press, 2003) and Melvin Stokes and Richard Maltby, eds., *American Movie Audiences: From the Turn of the Century to the Early Sound Era* (London: British Film Institute, 1999). In *Perverse Spectators: The Practices of Film Reception* (New York: New York University Press, 2000), Janet Staiger discusses how audiences and critics can respond to films in ways that the filmmakers could not have anticipated.

Many critics concentrate on ascribing implicit and symptomatic meanings to films—that is, interpreting them. A survey of interpretive approaches is offered in R. Barton Palmer, *The Cinematic Text: Methods and Approaches* (New York: AMS Press, 1989). David Bordwell's *Making Meaning: Inference and Rhetoric in the Interpretation of Cinema* (Cambridge, MA: Harvard University Press, 1989) reviews trends in film interpretation.

Linear Segmentation and Diagramming

When we're analyzing a scripted fiction film, creating a segmentation often amounts to retracing the screenwriter's creative steps. The writer typically builds a screenplay out of a list of scenes, sometimes noting each scene on a card and laying out the cards to assess how the plot is shaping up.

Because today's feature films tend to have short scenes (typically running one to three minutes each), there may be 60 or more sequences in a film. Older films seldom contain more than 40, and silent films may have only 10 or 20. Of course, sequences and scenes can also be further subdivided into smaller parts. In segmenting any film, use an outline format or a linear diagram to help you visualize formal relations (beginnings and endings, parallels, patterns of development). We employ an outline format in discussing *Citizen Kane* in the next chapter and in discussing modes of filmmaking in Chapter 10.

Websites

www.uca.edu/org/ccsmi/ A site devoted to the Center for Cognitive Studies of the Moving Image, which examines various aspects of psychological and emotional responses to film.

http://en.wikipedia.org/wiki/Art. A helpful introductory essay on the role of form in different art media.

Recommended DVD Supplements

The Warner Bros. two-disc special edition of *The Wizard of Oz* contains supplements documenting the film's production. See also Aljean Harmetz, *The Making of the Wizard of Oz* (New York: Limelight, 1984), and John Fricke, Jay Scarfone, and William Stillman, *The Wizard of Oz: The*

Official 50th Anniversary Pictorial History (New York: Warner Books, 1989).

While the film was in postproduction, MGM executives quarreled about whether the song "Over the Rainbow" should be dropped. Some thought it was too long and slowed the pace; others suggested that singing in a barnyard was undignified. Producer Arthur Freed argued passionately for retaining the ballad, and he won. His reasoning was expressed in an early memo, and its wording shows that he was conscious of the song's role in motivating Dorothy's journey:

> The whole love story in *Snow White* is motivated by the song "Some Day My Prince Will Come" as Snow White is looking into the well. Dialogue could not have accomplished this half as well. I make this illustration for the purpose that we plant our *Wizard of Oz* script in a similar way through a musical sequence on the farm. Doing it musically takes all the triteness out of a straight plot scene. (Quoted in Fricke, Scarfone, and Stillman, *The Wizard of Oz,* p. 30)

DVD supplements tend to focus on behind-the-scenes production information and on exposing how techniques such as special-effects and music were accomplished. Sometimes, though, such descriptions analyze formal aspects of the film. In "Sweet Sounds," the supplement on the music in *Charlie and the Chocolate Factory,* composer Danny Elfman discusses how the musical numbers that follow the disappearance of each of the obnoxious children created parallels among them and yet achieved variety by being derived from different styles of music.

"Their Production Will Be Second to None," on the *Hard Day's Night* DVD, includes an intelligent interview with director Richard Lester in which he talks about the overall form of the film. He remarks, for example, that in the first third, he deliberately used confined spaces and low ceilings to prepare for the extreme contrast of the open spaces into which the Beatles escape.

The "Production Design" supplement for *The Golden Compass* discusses motifs: circular elements in the sets and props associated with the heroine Lyra and the Oxford setting opposed to oval elements associated with the villainous Mrs. Coulter and the Magisterium.

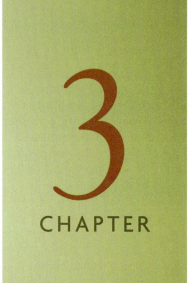

3
CHAPTER

Narrative as a Formal System

Principles of Narrative Construction

Stories surround us. In childhood, we learn fairy tales and myths. As we grow up, we read short stories, novels, history, and biography. Religion, philosophy, and science often present their doctrines through parables and tales. Plays tell stories, as do films, television shows, comic books, paintings, dance, and many other cultural phenomena. Much of our conversation is taken up with telling tales—recalling a past event or telling a joke. Even newspaper articles are called stories, and when we ask for an explanation of something, we may say, "What's the story?" We can't escape even by going to sleep, since we often experience our dreams as little narratives. Narrative is a fundamental way that humans make sense of the world.

The prevalence of stories in our lives is one reason that we need to take a close look at how films may embody **narrative form.** When we speak of "going to the movies," we almost always mean that we are going to see a narrative film—a film that tells a story.

Narrative form is most common in fictional films, but it can appear in all other basic types. For instance, documentaries often employ narrative form. *Primary* tells the story of how Hubert Humphrey and John F. Kennedy campaigned in the Wisconsin presidential primary of 1960. Many animated films, such as Disney features and Warner Bros. short cartoons, also tell stories. Some experimental and avant-garde films use narrative form, although the story or the way it is told may be quite unusual, as we shall see in Chapter 10.

Because stories are all around us, spectators approach a narrative film with definite expectations. We may know a great deal about the particular story the film will tell. Perhaps we have read the book on which a film is based, or we have seen the film to which this is a sequel. More generally, though, we have anticipations that are characteristic of narrative form itself. We assume that there will be characters and some action that will involve them with one another. We expect a series of incidents that will be connected in some way. We also probably expect that the problems or conflicts arising in the course of the action will achieve some final state—either they will be resolved or, at least, a new light will be cast on them. A spectator comes prepared to make sense of a narrative film.

As the viewer watches the film, she or he picks up cues, recalls information, anticipates what will follow, and generally participates in the creation of the film's form. The film shapes particular expectations by summoning up curiosity, suspense, and surprise. The ending has the task of satisfying or cheating the expectations prompted by the film as a whole. The ending may also activate memory by cueing the spectator to review earlier events, possibly considering them in a new light. When *The Sixth Sense* was released in 1999, many moviegoers were so intrigued by the surprise twist at the end that they returned to see the film again and trace how their expectations had been manipulated. Something similar happened with *The Prestige* (see pp. 302–303). As we examine narrative form, we consider at various points how it engages the viewer in a dynamic activity.

What Is Narrative?

We can consider a *narrative* to be *a chain of events linked by cause and effect and occurring in time and space*. A narrative is what we usually mean by the term *story*, although we shall be using *story* in a slightly different way later. Typically, a narrative begins with one situation; a series of changes occurs according to a pattern of cause and effect; finally, a new situation arises that brings about the end of the narrative. Our engagement with the story depends on our understanding of the pattern of change and stability, cause and effect, time and space.

All the components of our definition—causality, time, and space—are important to narratives in most media, but causality and time are central. A random string of events is hard to understand as a story. Consider the following actions: "A man tosses and turns, unable to sleep. A mirror breaks. A telephone rings." We have trouble grasping this as a narrative because we are unable to determine the causal or temporal relations among the events.

Consider a new description of these same events: "A man has a fight with his boss; he tosses and turns that night, unable to sleep. In the morning, he is still so angry that he smashes the mirror while shaving. Then his telephone rings; his boss has called to apologize."

We now have a narrative. We can connect the events spatially: the man is in the office, then in his bed; the mirror is in the bathroom; the phone is somewhere else in his home. More important, we can understand that the three events are part of a series of causes and effects. The argument with the boss causes the sleeplessness and the broken mirror. The phone call from the boss resolves the conflict; the narrative ends. In this example, time is important, too. The sleepless night occurs before the breaking of the mirror, which in turn occurs before the phone call; all of the action runs from one day to the following morning. The narrative develops from an initial situation of conflict between employee and boss, through a series of events caused by the conflict, to the resolution of the conflict. Simple and minimal as our example is, it shows how important causality, space, and time are to narrative form.

The fact that a narrative relies on causality, time, and space doesn't mean that other formal principles can't govern the film. For instance, a narrative may make use of parallelism. As Chapter 2 points out (pp. 68–70), parallelism presents a similarity among different elements. Our example was the way that *The Wizard of Oz* made the three Kansas farmhands parallel to Dorothy's three Oz companions. A narrative may cue us to draw parallels among characters, settings, situations, times of day, or any other elements. In Věra Chytilová's *Something Different*, scenes from the life of a housewife and from the career of a gymnast are presented in alternation. Since the two women never meet and lead entirely separate lives, there is no way that we can connect the two stories causally. Instead, we compare and contrast the two women's actions and situations—that is, we draw parallels.

The documentary *Hoop Dreams* makes even stronger use of parallels. Two high school students from Chicago's black ghetto dream of becoming professional basketball players, and the film follows as each one pursues his athletic career. The film's form invites us to compare and contrast their personalities, the obstacles they face, and the choices they make. In addition, the film creates parallels between their high schools, their coaches, their parents, and older male relatives who vicariously pursue their own dreams of athletic glory. Parallelism allows the film to become richer and more complex than it might have been had it concentrated on only one protagonist.

Yet *Hoop Dreams*, like *Something Different*, is still a narrative film. Each of the two lines of action is organized by time, space, and causality. The film suggests

"Narrative is one of the ways in which knowledge is organized. I have always thought it was the most important way to transmit and receive knowledge. I am less certain of that now—but the craving for narrative has never lessened, and the hunger for it is as keen as it was on Mt. Sinai or Calvary or the middle of the fens."
— Toni Morrison, author, *Beloved*

"I had actually trapped myself in a story that was very convoluted, and I would have been able to cut more later if I'd simplified it at the script stage, but I'd reached a point where I was up against a wall of story logic. If I had cut too much at that stage, the audience would have felt lost."
— James Cameron, director, *Aliens*

CONNECT TO THE BLOG For a more theoretical discussion of the concept of narrative, using the stories offered up during the 2008 presidential campaign, see "It was a dark and stormy campaign," at www.davidbordwell.net/blog/?p=2962.

some broad causal forces as well. Both young men have grown up in urban poverty, and because sports is the most visible sign of success for them, they turn their hopes in that direction.

Plot and Story

We make sense of a narrative, then, by identifying its events and linking them by cause and effect, time, and space. As viewers, we do other things as well. We often infer events that are not explicitly presented, and we recognize the presence of material that is extraneous to the story world. In order to describe how we manage to do these things, we can draw a distinction between *story* and *plot* (sometimes called *discourse*). This isn't a difficult distinction to grasp, but we still need to examine it in a little more detail.

We often make assumptions and inferences about events in a narrative. For instance, at the start of Alfred Hitchcock's *North by Northwest,* we know we are in Manhattan at rush hour. The cues stand out clearly: skyscrapers, bustling pedestrians, congested traffic **(3.1).** Then we watch Roger Thornhill as he leaves an elevator with his secretary, Maggie, and strides through the lobby, dictating memos **(3.2).** On the basis of these cues, we start to draw some conclusions. Thornhill is an executive who leads a busy life. We assume that before we saw Thornhill and Maggie, he was also dictating to her; we have come in on the middle of a string of events in time. We also assume that the dictating began in the office, before they got on the elevator. In other words, we infer causes, a temporal sequence, and another locale even though none of this information has been directly presented. We are probably not aware of having made these inferences, but they are no less firm for going unnoticed.

CONNECT TO THE BLOG

Sequels can extend a story and even jump back in time if a prequel is made. We discuss prequels in "Originality and origin stories."

See www.davidbordwell.net/blog/?p=44.

3.1 Hurrying Manhattan pedestrians in *North by Northwest.*

3.2 Maggie takes dictation from Roger Thornhill.

The set of *all* the events in a narrative, both the ones explicitly presented and those the viewer infers, constitutes the **story.** In our example, the story would consist of at least two depicted events and two inferred ones. We can list them, putting the inferred events in parentheses:

> (Roger Thornhill has a busy day at his office.)
>
> Rush hour hits Manhattan.
>
> (While dictating to his secretary, Maggie, Roger leaves the office, and they take the elevator.)
>
> Still dictating, Roger gets off the elevator with Maggie and they stride through the lobby.

The total world of the story action is sometimes called the film's *diegesis* (the Greek word for "recounted story"). In the opening of *North by Northwest,* the traffic, streets, skyscrapers, and people we see, as well as the traffic, streets, skyscrapers, and people we assume to be offscreen, are all diegetic because they are assumed to exist in the world that the film depicts.

The term *plot* is used to describe everything visibly and audibly present in the film before us. The plot includes, first, all the story events that are directly depicted. In our *North by Northwest* example, only two story events are explicitly presented in the plot: rush hour and Roger Thornhill's dictating to Maggie as they leave the elevator.

Note, though, that the film's plot may contain material that is extraneous to the story world. For example, while the opening of *North by Northwest* is portraying rush hour in Manhattan, we also see the film's credits and hear orchestral music. Neither of these elements is diegetic, since they are brought in from *outside* the story world. (The characters can't read the credits or hear the music.) Credits and such extraneous music are thus *nondiegetic* elements. In Chapters 6 and 7, we'll consider how editing and sound can function nondiegetically. At this point, we need only notice that the plot—the totality of the film—can bring in nondiegetic material.

3.3   A hopeful investor in the play enters the theater . . .

3.4   . . . and the camera moves in on a poster predicting success for the musical.

3.5   But three comic nondiegetic images reveal it to be a flop: ghostly figures on a boat . . .

3.6   . . . a skull in a desert . . .

3.7   . . . and an egg.

Nondiegetic material may occur elsewhere than in credit sequences. In *The Band Wagon,* we see the premiere of a hopelessly pretentious musical play. Eager patrons file into the theater **(3.3),** and the camera moves closer to a poster above the door **(3.4).** There then appear three black-and-white images **(3.5–3.7)** accompanied by a brooding chorus. These images and sounds are clearly nondiegetic, inserted from outside the story world in order to signal that the production bombed. The plot has added material to the story for comic effect.

In sum, story and plot overlap in one respect and diverge in others. The plot explicitly presents certain story events, so these events are common to both domains. The story goes beyond the plot in suggesting some diegetic events that we never witness. The plot goes beyond the story world by presenting nondiegetic images and sounds that may affect our understanding of the action. A diagram of the situation would look like this:

Story

Presumed and inferred events	Explicitly presented events	Added nondiegetic material
	Plot	

We can think about these differences between story and plot from two perspectives. From the standpoint of the storyteller—the filmmaker—the story is the sum total of all the events in the narrative. The storyteller can present some of these events directly (that is, make them part of the plot), can hint at events that are not presented, and can simply ignore other events. For instance, though we learn later in *North by Northwest* that Roger's mother is still close to him, we never learn what happened to his father. The filmmaker can also add nondiegetic material, as in the example from *The Band Wagon.* In a sense, then, the filmmaker makes a story into a plot.

From the perceiver's standpoint, things look somewhat different. All we have before us is the plot—the arrangement of material in the film as it stands. We create the story in our minds on the basis of cues in the plot. We also recognize when the plot presents nondiegetic material.

The story–plot distinction suggests that if you want to give someone a synopsis of a narrative film, you can do it in two ways. You can summarize the story, starting from the very earliest incident that the plot cues you to assume or infer and running chronologically to the end. Or you can tell the plot, starting with the first incident you encountered in watching the film and presenting narrative information as you received it while watching the movie.

Our initial definition and the distinction between plot and story constitute a set of tools for analyzing how narrative works. We shall see that the story–plot distinction affects all three aspects of narrative: causality, time, and space.

Cause and Effect

If narrative depends so heavily on cause and effect, what kinds of things can function as causes in a narrative? Usually, the agents of cause and effect are *characters*. By triggering and reacting to events, characters play roles within the film's formal system.

Most often, characters are persons, or at least entities like persons—Bugs Bunny or E.T. the extraterrestrial or even the singing teapot in *Beauty and the Beast.* For our purposes here, Michael Moore is a character in *Roger and Me* no less than Roger Thornhill is in *North by Northwest,* even though Moore is a real person and Thornhill is fictional. In any narrative film, either fictional or documentary, characters create causes and register effects. Within the film's formal system, they make things happen and respond to events. Their actions and reactions contribute strongly to our engagement with the film.

Unlike characters in novels, film characters typically have a visible body. This is such a basic convention that we take it for granted, but it can be contested. Occasionally, a character is only a voice, as when the dead Obi-Wan Kenobi urges the Jedi master Yoda to train Luke Skywalker in *The Empire Strikes Back.* More disturbingly, in Luis Buñuel's *That Obscure Object of Desire,* one woman is portrayed by two actresses, and the physical differences between them may suggest different sides of her character. Todd Solondz takes this innovation further in *Palindromes,* in which a 13-year-old girl is portrayed by male and female performers of different ages and races.

Along with a body, a character has *traits:* attitudes, skills, habits, tastes, psychological drives, and any other qualities that distinguish the character. Some characters, such as Mickey Mouse, may have only a few traits. When we say a character possesses several varying traits, some at odds with one another, we tend to call that character complex, or three-dimensional, or well developed. A memorable character such as Sherlock Holmes is a mass of traits. Some bear on his habits, such as his love of music or his addiction to cocaine, while others reflect his basic nature: his penetrating intelligence, his disdain for stupidity, his professional pride, his occasional gallantry.

As our love of gossip shows, we're curious about other humans, and we bring our people-watching skills to narratives. We're quick to assign traits to the characters onscreen, and often the movie helps us out. Most characters wear their traits far more openly than people do in real life, and the plot presents situations that swiftly reveal them to us. The opening scene of *Raiders of the Lost Ark* throws Indiana Jones's personality into high relief. We see immediately that he's bold and resourceful. He's courageous, but he can feel fear. By unearthing ancient treasures for museums, he shows an admirable devotion to scientific knowledge. In a few minutes, his essential traits are presented straightforwardly, and we come to know and sympathize with him.

It's not accidental that all of the traits that Indiana Jones displays in the opening scene are relevant to later scenes in *Raiders.* In general, a character is given traits that will play causal roles in the overall story action. The second scene of Alfred Hitchcock's *The Man Who Knew Too Much* (1934) shows that the heroine, Jill, is an excellent shot with a rifle. For much of the film, this trait seems irrelevant to the action, but in the last scene, Jill is able to shoot one of the villains when a police marksman cannot do it. This skill with a rifle is a trait that helps make up a character named Jill, and it serves a particular narrative function.

Not all causes and effects in narratives originate with characters. In the so-called disaster movies, an earthquake or tidal wave may precipitate a series of actions on the parts of the characters. The same principle holds when the shark in *Jaws* terrorizes a community. Still, once these natural occurrences set the situation up, human desires and goals usually enter the action to develop the narrative. A man escaping from a flood may be placed in the situation of having to decide whether to rescue his worst enemy. In *Jaws,* the townspeople pursue a variety of strategies to deal with the shark, propelling the plot as they do so.

In general, the spectator actively seeks to connect events by means of cause and effect. Given an incident, we tend to imagine what might have caused it or what it might in turn cause. That is, we look for causal motivation. We have mentioned an instance of this in Chapter 2: In the scene from *My Man Godfrey,* a scavenger hunt serves as a cause that justifies the presence of a beggar at a society ball (see p. 68).

Causal motivation often involves the planting of information in advance of a scene, as we saw in the kitchen scene of *The Shining* (2.7, 2.8). In *L.A. Confidential,* the idealistic detective Exley confides in his cynical colleague Vincennes that the murder of his father had driven him to enter law enforcement. He had privately named the unknown killer "Rollo Tomasi," a name that he has turned into an emblem of all unpunished evil. This conversation initially seems like a simple bit of psychological insight. Yet later, when the corrupt police chief Smith shoots Vincennes, the latter mutters "Rollo Tomasi" with his last breath. When the puzzled Smith asks Exley who Rollo Tomasi is, Exley's earlier conversation with Vincennes motivates his shocked realization that the dead Vincennes has given him a clue to his killer. Near the end, when Exley is about to shoot Smith, he says that the chief is Rollo Tomasi. Thus an apparently minor detail returns as a major causal and thematic motif. And perhaps the unusual name, Rollo Tomasi, functions to help the audience remember this motif.

Most of what we have said about causality pertains to the plot's direct presentation of causes and effects. In *The Man Who Knew Too Much,* Jill is shown to be a good shot, and because of this, she can save her daughter. But the plot can also lead us to *infer* causes and effects, and thus build up a total story. The detective film furnishes the best example of how we actively construct the story.

A murder has been committed. That is, we know an effect but not the causes—the killer, the motive, and perhaps also the method. The mystery tale thus depends strongly on curiosity—on our desire to know events that have occurred before the events that the plot presents to us. It's the detective's job to disclose, at the end, the missing causes—to name the killer, explain the motive, and reveal the method. That is, in the detective film, the climax of the plot (the action we see) is a revelation of prior incidents in the story (events we did not see). We can diagram this:

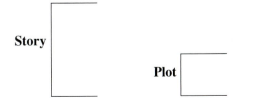

a. Crime conceived
b. Crime planned
c. Crime committed
d. Crime discovered
e. Detective investigates
f. Detective reveals a, b, and c

Although this pattern is most common in detective narratives, any film's plot can withhold causes and thus arouse our curiosity. Horror and science fiction films often leave us temporarily in the dark about what forces lurk behind certain events. Not

3.8   The final image of *The 400 Blows* leaves Antoine's future uncertain.

until three-quarters of the way through *Alien* do we learn that the science officer Ash is a robot conspiring to protect the alien. In *Caché,* a married couple receive an anonymous videotape recording their daily lives. The film's plot shows them trying to discover who made it and why it was made. In general, whenever any film creates a mystery, it suppresses certain story causes and presents only effects in the plot.

The plot may also present causes but withhold story *effects,* prompting suspense and uncertainty in the viewer. After Hannibal Lecter's attack on his guards in the Tennessee prison in *The Silence of the Lambs,* the police search of the building raises the possibility that a body lying on top of an elevator is the wounded Lecter. After an extended suspense scene, we learn that he has switched clothes with a dead guard and escaped.

A plot's withholding of effects can provide a vivid ending. A famous example occurs in the final moments of François Truffaut's *The 400 Blows.* The boy Antoine Doinel, having escaped from a reformatory, runs along the seashore. The camera zooms in on his face, and the frame freezes **(3.8).** The plot does not reveal if he is captured and brought back, leaving us to speculate on what might happen in Antoine's future.

Time

Causes and their effects are basic to narrative, but they take place in time. Here again our story–plot distinction helps clarify how time shapes our understanding of narrative action.

As we watch a film, we construct story time on the basis of what the plot presents. For example, the plot may present events out of chronological order. In *Citizen Kane,* we see a man's death before we see his youth, and we must build up a chronological version of his life. Even if events are shown in chronological order, most plots don't show every detail from beginning to end. We assume that the characters spend uneventful time sleeping, traveling from place to place, eating, and the like, but the story duration containing irrelevant action has simply been skipped over. Another possibility is to have the plot present the same story event more than once, as when a character recalls a traumatic incident. In John Woo's *The Killer,* an accident in the opening scene blinds a singer, and later we see the same event again and again as the protagonist regretfully thinks back to it.

Such options mean that in constructing the film's story out of its plot, the viewer is engaged in trying to put events in chronological *order* and to assign them some *duration* and *frequency.* We can look at each of these temporal factors separately.

Temporal Order   We are quite accustomed to films that present events out of story **order.** A flashback is simply a portion of a story that the plot presents out of chronological order. In *Edward Scissorhands,* we first see the Winona Ryder character as an old woman telling her granddaughter a bedtime story. Most of the film then shows events that occurred when she was a high school girl. Such reordering doesn't confuse us because we mentally rearrange the events into the order in which they would logically have to occur: childhood comes before adulthood. From the plot order, we infer the story order. If story events can be thought of as ABCD, then the plot that uses a flashback presents something like BACD. Similarly, a flash-forward—that is, moving from present to future then back to the present—would also be an instance of how plot can shuffle story order. A flash-forward could be represented as ABDC.

One common pattern for reordering story events is an alternation of past and present in the plot. In the first half of Terence Davies' *Distant Voices, Still Lives,* we see scenes set in the present during a young woman's wedding day. These alternate with flashbacks to a time when her family lived under the sway of an abusive, mentally disturbed father. Interestingly, the flashback scenes are arranged out of chronological story order: childhood episodes alternate with scenes of adolescence, further cueing the spectator to assemble a linear story.

Sometimes a fairly simple reordering of scenes can create complicated effects. The plot of Quentin Tarantino's *Pulp Fiction* begins with a couple deciding to rob the diner in which they're eating breakfast. This scene takes place fairly late in the story, but the viewer doesn't learn this until near the end of the film, when the robbery interrupts a dialogue involving other, more central, characters eating breakfast in the same diner. Just by pulling a scene out of order and placing it at the start, Tarantino creates a surprise. At another point in *Pulp Fiction,* a hired killer is shot to death. But he reappears alive in subsequent scenes, which show him and his partner trying to dispose of a dead body. Tarantino has shifted a block of scenes from the middle of the story (before the man was killed) to the end of the plot. By coming at the film's conclusion, these portions receive an emphasis they wouldn't have if they had remained in their chronological story order.

Temporal Duration   The plot of *North by Northwest* presents four crowded days and nights in the life of Roger Thornhill. But the story stretches back far before that, since information about the past is revealed in the course of the plot. The story events include Roger's past marriages, the U.S. Intelligence Agency's plot to create a false agent named George Kaplan, and the villain Van Damm's series of smuggling activities.

In general, a film's plot selects certain stretches of story **duration.** This could involve concentrating on a short, relatively cohesive time span, as *North by Northwest* does. Or it could involve highlighting significant stretches of time from a period of many years, as *Citizen Kane* does when it shows us the protagonist in his youth, skips over some time to show him as a young man, skips over more time to show him middle-aged, and so forth. The sum of all these slices of *story* duration yields an overall *plot* duration.

But we need one more distinction. Watching a movie takes time—20 minutes or two hours or eight hours (as in Hans Jürgen Syberberg's *Our Hitler: A Film from Germany*). There is thus a third duration involved in a narrative film, which we can call *screen* duration. The relationships among story duration, plot duration, and screen duration are complex (see "Where to Go from Here" for further discussion), but for our purposes, we can say this: the filmmaker can manipulate screen duration independently of the overall story duration and plot duration. For example, *North by Northwest* has an overall story duration of several years (including all relevant prior events), an overall plot duration of four days and nights, and a screen duration of about 136 minutes.

Just as plot duration selects from story duration, so screen duration selects from overall plot duration. In *North by Northwest,* only portions of the film's four days and nights are shown to us. An interesting counterexample is *Twelve Angry Men,* the story of a jury deliberating a murder case. The 95 minutes of the movie approximate the same stretch of time in its characters' lives.

At a more specific level, the plot can use screen duration to override story time. For example, screen duration can *expand* story duration. A famous instance is that of the raising of the bridges in Sergei Eisenstein's *October*. Here an event that takes only a few moments in the story is stretched out to several minutes of screen time by means of the technique of film editing. As a result, this action gains a tremendous emphasis. The plot can also use screen duration to compress story time, as when a process taking hours or days is condensed into a rapid series of shots. These examples suggest that film techniques play a central role in creating screen duration. We shall consider this in more detail in Chapters 5 and 6.

Temporal Frequency   Most commonly, a story event is presented only once in the plot. Occasionally, however, a single story event may appear twice or even more in the plot treatment. If we see an event early in a film and then there is a flashback to that event later on, we see that same event twice. Some films use multiple narrators, each of whom describes the same event; again, we see it occur several times. This increased **frequency** may allow us to see the same action in several ways. When a plot repeats a story event, the aim is often to provide new information. This occurs in *Pulp Fiction,* when the robbery of the diner, triggered at the start of the film, takes on its full significance only when it is repeated at the climax. In *Run Lola Run,* a single event is repeated many times after it first occurs: Lola's boyfriend reports by phone that he has lost a bag (*Tasche*) full of drug money, and we hear him and Lola shouting "Tasche" several times, even though we realize that they really say it only once or twice each. The repetition of their shouts underlines their terror in a way characteristic of this hyperkinetic movie. In our examination of *Citizen Kane,* we shall see another example of how repetition can recontextualize old information.

The various ways that a film's plot may manipulate story order, duration, and frequency illustrate how we actively participate in making sense of the narrative film. The plot supplies cues about chronological sequence, the time span of the actions, and the number of times an event occurs, and it's up to the viewer to make assumptions and inferences and to form expectations. In some cases, our understanding of temporal relations can get quite complicated. In *The Usual Suspects,* a seemingly petty criminal spins an elaborate tale of his gang's activities to an FBI agent. His recounting unfolds in many flashbacks, some of which repeat events we witnessed in the opening scene. Yet a surprise final twist reveals that some of the flashbacks must have contained lies, and we must piece together both the chronology of events and the story's real cause–effect chain. Such time scrambling has become more common in recent decades. (See "A Closer Look," p. 87.)

Often we must motivate manipulations of time by the all-important principle of cause and effect. For instance, a flashback will often be caused by some incident that triggers a character's recalling some event in the past. The plot may skip over years of story duration if they contain nothing important to the chains of cause and effect. The repetition of actions may also be motivated by the plot's need to communicate certain key causes very clearly to the spectator.

Space

In some media, a narrative might emphasize only causality and time. Many of the anecdotes we tell each other don't specify where the action takes place. In film narrative, however, **space** is usually an important factor. Events occur in well-defined locales, such as Kansas or Oz; the Flint, Michigan, of *Roger and Me;* or the Manhattan of *North by Northwest*. We shall consider setting in more detail when we examine mise-en-scene in Chapter 4, but we ought briefly to note how plot and story can manipulate space.

PLAYING GAMES WITH STORY TIME

For a spectator, reconstructing story order from the plot might be seen as a sort of game. Most Hollywood films make this game fairly simple. Still, just as we enjoy learning the rules of new games rather than playing the same one over and over, in unusual films, we can enjoy the challenge of unpredictable presentations of story events.

Since the 1980s, occasional films have exploited that enjoyment by using techniques other than straightforward flashbacks to tell their stories. For instance, the story events might be reordered in novel ways. *Pulp Fiction* (1994) begins and ends with stages of a restaurant holdup—seemingly a conventional frame story. Yet in fact the final event to occur in the story—the Bruce Willis character and his girlfriend fleeing Los Angeles—happens well *after* the final scene we see. The reordering of events is startling and confusing at first, but it is dramatically effective in the way the conclusion forces us to rethink events we have seen earlier.

The success of *Pulp Fiction* made such a play with story order more acceptable in American filmmaking. *GO* (Doug Liman, 1999) presents the events of a single night three times, each time from a different character's point of view. We cannot fully figure out what happened until the end, since various events are withheld from the first version and shown in the second or third.

Pulp Fiction and *GO* were independent films, but more mainstream Hollywood movies have also played with the temporal relations of story and plot. Steven Soderbergh's *Out of Sight* (1998) begins with the story of an inept bank robber who falls in love with the FBI agent who pursues him. As their oddball romance proceeds, there is a string of flashbacks not motivated by any character's memory. These seem to involve a quite separate story line, and their purpose is puzzling until the film's second half, when the last flashback, perhaps a character's recollection, loops back to the action that had begun the film and thus helps explain the main plot events.

Mainstream films may also use science fiction or fantasy premises to present alternative futures, often called "what if?" narratives. (The film industry website Box Office Mojo even lists "What If" as a separate genre and defines it as "Comedies About Metaphysical Questions That Come to Pass by Fantastical Means but in Realistic Settings.") Such films typically present a situation at the beginning, then show how the story might proceed along different cause–effect chains if one factor were to be changed. *Sliding Doors* (Peter Howitt, 1998), for example, shows the heroine, Helen, fired from her job and heading home to her apartment, where her boyfriend is in bed with another woman.

We see Helen entering the subway and catching her train, but then the action runs backward and she arrives on the platform again, this time bumping into a child on the stairs and missing the train. The rest of the film's plot moves between two alternative futures for Helen. By catching the train, Helen arrives in time to discover her boyfriend's affair and moves out. By missing the train, she arrives after the other woman has left and hence she stays with her faithless lover. The plot moves back and forth between these alternative cause–effect chains before neatly dovetailing them at the end.

Groundhog Day (Harold Ramis, 1993) helped to popularize "what if?" plots. On February 1, an obnoxious weatherman, Phil Connor, travels to Punxsutawney to cover the famous Groundhog Day ceremonies. He then finds himself trapped in February 2, which repeats over and over, with variants depending on how Phil acts each day, sometimes behaving frivolously, sometimes breaking laws **(3.9, 3.10),** and later trying to improve himself. Only after many such days does he become an admirable character, and the repetitions mysteriously stop.

3.9 During one repetition of February 2 in *Groundhog Day*, Phil tests whether he can get away with crimes, getting himself tossed in jail in the evening . . .

3.10 . . . only to find himself waking up, as on other Groundhog Days, back in bed at the bed-and-breakfast inn.

3.13   In *Exodus*, Dov Landau recounts his traumatic stay in a concentration camp. Instead of presenting this through a flashback, the narration dwells on his face, leaving us to visualize his ordeal.

"The multiple points of view replaced the linear story. Watching a repeated action or an intersection happen again and again . . . they hold the audience in the story. It's like watching a puzzle unfold."

— Gus van Sant, director, on *Elephant*

Normally, the place of the story action is also that of the plot, but sometimes the plot leads us to infer other locales as part of the story. We never see Roger Thornhill's office or the colleges that kicked Kane out. Thus the narrative may ask us to imagine spaces and actions that are never shown. In Otto Preminger's *Exodus*, one scene is devoted to Dov Landau's interrogation by a terrorist organization he wants to join. Dov reluctantly tells his questioners of life in a Nazi concentration camp **(3.13)**. Although the film never shows this locale through a flashback, much of the scene's emotional power depends on our using our imagination to fill in Dov's sketchy description of the camp.

Further, we can introduce an idea akin to the concept of screen duration. Besides story space and plot space, cinema employs screen space: the visible space within the frame. We'll consider screen space and offscreen space in detail in Chapter 5, when we analyze framing as a cinematographic technique. For now, it's enough to say that, just as screen duration selects certain plot spans for presentation, so screen space selects portions of plot space.

Openings, Closings, and Patterns of Development

In Chapter 2, our discussion of formal development in general within the film suggested that it's often useful to compare beginnings and endings. A narrative's use of causality, time, and space usually involves a change from an initial situation to a final situation.

A film does not just start, it *begins*. The opening provides a basis for what is to come and initiates us into the narrative. In some cases, the plot will seek to arouse curiosity by bringing us into a series of actions that has already started. (This is called opening *in medias res*, a Latin phrase meaning "in the middle of things.") The viewer speculates on possible causes of the events presented. *The Usual Suspects* begins with a mysterious man named Keyser Söze killing one of the main characters and setting fire to a ship. Much of the rest of the film deals with how these events came to pass. In other cases, the film begins by telling us about the characters and their situations before any major actions occur.

Either way, some of the actions that took place before the plot started will be stated or suggested so that we can start to connect up the whole story. The portion of the plot that lays out important story events and character traits in the opening situation is called the *exposition*. In general, the opening raises our expectations by setting up a specific range of possible causes for and effects of what we see. Indeed, the first quarter or so of a film's plot is often referred to as the *setup*.

As the plot proceeds, the causes and effects will define narrower patterns of development. There is no exhaustive list of possible plot patterns, but several kinds crop up frequently enough to be worth mentioning.

Most patterns of plot development depend heavily on the ways that causes and effects create a change in a character's situation. The most common general pattern is a *change in knowledge.* Very often, a character learns something in the course of the action, with the most crucial knowledge coming at the final turning point of the plot. In *Witness,* when John Book, hiding out on an Amish farm, learns that his partner has been killed, his rage soon leads to a climactic shoot-out.

A very common pattern of development is the *goal-oriented* plot, in which a character takes steps to achieve a desired object or state of affairs. Plots based on *searches* would be instances of the goal plot. In *Raiders of the Lost Ark,* the protagonists try to find the Ark of the Covenant; in *Le Million,* characters search for a missing lottery ticket; in *North by Northwest,* Roger Thornhill looks for George Kaplan. A variation on the goal-oriented plot pattern is the *investigation,* so typical of detective films, in which the protagonist's goal is not an object, but information, usually about mysterious causes. In more strongly psychological films, such as Fellini's *8½,* the search and the investigation become internalized when the protagonist, a noted film director, attempts to discover the source of his creative problems.

Time or space may also provide plot patterns. A framing situation in the present may initiate a series of flashbacks showing how events led up to the present situation, as in *The Usual Suspects'* flashbacks. *Hoop Dreams* is organized around the two main characters' high school careers, with each part of the film devoted to a year of their lives. The plot may also create a specific duration for the action—a *deadline.* In *Back to the Future,* the hero must synchronize his time machine with a bolt of lightning at a specific moment in order to return to the present. This creates a goal toward which he must struggle. Or the plot may create patterns of repeated action via cycles of events: the familiar "here we go again" pattern. Such a pattern occurs in Woody Allen's *Zelig,* in which the chameleon-like hero repeatedly loses his own identity by imitating the people around him.

Space can also become the basis for a plot pattern. This usually happens when the action is confined to a single locale, such as a train (Anthony Mann's *The Tall Target*) or a home (Sidney Lumet's *Long Day's Journey into Night*).

A given plot can, of course, combine these patterns. Many films built around a journey, such as *The Wizard of Oz* or *North by Northwest,* involve deadlines. *The Usual Suspects* puts its flashbacks at the service of an investigation. Jacques Tati's *Mr. Hulot's Holiday* uses both spatial and temporal patterns to structure its comic plot. The plot confines itself to a beachside resort and its neighboring areas, and it consumes one week of a summer vacation. Each day certain routines recur: morning exercise, lunch, afternoon outings, dinner, evening entertainment. Much of the film's humor relies on the way that Mr. Hulot alienates the other guests and the townspeople by disrupting their conventional habits **(3.14).** Although cause and effect still operate in *Mr. Hulot's Holiday,* time and space are central to the plot's formal patterning.

For any pattern of development, the spectator will create specific expectations. As the film trains the viewer in its particular form, these expectations become more and more precise. Once we comprehend Dorothy's desire to go home, we see her every action as furthering or delaying her progress toward her goal. Thus her trip through Oz is hardly a sightseeing tour. Each step of her journey (to the Emerald City, to the Witch's castle, to the Emerald City again) is governed by the same principle—her desire to go home.

In any film, the pattern of development in the middle portion may delay an expected outcome. When Dorothy at last reaches the Wizard, he sets up a new obstacle for her by demanding the Witch's broom. Similarly, in *North by Northwest,* Hitchcock's journey plot constantly postpones Roger Thornhill's discovery of the

3.14 In *Mr. Hulot's Holiday,* Hulot's aged, noisy car has a flat tire that breaks up a funeral.

Kaplan hoax, and this, too, creates suspense. The pattern of development may also create surprise, the cheating of an expectation, as when Dorothy discovers that the Wizard is a fraud or when Thornhill sees the minion Leonard fire point-blank at his boss Van Damm. Patterns of development encourage the spectator to form long-term expectations that can be delayed, cheated, or gratified.

A film doesn't simply stop; it *ends.* The narrative will typically resolve its causal issues by bringing the development to a high point, or *climax.* In the climax, the action is presented as having a narrow range of possible outcomes. At the climax of *North by Northwest,* Roger and Eve are dangling off Mount Rushmore, and there are only two possibilities: they will fall, or they will be saved.

Because the climax focuses possible outcomes so narrowly, it typically serves to settle the causal issues that have run through the film. In the documentary *Primary,* the climax takes place on election night; both Kennedy and Humphrey await the voters' verdict and finally learn the winner. In *Jaws,* several battles with the shark climax in the destruction of the boat, the death of Captain Quint, the apparent death of Hooper, and Brody's final victory. In such films, the ending resolves, or closes off, the chains of cause and effect.

Emotionally, the climax aims to lift the viewer to a high degree of tension or suspense. Since the viewer knows that there are relatively few ways the action can develop, she or he can hope for a fairly specific outcome. In the climax of many films, formal resolution coincides with an emotional satisfaction.

A few narratives, however, are deliberately anticlimactic. Having created expectations about how the cause–effect chain will be resolved, the film scotches them by refusing to settle things definitely. One famous example is the last shot of *The 400 Blows* (p. 84). In Michelangelo Antonioni's *L'Eclisse* ("The Eclipse"), the two lovers vow to meet for a final reconciliation but aren't shown doing so.

In such films, the ending remains relatively open. That is, the plot leaves us uncertain about the final consequences of the story events. Our response becomes less firm than it does when a film has a clear-cut climax and resolution. The form may encourage us to imagine what might happen next or to reflect on other ways in which our expectations might have been fulfilled.

Narration: The Flow of Story Information

A plot presents or implies story information. The opening of *North by Northwest* shows Manhattan at rush hour and introduces Roger Thornhill as an advertising executive; it also suggests that he has been busily dictating before we see him.

Filmmakers have long realized that the spectator's interest can be aroused and manipulated by carefully divulging story information at various points. In general, when we go to a film, we know relatively little about the story; by the end, we know a lot more, usually the whole story. What happens in between?

The plot may arrange cues in ways that withhold information for the sake of curiosity or surprise. Or the plot may supply information in such a way as to create expectations or increase suspense. All these processes constitute **narration,** the plot's way of distributing story information in order to achieve specific effects. Narration is the moment-by-moment process that guides us in building the story out of the plot. Many factors enter into narration, but the most important ones for our purposes involve the *range* and the *depth* of story information that the plot presents.

Range of Story Information

The plot of D. W. Griffith's *The Birth of a Nation* begins by recounting how slaves were brought to America and how people debated the need to free them. The plot then shows two families, the northern Stoneman family and the southern Camerons. The plot also dwells on political matters, including Lincoln's hope of averting civil war. From the start, then, our range of knowledge is very broad. The plot takes us across historical periods, regions of the country, and various groups of characters. This breadth of story information continues throughout the film. When Ben Cameron founds the Ku Klux Klan, we know about it at the moment the idea strikes him, long before the other characters learn of it. At the climax, we know that the Klan is riding to rescue several characters besieged in a cabin, but the besieged people do not know this. On the whole, in *The Birth of a Nation,* the narration is very *unrestricted:* We know more, we see and hear more, than any of the characters can. Such extremely knowledgeable narration is often called *omniscient narration.*

Now consider the plot of Howard Hawks's *The Big Sleep.* The film begins with the detective Philip Marlowe visiting General Sternwood, who wants to hire him. We learn about the case as he does. Throughout the rest of the film, Marlowe is present in every scene. With hardly any exceptions, we don't see or hear anything that he can't see and hear. The narration is thus *restricted* to what Marlowe knows.

Each alternative offers certain advantages. *The Birth of a Nation* seeks to present a panoramic vision of a period in American history (seen through peculiarly racist spectacles). Omniscient narration is thus essential to creating the sense of many destinies intertwined with the fate of the country. Had Griffith restricted narration the way *The Big Sleep* does, we would have learned story information solely through one character—say, Ben Cameron. We could not witness the prologue scene, or the scenes in Lincoln's office, or most of the battle episodes, or the scene of Lincoln's assassination, since Ben is present at none of these events. The plot would now concentrate on one man's experience of the Civil War and Reconstruction.

Similarly, *The Big Sleep* derives functional advantages from its restricted narration. By limiting us to Marlowe's range of knowledge, the film can create curiosity and surprise. Restricted narration is important to mystery films, since the films engage our interest by hiding certain important causes. Confining the plot to an investigator's range of knowledge plausibly motivates concealing other story information. *The Big Sleep* could have been less restricted by, say, alternating scenes of Marlowe's investigation with scenes that show the gambling boss, Eddie Mars, planning his crimes, but this would have given away some of the mystery. In each of the two films, the narration's range of knowledge functions to elicit particular reactions from the viewer.

Unrestricted and restricted narration aren't watertight categories but rather are two ends of a continuum. Range is a matter of degree. A film may present a broader range of knowledge than does *The Big Sleep* and still not attain the omniscience of *The Birth of a Nation.* In *North by Northwest,* for instance, the early scenes confine

"In the first section [of Reservoir Dogs], up until Mr. Orange shoots Mr. Blonde, the characters have far more information about what's going on than you have—and they have conflicting information. Then the Mr. Orange sequence happens and that's a great leveller. You start getting caught up with exactly what's going on, and in the third part, when you go back into the warehouse for the climax you are totally ahead of everybody—you know far more than any one of the characters."

— Quentin Tarantino, director

us pretty much to what Roger Thornhill sees and knows. After he flees from the United Nations building, however, the plot moves to Washington, where the members of the U.S. Intelligence Agency discuss the situation. Here the viewer learns something that Roger Thornhill will not learn for some time: the man he seeks, George Kaplan, does not exist. Thereafter, we have a greater range of knowledge than Roger does. In at least one important respect, we also know more than the Agency's staff: we know exactly how the mix-up took place. But we still do not know many other things that the narration could have divulged in the scene in Washington. For instance, the Agency's staff do not identify the real agent they have working under Van Damm's nose. In this way, any film may oscillate between restricted and unrestricted presentation of story information.

Across a whole film, narration is never completely unrestricted. There is always something we are not told, even if it is only how the story will end. Usually, we think of a typical unrestricted narration as operating in the way that it does in *The Birth of a Nation:* the plot shifts constantly from character to character to change our source of information.

Similarly, a completely restricted narration is not common. Even if the plot is built around a single character, the narration usually includes a few scenes that the character is not present to witness. Though *Tootsie*'s narration remains almost entirely attached to actor Michael Dorsey, a few shots show his acquaintances shopping or watching him on television.

The plot's range of story information creates a *hierarchy of knowledge*. At any given moment, we can ask if the viewer knows more than, less than, or as much as the characters do. For instance, here's how hierarchies would look for the three films we have been discussing. The higher someone is on the scale, the greater his or her range of knowledge:

The Birth of a Nation	*The Big Sleep*	*North by Northwest*
(unrestricted narration)	(restricted)	(mixed and fluctuating)
viewer	viewer—Marlowe	the Agency
all characters		viewer
		Thornhill

An easy way to analyze the range of narration is to ask, *Who knows what when?* The spectator must be included among the "whos," not only because we may get more knowledge than any one character but also because we may get knowledge that *no* character possesses. We shall see this happen at the end of *Citizen Kane.*

Our examples suggest the powerful effects that narration can achieve by manipulating the range of story information. Restricted narration tends to create greater curiosity and surprise for the viewer. For instance, if a character is exploring a sinister house, and we see and hear no more than the character does, a sudden revelation of a hand thrusting out from a doorway will startle us.

In contrast, as Hitchcock pointed out, a degree of unrestricted narration helps build suspense. He explained it this way to François Truffaut:

> We are now having a very innocent little chat. Let us suppose that there is a bomb underneath this table between us. Nothing happens, and then all of a sudden, "Boom!" There is an explosion. The public is surprised, but prior to this surprise, it has seen an absolutely ordinary scene, of no special consequence. Now, let us take a suspense situation. The bomb is underneath the table and the public knows it, probably because they have seen the anarchist place it there. The public is aware that the bomb is going to explode at one o'clock and there is a clock in the decor. The public can see that it is a quarter to one. In these conditions this innocuous conversation becomes fascinating because the public is participating in the scene. The audience is longing to warn the characters on the screen: "You shouldn't be talking about such trivial matters. There's a bomb beneath you and it's about to explode!"

CONNECT TO THE BLOG
Cloverfield uses an unusually restricted narration, confining itself to film shot by the main characters. See our analysis, "A behemoth from the Dead Zone," at
www.davidbordwell.net/blog/?p=1844.

In the first case we have given the public fifteen seconds of surprise at the moment of the explosion. In the second case we have provided them with fifteen minutes of suspense. The conclusion is that whenever possible the public must be informed. (François Truffaut, *Hitchcock* [New York: Simon & Schuster, 1967], p. 52)

Hitchcock put his theory into practice. In *Psycho*, Lila Crane explores the Bates mansion in much the same way as our hypothetical character is doing above. There are isolated moments of surprise as she discovers odd information about Norman and his mother. But the overall effect of the sequence is built on suspense because we know, as Lila does not, that Mrs. Bates is in the house. (Actually, as in *North by Northwest*, our knowledge isn't completely accurate, but during Lila's investigation, we believe it to be.) As in Hitchcock's anecdote, our superior range of knowledge creates suspense because we can anticipate events that the character cannot.

CONNECT TO THE BLOG

We present a more detailed discussion of the distinction between perceptual and mental subjectivity in narration in "Categorical coherence: A closer look at character subjectivity."

See www.davidbordwell.net/blog/?p=2927.

Depth of Story Information

A film's narration manipulates not only the range of knowledge but also the depth of our knowledge. Here we are referring to how deeply the plot plunges into a character's psychological states. Just as there is a spectrum between restricted and unrestricted narration, there is a continuum between objectivity and subjectivity.

A plot might confine us wholly to information about what characters say and do: their external behavior. Here the narration is relatively *objective*. Or a film's plot may give us access to what characters see and hear. We might see shots taken from a character's optical standpoint, the **point-of-view shot.** For instance, in *North by Northwest*, point-of-view editing is used as we see Roger Thornhill crawl up to Van Damm's window (**3.15–3.17**). Or we might hear sounds as the character would hear them, what sound recordists call *sound perspective*. Visual or auditory point of view offers a degree of subjectivity, one we might call *perceptual subjectivity*.

There is the possibility of still greater depth if the plot plunges into the character's mind. We can call this *mental subjectivity*. We might hear an internal voice reporting the character's thoughts, or we might see the character's inner images, representing memory, fantasy, dreams, or hallucinations. In *Slumdog Millionaire*, the hero is a contestant on a quiz show, but his concentration is often interrupted by brief shots of his memories, particularly one image of the woman he loves (**3.18–3.19**). Here Jamal's memory motivates flashbacks to earlier story events.

Either sort of subjectivity may be signaled through particular film techniques. If a character is drunk, or drugged, or disoriented, the narration may render those perceptual states through slow motion, blurred imagery, or distorted sound. Similar stylistic qualities may suggest a dream or hallucination.

But some imaginary actions may not be so strongly marked. A later scene in *Slumdog Millionaire* shows Jamal reuniting with his gangster brother Salim atop a skyscraper under construction. Jamal hurls himself at Salim, and we see shots of both falling from the building (**3.20–3.21**). But the next shot presents Jamal still on the skyscraper, glaring at Salim (**3.22**). Now we realize that the images of the falling men were purely mental, representing Jamal's rage. We briefly thought that their fall was really taking place because the shots lacked any marks of subjectivity.

Typically, either perceptual or mental subjectivity is embedded in a framework of objective narration. Point-of-view shots, like those of Roger Thornhill in *North by Northwest*, and flashbacks or fantasies are bracketed by more objective shots. We are able to understand Jamal's memory of Latika and his urge to kill Salim because those images are framed by shots of actions that we take to be really happening in the plot. Other sorts of films, however, may avoid this convention. Fellini's *8½*, Bunuel's *Belle de Jour*, Haneke's *Caché*, and Nolan's *Memento* mix objectivity and subjectivity in ambiguous ways.

3.15 In *North by Northwest*, Roger Thornhill looks in Van Damm's window (objective narration).

3.16 A shot from Roger's point of view follows (perceptual subjectivity).

3.17 This is followed by another shot of Roger looking (objectivity again).

3.18   Early in *Slumdog Millionaire,* it's established that during the quiz show Jamal recalls his past . . .

3.19   . . . most often, his glimpse of Latika at the train station.

3.20   Furious with Salim, Jamal grabs him and rushes toward the edge of the building.

3.21   Several shots present their fall.

3.22   Cut back to Jamal, glaring at Salim. The shot reveals that he only imagined killing both of them.

Does a restricted range of knowledge create a greater subjective depth? Not necessarily. *The Big Sleep* is quite restricted in its range of knowledge, as we've seen. But we very seldom see or hear things from Marlowe's perceptual vantage point, and we never get direct access to his mind. *The Big Sleep* uses almost completely objective narration. The omniscient narration of *The Birth of a Nation,* however, plunges to considerable depth with optical point-of-view shots, flashbacks, and the hero's final fantasy vision of a world without war. Hitchcock delights in giving us greater knowledge than his characters have, but at certain moments, he confines us to their perceptual subjectivity (usually relying on point-of-view shots). Range and depth of knowledge are independent variables.

Incidentally, this is one reason why the term *point of view* is ambiguous. It can refer to range of knowledge (as when a critic speaks of an "omniscient point of view") or to depth (as when speaking of "subjective point of view"). In the rest of this book, we will use point of view only to refer to perceptual subjectivity, as in the phrase "optical point-of-view shot," or POV shot.

Manipulating the depth of knowledge can achieve many purposes. Plunging to the depths of mental subjectivity can increase our sympathy for a character and can cue stable expectations about what the characters will later say or do. The memory sequences in Alain Resnais's *Hiroshima mon amour* and the fantasy sequences in

3.23 One of the early flashbacks in *Sansho the Bailiff* starts with the mother, now living in exile with her children, kneeling by a stream.

3.24 Her image is replaced by a shot of her husband in the past, about to summon his son Zushio.

3.25 At the climax of the scene in the past, the father gives Zushio an image of the goddess of mercy and admonishes him always to show kindness to others.

Fellini's *8½* yield information about the protagonists' traits and possible future actions that would be less vivid if presented objectively. A subjectively motivated flashback can create parallels among characters, as does the flashback shared by mother and son in Kenji Mizoguchi's *Sansho the Bailiff* (**3.23–3.26**). A plot can create curiosity about a character's motives and then use some degree of subjectivity—for example, inner commentary or subjective flashback—to explain the cause of the behavior. In *The Sixth Sense,* the child psychologist's odd estrangement from his wife begins to make sense when we hear his inner recollection of something his young patient had told him much earlier.

On the other hand, objectivity can be an effective way of withholding information. One reason that *The Big Sleep* does not treat Marlowe subjectively is that the detective genre demands that the detective's reasoning be concealed from the viewer. The mystery is more mysterious if we do not know the investigator's hunches and conclusions before he reveals them at the end.

A film need not be in the mystery genre in order to exploit objective and restricted narration. Julia Loktev's *Day Night Day Night* follows a young woman who has been recruited as a suicide bomber. We see her accepted into the group, awaiting orders, and eventually embarking on the mission. One scene utilizes optical point of view extensively, while another does so briefly. There are a few moments of auditory subjectivity, when the noises of street traffic drop out. Yet these flashes of subjective depth stand out against an overwhelmingly objective presentation. For nearly the entire film, we have to assess the woman's state of mind purely through her physical behavior. Moreover, our information about the story action is very limited. We are never told what political group has recruited her or why she has volunteered for the task. The woman herself does not know the plan, the members of the terrorist group, or the reasons she was picked. In fact, we know less than she does, because we get only hints about her past life. The impersonal, tightly restricted narration of *Day Night Day Night* not only creates suspense about her mission but also encourages curiosity about a rather large number of story events.

At any moment in a film, we can ask, "How deeply do I know the characters' perceptions, feelings, and thoughts?" The answer will point directly to how the narration is presenting or withholding story information in order to achieve a specific effect on the viewer.

In all of these examples, the filmmaker's choice about range or depth affects how the spectator responds to the film as it progresses.

3.26 Normal procedure would come out of the flashback showing the mother again, emphasizing it as her memory. Instead, we return to the present with a shot of Zushio, bearing the goddess's image. It is as if he and his mother have shared the memory of the father's gift.

The Narrator

Narration, then, is the process by which the plot presents story information to the spectator. This process may shift between restricted and unrestricted ranges of

WHEN THE LIGHTS GO DOWN, THE NARRATION STARTS

When we open a novel for the first time, we don't expect the story action to start on the copyright page. Nor do we expect to find the story's last scene on the back cover. But films can start emitting narrative information in the credit sequences and continue to the very last moments we're in the theater.

Credit sequences serve to identify the participants in a production, and today the list can run many minutes. In the late 1910s, filmmakers realized that credits could be enlivened by drawings and paintings keyed to the film **(3.27)**. Since the 1920s, the credits' graphic design and musical accompaniment have often quickly conjured up the time and place of the story **(3.28)**. The breezy credits of Truffaut's *Jules and Jim* offer glimpses of the action to come while firmly establishing the two young men's friendship in turn-of-the-century Paris.

An overall mood is often set simply by music playing over simple titles, as in *The Exorcist,* but the credits can take a more active role through type fonts, color, or movement. Saul Bass, a celebrated designer of corporate logos, gave Alfred Hitchcock's and Otto Preminger's films dynamic geometric designs **(3.29)**. Rainer Werner Fassbinder was famous for his imaginative credit sequences, some in homage to the 1950s Hollywood melodramas he admired. In a similar vein, the brash collages in Pedro Almodóvar's credit sequences lead us to expect sexy irreverence **(3.30)**.

Plot elements can be announced quite specifically. Illustrations can anticipate particular scenes **(3.31)**.

3.27 An early example of illustrated credits for the 1917 comedy *Reaching for the Moon.*

3.30 A collage design suggesting sophistication and glamorous lifestyles (*Women on the Verge of a Nervous Breakdown*).

3.28 *Raw Deal,* a crime film from 1948, begins in prison, and the credit sequence suggests the locale before the action begins.

3.31 Some of the stick-figure credits in *Bringing Up Baby* anticipate scenes that will take place in the story action.

3.29 Saul Bass's elegantly simple credits for *Advise and Consent* hint that the story will lift the lid off Washington scandals.

Se7en's scratchy glimpses of cutting, stitching, and defacement launched a cycle of nightmarish credit sequences showing violation and dismemberment. *Goldfinger*'s credits present a key motif and anticipate several scenes **(3.32)**. Many of the scenes in *Catch Me If You Can* are previewed in the title sequence, which pays affectionate homage to the animated credit sequences of the film's period **(3.33)**. More subtly, the opening of *The Thomas Crown Affair* (1999) hints at the method by which the hero will steal a painting.

Films often end their plot with an epilogue that celebrates the stable state that the characters have achieved, and that situation can be presented in tandem with the credits **(3.34)**. Sometimes key scenes will be replayed under the final credits, or new plot action will be shown. *Airplane!* began a fashion for weaving running gags into its final credits.

Occasionally, the filmmaker fools us. We think the plot has ended, and a long list of personnel crawls upward. But then the film tacks an image on the very end **(3.35)**. These "credit cookies" remind us that an enterprising filmmaker may exploit every moment of the film's running time to engage our narrative expectations.

3.32 *Goldfinger:* The gilded woman herself will reappear in the film, while other scenes to come are projected on areas of her body.

3.33 The streamlined animation of *Catch Me If You Can* evokes 1960s credit sequences while previewing story action and settings. Here the Tom Hanks character starts to trail Leonardo DiCaprio, who plays an impostor pretending to be an airline pilot.

3.34 In *Slumdog Millionaire,* the dance epilogue in the railway station is intercut with the major credits, which recall scenes from the film.

3.35 Takeshi Kitano's *Sonatine* follows its final credit sequence with desolate images of a beach, wistfully reminding us of earlier scenes showing childish gangsters at play.

knowledge and varying degrees of objectivity and subjectivity. Narration may also use a *narrator,* some specific agent who purports to be telling us the story.

The narrator may be a *character* in the story. We are familiar with this convention from literature, as when Huck Finn or Jane Eyre recounts a novel's action. In Edward Dmytryk's film *Murder, My Sweet,* the detective tells his story in flashbacks, addressing the information to inquiring policemen. In the documentary *Roger and Me,* Michael Moore frankly acknowledges his role as a character narrator. He starts the film with his reminiscences of growing up in Flint, Michigan, and he appears on camera in interviews with workers and in confrontations with General Motors security staff.

A film can also use a *noncharacter narrator.* Noncharacter narrators are common in documentaries. We never learn who belongs to the anonymous "voice of God" we hear in *The River, Primary,* or *Hoop Dreams.* A fictional film may employ this device as well. *Jules and Jim* uses a dry, matter-of-fact commentator to lend a flavor of objectivity, while other films might call on this device to lend a sense of realism, as in the urgent voice-over we hear during *The Naked City.*

A film may play on the character/noncharacter distinction by making the source of a narrating voice uncertain. In *Film About a Woman Who . . . ,* we might assume that a character is the narrator, but we cannot be sure because we cannot tell which character the voice belongs to. In fact, it may be coming from an external commentator.

Note that either sort of narrator may present various sorts of narration. A character narrator is not necessarily restricted and may tell of events that she or he did not witness, as the relatively minor figure of the village priest does in John Ford's *The Quiet Man.* A noncharacter narrator need not be omniscient and could confine the commentary to what a single character knows. A character narrator might be highly subjective, telling us details of his or her inner life, or might be objective, confining his or her recounting strictly to externals. A noncharacter narrator might give us access to subjective depths, as in *Jules and Jim,* or might stick simply to surface events, as does the impersonal voice-over commentator in *The Killing.* In any case, the viewer's process of picking up cues, developing expectations, and constructing an ongoing story out of the plot will be partially shaped by what the narrator tells or doesn't tell.

Summing Up Narration

We can summarize the shaping power of narration by considering George Miller's *The Road Warrior* (also known as *Mad Max II*). The film's plot opens with a voice-over commentary by an elderly male narrator who recalls "the warrior Max." After presenting exposition that tells of the worldwide wars that led society to degenerate into gangs of scavengers, the narrator falls silent. The question of his identity is left unanswered.

The rest of the plot is organized around Max's encounter with a group of peaceful desert people. They want to flee to the coast with the gasoline they have refined, but they're under siege by a gang of vicious marauders. The plot action involves Max's agreement to work for the settlers in exchange for gasoline. Later, after a brush with the gang leaves him wounded, his dog dead, and his car demolished, Max commits himself to helping the people escape their compound. The struggle against the encircling gang comes to its climax in an attempt to escape with a tanker truck, with Max at the wheel.

Max is at the center of the plot's causal chain; his goals and conflicts propel the developing action. Moreover, after the anonymous narrator's prologue, most of the film is restricted to Max's range of knowledge. Like Philip Marlowe in *The Big Sleep,* Max is present in every scene, and almost everything we learn gets funneled through him. The depth of story information is also consistent. The narration provides optical point-of-view shots as Max drives his car (**3.36**) or watches a skirmish

3.36 A point-of-view shot as Max drives up to an apparently abandoned gyro in *The Road Warrior.*

3.37 The injured Max's dizzy view of his rescuer uses double exposure.

through a telescope. When he is rescued after his car crash, his delirium is rendered as perceptual subjectivity, using the conventional cues of slow motion, superimposed imagery, and slowed-down sound **(3.37).** All of these narrational devices encourage us to sympathize with Max.

At certain points, however, the narration becomes more unrestricted. This occurs principally during chases and battle scenes, when we witness events Max probably does not know about. In such scenes, unrestricted narration functions to build up suspense by showing both pursuers and pursued or different aspects of the battle. At the climax, Max's truck successfully draws the gang away from the desert people, who escape to the south. But when his truck overturns, Max—and we—learn that the truck holds only sand. It has been a decoy. Thus our restriction to Max's range of knowledge creates a surprise.

There is still more to learn, however. At the very end, the elderly narrator's voice returns to tell us that he was the feral child whom Max had befriended. The desert people drive off, and Max is left alone in the middle of the highway. The film's final image—a shot of the solitary Max receding into the distance as we pull back **(3.38)**—suggests both a perceptual subjectivity (the boy's point of view as he rides away from Max) and a mental subjectivity (the memory of Max dimming for the narrator).

In *The Road Warrior,* then, the plot's form is achieved not only by causality, time, and space but also by a coherent use of narration. The main portion of the film channels our expectations through an attachment to Max, alternating with more unrestricted portions. In turn, this section is framed by the mysterious narrator who puts all the events into the distant past. The narrator's presence at the opening leads us to expect him to return at the end, perhaps explaining who he is. Thus both the cause–effect organization and the narrational patterning help the film give us a unified experience.

"Narrative tension is primarily about withholding information."

— Ian McEwan, novelist

3.38   As the camera tracks away from Max, we hear the narrator's voice: "And the Road Warrior? That was the last we ever saw of him. He lives now only in my memories."

The Classical Hollywood Cinema

The number of possible narratives is unlimited. Historically, however, fictional filmmaking has tended to be dominated by a single tradition of narrative form. We'll refer to this dominant mode as the "classical Hollywood cinema." This mode is called "classical" because of its lengthy, stable, and influential history, and "Hollywood" because the mode assumed its most elaborate shape in American studio films. The same mode, however, governs many narrative films made in other countries. For example, *The Road Warrior,* though an Australian film, is constructed along classical Hollywood lines. And many documentaries, such as *Primary,* rely on conventions derived from Hollywood's fictional narratives.

This conception of narrative depends on the assumption that the action will spring primarily from *individual characters as causal agents.* Natural causes (floods, earthquakes) or societal causes (institutions, wars, economic depressions) may affect the action, but the narrative centers on personal psychological causes: decisions, choices, and traits of character.

Typically what gets this sort of narragive going is someone's *desire.* A character wants something. The desire sets up a *goal,* and the course of the narrative's development will most likely involve the process of achieving that goal. In *The Wizard of Oz,* Dorothy has a series of goals, as we've seen: from saving Toto from Miss Gulch to getting home from Oz. The latter goal creates short-term goals along the way: getting to the Emerald City and then killing the Witch.

If this desire to reach a goal were the only element present, there would be nothing to stop the character from moving quickly to achieve it. But there is a counterforce in the classical narrative: an opposition that creates conflict. The protagonist comes up against a character with opposing traits and goals. As a result, the protagonist must seek to change the situation so that he or she can achieve the goal. Dorothy's desire to return to Kansas is opposed by the Wicked Witch, whose goal is to obtain the Ruby Slippers. Dorothy must eventually eliminate the Witch before she is able to use the slippers to go home. We shall see in *His Girl Friday* how the two main characters' goals conflict until the final resolution (pp. 444–445).

Cause and effect imply *change.* If the characters didn't desire something to be different from the way it is at the beginning of the narrative, change wouldn't occur. Therefore characters' traits and wants are a strong source of causes and effects.

But don't all narratives have protagonists of this sort? Actually, no. In 1920s Soviet films, such as Sergei Eisenstein's *Potemkin, October,* and *Strike,* no *individual* serves as protagonist. In films by Eisenstein and Yasujiro Ozu, many events are seen as caused not by characters but by larger forces (social dynamics in the former, an overarching nature in the latter). In narrative films such as Michelangelo Antonioni's *L'Avventura,* the protagonist is not active but passive. So the striving, goal-oriented protagonist, though common, doesn't appear in every narrative film.

"Movies to me are about wanting something, a character wanting something that you as the audience desperately want him to have. You, the writer, keep him from getting it for as long as possible, and then, through whatever effort he makes, he gets it."

— Bruce Joel Rubin, screenwriter, *Ghost*

In the classical Hollywood narrative, psychological causes tend to motivate most other narrative events. Time is subordinated to the cause–effect chain. The plot will omit significant durations in order to show only events of causal importance. (The hours Dorothy and her entourage spend walking on the Yellow Brick Road are omitted, but the plot dwells on the moments during which she meets a new character.) The plot will arrange story chronology so as to present the cause–effect chain most strikingly. For instance, in one scene of *Hannah and Her Sisters*, Mickey (played by Woody Allen) is in a suicidal depression. When we next see him several scenes later, he is bubbly and cheerful. Our curiosity about this abrupt change enhances his comic explanation to a friend, via a flashback, that he achieved a serene attitude toward life while watching a Marx Brothers film.

Specific devices make plot time depend on the story's cause–effect chain. The *appointment* motivates characters' encountering each other at a specific moment. The *deadline* makes plot duration dependent on the cause–effect chain. Throughout, motivation in the classical narrative film strives to be as clear and complete as possible—even in the fanciful genre of the musical, in which song-and-dance numbers become motivated as either expressions of the characters' emotions or stage shows mounted by the characters.

Narration in the classical Hollywood cinema exploits a variety of options, but there's a strong tendency for it to be objective in the way discussed on pages 95–97. It presents a basically objective story reality, against which various degrees of perceptual or mental subjectivity can be measured. Classical cinema also tends toward fairly unrestricted narration. Even if we follow a single character, there are portions of the film giving us access to things the character does not see, hear, or know. *North by Northwest* and *The Road Warrior* remain good examples of this tendency. This weighting is overridden only in genres that depend heavily on mystery, such as the detective film, with its reliance on the sort of restrictiveness we saw at work in *The Big Sleep*.

Finally, most classical narrative films display a strong degree of *closure* at the end. Leaving few loose ends unresolved, these films seek to complete their causal chains with a final effect. We usually learn the fate of each character, the answer to each mystery, and the outcome of each conflict.

Again, none of these features is necessary to narrative form in general. There is nothing to prevent a filmmaker from presenting the dead time, or narratively unmotivated intervals between more significant events. (Jean-Luc Godard, Carl Dreyer, and Andy Warhol do this frequently, in different ways.) The filmmaker's plot can also reorder story chronology to make the causal chain *more* perplexing. For example, Jean-Marie Straub and Danièle Huillet's *Not Reconciled* moves back and forth among three widely different time periods without clearly signaling the shifts. Dušan Makavejev's *Love Affair, or the Case of the Missing Switchboard Operator* uses flash-forwards interspersed with the main plot action; only gradually do we come to understand the causal relations of these flash-forwards to the present-time events. More recently, puzzle films (pp. 88–89) tease the audience to find clues to enigmatic narration or story events.

The filmmaker can also include material that is unmotivated by narrative cause and effect, such as the chance meetings in Truffaut's films, the political monologues and interviews in Godard's films, the intellectual montage sequences in Eisenstein's films, and the transitional shots in Ozu's work. Narration may be completely subjective, as in *The Cabinet of Dr. Caligari,* or it may hover ambiguously between objectivity and subjectivity, as in *Last Year at Marienbad*. Finally, the filmmaker need not resolve all of the action at the end; films made outside the classical tradition sometimes have quite open endings.

We'll see in Chapter 6 how the classical Hollywood mode also makes cinematic space serve causality through continuity editing. For now we can simply note that the classical mode tends to treat narrative elements and narrational processes in specific and distinctive ways. For all of its effectiveness, the classical

CONNECT TO THE BLOG
For a discussion of how characters' goals can be crucial to major transitions in the plot, see "Time goes by turns," at
www.davidbordwell.net/blog/?p=2448.

CONNECT TO THE BLOG
The classical approach to narrative is still very much alive, as we show in "Your trash, my treasure."
See www.davidbordwell.net/blog/?p=1781.

Hollywood mode remains only one system among many that can be used for constructing narrative films.

Narrative Form in *Citizen Kane*

With its unusual organizational style, *Citizen Kane* invites us to analyze how principles of narrative form operate across an entire film. *Kane*'s investigation plot carries us toward analyzing how causality and goal-oriented characters may operate in narratives. The film's manipulations of our knowledge shed light on the story–plot distinction. *Kane* also shows how ambiguity may arise when certain elements aren't clearly motivated. Furthermore, the comparison of *Kane*'s beginning with its ending indicates how a film may deviate from the patterns of classical Hollywood narrative construction. Finally, *Kane* clearly shows how our experience can be shaped by the way that narration governs the flow of story information.

Overall Narrative Expectations in *Citizen Kane*

We saw in Chapter 2 that our experience of a film depends heavily on the expectations we bring to it and the extent to which the film confirms them. Before you saw *Citizen Kane,* you may have known only that it is regarded as a film classic. Such an evaluation would not give you a very specific set of expectations. A 1941 audience would have had a keener sense of anticipation. For one thing, the film was rumored to be a disguised version of the life of the newspaper publisher William Randolph Hearst. Spectators would thus be looking for events and references keyed to Hearst's life.

Several minutes into the film, the viewer can form more specific expectations about pertinent genre conventions. The early "News on the March" sequence suggests that this film may be a fictional biography, and this hint is confirmed once the reporter, Thompson, begins his inquiry into Kane's life. The film does indeed follow the conventional outline of the fictional biography, which typically covers an individual's whole life and dramatizes certain episodes in the period. Examples of this genre would be *Anthony Adverse* (1936) and *The Power and the Glory* (1933). (The latter film is often cited as an influence on *Citizen Kane* because of its complex use of flashbacks.)

The viewer can also quickly identify the film's use of conventions of the newspaper reporter genre. Thompson's colleagues resemble the wisecracking reporters in *Five Star Final* (1931), *Picture Snatcher* (1933), and *His Girl Friday* (1940). In this genre, the action usually depends on a reporter's dogged pursuit of a story against great odds. We therefore expect not only Thompson's investigation but also his triumphant discovery of the truth. In the scenes devoted to Susan, there are also some conventions typical of the musical film: frantic rehearsals, backstage preparations, and, most specifically, the montage of her opera career, which parodies the conventional montage of singing success in films like *Maytime* (1937). More broadly, the film evidently owes something to the detective genre, since Thompson is aiming to solve a mystery (Who or what is Rosebud?), and his interviews resemble those of a detective questioning suspects in search of clues.

Note, however, that *Kane*'s use of genre conventions is somewhat equivocal. Unlike many biographical films, *Kane* is more concerned with psychological states and relationships than with the hero's public deeds or adventures. As a newspaper film, *Kane* is unusual in that the reporter fails to get his story. And *Kane* is not exactly a standard mystery, since it answers some questions but leaves others unanswered. *Citizen Kane* is a good example of a film that relies on genre conventions but often thwarts the expectations they arouse.

The same sort of equivocal qualities can be found in *Kane*'s relation to the classical Hollywood cinema. Even without specific prior knowledge about this film, we expect that, as an American studio product of 1941, it will obey guidelines of that tradition. In most ways, it does. We'll see that desire propels the narrative, causality is defined around traits and goals, conflicts lead to consequences, time is motivated by plot necessity, and narration is objective, mixing restricted and unrestricted passages. We'll also see some ways in which *Citizen Kane* is more ambiguous than most films in this tradition. Desires, traits, and goals are not always spelled out; the conflicts sometimes have an uncertain outcome; at the end, the narration's omniscience is emphasized to a rare degree. The ending in particular doesn't provide the degree of closure we would expect in a classical film. Our analysis will show how *Citizen Kane* draws on Hollywood narrative conventions but also violates some of the expectations that we bring to a Hollywood film.

Plot and Story in *Citizen Kane*

In analyzing a film, it's helpful to begin by segmenting it into sequences. Sequences are often demarcated by cinematic devices (fades, dissolves, cuts, black screens, and so on). In a narrative film, the sequences constitute the parts of the plot.

Most sequences in a narrative film are called *scenes.* The term is used in its theatrical sense, to refer to distinct phases of the action occurring within a relatively unified space and time. Our segmentation of *Citizen Kane* appears below. In this outline, numerals refer to major parts, some of which are only one scene long. In most cases, however, the major parts consist of several scenes, and each of these is identified by a lowercase letter. Many of these segments could be further divided, but this segmentation suits our immediate purposes.

Our segmentation lets us see at a glance the major divisions of the plot and how scenes are organized within them. The outline also helps us notice how the plot organizes story causality and story time. Let's look at these factors more closely.

CITIZEN KANE: **PLOT SEGMENTATION**

C. Credit title
1. **Xanadu: Kane dies**
2. **Projection room:**
      a. "News on the March"
      b. Reporters discuss "Rosebud"
3. **El Rancho nightclub: Thompson tries to interview Susan**
4. **Thatcher library:**

                      a. Thompson enters and reads Thatcher's manuscript
                      b. Kane's mother sends the boy off with Thatcher
First   **c.** Kane grows up and buys the *Inquirer*
flashback   **d.** Kane launches the *Inquirer's* attack on big business
                      e. The Depression: Kane sells Thatcher his newspaper chain
                      f. Thompson leaves the library

5. **Bernstein's office:**

                      a. Thompson visits Bernstein
                      b. Kane takes over the *Inquirer*
                      c. Montage: the *Inquirer's* growth
Second   **d.** Party: the *Inquirer* celebrates getting the *Chronicle* staff
flashback   **e.** Leland and Bernstein discuss Kane's trip abroad
                      f. Kane returns with his fiancée Emily
                      g. Bernstein concludes his reminiscence

6. **Nursing home:**

                      a. Thompson talks with Leland
Third   **b.** Breakfast table montage: Kane's marriage deteriorates
flashback   **c.** Leland continues his recollections

Third
flashback
(cont.)

   d. Kane meets Susan and goes to her room
   e. Kane's political campaign culminates in his speech
   f. Kane confronts Gettys, Emily, and Susan
   g. Kane loses the election, and Leland asks to be transferred
   h. Kane marries Susan
   i. Susan has her opera premiere
   j. Because Leland is drunk, Kane finishes Leland's review
k. Leland concludes his reminiscence

7. El Rancho nightclub:

   a. Thompson talks with Susan

Fourth
flashback

   b. Susan rehearses her singing
   c. Susan has her opera premiere
   d. Kane insists that Susan go on singing
   e. Montage: Susan's opera career
   f. Susan attempts suicide, and Kane promises she can quit singing
   g. Xanadu: Susan is bored
   h. Montage: Susan plays with jigsaw puzzles
   i. Xanadu: Kane proposes a picnic
   j. Picnic: Kane slaps Susan
   k. Xanadu: Susan leaves Kane
l. Susan concludes her reminiscence

8. Xanadu:

   a. Thompson talks with Raymond

Fifth
flashback

   b. Kane destroys Susan's room and picks up a paperweight, murmuring "Rosebud"
   c. Raymond concludes his reminiscence; Thompson talks with the other reporters; all leave
   d. Survey of Kane's possessions leads to a revelation of Rosebud; exterior of gate and of castle; the end

E. End credits

Citizen Kane's Causality

In *Citizen Kane,* two distinct sets of characters cause events to happen. On the one hand, a group of reporters seeks information about Kane. On the other hand, Kane and the characters who know him provide the subject of the reporters' investigations.

The initial causal connection between the two groups is Kane's death, which leads the reporters to make a newsreel summing up his career. But the newsreel is already finished when the plot introduces the reporters. The boss, Rawlston, supplies the cause that initiates the investigation of Kane's life. Thompson's newsreel fails to satisfy him. Rawlston's desire for an angle for the newsreel gets the search for Rosebud under way. Thompson thus gains a goal, which sets him digging into Kane's past. His investigation constitutes one main line of the plot.

Another line of action, Kane's life, has already taken place in the past. There, too, a group of characters has caused actions to occur. Many years before, a poverty-stricken boarder at Kane's mother's boardinghouse has paid her with a deed to a silver mine. The wealth provided by this mine causes Mrs. Kane to appoint Thatcher as young Charles's guardian. Thatcher's guardianship results (in somewhat unspecified ways) in Kane's growing up into a spoiled, rebellious young man.

Citizen Kane is an unusual film in that the object of the investigator's search is not an object but a set of character traits. Thompson seeks to know what aspects of Kane's personality led him to say "Rosebud" on his deathbed. This mystery motivates Thompson's detective-like investigation. Kane, a very complex character, has many traits that influence the other characters' actions. As we shall see, however, *Citizen Kane's* narrative does not ultimately define all of Kane's character traits.

Kane himself has a goal; he, too, seems to be searching for something related to Rosebud. At several points, characters speculate that Rosebud was something that Kane lost or was never able to get. Again, the fact that Kane's goal remains so vague makes this an unusual narrative.

Other characters in Kane's life provide causal material for the narrative. The presence of several characters who knew Kane well makes Thompson's investigation possible, even though Kane has died. Significantly, the characters provide a range of information that spans Kane's entire life. This is important if we are to be able to reconstruct the progression of story events in the film. Thatcher knew Kane as a child; Bernstein, his manager, knew his business dealings; his best friend, Leland, knew of his personal life (his first marriage in particular); Susan Alexander, his second wife, knew him in middle age; and the butler, Raymond, managed Kane's affairs during his last years. Each of these characters has a causal role in Kane's life, as well as in Thompson's investigation. Note that Kane's wife Emily does not tell a story, since Emily's story would largely duplicate Leland's and would contribute no additional information to the present-day part of the narrative, the investigation. Hence the plot simply eliminates her (via a car accident).

Time in *Citizen Kane*

The order, duration, and frequency of events in the story differ greatly from the way the plot of *Citizen Kane* presents those events. Much of the film's power to engage our interest arises from the complex ways in which the plot cues us to construct the story.

To understand this story in its chronological order and assumed duration and frequency, the spectator must follow an intricate tapestry of plot events. For example, in the first flashback, Thatcher's diary tells of a scene in which Kane loses control of his newspapers during the Depression (4e). By this time, Kane is a middle-aged man. Yet in the second flashback, Bernstein describes young Kane's arrival at the *Inquirer* and his engagement to Emily (5b, 5f). We mentally sort these plot events into a correct chronological story order, then continue to rearrange other events as we learn of them.

Similarly, the earliest *story* event about which we learn is Mrs. Kane's acquisition of a deed to a valuable mine. We get this information during the newsreel, in the second sequence. But the first event in the *plot* is Kane's death. Just to illustrate the maneuvers we must execute to construct the film's story, let's assume that Kane's life consists of these phases:

Boyhood

Youthful newspaper editing

Life as a newlywed

Middle age

Old age

Significantly, the early portions of the plot tend to roam over many phases of Kane's life, while later portions tend to concentrate more on particular periods. The "News on the March" sequence (2a) gives us glimpses of all periods. Thatcher's manuscript (4) shows us Kane in boyhood, youth, and middle age. Then the flashbacks become primarily chronological. Bernstein's recounting (5) concentrates on episodes showing Kane as newspaper editor and fiancé of Emily. Leland's recollections (6) run from newlywed life to middle age. Susan (7) tells of Kane as a middle-aged and an old man. Raymond's perfunctory anecdote (8b) concentrates on Kane in old age.

The plot becomes more linear in its ordering as it goes along, and this aids the viewer's effort to understand the story. If every character's flashback skipped around Kane's life as much as the newsreel and Thatcher's account do, the story would be much harder to reconstruct. As it is, the early portions of the plot show us the results of events we have not seen, while the later portions confirm or modify the expectations that we formed earlier.

By arranging story events out of order, the plot cues us to form specific anticipations. In the beginning, with Kane's death and the newsreel version of his life, the plot creates strong curiosity about two issues. What does "Rosebud" mean? And what could have happened to make so powerful a man so solitary at the end of his life?

There is also a degree of suspense. When the plot goes back to the past, we already have quite firm knowledge. We know that neither of Kane's marriages will last and that his friends will drift away. The plot encourages us to focus our interest on *how and when* a particular thing will happen. Thus many scenes function to delay an outcome that we already know is certain. For example, we know that Susan will abandon Kane at some point, so we are constantly expecting her to do so each time he bullies her. For several scenes (7b–7j), she comes close to leaving him, though after her suicide attempt he mollifies her. The plot could have shown her walking out (7k) much earlier, but then the ups and downs of their relations would have been less vivid, and there would have been no suspense.

This process of mentally rearranging plot events into story order might be quite difficult in *Citizen Kane* were it not for the presence of the "News on the March" newsreel. The very first sequence in Xanadu disorients us, for it shows the death of a character about whom we so far know almost nothing. But the newsreel gives us a great deal of information quickly. Moreover, the newsreel's own structure uses parallels with the main film to supply a miniature introduction to the film's overall plot:

A. Shots of Xanadu

B. Funeral; headlines announcing Kane's death

C. Growth of financial empire

D. Silver mine and Mrs. Kane's boardinghouse

E. Thatcher testimony at congressional committee

F. Political career

G. Private life; weddings, divorces

H. Opera house and Xanadu

I. Political campaign

J. The Depression

K. 1935: Kane's old age

L. Isolation of Xanadu

M. Death announced

A comparison of this outline with our segmentation for the whole film shows some striking similarities. "News on the March" begins by emphasizing Kane as "Xanadu's Landlord"; a short segment (A) presents shots of the house, its grounds, and its contents. This is a variation on the opening of the whole film (1), which consisted of a series of shots of the grounds, moving progressively closer to the house. That opening sequence had ended with Kane's death; now the newsreel follows the shots of the house with Kane's funeral (B). Next comes a series of newspaper headlines announcing Kane's death. In a comparison with the plot diagram of *Citizen Kane,* these headlines occupy the approximate formal position of the whole newsreel itself (2a). Even the title card that follows the headlines ("To forty-four million U.S. news buyers, more newsworthy than the names in his own headlines was Kane himself. . . .") is a brief parallel to the scene in the projection room, in which the reporters decide that Thompson should continue to investigate Kane's "newsworthy" life.

The order of the newsreel's presentation of Kane's life roughly parallels the order of scenes in the flashbacks related to Thompson. "News on the March" moves from Kane's death to a summary of the building of Kane's newspaper empire (C), with a description of the boardinghouse deed and the silver mine (including an old photograph of Charles with his mother, as well as the first mention of the sled). Similarly, the first flashback (4) tells how Thatcher took over the young Kane's guardianship from his mother and how Kane first attempted to run the *Inquirer*. The rough parallels continue: the newsreel tells of Kane's political ambitions (F), his marriages (G), his building of the opera house (H), his political campaign (I), and so on. In the main plot, Thatcher's flashback describes his own clashes with Kane on political matters. Leland's flashback (6) covers the first marriage, the affair with Susan, the political campaign, and the premiere of the opera *Salammbo*.

These are not all of the similarities between the newsreel and the overall film. You can tease out many more by comparing the two closely. The crucial point is that the newsreel provides us with a map for the investigation of Kane's life. As we see the various scenes of the flashbacks, we already expect certain events and have a rough chronological basis for fitting them into our story reconstruction.

Kane's many flashbacks allow us to see past events directly, and in these portions, story and plot duration are close to the same. We know that Kane is 75 years old at his death, and the earliest scene shows him at perhaps 10. Thus the plot covers roughly 65 years of his life, plus the week of Thompson's investigation. The single earlier story event of which we only hear is Mrs. Kane's acquisition of the mine deed, which we can infer took place a short time before she turned her son over to Thatcher. So the story runs a bit longer than the plot—perhaps closer to 70 years. This time span is presented in a screen duration of almost 120 minutes.

Like most films, *Citizen Kane* uses ellipses. The plot skips over years of story time, as well as many hours of Thompson's week of investigations. But plot duration also compresses time through montage sequences, such as those showing the *Inquirer*'s campaign against big business (4d), the growth of the paper's circulation (5c), Susan's opera career (7e), and Susan's bored playing with jigsaw puzzles (7h). Here long passages of story time are condensed into brief summaries quite different from ordinary narrative scenes. We will discuss montage sequences in more detail in Chapter 8, but we can already see the value of such segments in condensing story duration in a comprehensible way.

Citizen Kane also provides a clear demonstration of how events that occur only once in the story may appear several times in the plot. In their respective flashbacks, both Leland and Susan describe the latter's debut in the Chicago premiere of *Salammbo*. Watching Leland's account (6i), we see the performance from the front; we witness the audience reacting with distaste. Susan's version (7c) shows us the performance from behind and on the stage, to suggest her humiliation. This repeated presentation of Susan's debut in the plot doesn't confuse us, for we understand the two scenes as depicting the same story event. ("News on the March" has also referred to Susan's opera career, in parts G and H.) By repeating scenes of her embarrassment, the plot makes vivid the pain that Kane forces her to undergo.

Overall, *Citizen Kane*'s narrative dramatizes Thompson's search by means of flashbacks that encourage us to seek the sources of Kane's failure and to try to identify "Rosebud." As in a detective film, we must locate missing causes and arrange events into a coherent story pattern. Through manipulations of order, duration, and frequency, the plot both assists our search and complicates it in order to provoke curiosity and suspense.

Motivation in *Citizen Kane*

Some critics have argued that Welles's use of the search for "Rosebud" is a flaw in *Citizen Kane,* because the identification of the word proves it to be a trivial gimmick. If indeed we assume that the whole point of *Citizen Kane* is really to identify Rosebud, this charge might be valid. But in fact, Rosebud serves a very important motivating function in the film. It creates Thompson's goal and thus focuses our

CONNECT TO THE BLOG
The flashback tradition developed a rich history before *Citizen Kane*. For analysis of flashbacks in Hollywood films during the 1930s, and especially *The Power and the Glory*, which influenced Orson Welles, see "Grandmaster flashback."

See www.davidbordwell.net/blog/?p=3253.

attention on his delving into the lives of Kane and his associates. *Citizen Kane* becomes a mystery story; but instead of investigating a crime, the reporter investigates a character. So the Rosebud clues provide the basic motivation necessary for the plot to progress. (Of course, the Rosebud device serves other functions as well; for instance, the little sled provides a transition from the boardinghouse scene to the cheerless Christmas when Thatcher gives Charles a new sled.)

Citizen Kane's narrative revolves around an investigation into traits of character. As a result, these traits provide many of the motivations for events. (In this respect, the film obeys principles of the classical Hollywood narrative.) Kane's desire to prove that Susan is really a singer and not merely his mistress motivates his manipulation of her opera career. His mother's overly protective desire to remove her son from what she considers to be a bad environment motivates her appointment of Thatcher as the boy's guardian. Dozens of actions are motivated by character traits and goals.

At the end of the film, Thompson gives up his search for the meaning of Rosebud, saying he doesn't think "any word can explain a man's life." Up to a point, Thompson's statement motivates his acceptance of his failure. But if we as spectators are to accept this idea that no key can unlock the secrets of a life, we need further motivation. The film provides it. In the scene in the newsreel projection room, Rawlston suggests that "maybe he told us all about himself on his deathbed." Immediately, one of the reporters says, "Yeah, and maybe he didn't." Already the suggestion is planted that Rosebud may not provide any adequate answers about Kane. Later Leland scornfully dismisses the Rosebud issue and goes on to talk of other things. Characters' skepticism about the Rosebud clue helps justify Thompson's pessimistic attitude in the final sequence.

The presence of the scene in which Thompson first visits Susan at the El Rancho nightclub (3) might seem puzzling at first. Unlike the other scenes in which he visits people, no flashback occurs here. Thompson learns from the waiter that Susan knows nothing about Rosebud; he could easily learn this on his later visit to her. So why should the plot include the scene at all? One reason is that it evokes curiosity and deepens the mystery around Kane. Moreover, Susan's story, when she does tell it, covers events relatively late in Kane's career. As we've seen, the flashbacks go through Kane's life roughly in order. If Susan had told her story first, we would not have all of the material necessary to understand it. But it is plausible that Thompson should start his search with Kane's ex-wife, presumably the surviving person closest to him. In Thompson's first visit, Susan's drunken refusal to speak to him motivates the fact that her flashback comes later. By that point, Bernstein and Leland have filled in enough of Kane's personal life to prepare the way for Susan's flashback. This first scene functions partly to justify postponing Susan's flashback until a later part of the plot.

Motivation makes us take things for granted in narratives. Mrs. Kane's desire for her son to be rich and successful motivates her decision to entrust him to Thatcher, a powerful banker, as his guardian. We may just take it for granted that Thatcher is a rich businessman. Yet on closer inspection, this feature is necessary to motivate other events. It motivates Thatcher's presence in the newsreel; he is powerful enough to have been asked to testify at a congressional hearing. More important, Thatcher's success motivates the fact that he has kept a journal now on deposit at a memorial library that Thompson visits. This, in turn, justifies the fact that Thompson can uncover information from a source who knew Kane as a child.

Despite its reliance on psychological motivation, *Citizen Kane* also departs somewhat from the usual practice of the classical Hollywood narrative by leaving some motivations ambiguous. The ambiguities relate primarily to Kane's character. The other characters who tell Thompson their stories all have definite opinions of Kane, but these do not always tally. Bernstein still looks on Kane with sympathy and affection, whereas Leland is cynical about his own relationship with Kane. The reasons for some of Kane's actions remain unclear. Does he send Leland the

$25,000 check in firing him because of a lingering sentiment over their old friendship or from a proud desire to prove himself more generous than Leland? Why does he insist on stuffing Xanadu with hundreds of artworks that he never even unpacks? By leaving these questions open, the film invites us to speculate on various facets of Kane's personality.

Citizen Kane's Parallelism

Parallelism doesn't provide a major principle of development in *Citizen Kane*'s narrative form, but it crops up more locally. We've already seen important formal parallels between the newsreel and the film's plot as a whole. We've also noticed a parallel between the two major lines of action: Kane's life and Thompson's search. In a different sense, both men are searching for Rosebud. Rosebud serves as a summary of the things Kane strives for through his adult life. We see him repeatedly fail to find love and friendship, living alone at Xanadu in the end. His inability to find happiness parallels Thompson's failure to locate the significance of the word "Rosebud." This parallel doesn't imply that Kane and Thompson share similar character traits. Rather, it allows both lines of action to develop simultaneously in similar directions.

Another narrative parallel juxtaposes Kane's campaign for the governorship with his attempt to build up Susan's career as an opera star. In each case, he seeks to inflate his reputation by influencing public opinion. In trying to achieve success for Susan, Kane forces his newspaper employees to write favorable reviews of her performances. This parallels the moment when he loses the election and the *Inquirer* automatically proclaims a fraud at the polls. In both cases, Kane fails to realize that his power over the public is not great enough to hide the flaws in his projects: first his affair with Susan, which ruins his campaign; then her lack of singing ability, which Kane refuses to admit. The parallels show that Kane continues to make the same kinds of mistakes throughout his life.

Patterns of Plot Development in *Citizen Kane*

The order of Thompson's visits to Kane's acquaintances allows the series of flashbacks to have a clear pattern of progression. Thompson moves from people who knew Kane early in his life to those who knew him as an old man. Moreover, each flashback contains a distinct type of information about Kane. Thatcher establishes Kane's political stance; Bernstein gives an account of the business dealings of the newspaper. These provide the background to Kane's early success and lead into Leland's stories of Kane's personal life, where we get the first real indications of Kane's failure. Susan continues the description of his decline with her account of how he manipulated her life. Finally, in Raymond's flashback, Kane becomes a pitiable old man.

Thus, even though the order of events in the story varies greatly from that given in the plot, *Citizen Kane* presents Kane's life through a steady pattern of development. The present-day portions of the narrative—Thompson's scenes—also follow their own pattern of a search. By the ending, this search has failed, as Kane's own search for happiness or personal success had failed.

Because of Thompson's failure, the ending of *Citizen Kane* remains somewhat more open than was the rule in Hollywood in 1941. True, Thompson does resolve the question of Rosebud for himself by saying that it would not have explained Kane's life. To this extent, we have the common pattern of action leading to greater knowledge. Thompson has come to understand that a life cannot be summed up in one word. Still, in most classical narrative films, the main character reaches his or her initial goal, and Thompson is the main character of this line of action.

The line of action involving Kane himself has even less closure. Not only does Kane apparently not reach his goal, but the film never specifies what that goal is to start with. Most classical narratives create a situation of conflict. The character must struggle with a problem and solve it by the ending. Kane begins his adult life in a highly successful position (happily running the *Inquirer*), then gradually falls into a barren solitude. We are invited to speculate about exactly what, if anything, would make Kane happy. *Citizen Kane*'s lack of closure in this line of action made it a very unusual narrative for its day.

The search for Rosebud does lead to a certain resolution at the end. We the audience discover what Rosebud was. The ending of the film, which follows this discovery, strongly echoes the beginning. The beginning moved past fences toward the mansion. Now a series of shots takes us away from the house and back outside the fences, with the "No Trespassing" sign and large K insignia.

But even at this point, when we learn the answer to Thompson's question, a degree of uncertainty remains. Just because we have learned what Kane's dying word referred to, do we now have the key to his entire character? Or is Thompson's final statement *correct*—that no one word can explain a person's life? Perhaps the "No Trespassing" sign hints that neither Thompson nor we should have expected to explore Kane's mind. It is tempting to declare that all of Kane's problems arose from the loss of his sled and his childhood home life, but the film also suggests that this is too easy a solution. It is the kind of solution that the slick editor Rawlston would pounce on as an angle for his newsreel.

For years critics have debated whether the Rosebud solution does give us a key that resolves the entire narrative. This debate itself suggests the ambiguity at work in *Citizen Kane*. The film provides much evidence for both views and hence avoids complete closure. You might contrast this slightly open ending with the tightly closed narratives of *His Girl Friday* and *North by Northwest* in Chapter 11. You might also compare *Citizen Kane*'s narrative with that of another somewhat open-ended film, *Do The Right Thing*, also discussed in Chapter 11.

Narration in *Citizen Kane*

In analyzing how *Kane*'s plot manipulates the flow of story information, it's useful to consider a remarkable fact: The only time we see Kane directly and in the present is when he dies. On all other occasions, he is presented at one remove—in the newsreel or in various characters' memories. This unusual treatment makes the film something of a portrait, a study of a man seen from different perspectives.

The film employs five character narrators, the people whom Thompson tracks down: Thatcher (whose account is in writing), Bernstein, Leland, Susan, and the butler, Raymond. The plot thus motivates a series of views of Kane that are more or less restricted in their range of knowledge. In Thatcher's account (4b–4e), we see only scenes at which he is present. Even Kane's newspaper crusade is rendered as Thatcher learns of it, through buying copies of the *Inquirer*. In Bernstein's flashback (5b–5f), there is some deviation from what Bernstein witnesses, but in general his range of knowledge is respected. At the *Inquirer* party, for example, we follow Bernstein and Leland's conversation while Kane dances in the background. Similarly, we never see Kane in Europe; we merely hear the contents of Kane's telegram, which Bernstein delivers to Leland.

Leland's flashbacks (6b, 6d–6j) deviate most markedly from the narrator's range of knowledge. Here we see Kane and Emily at a series of morning breakfasts, Kane's meeting with Susan, and the confrontation of Kane with Boss Gettys at Susan's apartment. In scene 6j, Leland is present but in a drunken stupor most of the time. (The plot motivates Leland's knowledge of Kane's affair with Susan by having Leland suggest that Kane told him about it, but the scenes present detailed knowledge that Leland is unlikely to possess.) By the time we get to Susan's flashback (7b–7k), however, the range of knowledge again fits the character more snugly. (There remains one scene, 7f, in which Susan is unconscious for part of the action.) The last flashback (8b) is recounted by Raymond and plausibly accords with his range of knowledge; he is standing in the hallway as Kane wrecks Susan's room.

"Kane, we are told, loved only his mother—only his newspaper—only his second wife—only himself. Maybe he loved all of these, or none. It is for the audience to judge. Kane was selfish and selfless, an idealist, a scoundrel, a very big man and a very little one. It depends on who's talking about him. He is never judged with the objectivity of an author, and the point of the picture is not so much the solution of the problem as its presentation."

— Orson Welles, director

Using different narrators to transmit story information fulfills several functions. It offers itself as a plausible depiction of the process of investigation, since we expect any reporter to hunt down information through a series of inquiries. More deeply, the plot's portrayal of Kane himself becomes more complex by showing somewhat different sides of him, depending on who's talking about him. Moreover, the use of multiple narrators makes the film like one of Susan's jigsaw puzzles. We must put things together piece by piece. The pattern of gradual revelation enhances curiosity—what is it in Kane's past that he associates with Rosebud?—and suspense—how will he lose his friends and his wives?

This strategy has important implications for film form. While Thompson uses the various narrators to gather data, the plot uses them to furnish us with story information and to *conceal* information. The narration can motivate gaps in knowledge about Kane by appealing to the fact that no informant can know everything about anyone. If we were able to enter Kane's consciousness, we might discover the meaning of Rosebud much sooner—but Kane is dead. The multiple-narrator format appeals to expectations we derive from real life in order to motivate the bit-by-bit transmission of story information, the withholding of key pieces of information, and the arousing of curiosity and suspense.

Although each narrator's account is mostly restricted to his or her range of knowledge, the plot doesn't treat each flashback in much subjective depth. Most of the flashbacks are rendered objectively. Some transitions from the framing episodes use a voice-over commentary to lead us into the flashbacks, but these don't represent the narrators' subjective states. Only in Susan's flashbacks are there some attempts to render subjectivity. In scene 7c, we see Leland as if from her optical point of view on stage, and the phantasmagoric montage of her career (7e) suggests some mental subjectivity that renders her fatigue and frustration.

Against the five character narrators, the film's plot sets another purveyor of knowledge, the "News on the March" short. We've already seen the crucial function of the newsreel in introducing us both to *Kane*'s story and to its plot construction, with the newsreel's sections previewing the parts of the film as a whole. The newsreel also gives us a broad sketch of Kane's life and death that will be filled in by the more restricted behind-the-scenes accounts offered by the narrators. The newsreel is also highly objective, even more so than the rest of the film; it reveals nothing about Kane's inner life. Rawlston acknowledges this: "It isn't enough to tell us what a man did, you've got to tell us who he was." In effect, Thompson's aim is to add depth to the newsreel's superficial version of Kane's life.

Yet we still aren't through with the narrational manipulations in this complex and daring film. For one thing, all the localized sources of knowledge—"News on the March" and the five narrators—are linked together by the shadowy reporter Thompson. To some extent, he is our surrogate in the film, gathering and assembling the puzzle pieces.

Note, too, that Thompson is barely characterized; we can't even identify his face. This, as usual, has a function. If we saw him clearly, if the plot gave him more traits or a background or a past, he would become the protagonist. But *Citizen Kane* is less about Thompson than about his *search*. The plot's handling of Thompson makes him a neutral conduit for the story information that he gathers (though his conclusion at the end—"I don't think any word can explain a man's life"—suggests that he has been changed by his investigation).

Thompson is not, however, a perfect surrogate for us because the film's narration inserts the newsreel, the narrators, and Thompson within a still broader range of knowledge. The flashback portions are predominantly restricted, but there are other passages that reveal an overall narrational omniscience.

From the very start, we are given a god's-eye-view of the action. We move into a mysterious setting that we will later learn is Kane's estate, Xanadu. We might have learned about this locale through a character's journey, the way we acquaint ourselves with Oz by means of Dorothy's adventures there. Here, however, an

The Shot: Mise-en-Scene

Of all the techniques of cinema, **mise-en-scene** is the one with which we are most familiar. After seeing a film, we may not recall the cutting or the camera movements, the dissolves or the offscreen sound. But we do remember the costumes in *Gone with the Wind* and the bleak, chilly lighting in Charles Foster Kane's Xanadu. We retain vivid impressions of the misty streets in *The Big Sleep* and the labyrinthine, fluorescent-lit lair of Buffalo Bill in *The Silence of the Lambs*. We recall Harpo Marx clambering over Edgar Kennedy's peanut wagon (*Duck Soup*), Katharine Hepburn defiantly splintering Cary Grant's golf clubs (*The Philadelphia Story*), and Michael J. Fox escaping high-school bullies on an improvised skateboard (*Back to the Future*). In short, many of our most sharply etched memories of the cinema turn out to center on mise-en-scene.

What Is Mise-en-Scene?

In the original French, *mise en scène* (pronounced meez-ahn-sen) means "putting into the scene," and it was first applied to the practice of directing plays. Film scholars, extending the term to film direction, use the term to signify the director's control over what appears in the film frame. As you would expect, mise-en-scene includes those aspects of film that overlap with the art of the theater: setting, lighting, costume, and the behavior of the figures. In controlling the mise-en-scene, the director *stages the event* for the camera.

Mise-en-scene usually involves some planning, but the filmmaker may be open to unplanned events as well. An actor may add a line on the set, or an unexpected change in lighting may enhance a dramatic effect. While filming a cavalry procession through Monument Valley for *She Wore a Yellow Ribbon,* John Ford took advantage of an approaching lightning storm to create a dramatic backdrop for the action (**4.1**). The storm remains part of the film's mise-en-scene even though Ford neither planned it nor controlled it; it was a lucky accident that helped create one of the film's most affecting passages. Jean Renoir, Robert Altman, and other directors have allowed their actors to improvise their performances, making the films' mise-en-scene more spontaneous and unpredictable.

Realism

Before we analyze mise-en-scene in detail, one preconception must be brought to light. Just as viewers often remember this or that bit of mise-en-scene from a film, so they often judge mise-en-scene by standards of realism. A car may seem to be

4.1 *She Wore a Yellow Ribbon:* a thunderstorm in Monument Valley.

realistic for the period the film depicts, or a gesture may not seem realistic because "real people don't act that way."

Realism as a standard of value, however, raises several problems. Notions of realism vary across cultures, over time, and even among individuals. Marlon Brando's acclaimed realist performance in the 1954 film *On the Waterfront* looks stylized today. American critics of the 1910s praised William S. Hart's Westerns for being realistic, but equally enthusiastic French critics of the 1920s considered the same films to be as artificial as a medieval epic. Most important, to insist rigidly on realism for all films can blind us to the vast range of mise-en-scene possibilities.

Look, for instance, at the frame from *The Cabinet of Dr. Caligari* (**4.2**). Such a depiction of rooftops certainly does not accord with our conception of normal reality. Yet to condemn the film for lacking realism would be inappropriate, because the film uses stylization to present a madman's fantasy. *The Cabinet of Dr. Caligari* borrows conventions of Expressionist painting and theater, and then assigns them the function of suggesting a delusion.

4.2 An Expressionist rooftop scene created from jagged peaks and slanted chimneys in *The Cabinet of Dr. Caligari.*

It is best, then, to examine the *functions* of mise-en-scene in the films we see. While one film might use mise-en-scene to create an impression of realism, other films might seek very different effects: comic exaggeration, supernatural terror, understated beauty, and any number of other functions. We should analyze mise-en-scene's function in the total film—how it is motivated, how it varies or develops, how it works in relation to other film techniques.

The Power of Mise-en-Scene

Confining the cinema to some notion of realism would impoverish mise-en-scene. This technique has the power to transcend normal conceptions of reality, as we can see from a glance at the cinema's first master of the technique, Georges Méliès. Méliès's mise-en-scene enabled him to create a totally imaginary world on film.

A caricaturist and magician, Méliès became fascinated by the Lumière brothers' demonstration of their short films in 1895. (For more on the Lumières, see p. 186.) After building a camera based on an English projector, Méliès began filming unstaged street scenes and moments of passing daily life. One day, the story goes, he was filming at the Place de l'Opéra, and his camera jammed as a bus was passing. After some tinkering, he was able to resume filming, but by this time, the bus had gone and a hearse was passing in front of his lens. When Méliès screened the film, he discovered something unexpected: a moving bus seemed to transform

"When Buñuel was preparing The Discreet Charm of the Bourgeoisie, *he chose a tree-lined avenue for the recurring shot of his characters traipsing endlessly down it. The avenue was strangely stranded in open country and it perfectly suggested the idea of these people coming from nowhere and going nowhere. Buñuel's assistant said, 'You can't use that road. It's been used in at least ten other movies.' 'Ten other movies?' said Buñuel, impressed. 'Then it must be good.'"*

instantly into a hearse. Whether or not the anecdote is true, it at least illustrates Méliès's recognition of the magical powers of mise-en-scene. He would devote most of his efforts to cinematic conjuring.

To do so would require preparation, since Méliès could not count on lucky accidents like the bus–hearse transformation. He would have to plan and stage action for the camera. Drawing on his experience in theater, Méliès built one of the first film studios—a small, crammed affair bristling with theatrical machinery, balconies, trapdoors, and sliding backdrops. He sketched shots beforehand and designed sets and costumes. The correspondence between his detailed drawings and the finished shots is illustrated in **4.3** and **4.4**. As if this were not enough, Méliès starred in his own films (often in several roles per film). His desire to create magical effects led Méliès to control every aspect of his films' mise-en-scene.

Such control was necessary to create the fantasy world he envisioned. Only in a studio could Méliès produce *The Mermaid* (**4.5**). He could also surround himself (playing an astronomer) with a gigantic array of cartoonish cut-outs in *La Lune à un mètre* (**4.6**).

Méliès's "Star-Film" studio made hundreds of short fantasy and trick films based on such a control over every element in the frame, and the first master of mise-en-scene demonstrated the great range of technical possibilities it offers.

4.3   Georges Méliès's design for the rocket-launching scene in *A Trip to the Moon* and . . .

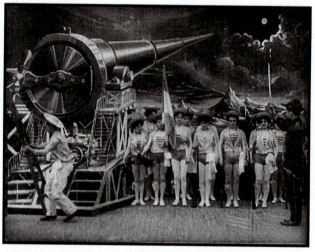

4.4   . . . the scene in the film.

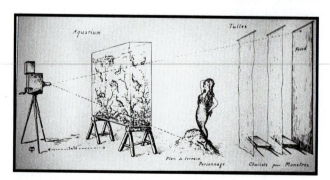

4.5   *The Mermaid* created an undersea world by placing a fish tank between the camera and an actress, some backdrops, and "carts for monsters."

4.6   The telescope, globe, and blackboard are all flat, painted cut-outs in *La Lune á une mètre.*

The legacy of Méliès's magic is a delightfully unreal world wholly obedient to the whims of the imagination.

Aspects of Mise-en-Scene

What possibilities for selection and control does mise-en-scene offer the filmmaker? We can mark out four general areas: setting, costumes and makeup, lighting, and staging.

Setting

Since the earliest days of cinema, critics and audiences have understood that setting plays a more active role in cinema than it usually does in the theater. André Bazin writes,

> The human being is all-important in the theatre. The drama on the screen can exist without actors. A banging door, a leaf in the wind, waves beating on the shore can heighten the dramatic effect. Some film masterpieces use man only as an accessory, like an extra, or in counterpoint to nature, which is the true leading character.

Cinema setting can come to the forefront; it need not be only a container for human events but can dynamically enter the narrative action. Kelly Reichardt's *Wendy and Lucy* begins with shots of a railroad yard as trains pass through (**4.7**). But we don't see any people. Wendy, who is making her way across the United States by car, is later seen walking her dog Lucy in a park. The opening shots of the rail yard suggest the sort of neighborhoods where she must stay. At later points in the film, the roar and whistle of rail traffic will increase suspense, but not until the ending will we come to understand why the opening emphasized the trains.

The filmmaker may control setting in many ways. One way is to select an already existing locale in which to stage the action, a practice stretching back to the earliest films. Louis Lumière shot his short comedy *L'Arroseur arrosé* ("The Waterer Watered," **4.8**) in a garden. At the close of World War II, Roberto Rossellini shot *Germany Year Zero* in the rubble of Berlin (**4.9**). Today filmmakers often go on location to shoot.

Alternatively, the filmmaker may construct the setting. Méliès understood that shooting in a studio increased his control, and many filmmakers followed his lead. In France, Germany, and especially the United States, the possibility of creating a wholly artificial world on film led to several approaches to setting.

Some directors have emphasized authenticity. For example, Erich von Stroheim prided himself on meticulous research into details of locale for *Greed* (**4.10**). *All the President's Men* (1976) took a similar tack, seeking to duplicate the *Washington Post* office on a soundstage (**4.11**). Even wastepaper from the actual office was scattered

4.8   *L'Arroseur arrosé.*

4.7   The railway yard at the opening of *Wendy and Lucy* is a setting that will take on significance later in the film.

4.9   *Germany Year Zero.*

4.10   Details like hanging flypaper and posters create a tavern scene in *Greed*.

4.11   Replicating an actual newsroom in *All the President's Men*.

4.12   The Babylonian sequences of *Intolerance* combined influences from Assyrian history, 19th-century biblical illustration, and modern dance.

4.13   In *Ivan the Terrible,* Part 2, the decor makes the characters seem to wriggle from one space to another.

4.14   In *Wings of Desire,* busy, colorful graffiti on a wall draw attention away from the man lying on the ground.

4.15   In *Bram Stoker's Dracula,* apart from the candles, the setting of this scene has been obliterated by darkness.

around the set. Other films have been less committed to historical accuracy. Though D. W. Griffith studied the various historical periods presented in *Intolerance*, his Babylon constitutes a personal image of that city (**4.12**). Similarly, in *Ivan the Terrible*, Sergei Eisenstein freely stylized the decor of the czar's palace to harmonize with the lighting, costume, and figure movement, so that characters crawl through doorways that resemble mouseholes and stand frozen before allegorical murals (**4.13**).

Setting can overwhelm the actors, as in Wim Wender's *Wings of Desire* (**4.14**), or it can be reduced to almost nothing, as in Francis Ford Coppola's *Bram Stoker's Dracula* (**4.15**).

The overall design of a setting can shape how we understand story action. In Louis Feuillade's silent crime serial *The Vampires*, a criminal gang has killed a courier on his way to a bank. The gang's confederate, Irma Vep, is also a bank employee, and just as she tells her superior that the courier has vanished, an imposter, in beard and bowler hat, strolls in behind them (**4.16**). They turn away from us in surprise as he comes forward (**4.17**). Working in a period when cutting to closer shots was rare in a French film, Feuillade draws our attention to the man by centering him in the doorway.

Something similar happens in a more crowded setting in Juzo Itami's *Tampopo*. The plot revolves around a widow who is trying to improve the food and service she offers in her restaurant. In one scene, a truck driver (in a cowboy hat) helps her by taking her to another noodle shop to study technique. Itami has staged the scene so that the kitchen and the counter serve as two arenas for the action. At first, the widow watches the noodle-man take orders, sitting by her mentor on the edge of the kitchen (**4.18**). Quickly, the counter fills with customers calling out orders. The truck driver challenges her to match the orders with the customers, and she steps closer to the center of the kitchen (**4.19**). After she calls out the orders correctly, she turns her back to us, and our interest shifts to the customers at the counter, who applaud her (**4.20**).

As the *Tampopo* example shows, color can be an important component of settings. The dark colors of the kitchen surfaces make the widow's red dress stand out. Robert Bresson's *L'Argent* creates parallels among its various settings by the recurrence of drab green backgrounds and cold blue props and costumes (**4.21–4.23**). In contrast, Jacques Tati's *Play Time* displays sharply changing color schemes. In the first portion of *Play Time*, the settings and costumes are mostly gray, brown, and black—cold, steely colors. Later in the film, however, beginning in the restaurant scene, the settings start to sport cheery reds, pinks, and greens. This change in the settings' colors supports a narrative development that shows an inhuman city landscape that is transformed by vitality and spontaneity.

A full-size setting need not always be built. Through much of the history of the cinema, filmmakers used miniature buildings to create fantasy scenes or simply to economize. Parts of settings could also be rendered as paintings and combined photographically with full-sized sections of the space. Now, digital special effects are used to fill in portions of the setting, such as cities in *The Phantom Menace* and *The Fifth Element* (**4.24**). Since such special effects also involve cinematography, we look at them in the next chapter.

In manipulating a shot's setting, the filmmaker may use a *prop*—short for *property*. This is another term borrowed from theatrical mise-en-scene. When an object in the setting has a function within the ongoing action, we can call it a prop. Films teem with examples: the snowstorm paperweight that shatters at the beginning of *Citizen Kane*, the little girl's balloon in *M*, the cactus rose in *The Man Who Shot Liberty Valance*, Sarah Connor's hospital bed turned exercise machine in *Terminator 2: Judgment Day*. Comedies often use props for humorous purposes (**4.25**).

Over the course of a narrative, a prop may become a motif. In Alexander Payne's *Election*, the fussy, frustrated high-school teacher begins his day by cleaning out the faculty refrigerator (**4.26**). Soon afterward, he picks up hallway litter (**4.27**). At a major turning point in the plot, he decides to conceal a decisive ballot, which he crumples and secretly drops into a wastebasket (**4.28**). Payne calls this the motif of

4.16   In *Les Vampires*, a background frame created by a large doorway . . .

4.17   . . . emphasizes the importance of an entering character.

"The best sets are the simplest, most 'decent' ones; everything should contribute to the feeling of the story and anything that does not do this has no place. Reality is usually too complicated. Real locations contain too much that is extreme or contradictory and always require some simplifying: taking things away, unifying colors, etc. This strength through simplicity is much easier to achieve on a built set than in an existing location."

— Stuart Craig, art director, *Notting Hill*

4.18 In *Tampopo,* at the start of the scene, the noodle counter, with only two customers, occupies the center of the action. The widow and her truck driver mentor stand inconspicuously at the left.

4.19 After the counter is full, the dramatic emphasis shifts to the kitchen when the widow rises and takes the challenge to name the customers' orders. Her red dress helps draw attention to her.

4.20 When she has triumphantly matched the orders, she gets a round of applause. By turning her away from us, Itami once more emphasizes the counter area, now filled with customers.

4.21 Color links the home in *L'Argent* . . .

4.22 . . . to the prison . . .

4.23 . . . and later to the old woman's home.

trash, "of throwing things away, since that's in fact the climax of the film. . . . So we establish it early on."

When the filmmaker uses color to create parallels among elements of setting, a color motif may become associated with several props, as in Souleymane Cissé's *Finye* (*The Wind,* **4.29–4.31**). In these and other scenes, the recurrent use of orange creates a cluster of nature motifs within the narrative. Later in this chapter, we shall examine in more detail how elements of setting can weave through a film to create motifs.

4.24 *The Fifth Element* creates a collagelike city using computer graphics to join images from various sources.

4.25 The irresponsible protagonist of *Groundhog Day* eats an enormous breakfast made up of props that dominate the foreground of the diner setting.

Costume and Makeup

Like setting, costume can have specific functions in the total film, and the range of possibilities is huge. Erich von Stroheim, for instance, was as passionately committed to authenticity of dress as of setting, and he was said to have created underwear that would instill the proper mood in his actors even though it was never to be seen in the film. In Griffith's *The Birth of a Nation,* a poignant moment occurs when the Little Sister decorates her dress with "ermine" made of cotton dotted with spots of soot **(4.32).** The costume displays the poverty of the defeated Southerners at the end of the Civil War.

In other films, costumes may be quite stylized, calling attention to their purely graphic qualities. Throughout *Ivan the Terrible,* costumes are carefully orchestrated with one another in their colors, their textures, and even their movements. One shot of Ivan and his adversary gives their robes a plastic sweep and dynamism **(4.33).** In *Freak Orlando,* Ulrike Ottinger (herself a costume designer) boldly uses costumes to display the spectrum's primary colors in maximum intensity **(4.34).**

Costumes can play important motivic and causal roles in narratives. The film director Guido in Fellini's *8½* persistently uses his dark glasses to shield himself from the world **(4.35).** When Hildy Johnson, in *His Girl Friday,* switches

4.26   In *Election,* as he discards spoiled leftovers, the teacher is suspiciously watched by the custodian—who will play an important role in his downfall.

4.27   He tosses a scrap of paper into the corridor trash bin.

4.28   A close-up of the teacher's hand discarding the crucial vote for student council president.

4.29 *Finye* begins with a woman carrying an orange calabash as the wind rustles through weeds.

4.30 Later, the vengeful grandfather prepares to stalk his grandson's persecutor by dressing in orange and making magic before a fire.

4.31 At the end, the little boy passes his bowl to someone offscreen—possibly the couple seen earlier.

4.32 In *The Birth of a Nation*, the Little Sister realizes how shabby her dress remains despite her attempts to add festive trimming.

4.33 The sweeping folds of a priest's lightweight black robe contrast with the heavy cloak and train of the czar's finery in *Ivan the Terrible*.

4.34 Stylized costumes in *Freak Orlando*.

4.35 In *8½*, sunglasses shield Marcello from the world.

4.36 Hildy's stylish hat with a low-dipping brim worn early in *His Girl Friday* . . .

4.37 . . . is replaced by a "masculine" hat with its brim pushed up, journalist-style, when she returns to work.

from her role of aspiring housewife to that of reporter, her hats change as well (**4.36, 4.37**). In the runaway bus section of *Speed*, during a phone conversation with Jack, the villain Howard refers to Annie as a "Wildcat"; Jack sees Annie's University of Arizona sweater and realizes that Howard has hidden a video camera aboard the bus. A costume provides the clue that allows Jack to outwit Howard.

As we have already seen in *Tampopo* and *L'Argent* (p. 124), costume is often coordinated with setting. Since the filmmaker usually wants to emphasize the human figures, setting may provide a more or less neutral background, while costume helps pick out the characters. Color design is particularly important here. The *Freak Orlando* costumes (**4.34**) stand out boldly against the neutral gray background of an artificial lake. In *The Night of the Shooting Stars*, luminous wheat fields set off the hard black-and-blue costumes of the fascists and the peasants (**4.38**). The director may instead choose to match the color values of setting and costume more closely. One shot in Fellini's *Casanova* creates a color gradation that runs from bright red costumes to paler red walls, the whole composition capped by a small white accent (**4.39**). This "bleeding" of the costume into the setting is carried to a kind of limit in the prison scene of *THX 1138*, in which George Lucas strips both locale and clothing to stark white on white (**4.40**).

Ken Russell's *Women in Love* affords a clear example of how costume and setting can contribute to a film's overall narrative progression. The opening scenes portray the characters' shallow middle-class life by means of saturated primary and complementary colors in costume and setting (**4.41**). In the middle portions of the film, as the characters discover love on a country estate, pale pastels predominate (**4.42**). The last section of *Women in Love* takes place around the Matterhorn, and the characters' ardor has cooled. Now the colors have become even paler, dominated by pure black and white (**4.43**). By integrating with setting, costume may function to reinforce narrative and thematic patterns.

Many of these points about costume apply equally to a closely related area of mise-en-scene, the actors' makeup. Makeup was originally necessary because actors' faces would not register well on early film stocks. Up to the present, it has been used in various ways to enhance the appearance of actors on the screen. Over the course of film history, a wide range of possibilities has emerged. Dreyer's *La Passion de Jeanne d'Arc* was famous for its complete avoidance of makeup (**4.44**). This film relied on close-ups and tiny facial changes to create an intense religious drama. On the other hand, Nikolai Cherkasov did not look particularly like Eisenstein's conception of Czar Ivan IV, so he wore a wig and false beard, nose, and eyebrows for *Ivan the Terrible* (**4.45**). Changing actors to look like historical personages has been one common function of makeup.

Today makeup usually tries to pass unnoticed, but it also accentuates expressive qualities of the actor's face. Since the camera may record cruel details that would pass unnoticed in ordinary life, any unsuitable blemishes, wrinkles, and sagging skin will have to be hidden. The makeup artist can sculpt the face, making it seem narrower or broader by applying blush and shadow. Viewers expect that female performers will wear lipstick and other cosmetics, but the male actors are often wearing makeup, too (**4.46, 4.47**).

Film actors rely on their eyes to a very great extent (see box, p. 134), and makeup artists can often enhance eye behavior. Eyeliner and mascara can draw attention to the eyes and emphasize the direction of a glance. Nearly every actor will also have expressively shaped eyebrows. Lengthened eyebrows can enlarge the face, while shorter brows make it seem more compact. Eyebrows plucked in a slightly rising curve add gaiety to the face, while slightly sloping ones hint at sadness. Thick, straight brows, commonly applied to men, reinforce the impression of a hard, serious gaze. Thus eye makeup can assist the actor's performance (**4.48, 4.49**).

4.38 The climactic skirmish of *The Night of the Shooting Stars.*

4.39 *Casanova:* subtle color gradations and a dramatic accent in the distance.

4.40 Heads seem to float in space as white costumes and settings blend in *THX 1138.*

4.41 Bright colors in an early scene of *Women in Love* give way . . .

4.42 . . . to the softer hues of trees and fields . . .

4.43 . . . and finally to a predominantly white-and-black scheme.

4.44 Light, blank backgrounds focus attention on the actors' faces in many shots of *La Passion de Jeanne d'Arc.*

4.45 In *Ivan the Terrible,* Part 1, makeup shapes the eyebrows and hollows the eye sockets to emphasize Ivan's piercing gaze.

4.46   In *Heat,* Al Pacino's makeup gives him slightly rounded eyebrows and, with the help of the lighting, minimizes the bags under his eyes.

4.47   In *The Godfather Part III,* made five years before *Heat,* Pacino looks older. Not only has his hair been whitened, but the makeup, again assisted by the lighting, gives him more sunken and baggy eyes, more hollow cheeks, and a longer, flatter chin.

4.48   In *Speed,* Sandra Bullock's eyeliner, shadow, and arched brows make her eyes vivid and give her an alert expression.

4.49   For the same scene, the eyeliner on Keanu Reeves makes the upper edges of his eyes stand out. Note also the somewhat fierce curve of the eyebrows, accentuating his slight frown.

In recent decades, the craft of makeup has developed in response to the popularity of horror and science fiction genres. Rubber and plasticine compounds create bumps, bulges, extra organs, and layers of artificial skin in such films as David Cronenberg's *The Fly* **(4.50).** In such contexts, makeup, like costume, becomes important in creating character traits or motivating plot action.

4.50 Jeff Goldblum, nearly unrecognizable under grotesque makeup, during his transformation into *The Fly*.

4.51 In *The Cheat*, Cecil B. DeMille suggests a jail cell by casting a bright light on a man's face and body through unseen bars.

4.52 Robert Bresson's *Pickpocket*.

Lighting

Much of the impact of an image comes from its manipulation of lighting. In cinema, lighting is more than just illumination that permits us to see the action. Lighter and darker areas within the frame help create the overall composition of each shot and thus guide our attention to certain objects and actions. A brightly illuminated patch may draw our eye to a key gesture, while a shadow may conceal a detail or build up suspense about what may be present. Lighting can also articulate textures: the curve of a face, the grain of a piece of wood, the tracery of a spider's web, the sparkle of a gem.

Lighting shapes objects by creating highlights and shadows. A highlight is a patch of relative brightness on a surface. The man's face in **4.51** and the edge of the fingers in **4.52** display highlights. Highlights provide important cues to the texture of the surface. If the surface is smooth, like glass or chrome, the highlights tend to gleam or sparkle; a rougher surface, like a coarse stone facing, yields more diffuse highlights.

There are two basic types of shadows, each of which is important in film composition: *attached* shadows, or *shading*, and *cast* shadows. An attached shadow occurs when light fails to illuminate part of an object because of the object's shape or surface features. If a person sits by a candle in a darkened room, patches of the face and body will fall into darkness. Most obviously, the nose often creates a patch of darkness on an adjoining cheek. This phenomenon is shading, or attached shadow. But the candle also projects a shadow on the wall behind. This is a cast shadow, because the body blocks out the light. The shadows in 4.51, for example, are cast shadows, made by bars between the actor and the light source. But in 4.52, the small, dark patches on the hand are attached shadows, for they are caused by the three-dimensional curves and ridges of the hand itself.

As these examples suggest, highlights and shadows help create our sense of a scene's space. In 4.51, a few shadows imply an entire prison cell. Lighting also shapes a shot's overall composition. One shot from John Huston's *Asphalt Jungle* welds the gang members into a unit by the pool of light cast by a hanging lamp (**4.53**). At the same time, it sets up a scale of importance, emphasizing the protagonist by making him the most frontal and clearly lit figure.

A shot's lighting affects our sense of the shape and texture of the objects depicted. If a ball is lit straight on from the front, it appears round. If the same ball is lit from the side, we see it as a half-circle. Hollis Frampton's short film *Lemon* consists primarily of light moving around a lemon, and the shifting shadows create dramatically changing patterns of yellow and black. This film almost seems designed to prove the truth of a remark made by Josef von Sternberg, one of the cinema's masters of film lighting: "The proper use of light can embellish and dramatize every object."

4.53 Attached shadows on faces create a dramatic composition in John Huston's *Asphalt Jungle*.

"*Light is everything. It expresses ideology, emotion, colour, depth, style. It can efface, narrate, describe. With the right lighting, the ugliest face, the most idiotic expression can radiate with beauty or intelligence.*"

— Frederico Fellini, director

4.54 In this shot from Satyajit Ray's *Aparajito,* Apu's mother and the globe she holds are emphasized by hard lighting, while . . .

4.55 . . . in another shot from the same film, softer lighting blurs contours and textures and makes for more diffusion and gentler contrasts between light and shade.

4.56 In *La Chinoise,* frontal lighting makes the actress's shadow fall directly behind her, where we cannot see it.

"Every light has a point where it is brightest and a point toward which it wanders to lose itself completely. . . . The journey of rays from that central core to the outposts of blackness is the adventure and drama of light."

— Josef von Sternberg

For our purposes, we can isolate four major features of film lighting: its quality, direction, source, and color.

Lighting *quality* refers to the relative intensity of the illumination. *Hard* lighting creates clearly defined shadows, crisp textures, and sharp edges, whereas *soft* lighting creates a diffused illumination. In nature, the noonday sun creates hard light, while an overcast sky creates soft light. The terms are relative, and many lighting situations will fall between the extremes, but we can usually recognize the differences (**4.54, 4.55**).

The *direction* of lighting in a shot refers to the path of light from its source or sources to the object lit. For convenience we can distinguish among frontal lighting, sidelighting, backlighting, underlighting, and top lighting.

Frontal lighting can be recognized by its tendency to eliminate shadows. In **4.56,** from Jean-Luc Godard's *La Chinoise,* the result of such frontal lighting is a fairly flat-looking image. Contrast **4.57,** from *Touch of Evil,* in which Orson Welles uses a hard **sidelight** (also called a *crosslight*) to sculpt the character's features.

Backlighting, as the name suggests, comes from behind the subject filmed. The light can be positioned at many angles: high above the figure, at various angles off to the side, pointing straight at the camera, or from below. Used with no other sources of light, backlighting tends to create silhouettes, as in **4.58.** Combined with more frontal sources of light, the technique can create an unobtrusively illuminated contour. This use of backlighting is called *edge lighting* or *rim lighting* (**4.59).**

As its name implies, **underlighting** suggests that the light comes from below the subject. Since underlighting tends to distort features, it is often used to create dramatic horror effects, but it may also simply indicate a realistic light source, such as a fireplace, or, as in **4.60,** a flashlight. As usual, a particular technique can function differently according to context.

Top lighting is exemplified by **4.61,** where the spotlight shines down from almost directly above Marlene Dietrich's face. Von Sternberg frequently used such a high frontal light to bring out the line of his star's cheekbones. (Our earlier example from *Asphalt Jungle* in 4.53 provides a less glamorous instance of top lighting.)

Lighting can also be characterized by its *source.* In making a documentary, the filmmaker may be obliged to shoot with the light available in the actual surroundings. Most fictional films, however, use extra light sources to obtain greater control of the image's look. In most fictional films, the table lamps and streetlights you see in the mise-en-scene are not the principal sources of illumination for the filming. But these visible sources of light will motivate the lighting decisions made in production. The filmmaker will usually strive to create a lighting design that is consistent with the sources in the setting. In **4.62,** from *The Miracle Worker,* the window in the rear and the lantern in the right foreground are purportedly the sources of

4.58 In Godard's *Passion,* the lamp and window provide backlighting that presents the woman almost entirely in silhouette.

4.57 In *Touch of Evil,* sidelight creates sharp attached shadows by the character's nose, cheek, and lips, while long cast shadows appear on the file cabinets at the left.

4.59 In *Wings,* a narrow line of light makes each actor's body stand out from the background.

4.60 In *The Sixth Sense,* a flashlight lights the boy's face from below, enhancing our empathy with his fright as he feels the presence of a ghost.

4.61 Top lighting in Josef von Sternberg's *Shanghai Express.*

4.62 Apparent and hidden light sources in *The Miracle Worker.*

illumination, but the many studio lights used in this shot are reflected as white dots in the glass lantern.

Directors and cinematographers manipulating the lighting of the scene will start from the assumption that any subject normally requires two light sources: a **key light** and a **fill light.** The key light is the primary source, providing the dominant illumination and casting the strongest shadows. The key light is the most

4.63   Strong key and soft fill light combined in *The Bodyguard.*

4.64   *Bezhin Meadow.*

directional light, and it usually corresponds to the motivating light source in the setting. A fill is a less intense illumination that "fills in," softening or eliminating shadows cast by the key light. By combining key and fill, and by adding other sources, lighting can be controlled quite exactly.

The key lighting source may be aimed at the subject from any angle, as our examples of lighting direction have indicated. As one shot from *Ivan the Terrible* shows (4.77), underlighting may be the key source, while a softer and dimmer fill falls on the setting behind the figure.

Lights from various directions can be combined in any way. A shot may use key and fill lights without backlighting. In the frame from *The Bodyguard* (**4.63),** a strong key light from offscreen left throws a dramatic shadow on the wall at the right. The dim fill light inconspicuously shows the back wall and ceiling of the set, but leaves the right side of the actor's head dark.

In **4.64,** from *Bezhin Meadow,* Eisenstein uses a number of light sources and directions. The key light falling on the figures comes from the left side, but it is hard on the face of the old woman in the foreground and softened on the face of the man because a fill light comes in from the right. This fill light falls on the woman's forehead and nose.

Classical Hollywood filmmaking developed the custom of using at least three light sources per shot: key light, fill light, and backlight. The most basic arrangement of these lights on a single figure is shown in **4.65.** The *backlight* comes from behind and above the figure, the *key light* comes diagonally from the front, and a *fill light* comes from a position near the camera. The key will usually be closer to the figure or brighter than the fill. Typically, each major character in a scene will have his or her own key light, fill light, and backlight. If another actor is added (as in the dotted figure in 4.65), the key light for one can be altered slightly to form the backlight for the other, and vice versa, with a fill light on either side of the camera.

In **4.66,** the Bette Davis character in *Jezebel* is the most important figure, and the **three-point lighting** centers attention on her. A bright backlight from the rear upper right highlights her hair and edge-lights her left arm. The key light is off left, making her right arm brightly illuminated. A fill light comes from just to the right of the camera. It is less bright than the key. This balanced lighting creates mild shading, modeling Davis's face to suggest volume rather than flatness. (Note the slight shadow cast by her nose.) Davis's backlight and key light serve to illuminate the woman behind her at the right, but less prominently. Other fill lights, called *background* or *set lighting,* fall on the setting and on the crowd at the left rear. Three-point lighting emerged during the studio era of Hollywood filmmaking, and it is still widely used, as in **4.67,** from *Amélie.*

You may have already noticed that this three-point lighting system demands that the lamps be rearranged virtually every time the camera shifts to a new framing of the scene. In spite of the great cost involved, most Hollywood films have a

"When taking close-ups in a colour picture, there is too much visual information in the background, which tends to draw attention away from the face. That is why the faces of the actresses in the old black and white pictures are so vividly remembered. Even now, movie fans nostalgically recall Dietrich . . . Garbo . . . Lamarr . . . Why? Filmed in black and white, those figures looked as if they were lit from within. When a face appeared on the screen over-exposed—the high-key technique, which also erased imperfections—it was as if a bright object was emerging from the screen."

— Nestor Almendros, cinematographer

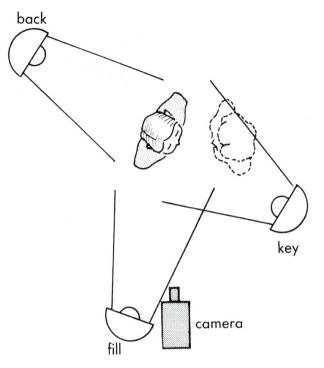

back

key

camera

fill

4.65 Three-point lighting, one of the basic techniques of
Hollywood cinema.

4.66 The three-point system's effect as it looks on the screen
in *Jezebel*.

4.67 In *Amélie*, the light-hearted romantic tone is enhanced by high-key,
three-point lighting.

4.68 *Back to the Future: day . . .*

4.69 *. . . versus night.*

different lighting arrangement for each camera position. Such variations in the light
sources do not conform to reality, but they do enable filmmakers to create clear
compositions for each shot.

Three-point lighting was particularly well suited for the high-key lighting used
in classical Hollywood cinema and other filmmaking traditions. **High-key lighting**
refers to an overall lighting design that uses fill light and backlight to create low
contrast between brighter and darker areas. Usually, the light quality is soft, making shadow areas fairly transparent. The frames from *Jezebel* (4.66) and *Amélie*
(4.67) exemplify high-key lighting. Hollywood directors and cinematographers
have relied on this for comedies, adventure films, and most dramas.

High-key lighting is not used simply to render a brightly lit situation, such
as a dazzling ballroom or a sunny afternoon. High-key lighting is an overall approach to illumination that can suggest different lighting conditions or times of
day. Consider, for example, two frames from *Back to the Future*. The first shot
(4.68) uses high-key illumination matched to daylight and a brightly lit malt shop.
The second frame **(4.69)** is from a scene set in a room at night, but it still uses the

4.70 In *Kanal*, low-key lighting creates a harsh highlight on one side of the woman's face, a deep shadow on the other.

"When I started watching films in the 1940s and 1950s, Indian cinematography was completely under the influence of Hollywood aesthetics, which mostly insisted on the 'ideal light' for the face, using heavy diffusion and strong backlight. I came to resent the complete disregard of the actual source of light and the clichéd use of backlight. Using backlight all the time is like using chili powder in whatever you cook."

— Subrata Mitra, cinematographer

high-key approach, as can be seen from the lighting's softness, its low contrast, and its detail in shadow areas.

Low-key illumination creates stronger contrasts and sharper, darker shadows. Often the lighting is hard, and fill light is lessened or eliminated altogether. The effect is of *chiaroscuro,* or extremely dark and light regions within the image. An example is **4.70,** from Andrzej Wajda's *Kanal.* Here the fill light and background light are significantly less intense than in high-key technique. As a result, shadow areas on the left third of the screen remain hard and opaque. In **4.71,** a low-key shot from Leos Carax's *Mauvais sang,* the key light is hard and comes from the side. Carax eliminates both fill and background illumination, creating very sharp shadows and a dark void around the characters.

As our examples indicate, low-key lighting has usually been applied to somber or mysterious scenes. It was common in horror films of the 1930s and films noirs (dark films) of the 1940s and 1950s. The low-key approach was revived in the 1980s in such films as *Blade Runner* and *Rumble Fish* and continued in the 1990s in films noirs like *Se7en* and *The Usual Suspects.* In *El Sur* **(4.72),** Victor Erice's low-key lighting yields dramatic chiaroscuro effects that portray the adult world as a child imagines it.

When the actors move, the director must decide whether to alter the lighting. By overlapping several different key lights, the filmmaker can maintain a constant intensity as actors move around the set. Although constant lighting is not particularly realistic, it has advantages, the main one being that distracting shadows and highlights do not move across actors. At the end of Fellini's *Nights of Cabiria,* for example, the heroine moves diagonally toward us, accompanied by a band of singing young people **(4.73, 4.74).** Alternatively, the filmmaker may have his or her figures move through patches of light and shadow. The sword fight in *Rashomon* is intensified by the contrast between the ferocious combat and the cheerfully dappled lighting pouring into the glade **(4.75).**

We tend to think of film lighting as limited to two colors—the white of sunlight or the soft yellow of incandescent interior lamps. In practice, filmmakers who choose to control lighting typically work with as purely white a light as they can. By use of filters placed in front of the light source, the filmmaker can color the on-screen illumination in any fashion. There may be a realistic source in the scene to motivate the hue of the light. For example, cinematographers often use filters over lighting equipment to suggest the orange tint of candlelight, as in François Truffaut's *The Green Room* **(4.76).** But colored light can also be unrealistic in its motivation. Eisenstein's *Ivan the Terrible,* Part 2, uses a blue light suddenly cast on an actor, nondiegetically, to suggest the character's terror and uncertainty **(4.77, 4.78).** Such a shift in stylistic function—using colored light to perform a function usually confined to acting—is all the more effective because it is so unexpected.

4.71 In *Mauvais sang,* a single key light without any fill on the actress's face leaves her expression nearly invisible.

4.72 Low-key lighting in *El Sur* suggests a child's view of the adult world as full of mystery and danger.

4.73 In *Nights of Cabiria,* the heroine is surrounded by a band of young street musicians.

4.74 As she walks, the lighting on her face does not change, enabling us to notice slight changes in her expression.

4.75 Dappled lighting in *Rashomon.*

4.76 An orange filter suggests that all the light in this scene from *The Green Room* comes from candles.

4.77 In *Ivan the Terrible,* a character's fear registers on his face . . .

4.78 . . . but a blue light also suddenly and briefly shines on it until it disappears and the scene continues.

4.79 In *The Golden Compass,* stark arctic sunshine from offscreen right falls as sidelight on the snow and the fighting bears. Simulated fill light was added to the onlookers and in areas of attached shadows on the foreground bears.

Most film lighting is arranged as part of preparation for live-action filmmaking. But what if the settings and figures are created with a computer? Scanning a model or motion-capturing a figure does not record the light falling on it, and it comes out a neutral gray all over. Animators add simulated light to a scene using special programs. Watch the credits for any special-effects-heavy film, and you will see long lists of names of people dealing with light and shade.

In *The Golden Compass,* the vicious combat between two armored polar bears was created entirely digitally. The fight takes place with a bright sun low in the sky, coming from off right, and the icy clearing contains shadows with bright stretches where the light shines between the surrounding crags **(4.79).** Simulated light is also used in cartoons, where all the mise-en-scene is created via computers. Pixar's

4.80   A virtuoso display of computer-simulated lighting, with colored neon signs reflecting in shiny, colored surfaces as the *Cars* cruise through their small-town street.

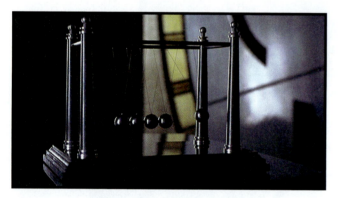

4.81   In *The Hudsucker Proxy,* when the mailboy Norville proposes his new toy idea, the clicking balls on his boss's desktop suddenly and inexplicably stop.

4.82   The abstract film *Parabola* uses lighting and a pure background to emphasize sculptural forms.

Cars experimented with the difficult challenge of rendering the look of colored lights reflected in metal and glass surfaces **(4.80).**

We are used to ignoring the illumination of our everyday surroundings, so film lighting is also easy to take for granted. Yet the look of a shot is centrally controlled by light quality, direction, source, and color. The filmmaker can manipulate and combine these factors to shape the viewer's experience in a great many ways. No component of mise-en-scene is more important than what Sternberg called "the drama and adventure of light."

Staging: Movement and Performance

The director may also control the behavior of various figures in the mise-en-scene. Here the word *figures* covers a wide range of possibilities, since the figure may represent a person but could also be an animal (Lassie, the donkey Balthasar, Donald Duck), a robot (R2D2 and C3PO in the *Star Wars* series), an object **(4.81),** or even a pure shape **(4.82).** Mise-en-scene allows such figures to express feelings and thoughts; it can also dynamize them to create various kinetic patterns.

In **4.83,** from *Seven Samurai,* the samurai have won the battle with the bandits. Virtually the only movement in the frame is the driving rain, but the slouching postures of the men leaning on their spears express their tense weariness. In contrast, in *White Heat,* explosive movements and ferocious facial expressions present an image of psychotic rage **(4.84).**

In cinema, facial expression and movement are not restricted to human figures. In one type of animated film, puppets are manipulated frame by frame through the technique of *stop-action* or *stop-motion* **(4.85).** The filmmakers can also stage action without three-dimensional objects moving through real space. Images of characters that never existed, like Shrek or Daffy Duck, can be used in animated cartoons. In science-fiction and fantasy movies, robots and fabulous monsters created as models can be scanned and movement added via computer manipulation (1.27). Sophisticated digital techniques also allow filmmakers to motion-capture many points of movement on actors' faces and transfer their performances to computer-generated creatures **(4.86).**

Acting and Actuality   Although abstract shapes and animated figures can become important in the mise-en-scene, the most intuitively familiar cases of figure expression and movement are actors playing roles. Like other aspects of mise-en-scene, the performance is created in order to be filmed. An actor's performance consists of visual elements (appearance, gestures, facial expressions) and sound (voice, effects). At times, of course, an actor may contribute only visual aspects, as in silent movies. Similarly, an actor's performance may sometimes exist only on the sound track of the film; in *A Letter to Three Wives,* Celeste Holm's character, Addie Ross, speaks a narration over the images but never appears on the screen.

Acting is often approached as a question of realism. But concepts of realistic acting have changed over film history. Today we may think that the performance of Hilary Swank in *Boys Don't Cry* or those given by Heath Ledger and Jake Gyllenhaal in *Brokeback Mountain* are reasonably close to people's real-life behavior. Yet in the early 1950s, the New York Actors Studio style, as exemplified by Marlon Brando's performances in *On the Waterfront* and *A Streetcar Named Desire,* was also thought to be extremely realistic. Fine though we may still find Brando's work in these films, it seems deliberate, heightened, and quite unrealistic. The same might be said of the performances, by professional and amateur actors alike, in post–World War II Italian neorealist films. These were hailed when they first appeared as almost documentary depictions of Italian life, but many of them now seem to us to contain polished performances suitable to Hollywood films. Already, major naturalistic performances of the 1970s, such as Robert De Niro's protagonist in *Taxi Driver,* seem quite stylized. Who can say what the acting in *The Insider, In the Bedroom, Frozen River,* and other films will look like in a few decades?

4.83   The actors strike weary poses in *Seven Samurai.*

4.84   In *White Heat,* Cody Jarrett (James Cagney) bursts up from the prison mess table after learning of his mother's death.

CONNECT TO THE BLOG
It's not easy to analyze film acting. We consider how it might be done and link to some close analyses of silent-film acting in "Acting up."
See www.davidbordwell.net/blog/?p=3763.

4.85   Ladislav Starevich's puppet film *The Mascot* includes a conversation between a devil and a thief, with subtle facial expressions and gestures created through animation.

4.86   *Pirates of the Caribbean: Dead Man's Chest*: Along with makeup around his eyes and mouth, actor Bill Nighy had white motion-capture dots applied to his face. His facial expressions were used to create virtual makeup, including a beard made of writhing tentacles, for his character, Davy Jones.

Changing views of realism are not the only reason to be wary of this as a concept for analyzing acting. Often, when people call a performance unrealistic, they are evaluating it as bad. But not all films try to achieve realism. Since the performance an actor creates is part of the overall mise-en-scene, films contain a wide variety of acting styles. Instead of assuming that acting must be realistic, we should try to understand what kind of acting style the film is aiming at. If the functions of acting in the film are best served by a nonrealistic performance, that is the kind that the skillful actor will strive to present. Obvious examples of nonrealistic acting style can be found in *The Wizard of Oz,* for fantasy purposes. (How would a real Wicked Witch behave?) Moreover, realistic performance will always be only one option in film acting. In mass-production filmmaking from Hollywood, India, Hong Kong, and other traditions, overblown performances are a crucial source of the audience's pleasure. Viewers do not expect narrowly realistic acting from Jim Carrey or from martial-arts stars such as Jet Li and Jackie Chan.

Finally, when we watch any fictional film, we are to some degree aware that the performances on the screen are the result of the actors' skills and decisions. (See "A Closer Look.") When we use the phrase "larger than life" to describe an effective performance, we seem to be tacitly acknowledging the actor's deliberate craft. In analyzing a particular film, it is usually necessary to go beyond assumptions about realism and consider the functions and purposes that the actor's craft serves.

Acting: Functions and Motivation   In 1985, Hollywood observers were surprised that Steve Martin wasn't nominated for an Academy Award for *All of Me.* In that film, Martin portrays a man whose body is suddenly inhabited on the right side by the soul of a woman who has just died. Martin used sudden changes of voice, along with acrobatic pantomime, to suggest a split body. In 1999, a similar outcry occurred when Jim Carrey was not nominated for an Oscar for *The Truman Show,* a comedy about a man who is unaware that his entire life has been broadcast as a sitcom on television. Neither Martin nor Carrey could be expected to perform realistically in the narrow sense of the word, since the situations they portray could not exist in the real world. Yet in these fantasy-comedies, the performances are completely appropriate.

In films like *All of Me* and *The Truman Show,* a more muted and superficially realistic performance would clearly be inappropriate to the context established by the genre, the film's narrative, and the overall mise-en-scene. This suggests that a performance, realistic or not, should be examined according to its *function* in the context of the film.

We can consider performance along two dimensions. A performance will be more or less *individualized,* and it will be more or less *stylized.* Often we have both in mind when we think of a realistic performance: it creates a unique character, and it does not seem too exaggerated or too underplayed. Marlon Brando's portrayal of Don Vito Corleone in *The Godfather* is quite individualized. Brando gives the Godfather a complex psychology, a distinctive appearance and voice, and a string of facial expressions and gestures that make him significantly different from the standard image of a gang boss. As for stylization, Brando keeps Don Vito in the middle range. His performance is neither flat nor flamboyant; he isn't impassive, but he doesn't chew the scenery either.

Yet this middle range, which we often identify with realistic performance, isn't the only option. On the individuality scale, films may create broader, more anonymous *types.* Classical Hollywood narrative was built on ideologically stereotyped roles: the Irish cop on the beat, the black servant, the Jewish pawnbroker, the wisecracking waitress or showgirl. Through *typecasting,* actors were selected and directed to conform to type. Often, however, skillful performers gave these conventions a freshness and vividness. In the Soviet cinema of the 1920s, several directors used a similar principle, called *typage.* Here the actor was expected to portray a typical representative of a social class or historical movement (**4.97, 4.98**).

THE FILM ACTOR'S TOOLKIT

We might think that the most important task facing an actor is speaking dialogue in a convincing and stirring way. Certainly, voice and delivery are very important in cinema, but considered in terms of mise-en-scene, the actor is always part of the overall visual design. Many film scenes contain little or no dialogue, but at every moment onscreen, the actor must be in character. The actor and director shape the performance pictorially.

At all times, film actors use their faces. This was most evident before movies had sound, and theorists of the silent film were full of praise for the subtle facial acting of Charlie Chaplin, Greta Garbo, and Lillian Gish. Since some basic facial expressions (happiness, fear, anger) are understood easily across cultures, it's not surprising that silent films could become popular around the world. Today, with mainstream fiction films using many close-ups (see p. 195), actors' faces are hugely enlarged, and the performers must control their expressions minutely.

The most expressive parts of the face are the mouth, eyebrows, and eyes. All work together to signal how the character is responding to the dramatic situation. In *Jerry Maguire,* the accountant Dorothy Boyd accidentally meets Jerry at an airport baggage conveyor. She has a crush on him, partly because she admires the courageous mission statement he has issued to the sports agency they work for. As he starts to back off from the statement, she eagerly quotes it from memory; Renee Zellwegger's earnest smile and steady gaze suggest that she takes the issues more seriously than Jerry does **(4.87).** This impression is confirmed when Jerry says, "Uh-huh," and studies her skeptically, his fixed smile signaling social politeness rather than genuine pride **(4.88).** This encounter sets up one premise of the film—that Jerry's idealistic impulses will need

constant shoring up, for he might at any moment slip back into being "a shark in a suit."

The eyes hold a special place in film. In any scene, crucial story information is conveyed by the direction of a character's glance, the use of eyelids, and the shape of the eyebrows. One of Chaplin's most heart-rending moments comes in *City Lights,* when the blind flower girl, now sighted, suddenly realizes that he's her benefactor. Chaplin twirls a flower in his teeth, so we can't see the shape of his mouth; we must read yearning in his brows and rapt, dark gaze **(4.89).**

Normally, we don't stare intently at the people we talk with. We glance away about half the time to gather our thoughts, and we blink 10–12 times a minute. But actors must learn to look directly at each other, locking eyes and seldom blinking. If an actor glances away from the partner in the conversation, it suggests distraction or evasion. If an actor blinks, it suggests a reaction to what is happening in the scene (surprise, or anxiety). Actors playing forceful characters often stare fixedly. Anthony Hopkins said this of playing Hannibal Lecter: "If you don't blink you can keep the audience mesmerized." (See 8.3, 8.5.) In our *Jerry Maguire* scene, the protagonists watch each other fixedly. When Jerry does close his eyes in response to Dorothy's praise, it indicates his nervousness about confronting the issues that his mission statement raised.

Actors act with their bodies as well. How a character walks, stands, or sits conveys a great deal about personality and attitude. In fact, during the 18th and 19th centuries, *attitude* was used to refer to the way a person stood. Stage acting gave early film a repertoire

4.87 Perky and sincere, Dorothy pledges allegiance to Jerry Maguire's idealistic memo.

4.88 Jerry smiles politely, but his sideways glance and brows suggest that he is a bit put off by her earnestness.

4.89 In the climax of *City Lights,* by concealing his mouth with the flower he twirls nervously, Chaplin obliges us to find his hope expressed in the upper part of his face.

of postures that could express a character's state of mind. In the 1916 Italian film *Tigre Reale* (*The Royal Tigress*), the diva Pina Menichelli plays a countess with a shady past. At one point, she confesses this in a florid attitude that expresses noble suffering **(4.90)**. While few actors today would resort to this stylized posture, early film audiences would have accepted it as vividly expressive, like a movement in dance. Menichelli plays the rest of the scene more quietly, but she still employs expressive attitudes **(4.91, 4.92)**.

Chaplin's and Menichelli's gestures show that hands are important tools of the film actor. Hands are to the body what eyes are to the face: They focus our attention and evoke the character's thoughts and feelings. Actress Maureen O'Hara said of Henry Fonda, "All he had to do was wag his little finger and he could steal a scene from anybody." A good example can be seen in the doomsday thriller *Fail-Safe*. Henry Fonda plays the U.S. president, who has learned that an American warplane has been accidentally sent to bomb the

4.90 In *Tigre Reale,* Menichelli's right hand seizes her hair, as if pulling her head back in agony; but her body still expresses defiance, thrust forward and standing firm as the left hand grips her waist.

4.91 As Menichelli begins to feel shame, she retreats toward the fireplace, turning from us and slumping in a way that suggests regret.

4.92 She keeps her back to the camera as she withdraws, now a pathetic figure.

4.97 The opening of Sergei Eisenstein's *Strike* presents the cartoonish cliché of the top-hatted capitalist . . .

4.98 . . . while in contrast the workers are later presented as earnest and resolute.

Whether more or less typed, the performance can also be located on a continuum of stylization. A long tradition of film acting strives for a resemblance to what is thought of as realistic behavior. This sense of realism may be created by giving the actors small bits of business to perform while they speak their lines. Frequent gestures and movements by the actors add plausibility to the humor of Woody Allen's films **(4.99)**. More intense and explicit emotions dominate *Winchester 73*, in which James Stewart plays a man driven by a desire for revenge **(4.100)**.

Psychological motivation is less important in a film like *Trouble in Paradise*, a sophisticated comedy of manners in which the main concern is with more stereotypical characters in a comic situation. In **4.101,** two women competing for the

Soviet Union. Fonda stands erect at the phone as he hears distressing news about the plane's progress, and he hangs up with his left hand (4.93–4.96). By keeping most of the shot still and bare, director Sidney Lumet has given Fonda's fingers the main role, letting them express the president's measured prudence but also suggesting the strain of the crisis.

4.93 In *Fail-Safe*, the president stands erect at the phone as he hears distressing news about the plane's progress, and he hangs up with his left hand.

4.94 The president pauses and rubs his fingers together thoughtfully . . .

4.95 . . . then he taps into the intercom with his right hand.

4.96 As he waits, for a brief moment his left fingers waggle anxiously.

4.99 Verisimilitude in acting: Mia Farrow as Hannah, Diane Wiest as her sister Holly, and Carrie Fisher as their friend April set a table, chatting about the other guests in *Hannah and Her Sisters*.

same man pretend to be friendly. Again, the performances are perfectly appropriate to the genre, narrative, and overall style of the film.

Comedy doesn't provide the only motivation for greater stylization. *Ivan the Terrible* is a film that heightens every element—music, costume, setting—to create a larger-than-life portrait of its hero. Nikolai Cherkasov's broad, abrupt gestures fit in perfectly with all of these other elements to create an overall unity of composition (4.102).

4.100   In *Winchester 73*, Jimmy Stewart's mild manner occasionally erupts into explosions of anger, revealing him as on the brink of psychosis.

4.101   The exaggerated smiles and gestures in *Trouble in Paradise* are amusing because we know that each woman is trying to deceive the other.

4.102   Nikolai Cherkasov's dramatically raised arm and thrown-back head are appropriate to the heightened style of *Ivan the Terrible*.

4.103   Playing the heroine of *Au Hasard Balthasar,* Anna Wiazemsky looks without expression at her would-be seducer, who wants her to get in his car . . .

4.104   . . . and glances downward, still without registering her thoughts, before getting into the car.

CONNECT TO THE BLOG
Sometimes critics concentrate on acting to the exclusion of a film's other qualities, as we complain in "Good actors spell good acting."

See www.davidbordwell.net/blog/?p=146.

For the conventions of award-winning performances, see "Good actors spell good acting, 2: Oscar bait," at

www.davidbordwell.net/blog/?p=205.

Some films may combine different degrees of stylization. *Amadeus* contrasts a grotesque, giggling performance by Tom Hulce as Mozart with Murray Abraham's suave Salieri. Here the acting sharpens the contrast between the older composer's decorous but dull music and the young man's irrepressible but offensive genius.

Films like *Caligari, Ivan the Terrible,* and *Amadeus* create stylized performances through extroversion and exaggeration. The director can also explore the possibilities of very muted performances. Compared to normal practice, highly restrained acting can seem quite stylized. Robert Bresson is noted for such restrained performances. Using nonprofessional actors and drilling them in the details of the characters' physical actions, Bresson makes his actors quite inexpressive by conventional standards **(4.103, 4.104)**. Although these performances may upset our expectations, we soon realize that such restraint focuses our attention on details of action we never notice in most movies.

Acting in the Context of Other Techniques   By examining how an actor's performance functions in the context of the overall film, we can also notice how acting cooperates with other film techniques. For instance, the actor is always a graphic element in the film, but some films underline this fact. In *The Cabinet of Dr. Caligari*, Conrad Veidt's dancelike portrayal of the somnambulist Cesare makes him blend in with the graphic elements of the setting **(4.105).** As we shall see in our examination of the history of film styles, the graphic design of this scene in *Caligari* typifies the systematic distortion characteristic of German Expressionism.

4.105 In *The Cabinet of Dr. Caligari*, Cesare's body echoes the tilted tree trunks, his arms and hands their branches and leaves.

4.106 Jean Seberg in *Breathless*, an inexpressive performance or an enigmatic one?

In *Breathless,* director Jean-Luc Godard juxtaposes Jean Seberg's face with a print of a Renoir painting (**4.106**). We might think that Seberg is giving a wooden performance, for she simply poses in the frame and turns her head. Indeed, her acting in the entire film may seem flat and inexpressive. Yet her face and general demeanor are visually appropriate for her role, a capricious American woman unfathomable to her Parisian boyfriend.

The context of a performance may also be shaped by the technique of film editing. Because a film is shot over a period of time, actors perform in bits. This can work to the filmmaker's advantage, since these bits can be selected and combined to build up a performance in ways that could never be accomplished on the stage. If a scene has been filmed in several shots, with alternate takes of each shot, the editor may select the best gestures and expressions and create a composite performance better than any one sustained performance is likely to be. Through the addition of sound and the combination with other shots, the performance can be built up still further. The director may simply tell an actor to widen his or her eyes and stare offscreen. If the next shot shows a hand with a gun, we are likely to think the actor is depicting fear quite effectively.

Camera techniques also create a controlling context for acting. Film acting, as most viewers know, differs from theatrical acting. At first glance, that suggests that cinema always call for more underplaying, since the camera can closely approach the actor. But cinema actually calls for a stronger interplay between restraint and emphasis.

In a theater, we are usually at a considerable distance from the actor on the stage. We certainly can never get as close to the theater actor as the camera can put us in a film. But recall that the camera can be at *any* distance from the figure. Filmed from very far away, the actor is a dot on the screen—much smaller than an actor on stage seen from the back of the balcony. Filmed from very close, the actor's tiniest eye movement may be revealed.

Thus the film actor must behave differently than the stage actor does, but not always by being more restrained. Rather, she or he must be able to *adjust to each type of camera distance.* If the actor is far from the camera, he or she will have to gesture broadly or move around to be seen as acting at all. But if the camera and actor are inches apart, a twitch of a mouth muscle will come across clearly. Between these extremes, there is a whole range of adjustments to be made.

Basically, a scene can concentrate on either the actor's facial expression or on pantomimic gestures of the body. Clearly, the closer the actor is to the camera, the more the facial expression will be visible and the more important it will be (although the filmmaker may choose to concentrate on another part of the body,

"You can ask a bear to do something like, let's say, 'Stand up,' and the bear stands up. But you cannot say to a bear, 'Look astonished.' So you have him standing up, but then you have to astonish him. I would bang two saucepans, or get a chicken from a cage, then shake it so it squawked, and the bear would think, 'What was that?' and 'click' I'd have that expression."

— Jean-Jacques Annaud, director, *The Bear*

4.107   In this long shot from *The Spider's Stratagem,* the stiff, upright way in which the heroine holds her parasol is one of the main facets of the actress's performance . .

4.108   . . . while in a conversation scene we can see details of her eye and lip movements.

4.109   A cat "acting" in *Aliens.*

excluding the face and emphasizing gesture). But if the actor is far away from the camera, or turned to conceal the face, his or her gestures become the center of the performance.

Thus both the staging of the action and the camera's distance from it determine how we will see the actors' performances. Many shots in Bernardo Bertolucci's *The Spider's Stratagem* show the two main characters from a distance, so that their manner of walking constitutes the actors' performances in the scene (**4.107**). In conversation scenes, however, we see their faces clearly, as in **4.108.**

Such factors of context are particularly important when the performers are not actors, or even human beings. Framing, editing, and other film techniques can make trained animals give appropriate performances. Jonesy, the cat in *Aliens,* seems threatening because his hissing movement has been emphasized by lighting, framing, editing, and the sound track (**4.109**). Editing makes it seem that the cat is reacting angrily to something within the scene where the shot appears, yet in reality it probably hissed at something quite different.

As with every element of a film, acting offers an unlimited range of distinct possibilities. It cannot be judged on a universal scale that is separate from the concrete context of the entire film's form.

Putting It All Together: Mise-en-Scene in Space and Time

Sandro and Claudia are searching for Anna, who has mysteriously vanished. Anna is Claudia's friend and Sandro's lover, but during their search, they've begun to drift from their goal of finding her. They've also begun a love affair. In the town of Noto, they stand on a church rooftop near the bells, and Sandro says he regrets giving up architectural design. Claudia is encouraging him to return to his art when suddenly he asks her to marry him.

She's startled and confused, and Sandro comes toward her. She is turned away from us. At first, only Sandro's expression is visible as he reacts to her plea "Why can't things be simpler?" (**4.110**). Claudia twists her arms around the bell rope, then turns away from him, toward us, grasping the rope and fluttering her hand. Now we can see that she's quite distraught. Sandro, a bit uneasy, turns away as she says anxiously, "I'd like to see things clearly" (**4.111**).

Brief though it is, this exchange in Michelangelo Antonioni's *L'Avventura* (*The Adventure*) shows how the tools of mise-en-scene—setting, costume, lighting, performance, and staging—can work together smoothly. We've considered them separately in order to examine the contribution each one makes, but in any shot, they mesh. They unfold on the screen in space and time, fulfilling several functions.

4.110   A striking instance of frontality in *L'Avventura:* The characters alternate . . .

4.111   . . . turning their backs on the camera.

Most basically, the filmmaker has to guide the audience's attention to the important areas of the image. We need to spot the items important for the ongoing action. The filmmaker also wants to build up our interest by arousing curiosity and suspense. And the filmmaker tries to add expressive qualities, giving the shot an emotional coloration. Mise-en-scene helps the filmmaker achieve all these purposes.

How did Antonioni guide our attention in the Claudia–Sandro exchange? First, we're watching the figures, not the railing behind them. Based on the story so far, we expect Sandro and Claudia to be the objects of interest. At other points in the film, Antonioni makes his couple tiny figures in massive urban or seaside landscapes. Here, however, his mise-en-scene keeps their intimate interchange foremost in our minds.

Consider the first image merely as a two-dimensional picture. Both Sandro and Claudia stand out against the pale sky and the darker railing. They're also mostly curved shapes—heads and shoulders—and so they contrast with the geometrical regularity of the posts. In the first frame, light strikes Sandro's face and suit from the right, picking him out against the rails. His dark hair is well positioned to make his head stand out against the sky. Claudia, a blonde, stands out against the railing and sky less vividly, but her polka-dot blouse creates a distinctive pattern. And considered only as a picture, the shot roughly balances the two figures, Sandro in the left half and Claudia in the right.

It's hard to think of the shot as simply two-dimensional, though. We instinctively see it as portraying a space that we could move around in. Claudia seems closer to us because her body masks things farther away, a spatial cue called *overlap*. She's also somewhat larger in the frame than Sandro, which reinforces our sense that she's closer. The rope slices across the bottom third of the frame, separating her from him (overlap again). Sandro himself overlaps the railing, which in turn overlaps the sky and the town. We get a sense of distinct planes of space, layers lying closer to or farther from us. Elements of mise-en-scene like costume, lighting, setting, and figure placement create this sense of a three-dimensional arena for the action.

Antonioni has used mise-en-scene to emphasize his characters and their interaction. But that interaction unfolds in time, and it gives him an opportunity to guide our attention while building up suspense and expressing emotion. Claudia is turned away from us when Sandro presses her to marry him, and the rope is taut between them (4.110). How will she respond?

Antonioni starts by giving Claudia a bit of business. She twists the rope around her arms and slips it over her back. This could be a hint that she's drawn to Sandro's proposal. At the same time, she hesitates. For as soon as he presses her, she turns away from him (4.111).

We know that faces give us access to characters' thoughts and emotions. Another filmmaker might have had Claudia already facing us when Sandro asked, so we'd see her response immediately. Antonioni instead makes things uncertain for a moment. He has concealed Claudia's reaction and then lets her turn toward us. To make sure that we watch her and not Sandro at this moment, Antonioni has him turn away when she gestures and speaks ("I'd like to see things clearly"). Our attention is riveted on her.

Soon enough, Sandro turns back toward the camera, so we can see his reaction, but already Claudia's anxiety has flashed out at us. Her complex relation to Sandro—attraction (sliding under the bell rope) and uncertainty (turning away tensely)—has been presented to us concretely.

This is only one moment in a complex scene, but it shows how various elements of mise-en-scene can cooperate to create a specific effect—the delayed revelation of a character's emotion. That revelation couldn't have occurred without the director's choices about what to show us at particular points. When we look at an image, we look purposefully. What we notice is guided by our expectations about what might be significant.

4.112   Narrative expectations guide our eye to the main characters in *Tootsie*.

Often the form of the whole film sets up our expectations. If a shot shows a crowd, we will tend to scan it looking for a character we recognize from earlier scenes. In **4.112,** although there are several people in the foreground of this shot from *Tootsie,* we will likely notice Julie (Jessica Lange) and Dorothy Michaels (Dustin Hoffman) quickly, since they are our main characters. Similarly, we notice Les, seen here for the first time, because he and Dorothy are exchanging smiles. Similarly, sound can become an important factor controlling our attention, as we shall see in Chapter 7. In addition to the film's story context, there are several ways directors can guide our expectations about what to notice. In the spirit of trying to grasp all the options on the mise-en-scene menu, let's look in more detail at the spatial and temporal possibilities.

Space

"The audience is only going to look at the most overriding thing in the frame. You must take charge of and direct their attention. It's also the principle of magic: what is the single important thing? Make it easy for them to see it, and you're doing your job."

— David Mamet, director

Screen Space   In many respects, a film shot resembles a painting. It presents a flat array of colors and shapes. Before we even start to read the image as a three-dimensional space, mise-en-scene offers many cues for guiding our attention and emphasizing elements in the frame.

Take something as simple as balancing the shot. Filmmakers often try to distribute various points of interest evenly around the frame. They assume that viewers will concentrate more on the upper half of the frame, probably because that's where we tend to find characters' faces. Since the film frame is a horizontal rectangle, the director usually tries to balance the right and left halves. The extreme type of such balancing is bilateral symmetry. In the battle scene in *Life on a String,* Chen Kaige stages one shot symmetrically **(4.113).**

4.113   A limited palette emphasizes this symmetrical composition in *Life on a String*.

4.114   *Mars Attacks!:* centering a single character . . .

4.115   . . . and balancing two.

More common than such near-perfect symmetry is a loose balancing of the shot's left and right regions. The simplest way to achieve compositional balance is to center the frame on the human body. Filmmakers often place a single figure at the center of the frame and minimize distracting elements at the sides, as in **4.114.** Many of our earlier illustrations display this flexible balance. Other shots may counterweight two or more elements, encouraging our eye to move back and forth, as in **4.115** and our *L'Avventura* dialogue (4.110, 4.111).

Balanced composition is the norm, but unbalanced shots can also create strong effects. In *Bicycle Thieves,* the composition emphasizes the father's new job by massing most of the figures on the right. They don't balance the son, but he seems even more vulnerable by being such an ineffective counterweight **(4.116).** A more drastic example occurs in Michelangelo Antonioni's *Il Grido* **(4.117),** where two strong elements, the hero and a tree trunk, are grouped on the right side of the shot. One could argue that the shot creates a powerful urge for the audience to see the woman's hidden face.

Sometimes the filmmaker will leave the shots a little unbalanced, in order to prime our expectation that something will change position in the frame. The cinema of the 1910s offers intriguing examples. Very often a doorway in the back of the set allowed the director to show that new characters were entering the scene, but then figures closer to the camera had to be rearranged to permit a clear entrance. The result was a subtle unbalancing and rebalancing of the composition **(4.118–4.121).** In Chapter 6, we'll see how cutting can create a balance between two shots with relatively unbalanced compositions.

The filmmaker can guide our attention by use of another time-tested strategy, the principle of contrast. Our eyes are biased toward registering differences and

4.116   This composition from *Bicycle Thieves* emphasizes the father's new job by massing most of the figures on the right.

4.117   In *Il Grido,* instead of balancing the couple, the composition centers the man. If there were no tree in the frame, the shot would still be somewhat weighted to the right, but the unexpected vertical of the trunk makes that side even heavier.

4.118   From quite early in cinema history, filmmakers used unbalanced compositions to prepare the viewer for new narrative developments. In Yevgenii Bauer's *The Dying Swan* (1916), the young ballerina receives a tiara from an admirer.

4.119   She admires herself in a mirror, in a notably decentered framing.

4.120   As the ballerina lowers her arm, the door opens and her father appears.

4.121   Her father comes to the front area and balances the composition.

4.122   In V. I. Pudovkin's *Mother,* the spectator concentrates on the man's face rather than on the darkness surrounding it.

changes. In most black-and-white films, light costumes or brightly lit faces stand out while darker areas tend to recede (**4.122**). If there are several light shapes in the frame, we'll tend to look from one to the other. But if the background is light, black elements will become prominent, as Sandro's hair does in our *L'Avventura* scene (4.110). The same principles work for color. A bright costume element shown against a more subdued setting is likely to draw the eye. Jiří Menzel exploits this principle in *Larks on a String* (**4.123**). Another pertinent principle is that when lightness values are equal, warm colors in the red-orange-yellow range tend to attract attention, while cool colors like purple and green are less prominent. In Yilmaz Güney's *Yol,* for example, the setting and the characters' outfits are already quite warm in hue, but the hot pink vest of the man in the central middle ground helps make him the primary object of attention (**4.124**).

Color contrasts don't have to be huge, because we're sensitive to small differences. What painters call a *limited palette* involves a few colors in the same range, as in our earlier example from Fellini's *Casanova* (4.39). Peter Greenaway's *The Draughtsman's Contract* employs a limited palette from the cooler end of the spectrum (**4.125**). An extreme case of the principle is sometimes called **monochromatic** color design. Here the filmmaker emphasizes a single color, varying it only in purity or lightness. We've already seen an example of monochromatic mise-en-scene in the white décor and costumes of *THX 1138* (4.40). In a monochromatic design, even a fleck of a contrasting color will catch the viewer's attention. The color design of *Aliens* is dominated by metallic tones, so even a dingy yellow can mark the stiltlike loader as an important prop in the narrative (**4.126**).

4.123   In *Larks on a String,* the junkyard setting provides earthy grays and blacks against which the characters' lighter clothes stand out sharply.

4.124   Warm colors guide the eye in *Yol.*

4.125 *The Draughtsman's Contract* uses a limited palette of green, black, and white.

4.126 *Aliens* uses warm colors like yellow sparingly.

Film has one resource that painting lacks. Our tendency to notice visual differences shifts into high gear when the image includes *movement*. In the *L'Avventura* scene, the turning of Claudia's head became a major event, but we are sensitive to far smaller motions in the frame. Normally, for instance we ignore the movement of scratches and dust on a film. But in David Rimmer's *Watching for the Queen*, in which the first image is an absolutely static photograph (**4.127**), the jumping bits of dust on the film draw our attention. In **4.128**, from Yasujiro Ozu's *Record of a Tenement Gentleman*, many items compete for our attention. But the moment that a scrap of newspaper flaps in the wind, it immediately attracts the eye because it is the only motion in the frame.

When several moving elements appear on the screen, as in a ballroom dance, we are likely to shift our attention among them, according to other cues or depending on our expectations about which one is most salient to the narrative action. In **4.129**, from John Ford's *Young Mr. Lincoln*, Lincoln is moving much less than the dancers we see in front of him. Yet he is framed centrally, as the major character, and the dancers pass rapidly through the frame. As a result, we are likely to concentrate on his gestures and facial expressions, however slight they might be compared to the energetic action in the foreground.

4.127 *Watching for the Queen* emphasizes scratches and dust.

Scene Space   Looking at a film image as a two-dimensional picture helps us appreciate the artistry of filmmakers, but it requires some effort. We find it easier to immediately see the edges and masses on the screen as a three-dimensional space, like the one we live in. The elements of the image that create this impression are called *depth cues*.

Depth cues are what enabled us to understand the encounter of Sandro and Claudia as taking place in a realistic space, with layers and volume. We develop our understanding of depth cues from our experience of real locales and from our earlier experience with pictorial media. In cinema, depth cues are provided by lighting, setting, costumes, and staging—that is, by all the aspects of mise-en-scene.

Depth cues suggest that a space has both *volume* and several distinct *planes*. When we speak of an object as having volume, we mean that it is solid and occupies a three-dimensional area. A film suggests volume by shape, shading, and movement. In 4.106 and **4.130**, we do not think of the actors' faces as flat cutouts, like paper dolls. The shapes of those heads and shoulders suggest solid people. The attached shadows on the faces suggest the curves and recesses of the actors' features and give a modeling effect. We assume that if Jean Seberg in 4.106 turned her head, we would see a profile. Thus we use our knowledge of objects in the world to discern volume in filmic space.

An abstract film, because it can use shapes that are not everyday objects, can create compositions without a sense of volume. The shapes in **4.131** give us no

4.128   A tiny movement in *Record of a Tenement Gentleman.*

4.129   Emphasizing a background figure in *Young Mr. Lincoln.*

4.130   Shading and shape suggest volume in Dreyer's *La Passion de Jeanne d'Arc.*

4.131   A flat composition in Norman McLaren's *Begone, Dull Care.*

CONNECT TO THE BLOG

Whether you see *Coraline* in a 3D or a 2D version, it has some fascinating use of depth cues to differentiate the heroine's real life and the alternative life she finds behind a door in her room. We take a look at these in "Coraline, cornered."

See www.davidbordwell.net/blog/?p=3789.

4.132   In *Sambizanga,* the heroine's dress has very warm and fairly saturated colors, making it stand out distinctly against the pale background.

4.133   Vivid colors emphasize the sense of extreme depth in *One Froggy Evening.*

depth cues for volume—they are unshaded, do not have a recognizable shape, and do not move in such a way as to reveal new views that suggest roundness.

Depth cues also pick out *planes* within the image. Planes are the layers of space occupied by persons or objects. Planes are described according to how close to or far away from the camera they are: foreground, middle ground, background.

Only a completely blank screen has a single plane. Whenever a shape—even an abstract one—appears, we will perceive it as being in front of a background. In 4.131, the four red S shapes are actually painted right on the frame surface, as is the lighter, textured area. Yet the textured area seems to lie behind the four shapes. The space here has only two planes, as in an abstract painting. This example, like our *L'Avventura* scene, suggests that one of the most basic depth cues is **overlap.** The curling S shapes have edges that overlap the background plane, block our vision of it, and thus seem to be closer to us.

Through overlap, a great many planes can be defined. In 4.56, from Jean-Luc Godard's *La Chinoise,* three distinct planes are displayed: the background of fashion cutouts, the woman's face that overlaps that background, and her hand, which overlaps her lower face. In the three-point lighting approach, edge-lighting accentuates the overlap of planes by emphasizing the contour of the object, thus sharply distinguishing it from the background. (See again 4.59, 4.64, and 4.66.)

Color differences also create overlapping planes. Because cool or pale colors tend to recede, filmmakers commonly use them for background planes such as setting. Similarly, because warm or saturated colors tend to come forward, such hues are often employed for costumes or other foreground elements, as in Sarah Maldoror's *Sambizanga* **(4.132).** (See also 4.29, 4.34, and 4.126.)

Animated films can achieve brighter and more saturated color than most live-action filming, so depth effects can be correspondingly more vivid. In Chuck Jones's *One Froggy Evening* **(4.133),** the luminous yellow of the umbrella and the frog's brilliant green skin make him stand out against the darker red of the curtain and the earth tones of the stage floor.

Because of the eye's sensitivity to differences, even quite muted color contrasts can suggest three-dimensional space. In *L'Argent* (4.21–4.23), Robert Bresson uses a limited, cool palette and relatively flat lighting. Yet the compositions pick out several planes by means of overlapping slightly different masses of black, tan, and light blue. Our shot from *Casanova* (4.39) articulates planes by means of slightly differing shades of red. By contrast, a filmmaker may want to minimize color differences and depth cues in order to create a flatter, more abstract composition **(4.134).**

In cinema, *movement* is one of the most important depth cues, since it strongly suggests both planes and volumes (4.129). **Aerial perspective,** or the hazing of more distant planes, is yet another depth cue. Typically, our visual system assumes that sharper outlines, clearer textures, and purer colors belong to foreground elements. In landscape shots, the blurring and graying of distant planes can be caused by actual atmospheric haze, as in Güney's *The Wall* **(4.135).** Even when such haze is a

4.134 Marjane Satrapi and Vincent Paronnaud's animated film *Persepolis* doesn't differentiate the schoolgirls' costumes by edge lighting or color differences. The result is a mass of black, and combined with the students' repetitive hand gestures, the image suggests that the school system demands conformity.

4.135 Fog emphasizes the distance between the foreground and background trees in *The Wall*.

4.136 In Michael Curtiz's *The Charge of the Light Brigade*, aerial perspective is artificially created through diffused lighting of the background and a lack of clear focus beyond the foreground character.

minor factor, our vision typically assigns strong color contrasts to the foreground, as in the *Sambizanga* shot (4.130). In addition, very often lighting is manipulated in conjunction with lens focus to blur the background planes **(4.136).**

In **4.137,** the mise-en-scene provides several depth cues: overlap of edges, cast shadows, and **size diminution.** That is, figures and objects farther away from us are seen to get proportionally smaller; the smaller the figure appears, the farther away we believe it to be. This reinforces our sense of there being a deep space with considerable distances between the various planes.

The same illustration dramatically displays *linear perspective.* We will consider perspective relations in more detail in the next chapter, since they derive as much from properties of the camera lens as they do from mise-en-scene. For now, we can simply note that a strong impression of depth emerges when parallel lines converge at a distant vanishing point. *Off-center* linear perspective is illustrated in 4.137; note that the vanishing point is not the geometrical center. *Central* perspective is exemplified in 4.125 from *The Draughtsman's Contract.*

All of these depth cues are *monocular,* which means that the illusion of depth requires input from only one eye. *Stereopsis* is a binocular depth cue. It results from the fact that our two eyes see the world from slightly different angles. In two-dimensional films, there is a single lens and thus no stereoptic effect. Three-dimensional cinema

4.137 Depth cues in Straub and Huillet's *The Chronicle of Anna Magdalena Bach.*

CONNECT TO THE BLOG

For our thoughts on some digital 3-D films, see "A turning point in digital projection?" at www.davidbordwell.net/blog/?p=1419; "Bwana Beowulf," at www.davidbordwell.net/blog/?p=1669;

and "Coraline, cornered," at www.davidbordwell.net/blog/?p=3789.

uses two lenses, imitating the separation of our eyes. The glasses used for viewing 3D films direct different visual information to each eye, creating a stronger illusion of depth than monocular depth cues can render. Stereopsis is a depth cue rendered by cinematography rather than mise-en-scene, though of course it involves arranging the material to be filmed in depth.

In many of the examples already given, you may have noticed that mise-en-scene serves not simply to direct our attention to foreground elements but rather to create a dynamic relation between foreground and background. In 4.56, for instance, Godard keeps our attention on the whole composition by using prominent backgrounds. Here the pictures behind the actress's head lead us to scan the various small shapes quickly.

The *La Chinoise* shot is a **shallow-space** composition. In such shots, the mise-en-scene suggests comparatively little depth, and the closest and most distant planes seem only slightly separated. The opposite tendency is **deep-space** composition, in which a significant distance seems to separate planes. Our example from *The Chronicle of Anna Magdalena Bach* (4.137) exemplifies deep-space mise-en-scene. Often a director creates a deep-space composition by making the foreground plane quite large and the background plane quite distant (**4.138**).

Shallow and deep mise-en-scene are relative concepts. Most compositions present a moderately deep space, falling between the extremes we have just considered. Sometimes a composition manipulates depth cues to make a space appear deeper or shallower than it really is—creating an optical illusion (**4.139**).

At this point, you might want to return to shots illustrated earlier in this chapter. You will notice that these images use depth cues of overlap, movement, cast shadows, aerial perspective, size diminution, and linear perspective to create distinctive foreground/background relations.

The fact that our vision is sensitive to differences allows filmmakers to guide our understanding of the mise-en-scene. All the cues to story space interact with one another, working to emphasize narrative elements, direct our attention, and set up dynamic relations among areas of screen space. We can see this interaction clearly in two shots from Carl Dreyer's *Day of Wrath*.

In the first shot, the heroine, Anne, is standing before a grillwork panel (**4.140**). She is not speaking, but since she is a major character in the film, the narrative already directs us to her. Setting, lighting, costume, and figure expression create pictorial cues that confirm our expectations. The setting yields a screen pattern of horizontal and vertical lines that intersect in the delicate curves of Anne's face and shoulders. The lighting yields a patch of brightness on the right half of the frame and a patch of darkness on the left, creating pictorial balance. Anne is the meeting

4.138   Several scenes of Wajda's *Ashes and Diamonds* create large foreground and distant background planes.

4.139   Leo Carax flattens space in *Boy Meets Girl* by making the actor in the foreground seem to blend into the advertisement on the wall behind.

point of these two areas. Her face becomes modeled by the relatively strong key lighting from the right, a little top lighting on her hair, and relatively little fill light. Coordinated with the lighting in creating the pattern of light and dark is Anne's costume—a black dress punctuated by a white collar, and a black cap edged with white—that again emphasizes her face.

4.140   *Day of Wrath:* concentrating on a single figure.

The shot is comparatively shallow, displaying two major planes with little distance between them. The background sets off the more important element, Anne. The rigid geometrical grid in the rear makes Anne's slightly sad face the most expressive element in the frame, thus encouraging our eye to pause there. In addition, the composition divides the screen space horizontally, with the grid pattern running across the top half and the dark, severe vertical of Anne's dress dominating the lower half. As is common, the upper zone is the stronger because the character's head and shoulders occupy it. Anne's figure is positioned slightly off center, but with her face turned to compensate for the vacant area on the right. (Imagine how unbalanced the shot would look if she were turned to face us squarely and the same amount of space were left empty on the right.) Thus compositional balance reinforces the shot's emphasis on Anne's expression. In all, without using motion, Dreyer has channeled our attention by means of lines and shapes, lights and darks, and the foreground and background relations in the mise-en-scene.

In the second example, also from *Day of Wrath,* Dreyer coaxes our attention into a to-and-fro movement (**4.141**). Again, the plot guides us, since the characters and the cart are crucial narrative elements. Sound helps too, since Martin is at the moment explaining to Anne what the cart is used for. But mise-en-scene also plays a role. Size diminution and cast shadows establish basic foreground/background relations, with Anne and Martin on the front plane and the cart of wood in the background. The space is comparatively deep (though the foreground is not as exaggeratedly close as that in *Ashes and Diamonds,* 4.138). The prominence of the couple and the cart is reinforced by line, shape, and lighting contrasts. The figures are defined by hard edges and by dark costumes within the predominantly bright setting. Unlike most shots, this puts the human figures in the lower half of the frame, which gives that zone an unusual importance. The composition thus creates a vertical balance, counterweighting the cart with the couple. This encourages us to glance up and down between the two objects of our attention.

4.141   *Day of Wrath:* dividing attention between foreground and background figures.

Similar processes are at work in color films. In one shot of Yasujiro Ozu's *An Autumn Afternoon* (**4.142**), our attention is concentrated on the bride in the center foreground. Here many depth cues are at work. Overlap locates the two figures in two foreground planes, setting them against a series of more distant planes. Aerial perspective makes the tree foliage somewhat out of focus. Movement creates depth when the bride lowers her head. Perspective diminution makes the more distant objects smaller. The figure and the bright silver, red, and gold bridal costume stand out strikingly against the muted, cool colors of the background planes. Moreover, the colors bring back a red-and-silver motif that began in the very first shot of the film (**4.143**).

4.142   A simple shot from *An Autumn Afternoon* employs several depth cues.

In all these cases, compositional elements and depth cues have functioned to focus our attention on the narrative elements. But this need not always be the case. Bresson's *Lancelot du Lac* uses a limited palette of dark and metallic hues, and warmer colors tend to stand out (**4.144**). Such a distracting use of color becomes a stylistic motif in the film.

Time

Cinema is an art of time as well as space. So we shouldn't be surprised to find that many of our examples of two-dimensional composition and three-dimensional scenic space have unfolded over time. The director's control over mise-en-scene governs not only *what* we see but *when* we see it and for how long. In our *L'Avventura* scene between Sandro and Claudia on the rooftop, the timing of the characters'

4.143   The striped smokestacks establish a color motif for *An Autumn Afternoon.*

4.144   In *Lancelot du Lac*, a group of conversing knights is centered and balanced in the foreground planes, yet a pinkish-purple saddle blanket on a passing horse momentarily draws our eyes away from the action.

4.145   Slow, quiet movement in *Jeanne Dielman, 23 quai du Commerce, 1080 Bruxelles*.

movements—Sandro turning away just as Claudia turns toward us—contributes to the effect of a sudden, sharp revelation of her anxiety.

The director shapes the speed and direction of movement within the shot. Since our eyes are attuned to noticing changes, we can pick up the slightest cues. In **4.145,** from Chantal Akerman's *Jeanne Dielman, 23 quai du Commerce, 1080 Bruxelles,* the protagonist simply peels potatoes. This feminist film traces, in painstaking detail, the everyday routines of a Belgian housewife. The composition of this shot strongly centers Jeanne, and no competing movements distract us from her steady and efficient preparation of a meal. The same rhythm is carried throughout the film, so that when she does start to vary her habits, we are prepared to notice even the slight errors she makes under emotional pressure.

A far busier shot is **4.146,** from Busby Berkeley's *42nd Street.* This overhead view presents strongly opposed movements. The central and outer rings of dancers circle in one direction, while the second ring turns in a contrary direction. The dancers also swing strips of shiny cloth back and forth. The result is a partially abstract composition, but it's easy to grasp because the movement of the wheels within wheels has a geometrical clarity.

The dancers in *42nd Street* are synchronized to a considerable degree, but **4.147,** from Jacques Tati's *Play Time,* contains movements of differing speeds, with different visual accents. Moreover, they occur on different planes and follow contrasting trajectories. These diverse movements accord with Tati's tendency to cram his compositions with gags that compete for our attention.

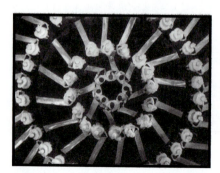

4.146   Synchronized rhythm in *42nd Street.*

4.147   Competing rhythms of movement in a busy shot from *Play Time.*

As we have already seen, we scan any film frame for information. This scanning brings time sharply into play. Only a very short shot forces us to try to take in the image all at once. In most shots, we get an initial overall impression that creates formal expectations. These expectations are quickly modified as our eye roams around the frame.

As we'd expect, our scanning of the shot is strongly affected by the presence of movement. A static composition, such as our first shot from *Day of Wrath* (4.140), may keep pulling our attention back to a single element (here, Anne's face). In contrast, a composition emphasizing movement becomes more time-bound because our glance may be directed from place to place by various speeds, directions, and rhythms of movements. In the second image from *Day of Wrath* (4.141), Anne and Martin are turned from us (so that expression and gesture are minimized), and they are standing still. Thus the single movement in the frame—the cart—catches our attention. But when Martin speaks and turns, we look back at the couple, then back at the cart, and so on, in a shuttling, dynamic shift of attention.

Our time-bound process of scanning involves not only looking to and fro across the screen but also, in a sense, looking into its depths. A deep-space composition will often use background events to create expectations about what is about to happen in the foreground. "Composing in depth isn't simply a matter of pictorial richness," British director Alexander Mackendrick has remarked. "It has value in the narrative of the action, the pacing of the scene. Within the same frame, the director can organize the action so that preparation for what will happen next is seen in the background of what is happening now."

Our example from *The Dying Swan* (4.118-4.121) illustrates MacKendrick's point. The same principle is used in **4.148–4.150,** from *Three Kings.* Here the frame starts off unbalanced, and the fact that it includes a background doorway prepares us for the scene's dramatic development. In addition, any movement from background to foreground is a strong attention-getter. At moments like these, the

4.148 In this shot from *Three Kings,* Chief Elgin comes in to tell the partying GIs that their superior is coming. Normally, when a character is looking offscreen left, he or she is set a little off center toward the right. But Elgin is set to the left, leaving the tent flap behind him prominent. Without being aware of it, we expect some action to develop there.

4.149 Confirming Elgin's warning, the superior officer bursts into the background.

4.150 The officer comes forward, which is always a powerful way to command the viewer's attention. He moves aggressively into close-up, ramping up the conflict as he demands to know where the men got alcohol.

4.151   In *Adam's Rib,* the wife who has shot her husband is given the greatest emphasis by three-point lighting, her animated gestures, and her frontal positioning. Interestingly, the exact center of the frame is occupied by a nurse in the background, but Cukor keeps her out of focus and unmoving so that she won't distract from Judy Holliday's performance.

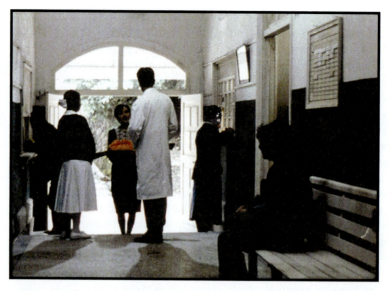

4.152   Although she is farther from the camera, the woman visiting the hospital in *City of Sadness* draws our eye partly because she is the only one facing front.

4.153   In a conversation in *The Bad and the Beautiful,* our attention fastens on the studio executive on the right because the other two characters are turned away from us . . .

4.154   . . . but when the producer turns to the camera, his centered position and frontal posture emphasize him.

mise-en-scene is preparing us for what will happen, and by arousing our expectations, the style engages us with the unfolding action.

The *Dying Swan* and *Three Kings* examples also illustrate the power of *frontality.* In explaining one five-minute shot in his film *Adam's Rib,* George Cukor signaled this. He remarked how the defense attorney was positioned to focus our attention on her client, who's reciting the reasons she shot her husband (**4.151**). Katharine Hepburn "had her back to the camera almost the whole time, but that had a meaning: she indicated to the audience that they should look at Judy Holliday. We did that whole thing without a cut."

All other things being equal, the viewer expects that more story information will come from a character's face than from a character's back. The viewer's attention will thus usually pass over figures that are turned away and fasten on figures that are positioned frontally. A more distant view can exploit frontality, too. In Hou Hsiao-hsien's *City of Sadness,* depth staging centers the Japanese woman coming to visit the hospital, and a burst of bright fabric also draws attention to her (**4.152**). Just as important, the other characters are turned away from us. It's characteristic of Hou's style to employ long shots with small changes in figure movement. The subdued, delicate effect of his scenes depends on our seeing characters' faces in relation to others' bodies and the overall setting.

Frontality can change over time to guide our attention to various parts of the shot. We've already seen alternating frontality at work in our *L'Avventura* scene, when Sandro and Claudia turn to and away from us (4.110, 4.111). When actors are in dialogue, a director may allow frontality to highlight one moment of one actor's performance, then give another performer more prominence (**4.153, 4.154**). This device reminds us that mise-en-scene can borrow devices from theatrical staging.

A flash of frontality can be very powerful. In the opening scene of *Rebel Without a Cause,* three teenagers are being held at the police station (**4.155**). They don't know one another yet. When Jim sees that Plato is shivering, he drunkenly comes forward to offer Plato his sport coat (**4.156, 4.157**). Jim's frontality, forward movement, bright white shirt, and central placement emphasize his gesture. Just as Plato takes the coat, Judy turns and notices Jim for the first time (**4.158**). Like Claudia's sudden turn to the camera in our *L'Avventura* example, this sudden revelation

4.155 Mise-en-scene in the widescreen frame in *Rebel Without a Cause*.

4.156 Jim comes forward, drawing our attention and arousing expectations of a dramatic exchange.

4.157 Jim offers Plato his jacket, his action centered and his brightly lit white shirt making him the dominant player. Judy remains a secondary center of interest, segregated by the office window but highlighted by her bright red coat.

4.158 Judy turns abruptly, and her face's frontal position signals her interest in Jim.

spikes our interest. It prepares us for the somewhat tense romance that will develop between them in later scenes. Overall, the scene's setting, lighting, costume, and staging cooperate to develop the drama.

The director can also achieve a strong effect by denying frontality, keeping us in suspense about what a character's face reveals. At a climactic moment in Kenji Mizoguchi's *Naniwa Elegy*, some of the cues for emphasis are reversed (**4.159**, **4.160**). We get a long shot rather than a closer view, and the character is turned from us and moving away from the camera, through patches of darkness. Ayako is confessing to her suitor that she's been another man's mistress. Her withdrawal conveys a powerful sense of shame, and we, like her friend, have to judge her sincerity based on her posture and voice. In this and our other examples, several techniques of mise-en-scene dovetail from moment to moment in order to engage us more vividly with the action.

4.159 At the height of the drama in *Naniwa Elegy*, Kenji Mizoguchi has the heroine move away from us, into depth . . .

Narrative Functions of Mise-en-Scene in *Our Hospitality*

Our Hospitality, like most of Buster Keaton's films, exemplifies how mise-en-scene can economically advance the narrative and create a pattern of motifs. Since the film is a comedy, the mise-en-scene also creates gags. *Our Hospitality*, then, exemplifies what we will find in our study of every film technique: An individual element almost always has *several* functions, not just one.

Consider, for example, how the settings function within the plot of *Our Hospitality*. For one thing, they help divide the film into scenes and to contrast those scenes. The film begins with a prologue showing how the feud between the McKays and the Canfields results in the deaths of the young Canfield and the husband of the McKay family. We are left in suspense about the fate of the baby, Willie. Willie's

4.160 . . . and as she passes through patches of distant darkness, our curiosity about her emotional state intensifies.

4.161   In *Our Hospitality,* when the elder McKay flings off his hat to douse the lamp, the illumination changes from a soft blend of key, fill, and backlight . . .

4.162   . . . to a stark key light from the fireplace.

mother flees with her son from their southern home to the North (action narrated to us mainly by an intertitle).

The plot jumps ahead many years to begin the main action, with the grown-up Willie living in New York. There are a number of gags concerning early-19th-century life in the metropolis, contrasting sharply with the prologue scene. We are led to wonder how this locale will relate to the southern scenes. Soon Willie receives word that he has inherited his parents' home in the South. A series of amusing short scenes follows as he takes a primitive train back to his birthplace. During these scenes, Keaton uses real locales, but by laying out the railroad tracks in different ways, he exploits the landscapes for surprising and unusual comic effects, which we shall examine shortly.

The rest of the film deals with Willie's movements in and around the southern town. On the day of his arrival, he wanders around and gets into a number of comic situations. That night he stays in the Canfield house itself. An extended chase occurs the next day, moving through the countryside and back to the Canfield house for the settling of the feud. Thus the action depends heavily on shifts of setting that establish Willie's two journeys, as baby and as man, and later his wanderings to escape his enemies' pursuit. The narration is relatively unrestricted after Willie reaches the South, shifting between him and members of the Canfield family. We usually know more about where they are than Willie does, and the narrative generates suspense by showing them coming toward the places where Willie is hiding.

Specific settings fulfill distinct narrative functions. The McKay estate, which Willie envisions as a mansion, turns out to be a tumbledown shack. The McKay house is contrasted with the Canfield's palatial plantation home. In narrative terms, the Canfield home gains even more functional importance when the Canfield father forbids his sons to kill Willie on the premises: "Our code of honor forbids us to shoot him while he is a guest in our house." (Once Willie overhears this, he determines *never* to leave.) Ironically, the home of Willie's enemies becomes the only safe spot in town, and many scenes are organized around the Canfield brothers' attempts to lure Willie outside. At the end of the film, another setting takes on significance: the landscape of meadows, mountains, riverbanks, rapids, and waterfalls across which the Canfields pursue Willie. Finally, the feud ends back in the Canfield house itself, with Willie now welcomed as the daughter's husband. The pattern of development is clear: from the opening shootout at the McKay house that breaks up Willie's family to the final scene in the Canfield house with Willie becoming part of a new family. In such ways, every setting becomes highly motivated by the narrative's system of causes and effects, parallels and contrasts, and overall development.

The same narrative motivation marks the film's use of costume. Willie is characterized as a city boy through his dandified suit, but the southern gentility of the elder Canfield is represented through his white planter's suit. Props become important here: Willie's suitcase and umbrella succinctly summarize his role as visitor and wanderer, and the Canfields' ever-present pistols remind us of their goal of continuing the feud. In addition, a change of costume (Willie's disguising himself as a woman) enables him to escape from the Canfield household. At the end, when the characters put aside their guns, the feud is over.

Like setting, lighting in *Our Hospitality* has both general and specific functions. The film alternates scenes in darkness with scenes in daylight. The feuding in the prologue takes place at night; Willie's trip South and wanderings through the town occur in daylight; that night Willie comes to dinner at the Canfield's and stays as a guest; the next day, the Canfields pursue him; and the film ends that night with the marriage of Willie and the Canfield daughter. More specifically, the bulk of the film is evenly lit in the three-point method. Yet the somber action of the prologue takes place in hard sidelighting (**4.161, 4.162**). Later, the murder scene is played out in flashes of light—lightning, gunfire—that fitfully punctuate the overall darkness. Because this sporadic lighting hides part of the action from us, it helps build

4.163   Within the same frame, we see both cause—the engineer's cheerful ignorance, made visible by frontality— and effect—the runaway cars.

4.164   The Canfield boys in the foreground make plans to shoot Willie, who overhears them in the background.

4.165   While Willie ambles along unsuspectingly in the background, one Canfield waits in the foreground to ambush him.

suspense. The gunshots themselves are seen only as flashes in the darkness, and we must wait to learn the outcome—the deaths of both opponents—until the next flash of lightning.

Most economically of all, virtually every bit of the acting functions to support and advance the cause–effect chain of the narrative. The way Canfield sips and savors his mint julep establishes his southern ways; his southern hospitality in turn will not allow him to shoot a guest in his house. Similarly, Willie's every move expresses his diffidence or resourcefulness.

Even more concise is the way the film uses staging in depth to present two narrative events simultaneously. While the engineer drives the locomotive, the other cars pass him on a parallel track (**4.163**). In other shots, Willie's awareness or ignorance of a situation is displayed through planes of depth (**4.164, 4.165**). Thanks to such spatial arrangements, Keaton is able to pack together two story events, resulting in a tight narrative construction and in a relatively unrestricted narration. In 4.164, we know what Willie knows, and we expect that he will probably flee now that he understands the sons' plans. But in 4.165, we are aware, as Willie is not, that danger lurks around the corner; suspense results, as we wonder whether the Canfield boys' ambush will succeed.

All of these devices for narrative economy considerably unify the film, but some other elements of mise-en-scene function as specific motifs. For one thing, there is the repeated squabble between the anonymous husband and wife. On his way to his estate, Willie passes a husband throttling his wife. Willie intervenes to protect her; the wife proceeds to thrash Willie for butting in. On Willie's way back, he passes the same couple, still fighting, but studiously avoids them. Nevertheless, the wife aims a kick at him as he passes. The mere repetition of the motif strengthens the film's narrative unity, but it functions thematically, too, as another joke on the contradictions surrounding the idea of hospitality.

Other motifs recur. Willie's first hat is too tall to wear in a jouncing railway coach. (When it gets crushed, he swaps it for the trademark flat Keaton hat.) Willie's second hat serves to distract the Canfields when Willie coaxes his dog to fetch it. There is also a pronounced water motif in the film. Rain conceals from us the murders in the prologue and later saves Willie from leaving the Canfield home after dinner. ("It would be the death of anyone to go out on a night like this!") A river functions significantly in the final chase. And a waterfall appears soon after Willie's arrival in the South (**4.166**). This waterfall initially protects Willie by hiding him (**4.167, 4.168**) but later threatens both him and the Canfield daughters as they are nearly swept over it (4.174).

Two specific motifs of setting help unify the narrative. First there is the recurrence of an embroidered sampler hanging on the Canfield wall: "Love Thy Neighbor." It appears initially in the prologue of the film, when seeing it motivates

4.166   After an explosion demolishes a dam, the water spills over a cliff and creates a waterfall.

4.167   The new waterfall begins to hide Willie as he sits fishing . . .

4.168   . . . and by the time the Canfields rush into the foreground, he is invisible.

Canfield's attempt to stop the feud. The sampler reappears at the end when Canfield, enraged that Willie has married his daughter, glances at the wall, reads the inscription, and resolves to halt the years of feuding. His change in attitude is motivated by the earlier appearance of the motif.

The film also uses gun racks as a motif. In the prologue, each feuder goes to his mantelpiece to get his pistol. Later, when Willie arrives in town, the Canfields hurry to their gun rack and begin to load their pistols. Near the end of the film, when the Canfields return home after failing to find Willie, one of the sons notices that the gun rack is now empty. And, in the final shot, when the Canfields accept the marriage and lay down their arms, Willie produces from all over his person a staggering assortment of pistols taken as a precaution from the Canfields' own supply. Thus mise-en-scene motifs unify the film through their repetition, variation, and development.

Yet *Our Hospitality* is more than a film whose narrative system relates economically to patterns of mise-en-scene. It is a comedy, and one of the funniest. We should not be surprised to find, then, that Keaton uses mise-en-scene for gags. Indeed, so unified is the film that most of the elements that create narrative economy also function to yield comic effects.

4.169   The tunnel cut to fit the old-fashioned train.

The mise-en-scene bristles with many individually comic elements. Settings are exploited for amusement—the ramshackle McKay estate, the Broadway of 1830, the specially cut train tunnel that just fits the old-fashioned train and its smokestack **(4.169)**. Costume gags also stand out. Willie's disguise as a woman is exposed by a gap in the rear of his skirt; later, Willie puts the same costume on a horse to distract the Canfields. Most strongly, comedy arises from the behavior of the figures. The railroad engineer's high kick unexpectedly swipes off his conductor's hat **(4.170)**. The elder Canfield sharpens his carving knife with ferocious energy, just inches from Willie's head. When Willie lands at the bottom of the river, he stands there looking left and right, his hand shading his eyes, before he realizes where he is. Later, Willie scuds down the river, leaping out of the water like a fish and slithering across the rocks.

4.170   As the engineer, Keaton's father, Joe, used his famous high-kick vaudeville stunt for this gag.

Perhaps the only aspect of mise-en-scene that competes with the comic brilliance of the figures' behavior is the film's use of deep space for gags. Many of the shots we have already examined function to create comedy as well: The engineer stands firmly oblivious to the separation of train cars from the engine (see 4.163) just as Willie is unaware that the Canfield boy is lurking murderously in the foreground (4.165).

Even more striking, though, is the deep-space gag that follows the demolition of the dam. The Canfield boys have been searching the town for Willie. In the meantime, Willie sits on a ledge, fishing. As the water bursts from the dam and sweeps over the cliff, it completely engulfs Willie (4.167). At that very instant, the Canfield brothers step into the foreground from either side of the frame, still looking for their victim (4.168). The water's concealment of Willie reduces him to a neutral background for the movement of the Canfields. This sudden eruption of new action into the scene surprises us, rather than generating suspense, since we were not aware that the Canfield sons were so close by. Here surprise is crucial to the comedy.

However appealing the individual gags are, *Our Hospitality* patterns its comic aspects as strictly as it does its other motifs. The film's journey pattern often arranges a series of gags according to a formal principle of theme and variations. For instance, during the train trip South, a string of gags is based on the idea of people encountering the train. Several people turn out to watch it pass, a tramp rides the rods, and an old man chucks rocks at the engine. Another swift series of gags takes the train tracks themselves as its theme. The variations include a humped track, a donkey blocking the tracks, curled and rippled tracks, and finally no tracks at all.

But the most complex theme-and-variations series can be seen in the motif of "the fish on the line." Soon after Willie arrives in town, he is angling and hauls up a minuscule fish. Shortly afterward, a huge fish yanks him into the water **(4.171)**.

4.171   The motif begins as Willie is jerked into the water.

4.172   Tied to Willie, the Canfield boy falls off the cliff . . .

4.173   . . . and Willie braces himself to be pulled after.

4.174   Willie dangles like a fish on the end of a pole.

Later in the film, through a series of mishaps, Willie becomes tied by a rope to one of the Canfield sons. Many gags arise from this umbilical-cord linkage, especially one that results in Canfield's being pulled into the water as Willie was earlier.

Perhaps the single funniest shot in the film occurs when Willie realizes that since the Canfield boy has fallen off the rocks **(4.172)**, so must he **(4.173)**. But even after Willie gets free of Canfield, the rope remains tied around his waist. So in the film's climax, Willie is dangling from a log over the waterfall **(4.174)**. Here again, one element fulfills multiple functions. The fish-on-the-line device advances the narrative, becomes a motif unifying the film, and takes its place in a pattern of parallel gags involving variations of Willie on the rope. In such ways, *Our Hospitality* becomes an outstanding example of the integration of cinematic mise-en-scene with narrative form.

SUMMARY

The viewer who wants to study mise-en-scene should look for it systematically. We should watch, first of all, for how setting, costume, lighting, and the behavior of the figures present themselves in a given film. As a start, we might trace only one sort of element—say, setting or lighting—through a scene.

We should also reflect on the patterning of mise-en-scene elements. How do they function? How do they constitute motifs that weave their ways through the entire film? In addition, we should notice how mise-en-scene is patterned in space and time to attract and guide our attention through the process of watching the film and to create suspense or surprise.

Finally, we should try to relate the system of mise-en-scene to the large-scale form of the film. Hard-and-fast prejudices about realism are of less value here than an openness to the great variety of mise-en-scene possibilities. Awareness of those possibilities will better help us to determine the functions of mise-en-scene.

WHERE TO GO FROM HERE

On the Origins of Mise-en-Scene

As a concept, mise-en-scene dates back to the 19th-century theater. For a historical introduction that is relevant to film, see Oscar G. Brockett and Robert R. Findlay, *Century of Innovation* (Englewood Cliffs, NJ: Prentice-Hall, 1973). The standard film works are Nicolas Vardac, *Stage to Screen* (Cambridge, MA: Harvard University Press, 1949), and Ben

Brewster and Lea Jacobs, *Theatre to Cinema: Stage Pictorialism and the Early Feature Film* (Oxford: Oxford University Press, 1997).

On Realism in Mise-en-Scene

Many film theorists have seen film as a realistic medium par excellence. For such theorists as Siegfried Kracauer, André

Bazin, and V. F. Perkins, cinema's power lies in its ability to present a recognizable reality. The realist theorist thus often values authenticity in costume and setting, naturalistic acting, and unstylized lighting. "The primary function of decor," writes Perkins, "is to provide a believable environment for the action" (*Film as Film* [Baltimore: Penguin, 1972], p. 94). Bazin praises the Italian neorealist films of the 1940s for "faithfulness to everyday life in the scenario, truth to his part in an actor" (*What Is Cinema?* vol. 2 [Berkeley: University of California Press, 1970], p. 25).

Though mise-en-scene is always a product of selection and choice, the realist theorist may value the filmmaker who creates a mise-en-scene that *appears* to be reality. Kracauer suggests that even apparently unrealistic song-and-dance numbers in a musical can seem impromptu (*Theory of Film* [New York: Oxford University Press, 1965]), and Bazin considers a fantasy film such as *The Red Balloon* realistic because here "what is imaginary on the screen has the spatial density of something real" (*What Is Cinema?* vol. 1 [Berkeley: University of California Press, 1966], p. 48).

These theorists set the filmmaker the task of representing some historical, social, or aesthetic reality through the selection and arrangement of mise-en-scene. Though this book postpones the consideration of this problem—it lies more strictly in the domain of film theory—the realist controversy is worth your examination. Christopher Williams, in *Realism and the Cinema* (London: Routledge & Kegan Paul, 1980), reviews many issues in the area.

Computer Imaging and Mise-en-Scene

Digital, or *3D,* animation typically involves a few widely used programs, such as Maya for creating movement and Renderman for adding surface texture. Animators deal with specific needs of their projects by developing new software for such effects as fire, water, and moving foliage. The figures to be animated are created either by scanning every surface of a maquette (a detailed model, such as the dinosaur in 1.29) or by using motion capture ("mocap"), filming actors or animals in neutrally colored costumes covered with dots, which are the only things visible to the camera. The dots are connected by lines to create a "wire-frame" moving image, and the computer gradually adds more detailed layers to build a textured, three-dimensional, moving figure. Backgrounds can also be created digitally, using matte-painting programs. For figure animation, see *The Art of Maya: An Introduction to 3D Computer Graphics,* 3d ed. (Alameda, CA: Sybex, 2007), which includes a CD-ROM with introductory material.

For fiction feature films, 3D animation became viable with *digital compositing,* used for the T-1000 cyborg in *Terminator 2: Judgment Day.* Here a grid was painted on the actor's body, and the actor was filmed executing movements. As the film was scanned, the changing grid patterns were translated into a digital code similar to that used on compact discs. Then new actions could be created on the computer frame by frame. For a discussion, see Jody Duncan, "A Once and Future War," *Cinefex* 47 (August 1991): 4–59. Since *Terminator 2,* sophisticated software programs have enabled directors to create "actors" wholly from models that can be scanned into a computer and then animated. The most famous early example is the gallimimus herd in *Jurassic Park.* The phases of the imaging process for this film are explained in Jody Duncan, "The Beauty in the Beasts," *Cinefex* 55 (August 1993): 42–95. Both analog image synthesis and digital compositing were used in *The Matrix;* for background, see Kevin H. Martin, "Jacking into the Matrix," *Cinefex* 79 (October 1999): 66–89. The rendering of realistic human and humanlike characters depended on finding a way to create the elusively translucent quality of skin. Such figures as Jar Jar Binks in *Star Wars Episode 1: The Phantom Menace* and especially Gollum in *The Lord of the Rings* finally achieved this goal. See *Cinefex* 78 (July 1999), completely devoted to *The Phantom Menace;* Joe Fordham, "Middle-Earth Strikes Back," *Cinefex* 92 (January 2003): 70–142; and Joe Fordham, "Journey's End," *Cinefex* 96 (January 2004): 55–142. Computer visual effects have become so common that any issue of *Cinefex* details the technology used in one or more recent films.

The combination of live-action filming with computer animation has created a fresh range of cinematic effects. Méliès' urge to dazzle the audience with the magical powers of mise-en-scene continues to bear fruit.

Particular Aspects of Mise-en-Scene

On costume, see Elizabeth Lees, *Costume Design in the Movies* (London: BCW, 1976), and Edward Maeder, ed., *Hollywood and History: Costume Design in Film* (New York: Thames & Hudson, 1987). See also Vincent J.-R. Kehoe, *The Technique of the Professional Make-Up Artist* (Boston: Focal Press, 1995).

Léon Barsacq, with careful assistance by Elliott Stein, has produced a wide-ranging history of setting, *Caligari's Cabinet and Other Grand Illusions: A History of Film Design* (New York: New American Library, 1976). Other major studies of decor in the cinema are Charles Affron and Mirella Jona Affron, *Sets in Motion: Art Direction and Film Narrative* (New Brunswick, NJ: Rutgers University Press, 1995); Dietrich Meumann, ed., *Film Architecture: Set Designs from "Metropolis" to "Blade Runner"* (Munich: Prestel, 1996); and C. S. Tashiro, *Pretty Pictures: Production Design and the History of Film* (Austin: University of Texas Press, 1998). For insightful interviews with set designers, see Vincent LoBrutto, *By Design* (New York: Praeger, 1992), and Peter Ettedgui, *Production Design & Art Direction* (Woburn, MA: Focal Press, 1999). An excellent overview is offered by Vincent LoBrutto in *The Filmmaker's Guide to Production Design* (New York: Allworth, 2002). See also Peter Ettedgui, *Production Design and Art Direction* (Woburn, MA: Focal Press, 1999). Pascal Pinteau's gorgeously illustrated *Special Effects: An Oral His-*

tory (New York: Abrams, 2003) covers not only models and digital effects but also make-up, setting, and even theme park rides.

A wide-ranging analysis of performance in film is Richard Dyer, *Stars* (London: British Film Institute, 1979). This book is complemented by Charles Affron, *Star Acting: Gish, Garbo, Davis* (New York: Dutton, 1977), and James Naremore, *Acting in the Cinema* (Berkeley: University of California Press, 1988). Useful practical guides are Patrick Tucker, *Secrets of Screen Acting* (New York: Routledge, 1994), and Tony Barr, *Acting for the Camera* (New York: Perennial, 1986). The ways in which a performance can be integrated with a film's overall form are considered in two other manuals: *The Film Director's Intuition: Script Analysis and Rehearsal Techniques,* by Judith Wilson (Studio City, CA: Michael Wiese, 2003), and Delia Salvi's *Friendly Enemies: Maximizing the Director–Actor Relationship* (New York: Billboard, 2003). Staging techniques in theater are comprehensively explained in Terry John Converse's *Directing for the Stage* (Colorado Springs: Meriwether, 2005). Michael Caine's *Acting in Film: An Actor's Take on Movie Making* (New York: Applause Books) offers excellent and detailed discussion; see also the accompanying video, *Michael Caine on Acting in Film.*

Two fine surveys of lighting are Kris Malkiewicz, *Film Lighting: Talks with Hollywood's Cinematographers and Gaffers* (New York: Prentice-Hall, 1986), and Gerald Millerson, *Lighting for Television & Film,* 3d ed. (Boston: Focal Press, 1999). John Alton's *Painting with Light* (New York: Macmillan, 1949) and Gerald Millerson's *Technique of Lighting for Television and Motion Pictures* (New York: Hastings House, 1972) are useful older discussions, with emphasis on classical Hollywood practices. See also John Jackman, *Lighting for Digital Video and Television,* 2d. ed. (San Francisco: CMP, 2004). A useful reference book is Richard K. Ferncase's *Film and Video Lighting Terms and Concepts* (Newton, MA: Focal Press, 1995).

Depth

Art historians have long studied how a two-dimensional image can be made to suggest a deep space. A comprehensive introductory survey is William V. Dunning, *Changing Images of Pictorial Space: A History of Spatial Illusion in Painting* (Syracuse: Syracuse University Press, 1991). Dunning's history of Western painting emphasizes the manipulation of five techniques we have considered in this chapter: linear perspective, shading, the separation of planes, atmospheric perspective, and color perspective.

Though film directors have of course manipulated the image's depth and flatness since the beginning of cinema, critical understanding of these spatial qualities did not emerge until the 1940s. It was then that André Bazin called attention to the fact that certain directors staged their shots in unusually deep space. Bazin singled out F. W. Murnau (for *Nosferatu* and *Sunrise*), Orson Welles (for *Citizen Kane*

and *The Magnificent Ambersons*), William Wyler (for *The Little Foxes* and *The Best Years of Our Lives*), and Jean Renoir (for practically all of his 1930s work). By offering us depth and flatness as analytical categories, Bazin increased our understanding of mise-en-scene. (See "The Evolution of the Language of Cinema," in *What Is Cinema?* vol. 1.) Interestingly, Sergei Eisenstein, who is often contrasted with Bazin, explicitly discussed principles of deep-space staging in the 1930s, as recorded by his faithful pupil, Vladimir Nizhny, in *Lessons with Eisenstein* (New York: Hill & Wang, 1962). Eisenstein asked his class to stage a murder scene in a single shot and without camera movement; the result was a startling use of extreme depth and dynamic movement toward the spectator. For a discussion, see David Bordwell, *The Cinema of Eisenstein* (Cambridge, MA: Harvard University Press, 1993), chaps. 4 and 6. For a general historical overview of depth in mise-en-scene, see David Bordwell's *On the History of Film Style* (Cambridge, MA: Harvard University Press, 1997), chap. 6.

Color Design

Two clear and readable discussions of color aesthetics in general are Luigina De Grandis, *Theory and Use of Color,* trans. John Gilbert (New York: Abrams, 1986), and Paul Zelanski and Mary Pat Fisher, *Colour for Designers and Artists* (London: Herbert Press, 1989).

For general discussion of the aesthetics of film color, see Raymond Durgnat, "Colours and Contrasts," *Films and Filming* 15, 2 (November 1968): 58–62; and William Johnson, "Coming to Terms with Color," *Film Quarterly* 20, 1 (Fall 1966): 2–22. The most detailed analysis of color organization in films is Scott Higgins, *Harnessing the Rainbow: Technicolor Design in the 1930s* (Austin: University of Texas Press, 2006).

Frame Composition and the Viewer's Eye

The film shot is like the painter's canvas: it must be filled up, and the spectator must be cued to notice certain things (and not to notice others). For this reason, composition in film owes much to principles developed in the graphic arts. A good basic study of composition is Donald L. Weismann, *The Visual Arts as Human Experience* (Englewood Cliffs, NJ: Prentice-Hall, 1974), which has many interesting things to say about depth as well. More elaborate discussions are to be found in Rudolf Arnheim, *Art and Visual Perception: A Psychology of the Creative Eye,* rev. ed. (Berkeley: University of California Press, 1974), and his *The Power of the Center: A Study of Composition in the Visual Arts,* 2d ed. (Berkeley: University of California Press, 1988). See also Peter Ward, *Picture Composition for Film and Television* (London: Focal Press, 1996).

André Bazin suggested that shots staged in depth and shot in deep focus give the viewer's eye greater freedom than do flatter, shallower shots: the viewer's eye can roam across the screen. (See Bazin, *Orson Welles* [New York: Harper & Row, 1978].) Noël Burch takes issue: "All the elements in any given film image are perceived as equal in importance" (Burch, *Theory of Film Practice* [Princeton, NJ: Princeton University Press, 1981], p. 34). Psychological research on pictorial perception suggests, however, that viewers do indeed scan images according to specific cues. In cinema, static visual cues for "when to look where" are reinforced or undermined by movement of figures or of camera, by sound track and editing, and by the overall form of the film. The psychological research is outlined in Robert L. Solso, *Cognition and the Visual Arts* (Cambridge, MA: MIT Press, 1994), pp. 129–56. In *Figures Traced in Light: On Cinematic Staging* (Berkeley: University of California Press, 2005), David Bordwell studies how the filmmaker uses staging and frame composition to guide the viewer's scanning of the shot.

Websites

www.thescenographer.com/ Website for *The Scenographer* magazine, which deals with production design and costume design; has some online articles.

www.makeupmag.com/ Website for *Make-Up Artist Magazine,* professional journal for film and television workers; has some online articles.

www.16-9.dk/2003-06/side11_minnelli.htm/ In a well-illustrated article, "Medium Shot Gestures: Vincente Minnelli and *Some Came Running,*" Joe McElhaney provides a very good example of close analysis of long-take staging. The page is hosted by the Danish online magazine *16:9.*

continuityboy.blogspot.com/2007/03/seeing-spots .html/ Visual researcher Tim Smith measures viewers' eye movements when they watch films.

Recommended DVD Supplements

DVDs often include galleries of designs for sets, costumes, and occasionally make-up. Documentaries on the subject include *Pulp Fiction*'s "Production Design Featurette." The unusually large, labyrinthine, enclosed spaceship interior in *Alien,* as well as the film's other sets, are discussed in the "Fear of the Unknown" and "The Darkest Reaches" segments. (The former also deals with costume design.) *Speed*'s "On Location" supplement deals with the 12 different buses that appeared at various stages of the film's action, as well as how the freeway locations were used. "Magical Places," a supplement for *The Da Vinci Code,* is an excellent demonstration of the logistics of going on location: permissions needed, technical challenges (such as lighting real interiors), and the substitution of one real building for another. Three supplements for *The Golden Compass*—"The Alethiometer,"

"Production Design," and "Costumes"—offer particularly detailed examples of prop, set, and costume design.

The DVD for *Hellboy II: The Golden Army* includes a lengthy documentary, "Hellboy: In Service of the Demon." In one lengthy segment, Doug Jones is made up as the Angel of Death while offering a fascinating discussion of makeup and acting—including how digital controls move the eyes in the wings of his costume!

Lighting is an area of mise-en-scene that receives relatively little coverage. An exception is "Painting with Light," a documentary on cinematographer Jack Cardiff's work on the extraordinary color film *Black Narcissus.* A brief but informative look at lighting comes in the "Shooting on Location: Annie's Office" supplement for *Collateral.* In the "Here to Show Everybody the Light" section of the "Working like a Dog" supplement for *A Hard Day's Night,* director of photography Gilbert Taylor talks about how high-key lighting on the Beatles achieved the characteristic look of the images and about such challenges as rigging lighting equipment in a real train. *Toy Story*'s "Shaders and Lighting" section reveals how computer animation can simulate rim and key lighting. *Hellboy* cinematographer Guillermo Navarro presents and discusses some lighting tests in "*Hellboy:* The Seeds of Creation."

Auditions are commonly included in DVD supplements, such as those for "The Making of *American Graffiti*" and especially *The Godfather*—where 72 minutes cover the casting, including many screen tests! Some discs go more deeply into aspects of acting. *Collateral*'s extras include a short segment, "Tom Cruise & Jamie Fox Rehearse." "The Stunts," included with *Speed,* shows how the drivers' maneuvers with the vehicles involved in the accidents and near-misses were choreographed using models, as well as covering how decisions are made about whether to let stars do their own stunts. "Becoming an Oompa-Loompa" details the training Deep Roy underwent to play all the Oompa-Loompas in *Charlie and the Chocolate Factory.* A detailed exploration of the distinctive acting in the films of Robert Bresson is offered by Babette Mangolte's "The Models of *Pickpocket,*" including lengthy interviews with the three main performers recalling the director's methods.

The *Dancer in the Dark* supplement "Choreography: Creating Vincent Paterson's Dance Sequences" takes an unusually close look at this particular type of staging. (This section can be best appreciated if you have watched the whole film or at least the musical numbers "Cvalda" [Track 9] and "I Have Seen It All" [Track 13].)

Detailed discussion of staging strategies can be found on a six-DVD set, *Hollywood Camera Work: The Master Course in High-End Blocking and Staging.* The exercises cover stationary scenes, actor movement, and camera movement. See http://www.hollywoodcamerawork.us/.

CHAPTER

5

The Shot: Cinematography

I n controlling mise-en-scene, the filmmaker stages an event to be filmed. But a comprehensive account of cinema as a medium cannot stop with simply what is put in front of the camera. The *shot* does not exist until patterns are inscribed on a strip of film. The filmmaker also controls the *cinematographic qualities* of the shot—not only *what* is filmed but also *how* it is filmed. This "how" factor involves three areas of choice: (1) the photographic aspects of the shot, (2) the framing of the shot, and (3) the duration of the shot. This chapter surveys these three areas.

The Photographic Image

Cinematography (literally, writing in movement) depends to a large extent on *photography* (writing in light). Sometimes the filmmaker eliminates the camera and simply works on the film itself; but even when drawing, painting, or scratching directly on film, punching holes in it, or growing mold on it, the filmmaker is creating patterns of light on celluloid. Most often, the filmmaker uses a camera to regulate how light from some object will be photochemically registered on the sensitized film. In digital video, the light activates a computer chip, which translates the pattern into ones and zeroes. In either case, the filmmaker can select the range of tonalities, manipulate the speed of motion, and transform perspective.

The Range of Tonalities

An image may seem all grays or stark black and white. It may display a range of colors. Textures may stand out clearly or recede into a haze. The filmmaker may control all these visual qualities by manipulating the film stock, exposure, and developing procedures.

Types of **film stocks** are differentiated by the chemical qualities of the emulsion. The choice of film stock has many artistic implications. For one thing, the image will have more or less *contrast* depending partly on the stock used. Contrast refers to the degree of difference between the darkest and lightest areas of the frame. A high-contrast image displays bright white highlights, stark black areas, and a narrow range of grays in between. A low-contrast image possesses a wide range of grays with no true white or black areas.

As we have already seen in Chapter 4, human vision is highly sensitive to differences in color, texture, shape, and other pictorial properties. Contrasts within the image enable filmmakers to guide the viewer's eye to important parts of the frame. Filmmakers control the degree of contrast in the image in various ways.

167

"Both [cinematographer] Floyd [Crosby] and I wanted [High Noon] to look like a documentary, or a newsreel from the period of the 1880s, if film had existed at that time—which, of course, it did not. I believe that we came close to our goal by using flat lighting, a grainy texture in the printing and an unfiltered white sky."

— Fred Zinnemann, director

In general, a very fast film stock, one that is very sensitive to reflected light, will produce a "low-contrast" look, while a slower, less light-sensitive one will be high in contrast. The amount of light used on the set during shooting will also affect the image's degree of contrast. Moreover, the cinematographer may use particular developing procedures that increase or decrease contrast. For example, the strength and temperature of the chemicals and the length of time the film is left in the developing bath affect contrast. By manipulating the film stock, lighting factors, and developing procedures, filmmakers can achieve enormous variety in the look of the film image (**5.1–5.3**). Most black-and-white films employ a balance of grays, blacks, and whites.

Jean-Luc Godard's *Les Carabiniers* (**5.4**) offers a good example of what post-filming manipulations of film stock can accomplish. The shot's newsreel-like quality is heightened by both the film stock and lab work that increased contrast. "The positive prints," Godard has explained, "were simply made on a special Kodak high contrast stock. . . . Several shots, intrinsically too gray, were duped again sometimes two or three times, always to their highest contrast." The effect suggests old combat footage that has been recopied or shot under bad lighting conditions; the high-contrast look suited a film about the grubbiness of war.

Different color film stocks yield varying color contrasts. Technicolor became famous for its sharply distinct, heavily saturated hues, as seen in such films as *Meet Me in St. Louis* (**5.5**). The richness of Technicolor was achieved by means of a specially designed camera and sophisticated printing process. To take another example, Soviet filmmakers used a domestically made stock that tends to lower contrast and give the image a murky greenish-blue cast. Andrei Tarkovsky exploited

5.1   Most black-and-white films employ a balance of grays, blacks, and whites, as in this shot from *Casablanca*.

5.2   In *Breaking the Waves,* color manipulation creates bleached-out images.

5.3   The dream sequence early in Ingmar Bergman's *Wild Strawberries* uses a combination of film stock, overexposure, and laboratory processing to create a bleached-out look.

5.4   This shot from *Les Carabiniers* achieves a newsreel-like quality heightened by both the film stock and lab work that increased contrast.

5.5   The trolley scene in *Meet Me in St. Louis* shows off the vivid colors possible with the Technicolor process.

5.6   The use of blues in *Stalker* makes the action seem almost to be taking place underwater.

5.7   Lye manipulated Gasparcolor paper stock to create pure, saturated silhouettes that split and recombine in *Rainbow Dance*.

just these qualities in the monochromatic color design of his shadowy *Stalker* (**5.6**). Len Lye's abstract *Rainbow Dance* uses specific features of the English stock Gasparcolor (**5.7**).

The tonalities of color stock may also be altered by laboratory processes. The person assigned the role of *color timer* or *grader* has a wide choice about the color range of a print. A red patch in the image may be printed as crimson, pink, or almost any shade in between. Often the timer consults with the director to select a key tone that will serve as a reference point for color relations throughout the film. Increasingly, cinematographers are using computer grading for selected shots or even an entire film. (See "A Closer Look," pp. 184–185.)

Certain procedures may also add color to footage originally shot in black and white. Before 1930, filmmakers often used tinting and toning. *Tinting* is accomplished by dipping the already developed film into a bath of dye. The dark areas remain black and gray, while the lighter areas pick up the color (**5.8**). *Toning* worked in an opposite fashion. The dye was added during the developing of the positive

5.8   Tinting creates a brownish color across the entire frame in the 1914 film *The Wrath of the Gods*.

5.9   In *Cenere,* the deep blue of the dark areas and the nearly white patches are characteristic of toning.

5.10   Toning in *Daisies.*

5.11   In *Innocence Unprotected,* stylized images are created by painting multiple colors within a shot.

5.12   By scratching the emulsion, Brakhage emphasizes the eye motif that runs through *Reflections on Black.*

5.13   Deliberate overexposure of windows in *Vidas Secas.*

print. As a result, darker areas are colored, while the lighter portions of the frame remain white or only faintly colored **(5.9).**

Certain conventions grew up around tinting and toning. Night scenes, as in 5.9 (from *Cenere,* a 1916 Italian film) were often colored blue. Firelight was frequently colored red, while interiors were commonly amber. *The Wrath of the Gods* (1914) uses a brown tint to suggest the glow of an erupting volcano (5.8). Some later filmmakers revived these processes. Vera Chytilova employs a crimson toning in *Daisies* **(5.10).**

A rarer method of adding color is the difficult process of *hand coloring.* Here portions of black-and-white images are painted in colors, frame by frame. The ship's flag in Sergei Eisenstein's *Potemkin* was originally hand colored red against a blue sky. A modern use of hand coloring may be seen in Makavejev's *Innocence Unprotected* **(5.11).**

There are many other ways in which the filmmaker can manipulate the image's tonalities after filming. In *Reflections on Black,* Stan Brakhage scratched off the emulsion in certain parts of the shot **(5.12).** Lars von Trier shot *Breaking the Waves* on 35mm film, then transferred the footage to video and used digital manipulation to drain out much of the color. He transferred the footage back to film, resulting in desaturated images that tremble and shimmer (5.2).

The range of tonalities in the image is most crucially affected by the *exposure* of the image during filming. The filmmaker usually controls **exposure** by regulating how much light passes through the camera lens, though images shot with correct exposure can also be overexposed or underexposed in developing and printing. We commonly think that a photograph should be well exposed—neither underexposed (too dark, not enough light admitted through the lens) nor overexposed (too bright, too much light admitted through the lens). But even correct exposure usually offers some latitude for choice; it is not an absolute.

The filmmaker can manipulate exposure for specific effects. American film noir of the 1940s sometimes underexposed shadowy regions of the image in keeping with low-key lighting techniques. In *Vidas Secas,* Nelson Pereira dos Santos overexposed the windows of the prison cell to sharpen the contrast between the prisoner's confinement and the world of freedom outside **(5.13).** In the Moria sequence, *The Lord of the Rings: The Fellowship of the Ring* used overexposure in several shots. In **5.14,** the white glare was achieved by digital grading that simulated photographic overexposure.

Choices of exposure are particularly critical in working with color. For shots of *Kasba,* Kumar Shahani chose to emphasize tones within shaded areas, and so he exposed them and let sunlit areas bleach out somewhat **(5.15, 5.16).**

Exposure can in turn be affected by **filters**—slices of glass or gelatin put in front of the lens of the camera or printer to reduce certain frequencies of light reaching the film. Filters thus alter the range of tonalities in quite radical ways.

5.14   In *The Fellowship of the Ring,* the overexposure of the wizard's staff makes the Fellowship a bright island threatened by countless orcs in the surrounding darkness.

5.15   In *Kasbah,* the vibrant hues of the store's wares stand out, while the countryside behind is overexposed . . .

5.16   . . . while at other moments underexposure for the shaded porches emphasizes the central outdoor area.

5.17   In *The Searchers,* this scene of the protagonists spying on an Indian camp from a bluff was shot in sunlight using day-for-night filters.

Before modern improvements in film stocks and lighting made it practical to shoot most outdoor night scenes at night, filmmakers routinely made such scenes by using blue filters in sunlight—a technique called *day for night* (**5.17**). Hollywood cinematographers since the 1920s have sought to add glamour to close-ups, especially of women, by means of diffusion filters and silks placed over light sources.

The Speed of Motion

A gymnast's performance seen in slow motion, ordinary action accelerated to comic speed, a tennis serve stopped in a freeze-frame—we are all familiar with the effects of the control of the speed of motion. Of course, the filmmaker who stages the

5.18   Cars become blurs of light when shot in fast motion for *Koyaanisqatsi.*

event to be filmed can (within limits) dictate the pace of the action. But that pace can also be controlled by a photographic power unique to cinema: the control of the speed of movement seen on the screen.

The speed of the motion we see on the screen depends on the relation between the rate at which the film was shot and the rate of projection. Both **rates** are calculated in frames per second. The standard rate, established when synchronized-sound cinema came in at the end of the 1920s, was 24 frames per second (fps). Today's 35mm cameras commonly offer the filmmaker a choice of anything between 8 and 64 fps, with specialized cameras offering still wider range of choice.

If the movement is to look accurate on the screen, the rate of shooting should correspond to the rate of projection. That's why silent films sometimes look jerky today: films shot at anywhere from 16 to 20 fps are speeded up when shown at 24 fps. Projected at the correct speed, silent films can look as smooth as movies made today.

As the silent films indicate, if a film is exposed at fewer frames per second than the projection, the screen action will look speeded up. This is the *fast-motion* effect sometimes seen in comedies. But fast motion has long been used for other purposes. In F. W. Murnau's *Nosferatu,* the vampire's coach rushes skittishly across the landscape, suggesting his supernatural power. In Godfrey Reggio's *Koyaanisqatsi,* delirious fast motion renders the hectic rhythms of urban life **(5.18).** More recent films have used fast motion to grab our attention and accelerate the pace, whisking us through a setting to the heart of the action.

The more frames per second shot, the slower the screen action will appear. The resulting *slow-motion* effect is used notably in Dziga Vertov's *Man with a Movie Camera* to render sports events in detail, a function that continues to be important today. The technique can also be used for expressive purposes. In Rouben Mamoulian's *Love Me Tonight,* the members of a hunt decide to ride quietly home to avoid waking the sleeping deer; their ride is filmed in slow motion to create a comic depiction of noiseless movement. Today slow-motion footage often functions to suggest that the action takes place in a dream or fantasy or to convey enormous power, as in a martial-arts film. Slow-motion scenes of lovers walking add a lyrical rhythm to Wong Kar-wai's *In the Mood for Love.* Slow motion is also used for emphasis, becoming a way of dwelling on a moment of spectacle or high drama.

To enhance expressive effects, filmmakers can change the speed of motion in the course of a shot. Often the change of speed helps create special effects. In *Die Hard* a fireball bursts up an elevator shaft toward the camera. During the filming, the fire at the bottom of the shaft was filmed at 100 fps, slowing down its progress, and then shot at faster speeds as it erupted upward, giving the impression of an explosive acceleration. For *Bram Stoker's Dracula,* director Francis Ford Coppola wanted his vampire to glide toward his prey with supernatural suddenness. Cinematographer Michael Ballhaus used a computer program to control the shutter and the speed of filming, allowing smooth and instantaneous changes from 24 fps to 8 fps and back again.

Digital postproduction allows filmmakers to create the effect of variable shooting speeds through *ramping,* shifting speed of movement very smoothly and rapidly. In an early scene of Michael Mann's *The Insider,* researcher Jeffrey Wigand leaves the tobacco company that has just fired him. As he crosses the lobby toward a revolving door, his brisk walk suddenly slows to a dreamlike drifting. The point of this very noticeable stylistic choice becomes apparent only in the film's last shot. Lowell Bergman, the TV producer who has helped Wigand reveal that addictive substances are added to cigarettes, has been dismissed from CBS. Bergman strides across the lobby, and as he passes through the revolving door, his movement glides into extreme slow motion. The repetition of the technique points out the parallels between two men who have lost their livelihoods as a result of telling the truth—two insiders who have become outsiders.

Extreme forms of fast and slow motion alter the speed of the depicted material even more radically. *Time-lapse* cinematography permits us to see the sun set in seconds or a flower sprout, bud, and bloom in a minute. For this, a very low shooting speed is required—perhaps one frame per minute, hour, or even day. For *high-speed* cinematography, which may seek to record a bullet shattering glass, the camera may expose hundreds, or even thousands, of frames per second. Most cameras can be used for time-lapse shooting, but high-speed cinematography requires specially designed cameras.

After filming, the filmmaker can still control the speed of movement on the screen through various laboratory procedures. Until the early 1990s, the most common means used was the optical printer. This device rephotographs a film, copying all or part of each original frame onto another reel of film. The filmmaker can use the optical printer to skip frames (accelerating the action when projected), reprint a frame at desired intervals (slowing the action by *stretch printing*), stop the action (repeating a frame over and over, to freeze the projected image for seconds or minutes), or reverse the action. Some silent films are stretch-printed with every other frame repeated, so that they may run more smoothly at sound speed. We are familiar with freeze-framing, slow-motion, and reverse-motion printing effects from the *instant replays* of sports coverage and investigative documentaries. Many experimental films have made striking use of the optical printer's possibilities, such as Ken Jacobs's *Tom Tom the Piper's Son,* which explores the images of an early silent film by enlarging portions of its shots. Today the optical printer has largely been replaced by digital manipulations of the speed of movement.

Perspective

You are standing on railroad tracks, looking toward the horizon. The tracks not only recede but also seem to meet at the horizon. You glance at the trees and buildings along the tracks. They diminish by simple, systematic rule: the closer objects look larger, the farther objects look smaller—even if they are actually of uniform size. The optical system of your eye, registering light rays reflected from the scene, supplies a host of information about scale, depth, and spatial relations among parts of the scene. Such relations are called *perspective* relations.

The **lens** of a photographic camera does roughly what your eye does. It gathers light from the scene and transmits that light onto the flat surface of the film to form an image that represents size, depth, and other dimensions of the scene. One difference between the eye and the camera, though, is that photographic lenses may be changed, and each type of lens will render perspective in different ways. If two different lenses photograph the same scene, the perspective relations in the resulting images could be drastically different. A wide-angle lens could exaggerate the depth

5.19 In *Don't Look Now*, as the camera swivels to follow the walking character, the wide-angle lens makes a street lamp he passes appear to lean rightward . . .

5.20 . . . and then leftward.

"I'm standing around waiting to see where the 50mm is going to be, or what size lens they're putting on, and in that unwritten book in my brain, I said, 'Don't ever let them shoot you full face, on a wide-angle lens, you'll end up looking like Dumbo.'"

— Tony Curtis, actor

you see down the track or could make the foreground trees and buildings seem to bulge; a telephoto lens could drastically reduce the depth, making the trees seem very close together and nearly the same size.

The Lens: Focal Length   Control of perspective in the image is very important to the filmmaker. The chief variable in the process is the **focal length** of the lens. In technical terms, the focal length is the distance from the center of the lens to the point where light rays converge to a point of focus on the film. The focal length alters the perceived magnification, depth, and scale of things in the image. We usually distinguish three sorts of lenses on the basis of their effects on perspective:

1. *The short-focal-length* (wide-angle) *lens*

In 35mm-gauge cinematography, a lens of less than 35mm in focal length is considered a wide-angle lens. Such lenses tend to distort straight lines lying near the edges of the frame, bulging them outward. Note the distortion in two frames from a shot in Nicholas Roeg's *Don't Look Now* (**5.19, 5.20**). When a wide-angle lens is used for a medium shot or close-up, the distortion of shape may become very evident (**5.21**).

The lens of short focal length has the property of exaggerating depth (**5.22**). Because distances between foreground and background seem greater, the wide-angle lens also makes figures moving to or from the camera seem to cover ground more rapidly.

2. *The middle-focal-length* (medium) *lens*

A common lens length for a medium lens is 50mm. This lens seeks to avoid noticeable perspective distortion. With a medium lens, horizontal and vertical lines are rendered as straight and perpendicular. (Compare the bulging effect of the wide-angle lens.) Parallel lines should recede to distant vanishing points, as in our railroad tracks example. Foreground and background should seem neither stretched apart (as with the wide-angle lens) nor squashed together (as with the telephoto lens). A medium lens was used for **5.23**; contrast the sense of distance among the figures achieved in 5.22.

3. *The long-focal-length* (telephoto) *lens*

Whereas wide-angle lenses distort space laterally, longer lenses flatten the space along the camera axis. Cues for depth and volume are reduced. The planes seem squashed together, much as when you look through a telescope or binoculars. In **5.24**, from Chen Kaige's *Life on a String*, the long lens pushes the crowd members almost to the same plane. It also makes the rapids behind the men virtually a two-dimensional backdrop.

5.21 Wide-angle distortion in Mikhail Kalatozov's *The Cranes Are Flying*.

5.22 In this scene from *The Little Foxes*, the lens makes the characters seem farther from one another than we would expect in so relatively tight a grouping.

5.23 A shot made with a medium lens in *His Girl Friday*.

5.24 The long lens in Chen Kaige's *Life on a String.*

5.25 In *Koyaanisqatsi*, an airport is filmed from a great distance, and the long lens makes it appear that a plane is landing on a crowded highway.

Today long lenses typically are 100mm or greater in length. They are commonly used in the filming or televising of sports events, since they allow the cinematographer to magnify action at a distance. (For this reason, long lenses are also called telephoto lenses.) In a baseball game, there will invariably be shots taken from almost directly behind the pitcher, using a camera located beyond the center field wall. You have probably noticed that such shots make the umpire, catcher, batter, and pitcher look unnaturally close to one another. What a very long lens can do to space is dramatically illustrated throughout Godfrey Reggio's *Koyaanisqatsi* **(5.25).**

A long-focal-length lens also affects subject movement, flattening depth. Thus a figure moving toward the camera takes more time to cover what seems to be a small distance. The running-in-place shots in *The Graduate* and other films of the 1960s and 1970s were produced by lenses of very long focal length. In *Tootsie*, the introduction of Michael Dorsey disguised as Dorothy Michaels occurs in a lengthy telephoto shot in order for us to recognize his altered appearance and to notice that none of the people around him finds "her" unusual **(5.26–5.28).**

Lens length can distinctly affect the spectator's experience. For example, expressive qualities can be suggested by lenses that distort objects or characters. We

"In New York, New York, we shot only with a 32mm lens, the whole movie. We tried to equate the old style of framing, the old style meaning 1946–53."

— Martin Scorsese, director

5.26 In *Tootsie*, Dorothy becomes visible among the crowd at a considerable distance from the camera . . .

5.27 . . . and after taking 20 steps seems only slightly closer until . . .

5.28 . . . "she" finally grows somewhat larger, after a total of about 36 steps.

5.29   In Ilya Trauberg's *China Express,* a wide-angle lens creates foreground distortion.

5.30   In *Eternity and a Day,* a long lens makes the beach and sea appear as two vertical blocks.

5.31   In Kurosawa's *Red Beard,* the mad patient in the background seems threateningly to approach the intern . . .

5.32   . . . until a cut reveals that she is across the room from him.

"I tend to rely on only two kinds of lenses to compose my frames: very wide angle and extreme telephoto. I use the wide angle because when I want to see something, I want to see it completely, with the most detail possible. As for the telephoto, I use it for close-ups because I find it creates a real 'encounter' with the actor. If you shoot someone's face with a 200-millimeter lens, the audience will feel like the actor is really standing in front of them. It gives presence to the shot. So I like extremes. Anything in between is of no interest to me."

— John Woo, director

tend to see the man in **5.29** as looming, even aggressive. Moreover, choice of the lens can make a character or object blend into the setting (5.26) or stand out in sharp relief (5.29). Filmmakers may exploit the flattening effects of the long-focal-length lens to create solid masses of space **(5.30),** as in an abstract painting.

A director can use lens length to surprise us, as Kurosawa does in *Red Beard.* When the mad patient comes into the intern's room, a long-focal-length lens filming from behind him initially makes her seem to be quite close to him **(5.31).** But a cut to a more perpendicular angle shows that the patient and the intern are actually several feet apart and that he is not yet in danger **(5.32).**

There is one sort of lens that offers the director a chance to manipulate focal length and to transform perspective relations during a single shot. A **zoom lens** is

5.33 In the opening of *The Conversation,* a long, slow zoom-in arouses considerable uncertainty about its target . . .

5.34 . . . until it finally centers on a mime and our protagonist, surveillance technician Harry Caul.

optically designed to permit the continuous varying of focal length. Originally created for aerial and reconnaissance photography, zoom lenses gradually became a standard tool for newsreel filming. It was not, however, the general practice to zoom during shooting. The camera operator varied the focal length as desired and then started filming. In the late 1950s, however, the increased portability of cameras led to a trend toward zooming while filming.

Since then, the zoom has sometimes been used to substitute for moving the camera forward or backward. Although the zoom shot presents a mobile framing, the camera remains fixed. During a zoom, the camera remains stationary, and the lens simply increases or decreases its focal length. Onscreen, the zoom shot magnifies or demagnifies the objects filmed, excluding or including surrounding space, as in **5.33** and **5.34,** from Francis Ford Coppola's *The Conversation.* The zoom can produce interesting and peculiar transformations of scale and depth, as we shall see when we examine Michael Snow's *Wavelength.*

The impact that focal length can have on the image's perspective qualities is dramatically illustrated in Ernie Gehr's abstract experimental film *Serene Velocity.* The scene is an empty corridor. Gehr shot the film with a zoom lens, but he did not zoom while filming the shot. Instead, the zoom permitted him to change the lens's focal length between takes. As Gehr explains,

> [I] divided the mm range of the zoom lens in half and starting from the middle I recorded changes in mm positions. . . . The camera was not moved at all. The zoom lens was not moved during recording either. Each frame was recorded individually as a still. Four frames to each position. To give an example: I shot the first four frames at 50mm. The next four frames I shot at 55mm. And then, for a certain duration, approximately 60 feet, I went back and forth, four frames at 50mm, four frames at 55mm; four frames at 50mm, four frames at 55mm; etc. . . . for about 60 feet. Then I went to 45–60 [mm] and did the same for about 60 feet. Then to 40–65, and so on.

The resulting film presents an image whose perspective relations pulsate rhythmically—first with little difference in size and scale, but gradually with greater tension between a telephoto image and a wide-angle image **(5.35)**. In a sense, *Serene Velocity* takes as its subject the effect of focal length on perspective.

The Lens: Depth of Field and Focus   Focal length not only affects how shape and scale are magnified or distorted. It also affects the lens's **depth of field**—the range of distances before the lens within which objects can be photographed in sharp **focus.** A lens with a depth of field of 10 feet to infinity will render any object in that range clearly, but the sharpness of the image will decrease when the object moves closer to the lens (say, to 4 feet). All other things being equal, a short-focal-length (wide-angle) lens has a relatively greater depth of field than does a long-focal-length (telephoto) lens.

5.35 In *Serene Velocity,* telephoto shots of a hallway are juxtaposed to wide-angle shots taken from the same spot.

5.36   In the first shot of *Simple Men*, the foreground railing and the man in the distance are out of focus, emphasizing the drama in focus in the middle ground.

5.37   Agnès Varda's *Vagabonde (Sans toi ni loi).*

Depth of field should not be confused with the concept of deep space, discussed in Chapter 4. *Deep space* is a term for the way the filmmaker has staged the action on several different planes, *regardless of whether all of these planes are in focus.* In the case of *Our Hospitality,* those planes usually are in sharp focus, but in other films, not every plane of deep space is in focus. In this shot from *Simple Men* **(5.36),** we can see three planes of depth, but deep focus isn't used. The robber and the security guard she holds at pistol point in the middle ground are in focus. But the yellow railing forming a distinct foreground plane is out of focus. In the distant background, visible between the rails, stands the female robber's partner. He's out of focus, too. The example shows that deep space is a property of mise-en-scene, the techniques that affect what is placed in front of the camera. Depth of field depends on the camera itself, with the lens determining what layers of the mise-en-scene are in focus.

As the *Simple Men* example suggests, selective focus is often used to call attention to the main action and to deemphasize less significant parts of the surroundings. Often this involves centering the main character in the foreground and throwing the background out of focus **(5.37).**

If depth of field controls perspective relations by determining which planes will be in focus, what choices are open to the filmmaker? He or she may opt for what is usually called *selective focus*—choosing to focus on only one plane and letting the other planes blur. This is what director Hal Hurtley does in the *Simple Men* example. Selective focus typically draws the viewer's attention to the main character or object (5.37). The technique can be used for a more abstract compositional effect as well **(5.38).**

In Hollywood during the 1940s, partly due to the influence of *Citizen Kane,* filmmakers began using faster film, shorter-focal-length lenses, and more intense lighting to yield a greater depth of field. The contract-signing scene from *Citizen Kane* **(5.39)** offers a famous example. This practice came to be called **deep focus.**

Deep-focus cinematography became a major stylistic option in the 1940s and 1950s. A typical usage is illustrated in **5.40.** The technique was even imitated in animated cartoons (4.133, from Chuck Jones's *One Froggy Evening*). During the 1970s and 1980s, deep-focus cinematography was revived in Steven Spielberg's work, notably *Jaws* and *Close Encounters of the Third Kind,* and in the films of Brian De Palma **(5.41).** Today, extreme deep-focus effects are common in digital video **(5.42).**

The filmmaker may also have the option of adjusting perspective while filming by **racking focus,** or *pulling focus.* A shot may begin with an object in the foreground sharply visible and the rear plane fuzzy, then rack focus so that the background elements come into crisp focus and the foreground becomes blurred. Alternatively, the focus can rack from background to foreground, as in **5.43** and **5.44,** from Bernardo Bertolucci's *Last Tango in Paris.*

"If I made big-budget films, I would do what the filmmakers of twenty years ago did: use 35, 40, and 50mm [lenses] with lots of light so I could have that depth of field, because it plays upon the effect of surprise. It can give you a whole series of little tricks, little hiding places, little hooks in the image where you can hang surprises, places where they can suddenly appear, just like that, within the frame itself. You can create the off-frame within the frame."

— Benoit Jacquot, director

5.38 Leos Carax's *Boy Meets Girl.*

5.39 In *Citizen Kane,* from one plane near the lens (Bernstein's head), through several planes in the middle ground, to the wall far in the distance, everything is in sharp focus.

5.40 Anthony Mann's *The Tall Target.*

5.41 In *The Untouchables,* a conversation scene is played in the foreground while setting and distant figures are also kept in focus.

5.42 The small size of the chip in a digital video camera yields extreme depth of field. If this shot, from Agnès Varda's *The Gleaners and I,* had been made on film, either Varda's hand or the truck would have been far more out of focus.

5.43 In this shot from *Last Tango in Paris,* the woman, bench, and wall in the distance are in focus, while the man in the foreground is not . . .

5.44 . . . but after the camera racks focus, the man in the foreground becomes sharp and the background fuzzy.

Special Effects The image's perspective relations may also be created by means of **special effects.** We have already seen (p. 123) that the filmmaker can create setting by use of models and computer-generated images. Alternatively, separately photographed planes of action may be combined on the same strip of film to create the illusion that the two planes are adjacent. The simplest way to do this is through **superimposition.** By double exposure either in the camera or in laboratory printing, one image is laid over another. Superimpositions have been used since

5.45   In the opening of Quentin Tarantino's *Kill Bill, Vol. 1*, the Bride sees the first victim of her revenge, and her memory of a violent struggle is superimposed over a tight framing of her eyes.

5.46   *Boom Town.*

the earliest years of the cinema. One common function is to render ghosts, which appear as translucent figures. Superimpositions also frequently provide a way of conveying dreams, visions, or memories. Typically, these mental images are shown against a close view of a face (**5.45**).

More complex techniques for combining strips of film to create a single shot are usually called **process,** or *composite,* **shots.** These techniques can be divided into *projection process work* and *matte process work.*

In projection process work, the filmmaker projects footage of a setting onto a screen, then films actors performing in front of the screen. Classical Hollywood filmmaking began this process in the late 1920s, as a way to avoid taking cast and crew on location. The Hollywood technique involved placing the actors against a translucent screen and projecting a film of the setting from behind the screen. The whole ensemble could then be filmed from the front (**5.46**).

Rear projection, as this system was known, seldom creates very convincing depth cues. Foreground and background tend to look starkly separate, partly because of the absence of cast shadows from foreground to background and partly because all background planes tend to seem equally diffuse (**5.47**).

5.47   In Hitchcock's *Vertigo,* the seascape in the rear plane was shot separately and used as a back-projected setting for an embrace filmed under studio lighting.

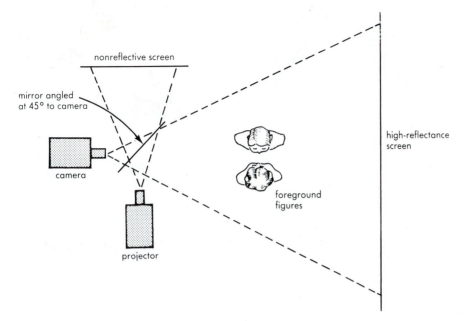

5.48 A front-projection system.

5.49 In Syberberg's film of Wagner's *Parsifal*, front projection conjures up colossal, phantasmagoric landscapes.

Front projection, which came into use in the late 1960s, projects the setting onto a two-way mirror, angled to throw the image onto a high-reflectance screen. The camera photographs the actors against the screen by shooting through the mirror **(5.48).** The results of front projection can be clearly seen in the "Dawn of Man" sequence of *2001: A Space Odyssey,* the first film to use front projection extensively. (At one moment, a saber-toothed tiger's eyes glow, reflecting the projector's light.) Because of the sharp focus of the projected footage, front projection blends foreground and background planes fairly smoothly. The nonrealistic possibilities of front projection have been explored by Hans-Jürgen Syberberg. In his film of Wagner's opera *Parsifal,* front projection conjures up colossal, phantasmagoric landscapes **(5.49).** Front and rear projection have largely been replaced by digital techniques. Here action is filmed in front of a large blue or green screen rather than a film image, with the background later added by digital manipulation.

Composite filming can also be accomplished by **matte work.** A *matte* is a portion of the setting photographed on a strip of film, usually with a part of the frame empty. Through laboratory printing, the matte is joined with another strip of film containing the actors. One sort of matte involves a painting of the desired areas of setting, which is then filmed. The footage is combined with footage of action, segregated in the blank portions of the painted scenery. In this way, a matte can create an entire imaginary setting for the film. Stationary mattes of this sort have made glass shots virtually obsolete and were so widely used in commercial cinema that until the late 1990s the matte painter was a mainstay of production. In recent years, matte paintings have been made using computer programs, but they are used in the same way to create scenery **(5.50).**

With a matte painting, however, the actor cannot move into the painted portions of the frame without seeming to disappear. To solve this problem, the filmmaker can use a *traveling matte.* Here the actor is photographed against a blank, usually blue, background. In laboratory printing, the moving outline of the actor is cut out of footage of the desired background. After further lab work, the shot of the actor is jigsawed into the moving gap in the background footage. It is traveling mattes that present shots of Superman's flight or of spaceships hurtling through space **(5.51).** The animated figures in *Who Framed Roger Rabbit?* **(5.52)** were matted into live-action footage shot separately.

5.50   In this shot from *The Fellowship of the Ring,* the distant part of the building, the cliffs, and the sky are all on a matte painting created by computer.

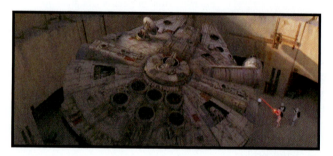

5.51   In *Star Wars: Episode IV—A New Hope,* the take-off of the *Millennium Falcon* was filmed as a model against a blue screen and matted into a shot of a building with imperial stormtroopers firing upward.

5.52   In *Who Framed Roger Rabbit?* a human director inhabits the same world as the cartoon characters starring in his film.

Before the perfecting of computer-generated imagery, traveling mattes were commonly used in all genres of mainstream cinema. Usually, they function to create a realistic-looking locale or situation. But they can also generate an abstract, deliberately unrealistic, image (**5.53**).

For many films, different types of special effects will be combined. The illustration from *The Fellowship of the Ring* in 5.50 includes a partial full-size set with an actor at the left, a miniature set in the middle ground, a matte painting of the background elements, and computer-animated waterfalls and falling leaves. A single shot of a science fiction film might animate miniatures or models through stop action, convey their movements by a traveling matte, and add animated ray bursts in superimposition while a matte painting supplies a background. For the train crash in *The Fugitive,* front and rear projection were used simultaneously within certain shots.

You may have noticed that superimpositions, projection process work, and matte work all straddle two general bodies of film techniques. These special effects all require arrangement of the material before the camera, so to some extent they are aspects of mise-en-scene. But they also require control of photographic choices (such as refilming and making laboratory adjustments) and affect perspective relations, so they involve cinematography as well. We have considered them here because, unlike effects employing models and miniatures, these effects are created

5.53 In *Rumble Fish*, a black-and-white film, Francis Ford Coppola uses traveling mattes to color the fish in an aquarium.

5.54 Computer-generated imagery created a gap in the freeway for the bus to leap in *Speed*.

CONNECT TO THE BLOG
CGI can create spectacle, and some critics claim that the special effects make the story unimportant. We argue the opposite and talk about a film historian who backs us up in "Classical cinema lives! New evidence for old norms."
See www.davidbordwell.net/blog/?p=412.

through specifically photographic tricks. The general term for them, *optical effects,* suggests their photographic nature.

With the rise of computer-generated effects, the fusion of mise-en-scene and cinematography became even more seamless. Digital compositing allows the filmmaker to shoot some action with performers and then add backgrounds, shadows, or movement that would previously have required photographed mattes, multiple exposures, or optical printing. In *Speed*, the audience sees a city bus leap a broken freeway. The stunt was performed on a ramp designed for the jump, and the highway background was drawn digitally as a matte painting (**5.54**). With the proliferation of specialized programs, computer-generated imagery (CGI) increasingly provides convincing effects that have all but replaced traditional optical printing. (See "A Closer Look.")

Like other film techniques, photographic manipulations of the shot are not ends in themselves. Rather, they function within the overall context of the film. Specific treatments of tonalities, speed of motion, or perspective should be judged less on criteria of realism than on criteria of function. For instance, most Hollywood filmmakers try to make their rear-projection shots unnoticeable. But in Jean-Marie Straub and Danièle Huillet's *The Chronicle of Anna Magdalena Bach,* the perspective relations are yanked out of kilter by an inconsistent rear projection (**5.55**). Since the film's other shots have been filmed on location in correct perspective, this blatantly artificial rear projection calls our attention to the visual style of the entire film.

Similarly, **5.58** looks unrealistic unless we posit the man as being about three feet long. But director Vera Chytilova has used setting, character position, and deep focus to make a comic point about the two women's treatment of men. Such trick

5.55 The foreground plane of this shot from *The Chronicle of Anna Magdalena Bach* shows Bach, shot straight on, playing a harpsichord—yet the back-projected building behind him is shot from a low angle.

A CLOSER LOOK

FROM MONSTERS TO THE MUNDANE:
Computer-Generated Imagery in *The Lord of the Rings*

The films adapted from J.R.R. Tolkien's trilogy *The Lord of the Rings* (*The Fellowship of the Ring, The Two Towers,* and *The Return of the King*) show how CGI can be used for impressive special effects: huge battle scenes, plausible monsters, and magical events. Less obviously, the films also indicate how CGI shapes many aspects of production, from the spectacular to the mundane.

CGI was used at every stage of production. In pre-production, a sort of animated storyboard (a *previz,* for "previsualization") was made, consisting of *animatics,* or rough, computer-generated versions of the scenes. Each of the three previzes was roughly as long as each finished film and helped to coordinate the work of the huge staff involved in both digital and physical tasks.

During production of the three films, CGI helped create portions of the mise-en-scene. Many shots digitally stitched together disparate elements, blending full-size settings, miniature sets, and matte paintings (5.50). A total of 68 miniature sets were built, and computer manipulation was required in each case to make them appear real or to allow camera movements through them. Computer paint programs could generate matte paintings for the sky, clouds, distant cliffs, and forests that appeared behind the miniatures.

Rings also drew on the rapidly developing capacity of CGI to create characters. The war scenes were staged with a small number of actual actors in costumes, while vast crowds of CGI soldiers appeared in motion alongside them. As happens for many films, new software programs were devised for *Rings.* A crucial program was Massive (for "Multiple Agent Simulation System in Virtual Environment"). Using motion-capture on a few *agents* (costumed actors), the team could build a number of different military maneuvers, assigning all of them to the thousands of crude, digitally generated figures. By giving each figure a rudimentary artificial intelligence—such as the ability to see an approaching soldier and identify it as friend or foe—Massive could generate a scene with figures moving differently from each other **(5.56).**

The monsters encountered by the characters during their quest were more elaborately designed and executed than the troops. A detailed three-dimensional model of each creature was captured with a new scanning wand that could read into recesses and folds to create a complete image from all angles. A new system, Character Mapper, captured motion from an actor, then adjusted the mass and musculature to imaginary skeletons. In the cave-troll sequence, the large, squat

5.56 Vast crowds of soldiers with individualized movements were generated by the Massive software program for *The Two Towers*.

creature swings its limbs and flexes its muscles in a believable fashion.

Most of the speaking characters (with the important exception of the skeletal Gollum) were played by actors, but even here CGI was used. The main characters had digital look-alikes who served as stunt doubles, performing actions that were dangerous or impossible. In the cave-troll fight, the actors playing Legolas, Merry, and Pippin were all replaced by their digital doubles when they climbed or jumped on the troll's shoulders. A requirement specific to this story was the juxtaposition of full-size actors playing three-foot-tall hobbits with other characters considerably taller than themselves. The size difference was often created during filming by using small doubles or by placing the hobbits farther from the camera in false-perspective sets.

In many cases, CGI created the kinds of special effects formerly generated on an optical printer. In *The Fellowship of the Ring,* such effects include Gandalf's fireworks, the flood at the Fords of Bruinen, the avalanche that hits the Fellowship on the mountain pass, and the flaming Eye of Sauron.

Cinematography also depended on CGI. For the cave-troll scene, director Peter Jackson donned a virtual-reality helmet and planned camera positions by moving around a virtual set and facing a virtual troll. The camera positions were motion-captured and reproduced in the actual filming of the sequence—which has a rough, handheld style quite different from the rest of the scenes.

In postproduction, animators erased telephone poles in location shots and helicopter blades dipping into the aerial shots of the Fellowship's voyage across mountains. Specialized programs added details, such as the ripples in the water in the Mirror of Galadriel.

Perhaps most important, digital grading altered the color of shots, giving each major location a distinctive look. Rivendell's scenes are in autumnal tones, while the early scenes in the Shire were given a yellow glow that enhanced the sunshine and green fields. The grading also utilized an innovative program, 5D Colossus, which allowed artists to adjust the color values of individual elements within a shot. Thus in the Lórien scene in which Galadriel shows Frodo her mirror, she glows bright white, contrasting with the deep blue tones of Frodo's figure and setting **(5.57).** Thanks to digital grading, CGI techniques can go beyond the creation of imaginary creatures and large crowds to shape the visual style of an entire film.

5.57 In *The Fellowship of the Ring,* selective digital color grading makes one figure bright white while the rest of the scene has a uniform muted blue tone.

5.58   In *Daisies,* perspective cues create a comic optical illusion.

5.59   The Lumière camera provided flexibility in framing.

5.60   The bulky camera of W.K.L. Dickson.

perspective was designed to be unnoticeable in *The Lord of the Rings,* where an adult actor playing a three-foot-tall hobbit might be placed considerably farther from the camera than an actor playing a taller character, yet the two appeared to be talking face to face. (See "A Closer Look," p. 184) The filmmaker chooses not only how to register light and movement photographically but also how those photographic qualities will function within the overall formal system of the film.

Framing

In any image, the frame is not simply a neutral border; it imposes a *certain vantage point* onto the material within the image. In cinema, the frame is important because it actively *defines* the image for us.

To obtain proof of the power of **framing,** we need only turn to the first major filmmaker in history, Louis Lumière. An inventor and businessman, Lumière and his brother Auguste devised one of the first practical cinema cameras **(5.59).** The Lumière camera, the most flexible of its day, also doubled as a projector. Whereas the bulky American camera invented by W.K.L. Dickson was about the size of an office desk **(5.60),** the Lumière camera weighed only 12 pounds and was small and portable. As a result of its lightness, the Lumière camera could be taken outside and could be set up quickly. Louis Lumière's earliest films presented simple events— workers leaving his father's factory, a game of cards, a family meal. But even at so early a stage of film history, Lumière was able to use framing to transform everyday reality into cinematic events.

Consider one of the most famous Lumière films, *The Arrival of a Train at La Ciotat* (1897). Had Lumière followed theatrical practice, he might have framed the shot by setting the camera perpendicular to the platform, letting the train enter the frame from the right side, broadside to the spectator. Instead, Lumière positioned the camera at an oblique angle. The result is a dynamic composition, with the train arriving from the distance on a diagonal **(5.61).** If the scene had been shot perpendicularly, we would have seen only a string of passengers' backs climbing aboard. Here, however, Lumière's oblique angle brings out many aspects of the passengers' bodies and several planes of action. We see some figures in the foreground and some in the distance. Simple as it is, this single-shot film, less than a minute long, aptly illustrates how choosing a position for the camera makes a drastic difference in the framing of the image and how we perceive the filmed event.

Consider another Lumière short, *Baby's Meal* (1895). Lumière selected a camera position that would emphasize certain aspects of the event. A long shot would have situated the family in its garden, but Lumière framed the figures at a medium distance, which downplays the setting but emphasizes the family's gestures and facial expressions **(5.62).** The frame's control of the scale of the event has also controlled our understanding of the event itself.

Framing can powerfully affect the image by means of (1) the size and shape of the frame; (2) the way the frame defines onscreen and offscreen space; (3) the way framing imposes the distance, angle, and height of a vantage point onto the image; and (4) the way framing can move in relation to the mise-en-scene.

Frame Dimensions and Shape

We are so accustomed to the frame as a rectangle that we should remember that it need not be one. In painting and photography, of course, images have frames of various sizes and shapes: narrow rectangles, ovals, vertical panels, even triangles and parallelograms. In cinema, the choice has been more limited. The primary choices involve the width of the rectangular image.

The ratio of frame width to frame height is called the **aspect ratio.** The rough dimensions of the ratio were set quite early in the history of cinema by Thomas

5.61 Louis Lumière's diagonal framing in *The Arrival of a Train at La Ciotat.*

5.62 *Baby's Meal.*

CONNECT TO THE BLOG
Can framings create humor? We show how they can in "Funny framings."
See www.davidbordwell.net/blog/?p=761.

Edison, Dickson, Lumière, and other inventors. The proportions of the rectangular frame were approximately four to three, yielding an aspect ratio of 1.33:1. Nonetheless, in the silent period, some filmmakers felt that this standard was too limiting. Abel Gance shot and projected sequences of *Napoleon* (1927) in a format he called *triptychs.* This was a widescreen effect composed of three normal frames placed side by side. Gance used the effect to show a single huge expanse or to put three distinct images side by side **(5.63).** In contrast, the Soviet director Sergei Eisenstein argued for a square frame, which would make compositions along horizontal, vertical, and diagonal directions equally feasible.

The coming of sound in the late 1920s altered the frame somewhat. Adding the sound track to the filmstrip required adjusting either the shape or the size of the image. At first, some films were printed in an almost square format, usually about 1.17:1 **(5.64).** But in the early 1930s, the Hollywood Academy of Motion Picture Arts and Sciences established the so-called **Academy ratio** of 1.37:1, a modification of the classic 1.33:1 format to allow room for a sound track on the filmstrip **(5.65).** The Academy ratio was standardized throughout the world until the mid-1950s.

Since then, a variety of *widescreen* ratios has dominated 35mm filmmaking. The most common format in North America today is 1.85:1 **(5.66).** The 1.66:1 ratio **(5.67)** is more frequently used in Europe than in North America. A less common ratio, also widely used in European films, is 1.75:1 **(5.68).** This ratio is approximated by widescreen (16 × 9) television monitors and many digital-video formats.

A 2.35:1 ratio **(5.69)** was standardized by the CinemaScope anamorphic process during the 1950s. The 2.2:1 ratio was chiefly used for 70mm presentation **(5.70),** though as film stocks have improved, 70mm filming and projecting have largely disappeared.

The simplest way to create a widescreen image is by **masking** it at some stage in production or exhibition **(5.71).** This masking is usually called a *hard matte.*

5.63 A panoramic view from *Napoleon* joined images shot with three cameras.

COMMON ASPECT RATIOS OF 35MM FILM

1.17:1

◄ **5.64** *Public Enemy* shows the squarish aspect ratio of some early sound films.

► **5.65** *The Rules of the Game* was shot in Academy ratio.

1.37 (modified 1.33:1)

1.85:1

1.66:1

5.66 *Me and You and Everyone We Know* uses a common North American ratio.

5.67 *Une chambre en ville.*

1.75:1

2.35:1 (35mm anamorphic)

5.68 *Last Tango in Paris.*

5.69 Anamorphic widescreen in *The Valiant Ones.*

2.2:1 (70mm)

5.70 *Ghostbusters.*

5.71 This frame from Agnès Varda's *Vagabond* was masked during filming or printing.

5.72 A full-frame image from Martin Scorsese's *Raging Bull*. Note the microphone visible at the top edge.

5.73 A frame from Nagisa Oshima's anamorphic film *Boy,* squeezed on the original film strip.

5.74 The same frame, unsqueezed as it would be in projection.

Alternatively, many contemporary films are shot full-frame (that is, between 1.33:1 and 1.17:1) in the expectation that they will be masked when the film is shown in theaters or transferred to video. Sometimes the full-frame option results in lights or sound equipment being visible. In **5.72** you can clearly see the microphone bobbing down into the shot. This would not be seen in the theater, where the top and bottom of the frame would be masked by the aperture plate in the projector. The colored lines in our illustration show a projection framing at 1.85:1.

Another way to create a widescreen image is by using an **anamorphic** process. Here a special lens squeezes the image horizontally, either during filming or in printing. A comparable lens is necessary to unsqueeze the image during projection. The image on the 35mm filmstrip is shown in **5.73,** while the image as projected on the screen is shown in **5.74.** The anamorphic aspect ratio established by Cinema-Scope was 2.35:1 until the 1970s; for technical reasons, it was adjusted to 2.40:1. This is the aspect ratio of Panavision, today's most frequently used anamorphic system.

Widescreen cinema, either masked or anamorphic, has significant visual effects. The screen becomes a band or strip, emphasizing horizontal compositions. The format was initially associated with genres of spectacle—Westerns, travelogues,

CONNECT TO THE BLOG

The subtleties of emphasis that can be achieved with anamorphic widescreen framings are discussed in "Gradation of emphasis."

See www.davidbordwell.net/blog/?p=2986.

musicals, historical epics—in which sweeping settings were important. But directors quickly learned that widescreen has value for more intimate subjects, too. The frame from Kurosawa's *Sanjuro* **(5.75)** shows how an anamorphic process (Tohoscope, the Japanese equivalent of CinemaScope) can be used to create significant foreground and background areas in a confined setting.

In some widescreen compositions, the mise-en-scene draws the audience's attention to only one area of the image. A common solution is to put the important information slightly off center **(5.76)**, or even sharply off center **(5.77).** Or the director may use the widescreen format to multiply points of interest. Many scenes in Im Kwon-Taek's *Chunhyang* fill the frame with bustle and movement **(5.78).**

The rectangular frame, while by far the most common, has not prevented filmmakers from experimenting with other image shapes within the rectangular frame. This has usually been done by attaching **masks** over either the camera's or the printer's lens to block the passage of light. Masks were quite common in the

5.75   Akira Kurosawa's *Sanjuro.*

5.76   Souleymare Cissé's *Yeelen.*

5.77   John McTiernan's *Die Hard.*

5.78 In this busy scene from *Chunhyang,* our eye shuttles around the widescreen frame according to who is speaking, who is facing us, and who responds to the speaker.

5.79 Gance's *La Roue.*

5.80 Griffith's *Intolerance.*

5.81 Welles's *The Magnificent Ambersons.*

5.82 Philips Smalley's 1913 *Suspense* uses a three-way split screen.

silent cinema. A moving circular mask that opens to reveal or closes to conceal a scene is called an **iris.** In *La Roue,* Gance employed a variety of circular and oval masks **(5.79).** In **5.80,** a shot from Griffith's *Intolerance,* most of the frame is boldly blocked out to leave only a thin vertical slice, emphasizing the soldier's fall from the rampart. A number of directors in the sound cinema have revived the use of irises and masks. In *The Magnificent Ambersons* **(5.81),** Orson Welles used an iris to close a scene; the old-fashioned device adds a nostalgic note to the sequence.

We also should mention experiments with *multiple-frame,* or *split-screen,* imagery. In this process, two or more images, each with its own frame dimensions and shape, appear within the larger frame. From the early cinema onward, this device has been used to present scenes of telephone conversations **(5.82).** Split-screen phone scenes were revived for phone conversations in *Bye Bye Birdie* **(5.83)** and other 1960s widescreen comedies. Multiple-frame imagery is also useful for building suspense, as Brian De Palma has shown in such films as *Sisters.* We gain a godlike omniscience as we watch two or more actions at exactly the same moment. Peter Greenaway used split screen more experimentally in *Prospero's Books,* juxtaposing images suggested by Shakespeare's *The Tempest* **(5.84).**

As usual, the filmmaker's choice of screen format can be an important factor in shaping the viewer's experience. Frame size and shape can guide the spectator's attention. It can be concentrated through compositional patterns or masking, or it can be dispersed by use of various points of interest or sound cues. The same possibilities exist with multiple-frame imagery, which must be carefully coordinated either to focus the viewer's attention or to send it ricocheting from one image to another.

Onscreen and Offscreen Space

Whatever its shape, the frame makes the image bounded or limited. From an implicitly continuous world, the frame selects a slice to show us, leaving the rest of the space *offscreen.* If the camera leaves an object or person and moves elsewhere, we assume that the object or person is still there, outside the frame. Even in an abstract film, we cannot resist the sense that the shapes and patterns that burst into the frame come from somewhere.

Film aesthetician Noël Burch has pointed out six zones of offscreen space: the space beyond each of the four edges of the frame, the space behind the set, and the space behind the camera. It is worth considering how many ways a filmmaker can imply the presence of things in these zones of offscreen space. A character can aim looks or gestures at something offscreen. As we'll see in Chapter 7, sound can offer potent clues about offscreen space. And, of course, something from offscreen can protrude partly into the frame. Virtually any film could be cited for examples of all

5.83   Teenagers share the latest gossip in *Bye Bye Birdie*'s split-screen conversation.

5.84   The actor playing Ariel in *Prospero's Books* hovers over the scene in a separate space.

5.85   In *Jezebel*, the heroine, Julie, greets some friends in medium shot . . .

5.86   . . . when suddenly a huge fist holding a glass appears in the left foreground.

these possibilities, but attractive instances are offered by films that use offscreen space for surprise effects.

In a party scene in William Wyler's *Jezebel*, the heroine, Julie, is the main focus of attention until a man's hand comes abruptly into the frame **(5.85–5.88)**. The intrusion of the hand abruptly signals us to the man's presence; Julie's glance, the camera movement, and the sound track confirm our new awareness of the total space. The director has used the selective powers of the frame to exclude something of great importance and then introduce it with startling effect.

More systematically, D. W. Griffith's *Musketeers of Pig Alley* makes use of sudden intrusions into the frame as a motif developing across the whole film. When a gangster is trying to slip a drug into the heroine's drink, we are not aware that the Snapper Kid has entered the room until a plume of his cigarette smoke wafts into the frame **(5.89)**. At the film's end, when the Snapper Kid receives a payoff, a mysterious hand thrusts into the frame to offer him money **(5.90).** Griffith has exploited the surprise latent in our sudden awareness that figures are offscreen.

The use of the fifth zone of offscreen space, that behind the rear plane, is of course common; characters go out a door and are now concealed by a wall or a staircase. Somewhat rarer is the use of the sixth zone—offscreen space behind and near the camera. One lengthy example occurs in Abbas Kiarostami's *Under the Olive Trees*. The crew is shooting a film scene, and we watch through the lens of the camera. As the tensions between two young actors spoil take after take, the action is repeated many times **(5.91)**. Eventually, shots begin to show the director and his crew behind the camera **(5.92)**. After several repetitions, the director walks in from that offscreen space behind the camera and tries to resolve

5.87 Julie looks off at its owner and comes forward . . .

5.88 . . . and the camera retreats slightly to frame her with the man who toasted her.

5.89 *The Musketeers of Pig Alley.*

5.90 *The Musketeers of Pig Alley.*

5.91 The actors return to their positions for one of many retakes of a shot for the film-within-a-film in *Under the Olive Trees.*

5.92 Finally, a reverse shot reveals the crew behind the camera, trying to figure out what is causing the problem.

5.93 Eventually, the director walks into camera range and tries to talk the actors into playing their roles as he wants them to.

the problem (**5.93**). Because of our awareness of the space behind the camera, throughout the many retakes, we remain aware of the crew's growing frustration. In such ways, a filmmaker can turn the necessary limitations of the frame edge to advantage.

Angle, Level, Height, and Distance of Framing

The frame implies not only space outside itself but also a position from which the material in the image is viewed. Most often, such a position is that of the camera filming the event. Even in an animated film, the shots may be framed as high or low

5.94   A straight-on angle in *The Chronicle of Anna Magdalena Bach.*

5.95   A high-angle framing from *Se7en.*

5.96   A low-angle view places sailors and a machine gun against the sky in *They Were Expendable.*

5.97   A canted framing in *Fallen Angels.*

5.98   A startling canted framing in *The End.*

angles, or long shots or close-ups, all of which simply result from the perspective of drawings selected to be photographed.

Angle   The frame positions us at some angle looking onto the shot's mise-en-scene. The number of such angles is infinite, since the camera might be placed anywhere. In practice, we typically distinguish three general categories: the straight-on angle, the high angle, and the low angle. The straight-on angle is the most common **(5.94)**. The high-angle positions us looking down at the material within the frame **(5.95)**. The low-angle framing positions us as looking up at the framed materials **(5.96)**.

Level   The frame can be more or less level—that is, parallel to the horizon. If the framing is tipped to one side or the other, it's said to be **canted.** Canted framing is relatively rare, although a few films make heavy use of it, such as Orson Welles's *Mr. Arkadin,* Carol Reed's *The Third Man,* and Wong Kar-wai's *Fallen Angels* **(5.97)**. In Christopher Maclaine's *The End,* a canted framing makes a steep street in the foreground appear level and renders the houses in the background grotesquely out of kilter **(5.98)**.

Height   The framing usually gives us a sense of being stationed at a certain height in relation to the settings and figures. Camera angle is, of course, partly related to height: To frame from a high angle entails being at a vantage point higher than the material in the image. But camera height is not simply a matter of camera angle. For instance, the Japanese filmmaker Yasujiro Ozu films from a low height with a straight-on angle (4.142, 6.130, 6.131), giving his work a distinctive visual style.

5.99 *The Third Man:* extreme long shot.

5.100 Long shot.

5.101 Medium long shot.

5.102 Medium shot.

5.103 Medium close-up.

5.104 Close-up.

5.105 Extreme close-up.

5.106 *La Passion de Jeanne d'Arc.*

Distance The framing of the image stations us at a certain distance. Framing supplies a sense of being far away or close to the mise-en-scene of the shot. This aspect of framing is usually called *camera distance*. In presenting the terms used for various distances, we'll use the standard measure: the human body. Our examples are all from *The Third Man.*

In the **extreme long shot,** the human figure is lost or tiny (**5.99**). This is the framing for landscapes, bird's-eye views of cities, and other vistas. In the **long shot,** figures are more prominent, but the background still dominates (**5.100**). Shots in which the human figure is framed from about the knees up are called **medium long shots (5.101).** These are common, since they permit a nice balance of figure and surroundings.

The **medium shot** frames the human body from the waist up (**5.102**). Gesture and expression now become more visible. The **medium close-up** frames the body from the chest up (**5.103**). The **close-up** is traditionally the shot showing just the head, hands, feet, or a small object. It emphasizes facial expression, the details of a gesture, or a significant object (**5.104**). The **extreme close-up** singles out a portion of the face or isolates and magnifies an object (**5.105**).

Note that the size of the photographed material within the frame is as important as any real camera distance. From the same camera distance, you could film a long shot of a person or a close-up of King Kong's elbow. We would not call the shot in **5.106** (from *La Passion de Jeanne d'Arc)* a close-up just because only Jeanne's head appears in the frame; the framing is that of a long shot because in scale her head is relatively small. (If the framing were simply adjusted downward, her whole body would be visible.) In judging camera distance, the relative proportion of the material framed determines how we identify the shot.

Categories of framing are obviously matters of degree. There is no universal measure of camera angle or distance. No precise cutoff point distinguishes between a long shot and an extreme long shot, or a slightly low angle and a straight-on angle. Moreover, filmmakers are not bound by terminology. They don't worry if a shot

5.107   In *Citizen Kane,* the low angle functions to isolate Kane and his friend against an empty background, his deserted campaign headquarters.

"I don't like close-ups unless you can get a kick out of them, unless you need them. If you can get away with attitudes and positions that show the feeling of the scene, I think you're better off using the close-up only for absolute punctuation—that's the reason you do it. And you save it—not like TV where they do everything in close-up."

— Howard Hawks, director, *His Girl Friday*

5.108   *North by Northwest.*

does not fit into traditional categories. (Nevertheless, abbreviations like MS for medium shot and CU for close-up are regularly used in screenplays, so filmmakers do find these terms useful in their work.) In most cases, the concepts are clear enough for us to use them in talking about films.

Functions of Framing   Sometimes we're tempted to assign absolute meanings to angles, distances, and other qualities of framing. It is easy to claim that framing from a low angle automatically presents a character as powerful and that framing from a high angle presents him or her as dwarfed and defeated. Verbal analogies are especially seductive: a canted frame seems to mean that "the world is out of kilter."

The analysis of film as art would be a lot easier if technical qualities automatically possessed such hard-and-fast meanings, but individual films would thereby lose much of their uniqueness and richness. The fact is that framings have no absolute or general meanings. In *some* films, angles and distance carry such meanings as mentioned above, but in other films—probably most films—they do not. To rely on formulas is to forget that meaning and effect always stem from the film, from its operation as a system. The context of the film determines the function of the framings, just as it determines the function of mise-en-scene, photographic qualities, and other techniques. Consider three examples.

At many points in *Citizen Kane,* low-angle shots of Kane do convey his looming power, but the lowest angles occur at the point of Kane's most humiliating defeat—his miscarried gubernatorial campaign (**5.107**). Note that angles of framing affect not only our view of the main figures but also the background against which those figures may appear.

If the cliché about high-angle framings were correct, **5.108,** a shot from *North by Northwest,* would express the powerlessness of Van Damm and Leonard. In fact, Van Damm has just decided to eliminate his mistress by pushing her out of a plane, and he says, "I think that this is a matter best disposed of from a great height." The angle and distance of Hitchcock's shot wittily prophesy how the murder is to be carried out.

Similarly, the world is hardly out of kilter in the shot from Eisenstein's *October* shown in **5.109.** The canted frame dynamizes the effort of pushing the cannon.

These three examples should demonstrate that we cannot reduce the richness of cinema to a few recipes. We must, as usual, look for the *functions* the technique performs in the particular *context* of the total film.

Camera distance, height, level, and angle often take on clear-cut narrative functions. Camera distance can establish or reestablish settings and character positions, as we shall see in the next chapter when we examine the editing of the first sequence of *The Maltese Falcon.* A framing can isolate a narratively important detail (**5.110, 5.111**).

Framing also can cue us to take a shot as subjective. In Chapter 3, we saw that a film's narration may present story information with some degree of psychological

5.109   A dramatic canted framing from *October.*

5.110   The tears of Henriette in *A Day in the Country* are visible in extreme close-up.

5.111   In *Day for Night,* a close framing emphasizes the precision with which the film director positions an actor's hands.

5.112 In *Fury*, the hero in his jail cell is seen through the bars from a slightly low angle . . .

5.113 . . . while the next shot, a high angle through the window toward the street outside, shows us what he sees, from his point of view.

5.114 In *The Maltese Falcon*, Kasper Gutman is frequently photographed from a low angle, emphasizing his obesity.

depth (p. 95), and one option is a perceptual subjectivity that renders what a character sees or hears. When a shot's framing prompts us to take it as seen through a character's eyes, we call it an optically subjective shot, or a point-of-view (POV) shot). (See also p. 200.) Fritz Lang's *Fury* provides a clear example (**5.112, 5.113**).

Framings may serve the narrative in yet other ways. Across an entire film, the repetitions of certain framings may associate themselves with a character or situation. That is, framings may become motifs unifying the film (**5.114**). Throughout *La Passion de Jeanne d'Arc,* Dreyer returns obsessively to extreme close-up shots of Jeanne (4.130).

Alternatively, certain framings in a film may stand out by virtue of their rarity. The ominously calm effect of the shot of the birds descending on Bodega Bay in Hitchcock's film *The Birds* arises from the abrupt shift from straight-on medium shots to an extreme long shot from very high above the town (6.32 and 6.33). In a film composed primarily of long shots and medium shots, an extreme close-up will obviously have considerable force. Similarly, the early scenes of Ridley Scott's *Alien* present few shots depicting any character's point of view. But when Kane approaches the alien egg, we see close views of it as if through his eyes, and the creature leaps straight out at us. This not only provides a sudden shock; the abrupt switch to framings that restrict us to one character's range of knowledge emphasizes a major turning point in the plot.

Apart from their narrative significance, framings can add a visual interest of their own. Close-ups can bring out textures and details we might otherwise ignore. We can see the surreptitious gestures of a thief in the medium close-up from Robert Bresson's *Pickpocket* (**5.115**); a string of similar close shots makes up a dazzling, balletlike scene in this film. Long shots can permit us to explore vistas. Much of the visual delight of Westerns, of David Lynch's *The Straight Story,* or of Werner Herzog's documentary *Lessons of Darkness* (**5.116**) arises from long shots that make

5.115 Bresson's *Pickpocket.*

CONNECT TO THE BLOG
One way to add visual interest is to shoot straight into the rear plane of the setting, as we explain in "Shot-consciousness."
See www.davidbordwell.net/blog/?p=275.

5.116 In *Lessons of Darkness,* helicopter shots give the desolate burning oilfields of Kuwait after the 1991 Gulf War an eerie, horrifying grandeur.

5.118   René Clair in *Entr'acte* frames a ballerina from straight below, transforming the figure into an expanding and contracting flower.

5.117   In Hou Hsiao-hsien's *Summer at Grandpa's,* the boy from the city visits his disgraced uncle, and the neighborhood is presented as a welter of rooftops sheltering a spot of bright red.

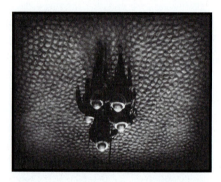

5.119   *La Passion de Jeanne d'Arc.*

CONNECT TO THE BLOG
We analyze subtleties of framing in films by two masters, William Wyler and Kenji Mizoguchi, in "Sleeves."

See www.davidbordwell.net/blog/?p=1549.

huge spaces manifest. By including a range of information, the long-shot framing encourages us to explore details or discover abstract patterns (**5.117**).

Our eye also enjoys the formal play presented by unusual angles on familiar objects (**5.118**). In *La Passion de Jeanne d'Arc,* the upside-down framings (**5.119**) are not motivated as a character's point of view; they express the frenzy of the massacre of the witnesses to Jeanne's death. "By reproducing the object from an unusual and striking angle," writes Rudolf Arnheim, "the artist forces the spectator to take a keener interest, which goes beyond mere noticing or acceptance. The object thus photographed sometimes gains in reality, and the impression it makes is livelier and more arresting."

Framing may be used for comic effect, as Charlie Chaplin, Buster Keaton, and Jacques Tati have all shown. We have seen that in *Our Hospitality* Keaton stages many gags in depth. Now we can see that well-chosen camera angles and distances are also vital to the gags' success. For example, if the railroad scene shown in 4.163 were shot from the side and in extreme long shot, we would not see so clearly that the two parts of the train are on parallel tracks. Moreover, we could not see the engineer's unconcerned posture, which indicates his failure to realize what has happened. Similarly, the use of framing to create offscreen space is vital to the gag shown in 4.172 and 4.173. Here the gag is laid out in time rather than space. First Willie tugs on the rope; then an unseen effect of that tug becomes visible as the Canfield son hurtles past and disappears. Finally, Willie reacts and is himself dragged down into the abyss below the frameline. Try to imagine these moments and others in *Our Hospitality* framed in a different way, and you will see how our reaction to Keaton's humor depends on the careful combination of mise-en-scene and framing.

Similarly, in Tati's *Play Time,* mise-en-scene and camera position cooperate to create pictorial jokes (**5.120**). The visual pun issues from the precisely chosen camera angle and distance, as well as from the mise-en-scene: the man's stooping posture and the door handles make him look like a goat. We cannot classify all the non-narrative functions of framing; we can only suggest that camera angle, level, height, and distance have the constant possibility of sharpening our awareness of purely visual qualities.

The Mobile Frame

All of the features of framing we have examined are present in paintings, photographs, comic strips, and other sorts of pictures. All images furnish instances of aspect ratios, in-frame and out-of-frame relations, angle, level, height, and distance

5.120 In *Play Time*, M. Hulot reacts with a start when he notices that a man locking a door seems suddenly to have sprouted horns (the door handles)

5.121 During a shot in Dreyer's *Ordet*, the camera pans right . . .

5.122 . . . to keep the figures in frame as they cross a room.

of the frame's vantage point. But there is one resource of framing that is specific to cinema (and video). In film, it is possible for the frame to *move* with respect to the framed material.

Mobile framing means that the framing of the object changes. The mobile frame changes the camera angle, level, height, or distance *during* the shot. Further, since the framing orients us to the material in the image, we often see ourselves as moving *along with* the frame. Through such framing, we may approach the object or retreat from it, circle it, or move past it.

Types of Mobile Framing We usually refer to the ability of the frame to be mobile as *camera movement*. A mobile frame is usually achieved by moving the camera physically during production. There are several kinds of camera movement, each a specific effect onscreen.

The **pan** (short for *panorama*) movement rotates the camera on a vertical axis. The camera as a whole does not move to a new position. Onscreen, the pan gives the impression of a frame horizontally scanning space. It is as if the camera "turns its head" right or left (**5.121, 5.122**).

The **tilt** movement rotates the camera on a horizontal axis. It is as if the camera's head were swiveling up or down. Again, the entire camera does not change position. Onscreen, the tilt movement yields the impression of unrolling a space from top to bottom or bottom to top (**5.123, 5.124**).

In the **tracking** or **dolly shot,** the camera as a whole does change position, traveling in any direction along the ground—forward, backward, circularly, diagonally, or from side to side (**5.125, 5.126**). Note how the figures remain in the same basic relationship to the frame as they stroll along a sidewalk, while the front of the house that they hope to buy remains visible behind them.

In the **crane shot,** the camera moves above ground level. Typically, it rises or descends, often thanks to a mechanical arm that lifts and lowers it. The mourning scene in *Ivan the Terrible* begins with a crane downward (**5.127, 5.128**). A crane shot may move not only up and down, like an elevator, but forward and backward or from side to side (**5.129, 5.130**). For *The Thin Red Line*, Terence Malick used a crane with a 72-foot arm to let the camera slither over tall grass during battle scenes. Variations of the crane shot are helicopter and airplane shots.

Pans, tilts, tracking shots, and crane shots are the most common framing movements, but virtually any kind of camera movement can be imagined (somersaulting, rolling, and so on). And as we shall see, types of camera movements can be combined.

Camera movements have held an appeal for filmmakers and audiences since the beginnings of cinema. Why? Visually, camera movements have several arresting

"I realized that if I could just get to the really good scripts, I could approach it the way I approach literature—why the camera moves this way because of this motif—and then it became fascinating."

—Jodie Foster, director, *Little Man Tate*

"It's a compulsion of mine to move the camera, and I now know why. It enhances three-dimensionality. It puts you in the space, and if you move the camera the audience becomes aware of the space."

— George Miller, director, *The Road Warrior*

5.123   François Truffaut's *The Bride Wore Black* begins with a tilt down a church spire . . .

5.124   . . . to the church door.

5.125   During this lateral tracking shot in Erich von Stroheim's *Greed,* the camera moves rightward . . .

5.126   . . . along with the two characters.

5.127   In *Ivan the Terrible,* from a high-angle view of the bier, the camera cranes down . . .

5.128   . . . to end with a straight-on framing of Ivan seated at the bier's base.

effects. They often increase information about the space of the image. Objects become sharper and more vivid than in stationary framings. New objects or figures are usually revealed. Tracking shots and crane shots supply continually changing perspectives on passing objects as the frame shifts its orientation. Objects appear more solid and three-dimensional when the camera arcs (that is, tracks along a curved path) around them. Pan and tilt shots present space as continuous, both horizontally and vertically.

Moreover, it is difficult not to see camera movement as a substitute for *our* movement. The objects do not seem to swell or shrink. We seem to approach or retreat from them. We are not, of course, completely fooled. We never forget that we are watching a film in a theater. But camera movement provides several convincing cues for movement through space. Indeed, so powerful are these cues that filmmakers often make camera movements subjective—motivated narratively to represent the view through the eyes of a moving character. That is, camera movement can be a powerful cue that we are watching a point-of-view shot.

In commercial film production today, many camera movements are made with the camera on a dolly. Before the 1970s, it was standard practice to mount the dolly on rails for lengthy movements (hence the term *tracking*). (See 1.33 for a production shot showing an elaborate dolly shot.)

While mounting the camera on tracks is still done today, body-mounted camera units have become common as well. These devices allow the camera to be an extension of the operator's normal walking or running. Servo mechanisms adjust for imbalances and jerkiness, so the camera seems to glide or float. The prototype of the body-worn camera stabilizer is the Steadicam, initially used on *Bound for Glory, Rocky,* and *The Shining.*

A body-worn camera can go places that would be difficult for a dolly. The operator can smoothly follow actors climbing stairs, riding vehicles, and walking great distances **(5.131, 5.132).** Some directors have taken advantage of the Steadicam to create lengthy shots moving through many locales, as in the opening scenes of Brian De Palma's *Bonfire of the Vanities* and Paul Thomas Anderson's *Boogie Nights.*

Sometimes the filmmaker does not want smooth camera movements, preferring a bumpy, jiggling image. Commonly, this sort of image is achieved through use of the **handheld** camera. That is, the operator does not anchor the machine on a tripod or dolly, but instead uses his or her body to act as the support without benefit of compensating equipment **(5.133).** This sort of camera movement became common in the late 1950s, with the growth of the *cinéma vérité* documentary. One of the most famous early handheld traveling shots was in *Primary,* when a cameraman held the camera above his head and followed John F. Kennedy through a milling crowd **(5.134).**

Handheld shots have appeared in many fiction films as well. Because the technique originated in documentary filming, it can lend an air of authenticity to pseudo-documentaries like *The Blair Witch Project.* In other instances, the handheld camera

5.129   At the end of Karel Reisz's *Morgan!* the camera moves diagonally up . . .

5.130   . . . and back to reveal that the hero's apparently innocuous flower garden proclaims his Communist sympathies.

5.131   In Martin Scorsese's *Raging Bull,* the Steadicam follows the protagonist out of his dressing room . . .

5.132   . . . and through a crowd up to the boxing ring.

5.133   Don Pennebaker hand-holds the camera while filming his *Keep on Rocking.*

5.134   John Kennedy greeting a Wisconsin crowd in *Primary.*

5.135   In Samuel Fuller's *The Naked Kiss,* a handheld subjective camera heightens the impact of a fight.

movement functions to create subjective point of view **(5.135).** Sometimes the hand-held shot intensifies a sense of abrupt movement, as if the action were glimpsed on the fly. For *julien donkey-boy,* Harmony Korine used lightweight, bouncy, mini-DV cameras to shoot Julian shuffling through his neighborhood **(5.136).**

A static camera can simulate frame mobility. In animation, the actual camera stays in one position, but by filming individual cels frame by frame, the animator can create the effect of camera movement **(5.137–5.139).** Alternatively, a mobile frame effect can be achieved by photographing a still picture or a stopped frame of film and gradually enlarging or reducing any portion of that image, as is frequently done in optical printing or with CGI. Iris masking can open up to reveal a vista or close down to isolate a detail.

5.136   As Julien walks, the handheld camera's jerky pace complements the explosions of color created by printing video up to 35mm.

5.137   A pan shot simulated by animation in *Peter Pan* begins with Peter and Captain Hook near a mast. Peter swings in to kick Hook . . .

5.138   . . . and the framing pans to follow as the two fly rightward . . .

5.139   . . . across the deck.

The zoom lens can also be used to provide a mobile framing while the camera stays fixed. How can we as viewers distinguish between a zoom and a tracking or craning movement? In general, animation, special effects, and the zoom lens reduce or blow up some portion of the image. Although the tracking shot and the crane shot do enlarge or reduce portions of the frame, this is not *all* that they do. In the genuine camera movement, static objects in different planes pass one another at different rates. We see different sides of objects, and backgrounds gain volume and depth.

In Alain Resnais's *La Guerre est finie,* a tracking shot (**5.140, 5.141**) gives the objects considerable volume. The wall has lost none of its bulk or solidity. Moreover, the street sign has not simply been enlarged. We also see it from a distinctly different angle.

5.140   In *La Guerre est finie,* a street sign tilted slightly up on its right side . . .

In contrast, with a zoom enlargement, the mobile frame does not alter the aspects or positions of the objects filmed. In **5.142** and **5.143,** from Theo Angelopoulos's *Ulysses' Gaze,* a zoom enlarges our view of a large, broken statue of Lenin floating on a barge. Our vantage point on the statue is the same at the end of the shot as at the beginning: The top of the statue is still seen against the bottom of a row of small

5.141   . . . is tilted up distinctly at the left by the end of the track-in.

5.142   A distant view of a statue on a barge in *Ulysses' Gaze* . . .

5.143   . . . is enlarged by a zoom-in.

trees, and its feet are in exactly the same place in relation to the railing on the ship's prow. As the zoom occurs, the barge gradually looks closer to the line of trees than it had at the beginning. In sum, when the camera moves, we sense our own movement through the space. In a zoom, a bit of the space seems magnified or demagnified.

So far, we have isolated these different sorts of mobile framings in fairly pure states. But filmmakers frequently combine such framings within a single shot: The camera may track and pan at the same time or crane up while zooming. Still, every instance can be identified as a combination of the basic types.

Functions of Frame Mobility   Our catalogue of the types of mobile framings is of little use without a consideration of how such framing strategies function systematically within films. How does mobile framing relate to cinematic space and time? How do mobile framings create patterns of their own? In short, how does mobile framing interact with the form of the film?

1. *The mobile frame and space*

The mobile frame affects onscreen and offscreen space considerably, as we've already seen in our earlier example from *Jezebel* (5.85–5.88). After the hand with the glass intrudes into close-up, the camera tracks back to frame the man standing in the foreground. The mobile frame also continually affects the angle, level, height, or distance of the framing. A crane up may change the angle from a low one to a high one; a track-in may change the distance from long shot to close-up.

We can ask several questions about how the mobile frame relates to space. Do the frame's movements depend on figure movement? For example, one of the commonest functions of camera movement is **reframing.** If a character moves in relation to another character, often the frame will slightly pan or tilt to adjust to the movement. In *His Girl Friday,* director Howard Hawks strives to balance his compositions through reframing **(5.144–5.146).** Since reframings are motivated by figure movement, they tend to be relatively unnoticeable. When you do start to notice them, you may be surprised at how frequently they appear. Almost any modern film is constantly reframing characters in conversation scenes.

Reframing is only one way that the mobile frame may depend on figure movement. The camera may also displace itself in order to follow figures or moving objects. A camera movement that is more than just a reframing and that follows a figure's movement is called—logically enough—a **following shot** (see 5.203–5.204, 5.210–5.211, and 5.215–5.224). A pan may keep a racing car centered, a tracking shot may follow a character from room to room, or a crane shot may pursue a rising balloon. In such cases, frame mobility functions primarily to keep our attention fastened on the subject of the shot, and it subordinates itself to that subject's movement.

The mobile frame can move independently of the figures, too. Often the camera moves away from the characters to reveal something of significance to the narrative.

> "I kept wondering, 'Can people talk this much in a feature film and anybody care?' And so I had to go through every moment in those dialogue scenes and look for the little events I would treat as large events. Like the ringing of a phone or the blinds being opened. . . . I had to treat those as fairly major events and have the moves of the camera be motivated by them, so that it would be organic to the scene yet still visually interesting."
>
> — John Patrick Shanley, writer and director, *Doubt*

CONNECT TO THE BLOG
One common function of tracking shots is to follow actors in conversation, as we discuss in "Walk the talk."
See www.davidbordwell.net/blog/?p=382.

5.144   In *His Girl Friday,* when Hildy crosses from the left . . .

5.145   . . . to sit on a desk, the camera pans right to reframe her . . .

5.146   . . . and when Walter swivels his chair to face her, the camera reframes slightly leftward.

A camera movement can point out an overlooked clue, a sign that comments on the action, an unnoticed shadow, or a clutching hand. The moving camera can establish a locale the characters will eventually enter. This is what happens at the start of Otto Preminger's *Laura,* when the camera glides through Waldo Lydecker's sitting room, establishing him as a man of wealth and artistic tastes, before revealing the detective MacPherson. Similarly, at the beginning of *Back to the Future,* the camera prowls through Doc's empty house, hinting at his character and the narrative to come. In Jean Renoir's *Crime of M. Lange,* the moving camera characterizes Lange by leaving him and panning around to survey his room (5.147–5.151). Lange is shown to be a fantasist, living in the world of Western lore he draws on for his cowboy stories.

Whether dependent on figure movement or independent of it, the mobile frame can profoundly affect how we perceive the space within the frame and offscreen. Different sorts of camera movements create different treatments of space. In *Last Year at Marienbad,* Resnais often tracks into corridors and through doorways, turning a fashionable resort hotel into a maze. Alfred Hitchcock has produced some of the most famous single-camera movements in film history. One track-and-crane shot moves from a high-angle long shot of a ballroom over the heads of the dancers to an extreme close-up of a drummer's blinking eyes (*Young and Innocent*). In *Vertigo,* an especially tricky combination track-*out* and zoom-*in* plastically distorts the shot's perspective and conveys the protagonist's dizziness. The device reappears in Spielberg's *Jaws,* when Sheriff Brody at the beach suddenly realizes that the shark has attacked a child. Simultaneously tracking and zooming in opposite directions has become common in modern Hollywood filmmaking (what director Sam Raimi calls the "warp-o cam"). In films such as *The Red and the White,* Miklós Jancsó specialized in lengthy camera movements that roam among groups of people moving across a plain. His shots use all of the resources of tracking, panning, craning, zooming, and racking focus to sculpt ever-changing spatial relations.

5.147   In *The Crime of M. Lange,* although the camera begins on Lange at work . . .

5.148   . . . it soon leaves him to show his cowboy pistols and hat . . .

5.149   . . . keeps going to show a map with Arizona outlined . . .

5.150   . . . pans past more guns . . .

5.151   . . . before returning to the excited author writing his Western tales.

All of these examples illustrate various ways in which frame mobility affects our sense of space. Of any mobile framing, we can ask, How does it function to reveal or conceal offscreen space? Is the frame mobility dependent on figure movement or independent of it? What particular trajectory does the camera pursue? Such questions will best be answered by considering how spatial effects of the camera movement function with respect to the film's overall form.

2. *The mobile frame and time*

Frame mobility involves time as well as space, and filmmakers have realized that our sense of duration and rhythm is affected by the mobile frame. The importance of duration in camera movement, for example, can be sensed by comparing two Japanese directors, Yasujiro Ozu and Kenji Mizoguchi. Ozu prefers short camera movements in a single direction, as in *Early Summer* and *The Flavor of Green Tea over Rice.* Mizoguchi, alternatively, cultivates the leisurely, drawn-out tracking shot, often combining it with panning.

Since a camera movement consumes time on screen, it can create an arc of expectation and fulfillment. If the camera pans quickly from an event, we may be prompted to wonder what has happened. If the camera abruptly tracks back to show us something in the foreground that we had not expected, as in our earlier *Jezebel* example (5.85–5.88), we are taken by surprise. If the camera slowly moves in on a detail, gradually enlarging it but delaying the fulfillment of our expectations, the camera movement has contributed to suspense. In the pan shot across M. Lange's study, Renoir makes us wonder why the camera strays from the main character, then answers the question by indicating Lange's fascination with the American West. Later in this chapter, we shall examine how our expectations are manipulated over time in the opening camera movements of Welles's *Touch of Evil.*

The velocity of frame mobility is important, too. A zoom or a camera movement may be relatively slow or fast. Richard Lester's *A Hard Day's Night* and *Help!* started a fad in the 1960s for very fast zoom-ins and -outs. In comparison, one of the most impressive early camera movements, D. W. Griffith's monumental crane shot in Belshazzar's feast in *Intolerance,* gains majesty and suspense through its inexorably slow descent toward the immense Babylonian set (4.12).

Sometimes the speed of the mobile framing functions rhythmically. In Will Hindle's *Pastorale d'été,* a gentle, bouncing beat is created by zooming in and slightly tilting up and down in time to Honegger's music. Often musical films make use of the speed of camera movement to underline qualities of a song or dance. During the "Broadway Rhythm" number in *Singin' in the Rain,* the camera cranes quickly back from Gene Kelly several times, and the speed of the movement is timed to accentuate the lyrics. Frame velocity can also create expressive qualities—a camera movement can be fluid, staccato, hesitant, and so forth. The entire plot of *Cloverfield* is presented as the video record of a monster's attack on Manhattan. At many points, the operator whips the camera around to capture a shocking incident, and our anxiety is intensified by the sudden speed of the panning movement **(5.152, 5.153).** In short, the duration and speed of the mobile frame can significantly control our perception of the shot over time.

3. *Patterns of mobile framing*

The mobile frame can create its own specific motifs within a film. For example, Hitchcock's *Psycho* begins and ends with a forward movement of the frame. In the film's first three shots, the camera pans right and then zooms in on a building in a cityscape **(5.154).** Two forward movements finally carry us under a window blind and into the darkness of a cheap hotel room **(5.155–5.157).** The camera's movement inward, the penetration of an interior, is repeated throughout the film, often motivated as a subjective point of view as when various characters move deeper and deeper into Norman Bates's mansion. The next-to-last shot of the film shows Norman sitting against a blank white wall, while we hear his interior monologue

"One thing I hate in films is when the camera starts circling characters. If three people are sitting at a table talking, you'll often see the camera circling them. I can't explain why, but I find it totally fake."

— Takeshi Kitano, director, *Sonatine*

5.152   *Cloverfield:* As the young partygoers run out into the street, their video camera records an explosion, and a whip pan to the right blurs the action.

5.153   While the framing becomes fixed again, we see that the blurry movement was roughly following the head of the Statue of Liberty rolling down the street.

5.154   The opening shot of *Psycho.*

5.155   The second shot concentrates on one building . . .

5.156   . . . as the camera moves lower and closer to a window . . .

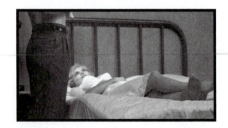

5.157   . . . and reveals the heroine and her boyfriend in a lunchtime tryst.

5.158   *Psycho*'s next-to-last shot begins at a distance from Norman . . .

5.159   . . . and moves in so that we see his expression as we hear his thoughts.

(5.158). The camera again moves forward into a close-up of his face **(5.159).** This shot is the climax of the forward movement initiated at the start of the film; the film has traced a movement into Norman's mind. Another film that relies heavily on a pattern of forward, penetrating movements is *Citizen Kane,* which depicts the same inexorable drive toward the revelation of a character's secret.

Other kinds of movements can repeat and develop across a film. Max Ophuls's *Lola Montès* uses both 360° tracking shots and constant upward and downward

5.160 A can used as a signal is initially seen sitting on a shelf . . .

5.161 . . . then is pulled over. It lands on a pillow and so makes no sound . . .

5.162 . . . and the camera pans left to reveal that the characters have not noticed it.

crane shots to contrast the circus arena with the world of Lola's past. In Michael Snow's ←→ (usually called *Back and Forth*), the constant panning to and fro across a classroom, Ping-Pong fashion, determines the basic formal pattern of the film. It comes as a surprise when, near the very end, the movement suddenly becomes a repeated tilting up and down. In these and many other films, the mobile frame sets up marked repetitions and variations.

Functions of Mobile Framing: Grand Illusion and Wavelength By way of summary, we can look at two contrasting films that illustrate possible relations of the mobile frame to narrative form. One uses the mobile frame in order to strengthen and support the narrative, whereas the other subordinates narrative form to an overall frame mobility.

Jean Renoir's *Grand Illusion* is a war film in which we almost never see the war. Heroic charges and doomed battalions, the staple of the genre, are absent. World War I remains obstinately offscreen. Instead, Renoir concentrates on life in a German POW camp to suggest how relations between nations and social classes are affected by war. The prisoners Maréchal and Boeldieu are both French; Rauffenstein is a German officer. Yet the aristocrat Boeldieu has more in common with Rauffenstein than with the mechanic Maréchal. The film's narrative form traces the death of the Boeldieu-Rauffenstein upper class and the precarious survival of Maréchal and his pal Rosenthal—their flight to Elsa's farm, their interlude of peace there, and their final escape back to France and presumably back to the war.

Within this framework, camera movement has several functions, all directly supportive of the narrative. First, and most typical, is its tendency to adhere to figure movement. When a character or vehicle moves, Renoir often pans or tracks to follow. The camera follows Maréchal and Rosenthal walking together after their escape; it tracks back when the prisoners are drawn to the window by the sound of marching Germans below. But it is the movements of the camera *independent* of figure movement that make the film more unusual.

When the camera moves on its own in *Grand Illusion,* we are conscious of it actively interpreting the action, creating suspense or giving us information that the characters do not have. For example, in one scene, a prisoner is digging in an escape tunnel and tugs a string signaling that he needs to be pulled out **(5.160)**. Independent camera movement builds suspense by showing that the other characters have missed the signal and do not realize that he is suffocating **(5.161, 5.162)**. Camera movement thus helps create a somewhat unrestricted narration.

Sometimes the camera is such an active agent that Renoir used repeated camera movements to create patterns of narrative significance. One such pattern is the movement to link characters with details of their environment. Often a sequence begins with a close-up of some detail, and the camera moves back to anchor this detail in its larger spatial and narrative context **(5.163, 5.164)**.

5.163 Renoir begins the scene of Boeldieu and Maréchal discussing escape plans by framing a close-up of a caged squirrel . . .

5.164 . . . before tracking back to reveal the men beside the cage, creating a clear narrative parallel.

5.165   As Rauffenstein moves to the geranium in the window . . .

5.166   . . . Renoir tracks in to a close shot of the flower as he cuts it.

More complicated is the scene of the Christmas celebration at Elsa's that begins with a close-up of the crèche and tracks back to show, in several stages, the interplay of reactions among the characters. Such camera movements are not simply decoration; beginning on a scenic detail before moving to the larger context makes narrative points economically, constantly emphasizing relationships among elements of Renoir's mise-en-scene. So does the rarer track-in to a detail at the *end* of a scene, as when after Boeldieu's death, Rauffenstein cuts the geranium, the one flower in the prison (**5.165, 5.166**).

Characters are tied to their environment by some even more ambitious moving-camera shots. These stress important narrative parallels. For example, tracking shots compare actions in two officers' bars—one French (**5.167–5.169**), one Ger-

5.167   In the first scene, as Maréchal leaves the French officers' bar . . .

5.168   . . . Renoir pans and tracks left from the door to reveal pinups (just coming into the frame at the right) . . .

5.169   . . . and a poster.

5.170   One scene later, in the German officers' bar, a similar camera movement, this time toward the right, leaves the characters . . .

5.171   . . . and explores on its own . . .

5.172   . . . discovering some similar decorations.

5.173   Renoir begins on a crucifix and . . .

5.174   . . . tilts down to a military portrait on an altar, underlining the irony of a chapel commandeered as a bivouac.

5.175   The camera tracks past whips, spurs, and swords . . .

5.176   . . . to a servant preparing Rauffenstein's gloves.

5.177   He then walks away from the camera to close a window before returning . . .

5.178   . . . into the foreground as the camera pans left and tracks back to reveal . . .

5.179   . . . a breakfast table . . .

5.180   . . . at which Rauffenstein is revealed to be sitting.

man **(5.170–5.172)**. Through his camera movements, Renoir indicates a similarity between the two warring sides, blurring their national differences and stressing common desires.

Or consider how two parallel tracking shots compare the war of the aristocrats and the war of the lower-class people. We are introduced to Rauffenstein's new position as commander of a POW camp through a lengthy tracking shot **(5.173–5.180)**. During this movement, Renoir presents, wordlessly, the military mystique of grace on the battlefield that characterizes the aristocrat's war.

Late in the film, however, a parallel shot criticizes this one **(5.181–5.183)**. Elsa's war has none of Rauffenstein's glory, and that is conveyed chiefly through a parallel created by the repeated camera movement. Moreover, these camera movements work together with mise-en-scene, as the narrative parallel is reinforced by the subtle use of objects as motifs—the crucifixes in 5.173 and 5.183, the photographs in

5.181   This shot also begins on an object, a photograph of Elsa's dead husband . . .

5.182   . . . before tracking left past Elsa, who remarks, "Now the table is too large" . . .

5.183   . . . to reveal the kitchen table, where her daughter Lotte sits alone.

5.184   As the lead "female" singer whips off his wig and requests the "Marseillaise" from the musicians . . .

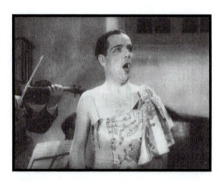

5.185   . . . the camera moves right as the singer turns toward the audience . . .

5.186   . . . and farther right as others onstage sing along.

5.187   A tilt down shows two worried German guards . . .

5.188   . . . and a track back to the left reveals a row of French prisoners in the audience on their feet, singing.

5.189   The camera tracks forward past them to the musicians and singer again . . .

5.190   . . . then pans quickly left to face the entire audience.

5.174 and 5.181, and the tables that end both shots. (Note the subtle use of the empty chairs upended on the table to reinforce the absence of Elsa's husband.)

Moving the camera independently of figure movement also links characters with one another. Again and again in the POW camp, the camera moves to join one man to his comrades, spatially indicating their shared condition. When the prisoners ransack the collection of women's clothes, one man decides to dress up in them. When he appears, a stillness falls over the men. Renoir tracks silently over the prisoners' faces, each one registering a reticent longing.

A more elaborate linking movement occurs in the scene of the prison vaudeville show, when the men learn that the French have recaptured a city. Renoir presents the shot as a celebration of spatial unity, with the camera moving among the men as they begin defiantly to sing the "Marseillaise" **(5.184–5.190).** This complex

5.191   As the Germans realize that Maréchal and Rosenthal have crossed over into Switzerland . . .

5.192   . . . Renoir pans to the right across the invisible border . . .

5.193   . . . to the two escapees, tiny dots in the huge landscape.

camera movement circulates freely among the prisoners, suggesting their patriotic courage and unity in disobeying their captors.

In Elsa's cottage as well as in the prison, camera movement links characters. After feeding a cow, Maréchal enters the house, and a pan with him reveals Elsa scrubbing the floor. The culmination of the linking movement comes near the film's end, when Renoir pans from the Germans on one side of the border (**5.191**) to the distant French escapees on the other (**5.192, 5.193**). Even on this scale, Renoir's camera refuses to honor national divisions.

The French film critic André Bazin remarked: "Jean Renoir found a way to reveal the hidden meaning of people and things without destroying the unity that is natural to them." By placing emphasis and making comparisons, the mobile frame in *Grand Illusion* becomes as important as the mise-en-scene. The camera movements carve into space to create connections that enrich the film's narrative form.

In Michael Snow's experimental film *Wavelength,* the relation of narrative to the mobile frame is quite different. Instead of supporting narrative form, frame mobility dominates narrative, even deflecting our attention from events. The film begins with a long-shot framing of a loft apartment, facing one wall and window (**5.194**). In the course of the film, the camera zooms in abruptly a short distance and then holds that framing. It zooms in a bit more and then holds that (**5.195**). And so it goes throughout the film's 45-minute length. By the end, a photograph of ocean waves on the distant wall fills the frame in close-up.

Thus *Wavelength* is structured primarily around a single kind of frame mobility—the zoom-in. Its pattern of progression and development is not a narrative one, but one of exploration, through deliberately limited means, of how the zoom transforms the space of the loft. The sudden zooms create frequent abrupt shifts of perspective relations. In excluding parts of the room, the zoom-in also magnifies and flattens what we see; every change of focal length gives us a new set of spatial relations. The zoom places more and more space offscreen. The sound track, for the most part, reinforces the basic formal progression by emitting a single humming tone that rises consistently in pitch as the zoom magnifies the space more and more.

Within *Wavelength*'s basic pattern, though, there are two contrasting systems. The first is a series of filtered tints that plays across the image as abstract fields of color. These tints often work against the depth represented in the shot of the loft.

A second system evokes a sketchy narrative. At various intervals, characters enter the loft and carry on certain activities (talking, listening to the radio, making phone calls). There is even a mysterious death (a body lies on the floor in **5.196**). But these events remain unexplained in cause–effect terms and inconclusive as to closure (although at the film's end we do hear a sound that resembles a police siren). Furthermore, none of these actions swerves the mobile framing from its predetermined course. The jerkily shifting and halting zoom continues, even when it

5.194   Early in *Wavelength,* much of the apartment is visible.

5.195   Near the end, the sporadic zoom-ins have made details of the far wall visible.

5.196   The zoom-ins in *Wavelength* will soon eliminate the body on the floor from the frame.

excludes important narrative information. Thus *Wavelength* pulls in bits and pieces of narrative, but these fragments of action remain secondary, operating within the temporal progression of the zoom.

From the standpoint of the viewer's experience, *Wavelength*'s use of frame mobility arouses, delays, and gratifies unusual expectations. What plot there is briefly arouses curiosity (What are the people up to? What has led to the man's death, if he does die?) and surprise (the apparent murder). But in general, a story-centered suspense is replaced by a *stylistic* suspense: What will the zoom eventually frame? From this standpoint, the colored tints and even the plot work with the spasmodic qualities of the zoom to delay the forward progress of the framing. When the zoom finally reveals its target, our stylistic anticipations have come to fulfillment. The film's title stands revealed as a multiple pun, referring not only to the steadily rising pitch of the sound track but also to the distance that the zoom had to cross in order to reveal the photo—a "wave length."

Grand Illusion and *Wavelength* illustrate, in different ways, how frame mobility can guide and shape our perception of a film's space and time. Frame mobility may be motivated by larger formal purposes, as in Renoir's film, or it may itself become the principal formal concern, motivating other systems, as in Snow's film. By examining how filmmakers use the mobile frame within specific contexts, we can gain a fuller understanding of how our experience of a film is created.

Duration of the Image: The Long Take

In our consideration of the film image, we have emphasized spatial qualities—how photographic transformations can alter the properties of the image, how framing defines the image for our attention. But cinema is an art of time as well as space, and we have seen already how mise-en-scene and frame mobility operate in temporal as well as spatial dimensions. What we need to consider now is how the duration of the shot affects our understanding of it.

There is a tendency to consider the shot as recording real duration. Suppose a runner takes three seconds to clear a hurdle. If we film the runner, our projected film will also consume three seconds—or so the assumption goes. One film theorist, André Bazin, made it a major tenet of his aesthetic that cinema records real time. But the relation of shot duration to the time taken by the filmed event is not so simple.

First, obviously, the duration of the event on the screen may be manipulated during filming or post-production, as we discussed earlier in this chapter. Slow-motion or fast-motion techniques may present the runner's jump in 20 seconds or 2. Second, narrative films often permit no simple equivalence of real duration with screen duration, even within one shot. As Chapter 3 pointed out (p. 86), story duration will usually differ considerably from plot duration and screen duration.

5.197   A scene in *The Only Son* moves from night . . .

5.198   . . . to day in a single shot.

Consider a shot from Yasujiro Ozu's *The Only Son*. It is well past midnight, and we have just seen a family awake and talking; this shot shows a dim corner of the family's apartment, with none of the characters onscreen (**5.197**). But soon the light changes. The sun is rising. By the end of the shot, it is morning (**5.198**). This transitional shot consumes about a minute of screen time. It plainly does not record the duration of the story events; that duration would be at least five hours. To put it another way, by manipulating screen duration, the film's plot has condensed a story duration of several hours into a minute or so.

Other films use tracking movements to compress longer passages of time in a continuous shot (**5.199, 5.200**). The final shot of *Signs* moves away from an autumn view through a window (itself an echo of the opening shot's track-back from a window) and through a room, to reveal a winter landscape outside another window. Months of story time have passed during the tracking movement.

5.199 In Roger Michell's *Notting Hill,* the protagonist's walk through the Portobello street market moves through autumn . . .

5.200 . . . winter, and spring.

Functions of the Long Take

Every shot has some measurable screen duration, but in the history of cinema, directors have varied considerably in their choice of short or lengthy shots. In general, early cinema (1895–1905) tended to rely on shots of fairly long duration, since there was often only one shot in each film. With the emergence of continuity editing in the period 1905–1916, shots became shorter. In the late 1910s and early 1920s, an American film would have an average shot length of about 5 seconds. After the coming of sound, the average stretched to about 10 seconds.

Throughout the history of the cinema, some filmmakers have consistently preferred to use shots of greater duration than the average. In various countries in the mid-1930s, directors began to experiment with very lengthy shots. These filmmakers' unusually lengthy shots—**long takes,** as they're called—represented a powerful creative resource.

Long take is not the same as *long shot,* which refers to the apparent distance between camera and object. As we saw in examining film production (pp. 16–17), a *take* is one run of the camera that records a single shot. Calling a shot of notable length a long take rather than a long shot prevents ambiguity, since the latter term refers to a distanced framing, not to shot duration. In the films of Jean Renoir, Kenji Mizoguchi, Orson Welles, Carl Dreyer, Miklós Jancsó, Hou Hsiao-hsien, and Bèla Tarr, a shot may go on for several minutes. It would be impossible to analyze these films without an awareness of how the long take can contribute to form and style. One long take in Andy Warhol's *My Hustler* follows the seductive exchange of two

5.201   A long take in *My Hustler.*

5.202   The final three-minute shot of *Hour of the Furnaces.*

CONNECT TO THE BLOG
Both *There Will Be Blood* and *The Most Beautiful* contain subtle staging in two unmoving long takes. We compare them in "Hands (and faces) across the table," at

www.davidbordwell.net/blog/?p=1944.

gay men as they groom themselves in a bathroom **(5.201)**. The shot, which runs for about 30 minutes, constitutes much of the film's second half.

Usually, we can regard the long take as an alternative to a series of shots. The director may choose to present a scene in one or a few long takes or to present the scene through several shorter shots. When an entire scene is rendered in only one shot, the long take is known by the French term *plan-séquence,* or *sequence shot.*

Most filmmakers use the long take selectively. One scene may rely heavily on editing, while another is presented in a long take. This permits the director to associate certain aspects of narrative or non-narrative form with the different stylistic options. A vivid instance occurs in the first part of Fernando Solanas and Octavio Getino's *Hour of the Furnaces.* Most of the film relies on editing of newsreel and staged shots to describe how European and North American ideologies penetrate developing nations. But the last shot of the film is a slow zoom-in to a photograph of the corpse of Che Guevara, symbol of guerrilla resistance to imperialism. Solanas made the shot a long take, holding it for three minutes to force the viewer to dwell on the cost of resistance **(5.202)**.

Alternatively, the filmmaker may decide to build the entire film out of long takes. Hitchcock's *Rope* is famous for containing only 11 shots, most running between 4 and 10 minutes. Similarly, each scene in *Winterwind, Agnus Dei, Red Psalm,* and other films by Miklós Jancsó is a single shot. In such cases, the long take becomes a large-scale part of a film. And in such a context, editing can have great force. After a seven- or eight-minute shot, an elliptical cut can prove quite disorienting. Gus van Sant's *Elephant* traces events around a high-school shooting rampage, and it presents most scenes in very long takes following students through the hallways. Moreover, *Elephant's* plot doesn't present the events in chronological order. The narration flashes back to show other school days, the boys' lives at home, and their preparations for the killings. So when a cut interrupts a long take, the audience must reflect for a moment to determine how the new shot's action fits into the plot. The effect of the editing is unusually harsh, because the cuts tend to break the smooth rhythm of the sustained traveling shots **(5.203–5.205)**.

Could a feature-length movie consist of one long take? Many directors have dreamed of this possibility, but the lengths of film reels have prevented it. A 35mm camera reel typically runs for only 11 minutes, so Hitchcock tried to hide some of *Rope's* obligatory cuts. Extended 16mm reels of the type Warhol used in *My Hustler* **(5.201)** can run up to 30 minutes. With digital video, however, it is possible to shoot for over two hours on a single tape, and the Russian director Aleksander Sokurov

5.203   In a shot lasting two minutes, the camera follows Michelle into the library, where she starts reshelving books. Many of the long takes in *Elephant* frame the walking characters from behind. This conceals their facial expressions from us and emphasizes the school environment they move through.

5.204   Michelle turns as we hear a rifle being cocked.

5.205   We expect a reverse shot to reveal what she sees. Instead, we get a flashback to earlier that day when the two boys showered together before going to school on their deadly mission.

5.206   In *Russian Ark,* one episode takes place in the palace theater, with Catherine the Great pronouncing the rehearsal satisfactory.

5.207   An hour or so later, still within the same shot, hundreds of aristocrats and officers descend a staircase toward the impending devastation of the Russian Revolution.

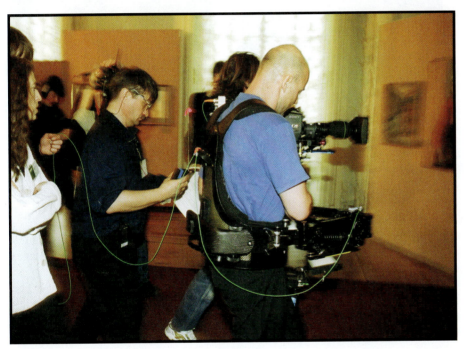

5.208   Crew members moving through the Hermitage Museum, filming *Russian Ark* with a digital camera mounted on a Steadicam (photography by Alexander Belenkiy).

seized this opportunity in his *Russian Ark.* The film consists of a single shot nearly 90 minutes long, as a Steadicam follows over 2000 actors in period costume through St. Petersburg's immense Winter Palace. *Russian Ark* takes us through several eras of Russian history, culminating in a stupendous ballroom dance and a crowd drifting off into a wintry night **(5.206–5.208).** Sokurov rehearsed *Russian Ark* for several months and completed the take used in the film on the fourth try.

The Long Take and the Mobile Frame

The *Elephant* example suggests that a long take is likely to rely on camera movement. Panning, tracking, craning, or zooming can be used to present continually changing vantage points that are comparable in some ways to the shifts of view supplied by editing.

Very often, frame mobility breaks the long-take shot into significant smaller units. In Mizoguchi's *Sisters of Gion,* one long take shows a young woman,

5.209 In *Sisters of Gion*, the long take begins with Omocha and the businessman seated. The camera follows as . . .

5.210 . . . she moves to the opposite end of the room . . .

5.211 . . . and sits at a small table facing him.

5.212 A second phase of the shot begins as she begins to appeal to his sympathy and he moves to the table . . .

5.213 . . . and sits down to console her.

5.214 Finally, the camera moves into a tighter shot as she sits beside him and he succumbs to her advances.

Omocha, luring a businessman into becoming her patron (**5.209–5.214**). Though there is no cutting, the camera and figure movements demarcate important stages of the scene's action.

As in this example, long takes tend to be framed in medium or long shots. The camera lingers on a fairly dense visual field, and the spectator has more opportunity to scan the shot for particular points of interest. This is recognized by Steven Spielberg, a director who has occasionally exploited lengthy takes:

> I'd love to see directors start trusting the audience to be the film editor with their eyes, the way you are sometimes with a stage play, where the audience selects who they would choose to look at while a scene is being played. . . . There's so much cutting and so many close-ups being shot today I think directly as an influence from television.

As we saw in the previous chapter, however, the director can guide the audience's scanning of the frame through all of the technical resources of mise-en-scene. This is another way of saying that using the long take often puts more emphasis on performance, setting, lighting, and other mise-en-scene factors.

The example from *Sisters of Gion* illustrates another important feature of the long take. Mizoguchi's shot reveals a complete internal logic—a beginning, middle, and end. As a part of a film, the long take can have its own formal pattern, its own development, its own trajectory and shape. Suspense develops; we start to ask how the shot will continue and when it will end.

The classic example of how the long take can constitute a formal pattern in its own right is the opening sequence of Welles's *Touch of Evil* (**5.215–5.226**). This opening shot makes plain most of the features of the long take. It offers an alternative to building the sequence out of many shots, and it stresses the cut that finally comes (occurring at the sound of the explosion of the car).

5.215 The opening shot of *Touch of Evil* begins with a close-up of a hand setting the timer of a bomb.

5.216 The camera tracks immediately right to follow first the shadow . . .

5.217 . . . and then the figure of an unknown assassin planting the bomb in a car.

5.218 The camera then cranes up to a high angle as the assassin flees and the victims arrive and set out in the car.

5.219 As the camera rounds the corner, it rejoins the car and tracks back to follow it.

5.220 The car passes Vargas and his wife, Susan, and the camera starts to follow them, losing the car and tracking diagonally backward with the couple through the crowd.

5.221 The camera tracks backward until both the occupants of the car and Susan and Vargas meet again . . .

5.222 . . . and a brief scene with the border guard ensues.

5.223 After tracking left with the car, the camera again encounters Susan and Vargas and tracks forward toward them . . .

5.224 . . . bringing them into medium shot as they begin to kiss.

5.225 Their embrace is interrupted by the offscreen sound of an explosion, and they turn to look leftward.

5.226 The next shot zooms in to show the car in flames.

Most important, the shot has its own internal pattern of development. We expect that the bomb shown at the beginning will explode at some point, and we wait for that explosion through the duration of the long take. The shot establishes the geography of the scene (the border between Mexico and the United States). The camera movement, alternately picking up the car and the walking couple, weaves together two lines of narrative cause and effect that intersect at the border station. Vargas and Susan are thus drawn into the action involving the bombing. Our expectation is fulfilled when the end of the shot coincides with the explosion (offscreen) of the bomb. The shot has guided our response by taking us through a suspenseful development.

The long take can present, in a single chunk of time, a complex pattern of events moving toward a goal, and this ability shows that shot duration can be as important to the image as photographic qualities and framing are.

SUMMARY

The film shot is a very complex unit. Mise-en-scene fills the image with material, arranging setting, lighting, costume, and staging within the formal context of the total film. Within that formal context, the filmmaker also controls the cinematographic qualities of the shot—how the image is photographed and framed, how long the image lasts on the screen.

You can sensitize yourself to these cinematographic qualities in much the same way that you worked on mise-en-scene. Trace the progress of a single technique—say, camera distance—through an entire scene. Notice when a shot begins and ends, observing how the long take may function to shape the film's form. Watch for camera movements, especially those that follow the action (since those are usually the hardest to notice). Once you are aware of cinematographic qualities, you can move to an understanding of their various possible functions within the total film.

Film art offers still other possibilities for choice and control. Chapters 4 and 5 focused on the shot. The filmmaker may also juxtapose one shot with another through editing, and that's the subject of Chapter 6.

WHERE TO GO FROM HERE

General Works

The standard reference book on cinematography is Stephen H. Burum, ed., *The American Cinematographer Manual,* 9th ed. (Hollywood: American Society of Cinematographers, 2007). Other good sources are Kris Malkiewicz, *Cinematography,* 3d ed. (New York: Fireside, 2005), and Paul Wheeler, *Practical Cinematography,* 2d ed. (Boston: Focal Press, 2005). On digital cinematography, see Scott Billups, *Digital Moviemaking 3.0* (Los Angeles: Michael Wiese Productions, 2008), and Paul Wheeler, *High Definition Cinematography,* 2d ed. (Boston: Focal Press, 2007). A monthly magazine, *American Cinematographer,* publishes detailed articles on current cinematography around the world.

Cinematographers can be articulate about their craft. See the conversations in Vincent LoBrutto, *Principal Photography: Interviews with Feature Film Cinematographers* (Westport, CT: Praeger, 1999); Pauline Rogers, *Contemporary Cinematographers on Their Art* (Boston: Focal Press, 1999); Benjamin Bergery, *Reflections: Twenty-One Cinematographers at Work* (Hollywood: ASC Press, 2002);

and Peter Ettedgui, *Cinematography: Screencraft* (Hove, England: RotoVision, 1998).

In the Rogers collection, Dean Cundey recalls that the camera movements in *Who Framed Roger Rabbit?* posed problems for adding animation. "If Roger was to go from one part of the room to another, hopping onto a chair, we had to find a way for the camera operator to track that movement. We developed full-size rubber characters to stage the action. The operator could then see movement in real time. He would associate movement with dialogue."

Alternative points of view on cinematography may be found in Stan Brakhage, "A Moving Picture Giving and Taking Book," in *Brakhage Scrapbook: Collected Writings 1964–1980,* ed. Robert A. Haller (New Paltz, NY: Documentext, 1982), pp. 53–77, and Dziga Vertov, *Kino-Eye: The Writings of Dziga Vertov,* ed. Annette Michelson (Berkeley: University of California Press, 1984).

Color Versus Black and White

Today most films are shot on color stock, and most viewers have come to expect that movies will be in color. At many points in film history, however, color and black-and-white film have been used to carry different meanings. In 1930s and 1940s American cinema, color tended to be reserved for fantasies (for example, *The Wizard of Oz*), historical films or films set in exotic locales (*Becky Sharp, Blood and Sand*), or lavish musicals (*Meet Me in St. Louis*). Black and white was then considered more realistic. But now that most films are in color, filmmakers can call on black and white to suggest a historical period (as witnessed by two such different films as Straub and Huillet's *Chronicle of Anna Magdalena Bach* and Tim Burton's *Ed Wood*). Such rules of thumb as "color for realism" have no universal validity; as always, it is a matter of context, the function of color or black-and-white tonalities within a specific film.

A basic history is R. T. Ryan, *A History of Motion Picture Color Technology* (New York: Focal Press, 1977). The most influential early process is considered in Fred E. Basten's *Glorious Technicolor: The Movies' Magic Rainbow* (Camarillo, CA: Technicolor, 2005). See also Scott Higgins, *Harnessing the Technicolor Rainbow: Color Design in the 1930s* (Austin: University of Texas Press, 2007). Len Lye explains the elaborate process behind the color design of *Rainbow Dance* in Wystan Curnow and Roger Horrocks, eds., *Figures of Motion: Len Lye/Selected Writings* (Auckland: Auckland University Press, 1984), pp. 47–49.

Film theorists have debated whether color film is artistically less pure than black and white. One argument against color may be found in Rudolf Arnheim, *Film as Art* (Berkeley: University of California Press, 1957). Arnheim's argument is disputed by V. F. Perkins in *Film as Film* (Baltimore: Penguin, 1972).

Special-Effects Cinematography

Part of the reason that major film studios tout themselves as "magic factories" is that special-effects cinematography demands the complexity and expense that only a big firm can support. Special effects require the time, patience, and rehearsal afforded by control over mise-en-scène. It is, then, no surprise that Méliès, the first person to exploit fully the possibilities of studio filmmaking, excelled at special-effects cinematography. Nor is it surprising that when UFA, the gigantic German firm of the 1920s, became the best-equipped film studio in Europe, it invested heavily in new special-effects processes. Similarly, as Hollywood studios grew from the mid-1910s on, so did their special-effects departments. Engineers, painters, photographers, and set designers collaborated to contrive fantastic visual novelties. In these magic factories, most of the history of special effects has been made.

But such firms were not motivated by sheer curiosity. The costs of elaborate back projection and matte work were good investments. First, expensive as they were, such tricks often saved money in the long run. Instead of building a huge set, one could photograph the actors through a glass with the setting painted on it. Instead of taking players to the desert, one could film them against a back projection

of the pyramids. Second, special effects made certain film genres possible. The historical epic—whether set in Rome, Babylon, or Jerusalem—was unthinkable unless special effects were devised to create huge vistas and crowds. The fantasy film, with its panoply of ghosts, flying horses, and invisible or incredibly shrinking people, demanded that superimposition and matte processes be improved. The science fiction film genre could scarcely exist without a barrage of special effects. For the major studios, the "factory" principle was responsible for the "magic."

A good survey of the subject is Richard Rickitt's sumptuously illustrated *Special Effects: The History and the Technique,* 2d ed. (New York: Billboard, 2007). Pascal Pintau offers a historical overview interspersed with interviews with 37 effects artists in his *Special Effects: An Oral History—Interviews with 37 Masters Spanning 100 Years* (New York: Harry N. Abrams, 2005). Illuminating case studies can be found in Linwood G. Dunn and George E. Turner, eds., *The ASC Treasury of Visual Effects* (Hollywood: American Society of Cinematographers, 1983). Patricia D. Netzley's *Encyclopedia of Movie Special Effects* (New York: Checkmark Books, 2001) provides entries on techniques, practitioners, and individual films. Aimed at low-budget filmmakers, Mark Sawicki's *Filming the Fantastic: A Guide to Visual Effects Cinematography* (Boston: Focal Press, 2007) introduces a wide range of physical and digital effects in language that readers of *Film Art* will largely be able to understand.

Studies of predigital effects include Mark Cotta Vaz and Craig Barron's *The Invisible Art: The Legends of Movie Matte Painting* (San Francisco: Chronicle Books, 2002). This extensive and well-illustrated history includes a CD-ROM with examples of matte paintings. Stan Winston was a master of physical effects, in particular puppets and creature creation; see Jody Duncan's *The Winston Effect: The Art & History of Stan Winston Studio* (London: Titan Books, 2006).

For histories of digital-effects firms, see Mark Cotta Vaz and Patricia Rose Duignan, *Industrial Light & Magic: Into the Digital Realm* (New York: Ballantine Books, 1996), and Piers Bizony, *Digital Domain: The Leading Edge of Visual Effects* (New York: Billboard Books, 2001). George Lucas has been a leading force in promoting digital technology, including special effects; Michael Rubin chronicles his career in *Droidmaker: George Lucas and the Digital Revolution* (Gainesville, FL: Triad Books, 2006).

Shilo T. McClean offers analyses of how digital special effects function in movies in her *Digital Storytelling: The Narrative Power of Visual Effects in Film* (Cambridge, MA: MIT Press, 2007).

Articles on particular films' use of special effects appear regularly in *American Cinematographer* and *Cinefex*.

Aspect Ratio

The aspect ratio of the film image has been debated since the inception of cinema. The Edison-Lumière ratio (1.33:1) was not generally standardized until 1911, and even after that other ratios were explored. Many cinematographers believed that 1.33:1 was the perfect ratio (perhaps not aware that it harks back to the "golden section" of academic painting). With the large-scale innovation of widescreen cinema in the early 1950s, cries of distress were heard. Most camera operators hated it. Lenses often were not sharp, lighting became more complicated, and as Lee Garmes put it, "We'd look through the camera and be startled at what it was taking in." Yet some directors—Nicholas Ray, Akira Kurosawa, Samuel Fuller, François Truffaut, and Jean-Luc Godard—created fascinating compositions in the widescreen ratio. The systems are exhaustively surveyed in Robert E. Carr and R. M. Hayes's *Wide Screen Movies: A History and Filmography of Wide Gauge Filmmaking* (Jefferson, NC: McFarland, 1988).

The most detailed defense of the aesthetic virtues of the widescreen image remains Charles Barr's "CinemaScope: Before and After," *Film Quarterly* 16, 4 (Summer 1963): 4–24. *The Velvet Light Trap* 21 (1985) contains several articles on the history and aesthetics of widescreen cinema, including an article on Barr's essay and second thoughts by Barr. On widescreen staging practices, see David Bordwell, "CinemaScope: The Modern Miracle You See Without Glasses," in *Poetics of Cinema* (New York: Routledge, 2007), pp. 281–325.

During the 1980s, two variants on traditional film gauges were designed in response to widescreen demands. One innovation was Super 35mm, which expands the image area within the traditional 35mm format. It allows filmmakers to make a release print at either 2.40:1 (anamorphic) ratio or 1.85:1 matted. For small-budget projects, there was Super 16mm, which can be blown up to make 35mm release prints more easily than from normal 16mm. Super 16mm provides 40 percent more image area and creates a wider frame that can be matted to the 1.85:1 aspect ratio favored in 35mm exhibition.

Widescreen Welles

The 2000 DVD release of Orson Welles's *Touch of Evil* created a controversy among admirers of the film. The film had originally been shot in 1.37, but by 1957, the widescreen revolution had made that format rare. Most films were shown in a wider ratio, such as 1.66 or 1.85. The producers of the DVD version of the film settled on 1.85 as the appropriate one. They explained that Welles would have expected the full-frame images to be cropped in projection and that he would have seen and approved the work print in that standard format.

But many observers argued that Welles didn't want his images cropped, having declared his distaste for widescreen formats. Many complained that the compositions looked too confining, and some older viewers recalled seeing the film in theaters in 1.37.

The controversy reached its peak when a new DVD box set was released in 2008. The debate can be followed online, at a website hosted by critic Dave Kehr (http://www.davekehr.com/?p=127) and at a site largely devoted to Criterion releases (http://www.criterionforum.org/forum/viewtopic.php?f=4&t=4223&start=150).

Welles's published comments on widescreen have been reprinted at http://www.wellesnet.com/?p=155. His remarks about *Touch of Evil* in a 1958 letter are ambiguous:

> Nowadays the eye is tamed, I think, by the new wide screens. These "systems" with their rigid technical limitations are in such monopoly that any vigorous use of the old black-and-white, normal aperture camera runs the risk of seeming tricky by comparison. The old camera permits use of a range of visual conventions as removed from "realism" as grand opera. This is a language not a bag of tricks. If it is now a dead language, as a candid partisan of the old eloquence, I must face the likelihood that I shall not again be able to put it to the service of any theme of my own choosing.

Welles registers his preference for the "normal" (1.37) aperture, but he indicates that it is now "dead." He also says that he won't be able to employ it "again." But does "again" mean, "after having employed it in *Touch of Evil*," or simply "since the widescreen revolution of the early 1950s"?

After consulting with Welles experts, we have decided to reproduce the *Touch of Evil* frames in this book in the wider-aspect ratio. But the matter is far from settled.

The Subjective Shot

Sometimes the camera, through its positioning and movements, invites us to see events through the eyes of a character. Some directors (Howard Hawks, John Ford, Kenji Mizoguchi, Jacques Tati) seldom use the subjective shot, but others use it constantly. As 5.135 indicated, Samuel Fuller's *Naked Kiss* starts with shocking subjective shots:

> We open with a direct cut. In that scene, the actors utilized the camera. They held the camera; it was strapped on them. For the first shot, the pimp has the camera strapped on his chest. I say to [Constance] Towers, "Hit the camera!" She hits the camera, the lens. Then I reverse it. I put the camera on her, and she whacks the hell out of him. I thought it was effective. (Quoted in Eric Sherman and Martin Rubin, *The Director's Event* [New York: Signet, 1969], p. 189)

Filmmakers began experimenting with the "first-person camera" or the "camera as character" quite early. *Grandma's Reading Glass* (1901) features subjective point-of-view shots. Keyholes, binoculars, and other apertures were often used to motivate optical point of view. In 1919, Abel Gance used many subjective shots in *J'accuse*. The 1920s saw many filmmakers taking an interest in subjectivity, seen in such films as E. A. Dupont's *Variety* (1925), F. W. Murnau's *The Last Laugh* (1924) with its famous drunken scene, and Abel Gance's *Napoleon* (1927). Some believe that in the 1940s, the subjective shot—especially subjective camera movement—got completely out of hand in Robert Montgomery's *Lady in the Lake* (1946). For almost the entire film, the camera represents the vision of the protagonist, Philip Marlowe; we see him only when he glances in mirrors. "Suspenseful! Unusual!" proclaimed the advertising. "YOU accept an invitation to a blonde's apartment! YOU get socked in the jaw by a murder suspect!"

The history of the technique has teased film theorists into speculating about whether the subjective shot evokes identification from the audience. Do we think we *are* Philip Marlowe? The problem of audience identification with a point-of-view shot remains a difficult one in film theory. A useful discussion is Edward Branigan's *Point of View in the Cinema: A Theory of Narration and Subjectivity in Classical Film* (New York: Mouton, 1984).

Real Time and the Long Take

When the camera is running, does it record real time? If so, what artistic implications follow from that?

André Bazin argued that cinema is an art that depends on actual duration. Like photography, Bazin claimed, cinema is a *recording process*. The camera registers, photochemically, the light reflected from the object. Like the still camera, the movie camera records space. But unlike the still camera, the movie camera can also record *time*. "The cinema is objectivity in time. . . . Now, for the first time, the image of things is likewise the image of their duration, change mummified as it were" (*What Is Cinema?* vol. 1 [Berkeley: University of California Press, 1966], pp. 14–15). On this basis, Bazin saw editing as an intrusive interruption of the natural continuity of duration. He thus praised long-take directors such as Jean Renoir, Orson Welles, William Wyler, and Roberto Rossellini as artists whose styles respected concrete moment-to-moment life.

Bazin should be credited with calling our attention to the possibilities latent in the long take at a time when other film theorists considered it theatrical and uncinematic. Yet the problem of real time in film seems more complicated than Bazin thought. For one thing, in the digital age, an apparent long take can be built up out of separate elements joined by special effects. In *The War of the Worlds,* for example, a shot of the hero and his children fleeing along a highway in a minivan lasts for 2 minutes and 22 seconds. As the family talks, screams, and shouts at each other about the attack they have just escaped, the camera circles the van, filming them through the windows. Yet in reality, the actors were performing in a studio against a bluescreen. The landscapes, people, and vehicles that whiz past them in the background were made with eight cameras mounted on a Jeep that drove along a stretch of highway. The circling camera filming the van on that same highway was mounted at times on the side of the vehicle and at other times on another vehicle that could pull quickly backward for long-shot views. All these elements were joined by animators into a single shot, using the upright frames of the windows as transition points where elements could be joined unnoticeably. To top it all off, the glass of the windows, which reflects the vehicles and lampposts whizzing by, were added digitally. (See Joe Fordham's "Alien Apocalypse," *Cinefex* 103 [October 2005]: 76.)

Bazin's claims about real time are also undermined by the fact that screen time does not always equal story time. For example, a five-minute long take may not present five minutes in the story. The shot that tracks the protagonist of *Notting Hill* through changing seasons lasts about 100 seconds on the screen, but it covers about a year of story time (p. 213). The 91-minute shot that constitutes *Russian Ark* shifts the viewer backward and forward through Russian history. Mise-en-scene cues can override the camera's recording of real duration, giving the film a flexible time frame. As usual, a film's overall formal context assigns concrete functions to particular stylistic elements.

Websites

www.theasc.com/ The official site of the American Society of Cinematographers, tied to this association's activities and its journal, *American Cinematographer.* Includes some on-line articles.

www.soc.org/magazine.html/ The official site of the Society of Operating Cameramen, with an archive of many articles. Especially good are Rick Meyer's essays on the history of widescreen processes.

www.cinematography.net/ An extensive discussion site about professional cinematography.

www.widescreenmuseum.com/ A vast site (950 pages, 3000 images) devoted to widescreen processes, past and present, as well as color and sound technology.

Recommended DVD Supplements

The 1993 documentary *Visions of Light: The Art of Cinematography,* which includes numerous interviews with cinematographers and brief clips from a wide variety of films, is available on DVD (Image Entertainment). In "Painting with Light," cinematographer Jack Cardiff talks about his use of Technicolor in *Black Narcissus.* Raoul Coutard discusses anamorphic widescreen and color processes in an interview on the *Contempt* DVD (which also includes a "Widescreen vs. Full-Frame Demonstration"). *Oklahoma!*'s disc contains a very good comparison featurette, "CinemaScope vs. Todd-AO," as well as a short originally shown in theaters before *Oklahoma!* to introduce the new widescreen process, "The Miracle of Todd-AO."

A rare demonstration of laboratory work comes in "Day 66: Journey of a Roll of Film," in *King Kong: Peter Jackson's Production Diaries,* which includes the use of a

Telecine machine to make a digital intermediate. The process of selective digital grading, which we discuss on page 185, is explained in "Digital Grading," on the *Lord of the Rings: The Fellowship of the Ring* supplements.

Discussions of perspective and depth cues are equally rare, but they receive fascinating coverage in "Little People, Big Effects," a supplement to the *Darby O'Gill and the Little People* DVD. It includes excellent footage of matte paintings for this film and for *Treasure Island.* There is a section on forced perspective, where actors are made to appear small by placing them farther away from the people they appear to be facing (the same technique used in many shots of *The Lord of the Rings* 40 years later). The importance of matching eyelines and of achieving deep focus is explained.

The "Outward Bound" chapter on the *Alien* disc provides a clear demonstration of how models were shot to look realistic in the pre-CGI, pre-green-screen era. *Speed*'s "Visual Effects" track covers motion control, the digital matte work and other tricks showing the bus jumping the freeway gap, and a huge miniature used for the final train crash. The "Special Effects Vignettes" for *Cast Away* do a particularly good job of tracing through the various layers that build up as CGI shots are created. "Visual FX: MTA Train" gives a brief but informative look at green-screen work in *Collateral*'s train scene; it shows how effects can be used not only for flashy action but also for such subtle purposes as varying the colors and lights seen through the windows as the mood of the scene shifts. "Designing the Enemy: Tripods and Aliens" (*War of the Worlds*) reveals how computers can be used to design digital figures. Each of the *Lord of the Rings* DVD sets contains extensive special-effects descriptions, and *The Return of the King* supplements include a segment on one of the most complex CGI scenes ever created: "Visual Effects Demonstration: 'The Mûmakil Battle.'"

"No Feat But What We Make," a *Terminator 2: Judgment Day* supplement, offers an excellent history of the early development of digital special effects in *The Abyss* and *Terminator 2,* and includes director James Cameron discussing perspective. "The Making of *Jurassic Park*" covers some of the same material and moves forward to the transitions from animation of shiny surfaces to the creation of realistic dinosaurs.

More recent developments in computer effects are dealt with in "Meet Davy Jones," a supplement on the *Pirates of the Caribbean: Dead Man's Chest* DVD; it demonstrates important advances in motion-capture technology. Good making-ofs for other effects-heavy films are "Wired: The Visual Effects of *Iron Man*" and "Daemons" and "Armoured Bears" in the *Golden Compass* supplements. The use of CGI to create less noticeable effects, like realistic settings and erasure of unwanted elements, is demonstrated in "The Visual Effects of *Zodiac*"; the "New York, New Zealand" section of *King Kong: Peter Jackson's Production Diaries*; and "In Camera: *The Dark Knight.*"

The Dark Knight was the first fiction feature to shoot some sequences using Imax cameras, as is explained in the supplement "Shooting Outside the Box."

With the recent increase in multiple-camera shooting in epic films, DVD supplements sometimes include sequences juxtaposing the views from those cameras shown in splitscreen. These tend not to provide much information about the process, but the "Interactive Multi-Angle Battle Scene Studies" for *Master and Commander* helpfully give readouts of lens length and shooting speed (revealing how common it has become for shots of violent action to be done with varying degrees of slow motion). Similarly, *Speed*'s "Action Sequences: Multi-angle Stunts," provides a frames-per-second readout in its demonstration. *Dancer in the Dark*'s extreme use of multiple-camera shooting for the music numbers is explained in "100 Cameras: Capturing Lars von Trier's Vision."

The ultimate supplement dealing with long takes is "In One Breath," which documents the filming of the single elaborate shot that makes up *Russian Ark.*

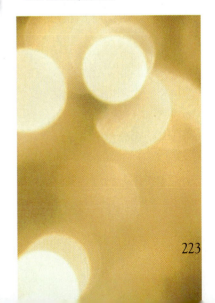

The Relation of Shot to Shot: Editing

Since the 1920s, when film theorists began to realize what **editing** can achieve, it has been the most widely discussed film technique. This hasn't been all to the good, for some writers have mistakenly found in editing the key to good cinema (or even *all* cinema). Yet many films, particularly in the period before 1904, consist of only one shot and hence do not depend on editing at all. There are major films from the 1910s, such as Victor Sjöström's *Ingeborg Holm,* that consist largely of single-take scenes that rely on subtle manipulations of mise-en-scene. Experimental films sometimes deemphasize editing by making each shot as long as the amount of film a camera will hold, as with Michael Snow's *La Région centrale* and Andy Warhol's *Eat, Sleep,* and *Empire.* Such films are not necessarily less "cinematic" than others that rely heavily on editing.

Still, we can see why editing has exercised such an enormous fascination for film aestheticians, for as a technique it's very powerful. The ride of the Klan in *The Birth of a Nation,* the Odessa Steps sequence in *Potemkin,* the hunt sequence in *The Rules of the Game,* the shower murder in *Psycho,* the diving sequence in *Olympia,* Clarice Starling's discovery of the killer's lair in *The Silence of the Lambs,* the tournament sequence in *Lancelot du Lac,* the reconstruction of the Dallas assassination in *JFK*—all of these celebrated moments derive much of their effect from editing.

Perhaps even more important, however, is the role of editing within an entire film's stylistic system. Today's Hollywood film typically contains between 1000 and 2000 shots; an action-based movie can have 3000 or more. This fact alone suggests that editing strongly shapes viewers' experiences, even if they aren't aware of it. Editing contributes a great deal to a film's organization and its effects on spectators.

> *"Editing is the basic creative force, by power of which the soulless photographs (the separate shots) are engineered into living, cinematographic form."*
>
> — V. I. Pudovkin, director

What Is Editing?

Editing may be thought of as the coordination of one shot with the next. As we have seen, in film production a shot is one or more exposed frames in a series on a continuous length of film stock. The film editor eliminates unwanted footage, usually by discarding all but the best take. The editor also cuts superfluous frames, such as those showing the clapboard (p. 21), from the beginnings and endings of shots. She or he then joins the desired shots, the end of one to the beginning of another.

These joins can be of different sorts. A **fade-out** gradually darkens the end of a shot to black, and a **fade-in** accordingly lightens a shot from black. A **dissolve** briefly superimposes the end of shot A and the beginning of shot B **(6.1–6.3)**. In a **wipe,** shot B replaces shot A by means of a boundary line moving across the screen **(6.4).** Here both images are briefly on the screen at the same time, but they do not blend, as in a dissolve. In the production process, fades, dissolves, and wipes are

6.1   The first shot of *The Maltese Falcon* leads to . . .

6.2   . . . a dissolve to . . .

6.3   . . . the second shot.

6.4   A wipe joins the last shot of one scene with the first of the next in *Seven Samurai*.

"You can definitely help performances in the cutting room, by intercutting reaction, maybe re-recording lines, adding lines over reaction shots. And you can help a film's structure by moving sequences about and dropping scenes that hold up pacing. And sometimes you can use bits and pieces from different takes, which also helps a lot. What you can do in the editing room to help a film is amazing."

— Jodie Foster, actor and director

optical effects and are marked as such by the editor. They are typically executed in the laboratory or, more recently, through digital manipulation.

The most common means of joining two shots is the **cut.** Until the rise of digital editing in the 1990s, a cut was made by splicing two shots together by means of film cement or tape. Some filmmakers "cut" during filming by planning for the film to emerge from the camera ready for final showing. Here the physical junction from shot to shot is created in the act of shooting. Such editing in the camera, however, is rare and is mainly confined to experimental and amateur filmmaking. Editing after shooting is the norm. Today most editing is done on computer, using footage stored on tape or a hard drive, so that the cuts (or *edits,* in video terminology) can be made without touching film. The final version of the film is prepared for printing by cutting and splicing the negative footage.

As viewers, we perceive a shot as an uninterrupted segment of screen time, space, or graphic configurations. Fades, dissolves, and wipes are perceived as gradually eliminating one shot and replacing it with another. Cuts are perceived as instantaneous changes from one shot to another.

Consider four shots from the first attack on Bodega Bay in Alfred Hitchcock's *The Birds* **(6.5–6.8):**

1. *Medium shot, straight-on angle.* Melanie, Mitch, and the Captain standing by the restaurant window talking. Melanie on extreme right, bartender in background (6.5).

2. *Medium close-up.* Melanie by the Captain's shoulder. She looks to right (out offscreen window) and up, as if following with her eyes. Pan right with her as she turns to window and looks out (6.6).

3. *Extreme long shot.* Melanie's point of view. Gas station across street, phone booth in left foreground. Birds dive-bomb attendant, right to left (6.7).

4. *Medium close-up.* Melanie, profile. The Captain moves right into shot, blocking out bartender; Mitch moves right into extreme foreground. All in profile look out window (6.8).

Each of these four shots presents a different segment of time, space, and pictorial information. The first shot shows three people talking. An instantaneous change—a cut—shifts us to a medium close-up shot of Melanie. Here space has changed (Melanie is isolated and larger in the frame), time is continuous, and the graphic configurations have changed (the arrangements of the shapes and colors vary). Another cut takes us instantly to what she sees. The gas station shot (6.7) presents a very different space, a successive bit of time, and a different graphic configuration. Another cut returns us to Melanie (6.8), and again we are shifted instantly to another space, the next slice of time, and a different graphic configuration. Thus the four shots are joined by three cuts.

Hitchcock could have presented the *Birds* scene without editing—as Jean Renoir might have done in a similar situation (5.170–5.172). Imagine a camera movement that frames the four people talking, tracks in and rightward to Melanie as she turns, pans rightward to the window to show the dive-bombing gull, and pans leftward back to catch the group's expressions. This would constitute one shot. The camera movements, no matter how fast, would not present the marked and abrupt shifts that cuts produce. Now imagine a deep-space composition of the sort that Orson Welles might have used (5.39), presenting Mitch in the foreground, Melanie and the window in the middle ground, and the gull attack in the distance. Again, the scene could now be played in one shot, for we would have no abrupt change of time or space or graphics. And the movements of the figures would not yield the jumps in time, space, and composition provided by editing.

Although many films today are shot with several cameras running simultaneously, throughout film history most sequences have been shot with only one camera. In the *Birds* scene, for example, the shots were taken at different times and places—one (shot 3) outdoors, the others in a sound stage (and these perhaps on different days). A film editor thus must assemble a large and varied batch of footage. To ease this task, most filmmakers plan for the editing phase during the preparation and shooting phases. Shots are filmed with an idea of how they will eventually fit together. In fictional filming, scripts and storyboards help plan editing, while documentary filmmakers often shoot with an eye to how the footage will be cut.

6.5 *The Birds:* shot 1.

6.6 *The Birds:* shot 2.

6.7 *The Birds:* shot 3.

6.8 *The Birds:* shot 4.

Dimensions of Film Editing

Editing offers the filmmaker four basic areas of choice and control:

1. Graphic relations between shot A and shot B
2. Rhythmic relations between shot A and shot B
3. Spatial relations between shot A and shot B
4. Temporal relations between shot A and shot B

Graphic and rhythmic relationships are present in the editing of any film. Spatial and temporal relationships may be irrelevant to the editing of films using abstract form (p. 368), but they are present in the editing of films built out of nonabstract images (that is, the great majority of motion pictures). Let's trace the range of choice and control in each area.

Graphic Relations Between Shot A and Shot B

The four shots from *The Birds* may be considered purely as graphic configurations, as patterns of light and dark, line and shape, volumes and depths, movement and stasis—*independent of* the shots' relation to the time and space of the story. For instance, Hitchcock did not drastically alter the overall brightness from shot to shot, because the scene takes place during the day. But if the scene had been set at night, he could have cut from the uniformly lit second shot in the bar (6.6, Melanie turning to the window) to a shot of the gas station swathed in darkness. Moreover, Hitchcock usually keeps the most important part of the composition roughly in the center of the frame. (Compare Melanie's position in the frame with that of the gas station in 6.7.) He could, however, have cut from a shot in which Melanie was in, say, upper frame left to a shot locating the gas station in the lower right of the frame.

Hitchcock also plays off certain color differences. Melanie's hair and outfit make her a predominantly yellow and green figure, whereas the shot of the gas station is dominated by drab grays set off by touches of red in the gas pumps. Alternatively, Hitchcock could have cut from Melanie to another figure composed of

6.9 A shot from *True Stories* showing the Texas horizon midway up the frame is graphically matched . . .

6.10 . . . with a shot where the waterline of ancient seas is in the same position.

similar colors. Furthermore, the movement in Melanie's shot—her turning to the window—does not blend into the movements of either the attendant or the gull in the next shot, but Hitchcock could have echoed Melanie's movement in speed, direction, or frame placement by movement in the next shot.

In short, editing together any two shots permits the interaction, through similarity and difference, of the *purely pictorial* qualities of those two shots. The four aspects of mise-en-scene (lighting, setting, costume, and the behavior of the figures in space and time) and most cinematographic qualities (photography, framing, and camera mobility) all furnish potential graphic elements. Thus every shot provides possibilities for purely graphic editing, and every cut creates some sort of graphic relationship between two shots.

Graphics may be edited to achieve smooth continuity or abrupt contrast. The filmmaker may link shots by graphic similarities, thus making a **graphic match.** Shapes, colors, overall composition, or movement in shot A may be picked up in the composition of shot B. A minimal instance is the cut that joins the first two shots of David Byrne's *True Stories* **(6.9, 6.10).** More dynamic graphic matches appear in Akira Kurosawa's *Seven Samurai.* After the samurai have first arrived at the village, an alarm sounds and they race to discover its source. Kurosawa cuts together six shots of different running samurai, which he dynamically matches by means of composition, lighting, setting, figure movement, and panning camera movement. (We show the first three in **6.11–6.13.**)

Filmmakers often call attention to graphic matches at transitional moments **(6.14–6.16).** Such precise graphic matching is relatively rare. Still, as in the *Birds* shots, an approximate graphic continuity from shot A to shot B is typical of most narrative cinema. The director will usually strive to keep the center of interest roughly constant across the cut, to maintain the overall lighting level, and to avoid strong color clashes from shot to shot. In Juzo Itami's *Tampopo,* an aspiring cook is trying to learn the secret of good noodles, and she questions a successful cook. Their confrontation is presented through head-on framings. Alternating shots keep each main character's face in the right center of each frame **(6.17, 6.18).**

Editing need not be graphically continuous. Mildly discontinuous editing may appear in widescreen compositions organized around characters facing one another.

6.11 *Seven Samurai.*

6.12 *Seven Samurai.*

6.13 *Seven Samurai.*

6.14 In *Aliens,* the curved outline of Ripley's sleeping face . . .

6.15 . . . is graphically matched by means of a dissolve . . .

6.16 . . . to the outline of the earth.

6.17   The woman and her friend, the cowboy truck driver . . .

6.18   . . . confront the enraged cook and his assistants. The key characters are made prominent by being placed in the same area of each shot.

6.19   As Tarantino cuts between Vincent and . . .

6.20   . . . Jules, our eye must move back and forth across the screen.

6.21   *Touch of Evil:* graphic discontinuity.

6.22   *Touch of Evil.*

A scene from Quentin Tarantino's *Pulp Fiction* places the two hitmen opposite each other in a restaurant booth, each framed distinctly off-center (**6.19, 6.20**). Compared to the *Tampopo* example, the cut here creates greater graphic discontinuity. Note, however, that the cut does balance the frame area from shot to shot: each man fills the space left empty in the previous shot. In addition, each man's face is just above the horizontal center of each frame, so that the spectator's eye can easily adjust to the changing composition.

Graphically discontinuous editing can be more noticeable. Orson Welles frequently sought a clash from shot to shot, as in *Citizen Kane* when the dark long shot of Kane's bedroom is followed by the bright opening title of the "News on the March" reel. Similarly, in *Touch of Evil,* Welles dissolves from a shot of Menzies looking out a window on frame right (**6.21**) to a shot of Susan Vargas looking out a different window on frame left (**6.22**). The clash is further accentuated by the contrasting screen positions of the window reflections. Alain Resnais's *Night and Fog* began something of a fad by utilizing an extreme but apt graphic conflict: color footage of an abandoned concentration camp today is cut together with black-and-white newsreel shots of the camps in the period 1942–1945. Resnais balanced the color/black-and-white contrasts by finding striking similarities in shape, as when a tracking shot of fence posts graphically matches a low-angle shot of marching Nazi legs.

Later in the *Birds* sequence, Hitchcock employs conflict of graphic qualities. Gasoline spurting from the pump has flowed across the street to a parking lot, and Melanie, along with several other people at the restaurant window, has seen a man accidentally set the gasoline alight. His car ignites, and an explosion of flame engulfs him. What we see next is Melanie watching helplessly as the flame races along the trail of gas toward the station. Hitchcock cuts the shots as shown in **6.23–6.33**:

Shot 30	(Long shot)	High angle. Melanie's POV. Flaming car, spreading flames (6.23).	73 frames
Shot 31	(Medium close-up)	Straight-on angle. Melanie, immobile, looking off left, mouth open (6.24).	20 frames
Shot 32	(Medium shot)	High angle. Melanie's POV. Pan with flames moving from lower right to upper left of trail of gasoline (6.25).	18 frames
Shot 33	(Medium close-up)	As 31. Melanie, immobile, staring down center (6.26).	16 frames
Shot 34	(Medium shot)	High angle. Melanie's POV. Pan with flames moving from lower right to upper left (6.27).	14 frames
Shot 35	(Medium close-up)	As 31. Melanie, immobile, looking off right, staring aghast (6.28).	12 frames
Shot 36	(Long shot)	Melanie's POV. Gas station. Flames rush in from right. Mitch, sheriff, and attendant run out left (6.29).	10 frames
Shot 37	(Medium close-up)	As 31. Melanie, immobile, stares off extreme right (6.30).	8 frames
Shot 38	(Long shot)	As 36. Melanie's POV. Cars at station explode (6.31).	34 frames
Shot 39	(Medium close-up)	As 31. Melanie covers face with hands (6.32).	33 frames
Shot 40	(Extreme long shot)	Extreme high angle on city, flaming trail in center. Gulls fly into shot (6.33).	

In graphic terms, Hitchcock has exploited two possibilities of contrast. First, although each shot's composition centers the action (Melanie's head, the flaming trail), the movements thrust in different directions. In shot 31, Melanie looks to the lower left, whereas in shot 32, the fire moves to the upper left. In shot 33, Melanie is looking down center, whereas in shot 34, the flames still move to the upper left, and so on.

More important—and what makes the sequence impossible to recapture on the printed page—is a crucial contrast of mobility and stasis. The shots of the flames present movement of both the subject (the flames rushing along the gas) and the camera (which pans to follow). But each shot of Melanie could be a still photograph, since each one is absolutely static. She does not turn her head in any shot, and the camera does not track in or away from her. We must infer the progress of her attention. By making movement conflict with countermovement and with stillness, Hitchcock has powerfully exploited the graphic possibilities of editing.

6.23   *The Birds:* shot 30.

6.24   *The Birds:* shot 31.

6.25   *The Birds:* shot 32.

6.26   *The Birds:* shot 33.

6.27   *The Birds:* shot 34.

6.28   *The Birds:* shot 35.

6.29   *The Birds:* shot 36.

6.30   *The Birds:* shot 37.

6.31   *The Birds:* shot 38.

6.32   *The Birds:* shot 39.

6.33   *The Birds:* shot 40.

Rhythmic Relations Between Shot A and Shot B

Each shot, being a strip of film, is of a certain length, measured in frames, feet, or meters. And the shot's physical length corresponds to a measurable duration on-screen. As we know, at sound speed, 24 frames last one second in projection. A shot can be as short as a single frame, or it may be thousands of frames long, running for many minutes when projected. Editing thus allows the filmmaker to determine the duration of each shot. When the filmmaker adjusts the length of shots in relation to one another, she or he is controlling the *rhythmic* potential of editing.

Cinematic rhythm as a whole derives not only from editing but from other film techniques as well. The filmmaker relies on movement in the mise-en-scene, camera position and movement, the rhythm of sound, and the overall context to determine the editing rhythm. Nevertheless, the patterning of shot lengths contributes considerably to what we intuitively recognize as a film's rhythm.

Sometimes the filmmaker will use shot duration to create a stressed, accented, moment. In one sequence of *The Road Warrior,* a ferocious gang member butts his head against that of a victim. At the moment of contact, director George Miller cuts in a few frames of pure white. The result is a sudden flash that suggests violent impact. Alternatively, a shot's duration can be used to deaccentuate an action. During test screenings of *Raiders of the Lost Ark,* Steven Spielberg discovered that after Indiana Jones shoots the gigantic swordsman, several seconds had to be added to allow the audience's reaction to die down before the action could resume.

More commonly, the rhythmic possibilities of editing emerge when several shot lengths form a discernible pattern. A steady beat can be established by making all of the shots approximately the same length. The filmmaker can also create a dynamic pace. Lengthening shots can gradually slow the tempo, while successively shorter shots can accelerate it.

Consider how Hitchcock handles the tempo of the first gull attack in *The Birds.* Shot 1, the medium shot of the group talking (6.5), consumes almost a thousand frames, or about 41 seconds. But shot 2 (6.6), which shows Melanie looking out the window, is much shorter—309 frames (about 13 seconds). Even shorter is shot 3 (6.7), which lasts only 55 frames (about 2⅓ seconds). The fourth shot (6.8), showing Melanie joined by Mitch and the Captain, lasts only 35 frames (about 1½ seconds). Clearly, Hitchcock is accelerating the pace at the beginning of what will be a tense sequence.

In what follows, Hitchcock makes the shots fairly short but subordinates the length of the shot to the rhythm of the dialogue and the movement in the images. As a result, shots 5–29 (not shown here) have no fixed pattern of lengths. But once the essential components of the scene have been established, Hitchcock returns to strongly accelerating cutting.

In presenting Melanie's horrified realization of the flames racing from the parking lot to the gas station, shots 30–40 (6.23–6.33) climax the rhythmic intensification of the sequence. As the description on page 228 shows, after the shot of the spreading flames (shot 30, 6.23), each shot decreases in length by 2 frames, from 20 frames (⅘ of a second) to 8 frames (⅓ of a second). Two shots, 38 and 39, then punctuate the sequence with almost identical durations (a little less than 1½ seconds apiece). Shot 40 (6.33), a long shot that lasts over 600 frames, functions as both a pause and a suspenseful preparation for the new attack. The scene's variations in rhythm alternate between rendering the savagery of the attack and generating suspense as we await the next onslaught.

We have had the luxury of counting frames on the actual strip of film. The theater viewer cannot do this, but she or he does feel the shifting tempo in this sequence because of the changing shot durations. In general, by controlling editing rhythm, the filmmaker controls the amount of time we have to grasp and reflect on what we see. A series of rapid shots, for example, leaves us little time to think about what we're watching. In the *Birds* sequence, Hitchcock's editing impels the viewer's

CONNECT TO THE BLOG
Some analysts study rhythm in film by calculating average shot lengths across sequences of films. For more on that, see "My name is David, and I'm a frame-counter," at
www.davidbordwell.net/blog/?p=230.

"I noticed a softening in American cinema over the last twenty years, and I think it's a direct influence of TV. I would even say that if you want to make movies today, you'd be better off studying television than film because that's the market. Television has diminished the audience's attention span. It's hard to make a slow, quiet film today. Not that I would want to make a slow, quiet film anyway!"

— Oliver Stone, director

perception to move at a faster and faster pace. Quickly grasping the progress of the fire and understanding Melanie's changes in position become essential factors in the rising excitement of the scene.

Hitchcock is not, of course, the only director to use rhythmic editing. Its possibilities were initially explored by such directors as D. W. Griffith (especially in *Intolerance*) and Abel Gance. In the 1920s, the French Impressionist filmmakers and the Soviet Montage school explored the rhythmic possibilities of strings of short shots (pp. 463–466, 467–469). When sound films became the norm, pronounced rhythmic editing survived in dramas such as Lewis Milestone's *All Quiet on the Western Front* and in musical comedies and fantasies such as René Clair's *À Nous la liberté* and *Le Million*, Rouben Mamoulian's *Love Me Tonight*, and Busby Berkeley's dance sequences in *42nd Street* and *Footlight Parade*.

Spatial Relations Between Shot A and Shot B

Editing usually serves not only to control graphics and rhythm but also to construct film space. Exhilaration in this newly discovered power can be sensed in the writings of such filmmakers as the Soviet director Dziga Vertov: "I am Kino-eye. I am builder. I have placed you . . . in an extraordinary room which did not exist until just now when I also created it. In this room there are twelve walls, shot by me in various parts of the world. In bringing together shots of walls and details, I've managed to arrange them in an order that is pleasing."

Such elation is understandable. Editing permits the filmmaker to juxtapose *any* two points in space and thus imply some kind of relationship between them.

The director might, for instance, start with a shot that establishes a spatial whole and follow this with a shot of a part of this space. This is what Hitchcock does in shot 1 and shot 2 of the *Birds* sequence (6.5, 6.6): a medium long shot of the group of people followed by a medium shot of only one, Melanie. Such analytical breakdown is a very common editing pattern.

Alternatively, the filmmaker could construct a whole space out of component parts. Hitchcock does this later in the *Birds* sequence. Note that in 6.5–6.8 and in shots 30–39 (6.23–6.32), we do not see an establishing shot including Melanie *and* the gas station. In production, the restaurant window need not have been across from the station at all; they could have been filmed in different towns or even countries. Yet we are compelled to believe that Melanie is across the street from the gas station. The bird cry offscreen and the mise-en-scene (the window and Melanie's sideways glance) contribute considerably as well. Still, the editing plays a major role in creating the spatial whole of restaurant-and-gas-station.

Such spatial manipulation through cutting is fairly common. In documentaries compiled from newsreel footage, for example, one shot might show a cannon firing, and another shot might show a shell hitting its target; we infer that the cannon fired the shell, though the shots may show entirely different battles. Again, if a shot of a speaker is followed by a shot of a cheering crowd, we assume a spatial coexistence.

The possibility of such spatial manipulation was examined by the Soviet filmmaker Lev Kuleshov. During the 1920s, Kuleshov conducted informal experiments by assembling shots of separate dramatic elements. The most famous of these experiments involved cutting neutral shots of an actor's face with other shots (variously reported as shots of soup, nature scenes, a dead woman, and a baby). The reported result was that the audience immediately assumed that the actor's expression changed and that the actor was reacting to things present in the same space as himself. Similarly, Kuleshov cut together shots of actors "looking at each other" but on Moscow streets miles apart, then meeting and strolling together—and looking at the White House in Washington. Although filmmakers had used such cutting before Kuleshov's work, film scholars call the *Kuleshov effect* any series of shots that *in the absence of an establishing shot* prompts the spectator to infer a spatial whole on the basis of seeing only portions of the space.

"[In editing The Dark Knight *for both 35mm and Imax presentation], we needed to extensively test to ensure that the cuts were not so quick that the audience would get disoriented, looking at that Imax screen, and at the same time not interfere with the pace of the standard cinema version.*"

— Lee Smith, editor

CONNECT TO THE BLOG

For more on why the Kuleshov effect works so well and on how it has been used in some older and more recent films, see "What happens between shots happens between your ears," at www.davidbordwell.net/blog/?p=1861.

The Kuleshov effect can conjure up robust cinematic illusions. In Corey Yuen's *Legend of Fong Sai-Yuk,* a martial-arts bout between the hero and an adept woman begins on a platform but then moves into the audience—or rather, onto the audience. The two fight while balancing on the heads and shoulders of the crowd. Yuen's rapid editing conveys the scene's point by means of the Kuleshov effect **(6.34, 6.35).** (In production, this meant that the combatants could be hung on wires or bars suspended outside the frame, as in 6.35.) Across many shots, Yuen provides only a few brief full-figure framings showing Fong Sai-Yuk and the woman.

While the viewer doesn't normally notice the Kuleshov effect, a few films call attention to it. Carl Reiner's *Dead Men Don't Wear Plaid* mixes footage filmed in the present with footage from Hollywood movies of the 1940s. Thanks to the Kuleshov effect, *Dead Men* creates unified scenes in which Steve Martin converses with characters who were originally featured in other films. In *A Movie,* Bruce Conner makes a joke of the Kuleshov effect by cutting from a submarine captain peering through a periscope to a woman gazing at the camera, as if they could see each other **(6.36, 6.37).**

In the Kuleshov effect, editing cues the spectator to infer a single locale. Editing can also emphasize action taking place in separate places. In *Intolerance,* D. W. Griffith cuts from ancient Babylon to Gethsemane and from France in 1572 to America in 1916. Such parallel editing, or **crosscutting,** is a common way films construct a variety of spaces.

More radically, the editing can present spatial relations as being ambiguous and uncertain. In Carl Dreyer's *La Passion de Jeanne d'Arc,* for instance, we know only that Jeanne and the priests are in the same room. Because the neutral white backgrounds and the numerous close-ups provide no orientation to the entire space, we can seldom tell how far apart the characters are or precisely who is beside whom. We'll see later how films can create even more extreme spatial discontinuities.

6.34   In *The Legend of Fong Sai-Yuk,* a shot of the woman's upper body is followed by . . .

6.35   . . . a shot of her legs and feet, supported by unwilling bystanders.

6.36   In *A Movie,* a shot from one film leads to . . .

6.37   . . . a shot from another, creating a visual joke.

Temporal Relations Between Shot A and Shot B

Like other film techniques, editing can control the time of the action denoted in the film. In a narrative film especially, editing usually contributes to the plot's manipulation of story time. You will recall that Chapter 3 pointed out three areas in which plot time can cue the spectator to construct the story time: order, duration, and frequency. Our *Birds* example (6.5–6.8) shows how editing reinforces all three areas of control.

First, there is the *order* of presentation of events. The men talk, then Melanie turns away, then she sees the gull swoop, then she responds. Hitchcock's editing presents these story events in the 1-2-3-4 order of his shots. But he could have shuffled the shots into any order at all, even reverse (4-3-2-1). This is to say that the filmmaker may control temporal succession through the editing.

Such manipulation of events leads to changes in story–plot relations. We are most familiar with such manipulations in **flashbacks,** which present one or more shots out of their presumed story order. In *Hiroshima mon amour,* Resnais uses the protagonist's memory to motivate a violation of temporal order. Three shots (**6.38–6.40**) suggest visually that the position of her current lover's hand triggers a recollection of another lover's death years before. In contemporary cinema, brief flashbacks to key events may brutally interrupt present-time action. *The Fugitive* uses this technique to return obsessively to the murder of Dr. Kimball's wife, the event that initiated the story's action.

A much rarer option for reordering story events is the **flash-forward.** Here the editing moves from the present to a future event and then returns to the present. A small-scale instance occurs in *The Godfather.* Don Vito Corleone talks with his sons Tom and Sonny about their upcoming meeting with Sollozzo, the gangster who is asking them to finance his narcotics traffic. As the Corleones talk in the present, shots of them are interspersed with shots of Sollozzo going to the meeting in the future (**6.41–6.43**). The editing is used to provide exposition about Sollozzo while also moving quickly to the Don's announcement, at the gangsters' meeting, that he will not involve the family in the drug trade.

Filmmakers may use flash-forwards to tease the viewer with glimpses of the eventual outcome of the story action. The end of *They Shoot Horses, Don't They?* is hinted at in brief shots that periodically interrupt scenes in the present. Such flashforwards create a sense of a narration with a powerful range of story knowledge.

We may assume, then, that if a series of shots traces a 1-2-3 order in the presentation of story events, it is because the filmmaker has chosen to do that, not because of any necessity of following this order.

Editing also offers ways for the filmmaker to alter the *duration* of story events as presented in the film's plot. **Elliptical editing** presents an action in such a way that it consumes less time on the screen than it does in the story. The filmmaker can create an *ellipsis* in three principal ways.

Suppose a director wants to show a man climbing a flight of stairs but doesn't want to show the entire duration of his climb. The director could use a conventional *punctuation* shot change, such as a dissolve or a wipe or a fade. In the classical filmmaking tradition, such a device signals that some time has been omitted. Our director could simply dissolve from a shot of the man starting at the bottom of the stairs to a shot of him reaching the top.

Alternatively, the filmmaker could show the man at the bottom of the staircase, let him walk up out of the frame, hold briefly on the empty frame, then cut to an empty frame of the top of the stairs and let the man enter the frame. The *empty frames* on either side of the cut cover the elided time.

Also, the filmmaker can create an ellipsis by means of a *cutaway:* a shot of another event elsewhere that will not last as long as the elided action. In our example, the director might start with the man climbing but then cut away to a woman in her apartment. We could then cut back to the man much farther along in his ascent.

6.38 In *Hiroshima mon amour,* a view of the protagonist's Japanese lover asleep is followed by . . .

6.39 . . . a shot of her looking at him, leading to . . .

6.40 . . . a flashback of her dead German lover's hand.

"I saw Toto the Hero, the first film of the Belgian ex-circus clown Jaco van Dormael. What a brilliant debut. He tells the story with the camera. His compression and ellipses and clever visual transitions make it one of the most cinematic movies in a long time. The story spans a lifetime and kaleidoscopic events with such a lightness and grace that you want to get up and cheer."

— John Boorman, director

6.41   In *The Godfather*, the Corleones discuss their upcoming meeting with Sollozzo.

6.42   Flash-forward: Sollozzo arrives at the meeting, greeted by Sonny.

6.43   The next few shots return us to the family conversation, where Don Vito ponders what he will tell Sollozzo.

"[In editing James Bond films], we also evolved a technique that jumped continuity by simple editing devices. Bond would take a half-step towards a door and you would pick him up stepping into the next scene. We also used inserts cleverly to speed up a scene."

— John Glen, editor and director

CONNECT TO THE BLOG

Sit in on an editing session for Johnnie To's *Mad Detective,* and see some of the final cuts from the film in "Truly madly cinematically."

See www.davidbordwell.net/blog/?p=2155.

It's also possible to expand story time. If the action from the end of one shot is partly repeated at the beginning of the next, we have **overlapping editing.** This prolongs the action, stretching it out past its story duration. The Russian filmmakers of the 1920s made frequent use of temporal expansion through such overlapping editing, and no one mastered it more thoroughly than Sergei Eisenstein. In *Strike,* when factory workers bowl over a foreman with a large wheel hanging from a crane, two shots expand the action (**6.44–6.46**). In *October,* Eisenstein overlaps several shots of rising bridges in order to stress the significance of the moment.

We're accustomed to seeing a scene present action only once. Occasionally, however, a filmmaker may go beyond expanding an action to repeat it in its entirety. The very rarity of this technique may make it a powerful editing resource. In Bruce Conner's *Report,* there is a newsreel shot of John and Jacqueline Kennedy riding a limousine down a Dallas street. The shot is systematically repeated, in part or in whole, over and over, building up tension in our expectations as the shot seems to move by tiny increments closer to the moment of the inevitable assassination. Occasionally in *Do The Right Thing,* Spike Lee cuts together two takes of the same action, as when we twice see a garbage can fly through the air and break the pizzeria window at the start of the riot. Jackie Chan often shows his most virtuosic stunts three or four times in a row from different angles to allow the audience to marvel at his daring (**6.47–6.49**).

Graphics, rhythm, space, and time, then, are at the service of the filmmaker through the technique of editing. They offer potentially unlimited creative possibilities. Yet most films we see make use of a very narrow set of editing possibilities—so narrow, indeed, that we can speak of a dominant editing style throughout film history. This is what is usually called **continuity editing.** Still, the most familiar way to edit a film isn't the only way to edit a film, and so we'll also consider some alternatives to continuity editing.

6.44   In *Strike,* a wheel swings toward the foreman . . .

6.45   . . . then swings toward him again . . .

6.46   . . . and then again before striking him.

6.47   In *Police Story,* chasing the gangsters through a shopping mall, Jackie Chan leaps onto a pole several stories above them . . .

6.48   . . . and slides down in a shower of exploding lights.

6.49   Cut to a new angle: Jackie leaps again, leading to an instant replay of the risky stunt.

Continuity Editing

Around 1900–1910, as filmmakers started to use editing, they sought to arrange their shots so as to tell a story coherently and clearly. Thus editing, supported by specific strategies of cinematography and mise-en-scene, was used to ensure *narrative continuity*. So powerful is this style that, even today, anyone working in narrative filmmaking around the world is expected to be familiar with it.

As its name implies, the basic purpose of the continuity system is to allow space, time, and action to flow over a series of shots. All of the possibilities of editing we have already examined are turned to this end. First, graphic qualities are usually kept roughly continuous from shot to shot. The figures are balanced and symmetrically deployed in the frame; the overall lighting tonality remains constant; the action occupies the central zone of the screen.

Second, the rhythm of the cutting is usually made dependent on the camera distance of the shot. Long shots are left on the screen longer than medium shots, and medium shots are left on longer than close-ups. The assumption is that the spectator needs more time to take in the shots containing more details. In scenes of physical action like the fire in *The Birds,* accelerated editing rhythms may be present, but in general, shorter shots will tend to be closer views.

Since the continuity style seeks to present a story, it's chiefly through the handling of space and time that editing furthers narrative continuity.

Spatial Continuity: The 180° System

In the continuity style, the space of a scene is constructed along what is called variously the **axis of action,** the *center line,* or the *180° line*. The scene's action—a person walking, two people conversing, a car racing along a road—is assumed to take place along a clear-cut vector. This axis of action determines a half-circle, or 180° area, where the camera can be placed to present the action. Consequently, the filmmaker will plan, film, and edit the shots so as to respect this center line. The camera work and mise-en-scene in each shot will be manipulated to establish and reiterate the 180° space.

Consider the bird's-eye view in **6.50.** We have a girl and a boy conversing. The axis of action is the imaginary line connecting the two people. Under the continuity system, the director would arrange the mise-en-scene and camera placement so as to establish and sustain this line. The camera can be put at any point as long as it stays on the same *side* of the line (hence the 180° term). A typical series of shots for coverage of the scene would be these: (1) a medium shot of the girl and boy, (2) a shot over the girl's shoulder, favoring the boy, and (3) a shot over the boy's shoulder, favoring the girl. But to cut to a shot from camera position X, or from any position within the tinted area, would be considered a violation of the system because it *crosses* the axis of action. Indeed, some handbooks of film directing call shot X flatly wrong. To see why, we need to examine what happens if a filmmaker follows the **180° system.**

The 180° system ensures that relative positions in the frame remain consistent. In the shots taken from camera positions 1, 2, and 3, the characters occupy the same areas of the frame relative to each other. Even though we see them from different angles, the girl is always on the left and the boy is always on the right. But if we cut to shot X, the characters will switch positions in the frame. An advocate of traditional continuity would claim that shot X confuses us: Have the two characters somehow swiveled around each other?

The 180° system ensures consistent eyelines. In shots 1, 2, and 3, the girl is looking right and the boy is looking left. Shot X violates this pattern by making the girl look to the left.

The 180° system ensures consistent screen direction. Imagine now that the girl is walking left to right; her path constitutes the axis of action. As long as our shots

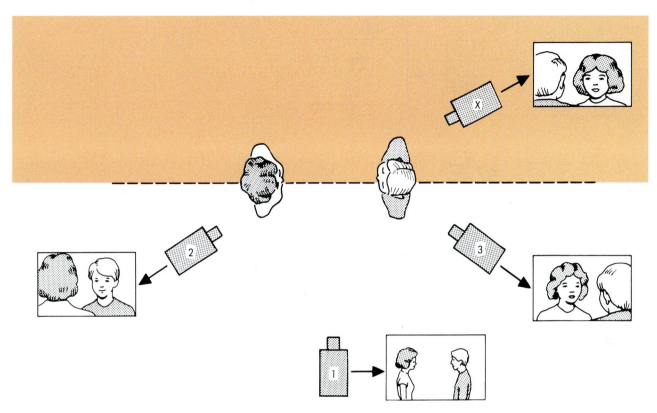

6.50   A conversation scene and the axis of action.

do not cross this axis, cutting them together will keep the **screen direction** of the girl's movement constant, from left to right. But if we *cross* the axis and film a shot from the other side, the girl will now appear on the screen as moving from *right to left*. Such a cut could be disorienting.

Consider a similar situation to that in 6.50, a standard scene of two cowboys meeting for a shootout on a town street **(6.51).** Cowboy A and cowboy B form the 180° line, but here A is walking from left to right and B is approaching from right to left, both seen in the shot taken from camera position 1. A closer view, from camera position 2, shows B still moving from right to left. A third shot, from camera position 3, shows A walking, as he had been in the first shot, from left to right.

But imagine that this third shot was instead taken from position X, on the opposite side of the line. A is now seen as moving from right to left. Has he taken fright and turned around while the second shot, of B, was on the screen? The filmmakers may want us to think that he is still walking toward his adversary, but the change in screen directions could make us think just the opposite. A cut to a shot taken from any point in the colored area would create this change in direction. Such breaks in continuity can be confusing.

Even more disorienting would be crossing the line while establishing the scene's action. In our shootout, if the first shot shows A walking from left to right and the second shot shows B (from the other side of the line) also walking left to right, we would probably not be sure that they were walking toward each other. The two cowboys would seem to be walking in the same direction at different points on the street, as if one were following the other. We would very likely be startled if they suddenly came face to face within the same shot.

The 180° system prides itself on delineating space clearly. The viewer should always know *where the characters are* in relation to one another and to the setting. More important, the viewer always knows *where he or she is* with respect to the story action. The space of the scene, clearly and unambiguously unfolded, does not

"... what I call 'new brutalism' in cinema ... is a form of naïveté, because it's made by people who I think don't really have a grasp of cinema's history. It's the MTV kind of editing, where the main idea is that the more disorienting it is, the more exciting. And you see it creeping into mainstream cinema more and more. You look at something like Armageddon and you see all the things that would have been forbidden in classical cinema, like crossing the line, camera jumping from side to side. It is a way to artificially generate excitement, but it doesn't really have any basis to it. And I find it kind of sad, because it's like an old man trying to dress like a teenager."

— John Boorman, director

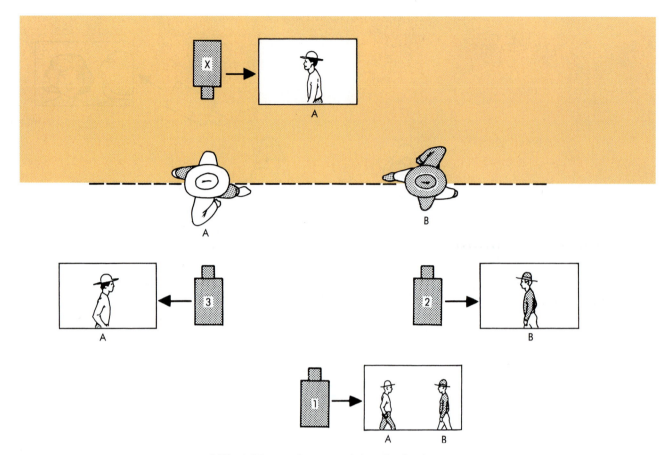

6.51 A Western shootout and the axis of action.

jar or disorient, because such disorientation, it is felt, will distract the viewer from the center of attention: the narrative chain of causes and effects.

Continuity Editing in *The Maltese Falcon*

We saw in Chapter 3 that the classical Hollywood mode of narrative subordinates time, motivation, and other factors to the cause–effect sequence. We also saw how mise-en-scene and camera work may present narrative material. Now we can note how, on the basis of the 180° principle, filmmakers have developed the continuity system as a way to build up a smoothly flowing space that remains subordinate to narrative action. Let's consider a concrete example: the opening of John Huston's film *The Maltese Falcon.*

The scene begins in the office of detective Sam Spade. In the first two shots, this space is established in several ways. First, there is the office window (shot 1a, **6.52**), from which the camera tilts down to reveal Spade (shot 1b, **6.53**) rolling a cigarette. As Spade says, "Yes, sweetheart?" shot 2 (**6.54**) appears. This is important in several respects. It is an **establishing shot,** delineating the overall space of the office: the door, the intervening area, the desk, and Spade's position. Note also that shot 2 establishes a 180° line between Spade and his secretary, Effie; Effie could be the girl in 6.50, and Spade could be the boy. The first phase of this scene will be built around staying on the same side of this 180° line.

Once laid out for us in the first two shots, the space is analyzed into its components. Shots 3 (**6.55**) and 4 (**6.56**) show Effie and Spade talking. Because the 180° line established at the outset is adhered to (each shot presents the two from the same side), we know their location and spatial relationships. In cutting together me-

6.52 *The Maltese Falcon:* shot 1a.

6.53 *The Maltese Falcon:* shot 1b.

6.54 *The Maltese Falcon:* shot 2.

6.55 *The Maltese Falcon:* shot 3.

6.56 *The Maltese Falcon:* shot 4.

dium shots of the two, however, Huston relies on two other common tactics within the 180° system.

The first is the **shot/reverse-shot** pattern. Once the 180° line has been established, we can show first one end point of the line, then the other. Here we cut back and forth from Effie to Spade. A reverse shot is not literally the reverse of the first framing. It's simply a shot of the opposite end of the axis of action, usually showing a three-quarters view of the subject. In our bird's-eye view diagram (6.50), shots 2 and 3 form a shot/reverse-shot pattern, as 6.55 and 6.56 do here. Earlier examples in this chapter of shot/reverse-shot cutting are 6.17, 6.18 and 6.19, 6.20.

The second tactic Huston uses here is the **eyeline match.** That is, shot A presents someone looking at something offscreen; shot B shows us what is being looked at. In neither shot are *both* looker and object present. In the *Maltese Falcon* opening, the cut from the shot of Effie (shot 3, 6.55) to the shot of Spade at his desk (shot 4, 6.56) is an eyeline match. The shots from *The Birds* of Melanie watching the bird attack and fire also create eyeline matches, as do the examples of editing balancing frame compositions (6.17, 6.18 and 6.19, 6.20).

Note that shot/reverse-shot editing need not employ eyeline matches. You could film both ends of the axis in a shot/reverse-shot pattern without showing the characters looking at each other. (In 6.56, Spade is not looking at Effie.) On the whole, however, most shot/reverse-shot cuts also utilize the eyeline match.

The eyeline match is a simple idea but a powerful one, since the *directional* quality of the eyeline creates a strong spatial continuity. To be looked at, an object must be near the looker. The eyeline match presumably created the effects Kuleshov identified in his construction of false spaces through editing. That is, the expressionless actor seems to be looking at whatever we see in the next shot, and the audience assumes that the actor is reacting accordingly.

Within the 180° system, the eyeline match, like constant screen direction, can stabilize space. Note how in shot 3, Effie's glance off right reiterates Spade's position even though he is not onscreen. And though Spade does not look up after the cut to shot 4, the camera position remains adamantly on the same side of the axis of action (indeed, the position is virtually identical to that in shot 1b). We know

CONNECT TO THE BLOG

For thoughts on the importance of eyeline directions in a very different art form, see "The eyeline match goes way, way back."

See www.davidbordwell.net/blog/?p=3518.

6.57   *The Maltese Falcon:* shot 5a.

6.58   *The Maltese Falcon:* shot 5b.

6.59   *The Maltese Falcon:* shot 6a.

6.60   *The Maltese Falcon:* shot 6b.

that Effie is offscreen left. Thus the breakdown of the scene's space is completely consistent. Thanks to the shot/reverse-shot pattern and the eyeline match, we understand the characters' locations even when they aren't in the same frame.

The spatial consistency is reaffirmed in shot 5, which presents the same framing as did shot 2. The office is shown again (shot 5a, **6.57**), when the new character, Brigid O'Shaughnessy, enters. Spade stands to greet her, and the camera reframes his movement by a slight tilt upward (shot 5b, **6.58**). Shot 5 is a **reestablishing shot,** since it reestablishes the overall space that was analyzed into shots 3 and 4. The pattern, then, has been *establishment/breakdown/reestablishment*—one of the most common patterns of spatial editing in the classical continuity style.

Let's pause to examine how this pattern has functioned to advance the narrative. Shot 1 has suggested the locale and, more important, has emphasized the protagonist by linking him to the sign on the window. Offscreen sound and Spade's "Yes, sweetheart?" motivate the cut to shot 2. This establishing shot firmly anchors shot 1 spatially. It also introduces the source of the offscreen sound—the new character, Effie. The shot changes at precisely the moment when Effie enters. We are thus unlikely to notice the cut, because our expectations lead us to want to see what happens next. The area near the door has been shown when the cause–effect chain makes it important, not before.

Shots 3 and 4 present the conversation between Spade and Effie, and the shot/reverse shot and the eyeline match reassure us as to the characters' locations. We may not even notice the cutting, since the style works to emphasize the dramatic flow of the scene—what Effie says and how Spade reacts. In shot 5, the overall view of the office is presented again, precisely at the moment when a new character enters the scene, and this in turn situates her firmly in the space. Thus narrative elements—the dialogue, the entrance of new characters—are emphasized by adhering to the 180° system. The editing subordinates space to action.

We can trace the same procedures, with one additional variation, in the shots that follow. In shot 5, Brigid O'Shaughnessy enters Spade's office. Shot 6 presents a reverse angle on the two of them as she comes toward him (shot 6a, **6.59**). She sits down alongside his desk (shot 6b, **6.60**). Up to this point, the 180° line has run between Spade and the doorway. Now the axis of action runs from Spade to the client's chair by his desk. Once established, this new line will not be violated.

The extra factor here is a third tactic for ensuring spatial continuity—the **match on action,** a very powerful device. Assume that a person starts to stand up in shot 1. We can wait until the character is standing up and has stopped moving before cutting to shot 2. But we can instead show the person's movement *beginning* in shot 1, and then we can cut to shot 2, which shows the continuation of the movement. We would then have a match on action, the editing device that carries a movement across the break between two shots.

To appreciate the skill involved in making a match on action, recall that most films are shot with a single camera. In filming shots whose action will be matched at the editing stage, it is possible that the first shot, in which the movement starts, will be filmed hours or days apart from the second, in which the movement is continued. Thus matching action is not simply a matter of cutting together two complete versions of the same scene from different vantage points. The director and the crew must keep notes about matters of camera work, mise-en-scene, and editing so that all the details can be fitted together in the assembly phase of production.

In the *Maltese Falcon* scene, the cut from the end of shot 5 (6.58) to the beginning of shot 6 (6.59) uses a match on action, the action being Brigid's walk toward Spade's desk. Again, the 180° system aids in concealing the match, since it keeps screen direction constant: Brigid moves from left to right in both shots. As you'd expect, the match on action is a tool of narrative continuity. It takes a practiced eye to spot a smooth match on action; so powerful is our desire to follow the action flowing across the cut that we ignore the cut itself.

6.61 *The Maltese Falcon:* shot 7.

6.62 *The Maltese Falcon:* shot 8.

6.63 *The Maltese Falcon:* shot 9.

6.64 *The Maltese Falcon:* shot 10.

6.65 *The Maltese Falcon:* shot 11.

6.66 *The Maltese Falcon:* shot 12.

6.67 *The Maltese Falcon:* shot 13.

6.68 *The Maltese Falcon:* shot 14.

6.69 *The Maltese Falcon:* shot 15.

Except for the match on action, the editing in the rest of the scene uses the same tactics we have already seen. When Brigid sits down, a new axis of action has been established (shot 6b, 6.60). This enables Huston to break down the space into closer shots (shots 7–13, **6.61–6.67**). All of these shots use the shot/reverse-shot tactic: the camera frames, at an oblique angle, one end point of the 180° line, then frames the other. (Note the shoulders in the foreground of shots 7, 8, and 10—6.61, 6.62, and 6.64.) Here again, the editing of space presents the dialogue action simply and unambiguously.

Beginning with shot 12, Huston's cuts also create eyeline matches. Spade looks off left at Brigid (shot 12, 6.66). She looks off left as the door is heard opening (shot 13, 6.67). Archer, just coming in, looks off right at them (shot 14, **6.68**), and they both look off at him (shot 15, **6.69**). The 180° rule permits us always to know who is looking at whom.

Huston could have played the entire conversation in one long take, remaining with shot 6b (6.60). Why has he broken the conversation into seven shots? Most evidently, the analytical cutting controls our attention. We'll look at Brigid or Spade at exactly the moment Huston wants us to. In the long take and the more distant

6.70   *The Maltese Falcon:* shot 16a.

6.71   *The Maltese Falcon:* shot 16b.

6.72   *The Maltese Falcon:* shot 17.

6.73   In Ron Howard's *Parenthood,* eyeline-matched shot/reverse shots present a conversation . . .

6.74   . . . with the women in the foreground establishing the axis of action.

CONNECT TO THE BLOG
Shots showing characters' reactions are often important to the narrative. We talk about how in "They're looking for us."

See www.davidbordwell.net/blog/?p=2743.

framing, Huston would have to channel our attention in other ways, perhaps through staging or sound.

Furthermore, the shot/reverse-shot pattern emphasizes the development of Brigid's story and Spade's reaction to it. As she gets into details, the cutting moves from over-the-shoulder shots (6.61, 6.62) to framings that isolate Brigid (6.63 and 6.65) and eventually one that isolates Spade (6.66). These shots come at the point when Brigid, in an artificially shy manner, tells her story, and the medium close-ups arouse our curiosity about whether she's telling the truth. The shot of Spade's reaction (6.66) suggests that he's skeptical. In short, the analytical editing cooperates with framing and figure behavior to focus our attention on Brigid's tale, to let us study her demeanor, and to get a hint as to Spade's response.

When Archer enters, the breakdown of the space stops for a moment, and Huston reestablishes the locale. Archer is integrated into the action by means of a right-ward pan shot (shots 16a and 16b, **6.70** and **6.71**). His path is consistent with the scene's first axis of action, that running between Spade and the doorway. Moreover, the framing on him is similar to that used for Brigid's entrance earlier. (Compare shot 16b with 6a [6.71 and 6.59].) Such repetitions allow the viewer to concentrate on the new information, not the manner in which it is presented.

Now firmly established as part of the scene, Archer hitches himself up onto Spade's desk. His position puts him at Spade's end of the axis of action (shot 17, **6.72**). The rest of the scene's editing analyzes this new set of relationships without ever crossing the 180° line.

The viewer is not supposed to notice all this. Throughout, the shots present space to emphasize the cause–effect flow—the characters' actions, entrances, dialogue, reactions. The editing has economically organized space to convey narrative continuity.

The continuity system, in exactly these terms, remains in force today. Most narrative films still draw on 180° principles (**6.73, 6.74**).

Continuity Editing: Some Fine Points

The continuity system can be refined in various ways. If a director arranges several characters in a circular pattern—say, sitting around a dinner table—then the axis of action will probably run between the characters of greatest importance at the moment. In **6.75** and **6.76,** from Howard Hawks's *Bringing Up Baby,* the important interaction is occurring between the two men, so we can cut from one side of the woman in the foreground to the other side in order to get consistent shot/reverse shots. When one man leaves the table, however, a semicircular arrangement of figures in space is created, so that a new axis of action can be established between the two women. Now we can get shot/reverse-shot exchanges running down the length of the table (**6.77, 6.78**).

Both the *Maltese Falcon* and the *Bringing Up Baby* examples show that in the course of a scene the 180° line may shift as the characters move around the setting.

6.75   In *Bringing Up Baby,* the shot/reverse shot between the man on the right . . .

6.76   . . . and the one on the left gives way to . . .

6.77   . . . a shot/reverse shot between the woman on the left . . .

6.78   . . . and the one on the right.

"The way [Howard] Hawks constructs a continuity of space is remarkable, and generally holds you 'inside' it. There is no possible way of escape, unless the film decides to provide you with one. My theory is that his films are captivating because they build a sense of continuity which is so strong that it allows the complete participation of the audience."

— Slobodan Sijan, director

In some cases, the filmmaker may create a new axis of action that allows the camera to take up a position that would have crossed the line in an earlier phase of the scene.

The power of the axis of action and the eyelines it can create is so great that the filmmaker may be able to eliminate an establishing shot, thus relying on the Kuleshov effect. In Spike Lee's *She's Gotta Have It,* Nola Darling holds a Thanksgiving dinner for her three male friends. Lee never presents a shot showing all four in the same frame. Instead, he uses medium long shots including all the men (for example, **6.79**), over-the-shoulder shot/reverse shots among them (for example, **6.80**), and eyeline-matched medium close-ups of them. Nola is given her own medium close-ups (**6.81**).

Through eyelines and body orientations, Lee's editing keeps the spatial relations completely consistent. For example, each man looks in a different direction when addressing Nola (**6.82, 6.83**). This cutting pattern enhances the dramatic action by making all the men equal competitors for her. They are clustered at one end of the table, and none is shown in the same frame with her. In addition, by organizing the angles around her overall orientation to the action (as in **6.84,** an optical point-of-view shot), Lee keeps Nola the pivotal character. Further, the longer shot and her separate medium close-ups intensify the progression of the scene: the men are on display, and Nola is coolly judging each one's behavior.

Another felicity in the 180° system is the **cheat cut.** Sometimes a director may not have perfect continuity from shot to shot because he or she has composed each shot for specific reasons. Must the two shots match perfectly? Again, narrative motivation decides the matter. Given that the 180° system emphasizes story action, if we're paying attention to that, the director has some freedom to "cheat" mise-en-scene from shot to shot—that is, to mismatch slightly the positions of characters or objects.

Consider two shots from William Wyler's *Jezebel.* Neither character moves during either shot, but Wyler has blatantly cheated the position of Julie (**6.85, 6.86**). Yet most viewers would not notice the discrepancy since it's the dialogue that is

CONNECT TO THE BLOG
Another refinement: What happens if the reverse shot is withheld? We show some examples and discuss their functions in "Angles and perceptions."

See www.davidbordwell.net/blog/?p=744.

6.79   *She's Gotta Have It.*

6.80   *She's Gotta Have It.*

6.81   *She's Gotta Have It.*

6.82   *She's Gotta Have It.*

6.83   *She's Gotta Have It.*

6.84   *She's Gotta Have It.*

6.85   In this shot from *Jezebel,* the top of Julie's head is even with the man's chin . . .

6.86   . . . but in the second shot she seems to have grown several inches.

CONNECT TO THE BLOG
For more examples of point-of-view editing and an analysis of a scene, see "Three nights of a dreamer," at
www.davidbordwell.net/blog/?p=1457.

paramount in the scene; here again, the similarities between shots outweigh the differences of position. Moreover, a change from a straight-on angle to a slightly high angle helps hide the cheat. There is, in fact, a cheat in the *Maltese Falcon* scene, too, between shots 6b and 7. In 6b (6.60), as Spade leans forward, the back of his chair is not near him. Yet in shot 7 (6.61), it has been cheated to be just behind his left arm. Here again, the primacy of the narrative flow overrides such a cheat cut.

One more fine point in spatial continuity is particularly relevant to a film's narration. We have already seen that a camera framing can strongly suggest a character's optical point of view, rendering the narration subjective. We see this in our earlier example from *Fury* (5.112, 5.113). That example depends on a cut from the person looking (5.112) to what he sees (5.113). We have also seen an instance of POV cutting in the *Birds* sequence discussed on pp. 228–231. Now we are in a position to see how optical POV is consistent with continuity editing, creating a variety of eyeline-match editing known as *point-of-view cutting.*

Alfred Hitchcock's *Rear Window* is built around the situation of the solitary photographer Jeff watching events taking place in an apartment across the courtyard. Hitchcock uses a standard eyeline-match pattern, cutting from a shot of Jeff looking (**6.87**) to a shot of what he sees (**6.88**). Since there is no establishing shot that shows both Jeff and the opposite apartment, the Kuleshov effect operates here: our mind connects the two images. More specifically, the second shot represents Jeff's optical viewpoint, and this is filmed from a position on his end of the axis of action (**6.89**). The camera has not crossed the line. We are strongly restricted to what Jeff sees and what (he thinks) he knows.

As *Rear Window* goes on, the subjectivity of the POV shots intensifies. Becoming more eager to examine the details of his neighbor's life, Jeff begins to use binoculars and a photographic telephoto lens to magnify his view. By using shots taken with lenses of different focal lengths, Hitchcock shows how each new tool enlarges what Jeff can see (**6.90–6.93**). Hitchcock's cutting adheres to spatial continuity rules and exploits their POV possibilities in order to arouse curiosity and suspense.

More Refinements: Crossing the Axis of Action

Most continuity-based filmmakers prefer not to cut across the axis of action. They would rather move the actors around the setting and create a new axis. Still, can

◀ **6.87** In *Rear Window,* Jeff looks out his window and . . .

▶ **6.88** . . . the next shot shows what he sees from his optical POV.

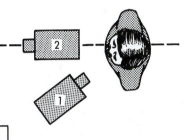

6.89 An overhead diagram of the *Rear Window* POV shot.

◀ **6.90** When Jeff looks through his binoculars . . .

▶ **6.91** . . . we see a telephoto POV shot of his neighbor.

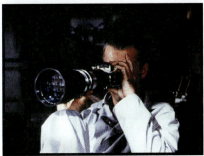

◀ **6.92** When he employs a powerful photographic lens . . .

▶ **6.93** . . . the resulting POV shot enlarges his neighbor's activities even more.

you ever legitimately cut across an established axis of action? Yes, sometimes. A scene occurring in a doorway, on a staircase, or in other symmetrical settings may occasionally break the line. Sometimes, too, the filmmakers can get across the axis by taking one shot *on the line itself* and using it as a transition. This strategy is rare in dialogue sequences, but it can be seen in chases and outdoor action. By filming on the axis, the filmmaker presents the action as moving directly toward the camera (a *head-on* shot) or away from it (a *tail-on* shot). The climactic chase of *The Road Warrior* offers several examples. As marauding road gangs try to board a fleeing gasoline truck, George Miller uses many head-on and tail-on shots of the vehicles **(6.94–6.98).**

Also, we should note that continuity-based films occasionally violate screen direction without confusing the viewer. This usually occurs when the scene's action is very well defined. For example, during a chase in John Ford's *Stagecoach*, there is no ambiguity about the Ringo Kid's leaping from the coach to the horses **(6.99, 6.100).** We wouldn't be likely to assume that the coach had turned around suddenly, as in the possible misinterpretation of the shootout scene with the two cowboys (6.51).

Crosscutting

The continuity system shows that editing can endow the film's narration with a great range of knowledge. A cut can take us to any point on the correct side of the axis of action. Editing can even create omniscience, that godlike knowledge that some films seek to present. The outstanding technical device here is *crosscutting*, first extensively explored by D. W. Griffith in his last-minute rescue scenes. In *The Battle at Elderbush Gulch*, a cavalry troop is riding to rescue some settlers trapped

6.94   Near the climax of the chase in *The Road Warrior*, Max is driving left to right along the road . . .

6.95   . . . and in later shots he is still driving toward the right. An attacking thug perched on the front of the truck turns and looks off right in horror . . .

6.96   . . . realizing that another vehicle, moving right to left, is coming toward them on a collision course.

6.97   Several quick shots facing head-on to the vehicles show the crash . . .

6.98   . . . and a long shot shows the truck again, now moving right to left.

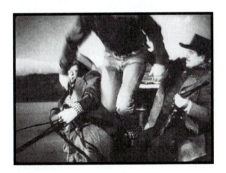

6.99   In *Stagecoach,* in a long shot where all movement is toward the right, the hero begins leaping from the driver's seat down onto the horse team . . .

6.100   . . . and in the next shot both he and the coach are moving leftward.

6.101   In *The Battle of Elderbush Gulch,* Griffith cuts from a shot of the cavalry . . .

6.102   . . . to a view inside the besieged cabin . . .

6.103   . . . back to the cavalry . . .

6.104   . . . and then back to the cabin.

in a cabin and battling the Indians outside **(6.101–6.104).** After 11 additional shots of the cavalry, various parts of the cabin interior, and the Indians outdoors, a 12th shot shows the cavalry riding in from the distance behind the cabin.

Crosscutting gives us an unrestricted knowledge of causal, temporal, or spatial information by alternating shots from one line of action in one place with shots of other events in other places. Crosscutting thus creates some spatial discontinuity, but it binds the action together by creating a sense of cause and effect and simultaneous time. In *Jerry Maguire,* for example, crosscutting interweaves the action of sports agent Jerry and his rival racing to sign up the same clients **(6.105–6.108).**

Fritz Lang's *M* goes further, intercutting three lines of action. While the police seek the child murderer, gangsters prowl the streets looking for him as well, and we also occasionally see the murderer himself. Crosscutting ties together the different lines of action, bringing out a temporal simultaneity and the causal process of the pursuit. The crosscutting also gives us a range of knowledge greater than that of any one character. We know that the gangsters are after the murderer, but the police and the murderer do not. Crosscutting also builds up suspense, as we form expectations that are only gradually clarified and fulfilled. It may create parallels as well, and Lang exploits this possibility by suggesting analogies between the police and the crooks. Whatever other functions it may have, though, crosscutting remains primarily a means of presenting narrative actions that are occurring in several locales at roughly the same time.

All the devices of spatial continuity show how film technique draws the spectator into an active process. We assume that setting, character movement, and character position will be consistent and coherent. Our prior knowledge of filmic conventions lets us form strong expectations about what shot will follow the one we are seeing. We also make inferences on the basis of cues, so that when Brigid and Spade look off left, we infer that someone is entering the room, and we expect to see a shot of that person.

What makes the continuity system invisible is its ability to draw on a range of skills that we have learned so well that they seem automatic. This makes spatial continuity editing a powerful tool for the filmmaker who wishes to reinforce habitual expectations. In recent decades, Hollywood filmmakers have developed ways to make traditional continuity techniques more forceful. (See "A Closer Look.") Because continuity editing has been so widely used for so long, it also becomes a central target for the filmmaker who wants to use film style to challenge or change our normal viewing activities.

Temporal Continuity: Order, Frequency, and Duration

In the classical continuity system, time, like space, is organized according to the development of the narrative. We know that the plot's presentation of the story typically involves manipulation of time. Continuity editing seeks to support and sustain this temporal manipulation.

6.105 In *Jerry Maguire*, from a shot of Jerry seething with tension . . .

6.106 . . . there is a cut to his confident rival and his assistant.

6.107 We cut back to Jerry placing a phone call . . .

6.108 . . . and his rival doing the same.

To get specific, recall our distinction among temporal order, frequency, and duration. Continuity editing typically presents the story events in a 1-2-3 order. Spade rolls a cigarette, then Effie comes in, then he answers her, and so on. The most common violation of 1-2-3 order is a flashback, signaled by a cut or dissolve. Furthermore, classical editing also often presents only *once* what happens *once* in the story; in continuity style, it would be a gross mistake for Huston to repeat the shot of, say, Brigid sitting down (6.60). Again, though, flashbacks are the most common way of motivating the repetition of a scene already witnessed. So chronological sequence and one-for-one frequency are the standard methods of handling order and frequency within the continuity style of editing. There are occasional exceptions, as we saw in our examples from *Hiroshima mon amour, The Godfather,* and *Police Story* (pp. 233–235).

What of duration? In the classical continuity system, story duration is seldom expanded; that is, screen time is seldom made greater than story time. Usually, duration is in complete continuity (plot time equaling story time) or is elided (story time being greater than plot time). Let's first consider complete continuity, the most common possibility. Here a scene occupying five minutes in the story also occupies five minutes when projected on the screen.

The first scene of *The Maltese Falcon* displays three cues for *temporal continuity*. First, the narrative progression of the scene has no gaps. Every movement by the characters and every line of dialogue is presented. Second, there is the sound track. Sound issuing from the story space (what we call *diegetic* sound) is a standard indicator of temporal continuity, especially when, as in this scene, the sound bleeds over each cut. Third, there is the match on action between shots 5 and 6. So powerful is the match on action that it creates both spatial *and* temporal continuity. The reason is obvious: if an action carries across the cut, the space and time are assumed to be continuous from shot to shot. In all, an absence of ellipses in the

"Now nobody trusts the actor's performance. If an actor has a scene where they are sitting in the distance, everybody says, 'What are you shooting? It has to be close-up!' This is ridiculous. You have the position of the hand, the whole body—this is the feeling of a movie. I hate movies where everybody has big close-ups all the time. . . . This is television. I have talking heads on my television set in my home all the time."

— Miroslav Ondříček, editor

INTENSIFIED CONTINUITY: *L.A. Confidential* and Contemporary Editing

By the 1930s, the continuity system was the standard approach to editing in most of the world's commercial filmmaking. But it underwent changes over the years. Today's editing practices abide by the principles of continuity but amplify them in certain ways.

Most obviously, mainstream films are now cut much faster than in the period between 1930 and 1960. Then, a film typically consisted of 300–500 shots, but in the years after 1960, the cutting pace picked up. Today a two-hour film might have over 2000 shots, and action films routinely contain 3000 or more. The average shot in *The Bourne Ultimatum* lasts about two seconds. Partly because of the faster editing, scenes are built out of relatively close views of individual characters, rather than long-shot framings. Establishing shots tend to be less common, sometimes appearing only at the end of a scene. Telephoto lenses, which enlarge faces, help achieve tight framings, and modern widescreen formats allow two or more facial close-ups to occupy the screen. Also, the camera tends to move very frequently, picking out one detail after another.

The accompanying shots from *L.A. Confidential* show several of these tendencies at work. After arresting three black suspects, Lieutenant Ed Exley prepares to wring a confession from them. The scene takes less than a minute but employs nine shots, two with significant camera movement. (The film contains nearly 2000 shots, an average of four seconds apiece.) Director Curtis Hanson shifts the emphasis among several key characters by coordinating his editing with anamorphic widescreen, staging in depth, close-ups and medium close-ups, rack-focus, and mobile framing **(6.109–6.120)**. Interestingly, the actors make no expressive use of their hands or bodies; the performances are almost completely facial.

CONNECT TO THE BLOG

After you've read about *L.A. Confidential,* check out our blog entries on the Bourne trilogy, in "Unsteadicam chronicles"
www.davidbordwell.net/blog/?p=1175,
"[insert your favorite Bourne pun here]"
www.davidbordwell.net/blog/?p=1230,
and "I broke everything new again"
www.davidbordwell.net/blog/?p=1285.
We also compare a scene in *The Shop Around the Corner* with the same one in the remake, *You've Got Mail,* in "Intensified continuity revisited,"
www.davidbordwell.net/blog/?p=859.
For thoughts on multiple-camera shooting and continuity, see "Cutting remarks: On *The Good German,* classical style, and the police tactical unit"
www.davidbordwell.net/blog/?p=91.

Why did this intensified form of continuity become so common? Some historians trace it to the influence of television. Recent movies were broadcast by TV networks in the 1960s, transmitted by cable and satellite in the 1970s, and available on home video in the 1980s and 1990s. As people saw movies on home screens rather than in theaters, filmmakers reshaped their techniques. Constantly changing the image by cutting and camera movement could keep the viewer from switching channels or picking up a magazine. On smaller screens, faster cutting is easier to follow, and closer views look better than long shots, which tend to lose detail. Intensified continuity was shaped by many factors, such as the arrival of computer-based editing, but television was a major influence.

6.109   Shot 1: The scene begins by presenting only a portion of the space. A reflection shows Exley waiting and his colleagues milling about outside the interrogation room. This image singles out the core dramatic action to come—Exley's brutal confrontation with the suspects.

6.110 Shot 2: A match on Exley's action of turning gives us a fuller view of the policemen and establishes two other main characters: Jack Vincennes on the left and Bud White in the background, watching. This is only a partial establishing shot; a later camera movement will acquaint us with the layout of the interrogation rooms.

6.111 Shot 3: Hanson underscores White's presence by cutting to a telephoto shot of him saying that the suspects killed his partner.

6.112 Shot 4: In an echo of the opening framing, Exley now stands at the second interrogation room, seen in another reflection. The shot also reiterates Vincennes's presence, which will provide an important reaction later.

6.113 The camera tracks with Exley moving right to study the suspect in the third room. White's reflection can be seen in frame center. The camera movement has linked the three main detectives on the case while also establishing the three rooms as being side by side. At the end of the camera movement, Exley turns, and . . .

6.114 Shot 5: . . . a two-shot establishes his superior, Smith, on the scene. As Smith explains that the suspects' shotguns put them at the murder scene, the camera racks focus to him, putting Exley out of focus.

6.115 Shot 6: A cutaway to White listening—again, a tight facial shot taken with a telephoto lens—reminds us of his presence. He is only an observer in this phase of the scene, but as the questioning heats up, he will burst in to attack a suspect.

6.116 Shot 7: Returning to the two-shot shows Smith demanding that Exley make the men confess.

6.117 Shot 8: A reverse-angle on Exley, the first shot in the scene devoted to his face alone, underscores his determination: "Oh, I'll break them, sir."

6.118   Shot 9: A cut back to the two-shot supplies Smith's satisfied reaction.

6.119   Exley turns away. The lens shifts focus to catch his grim face in the foreground, preparing us for the brutality he will display.

6.120   Exley walks out of the shot. The camera tilts down slightly and racks focus to display Vincennes's skeptical expression. The telephoto lens, accentuated by the rack-focus, has supplied facial views of Smith, then Exley, and then Vincennes in a single shot.

story action, diegetic sound overlapping the cuts, and matching on action are three primary indicators that the duration of the scene is continuous.

Sometimes, however, a second possibility will be explored: *temporal ellipsis.* The ellipsis may omit seconds, minutes, hours, days, years, or centuries. Some ellipses are of no importance to the narrative development and so are concealed. A classical narrative film doesn't show the entire time it takes a character to dress, wash, and breakfast in the morning. Shots of the character going into the shower, putting on shoes, or frying an egg might be combined so as to eliminate the unwanted bits of story time. As we saw on pp. 233–234, optical punctuations, empty frames, and cutaways are frequently used to cover short temporal ellipses.

But other ellipses are important to the narrative. The viewer must recognize that time has passed. For this task, the continuity style has built up a varied repertoire of devices. In films made before the 1960s, dissolves, fades, or wipes are typically used to indicate an ellipsis between shots, usually the end of one scene and the beginning of the next. The Hollywood rule is that a dissolve indicates a brief time lapse and a fade indicates a much longer one.

Contemporary filmmakers usually employ a cut for such transitions. For example, in *2001,* Stanley Kubrick cuts directly from a bone spinning in the air to a space station orbiting the earth, one of the boldest graphic matches in narrative cinema. The cut eliminates millions of years of story time. Less drastically, most contemporary films indicate the passage of time through direct cuts. Changes in lighting, locale, or character position cue us that story time has passed **(6.121–6.123).**

In other cases, it's necessary to show a large-scale process or a lengthy period—a city waking up in the morning, a war, a child growing up, the rise of a singing star. Here classical continuity uses another device for temporal ellipsis: the **montage sequence.** (This should not be confused with the concept of *montage* in Sergei Eisenstein's film theory.) Brief portions of a process, informative titles (for example, "1865" or "San Francisco"), stereotyped images (such as the Eiffel Tower), newsreel footage, newspaper headlines, and the like can be joined by dissolves and music to create a quick, regular rhythm and to compress a lengthy series of actions into a few moments.

American studio films of the 1930s established some montage clichés—calendar pages fluttering away, newspaper presses pounding out an Extra—but in the hands of deft editors, such sequences became small virtuoso pieces. The driving pace of gangster films like *Scarface* and *The Roaring Twenties* owes a lot to dynamic montage sequences. Slavko Vorkapich, an experimental filmmaker, created somewhat abstract, almost delirious summaries of wide-ranging actions such as stock market crashes, political campaigns, and an opera singer's career **(6.124).**

Montage sequences have been a mainstay of narrative filmmaking ever since. *Jaws* employs montage to summarize the start of tourist season through brief shots of vacationers arriving at the beach. A montage sequence in *Spider-Man* shows Peter Parker sketching his superhero costume, inspired by visions of the girl he loves **(6.125, 6.126).** All these instances also remind us that because montage sequences usually lack dialogue, they tend to come wrapped in music. In *Tootsie,* a song accompanies a series of magazine covers showing the hero's rise to success as a soap opera star.

In sum, the continuity style uses the temporal dimension of editing primarily for narrative purposes. Through prior knowledge, the spectator expects the editing to present story events in chronological order, with only occasional rearrangement through flashbacks. The viewer expects that editing will respect the frequency of story events. And the viewer assumes that actions irrelevant to story causality will be omitted or at least abridged by judicious ellipses. All these expectations allow the viewer to follow the story with minimal effort.

Like graphics, rhythm, and space, time is organized to permit the unfolding of cause and effect, and the arousal of curiosity, suspense, and surprise. But there are many alternatives to the continuity style of editing, and these are worth a look.

6.121 *Wendy and Lucy:* Arrested for shoplifting, Wendy is being fingerprinted, and she glances up at the clock. She's worried about having left her dog Lucy at the supermarket.

6.122   The clock shot has functioned as a cutaway to cover a time gap. This shot of Wendy in a cell indicates that some minutes have elapsed since she was fingerprinted.

6.123   Wendy's marked change of position from the previous shot suggests that still more time has passed. An older film would have implied the passage of time through dissolves, but here the abrupt changes of locale and character position suggest the same thing. A later shot of the clock will show that Wendy has been held for at least two hours.

6.124   In *May Time,* Slavko Vorkapich uses superimpositions (here, the singer, sheet music, and a curtain rising) and rapid editing to summarize an opera singer's triumphs. *Citizen Kane* ironically refers to this passage in the montage sequences showing Susan Alexander's failures.

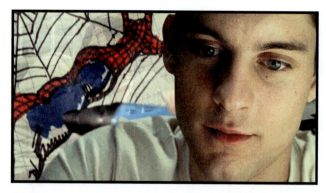

6.125   For a montage sequence in *Spider-Man*, CGI technique creates a split image, showing both Peter's expression and a close-up of the costume he's designing.

6.126   The *Spider-Man* sequence also uses a more traditional linking device, a dissolve that briefly superimposes two shots.

Alternatives to Continuity Editing

Graphic and Rhythmic Possibilities

Powerful and pervasive as it is, the continuity style remains only *one* style, and many filmmakers have explored other editing possibilities.

Films using abstract or associational form have frequently granted the graphic and rhythmic dimensions of editing great weight. Instead of joining shot 1 to shot 2 primarily on the basis of the spatial and temporal functions that the shot fulfills in presenting a story, you could join them on the basis of purely graphic or rhythmic qualities—independent of the time and space they represent. In films such as *Anticipation of the Night, Scenes from Under Childhood,* and *Western History,* experimentalist Stan Brakhage uses purely graphic means of joining shot to shot. Continuities and discontinuities of light, texture, and shape motivate the editing. Similarly, parts of Bruce Conner's *Cosmic Ray, A Movie,* and *Report* cut together newsreel footage, old film clips, film leader, and black frames on the basis of graphic patterns of movement, direction, and speed.

Many non-narrative films have completely subordinated the space and time presented in each shot to the rhythmic relations among shots. *Single-frame films* (in which each shot is only one frame long) are the most extreme examples of this overriding rhythmic concern. Two famous examples are Robert Breer's *Fist Fight* (**6.127**) and Peter Kubelka's *Schwechater.*

As early as 1913, some painters were contemplating the pure-design possibilities offered by film, and many works of the European avant-grade movements of the 1920s combined an interest in abstract graphics with a desire to explore rhythmic editing. Perhaps the most famous of these is the Fernand Léger–Dudley Murphy film *Ballet mécanique.* In Chapter 10, we'll see how *Ballet mécanique* juxtaposes its shots on the basis of graphic and rhythmic qualities.

The graphic and rhythmic possibilities of editing haven't been neglected in the story film, either. Some narrative filmmakers occasionally subordinate narrative concerns to graphic pattern. The most famous examples are probably the films for which Busby Berkeley choreographed elaborate dance numbers. In *42nd Street, Gold Diggers of 1933, Footlight Parade, Gold Diggers of 1935,* and *Dames,* the narrative periodically grinds to a halt, and the film presents intricate dances that are arranged, shot, and edited with a concern for the pure configuration of dancers and background (4.146, from *42nd Street*).

More complex is the graphic editing of Yasujiro Ozu. Ozu's cutting is often dictated by a much more precise graphic continuity than we find in the classical continuity style. In a scene from *An Autumn Afternoon,* Ozu creates close graphic

6.127   The stretches of single-frame shots in *Fist Fight* create a flickering effect on the screen.

6.128 In *An Autumn Afternoon,* Ozu cuts from one man drinking sake directly . . .

6.129 . . . to another caught in almost exactly the same position, costume, and gesture.

6.130 In *Ohayu,* Ozu creates a playful graphic match by cutting from an outdoor scene with a bright red sweater in the upper left . . .

matches on two men seated at a table drinking sake **(6.128, 6.129).** In *Ohayu,* Ozu uses color for the same purpose, cutting from laundry on a line to a domestic interior and matching on a red shape in the upper left of each shot (a shirt, a lamp; **6.130, 6.131).**

6.131 . . . to an interior with a vivid red lampshade in the same position.

Some narrative films have momentarily subordinated spatial and temporal editing to rhythmic cutting. In the 1920s, both the French Impressionist school and the Soviet avant-garde frequently made story progression secondary to purely rhythmic editing. In such films as Abel Gance's *La Roue,* Jean Epstein's *Coeur fidèle* and *La Glace à trois faces,* and Alexandre Volkoff's *Kean,* accelerated editing renders the tempo of an onrushing train, a whirling carousel, a racing automobile, and a drunken dance. Kuleshov's *The Death Ray* and, as we shall see, Eisenstein's *October* occasionally make rhythm dominate narrative space and time. We can find strong passages of rhythmic editing in Rouben Mamoulian's *Love Me Tonight,* René Clair's *Le Million,* and several films of Ozu and Hitchcock, as well as in *Assault on Precinct 13* and *The Terminator.* Pulsating rhythmic editing is prominent in films influenced by music videos, such as *The Crow* and *Romeo + Juliet.* As we saw with graphics, rhythmic editing may override the spatial and temporal dimensions; when this happens, narrative usually becomes less important.

Spatial and Temporal Discontinuity

How can you tell a story without adhering to the continuity rules? Let's sample some ways filmmakers have created distinct editing styles by use of what might be considered spatial and temporal discontinuities.

One option is to use spatial continuity in ambiguous ways. In *Mon Oncle d'Amérique,* Resnais intercuts the stories of his three main characters with shots of each character's favorite star, taken from French films of the 1940s. At one point, as René's pesky office mate calls to him, we get the coworker in one shot **(6.132).** But Resnais cuts to a shot of Jean Gabin in an older film, turning in reverse shot **(6.133).** Only then does Resnais supply a shot of René turning to meet his questioner **(6.134).** The film does not definitely present the Gabin shot as a fantasy image; we can't tell whether René imagines himself as his favorite star confronting his coworker, or whether the film's narration draws the comparison independent of René's state of mind. The cut relies on the cues of shot/reverse shot but uses them to create a momentarily jarring discontinuity that triggers ambiguity.

More drastically, a filmmaker may violate or ignore the 180° system. The editing choices of filmmakers Jacques Tati and Yasujiro Ozu are based on what we might call 360° space. Instead of an axis of action that dictates that the camera be placed within an imaginary semicircle, these filmmakers work as if the action were not a line but a point at the center of a circle and as if the camera could be placed

6.132   *Mon Oncle d'Amérique.*

6.133   *Mon Oncle d'Amérique.*

6.134   *Mon Oncle d'Amérique.*

6.135   In *Early Summer,* Ozu cuts on the grandfather's gesture of drinking . . .

6.136   . . . directly to the opposite side of the characters.

at any point on the circumference. In *Mr. Hulot's Holiday, Play Time,* and *Traffic,* Tati systematically films from almost every side; edited together, the shots present multiple spatial perspectives on a single event. Similarly, Ozu's scenes construct a 360° space that produces what the continuity style would consider grave editing errors. Ozu's films often do not yield consistent relative positions and screen directions; the eyeline matches are out of joint, and the only consistency is the *violation* of the 180° line. One of the gravest sins in the classical continuity style is to match on action while breaking the line, yet Ozu does this comfortably in *Early Summer* **(6.135, 6.136).**

Such spatially discontinuous cutting affects the spectator's experience as well. The defender of classical editing would claim that spatial continuity rules are necessary for the clear presentation of a narrative. But anyone who has seen a film by Ozu or Tati can testify that no narrative confusion arises from their continuity violations. Though the spaces do not flow as smoothly as in the Hollywood style (this is indeed part of the films' fascination), the causal developments remain intelligible. The likeliest conclusion is that the continuity system is only *one* way to tell a story. Historically, this system has been the dominant one, but artistically, it isn't a necessity.

There are two other notable devices of discontinuity. In *Breathless,* Jean-Luc Godard violates conventions of spatial, temporal, and graphic continuity by his systematic use of the **jump cut.** Though this term is often loosely used, its primary meaning is this: when two shots of the same subject are cut together but are not sufficiently different in camera distance and angle, there will be a noticeable jump on the screen. Classical continuity avoids such jumps by generous use of shot/reverse shots and by the *30° rule* (advising that every camera position be varied by at least

6.137 In *Breathless,* in the jump cut from this shot of Patricia . . .

6.138 . . . to this one, the background has changed and some story time has gone by.

6.139 In *Fury,* Lang cuts from house-wives gossiping . . .

6.140 . . . to shots of clucking hens.

30° from the previous one). An examination of shots from *Breathless* suggests the consequences of Godard's jump cuts **(6.137, 6.138).** Far from flowing unnoticeably, such cuts are very visible.

Jump cuts should not be confused with those elliptical cuts that convey the passage of time by showing a person in different positions. We saw an instance earlier (6.121–6.123) in which Wendy is sitting in two positions on her cell bunk. In cuts like this one, we have two distinct angles on the subject, in accordance with the 30° rule. The jump cut shows the action from a single angle.

Today's mainstream films have somewhat domesticated the jump cut. It can now be found in montage sequences and during moments of surprise or violence. Ridley Scott's *Matchstick Men* is one film that exploits the technique as extensively as *Breathless* does.

A second violation of continuity is created by the **nondiegetic insert.** Here the filmmaker cuts from the scene to a metaphorical or symbolic shot that is not part of the space and time of the narrative. Clichés abound here **(6.139, 6.140).** More complex examples occur in the films of Eisenstein and Godard. In Eisenstein's *Strike,* the massacre of workers is intercut with the slaughter of a bull. In Godard's *La Chinoise,* Henri tells an anecdote about the ancient Egyptians, who, he claims, thought that "their language was the language of the gods." As he says this **(6.141),** Godard cuts in two close-ups of relics from the tomb of King Tutankhamen **(6.142, 6.143).** As nondiegetic inserts, coming from outside the story world, these shots construct a running, often ironic, commentary on the action, and they prompt the spectator to search for implicit meanings. Do the relics corroborate or challenge what Henri says?

There are still other alternatives to classical continuity, especially with respect to time. Although the classical approach to order and frequency of story events may

6.141 A diegetic shot in *La Chinoise* is followed by . . .

6.142 . . . nondiegetic shots of the lion bed of King Tutankhamen . . .

6.143 . . . and his golden mask.

6.144   This external shot from *Caché* seems at first to be in temporal order, but later it's revealed to be a replayed videotape.

6.145   The glimpse of the watching boy is also misleading. He seems to be watching the house, but in fact this shot is a flashback, and he is watching something very different.

seem the best option, it is only the most familiar. Story events do not have to be edited in 1-2-3 order.

Modern audiences have become accustomed to scenes that are interrupted by brief flashbacks. But some filmmakers create greater uncertainty by inserting a shot that may or may not be out of story order. Michael Haneke's *Caché* repeatedly shows a luxurious apartment building seen from across the street. After one nighttime view, there is a two-second shot of a boy watching, also at night **(6.144, 6.145)**. At first, this shot seems to be in correct order, like the shots of Jeff looking at his neighbors in *Rear Window* (6.87, 6.88, 6.90–6.93). Later we'll learn that *Caché*'s narration has misled us severely.

More insistently, in Resnais's *La Guerre est finie,* scenes cut in conventional continuity are interrupted by images that may represent flashbacks, or fantasy episodes, or even future events. Editing can also play with variable frequency for narrative purposes; the same event can be shown repeatedly. In *La Guerre est finie,* the

6.146   In *Pierrot le fou,* initially, Ferdinand jumps into the car as Marianne pulls away . . .

6.147   . . . but then the couple are seen back in their apartment.

6.148   Next the car races down a street . . .

6.149   . . . and then Marianne and Ferdinand climb onto a rooftop, an event that occurred before they drove off.

same funeral is depicted in different hypothetical ways, with the protagonist either present or absent.

Again, Godard offers a striking example of how editing can manipulate both order and frequency. In *Pierrot le fou,* as Marianne and Ferdinand flee her apartment, Godard scrambles the order of the shots **(6.146–6.149).** Godard also plays with frequency by repeating one gesture—Ferdinand jumping into the car—but showing it *differently* each time. Such manipulation of editing blocks our normal expectations about story action and forces us to concentrate on the very process of piecing together the film's narrative.

The editing may take liberties with story duration as well. Although complete continuity and ellipsis are the most common ways of rendering duration, expansion—stretching a moment out, making screen time greater than story time—remains a distinct possibility. François Truffaut uses such expansions in *Jules and Jim* to underscore narrative turning points, as when the heroine Catherine lifts her veil or jumps off a bridge.

Filmmakers have found creative ways to rework the most basic tenets of the continuity system. We've indicated, for example, that a match on action strongly suggests that time continues across the cut. Yet Alain Resnais creates an impossible continuous action in *Last Year at Marienbad.* Small groups of guests are standing around the hotel lobby; one medium shot frames a blonde woman beginning to turn away from the camera **(6.150).** In the middle of her turn, there is a cut to her, still turning but in a different setting **(6.151).** The smooth match on action, along with the woman's graphically matched position in the frame, implies that she is moving continuously, yet the change of setting contradicts this impression. As we'll see in Chapter 10, experimental films push ambiguous or contradictory editing even further.

Our examples indicate that some discontinuities of order, duration, and frequency can become perfectly intelligible in a narrative context. On the other hand, with the jump cut, the nondiegetic insert, and the inconsistent match on action,

CONNECT TO THE BLOG
Early Japanese swordplay movies display some daring editing, as we demonstrate in "Bando on the run."

See www.davidbordwell.net/blog/?p=911.

6.150   In *Last Year at Marienbad,* a match on action . . .

6.151   . . . across two settings.

temporal dislocations can also push away from traditional notions of story altogether and create ambiguous relations among shots.

As an example of the power of spatial and temporal discontinuities in editing, let's look at a famous example: Sergei Eisenstein's *October.*

Functions of Discontinuity Editing: *October*

For many Soviet filmmakers of the 1920s, editing was a major means of organizing the entire form of the film; it did not simply serve the narrative progression, as in the continuity system. Eisenstein's *Strike, Potemkin, October,* and *Old and New* tried to build a film on the basis of certain editing devices. Rather than subordinate his editing patterns to the mapping out of a story, Eisenstein conceived of these films as editing constructions.

Eisenstein deliberately opposed himself to continuity editing, seeking out and exploiting what Hollywood would consider discontinuities. He often staged, shot, and cut his sequences for the maximum *collision* from shot to shot and sequence to sequence. He believed that by being forced to synthesize such conflicts the viewer would participate in actively understanding the film.

No longer bound by conventional dramaturgy, Eisenstein's films roam freely through time and space. They construct intricate patterns of images calculated to stimulate the viewer's senses, emotions, and thinking. A short passage from *October* can illustrate how he uses editing discontinuities.

The sequence is the third one in the film (and comprises over 125 shots). The story action is simple. The bourgeois Provisional Government has taken power in Russia after the February Revolution, but instead of withdrawing from World War I, the government has continued to support the Allies. This maneuver has left the Russian people no better off than under the czar. In classical Hollywood cinema, this story might have been shown through a montage sequence of newspaper headlines smoothly linked to a scene wherein a protagonist complains that the Provisional Government has not solved people's problems. *October*'s protagonist, though, is not one person but the entire Russian people, and the film does not usually use dialogue scenes to present its story points. Rather, *October* seeks to go beyond a simple presentation of story events by making the audience actively assemble those events. So the film confronts us with a disorienting and disjunctive set of images.

The sequence begins with shots showing the Russian soldiers on the front casting down their rifles and fraternizing freely with German soldiers (**6.152**). Eisenstein then cuts back to the Provisional Government, where a flunky extends a document to an unseen ruler (**6.153**); this document pledges the government to aid the Allies. The soldiers' fraternization is suddenly disrupted by a bombardment (**6.154**). The soldiers run back to the trenches and huddle as dirt and bomb fragments rain down on them. Eisenstein then cuts to a series of shots of a cannon being lowered off a factory assembly line. For a time, the narration crosscuts these images with the soldiers on the battlefield (**6.155, 6.156**). In the last section of the sequence, the shots of the cannon are crosscut with hungry women and children standing in breadlines

6.152 In *October*, Russian and German soldiers talk, drink, and laugh together on the battlefield.

6.153 *October:* at the Provisional Government's headquarters.

6.154 *October:* a bombardment at the front.

6.155 In *October*, a cannon in a factory intercut . . .

6.156 . . . with soldiers at the front.

6.157 In *October*, a breadline intercut with the war scenes.

in the snow **(6.157)**. The sequence ends with two intertitles: "All as before . . . "/ "Hunger and war."

Graphically, there are some continuities. When the soldiers fraternize, many shots closely resemble one another graphically, and one shot of a bursting bomb is graphically matched in its movement with men bustling into a trench. But the *discontinuities* are more noteworthy. Eisenstein cuts from a laughing German soldier facing right to a menacing eagle statue, facing left, at the government headquarters **(6.158, 6.159)**. There is a bold jump cut: The flunky is bowing; then suddenly he is standing up **(6.160, 6.161)**. A static shot of rifles thrust into the snow cuts to a long shot of a bursting shell **(6.162, 6.163).** When the soldiers race back to the trenches, Eisenstein often opposes their direction of movement from shot to shot.

Moreover, the cutting contrasts shots of the cannon slowly *descending* with shots of the men crouching in the trenches looking *upward* (6.155, 6.156). In the last phase of the sequence, Eisenstein juxtaposes the misty, almost completely static shots of the women and children with the sharply defined, dynamically moving shots of factory workers lowering the cannon **(6.164).** Such graphic discontinuities recur throughout the film, especially in scenes of dynamic action, and stimulate perceptual conflict in the audience. To watch an Eisenstein film is to submit oneself to such percussive, pulsating graphic editing.

Eisenstein also makes vigorous use of temporal discontinuities. The sequence as a whole is opposed to Hollywood rules in its refusal to present the order of events unambiguously. Does the crosscutting of battlefield and government, and factory and street indicate simultaneous action? (Consider, for example, that the women and children are seen at night, whereas the factory appears to be operating in the daytime.) It is impossible to say if the battlefield events take place before or after or during the women's vigil. Eisenstein has sacrificed the delineation of 1-2-3 order so that he can present the shots as emotional and conceptual units.

6.158 *October.*

6.159 *October.*

6.160 *October.*

6.161 *October.*

6.162 *October.*

6.163 *October.*

6.164 *October.*

Duration is likewise variable. The soldiers fraternize in fairly continuous time, but the Provisional Government's behavior presents drastic ellipses; this permits Eisenstein to identify the government as the unseen cause of the bombardment that ruptures the peace. At one point, Eisenstein uses one of his favorite devices, a temporal expansion: there is an overlapping cut as a soldier drinks from a bottle. The cut recalls the expanded sequence of the wheel knocking over the foreman in *Strike* (6.44–6.46). At another point, the gradual collapse of the women and children waiting in line is elided. We see them standing, then later lying on the ground. Even frequency is made discontinuous: it is difficult to say whether we are seeing several cannons lowered off the assembly line or only one descending cannon shown several times. Again, Eisenstein seeks a specific *juxtaposition* of elements, not obedience to a time line. Editing's manipulation of order, duration, and frequency subordinates straightforward story time to specific conceptual relationships. Eisenstein creates these relations by juxtaposing disparate lines of action through editing.

Spatially, the *October* sequence runs from rough continuity to extreme discontinuity. Although at times the 180° rule is respected (especially in the shots of women and children), never does Eisenstein begin a section with an establishing shot. Reestablishing shots are rare, and seldom are the major components of the locales shown together in one shot.

Throughout, the classical continuity of space is broken by the intercutting of the different locales. To what end? By violating space in this manner, the film invites us to make emotional and conceptual connections. For example, crosscutting to the Provisional Government makes it the source of bombardment, a meaning reinforced by the way the first explosions are followed by the jump cut of the government flunky.

More daringly, by cutting from the crouching soldiers to a descending cannon, Eisenstein powerfully depicts the men being crushed by the war-making apparatus of the government. This is reinforced by a false eyeline match from soldiers looking upward, *as if* at the lowering cannon—false because, of course, the two ele-

CONNECT TO THE BLOG
We give several examples of striking and effective cuts in "Some cuts I have known and loved," at
www.davidbordwell.net/blog/?p=2346.

ments are in entirely separate settings (6.155, 6.156). By later showing the factory workers lowering the cannon (6.164), the cutting links the oppressed soldiers to the oppressed proletariat. Finally, as the cannon hits the ground, Eisenstein crosscuts images of it with the shots of the starving families of the soldiers and the workers. They, too, are shown as crushed by the government machine. As the cannon wheels come ponderously to the floor, Einstein cuts to the women's feet in the snow, and the machine's heaviness is linked by titles ("one pound," "half a pound") to the steady starvation of the women and children. Although all of the spaces are in the story, such discontinuities create a running political commentary on the story events.

In all, then, Eisenstein's spatial editing, like his temporal and graphic editing, constructs correspondences, analogies, and contrasts that ask us to *interpret* the story events. The interpretation is not simply handed to the viewer; rather, the editing discontinuities push the viewer to work out implicit meanings. This sequence, like others in *October,* demonstrates that there are powerful alternatives to the principles of classical continuity.

SUMMARY

When any two shots are joined, we can ask several questions:

1. How are the shots graphically continuous or discontinuous?

2. What rhythmic relations are created?

3. Are the shots spatially continuous? If not, what creates the discontinuity? (Crosscutting? Ambiguous cues?) If the shots are spatially continuous, how does the 180° system create the continuity?

4. Are the shots temporally continuous? If so, what creates the continuity? (For example, matches on action?) If not, what creates the discontinuity? (Ellipsis? Overlapping cuts?)

More generally, we can ask the question we ask of every film technique: How does this technique *function* with respect to the film's narrative form? Does the film use editing to lay out the narrative space, time, and cause–effect chain in the manner of classical continuity? How do editing patterns emphasize facial expressions, dialogue, or setting? Do editing patterns withhold narrative information? In general, how does editing contribute to the viewer's experience of the film?

Some practical hints: You can learn to notice editing in several ways. If you are having trouble noticing cuts, try watching a film or TV show and tapping with a pencil each time a shot changes. Once you recognize editing easily, watch any film with the sole purpose of observing one editing aspect—say, the way space is presented or the control of graphics or time. Sensitize yourself to rhythmic editing by noting cutting rates; tapping out the tempo of the cuts can help.

Watching 1930s and 1940s American films can introduce you to classical continuity style; try to predict what shot will come next in a sequence. (You'll be surprised at how often you're right.) When you watch a film on video, try turning off the sound; editing patterns become more apparent this way. When there is a violation of continuity, ask yourself whether it is accidental or serves a purpose. When you see a film that does not obey classical continuity principles, search for its unique editing patterns. Use the slow-motion, freeze, and reverse controls on a DVD player to analyze a film sequence as this chapter has done. (Almost any film will do.) In such ways as these, you can considerably increase your awareness and understanding of the power of editing.

WHERE TO GO FROM HERE

What Editing Is

Professional reflections on the work of the film editor include Ralph Rosenblum, *When the Shooting Stops . . . The Cutting Begins: A Film Editor's Story* (New York: Penguin, 1980); Edward Dmytryk, *On Film Editing* (Boston: Focal Press, 1984); Vincent Lo Brutto, *Selected Takes: Film Editors on Film Editing* (New York: Praeger, 1991); Gabriella Oldham, *First Cut: Conversations with Film Editors* (Berkeley: University of California Press, 1992); and Declan

McGrath, *Editing and Post-Production* (Hove, England: RotoVision, 2001). See also Ken Dancyger, *The Technique of Film and Video Editing: History, Theory, and Practice,* 4th ed. (Boston: Focal Press, 2007), and "The Art and Craft of Film Editing," *Cineaste* 34, 2 (Spring 2009): 27–64.

Walter Murch, one of the most thoughtful and creative editors in history, provides a rich array of ideas in *In the Blink of an Eye: A Perspective on Film Editing,* 2d ed. (Los Angeles: Silman-James, 2001). Murch, who worked on *American Graffiti, The Godfather, Apocalypse Now,* and *The English Patient,* has always conceived of image and sound editing as part of the same process. He shares his thoughts in an extended dialogue with prominent novelist Michael Ondaatje in *The Conversations: Walter Murch and the Art of Editing Film* (New York: Knopf, 2002). Ever the experimenter, Murch tried using an inexpensive digital program to edit a theatrical feature. The result is traced in detail in Charles Koppelman, *Behind the Seen: How Walter Murch Edited* Cold Mountain *Using Apple's Final Cut Pro and What This Means for Cinema* (Berkeley, CA: New Riders, 2005). You can listen to Murch discussing his work on the National Public Radio program *Fresh Air,* available at www.npr.org.

We await a large-scale history of editing, but André Bazin sketches a very influential account in "The Evolution of Film Language," in *What Is Cinema?* vol. 1 (Berkeley: University of California Press, 1967), pp. 23–40. Editing in early U.S. cinema is carefully analyzed by Charlie Keil in *Early American Cinema in Transition: Story, Style, and Filmmaking, 1907–1913* (Madison: University of Wisconsin Press, 2001). Professional editor Don Fairservice offers a thoughtful account of editing in the silent and early sound eras in *Film Editing: History, Theory and Practice* (Manchester: Manchester University Press, 2001). Several sections of Barry Salt's *Film Style and Technology: History and Analysis* (London: Starword, 1992) are devoted to changes in editing practices.

Documentary films characteristically rely on editing, perhaps more than fictional films do. A set of cutting conventions has developed. For example, it is common to intercut talking-head shots of conflicting experts as a way of representing opposing points of view. Interestingly, in making *The Thin Blue Line,* Errol Morris instructed his editor, Paul Barnes, to avoid cutting between the two main suspects. "He didn't want the standard documentary good guy/ bad guy juxtaposition. . . . He hated when I intercut people telling the same story, or people contradicting or responding to what someone has just said" (Oldham, *First Cut,* p. 144). Morris apparently wanted to give each speaker's version a certain integrity, letting each stand as an alternative account of events.

Dimensions of Film Editing

Very little has been written on graphic aspects of editing. See Vladimir Nilsen, *The Cinema as a Graphic Art* (New York: Hill & Wang, 1959), and Jonas Mekas, "An Interview with Peter Kubelka," *Film Culture* 44 (Spring 1967): 42–47.

What we are calling rhythmic editing incorporates the categories of metric and rhythmic montage discussed by Sergei Eisenstein in "The Fourth Dimension in Cinema," in *Selected Works,* vol. I, pp. 181–94. For a sample analysis of a film's rhythm, see Lewis Jacobs, "D. W. Griffith," in *The Rise of the American Film* (New York: Teachers College Press, 1968), chap. 11, pp. 171–201. Television commercials are useful to study for rhythmic editing, for their highly stereotyped imagery permits the editor to cut the shots to match the beat of the jingle on the sound track.

The Kuleshov experiments have been variously described. The two most authoritative accounts are in V. I. Pudovkin, *Film Technique* (New York: Grove Press, 1960), and Ronald Levaco, trans. and ed., *Kuleshov on Film: Writings of Lev Kuleshov* (Berkeley: University of California Press, 1974), pp. 51–55. For a summary of Kuleshov's work, see Vance Kepley, Jr., "The Kuleshov Workshop," *Iris* 4, 1 (1986): 5–23. Can the effect actually suggest an expressionless character's emotional reaction? Two film researchers tried to test it, and their skeptical conclusions are set forth in Stephen Prince and Wayne E. Hensley, "The Kuleshov Effect: Recreating the Classic Experiment," *Cinema Journal* 31, 2 (Winter 1992): 59–75. During the 1990s, two Kuleshov experiments, one complete and one fragmentary, were discovered. For a description and historical background on one of them, see Yuri Tsivian, Ekaterina Khokhlova, and Kristin Thompson, "The Rediscovery of a Kuleshov Experiment: A Dossier," *Film History* 8, 3 (1996): 357–67.

Continuity Editing

For a historical discussion of continuity editing, see Chapter 12 and the chapter's bibliography. The hidden selectivity that continuity editing can achieve is well summarized in a remark from Thom Noble, who edited *Fahrenheit 451* and *Witness:* "What usually happens is that there are maybe seven moments in each scene that are brilliant. But they're all on different takes. My job is to try and get all those seven moments in and yet have it look seamless, so that nobody knows there's a cut in there" (quoted in David Chell, ed., *Moviemakers at Work* [Redmond, WA: Microsoft Press, 1987], pp. 81–82).

Many sources spell out the rules of continuity. See Karel Reisz and Gavin Millar, *The Technique of Film Editing* (New York: Hastings House, 1973); Daniel Arijohn, *A Grammar of the Film Language* (New York: Focal Press, 1978); Edward Dmytryk, *On Screen Directing* (Boston: Focal Press, 1984); and Stuart Bass, "Editing Structures," in *Transitions: Voices on the Craft of Digital Editing* (Birmingham, England: Friends of ED, 2002), pp. 28–39; and Richard D. Pepperman, *The Eye Is Quicker: Film Editing: Making a Good Film Better* (Los Angeles: Michael Wiese

Productions, 2004). Our diagram of a hypothetical axis of action has been adapted from Edward Pincus's concise discussion in his *Guide to Filmmaking* (New York: Signet, 1969), pp. 120–25.

For analyses of the continuity style, see Ramond Bellour, "The Obvious and the Code," *Screen* 15, 4 (Winter 1974–75): 7–17, and André Gaudreault, "Detours in Film Narrative: The Development of Cross-Cutting," *Cinema Journal* 19, 1 (Fall 1979): 35–59. Joyce E. Jesionowski presents a detailed study of Griffith's distinctive version of early continuity editing in *Thinking in Pictures: Dramatic Structure in D. W. Griffith's Biograph Films* (Berkeley: University of California Press, 1987). David Bordwell's *Planet Hong Kong: Popular Cinema and the Art of Entertainment* (Cambridge, MA: Harvard University Press, 2000) considers how Hollywood continuity was used by another national cinema.

Professional editor Bobbie O'Steen analyzes sequences from 10 Hollywood classics shot by shot in *The Invisible Cut: How Editors Make Movie Magic* (Studio City, CA: Michael Wiese Productions, 2009).

Contemporary Editing and Intensified Continuity

Taught in film schools and learned on the job by beginning filmmakers, the principles of continuity editing still dominate cinema around the world. As we suggested on p. 250, however, there have been some changes in the system. Shots tend to be shorter (*Moulin Rouge* contains over 4000) and framed closer to the performers. The medium shots in older filmmaking traditions display the hands and upper body fully, but intensified continuity concentrates on faces, particularly the actor's eyes. Film editor Walter Murch says, "The determining factor for selecting a particular shot is frequently: 'Can you register the expression in the actor's eyes?' If you can't, the editor will tend to use the next closer shot, even though the wider shot may be more than adequate when seen on the big screen."

There's some evidence that today's faster cutting pace and frequent camera movements allow directors to be a bit loose in matching eyelines. In several scenes of *Hulk, Mystic River, 8 Mile,* and *Syriana,* the axis of action is crossed, sometimes repeatedly. If viewers aren't confused by these cuts, it's perhaps because the actors don't move around the set very much and so the overall spatial layout remains clear. More complex spatial layouts may require more cutaways and sound cues, as editor Alan Heim explains with respect to one scene in *The Notebook.* See the Editors Guild website at www.editorsguild.com/v2/magazine/Newsletter/JulAug04/julaug04_notebook.html.

For more on intensified continuity, see David Bordwell, *The Way Hollywood Tells It: Story and Style in Modern Movies* (Berkeley: University of California Press, 2006), pp. 117–89.

Alternatives to Continuity Editing

Eisenstein remains the chief source in this area. A highly introspective filmmaker, he bequeathed us a rich set of ideas on the possibilities of non-narrative editing; see the essays in *Selected Works,* vol. 1. For further discussion of editing in *October,* see the essays by Annette Michelson, Noël Carroll, and Rosalind Krauss in the special "Eisenstein/Brakhage" issue of *Artforum* 11, 5 (January 1973): 30–37, 56–65. For a more general view of Eisenstein's editing, see David Bordwell, *The Cinema of Eisenstein* (Cambridge, MA: Harvard University Press, 1993). The writings of another Russian, Dziga Vertov, are also of interest. See Annette Michelson, ed., *Kino-Eye: The Writings of Dziga Vertov* (Berkeley: University of California Press, 1984). On Ozu's manipulation of discontinuities, see David Bordwell, *Ozu and the Poetics of Cinema* (Princeton, NJ: Princeton University Press, 1988).

Websites

www.editorsguild.com/v2/index.aspx/ A website supporting *Editors Guild* magazine, with many articles and interviews discussing editing in current films.

www.uemedia.com/CPC/editorsnet/ Offers articles on contemporary problems of editing.

www.cinemetrics.lv/ Want to study cutting rhythms in a movie of your choice? This nifty software allows you to come up with a profile of editing rates.

Recommended DVD Supplements

Watching people editing is not very exciting, and this technique usually gets short shrift in DVD supplements. Each film in the *Lord of the Rings* trilogy, however, has an "Editorial" section, and *The Fellowship of the Ring* includes an "Editorial Demonstration," juxtaposing the raw footage from six cameras in an excerpt from the Council of Elrond scene and showing how sections from each were fitted together. (An instructive exercise in learning to notice continuity editing would be to watch the Council of Elrond scene in the film itself with the sound turned off. Here a complex scene with many characters is stitched together with numerous correct eyeline matches and occasional matches on action. Imagine how confusing the characters' conversations could have been if no attention had been paid to eyeline direction.)

The DVD release of Lodge Kerrigan's *Keane* includes not only the theatrical version but a completely recut version of the film by producer Steven Soderberg. Soderberg calls his cut his "commentary track" for the disc.

In "Tell Us What You See," the camera operator for *A Hard Day's Night* discusses continuity of screen direction, and in "Every Head She's Had the Pleasure to Know," the film's hairdresser talks about having to keep hair length consistent for continuity.

"15-Minute Film School with Robert Rodriguez," one of the *Sin City* supplements, provides a clear instance of the Kuleshov effect in use. Although Rodriguez does not use that term, he demonstrates how he could cut together shots of characters interacting with each other via eyeline matches even though several of the actors never worked together during the filming.

A brief section of *Toy Story*'s supplements entitled "Layout Tricks" demonstrates how continuity editing principles are adhered to in animation as well as live-action filming. In a shot/reverse-shot sequence involving Buzz and Woody, the filmmakers diagram (as we do on p. 238) where a camera can be placed to maintain the axis of action (or "stage line," as it is termed here). The segment also shows how a camera movement can be used to shift the axis of action just before an important character enters the scene.

"Destination Yuma," a short making-of for *3:10 to Yuma*, contains an excellent demonstration of multiple-camera shooting for a scene of a stagecoach flipping over; the shooting and views from different cameras are immediately followed by the scene as edited in the final film. The audio commentary for *El Mariachi* (Sony "Special Edition") describes editing scenes using the Kuleshov effect.

Sound in the Cinema

M
ost films create the impression that the people and things onscreen simply produce an appropriate noise. But, as we saw in Chapter 1, in the process of film production, the sound track is constructed separately from the images, and it can be manipulated independently. This makes sound as flexible and wide-ranging as other film techniques.

Yet sound is perhaps the hardest technique to study. We're accustomed to ignoring many of the sounds in our environment. Our primary information about the layout of our surroundings comes from sight, and so in ordinary life, sound is often simply a background for our visual attention. Similarly, we speak of *watching* a film and of being movie *viewers* or *spectators*—all terms that suggest the sound track is a secondary factor. We're strongly inclined to think of sound as simply an accompaniment to the real basis of cinema: the moving images.

Moreover, we can't stop the film and freeze an instant of sound, as we can study a frame to examine mise-en-scene and cinematography. Nor can we lay out the sound track for our inspection as easily as we can examine the editing of a string of shots. In film, the sounds and the patterns they form are elusive. This elusiveness accounts for part of the power of this technique: sound can achieve very strong effects and yet remain quite unnoticeable. To study sound, we must learn to *listen* to films.

Fortunately, filmgoers have become more sensitive. *Star Wars* and other hits of the 1970s introduced the broad public to new technologies of sound recording and reproduction. Audiences came to expect Dolby noise reduction processes, expanded frequency and dynamic range, and four- and six-track theater playback. During the early 1990s, digital sound became routine for big-budget pictures, and now virtually all releases have crisp, dense sound tracks. "An older film like *Casablanca* has an empty soundtrack compared with what we do today," remarks sound designer Michael Kirchberger, supervising sound editor for *Lost in Translation*. "Tracks are fuller and more of a selling point." Multiplex theaters upgraded their sound systems to meet the challenge, and the popularity of DVDs prompted consumers to set up home theaters with ravishing sound. Viewers' new sensitivity to sound is apparent in the recent habit of starting a film's sound track with dialogue or sound effects, before the images appear. You can argue that this device serves to quiet down the audience so that the imagery gets the proper attention, but often the sonic information is important to the story as well. In any event, not since the first talkies of the late 1920s have filmgoers been so aware of what they hear.

7

CHAPTER

The Powers of Sound

Whether noticed or not, sound is a powerful film technique for several reasons. For one thing, it engages a distinct sense mode. Even before recorded sound was introduced in 1926, silent films were accompanied by orchestra, organ, or piano. At a minimum, the music filled in the silence and gave the spectator a more complete perceptual experience. More significantly, the engagement of hearing opens the possibility of what the Soviet director Sergei Eisenstein called "synchronization of senses"—making a single rhythm or expressive quality unify both image and sound.

The meshing of image and sound appeals to something quite deep in human consciousness. Babies spontaneously connect sounds with what they see. The most basic condition involves timing: if a sound and image occur at the same moment, they are perceived as one event, not two. Just as our minds search for patterns in a shot or for causal patterns in a narrative, we are inclined to seek out patterns that will fuse lip movements and speech, and even musical rhythms with visual ones. Our bias toward audio-visual patterning governs both our everyday activities (imagine hearing a friend's talk out of synch) and our experiences of arts like music, theater, and film.

Sound is often treated as an accompaniment to the images, but we need to recognize that it can actively shape how we understand them. In one sequence of *Letter from Siberia* **(7.1–7.4),** Chris Marker demonstrates the power of sound to alter our understanding of images. Three times Marker shows the same footage—a shot of a bus passing a car on a city street, three shots of workers paving a street. But each time the footage is accompanied by a completely different sound track. Compare the three versions tabulated alongside the sequence in Table 7.1. The first one is heavily affirmative, the second is harshly critical, and the third mixes praise and criticism. The audience will construe the same images differently, depending on the sound track.

The *Letter from Siberia* sequence demonstrates another advantage of sound: film sound can direct our attention quite specifically within the image. When the commentator describes the "blood-colored buses," we are likely to look at the bus and not at the car. When Fred Astaire and Ginger Rogers are executing an intricate step, chances are that we watch their bodies and not the silent nightclub spectators looking on. In such ways, sound can guide us through the images.

This possibility becomes even more fertile when you consider that the sound cue for some visual element may *anticipate* that element and relay our attention to it. Suppose we have a close-up of a man in a room and hear the creaking of a door opening. If the next shot shows the door, now open, our attention will probably shift to that door, the source of the offscreen sound. But if the second shot shows the door still closed, we will likely ponder our interpretation of the sound. (Maybe it wasn't a door, after all?) Thus the sound track can clarify image events, contradict them, or render them ambiguous. In all cases, the sound track can enter into an active relation with the image track.

This example of the door opening suggests another advantage of sound. It cues us to form expectations. If we hear a door creaking, we anticipate that someone has entered a room and that we will see the person in the next shot. But if the film draws on conventions of the horror genre, the camera might stay on the man, staring fearfully. We would then be in suspense awaiting the appearance of something frightful offscreen. Horror and mystery films often use the power of sound from an unseen source to engage the audience's interest, but all types of films can take advantage of this aspect of sound. During the town meeting in *Jaws,* the characters hear a grating sound and turn to look offscreen; a cut reveals Quint's fingers scraping on a blackboard—creating a dramatic introduction to this character. We'll see several other cases in which the use of sound can creatively cheat or redirect the viewer's expectations.

In addition, sound gives a new value to silence. A quiet passage in a film can create almost unbearable tension, forcing the viewer to concentrate on the screen.

"The most exciting moment is the moment when I add the sound.... At this moment, I tremble."

— Akira Kurosawa, director

TABLE 7.1   *Letter From Siberia* Footage

Images	First Commentary	Second Commentary	Third Commentary
 7.1	Yakutsk, capital of the Yakutsk Autonomous Soviet Socialist Republic, is a modern city in which comfortable buses made available to the population share the streets with powerful Zyms, the pride of the Soviet automobile industry. In the	Yakutsk is a dark city with an evil reputation. The population is crammed into blood-colored buses while the members of the privileged caste brazenly display the luxury of their Zyms—costly and uncomfortable cars at best. Bending	In Yakutsk, where modern houses are gradually replacing the dark older sections, a bus, less crowded than its London or New York equivalent at rush hour, passes a Zym, an excellent car reserved for public utilities departments on account of its scarcity.
 7.2	joyful spirit of socialist emulation, happy Soviet workers, among them this picturesque denizen	to the task like slaves, the miserable Soviet workers, among them this sinister-looking Asiatic,	With courage and tenacity under extremely difficult conditions, Soviet workers, among them this Yakut
 7.3	of the Arctic reaches, apply themselves	apply themselves to the primitive labor	afflicted with an eye disorder, apply themselves to
 7.4	to making Yakutsk an even better place to live. Or else:	of grading with a drag beam. Or simply:	improving the appearance of their city, which could certainly use it.

7.5   In *Babel,* when the deaf teenage girl enters the disco, the club music is about to climax.

7.6   Instead, it drops out when we cut to her optical point-of-view on the boy she's following. Instead of subjective sound, we get subjective silence, and this sharply dramatizes her isolation from what is happening around her.

An abrupt silence can jolt us and arrest our attention **(7.5, 7.6).** Just as color film turns black and white into grades of color, so the use of sound in film will include all the possibilities of silence.

One more advantage: sound bristles with as many creative possibilities as editing. Through editing, one may join shots of any two spaces to create a meaningful relation. Similarly, the filmmaker can mix any sonic phenomena into a whole. With the introduction of sound cinema, the infinity of visual possibilities was joined by the infinity of acoustic events.

Fundamentals of Film Sound

Perceptual Properties

Several aspects of sound as we perceive it are familiar to us from everyday experience and are central to film's use of sound.

Loudness The sound we hear results from vibrations in the air. The amplitude, or breadth, of the vibrations produces our sense of *loudness,* or volume. Film sound constantly manipulates volume. For example, in many films, a long shot of a busy street is accompanied by loud traffic noises, but when two people meet and start to speak, the volume of the traffic drops. Or a dialogue between a soft-spoken character and a blustery one is characterized as much by the difference in volume as by the substance of the talk.

Loudness is also related to perceived distance; often the louder the sound, the closer we take it to be. This sort of assumption seems to be at work in the street traffic example already mentioned: the couple's dialogue, being louder, is sensed as in the acoustic foreground, while the traffic noise recedes to the background. In addition, a film may startle the viewer by exploiting abrupt and extreme shifts in volume (usually called changes in *dynamics*), as when a quiet scene is interrupted by a very loud noise.

Pitch The frequency of sound vibrations affects *pitch,* or the perceived highness or lowness of the sound. Certain instruments, such as the tuning fork, can produce pure tones, but most sounds, in life and on film, are complex tones, batches of different frequencies. Nevertheless, pitch plays a useful role in helping us pick out distinct sounds in a film. It helps us distinguish music and speech from noises. It also serves to distinguish among objects. Thumps can suggest hollow objects, while higher-pitched sounds (like those of jingle bells) suggest smoother or harder surfaces and denser objects.

Pitch can also serve more specific purposes. When a young boy tries to speak in a man's deep voice and fails, as in *How Green Was My Valley,* the joke is based primarily on pitch. Marlene Dietrich's vocal delivery often depends on a long upward-gliding intonation that makes a statement sound like a question. In the coronation scene of *Ivan the Terrible,* Part I, a court singer with a deep bass voice begins a song of praise to Ivan, and each phrase rises dramatically in pitch **(7.7–7.9)**. When Bernard Herrmann obtained the effects of shrill, birdlike shrieking in Hitchcock's *Psycho,* even many musicians could not recognize the source: violins played at extraordinarily high pitch.

When Julianne Moore was planning her performance as the protagonist of Todd Haynes's *Safe,* she took pitch and other vocal qualities into account:

> My first key to her was her voice, her vocal patterns. I started with a very typical Southern California speech pattern. It's almost a sing-song rhythm, you know—it's referred to as the "Valley quality" that travelled across the country and became a universal American vocal pattern. It was important to me that her voice would have that kind of melody to it. And then I would put question marks at the end of the sentence all the time—that way she never makes a statement; it makes her very unsure and very undefined. I also went above my own chords, because I wanted the sensation of her voice not being connected at all to her body—that's why her voice is so high. This is someone who's completely disconnected from any kind of physicality, from any sense of being herself, from really knowing herself. In that sense, I guess the vocal choices are somewhat metaphorical.

Timbre The harmonic components of sound give it a certain color, or tone quality—what musicians call *timbre.* When we call someone's voice nasal or a certain musical tone mellow, we're referring to timbre. Timbre is actually a less fundamental acoustic parameter than amplitude or frequency, but it's indispensable in describing the texture or "feel" of a sound. In everyday life, the recognition of a familiar sound is largely a matter of various aspects of timbre.

Filmmakers manipulate timbre continually. Timbre can help articulate portions of the sound track, as when it differentiates musical instruments from one another. Timbre also comes forward on certain occasions, as in the clichéd use of oleaginous saxophone tones behind seduction scenes. More subtly, in the opening sequence of

7.7 In *Ivan the Terrible,* Eisenstein emphasizes changes in vocal pitch by cutting from a medium-long shot . . .

7.8 . . . to a medium shot . . .

7.9 . . . to a close-up of the singer.

Rouben Mamoulian's *Love Me Tonight,* people starting the day on a street pass a musical rhythm from object to object—a broom, a carpet beater—and the humor of the number springs in part from the very different timbres of the objects. In preparing the sound track for Peter Weir's *Witness,* the editors drew on sounds recorded 20 or more years before, so that the less modern timbre of the older recordings would evoke the rustic seclusion of the Amish community.

Loudness, pitch, and timbre interact to define the overall sonic texture of a film. For example, these qualities enable us to recognize different characters' voices. Both John Wayne and James Stewart speak slowly, but Wayne's voice tends to be deeper and gruffer than Stewart's querulous drawl. This difference works to great advantage in *The Man Who Shot Liberty Valance,* where their characters are sharply contrasted. In *The Wizard of Oz,* the disparity between the public image of the Wizard and the old charlatan who rigs it up is marked by the booming bass of the effigy and the old man's higher, softer, more quavering voice.

Loudness, pitch, and timbre also shape our experience of a film as a whole. *Citizen Kane,* for example, offers a wide range of sound manipulations. Echo chambers alter timbre and volume. A motif is formed by the inability of Kane's wife, Susan, to sing pitches accurately. Moreover, in *Citizen Kane,* the plot's shifts between times and places are covered by continuing a sound thread and varying the basic acoustics. A shot of Kane applauding dissolves to a shot of a crowd applauding (a shift in volume and timbre). Leland beginning a sentence in the street cuts to Kane finishing the sentence in an auditorium, his voice magnified by loudspeakers (a shift in volume, timbre, and pitch).

Recent noise reduction techniques, multitrack reproduction, and digital sound yield wider ranges of frequency and volume, as well as crisper timbres than filmmakers could achieve in the studio years. Today sound editors can individualize voice or noise to a surprising degree. For *The Thin Red Line,* every character's distinctive breathing sounds were recorded for use as ambient noise. Randy Thoms, sound designer for *Cast Away,* sought to characterize different sorts of wind—breezes from the open sea, winds in a cave. Sound even announces a shift in wind direction crucial to one of the hero's plans. "We can use the wind in a very musical way," Thoms notes.

Selection, Alteration, and Combination

Sound in the cinema is of three types: speech, music, and noise (also called *sound effects*). Occasionally, a sound may cross categories—Is a scream speech or noise? Is electronic music also noise?—and filmmakers have freely exploited these ambiguities. In *Psycho,* when a woman screams, we expect to hear a human voice and instead hear screaming violins. Nevertheless, in most cases, the distinctions hold. Now that we have an idea of some basic acoustic properties, how are speech, music, and noise selected and combined for specific purposes?

Choosing and Manipulating Sounds   The creation of the sound track resembles the editing of the image track. Just as the filmmaker may pick the best image from several shots, he or she may choose what exact bit of sound will best serve the purpose. Just as footage from disparate sources may be blended into a single visual track, so too sound that was not recorded during filming may be added freely. Moreover, a shot may be rephotographed or tinted in color or jigsawed into a composite image, and a bit of sound be processed to change its acoustic qualities. And just as the filmmaker may link or superimpose images, so may he or she join any two sounds end to end or place one over another. Though we aren't usually as aware of sonic manipulations, the sound track demands as much choice and control as does the visual track.

Sometimes the sound track is conceived before the image track. Studio-made animated cartoons typically record music, dialogue, and sound effects before the

"The Empire spaceship sounded a certain way as compared to the Imperial fleet; that was a deliberate style change. Everybody in the Empire had shrieking, howling, ghostlike, frightening sounds. . . . You hear it—you jump with fear. Whereas the rebel forces had more junky-sounding planes and spaceships. They weren't quite as powerful; they tended to pop and sputter more."

— Ben Burtt, sound editor, *Star Wars*

"Too many films seem essentially designed to be heard in the mixing studios. I always fight against recording every single footstep, and would rather lose the sound of people settling into armchairs, etc., and fade out a particular atmosphere sound once the emotional impact has been achieved, even at the cost of realism. You have to know how to play with silence, to treat sound like music."

— Bernard Tavernier, director

images are filmed, so that the figures may be synchronized with the sound frame by frame. For many years, Carl Stalling created frantically paced jumbles of familiar tunes, weird noises, and distinctive voices for the adventures of Bugs Bunny and Daffy Duck. Experimental films also frequently build their images around a preexisting sound track. Some filmmakers have even argued that abstract cinema is a sort of "visual music" and have tried to create a synthesis of the two media.

Not all the sounds we hear in a film are generated specifically for that project. Editors tend to build their own collections of sounds that intrigue them, but sometimes they reuse music or effects stored in sound libraries. Most famous is the "Wilhelm scream," first heard in a 1951 American film when an alligator bites off a cowboy's arm. The scream was recycled in *Star Wars, Raiders of the Lost Ark, Reservoir Dogs, Transformers,* and over a hundred other films.

As with other film techniques, sound guides the viewer's attention. Normally, the sound track is clarified and simplified so that important material stands out. Dialogue, as a transmitter of story information, is usually recorded and reproduced for maximum clarity. Important lines should not have to compete with music or background noise. Sound effects are usually less important. They supply an overall sense of a realistic environment and are seldom noticed; if they were missing, however, the silence would be distracting. Music is usually subordinate to dialogue as well, entering during pauses in conversation or effects.

Dialogue doesn't always rank highest in importance, though. Sound effects are usually central to action sequences, while music can dominate dance scenes, transitional sequences, or emotion-laden moments without dialogue. And some filmmakers have shifted the weight conventionally assigned to each type of sound. Charlie Chaplin's *City Lights* and *Modern Times* eliminate dialogue, letting sound effects and music come to the fore. The films of Jacques Tati and Jean-Marie Straub retain dialogue but still place great emphasis on sound effects. In Robert Bresson's *A Man Escaped,* music and noise fill out a sparse dialogue track by evoking offscreen space and creating thematic associations.

In creating a sound track, then, the filmmaker must select sounds that will fulfill a particular function. In order to do this, the filmmaker usually will provide a clearer, simpler sound world than that of everyday life. Normally, our perception filters out irrelevant stimuli and retains what is most useful at a particular moment. As you read this, you are attending to words on the page and (to various degrees) ignoring certain stimuli that reach your ears. But if you close your eyes and listen attentively to the sounds around you, you will become aware of many previously unnoticed sounds—traffic, footsteps, distant voices. Any amateur recordist knows that if you set up a microphone and recorder in what seems to be a quiet environment, those normally unnoticed sounds suddenly become obtrusive. The microphone is unselective; like the camera lens, it doesn't automatically filter out what is distracting. Sound studios, camera blimps to absorb motor noise, directional and shielded microphones, sound engineering and editing, and libraries of stock sounds—all allow the filmmaker to choose exactly what the sound track requires.

By choosing certain sounds, the filmmaker guides our perception of the image and the action. In one scene from Jacques Tati's *Mr. Hulot's Holiday,* vacationers at a resort hotel are relaxing (**7.10**). Early in the scene, the guests in the foreground are murmuring quietly, but Hulot's Ping-Pong game is louder; the sound cues us to watch Hulot. Later in the scene, however, the same Ping-Pong game makes no sound at all, and our attention is drawn to the muttering cardplayers in the foreground. The presence and absence of the sound of the Ping-Pong ball guides our expectations. If you start to notice how such selection of sound shapes our perception, you will also notice that filmmakers often use sound quite unrealistically, in order to shift our attention to what is narratively or visually important.

Our scene from *Mr. Hulot's Holiday* also points up the importance of how a chosen sound may have its acoustic qualities transformed for a particular purpose. Thanks to a manipulation of volume and timbre, the Ping-Pong game gains in

"We were going for a documentary feel. We came up with a way for the loop group actors to say lines in a way we called 'nondescript dialogue.' They said lines, but they didn't say the actual words. If you put it behind people speaking, you just think it's people talking offscreen, but your ear isn't drawn to it. It would just lie there as a bed, and you can play it relatively loudly and it just fits in with the scenes."

— Hugh Waddell, ADR supervisor, on *The Thin Red Line*

7.10 In *Mr. Hulot's Holiday,* in the foreground, guests quietly play cards while in the depth of the shot, Mr. Hulot is frantically playing Ping-Pong.

vividness. When two sounds are of the same frequency or loudness, contemporary sound designers freely adjust one to make it stand out more clearly. During the jungle chase in *Indiana Jones and the Kingdom of the Crystal Skull,* the skull's thump was altered. "I changed its pitch so that it would coexist with the music," sound designer Ben Burtt explained.

At the limit, wholly new sounds may be made of old ones. The noises emitted by the demonically possessed girl in *The Exorcist* blended screams, animal thrashings, and English spoken backward. To create the roar of a *Tyrannosaurus rex* for *Jurassic Park,* sound engineers fused a tiger's roar, a baby elephant's trumpeting at midrange frequencies, and an alligator's growl for the lower tones. On film, even jet planes' roars typically include cries of animals—not only lions and elephants but monkeys as well.

Nowadays, film sound is normally reprocessed to yield exactly the qualities desired. A *dry recording* of the sound in a fairly nonreflective space will be manipulated electronically to yield the desired effect. For instance, the voice of someone on the telephone is typically treated with filters to make it more tinny and muffled. (In Hollywood parlance, this is called "futzing" the sound.) The almost nonstop rock-and-roll music of *American Graffiti* used two recordings of the music. A dry one was prepared for moments when the music was to dominate the scene and had to be of high quality. A more ambient one for background noise was derived from a tape recorder simply playing the tune in a backyard.

Sound Mixing   Guiding the viewer's attention, then, depends on selecting and reworking particular sounds. It also depends on **mixing,** or combining them. It is useful to think of the sound track not as a set of discrete sound units but as an ongoing *stream* of auditory information. Each sonic event takes its place in a specific pattern. This pattern both links events in time and layers them at any given moment.

We can easily see how the sound track offers a stream of auditory information by considering a scene cut according to classical continuity principles. When filmmakers edit conversations in shot/reverse shot, they often use a **dialogue overlap** to smooth down the visual change of shot. In a dialogue overlap, the filmmaker continues a line of dialogue across a cut. During a conversation in John McTiernan's *The Hunt for Red October,* we get the following shots and dialogue:

1. (ms) Over the political officer's shoulder, favoring Captain Ramius (**7.11**)

    Officer: "Captain Tupalev's boat."

    Ramius: "You know Tupalev?"

    Officer: "I know he descends . . ."

2. (ms) Reverse angle over Ramius's shoulder, favoring the officer (**7.12**)

    Officer (continuing): ". . . from aristocracy, and that he was your student. It's rumored he has a special . . ."

3. (mcu) Reverse angle on Ramius (**7.13**)

    Officer (continuing): ". . . place in his heart for you."

    Ramius: "There's little room in Tupalev's heart for anyone but Tupalev."

Here the political officer's chatter provides an auditory continuity that distracts from the shot changes. Moreover, by cutting to a closer view of the listener before a sentence is finished, the sound and editing concentrate our attention on Ramius's response. As a Hollywood editor puts it, "The minute a telling word or a question is posed . . . I go for a reaction to see . . . how they are trying to formulate the answer in their face or dialogue." The principle of dialogue overlap can be used with noise as well. In the *Hunt for Red October* scene just mentioned, sounds of a spoon clinking in a tea cup and of papers being riffled also carry over certain cuts, providing a continuous stream of sonic information.

"Is it better to say, 'I love you,' bang, then cut to the reaction? Or is it better to say, 'I love you,' hang on it a beat to show the emotion of the person delivering the line, then go for the reaction? It's a matter of choice. Either way, there's a different result for the audience looking at it. Are their sympathies with the guy who said the line, or the girl who said the line? Or is the audience saying, 'Don't believe him, he's going to screw you over!' . . . If you find the frame to cut on at that right moment, the audience will be totally satisfied."

— Tom Rolf, editor

CONNECT TO THE BLOG
We've been fortunate enough to sit in on some mixing sessions and learn from people who mix sound. See "Christian Bale picks up a rail" www.davidbordwell.net/blog/?p=963, "What does a Water Horse sound like?" www.davidbordwell.net/blog/?p=1718, and "The boy in the Black Hole" www.davidbordwell.net/blog/?p=2212.

7.11 *The Hunt for Red October:* shot 1.

7.12 *The Hunt for Red October:* shot 2.

7.13 *The Hunt for Red October:* shot 3.

7.14 In *Jurassic Park,* although Hammond and Ellie are closer to the camera than is anything else in the shot, their dialogue is an unintelligible murmur, while the exposition about velociraptors given by the hunter in the background is clearly audible.

This auditory stream can involve more than simply linking one line of dialogue or bit of noise to another. We have already seen that in production, combining sounds is usually done after shooting, in the mixing process. For example, in *Jurassic Park,* Steven Spielberg manipulates volume unrealistically for purposes of narrative clarity. After a live cow has been lowered into the velociraptors' pen, the South African hunter gives important information about the habits of these predators, and his voice comes through louder than those of characters closer to the camera (**7.14**). The mixer can precisely control the volume, duration, and tone quality of each sound. In modern filmmaking, a dozen or more separate tracks may be mixed in layers at any moment. The mix can be quite dense, as when an airport scene combines the babble of several distinct voices, footsteps, luggage trolleys, Muzak, and plane engines. Or the mix can be very sparse, with an occasional sound emerging against a background of total silence. Most cases will fall somewhere between these extremes. In our *Hunt for Red October* scene, a distant throbbing engine and slight brushings of fabric form a muted background to the dialogue exchange.

The filmmaker may create a mix in which each sound blends smoothly with the others. This is commonly the case when music and effects are mixed with speech. In classical Hollywood cinema of the 1930s, the musical score may become prominent in moments in which there is no dialogue, and then it's likely to fade unnoticeably down just as the characters begin to talk. (In studio parlance, this is called *sneaking in* and *sneaking out.*) Sometimes the mix will associate sounds evocatively. In *The English Patient,* when the nurse feeds the patient a plum, a distant churchbell rings, suggesting a peaceful refuge from the war.

Alternatively, the acoustic stream may contain much more abrupt contrasts. Contemporary Hollywood films often exploit the dynamic range of Dolby technology to fill chase sequences with startling shifts between low, rumbling engines and whining sirens or squealing tires. In *The Godfather,* just as Michael Corleone is steeling himself to shoot the rival gangster Sollozzo, we hear a loud, metallic

"For the last few years—since Blue Velvet, *I think—I have tried to do most of the music before the shoot. I discuss the story with my composer, Angelo Badalamenti, and record all sorts of music that I listen to as I'm shooting the film, either on headphones during dialogue scenes or on loudspeakers, so that the whole crew gets in the right mood. It's a great tool. It's like a compass helping you find the right direction."*

— David Lynch, director

7.15   As Michael sits opposite Sollozzo, the sudden rumble and whine of an offscreen train sound all the more harsh when compared with the calm expression on Michael's face.

screech, presumably from a nearby elevated train. The sound suggests impending danger, both for the victim and for Michael himself: after the murder, his life will change irrevocably **(7.15).**

Yet another alternative is explored in Alexander Sokurov's *Alexandra*. A soldier's grandmother visits him at his camp and wanders freely among the men preparing for war. The sound track includes naturalistic dialogue and effects. But these conventional elements are wrapped in a flow of soft voices, orchestral chords, and snatches of rising and falling soprano singing. The murmuring auditory collage suggests a collective dimension to the old lady's stay, as if she is visiting on behalf of the unseen families of all the men, perhaps all soldiers' families throughout history.

A Dramatic Sound Stream: *Seven Samurai*   The ways in which sounds may combine to create an ongoing stream of information is well illustrated by the final battle sequence of Akira Kurosawa's *Seven Samurai*. In a heavy rain, marauding bandits charge into a village defended by the villagers and the samurai. The torrent and wind form a constant background noise throughout the scene. Before the battle, the conversation of the waiting men, the tread of footsteps, and the sound of swords being drawn are punctuated by long pauses in which we hear only the drumming rain. Suddenly distant horses' hooves are heard offscreen. This draws our attention from the defenders to the attackers. Then Kurosawa cuts to a long shot of the bandits; their horses' hooves become abruptly louder. (The scene employs vivid **sound perspective:** The closer the camera is to a source, the louder the sound.) When the bandits burst into the village, yet another sound element appears—the bandits' harsh battle cries, which increase steadily in volume as they approach.

The battle begins. The muddy, storm-swept mise-en-scene and rhythmic cutting gain impact from the way in which the incessant rain and splashing are explosively interrupted by brief noises—the screams of the wounded, the splintering of a fence a bandit crashes through, the whinnies of horses, the twang of a samurai's bowstring, the gurgle of a speared bandit, the screams of women when the bandit chieftain breaks into their hiding place. The sudden intrusion of certain sounds marks abrupt developments in the battle. Such frequent surprises heighten our tension, since the narration frequently shifts us from one line of action to another.

The scene climaxes after the main battle has ended. Offscreen the pounding of horses' hooves is cut short by a new sound—the sharp crack of a bandit's rifle shot, which fells one samurai. A long pause, in which we hear only the driving rain, emphasizes the moment. The samurai furiously flings his sword in the direction of the shot and falls dead into the mud. Another samurai splashes toward the bandit chieftain, who has the rifle; another shot cracks out and he falls back, wounded; another pause, in which only the relentless rain is heard. The wounded samurai kills the chieftain. The other samurai gather. At the scene's end, the sobs of a young samurai, the distant whinnies and hoofbeats of riderless horses, and the rain all fade slowly out.

The relatively dense mix of this sound track gradually introduces sounds that turn our attention to new narrative elements (hooves, battle cries) and then modulates these sounds into a harmonious stream. This stream is then punctuated by abrupt sounds of unusual volume or pitch associated with crucial narrative actions (the archery, women's screams, the gunshots). Overall, the combination of sounds enhances the unrestricted, objective narration of this sequence, which shows us what happens in various parts of the village rather than confining us to the experience of a single participant.

Sound and Film Form   The choice and combination of sonic materials can also create patterns that run through the film as a whole. We can study this most readily by examining how the filmmaker uses a musical score. Sometimes the filmmaker will select preexisting pieces of music to accompany the images, as Bruce Conner does in using portions of Respighi's *Pines of Rome* as the sound track for *A Movie*. (See pp. 376–377.) In other cases, the music will be composed for the film, and here the filmmaker and the composer make several choices.

The rhythm, melody, harmony, and instrumentation of the music can strongly affect the viewer's emotional reactions. In addition, a melody or musical phrase can be associated with a particular character, setting, situation, or idea. *Local Hero,* a film about a confused young executive who leaves Texas to close a business deal in a remote Scottish village, uses two major musical themes. A rockabilly tune is heard in the urban Southwest, while a slower, more poignantly folkish melody is associated with the seaside village. In the final scenes, after the young man has returned to Houston, he recalls Scotland with affection, and the film plays the two themes simultaneously.

In contrast, a single musical theme can change its quality when associated with different situations. In *Raising Arizona,* the hapless hero has a terrifying dream in which he envisions a homicidal biker pursuing him, and the accompanying music is appropriately ominous. But at the film's end, the hero dreams of raising dozens of children, and now the same melody, reorchestrated and played at a calm tempo, conveys a sense of peace and comfort.

By reordering and varying musical motifs, the filmmaker can subtly compare scenes, trace patterns of development, and suggest implicit meanings. A convenient example is Georges Delerue's score for François Truffaut's *Jules and Jim.* Overall, the film's music reflects the Paris of 1912–1933, the years during which the action takes place; many of the melodies resemble works by Claude Debussy and Erik Satie, two of the most prominent French composers of that era. Virtually the entire score consists of melodies in ¾ meter, many of them in waltz time, and all the main themes are in keys related to A major. These rhythmic and harmonic decisions help unify the film.

More specifically, musical themes are associated with particular aspects of the narrative. For instance, Catherine's constant search for happiness and freedom outside conventional boundaries is conveyed by her singing the "Tourbillon" ("Whirlwind") song, which says that life is a constant changing of romantic partners. Settings are also evoked in musical terms. One tune is heard every time the characters are in a café. As the years go by, the tune changes from a mechanical player-piano rendition to a jazzier version played by a black pianist.

The characters' relations become more strained and complicated over time, and the score reflects this in its development of major motifs. A lyrical melody is first heard when Jules, Jim, and Catherine visit the countryside and bicycle to the beach **(7.16).** This "idyll" tune will recur at many points when the characters reunite, but as the years pass, it will become slower in tempo and more somber in instrumentation, and will shift from a major to a minor mode. Another motif that

"It's a lot like writing an opera. There's a lot of form and structure. We're very conscious that LOTR is one story that has been broken into three parts. My score is a complex piece that has to be structured carefully, musically and thematically, so that all the parts relate to one another."

— Howard Shore, composer, *The Lord of the Rings*

7.16 In *Jules and Jim*, an idyllic bicycle ride in the country introduces the main musical theme associated with the three characters' relations.

7.17 Catherine discards the vitriol, which she has said is "for lying eyes."

reappears in different guises is a "dangerous love" theme associated with Jim and Catherine. This grave, shimmering waltz is first heard when he visits her apartment and watches her pour a bottle of vitriol down the sink (**7.17**). (The acid, she says, is "for lying eyes.") Thereafter, this harmonically unstable theme, which resembles one of Satie's *Gymnopédies* for piano, is used to underscore Jim and Catherine's vertiginous love affair. At times it accompanies scenes of passion, but at other times it accompanies their growing disillusionment and despair.

The most varied theme is a mysterious phrase first heard on the flute when Jules and Jim encounter a striking ancient statue (**7.18**). Later they meet Catherine and discover that she has the statue's face; a repetition of the musical motif confirms the comparison. Throughout the film, this brief motif is associated with the enigmatic side of Catherine. In the film's later scenes, this motif is developed in an intriguing way. The bass line (played on harpsichord or strings) that softly accompanied the woodwind tune now comes to the fore, creating a relentless, often harsh, pulsation. This "menace" waltz underscores Catherine's fling with Albert and accompanies her final vengeance on Jim: driving her car, with him as passenger, into the river.

Once musical motifs have been selected, they can be combined to evoke associations. During Jim and Catherine's first intimate talk after the war, the bass-line-dominated version of the enigma waltz is followed by the love theme, as if the latter could drown out the menacing side of Catherine's character. The love theme accompanies long tracking shots of Jim and Catherine strolling through the woods. But at the scene's end, as Jim bids Catherine farewell, the original woodwind version of her theme recalls her mystery and the risk he is running by falling in love with her. Similarly, when Jim and Catherine lie in bed, facing the end of their affair, the voice-over narrator says, "It was as if they were already dead" as the dangerous love theme plays. This sequence associates death with their romance and foreshadows their fate at the film's end.

A similar sort of blending can be found in the film's final scene. Catherine and Jim have drowned, and Jules is overseeing the cremation of their bodies. As shots of the coffins dissolve into detailed shots of the cremation process, the enigma motif segues into its sinister variant, the menace motif. But as Jules leaves the cemetery and the narrator comments that Catherine had wanted her ashes to be cast to the winds, the string instruments glide into a sweeping version of the whirlwind waltz (**7.19**). The film's musical score thus concludes by recalling the three sides of Catherine that attracted the men to her: her mystery, her menace, and her vivacious openness to experience. In such ways, a musical score can create, develop, and associate motifs that enter into the film's overall form.

"So, given this mood-altering potential of music, it becomes a great source of fun, as well as a chance to make a scene that works OK work a whole lot better—to bring out the point of a scene that you haven't captured in the shooting of it, to excite the audience, to create the impression that something is happening when something isn't, and also to create little emotional touchstones which you can draw upon as the story changes—so that the music that seemed so innocent and sweet earlier, in new circumstances brings on a whole other set of feelings."

— Jonathan Demme, director

Dimensions of Film Sound

We've seen what sounds consist of and how the filmmaker can take advantage of the widely different kinds of sounds available. In addition, the way in which the

7.18 The camera slowly arcs around the statue as a new musical motif is introduced.

7.19 The sadness of the ending is undercut by the lilting whirl-wind waltz.

sounds relate to other film elements gives them several other dimensions. First, because sound occupies a duration, it has a *rhythm*. Second, sound can relate to its perceived source with greater or lesser *fidelity*. Third, sound conveys a sense of the *spatial* conditions in which it occurs. And fourth, the sound relates to visual events that take place in a specific time, and this relationship gives sound a *temporal* dimension. These categories reveal that sound in film offers many creative possibilities to the filmmaker.

Rhythm

Rhythm is one of the most powerful aspects of sound, for it works on our bodies at deep levels. We have already considered it in relation to mise-en-scene (p. 156) and editing (p. 230). Rhythm involves, minimally, a *beat,* or pulse; a *tempo,* or pace; and a pattern of *accents,* or stronger and weaker beats. In the realm of sound, all of these features are naturally most recognizable in film music, since there beat, tempo, and accent are basic compositional features. In our examples from *Jules and Jim,* the motifs can be characterized as having a ¾ metrical pulse, putting an accent on the first beat, and displaying variable tempo—sometimes slow, sometimes fast.

We can find rhythmic qualities in sound effects as well. The plodding hooves of a farmhorse differ from a cavalry mount galloping at full speed. The reverberating tone of a gong may offer a slowly decaying accent, while a sudden sneeze provides a brief one. In a gangster film, a machine gun's fire creates a regular, rapid beat, while the sporadic reports of pistols may come at irregular intervals.

Speech also has rhythm. People can be identified by voice prints that show not only characteristic frequencies and amplitudes but also distinct patterns of pacing and syllabic stress. In *His Girl Friday,* our impression is of very rapid dialogue, but the scenes actually are rhythmically subtler than that. In the start of each scene, the pace is comparatively slow, but as the action develops, characters talk at a steadily accelerating rate. As the scene winds down, the conversational pace does as well. This rise-and-fall rhythm matches the arc of each scene, giving us a bit of a rest before launching the next comic complication.

Rhythm in Sound and Image: Coordination   Any consideration of the rhythmic uses of sound is complicated by the fact that the movements in the images have a rhythm as well, distinguished by the same principles of beat, tempo, and accent. In addition, the editing has a rhythm. As we have seen, a succession of short shots helps create a rapid tempo, whereas shots held longer tend to slow down the rhythm.

In most cases, the rhythms of editing, of movement within the image, and of sound all cooperate. Possibly the most common tendency is for the filmmaker to match visual and sonic rhythms to each other. In a dance sequence in a musical, the figures move about at a rhythm determined by the music. But variation is always possible. In the "Waltz in Swing Time" number in *Swing Time,* the dancing of Fred Astaire and Ginger Rogers moves quickly in time to the music. Yet no fast cutting accompanies this scene. Indeed, the scene consists of a single long take from a long-shot distance.

Another prototype of close coordination between screen movement and sound comes in the animated films of Walt Disney in the 1930s. Mickey Mouse and other Disney characters often move in exact synchronization with the music, even when they aren't dancing. (As we have seen, such exactness was possible because the sound track was recorded before the drawings were made.) Matching movement to music came to be known as *Mickey-Mousing.*

Films other than musicals and cartoons exploit correspondences among musical and pictorial rhythms. Michael Mann's *The Last of the Mohicans* culminates in a chase and a fight along a mountain ridge. Alice has been captured by the renegade Magua, and Hawkeye, Uncas, and Chingachgook race up the trail to rescue her. We might expect, then, the standard thunderous action score, but what we hear is a quick, grave Scottish dance, initially played on fiddle, mandolin, and harpsichord. The tune was heard in an earlier dance scene at the fort, so it functions to recall the two couples' romances, but here it gives the scene a propulsive energy. Hand-to-hand struggles stand out against the throbbing music. Eventually, the theme swells to the full orchestra, but the same implacable beat governs the action. When Alice hovers on the cliff edge, about to jump off, somber chords repeat a seesaw pulse, as if time is standing still.

At the scene's climax, Chingachgook sprints urgently into the fray, and faster musical figures played by stringed instruments recall the early dance tune. His attack on Magua consists of four precise blows from his battle-axe; each blow coincides with the third beat in a series of musical measures. In the final moment of combat, the two warriors stand frozen opposite each other. The shot lasts three beats. On the fourth beat, Chingachgook launches the fatal blow. As Magua topples over, the music's pulse is replaced by a sustained string chord. *The Last of the Mohicans* has synchronized dance music with visual rhythms, but the result doesn't feel like Mickey-Mousing. The throbbing 4/4 meter, the accented beats, and the leaping melody give the heroes' precise movements a choreographic grace.

Rhythm in Sound and Image: Disparities   The filmmaker may also choose to create a disparity among the rhythms of sound, editing, and image. One of the most common options is to edit dialogue scenes in ways that cut against natural speech rhythms. In our specimen of dialogue overlap from John McTiernan's *The Hunt for Red October* (7.11–7.13), the editing does not coincide with accented beats, cadences, or pauses in the officer's speech. Thus, the editing smoothes over the changes of shot and emphasizes the words and facial expressions of Captain Ramius. If a filmmaker wants to emphasize the speaker and the speech, the cuts usually come at pauses or natural stopping points in the line. McTiernan uses this sort of rhythmic cutting at other points in the film.

The filmmaker may contrast the rhythm of sound and picture in more noticeable ways. For instance, if the source of sound is primarily offscreen, the filmmaker can utilize the behavior of onscreen figures to create an expressive counterrhythm. Toward the end of John Ford's *She Wore a Yellow Ribbon,* the aging cavalry captain, Nathan Brittles, watches his troops ride out of the fort just after he has retired. He regrets leaving the service and desires to go with the patrol. The sound of the scene consists of two elements: the cheerful title song sung by the departing riders, and the quick hoofbeats of their horses. Yet only a few of the shots show the horses and singers, who ride at a rhythm matched to the sound. Instead, the scene concentrates our attention on Brittles, standing almost motionless by his own horse. The contrast of brisk musical rhythm and the static images of the solitary Brittles functions expressively to emphasize his regret at having to stay behind for the first time in many years.

At times, accompanying music might even seem rhythmically inappropriate to the images. At intervals in *Four Nights of a Dreamer,* Robert Bresson presents shots of a large, floating nightclub cruising the Seine. The boat's movement is slow and smooth, yet the sound track consists of lively calypso music. (Not until a later scene do we discover that the music comes from a band aboard the boat.) The strange combination of fast sound tempo with the slow passage of the boat creates a languorous, mysterious effect.

Jacques Tati does something similar in *Play Time*. In a scene outside a Parisian hotel, tourists climb aboard a bus to go to a nightclub. As they file slowly up the steps, raucous jazzy music begins. The music startles us because it seems inappropriate to the images. In fact, it primarily accompanies action in the next scene, in which some carpenters awkwardly carrying a large plateglass window seem to be dancing to the music. By starting the fast music over an earlier scene of slower visual rhythm, Tati creates a comic effect and prepares for a transition to a new locale.

In Chris Marker's *La Jetée,* the contrast between image and sound rhythms dominates the entire film. *La Jetée* is made up almost entirely of still shots; except for one tiny gesture, all movement within the images is eliminated. Yet the film utilizes voice-over narration, music, and sound effects of a generally rapid, constantly accented rhythm. Despite the absence of movement, the film doesn't seem uncinematic, partly because it offers a dynamic interplay of audio-visual rhythms.

These examples suggest some of the ways in which rhythms may be combined. But of course, most films also vary their rhythms. A change of rhythm may function to shift our expectations. In the famous battle on the ice in *Alexander Nevsky,* Sergei Eisenstein develops the sound from slow tempos to fast and back to slow. The first 12 shots of the scene show the Russian army anticipating the attack of the German knights. The shots are of moderate length, and they contain very little movement. The music is comparably slow, consisting of short, distinctly separated, chords. Then, as the German army rides into sight over the horizon, both the visual movement and the tempo of the music increase quickly, and the battle begins. At the end of the battle, Eisenstein creates another contrast with a long passage of slow, lamenting music and majestic tracking shots but little figure movement.

Fidelity

By *fidelity,* we don't mean the quality of recording. In our sense, fidelity refers to the extent to which the sound is faithful to the source as we conceive it. If a film shows us a barking dog and we hear a barking noise, that sound is faithful to its source; the sound maintains fidelity. But if the image of the barking dog is accompanied by the sound of a cat meowing, there enters a disparity between sound and image—a lack of fidelity.

From our standpoint, fidelity has nothing to do with what originally made the sound in production. As we have seen, the filmmaker may manipulate sound independently of image. Accompanying the image of a dog with the meow is no more difficult than accompanying the image with a bark. If the viewer takes the sound to be coming from its source in the diegetic world of the film, then it is faithful, regardless of its actual source in production.

Fidelity is thus purely a matter of expectation. Even if our dog emits a bark on screen, perhaps in production the bark came from a different dog or was electronically synthesized. We do not know what laser guns really sound like, but we accept the whang they make in *Return of the Jedi* as plausible. (In production, their sound was made by hammering guy wires that anchored a radio tower.)

When we do become aware that a sound is unfaithful to its source, that awareness is usually used for comic effect. In Jacques Tati's *Mr. Hulot's Holiday,* much humor arises from the opening and closing of a dining room door. Instead of simply recording a real door, Tati inserts a twanging sound like a plucked cello string each time the door swings. Aside from being amusing in itself, this sound functions to emphasize the rhythmic patterns created by waiters and diners passing through the door. Because many of the jokes in *Mr. Hulot's Holiday* and other Tati films are based on quirkily unfaithful noises, his films are good specimens for the study of sound.

As with low- or high-angle framings, we have no recipe that will allow us to interpret every manipulation of fidelity as comic. Some nonfaithful sounds have serious functions. In Alfred Hitchcock's *The Thirty-Nine Steps,* a landlady discovers a corpse in an apartment. A shot of her screaming face is accompanied by a train whistle; then the scene shifts to an actual train. Though the whistle is not a faithful sound for an image of a screaming person, it provides a dramatic transition.

In some cases, fidelity may be manipulated by a change in volume. A sound may seem unreasonably loud or soft in relation to other sounds in the film. Curtis Bernhardt's *Possessed* alters volume in ways that are not faithful to the sources. The central character is gradually falling deeper into mental illness. In one scene, she is alone, highly distraught, in her room on a rainy night, and the narration restricts us to her range of knowledge. But sound devices enable the narration to achieve subjective depth as well. We begin to hear things as she does; a ticking clock and dripping raindrops gradually magnify in volume. Here the shift in fidelity functions to suggest a psychological state, a movement from the character's heightened perception into sheer hallucination.

Space

Sound has a spatial dimension because it comes from a *source.* Our beliefs about that source have a powerful effect on how we understand the sound.

Diegetic Versus Nondiegetic Sound   For purposes of analyzing narrative form, we described events taking place in the story world as *diegetic* (p. 249). For this reason, **diegetic sound** is sound that has a source in the story world. The words spoken by the characters, sounds made by objects in the story, and music represented as coming from instruments in the story space are all diegetic sound.

Diegetic sound is often hard to notice as such. It may seem to come naturally from the world of the film. But as we saw in the sequence of the Ping-Pong game in *Mr. Hulot's Holiday,* when the game becomes abruptly quiet to allow us to hear action in the foreground, the filmmaker may manipulate diegetic sound in ways that aren't at all realistic.

Alternatively, there is **nondiegetic sound,** which is represented as coming from a source outside the story world. Music added to enhance the film's action is the most common type of nondiegetic sound. When Roger Thornhill is climbing Mount Rushmore in *North by Northwest* and tense music comes up, we don't expect to see an orchestra perched on the side of the mountain. Viewers understand that movie music is a convention and does not issue from the world of the story. The same holds true for the so-called omniscient narrator, the disembodied voice that gives us information but doesn't belong to any of the characters in the film. An example is *The Magnificent Ambersons,* in which the director, Orson Welles, speaks the nondiegetic narration.

Nondiegetic sound effects are also possible. In *Le Million,* various characters pursue an old coat with a winning lottery ticket in the pocket. The chase converges backstage at the opera, where the characters race and dodge around one another, tossing the coat to their accomplices. But instead of putting in the sounds coming from the actual space of the chase, director René Clair fades in the sounds of a football game. Because the maneuvers of the chase do look like a scrimmage, with the coat serving as a ball, this enhances the comedy of the sequence **(7.20).** Although we hear a crowd cheering and a referee's whistle, we do not assume that the characters present are making these sounds.

Entire films may be made with completely nondiegetic sound tracks. Conner's *A Movie,* Kenneth Anger's *Scorpio Rising,* and Derek Jarman's *War Requiem* use

7.20 Nondietetic sound effects create comedy in *Le Million* by creating a sort of audio-visual pun.

only nondiegetic music. Similarly, many compilation documentaries include no diegetic sound; instead, omniscient voice-over commentary and orchestral music guide our response to the images.

As with fidelity, the distinction between diegetic and nondiegetic sound doesn't depend on the real source of the sound in the filmmaking process. Rather, it depends on our understanding of the conventions of film viewing. We know that certain sounds are represented as coming from the story world, while others are represented as coming from outside the space of the story events. Such viewing conventions are so common that we usually don't have to think about which type of sound we are hearing at any moment.

At many times, however, a film's narration deliberately blurs boundaries between different spatial categories. Such a play with convention can be used to puzzle or surprise the audience, to create humor or ambiguity, or to achieve other purposes.

Resources of Diegetic Sound   We know that the space of the narrative action isn't limited to what we can see on the screen at any one moment. The same thing holds true for sound. In the last shot of our *The Hunt for Red October* scene, we hear the officer speaking while we see a shot of just Captain Ramius, listening (7.13). Early in the attack on the village in *The Seven Samurai,* we, along with the samurai, hear the hoofbeats of the bandits' horses before we see a shot of them. These instances remind us that diegetic sound can be either *onscreen* or *offscreen,* depending on whether its source is inside the frame or outside the frame.

Offscreen sound is crucial to our experience of a film, and filmmakers know that it can save time and money. A shot may show only a couple sitting together in airplane seats, but if we hear a throbbing engine, other passengers chatting, and the creak of a beverage cart, we'll conjure up a plane in flight. Offscreen sound can create the illusion of a bigger space than we actually see, as in the cavernous prison sequences of *The Silence of the Lambs.* It can also shape our sense of how a scene will develop **(7.21–7.23).**

The technique can fill in information very economically. In *Zodiac,* we see the alcoholic reporter Avery wake up after sleeping in his car. As he abruptly sits up, we hear the clink of bottles on the floor; the sound confirms our suspicion that he has spent another night drinking.

Used with optical point-of-view shots, offscreen sound can create restricted narration, guiding us toward what a character is noticing. In *No Country for Old Men,* Llewelyn Moss is holed up in a hotel room with a bag of cash, hiding from his implacable pursuer Anton Chigurh. When he realizes that a tracking device has been hidden among the bills, the narration is limited solely to what Moss sees and hears. He tries calling the downstairs desk; we dimly hear the distant phone ringing, so like him we infer that Chigurh has killed the clerk.

The sonic texture is very detailed, highlighting the slight noises of Moss shifting on the bed and switching off the lamp. Then, against a muted background of wind, we hear steadily approaching footsteps in the hall, accompanied by rapid pinging on a homing device. Optical point-of-view confirms Chigurh's arrival: we see the shadows of his feet in the crack under the door. Moss cocks his shotgun, creating a click that seems abnormally loud and close. The shadows move away, and we hear the slight creaking of a lightbulb being unscrewed in the hall, eliminating the streak of illumination under the door. The auditory climax of the scene is the metallic burst of the door lock rocketing into the room. *No Country's* narration has created suspense by restricting both vision and sound to Moss's range of knowledge. (For a more complex instance, see "A Closer Look.")

Sometimes offscreen sound can make the film's narration less restricted. In John Ford's *Stagecoach,* the stagecoach is desperately fleeing from a band of Indians. The ammunition is running out, and all seems lost until a troop of cavalry suddenly arrives. Yet Ford does not present the situation this baldly. He shows a

7.21   In *His Girl Friday,* Hildy goes into the pressroom to write her final story. As she chats with the other reporters, a loud clunk comes from an offscreen source, and they glance to the left.

7.22   Hildy and another reporter walk to the window . . .

7.23   . . . and see a gallows being prepared for a hanging.

A CLOSER LOOK

OFFSCREEN SOUND AND OPTICAL POINT OF VIEW:
The Money Exchange In *Jackie Brown*

Optical point-of-view cutting can be very powerful, as we saw in examining *Rear Window* (p. 245). Now we're in a position to see—and hear—how it can be coordinated with onscreen and offscreen sound. Quentin Tarantino's *Jackie Brown* offers an illuminating example because, somewhat in the spirit of our sequence from *Letter from Siberia* (pp. 270–271), it runs the same sequence of actions three times, with varying sound tracks. Unlike Chris Marker's film, however, *Jackie Brown* shows the scene as different characters experience it.

Jackie is supposed to deliver over half a million dollars in cash to the dangerous arms dealer Ordell. Ordell has sent his girlfriend, Melanie, and his partner, Louis, to pick up the money from a fitting room in a dress shop. Jackie, however, is playing her own game. She's agreed to help federal agents arrest Ordell, but she has also recruited the bail bondsman Max Cherry to help her switch shopping bags and leave Ordell empty-handed. This story action is presented three times in the plot, each time adding a layer to our understanding of what's really happening. It would be worthwhile to study the careful auditory touches in these three sequences, such as the replay of the shop's Muzak and the delicate Foley work on footsteps, fabric, and other noises. Here we'll concentrate on optical subjectivity and offscreen sound, because these techniques are crucial in making the triple play clear to the audience. They also serve to contrast the squabbling, inept go-betweens whom Ordell is relying on and the self-possessed Jackie and Max.

The first run-through confines us to Jackie's range of knowledge. She tries on a pantsuit, and the saleswoman says, "Wow, you look really cool!" **(7.24)**. Jackie goes back to the fitting rooms and waits for Melanie. We hear Melanie arrive offscreen, and Tarantino shows

7.24 The first run-through: The sales clerk tells Jackie, "Wow, you look really cool!"

7.25 After Jackie has left the money in the fitting room, she hurries away, pretending to be distraught. The clerk calls after her, "Wait, your change!"

7.26 The second version: As Melanie and Louis head toward the shop, the camera tracks rightward with them, passing Max Cherry in the foreground.

7.27 As Melanie and Louis approach, we hear, "Wow, you look really cool!" fairly softly.

us her shoes from Jackie's viewpoint. After Melanie has left, Jackie repacks the money in a shopping bag she leaves in the cubicle and hurries out. She hastily pays the sales clerk, who calls after her, "Wait, your change!" and waves her bills **(7.25)**. Jackie rushes out to the mall and summons the federal agents, shouting that Melanie stole the bag from her.

Tarantino flashes back to an earlier phase of the action, with Louis and Melanie arriving at the shop. As the camera follows them **(7.26, 7.27),** we hear the saleswoman say from offscreen, "Wow, you look really cool!" The camera pans to Jackie and the clerk **(7.28).** The offscreen sound has motivated showing this dialogue again, and its unnatural loudness assures that we understand that we're entering the scene at a point we've already witnessed. Louis and Melanie try to look inconspicuous, with Melanie distracted by Jackie's striking outfit. When Melanie teases Louis about his nervousness, he twists her arm, and she blurts out, "Hey, would you let go!" **(7.29).**

Tarantino now uses offscreen sound to test Louis's dull wits. Louis looks down at the shirts he's riffling through **(7.30),** and we hear an offscreen phone ring. Louis doesn't look up, but we are given a shot of the clerk answering **(7.31).** What does get Louis's attention is Melanie, who abruptly strides into the fitting rooms. Looking uneasily this way and that, Louis sees Max, whom he dimly recognizes, and the two men exchange glances in shot/reverse shot. Then Melanie hustles out of the fitting rooms, and Louis catches up with her. They leave quarreling about who should carry the bag.

The scene runs a third time, now attaching us to Max's range of knowledge. The second version hinted at his presence in the shop, when the tracking shot following Melanie and Louis glided past him in the foreground (7.26). We see him enter and browse, waiting calmly for the scam to begin. Once more Jackie comes out wearing the outfit, and the sales clerk says, "Wow, you look really cool!" But now the exchange is observed from Max's point of view **(7.32, 7.33).** The sound track fades out the dialogue between the clerk and Jackie and fades up the quarrel between Melanie and Louis. Max turns his attention to them and then back to Jackie and the clerk. Here the sound mixing is

7.28   The camera pans to pick up Jackie and the clerk, as Jackie says she'll buy the outfit. Sound perspective makes the dialogue louder and clearer, emphasizing that this is a repetition of the scene we've just witnessed. Compare 7.22.

7.29   Quarreling at the garment racks, Louis grabs Melanie's arm and she snaps, "Hey, would you let go!"

7.30   Louis browses through shirts. At the end of the shot, a telephone rings offscreen.

7.31   The clerk answers the phone, but this isn't Louis's point of view; it's close to what he might have seen if he *had* looked up.

quite subjective, conveying Max's shifting attention between the two conversations.

While Max is watching the action at the counter, we hear Louis and Melanie quarreling, and this motivates another switch in Max's attention, in time for him to observe her exclaiming, "Hey, would you let go!" **(7.34, 7.35)**. The ringing phone drives his eyes back to the clerk **(7.36, 7.37)**, but he keeps Melanie in mind, too. A little before Louis notices, Max watches Melanie set off on her mission. Louis clumsily scans the shop, but Max is calm and purposeful. Each offscreen sound snaps his attention to what is crucial to the plan. After Melanie and Louis leave, it's through Max's eyes that we see Jackie's departure, with the shopwoman calling, "Wait, your change!" **(7.38)**. Max pauses, then heads for the fitting room to retrieve the shopping bag and the fortune.

By repeating key actions, noises, and lines of dialogue, the replays lay out the mechanics of the exchange cogently. The variations between the second and third sequences allow Tarantino to characterize the thieves. Max is more alert than Louis and Melanie,

and offscreen sounds prompt him to shift his attention precisely. Moreover, each version of story events is nested neatly inside the next one: Jackie and the clerk, then Jackie and the clerk watched by Melanie and Louis, then all the others watched by Max, who completes the money exchange. Sound and image work together to peel back each layer and expand our appreciation of Jackie's intricate double-cross.

7.32 Third run-through: Pretending to be killing time in the shop, Max turns his attention to Jackie . . .

7.33 . . . just as the clerk exclaims, "Wow, you look really cool!" The repeated line anchors us in action we know. The framing from Max's optical point of view varies what we saw in 7.24 and 7.28.

7.34 After Jackie leaves for the changing room, Max shifts his attention to Melanie and Louis, in time to hear her say, "Hey, would you let go!"

medium close-up of one of the passengers, Hatfield, who has just discovered that he is down to his last bullet **(7.39)**. He glances off right and raises his gun **(7.40)**. The camera pans right to a woman, Lucy, praying. During all this, orchestral music, including bugles, plays nondiegetically. Unseen by Lucy, the gun comes into the frame from the left as Hatfield prepares to shoot her to prevent her from being captured by the Indians **(7.41)**. But before he shoots, an offscreen gunshot is heard, and Hatfield's hand and gun drop down out of the frame **(7.42)**. Then bugle music becomes somewhat more prominent. Lucy's expression changes as she says, "Can you hear it? Can you hear it? It's a bugle. They're blowing the charge" **(7.43)**. Only then does Ford cut to the cavalry itself racing toward the coach.

7.35 His switch in attention is conveyed through a point-of-view shot. Compare 7.29.

7.36 Max has been studying the couple, but the sound of a ringing phone offscreen makes him shift his glance.

7.37 The clerk answers the phone. (Compare 7.31). This diversion impels Melanie to seize the moment and stride into the changing room, watched by Max and, eventually, Louis.

7.38 After the bogus switch has been made, Jackie comes out and hurries to the counter. Max watches the transaction, and from his point of view we see Jackie rush off, with the clerk calling after, "Wait, your change!" Compare 7.25. Now Max walks to the counter. His approach will be presented, in keeping with the rest of the sequence, as his optical point-of-view.

Rather than showing the cavalry riding to the rescue, the film's narration uses offscreen sound to restrict our awareness to the initial despair of the passengers and their growing hope as they hear the distant sound. The sound of the bugle also emerges imperceptibly out of the nondiegetic music. Only Lucy's line tells us that this is a diegetic sound that signals their rescue, at which point the narration becomes far less restricted.

Diegetic sound harbors other possibilities. Often a filmmaker uses sound to represent what a character is thinking. We hear the character's voice speaking his or her thoughts even though that character's lips do not move; presumably, other characters cannot hear these thoughts. Here the narration uses sound to achieve

7.39 *Stagecoach.*

7.40 *Stagecoach.*

7.41 *Stagecoach.*

7.42 *Stagecoach.*

7.43 *Stagecoach.*

subjectivity, giving us information about the mental state of the character. Such spoken thoughts are comparable to mental images on the visual track. A character may also remember words, snatches of music, or events as represented by sound effects. In this case, the technique is comparable to a visual flashback.

The use of sound to enter a character's mind is so common that we need to distinguish between internal and external diegetic sound. **External diegetic sound** is that which we as spectators take to have a physical source in the scene. **Internal diegetic sound** is that which comes from inside the mind of a character; it is subjective. Nondiegetic and internal diegetic sounds are often called **sound over** because they do not come from the real space of the scene. Internal diegetic sound can't be heard by other characters.

In the Laurence Olivier version of *Hamlet,* for example, the filmmaker presents Hamlet's famous soliloquies as interior monologues. Hamlet is the source of the thoughts we hear represented as speech, but the words are only in his mind, not in his objective surroundings. Gus Van Sant employs a similar tactic in *Paranoid Park.* A teenage boy fleeing from a horrific accident is plagued by inner voices, some of them auditory flashbacks. By having snatches of dialogue burst in from different stereo channels and with different degrees of clarity, Van Sant presents the boy as engulfed by confusion about what to do next.

David Lynch makes interior monologue a central device in *Dune,* in which nearly every major character is given passages of internal diegetic observations. These aren't lengthy soliloquies but rather brief phrases slipped into pauses in normal conversation scenes. The result is an omniscient narration that unexpectedly plunges into mental subjectivity. The characters' voiced thoughts sometimes interweave with the external dialogue so tightly that they create a running commentary on a scene's action.

Recent films have reshaped the conventions of internal diegetic sound even more. Now an inner monologue may not be signaled by close shots of a character who's thinking, as in *Hamlet* and *Dune.* Wong Kar-wai and Terrence Malick will sometimes inject a character's voiced thoughts into scenes in which the character isn't prominent, or even visible. As the voice of a paid killer reflects on his job in Wong's *Fallen Angels,* we see distant shots of him mixed with several shots of the woman who arranges his contracts. In Malick's *The Thin Red Line* and *The New World,* characters are heard musing during lengthy montage sequences in which they don't even appear. These floating monologues come to resemble a more traditional voice-over narration. This impression is reinforced when the inner monologue uses the past tense, as if the action we're seeing onscreen is being recalled from a later time.

A different sort of internal diegetic sound occurs in Wim Wenders's *Wings of Desire.* Dozens of people are reading in a large public library **(7.44).** Incidentally, this sequence also constitutes an interesting exception to the general rule that one character cannot hear another's internal diegetic sound. The film's premise is that Berlin is patrolled by invisible angels who *can* tune in to humans' thoughts. This is

7.44 As the camera tracks past the readers in *Wings of Desire,* we hear their thoughts as a throbbing murmur of many voices in many languages.

7.45 The hero of *Blazing Saddles* rides jauntily through the desert accompanied by apparently nondiegetic music . . .

7.46 . . . until he passes Count Basie's orchestra, playing within the world of the narrative.

a good example of how the conventions of a genre (here, the fantasy film) and the film's specific narrative context can modify a traditional device.

To summarize: sound may be diegetic (in the story world) or nondiegetic (outside the story world). If it is diegetic, it may be onscreen or offscreen, and internal (subjective) or external (objective).

Playing with the Diegetic/Nondiegetic Distinction In most sequences, the sources of the sounds are clearly diegetic or nondiegetic. But some films blur the distinction between diegetic and nondiegetic sound, as we saw in the cavalry rescue scene from *Stagecoach.* Since we're used to identifying a sound's source easily, a film may try to cheat our expectations.

In Mel Brooks's *Blazing Saddles,* we hear what we think is nondiegetic musical accompaniment for a cowboy's ride across the prairie—until he rides past Count Basie and his orchestra **(7.45, 7.46).** This joke depends on a reversal of our expectations about the convention of nondiegetic music. A more elaborate example is the 1986 musical version of *Little Shop of Horrors.* There a trio of female singers strolls through many scenes, providing musical commentary on the action without any of the characters noticing them. (To complicate matters, the three singers also appear in minor diegetic roles, and then they do interact with the main characters.)

More complicated is a moment in *The Magnificent Ambersons* when Orson Welles creates an unusual interplay between the diegetic and nondiegetic sounds. A prologue to the film outlines the background of the Amberson family and the birth of the son, George. We see a group of townswomen gossiping about the marriage of Isabel Amberson, and one predicts that she will have "the worst spoiled lot of children this town will ever see" **(7.47).** This scene presents diegetic dialogue. After this conversation ends, the nondiegetic narrator resumes his description of the family history. Over a shot of the empty street, he says, "The prophetess proved to be mistaken in a single detail merely; Wilbur and Isabel did not have *children.* They had only one." But at this point, still over the shot of the street, we hear the

7.47 In this scene from *The Magnificent Ambersons,* the woman with the teacup makes a remark about Isabel Amberson's future children . . .

7.48 . . . that the nondiegetic narrator's voice corrects in the next shot.

7.49 As the woman seems to reply to the narrator, Isabel's son moves into view.

gossiper's voice again: "Only one! But I'd like to know if he isn't spoiled enough for a whole carload" **(7.48)**. After her line, the narrator goes on, "Again, she found none to challenge her. George Amberson Minifer, the Major's one grandchild, was a princely terror." During this description, a pony cart comes up the street, and we see George for the first time **(7.49)**. In this exchange, the woman seems to reply to the narrator, even though we must assume that she can't hear what he says. (After all, she's a character in the story and he isn't.) Here Welles playfully departs from conventional usage to emphasize the arrival of the story's main character and the hostility of the townspeople to him.

This passage from *The Magnificent Ambersons* juxtaposes diegetic and nondiegetic sounds in a disconcerting way. In other films, a single sound may be ambiguous because it could fall into either category. In the opening of *Apocalypse Now,* the throbbings of the ceiling fan and the helicopter blades are clearly diegetic, but Francis Ford Coppola accompanies these with The Doors' song "The End." This might be taken either as a subjective part of the character's Vietnam fantasy or as nondiegetic—an external commentary on the action in the manner of normal movie music.

Similarly, at a major point in Paul Thomas Anderson's *Magnolia,* several characters are shown in different locations, each singing softly along to the Aimee Mann song "Wise Up." When the sequence begins in Claudia's apartment, the song might be taken as diegetic and offscreen, since she has been listening to Aimee Mann music in an earlier scene. But then Anderson cuts to other characters elsewhere singing along, even though they cannot be hearing the music in Claudia's apartment. It would seem that the sound is now nondiegetic, with the characters accompanying it as they might do in a musical. The sequence underlines the parallels among several suffering characters and conveys an eerie sense of disparate people for once on the same emotional wavelength. The sound also works with the crosscutting to pull the characters together before the climax, when their lives will converge more directly.

A more disturbing uncertainty about whether a sound is diegetic often crops up in the films of Jean-Luc Godard. He narrates some of his films in nondiegetic voice-over, but in other films, such as *Two or Three Things I Know About Her,* he seems also to be in the story space, whispering questions or comments whose sound perspective makes them seem close to the camera. Godard does not claim to be a character in the action, yet the characters on the screen sometimes behave as though they hear him. This uncertainty as to diegetic or nondiegetic sound sources enables Godard to stress the conventionality of traditional sound usage.

Sound Perspective   One characteristic of diegetic sound is the possibility of suggesting the **sound perspective.** This is a sense of spatial distance and location analogous to the cues for visual depth and volume that we get with visual perspective. "I like to think," remarks sound designer Walter Murch, "that I not only record a sound but the space between me and the sound: The subject that generates the sound is merely what causes the surrounding space to resonate."

Sound perspective can be suggested by volume. A loud sound tends to seem near; a soft one, more distant. The horses' hooves in the *Seven Samurai* battle and the bugle call from *Stagecoach* exemplify how rising volume suggests closer distance. Sound perspective is also created by timbre. The combination of directly registered sounds and sounds reflected from the environment creates a timbre specific to a given distance. Timbre effects are most noticeable with echoes. In *The Magnificent Ambersons,* the conversations that take place on the baroque staircase have a distinct echo, giving the impression of huge, empty spaces around the characters.

As the camera follows a character, changes in sound perspective may suggest the character's movement through space, a sort of sonic point of view. But many uses of sound perspective don't try to be realistic. In a long shot, a character's voice will usually be clearer than if we were the same distance from her or him in reality, and when we cut to a close-up, that character's voice will not be significantly louder or crisper. In a conversation with sound overlaps, like the one in *The Hunt for Red October* (p. 277), the voices don't change perspective when the camera shifts to show the listener.

Sound perspective is particularly marked in telephone conversations. Typically, the film's narration cuts back and forth between the people talking, and the sound perspective varies accordingly. When the person on camera is speaking, the lines are clear and enhanced by natural ambient sounds. The voice heard over the receiver is usually more coarsely rendered and more reverberant, carrying lower pitches and providing little ambient sound. Sound editors call this disparity the *telephone split.* It represents the fact that the listener is hearing a voice on the line, but it seldom matches what a phone call sounds like in reality.

Like all conventions, the telephone split can be adjusted for expressive possibilities. In *Phone Booth,* a publicist is trapped in a booth, pinned down by an unseen sniper who keeps him talking on the phone. Here the telephone split takes an unusual form. The PR man is heard normally, with ambient sound, but we don't hear the sniper as a crackling telephone voice. Instead, we hear soft, closely miked speech in a dry sound envelope. It does not change when the camera moves toward or away from the booth. The voice has a slight electronic twang, so it doesn't sound as neutral as a narrator's voice-over, but it remains closer to our perspective than to the protagonist's. Whispering, laughing, making rude remarks about what's happening around the booth, the sniper's voice hovers in a realm somewhere between us and the street. It enhances the sense that the protagonist is being watched by a distant, somewhat ghostly threat.

Sound Perspective in the Theater Space Multichannel recording and reproduction tremendously increase the filmmaker's ability to suggest sound perspective. In most 35mm theaters equipped with multitrack sound systems, three speakers are located behind the screen. The center speaker transmits most of the onscreen dialogue, as well as the most important effects and music. The left and right speakers are stereophonic, adding their sound effects, music, and minor dialogue. These channels can suggest a region of sound within the frame or just offscreen. Surround channels principally carry minor sound effects and some music, and they are divided among several speakers arranged along the sides and in the back of the theater. The "inner dialogue" shot in *Paranoid Park* is unusual in spreading more important dialogue to subsidiary channels.

By using stereophonic and surround tracks, a film can more strongly imply a sound's distance and placement. In farcical comedies like *The Naked Gun* and *Hot Shots,* stereophonic sound can suggest collisions and falls outside the frame. Without the greater localization offered by the stereophonic channels, we might scan the frame for sources of the sounds. Even the center channel can be used to localize an offscreen object. In the climactic scene of *The Fugitive,* Richard Kimble is sneaking up on the friend who has betrayed him, and he reaches down past the lower frame line. As he slides his arm to the right, a rolling clank in the center track tells us that there is an iron pipe at his feet.

In addition, stereo reproduction can specify a moving sound's direction. In David Lean's *Lawrence of Arabia,* for instance, the approach of planes to bomb a camp is first suggested through a rumble occurring only on the right side of the screen. Lawrence and an officer look off right, and their dialogue identifies the source of the sound. Then, when the scene shifts to the besieged camp itself, the sound slides from channel to channel, suggesting the planes swooping overhead.

With stereophonic and surround channels, a remarkably convincing three-dimensional sound environment may be created within the theater. Sound sources can alter in position as the camera pans or tracks through a locale. The *Star Wars* series uses multiple-channel sound to suggest space vehicles whizzing not only across the screen but also above and behind the spectators.

"She first hears the music at a bit of a distance, coming from the house, and as she walks in—the music is getting closer, step-by-step—she goes from the entrance way up the stairs—the music is still growing—and she finally passes by a guitarist on the stairs."

—Tony Volante, re-recording mixer, *Rachel Getting Married*

Like other techniques, sound localization in the theater needn't be used for realistic purposes. *Apocalypse Now* divides its six-track sound among three channels in the rear of the theater and three in the front. In the film's first sequence, mentioned above, the protagonist Ben Willard is seen lying on his bed. Shots of his feverish face are superimposed on shots of U.S. helicopters dropping napalm on the Vietnamese jungle. The sound oscillates between internal and external status, as Willard's mind turns the whoosh of a ceiling fan into the whir of helicopter blades. These subjective sounds issue from both the front and back of the theater, engulfing the audience.

Abruptly, a POV shot tracking toward the window suggests that Willard has gotten to his feet and is walking. As the camera moves, the noises fade from all rear speakers and become concentrated in the front ones at screen left, right, and center. Then, as Willard's hand opens the venetian blinds to reveal his vision of the street outside, the sound fades out of the left and right front speakers and comes only from the center channel. Our attention has been narrowed: as we leave Willard's mind, the sound steers us back to the outside world, which is rendered as unrealistically monophonic. In addition, the disparity in acoustic dimensions suggests that the protagonist's wraparound memory of jungle destruction is more powerful than the pallid environment of Saigon.

Time

Sound also permits the filmmaker to represent time in various ways. This is because the time represented on the sound track may or may not be the same as that represented in the image.

The most straightforward audio-visual relations involve sound–image synchronization. The matching of sound with image in projection creates **synchronous sound.** In that case, we hear the sound at the same time as we see the source produce the sound. Dialogue between characters is normally synchronized so that the lips of the actors move at the same time that we hear the appropriate words.

When the sound does go out of synchronization during a viewing (often through an error in projection or lab work), the result is quite distracting. But some filmmakers have obtained imaginative effects by putting **asynchronous,** or out-of-sync, **sound** into the film itself. One such effect occurs in a scene in the musical by Gene Kelly and Stanley Donen, *Singin' in the Rain.* In the early days of Hollywood sound filming, a pair of silent screen actors have just made their first talking picture, *The Dueling Cavalier.* Their film company previews the film for an audience at a theater. In the earliest talkies, sound was often recorded on a phonograph disc to be played along with the film, and the sound sometimes fell out of synchronization with the picture. This is what happens in the preview of *The Dueling Cavalier.* As the film is projected, it slows down momentarily, but the record keeps running. From this point, all the sounds come several seconds before their sources are seen in the image. A line of dialogue begins, *then* the actor's lips move. A woman's voice is heard when a man moves his lips, and vice versa. The humor of this disastrous preview in *Singin' in the Rain* depends on our realization that a film's synchronization of sound and image is an illusion produced by mechanical means.

A lengthier play with our expectations about synchronization comes in Woody Allen's *What's Up, Tiger Lily?* Allen has taken an Asian spy film and dubbed a new sound track on, but the English-language dialogue is not a translation of the original. Instead, it creates a new story in comic juxtaposition with the original images. Much of the humor results from our constant awareness that the words are not perfectly synchronized with the actors' lips. Allen has turned the usual problems of the dubbing of foreign films into the basis of his comedy.

Synchronization relates to screen duration, or *viewing* time. As we saw in Chapter 3, narrative films can also present *story* and *plot* time. To recall the distinction: story time consists of the order, duration, and frequency of all the events pertinent to the narrative, whether they are shown to us or not. Plot time consists of the order,

TABLE 7.2 Temporal Relations of Sound in Cinema

Time	Space of Source	
	Diegetic (Story space)	Nondiegetic (Nonstory space)
1. Nonsimultaneous; sound from *earlier* in story than image	Sound flashback; image flash-forward; sound bridge	Sound marked as past put over images (e.g., sound of John Kennedy speech put over images of United States today)
2. Sound *simultaneous* in story with image	*External:* dialogue, effects, music *Internal:* thoughts of character heard	Sound marked as simultaneous with images put over images (e.g., narrator describing events in present tense)
3. Nonsimultaneous; sound from *later* in story than image	Sound of flash-forward; image flashback with sound continuing in present; character narrates earlier events; sound bridge	Sound marked as later put over images (e.g., reminiscing narrator of *The Magnificent Ambersons*)

duration, and frequency of the events actually represented in the film. Plot time shows us selected story events but skips over or only suggests others.

Story and plot time can be manipulated by sound in two principal ways. If the sound takes place at the same time as the image in terms of the story events, it is **simultaneous sound.** This is overwhelmingly the most common usage. When characters speak onscreen, the words we hear are occurring at the same moment in the plot's action as in story time.

But it is possible for the sound we hear to occur earlier or later in the story than the events we see in the image. In this manipulation of story order, the sound becomes **nonsimultaneous.** The most common example of this is the sonic flashback. For instance, we might see a character onscreen in the present but hear another character's voice from an earlier scene. By means of nonsimultaneous sound, the film can give us information about story events without presenting them visually. And nonsimultaneous sound may, like simultaneous sound, have either an external or an internal source—that is, a source in the objective world of film or the subjective realms of the character's mind.

So temporal relationships in the cinema can get complicated. To help distinguish them, Table 7.2 sums up the possible temporal and spatial relationships that image and sound can display.

Diegetic Sound   Because the first and third of these possibilities are rare, we start by commenting on the second, most common, option:

2. *Sound simultaneous in story with image.* This is by far the most common temporal relation that sound has in fiction films. Noise, music, or speech that comes from the space of the story almost invariably occurs at the same time as the image. Like any other sort of diegetic sound, simultaneous sound can be either external (objective) or internal (subjective).

1. *Sound earlier in story than image.* Here the sound comes from an earlier point in the story than the action currently visible onscreen. A clear example occurs at the end of Joseph Losey's *Accident.* Over a shot of a driveway gate,

7.50 One scene of *The Silence of the Lambs* ends with Clarice Starling on the telephone, as she mentions a location called the "Your Self Storage facility . . ."

7.51   . . . and her voice continues, ". . . right outside central Baltimore" over the first shot of the next scene, the sign for the Your Self warehouse.

we hear a car crash. The sound represents the crash that occurred at the *beginning* of the film. Now if there were cues that the sound was internal—that is, that a character was recalling it—it would not strictly be coming from the past, since the *memory* of the sound would be occurring in the present. Late in *The Sixth Sense,* for example, the protagonist recalls a crucial statement that his young patient had made to him, causing him to realize something that casts most of the previous action in an entirely new light. The boy's voice is clearly coming from the protagonist's mind at the moment of his recollection. But in the scene from *Accident,* no character is remembering the scene, so we have a fairly pure case of a sonic flashback. In this film, an unrestricted narration makes an ironic final comment on the action.

Sound may belong to an earlier time than the image in another way. The sound from the previous scene may linger briefly while the image is already presenting the next scene. This common device is called a **sound bridge.** Sound bridges of this sort may create smooth transitions by setting up expectations that are quickly confirmed, as in a scene change in Jonathan Demme's *The Silence of the Lambs* (**7.50, 7.51**).

Sound bridges can also make our expectations more uncertain. In Tim Hunter's *The River's Edge,* three high-school boys are standing outside school, and one of them confesses to having killed his girlfriend. When his pals scoff, he says, "They don't believe me." There is a cut to the dead girl lying in the grass by the river, while on the sound track we hear one of his friends respond to him by calling it a crazy story that no one will believe. For an instant, we cannot be sure whether a new scene is starting or we are seeing a cutaway to the corpse, which could be followed by a shot returning to the three boys at school. But the shot dwells on the dead girl, and after a pause, we hear, with a different sound ambience, "If you brought us . . ." Then there is a cut to a shot of the three youths walking through the woods to the river, as the same character continues, ". . . all the way out here for nothing. . . ." The friend's remark about the crazy story belongs to an earlier time than the shot of the corpse, and it is used as an unsettling sound bridge to the new scene.

3. *Sound later in story than image.* Nonsimultaneous sound may also occur at a time later than that depicted by the images. Here we are to take the images as occurring in the past and the sound as occurring in the present or future.

A simple prototype occurs in many trial dramas. The testimony of a witness in the present is heard on the sound track, while the image presents a flashback to an earlier event. The same effect occurs when the film employs a reminiscing narrator, as in John Ford's *How Green Was My Valley.* Aside from a glimpse at the beginning, we do not see the protagonist Huw as a man, only as a boy, but his narration accompanies the bulk of the plot, which is set in the distant past. Huw's present-time voice on the sound track creates a strong sense of nostalgia for the past and constantly reminds us of the pathetic decline that the characters will eventually suffer.

Since the late 1960s, it has become somewhat common for the sound from the next scene to begin while the images of the last one are still on the screen. Like the instances mentioned above, this transitional device is a *sound bridge.* In Wim Wenders's *American Friend,* a nighttime shot of a little boy riding in the back seat of a car is accompanied by a harsh clacking. There is a cut to a railroad station, where the timetable board flips through its metal cards listing times and destinations. Since the sound over the shot of the boy comes from the later scene, this portion is nonsimultaneous.

If the sound bridge isn't immediately identifiable, it can surprise or disorient the audience, as in the *American Friend* transition. A more recognizable sonic lead-in can create more clear-cut expectations about what we will see in the next scene. Federico Fellini's *8½* takes place in a town famous for its health spa and natural springs, and several scenes have shown an outdoor orchestra playing to entertain the guests. Midway through the film, a scene ends with the closing of a window on a steam bath. Near the end of the shot, we hear an orchestral version of the song "Blue Moon." There is a cut to an orchestra playing the tune in the center of the town's shopping area. Even before the new scene has established the exact locale of the action, we can reasonably expect that the musical bridge is bringing us back to the public life of the spa.

In principle, one could also have a sound *flash-forward.* The filmmaker could, say, use the sounds that belong with scene 5 to accompany the images in scene 2. In practice, such a technique is almost unknown. In Godard's *Contempt,* a husband and wife quarrel, and the scene ends with her swimming out to sea while he sits quietly on a rock formation. On the sound track, we hear her voice, closely miked, reciting a letter in which she tells him she has driven back to Rome with another man. Since the husband has not yet received the letter, and perhaps the wife has not yet written it, the letter and its recitation presumably come from a later point in the story. Here the sound flash-forward sets up strong expectations that a later scene confirms: We see the wife and the husband's rival stopping for gas on the road. In fact, we never see a scene in which the husband receives the letter.

Nondiegetic Sound Most nondiegetic sound has no relevant temporal relationship to the story. When mood music comes up over a tense scene, it would be irrelevant to ask if it is happening at the same time as the images, since the music has no existence in the world of the action. But occasionally, the filmmaker uses a type of nondiegetic sound that does have a defined temporal relationship to the story. Welles's narration in *The Magnificent Ambersons,* for instance, speaks of the action as having happened in a long-vanished era of American history.

As we watch a film, we don't mentally slot each sound into each of these spatial and temporal categories. But our categories do help us understand our viewing experience. They offer us ways of noticing important aspects of films—especially films that play with our expectations about sounds. By becoming aware of the rich range of possibilities, we're less likely to take a film's sound track for granted and likelier to notice unusual sound manipulations.

At the start of Alain Resnais's *Providence,* we see a wounded old man. Suddenly, we are in a courtroom, where a prosecutor is interrogating a young man **(7.52).** The scene then returns to the hunt, during which the old man was apparently murdered **(7.53).** A cut returns us to the courtroom, where the prosecutor continues his sarcastic questioning **(7.54).** The young man justifies his act by saying that the man was dying and turning into an animal **(7.55);** in 7.53, we had seen the man's hairy face and clawlike hands, so now we begin to see the links between the scenes. The prosecutor pauses, astonished, "Are you suggesting some kind of actual metamorphosis?" He pauses again, and a man's voice whispers, "A werewolf." The prosecutor then asks, "A werewolf, perhaps?" **(7.56).**

7.52 The prosecuting attorney in *Providence* questions a man accused of murder . . .

7.53 . . . and we see the accused confronting the old man who was killed.

7.54 The prosecutor is seen again . . .

7.55 . . . and then the accused man, who explains his actions.

7.56 The prosecutor seems to respond to a mysterious whispered voice—"A werewolf"—that no one else hears.

The whispered words startle us, for we cannot immediately account for them. Are they whispered by an unseen character offscreen? Are they subjective, conveying the thoughts of the prosecutor or witness? Are they perhaps even nondiegetic, coming from outside the story world? Only much later in the film do we find out whose voice whispered these words, and why. The whole opening of *Providence* provides an excellent extended case of how a filmmaker can play with conventions about sound sources.

In the *Providence* sequence, we are aware of the ambiguity immediately, and it points our expectations forward, arousing curiosity as to how the whisperer can be identified. The filmmaker can also use sound to create a retrospective awareness of how we have *mis*interpreted something earlier. This occurs in Francis Ford Coppola's *The Conversation,* a film that is virtually a textbook on the manipulation of sound and image.

The plot centers on Harry Caul, a sound engineer specializing in surveillance. Harry is hired by a mysterious corporate executive to tape a conversation between a young man and woman in a noisy park. Harry cleans up the garbled tape, but when he goes to turn over the copy to his client, he suspects foul play and refuses to relinquish it.

Now Harry obsessively replays, refilters, and remixes all his tapes of the conversation. Flashback images of the couple—perhaps in his memory, perhaps not—accompany his reworking of the tape. Finally, Harry arrives at a good dub, and we hear the man say, "He'd kill us if he could."

The overall situation is quite mysterious. Harry does not know who the young couple are (is the woman his client's wife or daughter?). Nevertheless, Harry suspects that they are in danger from the executive. Harry's studio is ransacked, the tape is stolen, and he later finds that the executive has it. Now more than ever, Harry feels that he is involved in a murder plot. After a highly ambiguous series of events, including Harry's bugging of a hotel room during which a killing seems to take place, Harry learns that the situation is not as he had thought.

Without giving away the revelation of the mystery, we can say that in *The Conversation* the narration misleads us by suggesting that certain sounds are objective when at the film's end we are inclined to consider them subjective, or at least ambiguous. The film's surprise, and its lingering mysteries, rely on unsignaled shifts between external and internal diegetic sound.

Providence and *The Conversation* show that distinguishing different types of sound can help us analyze filmmakers' creative choices. They and other examples also suggest that our categories correspond fairly well to how viewers understand what they hear. We tacitly learn to distinguish between diegetic and nondiegetic, internal and external, simultaneous and nonsimultaneous sound. We're surprised or amused or puzzled when a sound crosses these boundaries. Because the distinctions more or less tally with our assumptions, the sound bumps in *Providence, The Conversation,* and many other films can undermine our expectations, creating suspense or surprise or ambiguity. The categories we've reviewed point to ways in which sound, often without our awareness, shapes our experience of a film.

Functions of Film Sound: *The Prestige*

In London around 1900, two magicians are locked in desperate competition, each trying for ever more baffling illusions. As they deceive each other and their audiences, the film tries to deceive us as well.

A story of crime, professional rivalry, personal jealousy, and grand aspirations, *The Prestige* sets itself a difficult task. The film seeks to be as tantalizing as a magic trick, but one that can eventually be explained. As a result, director Christopher Nolan and his screenwriter (and brother) Jonathan Nolan have the job of both revealing and concealing. The film must present us just enough of the story to keep us engaged, while holding back the answers to the puzzles—and sometimes, like a magician, distracting us from what is really going on. Throughout *The Prestige,* sound takes part in an elaborate choreography of misdirection.

Transported Men

The conflict between the eager Robert Angier (Hugh Jackman) and the more sinister Alfred Borden (Christian Bale) begins when both are apprentice magicians. Robert's wife, Julia, dies in an immersion tank as a result of Borden's faulty rope-knot. As the two men grow in fame, their feud escalates. Robert shoots off two of Alfred's fingers in a botched "bullet catch." In response, Alfred sabotages one of Robert's illusions. Then Alfred mounts an amazing trick, the Transported Man: Alfred seems to disappear from one end of the stage and reappear instantly at the other. Vowing to surpass him, Robert finds a double of himself and creates a similar illusion. But Alfred unmasks the stunt, breaking Robert's leg and humiliating him before his audience.

Robert vows to find the secret behind Alfred's Transported Man. After consulting with Nicola Tesla, the great experimenter with electricity, Robert returns to London with a stunning illusion. He stands onstage in a crackling field of lightning bolts and disappears, reappearing a few seconds later in the balcony. Alfred, usually quick to unravel a trick, is baffled. He resigns himself to quitting the trade. Nonetheless, he shows up in disguise at one of Robert's performances and penetrates the area below stage. At the climax of the trick, Alfred sees Robert fall through a trapdoor into a tank of water below. He watches Robert drown. Alfred is arrested for murder and condemned to death.

At the climax of the film, the original Transported Man illusion is revealed as a simple trick: There are two Bordens, identical twins. At any moment, one takes the Alfred identity, while the other is disguised as Fallon, Alfred's designer of illusions (*ingénieur*). So when Alfred seems to change his mind about quitting magic, in fact one Borden twin does quit; but the other obstinately attends Robert's performance. As a result, while one Alfred is hanged, the other can stalk Robert for a final act of vengeance.

Somewhat earlier, and more gradually, we learn that Robert's version of the Transported Man is no illusion. Tesla has created a cloning machine, which makes an identical copy of Robert and deposits that at some distance from the original. At every performance, one Robert falls through the trapdoor and into a waiting tank, where he drowns. The reconstituted Robert, projected elsewhere in the theater, takes the crowd's applause—only to be sacrificed under the stage the following night.

The rising conflict between Robert and Alfred reveals contrasting aspects of each man's personality. Robert is a smooth showman, one whose highest goal is to amaze an audience. Alfred, less concerned with ornate effects, builds his original Transported Man illusion out of two simple doors and a child's red ball. He believes that a magician has a duty to come up with the most mind-bending trick possible, one that will puzzle not just the public but other professionals. To achieve that, the magician should be prepared to "live his act," to give up a full personal life if that helps him purify his art. So when one Borden brother loses two fingers to the bullet catch, the other must slice off his own to allow them to continue their charade.

Gradually, the personalities of Robert and Alfred move closer together, and our sympathies shift. At first Robert's love of magic is sensibly balanced by his love for Julia. Her death increases our sense that Alfred is treacherous and Robert a victim. But as Robert launches an all-out effort to destroy his rival, he comes to seem possessed. Both Tesla and Robert's *ingénieur* Cutter warn him that he is becoming obsessive. At the other pole, one of the Borden twins falls in love with Sarah, a young governess. He risks giving his secret away in order to have something like a normal life with her and their daughter Jess. The other, more cynical twin takes up an affair with Olivia, who becomes the act's assistant. The price of finding a woman to love is that sometimes one twin must stand in for the other. These substitutions create emotional discontinuities that each woman detects. To the art of magic, the two Alfreds sacrifice not only themselves but also their loved ones.

The Sounds of Magic

The basic story of *The Prestige* is complicated, but it could have been presented in linear order, letting us in on secrets behind the illusions. The plot might have made Robert the protagonist, withholding the information about Albert's personal and professional life that Robert never learns. Alternatively, the plot could have stuck to Borden's range of knowledge and shown the twins pulling off their stratagems. (David Cronenberg's *Dead Ringers* provides a rough example.) Instead, *The Prestige* wants to mystify us as much as the illusions mystify the magicians and their audiences. The competing magicians are driven by curiosity about how the tricks are done, and this curiosity is central to our experience as well.

Accordingly, the story is presented via unrestricted narration, but it is manipulated through many techniques of plot construction. The plot shuffles story order, plays with levels of knowledge, replays some scenes, and cuts off others, withholding their consequences. All these tactics do not confuse us about the basic story progression, however. They arouse curiosity (what has led up to this turn of events?) and suspense (what will happen next?). At the same time, the plot maneuvers misdirect our attention, suppressing key information about the magicians' secrets.

The overall dramatic progression is framed by present-time action, that of the climactic performance of Robert's Tesla-driven illusion. This stage spectacle leads to one of the Borden twins being arrested, condemned, and hanged, while the other faces Robert one last time. Most of the plot consists of layered flashbacks showing different stages of the two men's struggle. Our understanding is eased by the fact that most of the story strands are presented chronologically, as in *Citizen Kane* (pp. 107–109). In addition, the basic conflict is maintained through familiar means—scenes of confrontation, or backstage plotting, or confidences shared between the protagonists and their families and friends. Occasionally, there are personalized flashbacks illustrating what a character is recalling, as when in prison Alfred remembers his romance with Sarah. And when the second Alfred confronts Robert at the climax, more impersonal flashbacks show us what was really happening in scenes we thought we understood earlier.

Along with visual techniques, sound choices help smooth our understanding of the ongoing action. Characters are differentiated through their voices, especially the contrast between Alfred's London working-class accent and Robert's American accent (which turns out to be fake). A sketchy piano motif in the score is associated with Alfred's life with his wife and child. Each locale has its characteristic ambience—the prison with distant scuffling and slamming, the less cavernous echo of the warehouse that becomes Robert's workshop, the warmer sound of the theaters, the crunching snow surrounding Tesla's compound in Colorado.

The sound track is often expressive as well. David Julyan's score consists largely of prolonged notes shifting slightly up or down the scale, creating a moody, layered drone. Julyan leads into Robert's Real Transported Man by layering string chords and soft booms reminiscent of Tesla's lab. The score even makes use of an electronically generated Shepard tone, which creates an illusory sense of continually rising or falling pitch. The danger inherent in the giant Tesla coils is conveyed through brittle, harsh crackling that often cuts off menacingly, as if it had atomized its target. Indeed, from the very start, abrupt silences jolt the viewer into paying attention to the imagery.

As in most modern films, sound plays an important role in linking scenes. A sustained musical chord links a shot of Robert looking out of his coach with a shot of him already striding along the ground. There are many sound bridges as well. At the close of one performance, we hear Alfred saying, "He's complacent, he's pre-

"With The Prestige *I was using electronics to achieve effects I couldn't get with the orchestra. . . . There's a lot of stuff in tracks such as 'Colorado Springs' where in the background there is a Shepard's Tone. That's the audio equivalent of an optical illusion so that it appears to rise constantly. It's a very nice effect that Chris and I settled on. It also allows me to produce a very textural bed to lay under the orchestra."*

— David Julyan, composer for *The Prestige*

dictable," and this carries us to the next scene, in which he continues to complain about the magician who employs the two men. Robert is musing on a name for his act, and we hear him ask, "How about the New Transported Man?" as crowds arrive to see his show.

Nolan and Nolan also employ the **dialogue hook,** the technique of ending a scene with a line that prepares for the next scene. (This isn't a sound bridge, because the line is completed in the initial scene.) A simple instance occurs when Tesla asks Robert, "Have you eaten, Mr. Angier?" Cut to the two men at lunch. More dramatically, at a Colorado Springs hotel, the clerk remarks that Tesla has left a box for Robert. Robert: "What box?" Cut to the crate in the hotel ballroom. Dialogue hooks propel the story briskly and can call the viewer's attention to salient aspects of the scene to come, as the box example does.

Naturally, dialogue can mislead as well. Olivia, Robert's spy in his rival's camp, assures him that Alfred doesn't use a double because the man onstage is lacking two fingers; we later learn that one Alfred cut off his fingers so the two would continue to be identical. In retrospect, many lines prove to have hinted at the Borden twins' secret. In a quarrel with Olivia, Alfred says, "part of me" had a child with Sarah but "part of me" didn't, "the part that found you, the part that's sitting here right now." At the prison, bidding farewell to Fallon (his disguised twin), Alfred refers to the other's urge to quit. "You were right. I should have left him to his damn trick. . . . You go live your life in full now." Robert's own cloning stratagem is predicted when he tries to hire a double: "I don't need him to be my brother. I need him to be me." Few films contain so many lines of dialogue that can be understood in two equally valid ways.

Echoes, Visual and Auditory

Parallelism, a common narrative strategy, is important for advancing the film's action, tracing character development, and maintaining the mysteries. *The Prestige* is based on parallels: two magicians, each with a double and an *ingénieur*. Each magician wounds his counterpart, and each falls in love with a woman but loses her. Other parallels depend on the show business milieu. Acts are rehearsed and reperformed, each time with variations, as when Robert's double becomes more drunk and heedless. The stage trapdoors that we see so often point toward the gallows trapdoor that will end the life of the brusque Borden twin. Julia's drowning in the tank onstage is mirrored in Robert's drowning below stage, and the motif recurs up to the very last image **(7.57–7.59).**

There are auditory motifs as well. The harsh sound of iron, suggesting an age of lumbering mechanical objects, is first heard in the opening, when the top of the tank slams down with a shudder. From then on, we frequently hear rasping metal—chains in Alfred's prison, the buzzing shock Robert gets from Tesla's fence, the clank when the Tesla coil is switched off (but not concealing the snick of Robert's trapdoor), and the groaning spring that locks a dove into a trick apparatus. When Sarah hangs herself, some metallic clashing is heard, and later, when Alfred kneels to his daughter behind prison bars, we see little of his gestures but judge from the frantic clanking of his chains that he is desperate. This sound motif informs the final sequence, which crosscuts Alfred's hanging with Robert's disposal of Tesla's machine: while Cutter winds a creaking winch, the prisoner's chains clank and drag as he mounts the gallows.

A less harsh motif dominates the scenes involving Julia's immersion stunt. When she is first bound and submerged in the tank, a soft snare drum taps out a pulse. Later, when she is tied and can't escape, the tick of Cutter's stopwatch takes over the sound track, as if measuring her heartbeat; the sound stops when she is dead. At the film's climax, when Robert's opening act is replayed, a similar pulsation is heard in the nondiegetic music as he drowns—creating a parallel to Julia not unlike the one we've seen in the images (7.57–7.59).

7.57 The trauma that sets off Robert's obsession: He watches his wife drown in a failed illusion.

7.58 In his own version of the Transported Man, Robert drowns every night, replaced by a duplicate that appears in the auditorium.

7.59 One of the duplicate Roberts is seen submerged in the last shot.

In many films, parallels are carried by dialogue, and *The Prestige* makes constant use of recurring lines. Julia says that calling the act The Great Danton is "sophisticated," and after her death, Robert honors her by using the name: "It's sophisticated." Tesla's remark that "Man's grasp should exceed his nerve" is modified by Robert as his new tagline: "Man's reach exceeds his imagination." The most vivid dialogue motif is probably the one launched by Cutter, when he talks of "getting your hands dirty." At various points, Cutter and Alfred invoke this line to taunt Robert's reluctance to risk everything for his magic. At the end, however, confronting Robert's elaborate revenge scheme, both Alfreds admit that he has finally gotten his hands dirty.

As with other techniques, some of these dialogue motifs not only clarify the story but also drop hints. One striking instance occurs when at the climax we hear the warden intone, "Alfred Borden" during the hanging scene but see the mysterious assistant Fallon making his way to Robert. The juxtaposition prepares us for Fallon's unmasking as one of the twins. At various points, Robert says that in a disappearing act "no one cares about the man who goes into the box. They care about the man who comes out the other side." The motif points toward his method of callously killing the performer in the Tesla machine so that his double can be reborn elsewhere. It also anticipates the ending, in which Alfred, apparently hanged, returns home to Jessie and Cutter.

Two Diaries

The Prestige uses Robert's and Alfred's journals to frame certain parts of the past. One man reads the other man's diary, which will lead us into or out of a flashback.

In itself, the diary device is quite familiar, but *The Prestige* gives it a special emphasis by embedding one diary within another. In the past, Robert stole Alfred's notebook, and as he deciphered it, Robert recorded his reactions and memories in his own diary during his trip to Colorado. Robert's diary comments on Alfred's journal are later read by Alfred in his cell during his trial.

The embedded diaries help keep us oriented in time, guiding us from present to past and back again. Again, sound plays a crucial role in acclimating us to the device. The convention of letting us hear the diarist's voice as the reader reads the lines is a very helpful guide.

After the imprisoned Alfred is given Robert's diary, he starts to read it, and we hear Robert's voice-over, representing what he has written. "A cipher—an enigma—a search." The line leads us into the first of several flashbacks to Robert's trip to Tesla. Early in his stay, Robert begins to decipher Borden's notebook. Robert's diary voice-over describes a passage as taking place "just days after he first met me." This segues into Alfred's voice-over, representing what Robert has just deciphered: "We were two young men devoted to an illusion." The transition to a flashback within a flashback is made clear through the smooth transfers from one voice-over to the next.

The conflict between the men gets sharpened when even the diary entries seem to quarrel. As we see Alfred double over in pain from the botched bullet catch, we hear his diary voice-over explaining that he didn't really know what knot he had tied to bind Robert's wife. "I told him the truth" is followed by a cut back to Colorado, showing Robert reading Alfred's diary as the voice continues: ". . . that I have fought with myself over that night." Robert looks up from the diary and cries out, "How could he not know?" That external line of dialogue is repeated, but now as a voice-over: "How could he not know?" Cut to Alfred reading the line in his cell. The embedded diaries and blended voice-overs create a tense conversation across time and space.

Once the early transitions have established the nested time frames, however, the film starts to shift among them without showing the diaries or employing a voice-over. Instead, the voice-overs of Robert and Alfred are used to punctuate certain scenes, supplying private thoughts in the manner of an internal diegetic monologue. For example, on the street, Robert spies on Alfred and his family. Robert's voice-over bursts out, "I saw happiness—happiness that should have been mine."

Above all, it is Robert's diary voice-over that helps shift among time frames. His summaries of what he reads in Alfred's diary substitute for Alfred's direct voice-over. This prepares us for a surprise when Robert skips to the end of the diary and Albert's voice-over returns ominously:

> Today Olivia proves her love for me—to you, Angier. Yes, Angier, she gave you this notebook at my request. And Tesla is merely the key to my diary, not to my trick. Did you really think I'd part with my secret so easily, after so much? Good-bye, Angier. May you find solace for your thwarted ambition back in your American home.

But in a film of many parallels, even this mocking challenge is surpassed by another. Alfred, reading Robert's journal in his cell, confronts this on the last page:

> But here, at the turn, I must leave you, Borden. Yes, you, Borden. Sitting there in your cell, reading my diary. Awaiting your death, for my murder.

Alfred is as baffled as we are. How could Robert have known that he would die and that Alfred would be accused of his murder?

In retrospect, we realize that Robert (the clone who survived that night in the theater but didn't reveal himself) has prepared the final entry, and perhaps the whole journal, after Alfred's arrest as a way of tormenting him. The power of these surprises derives from a subtle shift in the voice-over convention. Going beyond simply giving us information, the diary-driven voices have misled us.

Hinting at Secrets

By weaving parallels and journal entries into the plot, the film propels the action forward while enhancing the mysteries. We are continually confronted with new information that has to be fitted into what we have already seen and heard. Yet the film also hints at what is concealed. Most centrally, the secret of both illusions is substitution of a double, and this is suggested by a visual motif. We learn that, since canaries look alike, magicians make canaries vanish and reappear by killing one and substituting another. This is a prototype of Robert's cloning technique, but it also foreshadows the consequences of the Borden twins' decision to live out their act, with one eventually sacrificed for the other.

As we've seen, hinting occurs throughout the dialogue and the voice-overs. As a single character, Alfred seems contradictory, alternately considerate and brusque. He speaks often of his secret, of being torn in two. His wife, Sarah, says that when he says he loves her, some days he does and some days he doesn't. In the climactic quarrel between the couple, she says she knows "what you really are," which panics the cold twin. Perhaps she suspects that there are two Alfreds? Sarah asks if he loves her. "Not today." She hangs herself.

More subtly, offscreen sound is used to withhold the "Prestige," or the payoff, of each man's greatest trick. (Originally, the word *prestige* meant "illusion," especially one that dazzles the eyes.) Alfred's first, minimal version of the Transported Man is shown only in part. We see the setup with Robert watching avidly and Cutter elsewhere in the audience, skeptical. But we don't see the Prestige phase of the trick. Nolan keeps the camera on Cutter while we hear the second door open and the bouncing ball being caught by the duplicate Alfred. Nolan thereby makes the trick itself mysterious, to be revealed in full later. Conveying the illusion through offscreen sound also emphasizes the contrasting reactions of Cutter, who is unimpressed, and Robert, who considers it "the greatest magic trick I've ever seen."

Another parallel, then: when Robert demonstrates his Real Transported Man before a world-weary theatrical agent, he vanishes from the stage in jagged blasts of the Tesla coil. The agent protests, "He has to come back. There has to be—" "A Prestige?" says a voice from offscreen. The agent turns automatically to see Robert behind him, stepping down from the back of the balcony. We will see the same stunt presented more fully and with panache in the first performance, but the momentary channeling of story information through the agent emphasizes what Robert values as a performer: watching the viewer's stunned expression when confronted with what appears to be a miracle.

The Opening

The use of sound to both reveal and conceal story information, in conjunction with other film techniques, comes at the very start of the film. Here sound and image must orient us to the narrative world, introducing the main characters and dramatic issues. The opening must also plant details that may seem unimportant or puzzling but that will later play major roles. The opening of *The Prestige* also introduces us to one of the film's major storytelling techniques, that of the voice-over commentary we encounter in the diaries. And some clues tantalize us but become comprehensible once we have penetrated the film's secrets. Once more, we find that sound assists both clear storytelling and bold misdirection.

The most dramatic portions of the opening involve a performance of Robert's Tesla-inspired version of the Transported Man. Alfred, disguised in the audience, goes onstage to inspect the gadget and then dodges into the wings and down under the stage. There he finds the tank awaiting Robert. As the trick is consummated, Robert plummets into the water and starts to drown before Alfred's eyes.

The performance is played with no dialogue, apart from the moment when Alfred assures a stagehand that he's part of the act. There is a soft but ominous drone from the musical score, overridden by fierce crackling as the Tesla coil fires up. As with the other major illusions, the act's payoff takes place offscreen; we see the result when Robert falls through the trapdoor. The coil's crackling and the musical score stop abruptly, in a harsh cutoff that will be typical of the rest of the film, and we hear a splash as Robert is submerged. The top of the tank snaps shut with a whang. Then another long silence, enhancing suspense.

The audience stirs restlessly; where has Robert gone? Meanwhile, below stage, Alfred approaches the drowning Robert and we hear the heartbeat pulse in the orchestra, foreshadowing Cutter's ticking stopwatch. As Robert thrashes underwater, the nondiegetic music turns into frantic string twitterings. The image fades to black, the music dies, and the next sequence, at Alfred's trial, begins.

But this highly dramatic scene, showing a magic trick apparently gone wrong, is crosscut with a more mundane, even trivial moment, taking place in an unidentified time. We see Cutter stroll past a row of cages, select one canary, put it into a cage, and make it disappear. He then makes it reappear to the delight of a little girl, who we'll later learn is Alfred's daughter Jessie. There is no dialogue from within this scene, only the chirping of the birds and the sound of Cutter performing the trick; the tense, somber music starts in this sequence and continues until the moment of Robert's immersion.

Two magic tricks, one of great simplicity and the other of lethal complexity, are shown in alternation. In three minutes, the film has aroused all manner of questions about what has led up to these events and what will follow. The narration also asks us what connection we are to make between the canary trick and the elaborate stage show. The answer, itself partial and teasing, is provided by a voice-over commentary.

We hear Cutter's voice explaining that every magic trick has three parts, and his layout of the phases corresponds to both crosscut lines of action. His description of the Pledge, the promise that things work in the ordinary way, is heard in his voice-over as he silently shows Jessie the canary and puts it in the cage. Cut to Robert displaying himself and his machine. Spectators, including Alfred, climb onstage to inspect the gadget.

Then, Cutter explains, comes the Turn, the moment when the ordinary becomes extraordinary. Covering the birdcage with a scarf, he flattens it. Cutter's commentary coincides with Robert stepping into the electrical field while Alfred explores the trapdoor area below stage. Finally, after the canary and Robert have disappeared, Cutter's voice-over says:

> But you wouldn't clap yet. Because making something disappear isn't enough. You have to bring it back. That's why every magic trick has a third act—the hardest part. The part we call the Prestige.

As we hear these words, we see him showing Jessie the revived canary—a successful feat of legerdemain—crosscut with Robert's uneasy audience and shots of Alfred staring at Robert struggling underwater.

Cutter's voice has been closely miked in a dry recording, lending it the sort of intimate, direct-address perspective we'll encounter in the diary voice-overs. But now, at the fade-out, in a more hollow timbre, another man's voice repeats, "The Prestige." As the new scene fades up, Cutter is in the witness box. His dialogue is now anchored in a more reverberant sound field, suitable to a large courtroom. We realize that his explanation of a trick's three acts is motivated as his testimony at Alfred's trial.

Cutter's voice-over introduces some central themes, such as the idea that a magic trick has an artistic structure that demands both skill and showmanship—the two components that distinguish Alfred and Robert. Cutter also stresses the need to

7.60   As Cutter's voice-over talks about a magician showing us something ordinary, his mention of "a man" is synchronized with the first shot of Alfred, disguised in the audience.

7.61   But Alfred is not the man central to the Pledge. That is Robert himself, seen in the next shot. Along with the editing, the commentary subtly establishes these two as the central antagonists.

distract the audience, because, he says, the spectator wants to be fooled. This could be taken as a commentary on our own urge to overlook details in watching the film. And Cutter's stress on bringing back the vanished object establishes the motif that when the Prestige arrives, no one cares about the man in the box.

With respect to plot construction, Cutter's commentary makes the death of Robert a flashback from the present time of the court proceedings. At the film's close, we will learn that the canary trick Cutter performs is a sort of flash-forward, referring to a still "later" present time enclosing the whole film. The crosscutting has shuttled us between two moments of story time, while the voice-over has put us in yet a third, the court testimony. That testimony is nonsimultaneous with respect to both lines of visual action; it takes place after the death of Robert but long before the scene with Jessie. This opening not only introduces us to major characters and themes but also establishes the time-juggling shifts that we'll encounter in the film to come.

Cutter's voice-over also prepares us for the tight image/sound synchronization that will carry the plot forward. His voice speaks of showing the Pledge object; he shows the canary; cut to Robert displaying his machine. When Cutter says the object probably isn't normal, we see Alfred tear off his false beard to prove he's part of the performance. Cutter explains the second phase, and as his voice says, "The Turn," cut to Robert literally turning to us. Cutter flattens the birdcage as his voice speaks of the "extraordinary"; cut to Robert seized by electricity.

The commentary drops a few hints, too, as when Cutter indirectly introduces the film's protagonists **(7.60, 7.61)**. Later, as Alfred prowls in the stage cellar, studying the water tank, Cutter speaks of the audience "not really looking" at what is going on in the trick. Robert plummets into the tank, the lock snaps shut, and Cutter says, "You want to be—" Cut to him snatching the scarf away, showing that the birdcage has vanished as his voice-over finishes: "—fooled." Indeed, Alfred will be fooled, since he does not understand Robert's manipulation of his clones until the end. Cutter's calm delivery about "bringing back" the ordinary object, timed to his presentation of the canary, serves as an upbeat contrast to the stage act. Jessie applauds, but Robert's audience doesn't, because the Prestige ("the hardest part") is missing. Robert, flailing underwater, will not be brought back—at least, not for some time.

This opening could not be as economical and intriguing as it is without Cutter's voice-over narration. The crosscutting and juxtapositions of dialogue will reappear in the climax and be finally explained in the final shots. Yet there is one more element in the opening passage to consider.

The very first shot of the film fades in on a leftward tracking shot across a field of top hats **(7.62)**. Later we will learn that those are the hats that Tesla has inadver-

7.62   The opening shot of *The Prestige:* The camera tracks over the scattered top hats . . .

7.63   . . . and continues to move along several parakeet cages, creating a parallel based on the idea of identical copies.

7.64   Addressing Jessie, Cutter also invites us to consider how a magic trick may mislead the audience.

tently cloned in his experiments. The next shot shows a row of canaries in cages (**7.63**); one of these will be the star of Cutter's trick for Jessie (**7.64**). In hindsight, we can see that these two shots hint at how both Alfred and Robert accomplish their magic—by using exact copies. In addition, just as a canary has to die in order to disappear, death will haunt each magician's double. Alfred has given up a great deal for his art, with each twin living only half a life. But Robert has wound up devoting himself to his craft just as passionately. In dying and being reborn every night, he has embraced what Alfred calls "total self-sacrifice."

But as usual, sound plays a role, too. At three points in the rest of the film, Alfred will ask someone, "Are you watching closely?" It's his mocking warning that he will practice some deceptive sleight of hand. At the very start, however, as the camera coasts over the top hats, we hear this line for the first time. Shifted out of its story position, spoken by a character we don't yet know, the question becomes a challenge and warning to the viewer. As a film inviting us to unmask its own legerdemain, *The Prestige* could just as easily start with the question "Are you listening closely?"

SUMMARY

As usual, both extensive viewing and intensive scrutiny will sharpen your capacity to notice the workings of film sound. You can get comfortable with the analytical tools we have suggested by asking several questions about a film's sound:

1. What sounds are present—music, speech, noise? How are loudness, pitch, and timbre used? Is the mixture sparse or dense? Modulated or abruptly changing?

2. Is the sound related rhythmically to the image? If so, how?

3. Is the sound faithful or unfaithful to its perceived source?

4. *Where* is the sound coming from? In the story's space or outside it? Onscreen or offscreen? If offscreen, how is it shaping your response to what you're seeing?

5. *When* is the sound occurring? Simultaneously with the story action? Before? After?

6. How are the various sorts of sounds organized across a sequence or the entire film? What patterns are formed, and how do they reinforce aspects of the film's overall form?

7. For each of questions 1–6, what *purposes* are fulfilled and what *effects* are achieved by the sonic manipulations?

Practice at trying to answer such questions will familiarize you with the basic uses of film sound.

As always, it isn't enough to name and classify. These categories and terms are most useful when we take the next step and examine how the types of sound we identify *function* in the total film.

WHERE TO GO FROM HERE

David Lewis Yewdall's *Practical Art of Motion Picture Sound,* 3d ed. (Boston: Focal Press, 2007), is an excellent overview and includes a very instructive DVD. A delightful essay on the development of film sound is Walter Murch's "Sound Design: The Dancing Shadow," in John Boorman et al., eds., *Projections 4* (1995), pp. 237–51. The essay includes a behind-the-scenes discussion of sound mixing in *The Godfather.*

Articles on particular aspects of sound recording and reproduction in Hollywood are published in *Recording Engineer/Producer* and *Mix.* See also Jeff Forlenza and Terri Stone, eds., *Sound for Picture* (Winona, MN: Hal Leonard, 1993), and Tom Kenny, *Sound for Picture: Film Sound Through the 1990s* (Vallejo, CA: Mix Books, 2000). For many practitioners' comments, see Vincent Lo Brutto, *Sound-on-Film: Interviews with Creators of Film Sound* (New York: Praeger, 1994). Walter Murch, Hollywood's principal sound designer, explains many contemporary sound techniques in Roy Paul Madsen, *Working Cinema: Learning from the Masters* (Belmont, CA: Wadsworth, 1990), pp. 288–313. Our quotation on p. 284 comes from this source, p. 000.

A useful introduction to the psychology of listening is Robert Sekuler and Randolph Blake, *Perception,* 4th ed. (New York: McGraw-Hill, 2002). See as well R. Murray Schafe, *The Soundscape: Our Sonic Environment and the Tuning of the World* (Rochester, VT: Destiny, 1994), and David Toop, *Ocean of Sound: Aether Talk, Ambient Sound and Imaginary Worlds* (London: Serpent's Tail, 2001).

The Power of Sound

The psychologists' term for our spontaneous merging of information from different senses is "cross-modal perception." It has been observed in newborn babies and in children as young as four months. Joseph D. Anderson, *The Reality of Illusion: An Ecological Approach to Cognitive Film Theory* (Carbondale: University of Illinois Press, 1996), chap. 5, provides a compact introduction to how our bias toward cross-model pickup shapes our understanding of films.

Of all directors, Sergei Eisenstein has written most prolifically and intriguingly about sound technique. See in particular his discussion of audio-visual polyphony in *Non-Indifferent Nature,* trans. Herbert Marshall (Cambridge: Cambridge University Press, 1987), pp. 282–354. (For his discussion of music, see below.) In addition, there are intriguing comments in Robert Bresson's *Notes on Cinematography,* trans. Jonathan Griffin (New York: Urizen, 1977).

The artistic possibilities of film sound are discussed in many essays. See John Belton and Elizabeth Weis, eds., *Film Sound: Theory and Practice* (New York: Columbia University Press, 1985); Rick Altman, ed., *Sound Theory Sound Practice* (New York: Routledge, 1992); Larry Sider, Diane Freeman, and Jerry Sider, eds., *Soundscape: The School of Sound Lectures 1998–2001* (London: Wallflower, 2003); "Sound and Music in the Movies," *Cinéaste* 21, 1–2 (1995): 46–80; and Jay Beck and Tony Grajeda, eds., *Lowering the Boom: Critical Studies in Film Sound* (Urbana:

University of Illinois Press, 2008). Three anthologies edited by Philip Brophy have been published under the general title *CineSonic* (New South Wales: Australian Film Television and Radio School, 1999–2001).

The most prolific researcher in the aesthetics of film sound is Michel Chion, whose ideas are summarized in his *Audio Vision,* trans. Claudia Gorbman (New York: Columbia University Press, 1994). Sarah Kozloff has written extensively on speech in cinema; see *Invisible Storytellers: Voice-Over Narration in American Fiction Film* (Berkeley: University of California Press, 1988) and *Overhearing Film Dialogue* (Berkeley: University of California Press, 2000). Lea Jacobs analyzes several dialogue patterns in "Keeping Up with Hawks," *Style* 32, 3 (Fall 1998): 402–26, from which our mention of accelerating and decelerating rhythm in *His Girl Friday* is drawn.

On sound and picture editing, see John Purcell, *Dialogue Editing for Motion Pictures: A Guide to the Invisible Art* (Boston: Focal Press, 2007). Dialogue overlap is explained in detail in Edward Dmytryk, *On Film Editing* (Boston: Focal Press, 1984), pp. 47–70.

As the *Letter from Siberia* extract suggests, documentary filmmakers have experimented a great deal with sound. For other cases, watch Basil Wright's *Song of Ceylon* and Humphrey Jennings's *Listen to Britain* and *Diary for Timothy.* Analyses of sound in these films may be found in Paul Rotha, *Documentary Film* (New York: Hastings House, 1952), and Karel Reisz and Gavin Millar's *Technique of Film Editing* (New York: Hastings House, 1968), pp. 156–70.

Stephen Handzo provides a wide-ranging discussion of systems for recording and reproducing film sound in "A Narrative Glossary of Film Sound Technology," in Belton and Weis, *Film Sound: Theory and Practice.* An updated survey is available in Gianluca Sergi, *The Dolby Era: Film Sound in Contemporary Hollywood* (Manchester: Manchester University Press, 2005). See also William Whittington, *Sound Design and Science Fiction* (Austin: University of Texas Press, 2007).

Silent Film Versus Sound Film

It's long been assumed that cinema is predominantly a visual medium, with sound forming at best a supplement and at worst a distraction. In the late 1920s, many film aestheticians protected against the coming of talkies, feeling that synchronized sound spoiled a pristine mute art. In the bad sound film, René Clair claimed, "The image is reduced precisely to the role of the illustration of a phonograph record, and the sole aim of the whole show is to resemble as closely as possible the play of which it is the 'cinematic' reproduction. In three or four settings there take place endless scenes of dialogue which are merely boring if you do not understand English but unbearable if you do" (*Cinema Yesterday and Today* [New York: Dover, 1972], p. 137). Rudolf Arnheim asserted that "the introduction of the sound film

smashed many of the forms that the film artists were using in favor of the inartistic demand for the greatest possible 'naturalness' (in the most superficial sense of the word)" (*Film as Art* [Berkeley: University of California Press, 1957], p. 154).

Today we find such beliefs silly, but we must recall that many early sound films relied simply on dialogue for their novelty; both Clair and Arnheim welcomed sound effects and music but warned against chatter. In any event, the inevitable reaction was led by André Bazin, who argued that a greater realism was possible in the sound cinema. See his *What Is Cinema?* vol. 1 (Berkeley: University of California Press, 1967). Even Bazin, however, seemed to believe that sound was secondary to the image in cinema. This view is also put forth by Siegfried Kracauer in *Theory of Film* (New York: Oxford University Press, 1965). "Films with sound live up to the spirit of the medium only if the visuals take the lead in them" (p. 103).

Today, many filmmakers and filmgoers would agree with Francis Ford Coppola's remark that sound is "half the movie . . . at least." One of the major advances of film scholarship of the 1970s and 1980s was the increased and detailed attention to the sound track.

On the transition from silent to sound film in American cinema, see Harry M. Geduld, *The Birth of the Talkies: From Edison to Jolson* (Bloomington: Indiana University Press, 1975); Alexander Walker, *The Shattered Silents* (New York: Morrow, 1979); chap. 23 of David Bordwell, Janet Staiger, and Kristin Thompson, *The Classical Hollywood Cinema: Film Style and Mode of Production to 1960* (New York: Columbia University Press, 1985); James Lastra, *Sound Technology in the American Cinema: Perception, Representation, Modernity* (New York: Columbia University Press, 2000); and Charles O'Brien, *Cinema's Conversion to Sound: Technology and Film Style in France and the U.S.* (Bloomington: Indiana University Press, 2005). Douglas Gomery's *The Coming of Sound* (New York: Routledge, 2005) provides a U.S. industry history.

David Julyan's discussion of scoring *The Prestige* can be found at www.aintitcool.com/node/31031.

Film Music

Of all the kinds of sound in cinema, music has been the most extensively discussed. The literature is voluminous, and with a recent surge of interest in film composers, many more recordings of film music have become available.

A basic introduction to music useful for film study is William S. Newman, *Understanding Music* (New York: Harper, 1961). An up-to-date and detailed production guide is Fred Karlin and Rayburn Wright's *On the Track: A Guide to Contemporary Film Scoring,* 2d ed. (New York: Schirmer, 1990). Karlin's *Listening to Movies* (New York: Routledge, 2004) offers a lively discussion of the Hollywood tradition.

The history of film scoring is handled in lively and unorthodox ways in Russell Lack, *Twenty-Four Frames Under: A Buried History of Film Music* (London: Quartet, 1997). For Hollywood-centered histories, see Roy M. Prendergast, *Film Music: A Neglected Art* (New York: Norton, 1977), and Gary Marmorstein, *Hollywood Rhapsody: Movie Music and Its Makers 1900–1975* (New York: Schirmer, 1997). Somewhat wider coverage is provided in Mervyn Cooke, *A History of Film Music* (Cambridge: Cambridge University Press, 2008). See also Martin Miller Marks, *Music and the Silent Film: Contexts and Case Studies 1895–1924* (New York: Oxford University Press, 1997), and Rick Altman, *Silent Film Sound* (New York: Columbia University Press, 2005). Contemporary film composers are interviewed in Michael Schelle, *The Score* (Los Angeles: Silman-James, 1999); David Morgan, *Knowing the Score* (New York: HarperCollins, 2000); and Mark Russell and James Young, *Film Music* (Hove, England; Rota, 2000).

The principal study of the theory of film music is Claudia Gorbman, *Unheard Melodies: Narrative Film Music* (Bloomington: Indiana University Press, 1987). A highly informed, wide-ranging meditation on the subject is Royal S. Brown, *Overtones and Undertones: Reading Film Music* (Berkeley: University of California Press, 1994). Jonathan Romney and Adrian Wootton's *Celluloid Jukebox: Popular Music and the Movies Since the 50s* (London: British Film Institute, 1995) is an enjoyable collection of essays. See also Chuck Jones, "Music and the Animated Cartoon," *Hollywood Quarterly* 1, 4 (July 1946): 364–70. A sampling of Carl Stalling's amazing cartoon sound tracks (p. 275) is available on two compact discs (Warner Bros. 9-26027-2 and 9-45430-2).

Despite the bulk of material on film music, there have been fairly few analyses of music's functions in particular films. The most famous (or notorious) is Sergei Eisenstein's "Form and Content: Practice," in *The Film Sense* (New York: Harcourt, Brace, 1942), pp. 157–216, which examines sound/image relations in a sequence from *Alexander Nevsky*. For sensitive analyses of film music, see Graham Bruce, *Bernard Herrmann: Film Music and Narrative* (Ann Arbor: University of Michigan, 1985); Kathryn Kalinak, *Settling the Score: Music and the Classical Hollywood Film* (Madison: University of Wisconsin Press, 1992); Jeff Smith, *The Sounds of Commerce: Marketing Popular Film Music* (New York: Columbia University Press, 1998); and Pamela Robertson Wojcik and Arthur Knight, eds., *Soundtrack Available: Essays on Film and Popular Music* (Durham, NC: Duke University Press, 2001).

Dubbing and Subtitles

People beginning to study cinema may express surprise (or annoyance) that films in foreign languages are usually shown with subtitled captions translating the dialogue. Why not, some viewers ask, use dubbed versions of the films—that is, versions in which the dialogue has been rerecorded in the audience's language? In many countries, dubbing is very common. (Germany and Italy have traditions of dubbing almost every imported film.) Why, then, do most people who study movies prefer subtitles?

There are several reasons. Dubbed voices usually have a bland studio sound. Elimination of the original actors' voices wipes out an important component of their performance. (Partisans of dubbing ought to look at dubbed versions of English-language films to see how a performance by Katharine Hepburn, Orson Welles, or John Wayne can be hurt by a voice that does not fit the body.) With dubbing, all of the usual problems of translation are multiplied by the need to synchronize specific words with specific lip movements. Most important, with subtitling, viewers still have access to the original sound track. By eliminating the original voice track, dubbing simply destroys part of the film.

For a survey of subtitling practice, see Jan Ivarsson and Mary Carroll, *Subtitling* (Simrishamn, Sweden: TransEdit, 1998).

Recommended Websites

www.filmsound.org The most comprehensive and detailed website on sound in cinema, with many interviews and links to other sites.

www.mixonline.com The site for *Mix Magazine,* devoted to all aspects of film and video sound production. Offers many free articles and original web content.

widescreenmuseum.com/sound/sound01.htm A review of the history of sound systems, illustrated with original documents.

www.filmmusic.com News of current releases, along with interviews with composers and music crew.

www.filmscoremonthly.com magazine site with some free articles.

www.geocities.com/Hollywood/Academy/4394/sync .htm In this 1995 article, "Sync Takes: The Art and Technique of Postproduction Sound," Elizabeth Weis concisely explains the creative choices involved in sound mixing. Our quotation from Michael Kirchberger is taken from one of the comments Weis presents here.

www.npr.org/templates/story/story.php?storyId= 1126863 A streaming audio interview with Walter Murch on the National Public Radio program *Fresh Air.*

Recommended DVD Supplements

ADR, the postdubbing of dialogue, seldom finds its way onto DVD supplements. An exception comes in "Peter Lorre's ADR Tracks" on the *20,000 Leagues Under the Sea* DVD. (The track is well hidden: in the "Bonus Material" section, click right to "Lost Treasures" and then choose "Audio Archives #2.") The opposite technique, recording songs for playback and lip-synching on set during the filming of musical numbers, is demonstrated in "Scoring Stage Sessions" on the *Singin' in the Rain* disc.

An excellent survey of how sound tracks are built up is "On Sound Design," for *Master and Commander,* where a dense ambient mix had to support the portrayal of a crowded ship. This supplement shows why so much dialogue recorded during filming is not usable and must be replaced by ADR. Sound-effects specialists demonstrate the subtleties of re-creating the noises from firing from various types of weapons.

The "Sound Design" section of "Music and Sound" on the *Toy Story 2* supplements includes a clear example of how sound functions within scenes. In the scene where the band of toys crosses a street full of traffic, the filmmakers' goal was to create extreme contrasts between movement and stasis. One technique was to stop and start the music as the toys froze and then moved on. The scene is played through with only sound effects, only music, and the final mix.

Each volume of *The Lord of the Rings* offers a supplement called "The Soundscapes of Middle-Earth," with the three adding up to about an hour. The *Fellowship of the Ring* documentary discusses ADR as well as sound effects. Each volume also contains a segment, "Music for Middle-Earth," totaling about an hour. The *Two Towers* DVD set contains a demonstration of sound mixing, with eight versions of the same clip from the Helm's Deep battle: one with the sound recorded on-set during filming, six with selected parts of the sound (music in one, weapon sounds in another, and so on), and the final mix. The six incomplete tracks have already been partially mixed from separate recordings. Originally, each sound was recorded separately. Early in *The Return of the King,* for example, as Gandalf leads the group through the woods to visit Isengard, one track was made just for the clicking of Legolas's arrows in his quiver—a sound barely distinguishable in the final mix.

Discussions of musical scores are among the most common of making-of supplements. In a particularly detailed and systematic discussion, "Scoring *War of the Worlds,*" John Williams comments extensively on the narrative functions of his music. The supplement was directed by Steven Spielberg. In the "Music" supplement for *The Golden Compass,* composer Alexandre Desplat discusses musical motifs; he also talks about the exotic instruments he chose to characterize the various ethnic groups in the story. Hans Zimmer, composer for *The Dark Knight,* describes the dissonant music associated with the Joker character in "The Sound of Anarchy" supplement.

Sergio Leone's Westerns are often called "operatic," and film music historian Jon Burlingame explains why in "Il Maestro: Ennio Morricone and *The Good, the Bad, and the Ugly.*" Unlike most movie music, the scores for Leone's films were written in advance, and this supplement explains how the music guided the director during shooting and editing.

8

"The choices you make push you
in a certain direction, and that
becomes what people call style."

—Chris Doyle, cinematographer,
Chungking Express

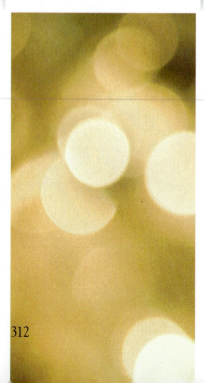

Summary: Style as a Formal System

The Concept of Style

At the beginning of Part Two, we saw how the different parts of a film relate to one another dynamically within its overall *form*. Now, having examined each category of techniques of the film medium, we may go on to see how these techniques interact to create another formal system of the film, its **style.** These two systems—style and narrative/non-narrative form—in turn interact with each other.

Stylistic patterns are a major part of any film. Sometimes, though, we talk about style in several films by the same filmmaker. We looked at *Our Hospitality* in terms of how its comic mise-en-scene is organized around a consistent use of long shots; this is part of Buster Keaton's style in other films, too. Many filmmakers have distinctive styles, and we can become familiar with those styles by analyzing the way in which they utilize techniques within whole filmic systems.

Further, we can also speak of a *group style*—the consistent use of techniques across the work of several filmmakers. We can speak of a German Expressionist style, or a Soviet montage style. In Part Six, we will consider some significant group styles that have emerged in film history.

Style and the Filmmaker

No single film uses all the technical possibilities we've discussed. For one thing, historical circumstances limit the choices that filmmakers have open to them. Before 1928, for example, filmmakers did not have the option of using synchronized dialogue. Even today, when the range of technical choices seems far broader, there are limits. Filmmakers cannot use the now obsolete orthochromatic film stock of the silent era, although in some respects it was superior to contemporary stocks. Similarly, a successful system for creating three-dimensional cinema images without the necessity for spectators to wear special glasses has yet to be invented.

There is another reason only some technical possibilities may be realized in a single film. As we saw in Chapter 1, working in a concrete production situation, the filmmaker must choose what techniques to employ. Typically, the filmmaker makes certain technical choices and adheres to them throughout the film. Across the film, a filmmaker will characteristically use three-point lighting, or continuity editing, or diegetic sound. A few segments might stand out as varying from the film's normal usage, but in general, a film tends to rely on consistent usage of certain techniques. The film's style results from a combination of historical constraints and deliberate choices.

Filmmakers also deliberately select techniques that will point out story parallels. Piotr Sobocinski, cinematographer for Krystyf Kieslowski, says that in *Three*

Colors: Red, a crane shot down to a fashion show was designed to recall an earlier camera movement, when the camera craned down as a book fell into the street. Similarly, in filming *Viva Zapata!* Elia Kazan tracked in on Zapata, who is ignoring the fact that a crowd of peasants is marching with him: "We had to go close on that shot and dolly [i.e., track] because what I wanted to show was his expression or lack of expression. We later contrasted that with a similar dolly shot on the police chief beginning to notice what was happening. The point was to contrast those two attitudes."

Films setting up strong narrative contrasts will often reinforce them with sharp stylistic differences. Jacques Tati's *Mon Oncle* opposes the charm of old Parisian neighborhoods to the sterility of the new buildings that replace them. Mr. Hulot lives in a ramshackle apartment building on a quiet little square, while the Arpel family—Hulot's sister, brother-in-law, and nephew—have just moved into an ultramodern house full of high-tech gadgets and chic but uncomfortable furniture. Scenes in Hulot's neighborhood tend to be accompanied by jaunty music, except when sound effects or dialogue become important. In this locale, the camera stays outside his apartment, stressing the interactions of the many people living and working around the square **(8.1).** By contrast, the Arpel scenes contain no music. Instead, we hear the tapping of shoes on stone floors and the clicks and whirs of the absurd appliances. There are frequent shots inside the house, and the street is almost invisible behind the family's metal security fence **(8.2).**

Many filmmakers plan the overall style of the film to reflect the progression of the story. For *Dead Man Walking,* Tim Robbins and his cinematographer, Roger Deakins, worked out a visual pattern to convey the increasing intimacy between the characters played by Susan Sarandon and Sean Penn, who talk to each other in a string of interviews spread across the film. Early scenes were shot to emphasize the wire mesh between the two, keeping it in focus and the Penn character more distant. Later, using longer lenses and slow tracking shots, the scenes minimize the barrier. Ultimately, when the characters are communicating through a cell door, reflections in the window make each one visible in the other's shot. As usual, repetitions and differences are used to shape our experience of the film.

Style and the Viewer

The spectator has a relation to style as well. Although we're seldom conscious of the fact, we tend to have expectations about style. If we see two characters in a long shot, we expect a cut-in to a closer view. If the actor walks rightward, as if about to leave the frame, we expect the camera to pan or track right to keep the person in the shot. If a character speaks, we expect to hear diegetic sound that is faithful to its source.

Like other kinds of expectations, stylistic ones derive from both our experience of the world generally (people talk; they don't chirp) and our experience of film and other media. The specific film's style can confirm our expectations, or modify them, or cheat, or challenge them.

Many films use techniques in ways that conform to our expectations. For example, the conventions of the classical Hollywood cinema and of specific genres provide a firm basis for reinforcing our prior assumptions. Other films ask us to narrow our expectations somewhat. Keaton's *Our Hospitality* accustoms us to expect deep-space manipulations of figures and objects, while Jean Renoir's *Grand Illusion* builds up specific expectations about the likelihood of camera movements. Still other films make highly unusual technical choices, and to follow them we must construct new stylistic expectations. The editing discontinuities in Sergei Eisenstein's *October* and the use of voice-over narration in *The Prestige* in effect teach us how to understand the style.

In other words, a director directs not only the cast and crew. A director also directs us, directs our attention, shapes our reaction. Thus the filmmaker's technical decisions make a difference in what we perceive and how we respond.

CONNECT TO THE BLOG
We trace the stylistic and formal development of a major contemporary filmmaker in "The sarcastic laments of Béla Tarr," at www.davidbordwell.net/blog/?p=1315. For the style of two art film directors of the previous generation, see "Bergman, Antonioni, and the stubborn stylists," at www.davidbordwell.net/blog/?p=1139.

8.1 *Mon Oncle.* Mr. Hulot chats with a neighbor while other people pass nearby.

8.2 The Arpels' inconveniently laid-out garden, with a giant metal security door that blots out their view of the street.

Style, then, is the patterned use of techniques across the film. Any one film will tend to rely on particular technical options in creating its style, and these are chosen by the filmmaker within the constraints of historical circumstances. We may also extend the term *style* to describe the characteristic use of techniques made by a single filmmaker or group of filmmakers. The spectator may not consciously notice film style, but it nonetheless contributes to his or her experience of the film.

Analyzing Film Style

As viewers, we register the effects of film style but seldom notice it. If we want to understand how these effects are achieved, we need to look and listen carefully. Since the previous four chapters have shown how we can pay attention to stylistic features, let's consider four general steps in analyzing style.

Step 1: Determine the Organizational Structure

The first step is to understand how the film is put together as a whole. If it is a narrative film, it will draw on all the principles discussed in Chapter 3. That is, it will have a plot that cues us to construct a story; it will manipulate causality, time, and space; it will have a distinct pattern of development from opening to closing; it may use parallelism; and its narration will choose between restricted and more unrestricted knowledge at various points. (Not all films tell stories. We'll discuss other types of form in Chapter 10.)

Step 2: Identify the Salient Techniques Used

Here the analysis will draw on our survey of technical possibilities in Chapters 4–7. You need to be able to spot things such as color, lighting, framing, cutting, and sound, which most viewers don't consciously notice. Once you notice them, you can identify them as techniques—such as nondiegetic music or a low-angle framing.

But noting and naming are only the beginning of stylistic analysis. The analyst must develop an eye for *salient* techniques. Salience will partly be determined by what techniques the film relies heavily on. The jerky forward zoom in *Wavelength* and the rapid, discontinuous editing of *October* invite scrutiny because they play a central role in the overall effect of each film.

In addition, what is salient depends partly on the analyst's purpose. If you want to show that a film's style is typical of one approach to filmmaking, you may focus on how the technique conforms to stylistic expectations. The 180-degree editing of *The Maltese Falcon* isn't obvious or emphasized, but adherence to rules of classical continuity is a characteristic of the film's style. Our purpose in Chapter 6 was to show that the film is typical in this respect. If, however, you want to stress unusual qualities of the film's style, you can concentrate on the more unexpected technical devices. Eisenstein's use of editing in *October* is unusual, representing choices that few filmmakers would make. It was the originality of these devices that we chose to stress in Chapter 6. From the standpoint of originality, costume in *October* is not as salient a stylistic feature as editing because it is more in accord with conventional practice. The analyst's decision about what techniques are salient will thus be influenced partly by what the film emphasizes and partly by the analyst's purpose.

Step 3: Trace Out Patterns of Techniques

Once you've identified salient techniques, you can notice how they are patterned. Techniques will be repeated and varied, developed and paralleled, across the whole

CONNECT TO THE BLOG
We discuss *Indiana Jones and the Kingdom of the Crystal Skull* and some aspects of Steven Spielberg's editing and use of light in "Reflections in a crystal eye," at
www.davidbordwell.net/blog/?p=2379.

film or within a single segment. Chapters 4–7 have shown how this occurs in some films.

You can zero in on stylistic patterns in two ways. First, you can reflect on your responses. If a scene begins with a track-in, do you expect that it will end with a track-out? If you see a character looking left, do you assume that someone or something is offscreen and will be revealed in the next shot? If you feel a mounting excitement in an action scene, is that traceable to a quickening tempo in the music or to accelerating editing?

A second tactic for noticing stylistic patterns is to look for ways in which style reinforces patterns of formal organization. Filmmakers often deliberately design the film's stylistic system to underscore developments in the drama. We have seen how shifting color schemes reflect three stages of the plot's development in *Women in Love* (4.41–4.43). For *Amistad,* Steven Spielberg and his cinematographer, Janusz Kaminski, traced the slaves' progress toward freedom by lighting and shooting the four courtroom scenes in markedly different ways, from greenish, smoky light and somewhat scattershot camera work to a final scene in the Supreme Court, with crisp illumination and smooth camera movements.

In designing *Portrait of a Lady,* Jane Campion and her cinematographer, Stuart Dryburgh, keyed colors to the protagonist's maturation. Isabel starts as an idealistic and somewhat headstrong young woman, and the background is an English summer, with bright green and yellow tones dominating. In Siena, as she becomes captivated by the sinister fortune hunter Osmond, the palette is richer and warmer, with orange and coral dominant. Years later, she is unhappily married to Osmond, and the color scheme is steeped in pale blues. The closing scenes return to the English countryside, recalling the opening, but now, as the wiser, remorseful Isabel confronts her future, the snowy landscape is bathed slightly in blue, suggesting that memories of her marriage still haunt her.

Even within a shorter span, style can create a subtle sense of narrative progression. A scene will usually have a dramatic pattern of encounter, conflict, and outcome, and the style will often reflect this, with the cutting becoming more marked and the shots coming closer to the characters as the scene progresses. In *The Silence of the Lambs,* for example, the scenes between Clarice Starling and Hannibal Lecter tend to begin with conventional shot/reverse-shot conversations. The characters, filmed in medium shot, look off to the right or the left of the camera (**8.3, 8.4**). As their conversations become more intense and intimate, the camera positions move closer to each one and shift subtly toward the axis of action until each person is looking directly into the lens (**8.5, 8.6**).

As we saw in *Grand Illusion* (pp. 208–210), style may create associations between situations, as when the camera movements suggest the prisoners' unity. It may also reinforce parallels, as do the tracking shots comparing Rauffenstein's war trophies and Elsa's. Later we'll see how style can also reinforce the organization of non-narrative films.

Sometimes, however, stylistic patterning will not respect the overall structure of the film. Style can claim our attention in its own right. Since most stylistic devices have several functions, a technique may interest the analyst for different reasons. In 6.130 and 6.131, a cut from a washline to a living room acts as a transition between scenes. But the cut is of more interest for other reasons, since we don't expect a narrative film to treat objects as flat patches of color to be compared across shots. Such attention to graphic play is a convention of abstract form. Here, in a passage from Ozu's *Ohayo,* a stylistic choice comes forward because it goes beyond its narrative function. Even here, though, stylistic patterns continue to call on the viewer's expectations and to draw the spectator into a dynamic process. Anyone who notices the graphic match on red objects in *Ohayu* will most likely be intrigued at such an unconventional way of editing. And, if stylistic patterns do swerve off on their own, we still need a sense of the film's narrative organization in order to show how and when that happens.

8.3   During the initial conversation in *The Silence of the Lambs,* shooting in depth with the foreground character's head prominent in the frame . . .

8.4   . . . emphasizes the distance between the pair.

8.5   Later in the scene, closer shots . . .

8.6   . . . deemphasize that distance.

CONNECT TO THE BLOG

For a discussion of how various techniques of film style can function to call our attention to things, see "Gradations of emphasis, starring Glenn Ford," at

www.davidbordwell.net/blog/?p=2986.

"There's no scene in any movie that 50 different directors couldn't have done 50 different ways."

— Paul Mazursky, director

CONNECT TO THE BLOG

Subtle stylistic echoes enrich *The Prestige*, as we show in "Niceties: How classical filmmaking can be at once simple and precise."

See www.davidbordwell.net/blog/?p=3878.

Step 4: Propose Functions for the Salient Techniques and the Patterns They Form

Here the analyst looks for the role that style plays in the film's overall form. Does the use of camera movement tend to create suspense by delaying the revelation of story information, as in the opening of *Touch of Evil* (pp. 132–133)? Does the use of discontinuous editing create a narrational omniscience, as in the sequence we analyzed in *October* (pp. 263–264)? Does the composition of the shot tend to make us concentrate on a particular detail (4.140, the shot of Anne's face in *Day of Wrath*)? Does the use of music or noise create surprise?

A direct route to noticing function is to notice the effects of the film on our viewing experience. Style may enhance *emotional* aspects of the film. Rapid cutting in *The Birds* evokes shock and horror, while the fluctuating drone of the score in *The Prestige* creates a tense but also melancholy tone.

Style also shapes *meaning.* We should, however, avoid reading isolated elements atomistically, taking them out of context. As we argued on p. 196, a high angle does not automatically mean "defeat," just as a low angle does not automatically mean "power." There is no dictionary that specifies the meaning of a specific stylistic element. Instead, the analyst must scrutinize the whole film, the patterns of the techniques in it, and the specific effects of film form. For example, in *Grand Illusion,* the contrast between Rauffenstein and Elsa is heightened by Renoir's parallel tracking shots.

Meaning is only one type of effect, and there is no reason to expect that every stylistic feature will possess a thematic significance. One part of a director's job is to direct our attention, and so style will often function simply *perceptually*—to get us to notice things, to emphasize one thing over another, to misdirect our attention, to clarify, intensify, or complicate our understanding of the action. (See "A Closer Look.")

One way to sharpen our sense of the functions of specific techniques is to *imagine alternatives* and reflect on what differences would result. Suppose the director had made a different technical choice; how would this create a different effect? Suppose in the scene from *Shadow of a Doubt* that Hitchcock had cut away to Little Charlie when she blurted out, "But they're people too!" Switching our attention to her reaction might have relieved the dramatic pressure created by Uncle Charlie's escalating bitterness, and it would have broken the steady buildup we feel in the camera movement that gradually enlarges his face.

To recall another example, *Our Hospitality* creates its gags by putting two elements into the same shot and letting us observe the comic juxtaposition. Suppose Keaton had instead isolated each element in a single shot and then linked the two elements by editing. The meaning might be the same, but the perceptual effects would vary: instead of a simultaneous presentation that lets our attention shuttle to and fro, we would have a more "programmed" pattern of building up the gags and paying them off. Or, suppose that John Huston had handled the opening scene of *The Maltese Falcon* as a single take with camera movement. How would he then have drawn our attention to Brigid O'Shaughnessy's and Sam Spade's facial reactions, and how would this have affected our expectations? By focusing on effects and imagining alternatives to the technical choices that were made, the analyst can gain a sharp sense of the particular functions of style in the given film.

The rest of this chapter provides an illustration of how we can analyze film style. Our example is the film whose narrative system we analyzed in Chapter 3: *Citizen Kane*. Here we follow all four steps in stylistic analysis. Since Chapter 3 discussed *Citizen Kane*'s organizational structures, we will concentrate here on identifying salient techniques, locating patterns, and proposing some functions for style in each case.

FILM STYLE IN *SHADOW OF A DOUBT*

Uncle Charlie has come to visit his sister's family in Santa Rosa, California. Charlie is a man of the world, flashing money freely. His sister Emmy adores him and has even named her daughter Charlie in his honor. But as Uncle Charlie lingers in town, Little Charlie begins to suspect that he's a serial killer who preys on rich widows. She can't prove it—the film's title is *Shadow of a Doubt*—but she now sees his menacing side. In many scenes, director Alfred Hitchcock uses film style to link our perception and understanding of events to those of Little Charlie.

One key moment in this process comes in a scene of the family having dinner. Uncle Charlie praises small-town living. Women keep busy in towns like Santa Rosa, he says, not like the rich, spoiled women one finds in cities. He slowly slips into a venomous monologue:

> "And what do the wives do, these useless women? You see them in the hotels, the best hotels, every day by the thousands. Drinking the money, eating the money, losing the money at bridge, playing all day and all night. Smelling of money. Proud of their jewelry but nothing else. Horrible . . . fat, faded, greedy women."

Reacting to this, Little Charlie blurts out, "But they're alive! They're human beings!" Uncle Charlie replies, "Are they? Are they, Charlie? Are they human or are they fat, wheezing animals?" As if realizing he's gone too far, Uncle Charlie smiles and switches back to his ingratiating manner.

This powerful scene depends on many stylistic decisions about how to affect the audience. The dialogue constitutes a step in the process of strengthening Little Charlie's suspicions that her uncle is a murderer. Since we in the audience have the same suspicions, the scene nudges us closer to the same belief. The scene suggests that he's slightly mad; his killing proceeds not only from a larcenous bent but also from a deep-seated hatred of women. We gain a better understanding of his personality. Our response has an emotional dimension, too, since in his description of the women he dehumanizes them to chilling effect.

Within the context of the film, this scene serves several functions. The development of the story depends on Uncle Charlie's visit to his family and Little Charlie's growing suspicions about his murderous instincts. As Uncle Charlie points out, however, she can't tell anyone the truth, since doing so would devastate her mother. This creates a powerful conflict, not only between Little Charlie and her uncle but also within her mind. Similarly, as she learns the truth, her attitude changes. Initially, she worships her uncle, but eventually, she becomes bitterly aware of his real nature, and her trust in the world starts to crack. The dinner scene, then, contributes to a growth in Little Charlie's character.

Even the fact that the scene occurs at dinner is important. More cheerful scenes have taken place at the same table. At one point, Uncle Charlie gives Emmy restored photographs of their parents, which seems to convey his sincere love for her and their family. Little Charlie is exuberant **(8.7)**. In these early scenes, we're told of a special rapport that uncle and niece share, and he even presents here with an elegant ring **(8.8)**. The ring plays an important role in the plot, since Little Charlie discovers an inscription on it (a clue that it came from one of her uncle's victims). So Uncle Charlie's hateful monologue creates a formal pattern alongside other moments we've already seen.

Hitchcock firmly believed in using the medium to arouse the viewer's mind and feelings. So, as Uncle Charlie launches into his monologue, Hitchcock presents us with an establishing shot of the entire table **(8.9)**. We've seen similar shots in earlier scenes, and it

8.7 In *Shadow of a Doubt*, Little Charlie is delighted when Uncle Charlie presents pictures of her grandparents.

8.8 In an eerie parallel to a lovers' engagement, Uncle Charlie presents his niece with a ring.

8.9 A general shot shows the family at table, with the two Charlies most visible.

orients us to the positions of the scene's major characters. At the same time, Hitchcock stages the scene so that Uncle Charlie rather than Emmy's husband sits at the head of the table. His domination of the household is presented visually. As Charlie starts to talk, after a shot of Emmy we get a brief shot of Little Charlie, eying him anxiously **(8.10)**. When he begins to denounce the "useless women," we see a close view of him as he continues his attack **(8.11)**.

Joseph Cotten's performance is very important here. He seethes with resentment of the "fat, faded, greedy women." He delivers the speech without blinking, as if musing to himself rather than talking to others. Hitchcock magnifies the effect of Cotten's performance with a tracking shot that eliminates everyone else at the table. The camera comes steadily forward, filling the frame with Uncle Charlie's face as his monologue increases in anger and intensity **(8.12)**.

Hitchcock could have used other techniques. He could have filmed Uncle Charlie from the rear, concealing his face but showing us the reactions of others at the table. He could have interrupted shots of Uncle

Charlie with the reactions of Emmy, her husband, and her children. But Hitchcock achieves a specific effect by the slow, riveting movement toward Uncle Charlie's face as his hatred for women surfaces. Even though he's speaking the lines aloud, the relentless forward tracking movement suggests that we're getting a glimpse into his mind.

Most directors would have shown Little Charlie objecting, "But they're alive! They're human beings!" by cutting to a shot of her face. But Hitchcock leaves her outburst offscreen. Then he adds an unexpected and eerie touch. As the tracking shot ends on an extremely tight close-up, Uncle Charlie turns slightly and looks into the camera as he replies, "Are they, Charlie?" **(8.13)**.

Suddenly, we're put in the young woman's place, seeing the full force of her uncle's hatred. (We've just seen Jonathan Demme employing a comparable technique in filming Hannibal Lecter in *The Silence of the Lambs* [8.3–8.6]. Like Little Charlie, we begin to realize that he's a sociopath, made all the more frightening by his steady gaze and controlled speech. Hitchcock's decisions about staging, framing, sound, and editing

8.10 After a shot of Emmy, Hitchcock cuts to Little Charlie looking uneasily at her uncle.

8.11 Uncle Charlie begins his monologue about useless women.

8.12 The camera moves closer to him . . .

Style in *Citizen Kane*

In analyzing *Citizen Kane*'s narrative, we discovered that the film is organized as a search; a detective-like figure, the reporter Thompson, tries to find the significance of Kane's last word, "Rosebud." But even before Thompson appears as a character, we, the spectators, are invited to ask questions about Kane and to seek the answers.

The very beginning of the film sets up a mystery. After a fade-in reveals a "No Trespassing" sign, in a series of craning movements upward, the camera travels over a set of fences, all matched graphically in the slow dissolves that link the shots. There follows a series of shots of a huge estate, always with the great house in the distance **(8.16)**. (This sequence depends largely on special effects; the house have intensely engaged our minds and emotions in the story.

Hitchcock's style here is related to technical choices in the movie as a whole. For one thing, the shot of Uncle Charlie is the closest we ever come to him, so this tight framing gives the scene particular force. More generally, Hitchcock employs techniques that put us in the position of the characters. Throughout the film, he uses optical point of view, most often allowing us to share Little Charlie's vantage point **(8.14, 8.15).**

This pattern of stylistic choices is sustained throughout the dinner table monologue. The brief shot of Little Charlie reminds us of her position beside her uncle (8.10). But rather than have Uncle Charlie start his monologue by glancing at her, Hitchcock lets him speak to the others at the table, or perhaps only to himself (8.11, 8.12). Only after Little Charlie's offscreen outburst does Uncle Charlie turn to her—and us (8.13). Hitchcock has saved the most startling point-of-view moment for the end of the shot.

The style of this scene enhances the film's pattern of restricted narration. After Uncle Charlie arrives in Santa Rosa, we get some private glimpses into his activities, but the scenes concentrate largely on Emmy's family and particularly on Little Charlie. We know a bit more than she knows about her uncle. For example, from the start, we suspect that he's being sought by the police, but we don't know what they're investigating. Later we learn that Uncle Charlie has torn a story out of the newspaper, but not until his niece finds it do we discover what he was trying to conceal. Slowly, along with Little Charlie, we discover that the Merry Widow Murderer is at large and that Uncle Charlie is a prime suspect.

So the overall form of the story's development and the stylistic presentation in each scene work to put us close to Little Charlie. We know roughly what she knows, and we learn some key information when she does. In the dinner table scene, the developing story line and Hitchcock's style combine to tie us even more tightly to Little Charlie. The moment when Uncle Charlie turns challengingly to the camera becomes a high point of this pattern.

8.13 ... and is very close when he turns and replies to Little Charlie's protests that these women are human; he asks, "Are they, Charlie?"

8.14 Earlier in the film, when Little Charlie has begun to suspect her uncle, she pauses on the front doorstep.

8.15 Hitchcock then gives us an optical point-of-view shot of what makes her hesitate: Uncle Charlie holding her mother spellbound.

itself is a series of paintings, combined through matte work with three-dimensional miniatures in the foreground.) The gloomy lighting, the deserted setting, and the ominous music give the opening of the film the eerie uncertainty that we associate with mystery stories. These opening shots are connected by dissolves, making the camera seem to draw closer to the house although there is no forward camera movement. From shot to shot, the foreground changes, yet the lighted window remains in almost exactly the same position on the screen. Graphically matching the window from shot to shot already focuses our attention on it; we assume (rightly) that whatever is in that room will be important in initiating the story.

This pattern of our penetration into the space of a scene returns at other points in the film. Again and again, the camera moves toward things that might reveal the

8.16   The opening of *Citizen Kane*.

8.17   As this scene of *Citizen Kane* begins, the camera frames a poster of Susan Alexander on an outside wall of the nightclub . . .

8.18   . . . then moves up the wall to the roof . . .

8.19   . . . forward and through the "El Rancho" sign . . .

8.20   . . . and over to the skylight.

secrets of Kane's character, as in the spectacular crane up the side of a nightclub to a skylight as Thompson goes to interview Susan Alexander **(8.17–8.20).** As the camera reaches the skylight, a dissolve and a crack of lightning shift the scene inside to another craning movement down to Susan's table. (Actually, some of what seem to be camera movements were created in the laboratory using special effects; see "Where to Go from Here" at the end of the chapter.)

The opening scene and the introduction to El Rancho have some striking similarities. Each begins with a sign ("No Trespassing" and the publicity poster), and each moves us into a building to reveal a new character. The first scene uses a series of shots, whereas the second depends more on camera movement, but these different techniques are working to create a consistent pattern that becomes part of the film's style. Later, Thompson's second visit to Susan repeats the crane shots of the first. The second flashback of Jed Leland's story begins with yet another movement into a scene. The camera is initially pointed at wet cobblestones. Then it tilts up and tracks in toward Susan coming out of a drugstore. Only then does the camera pan right to reveal Kane standing, splashed with mud, on the curb. This pattern of gradual movement into the story space not only suits the narrative's search pattern but also creates curiosity and suspense.

As we have seen, films' endings often contain variations of their beginnings. Toward the end of *Citizen Kane,* Thompson gives up his search for Rosebud. But after the reporters leave the huge storeroom of Xanadu, the camera begins to move over the great expanse of Kane's collections. It cranes forward high above the crates

8.21 A crane shot near the end of *Citizen Kane* . . .

8.22 . . . moves down to center on Kane's sled.

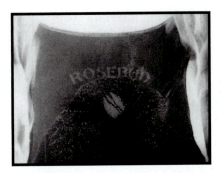

8.23 Another forward camera movement brings the sled into close-up.

and piles of objects **(8.21)**, then moves down to center on the sled from Kane's childhood **(8.22)**. Then there is a cut to the furnace, and the camera again moves in on the sled as it is tossed into the fire. At last we are able to read the word "Rose-bud" on the sled **(8.23)**. The ending continues the pattern set up at the beginning; the film techniques create a penetration into the story space, probing the mystery of the central character.

After our glimpse of the sled, however, the film reverses the pattern. A series of shots linked by dissolves leads us back outside Xanadu, the camera travels down to the "No Trespassing" sign again, and we are left to wonder whether this discovery really provides a resolution to the mystery about Kane's character. Now the beginning and the ending echo each other explicitly.

Our study of *Citizen Kane*'s organization in Chapter 3 also showed that Thompson's search was, from the standpoint of narration, a complex one. At one level, our knowledge is restricted principally to what Kane's acquaintances know. Within the flashbacks, the style reinforces this restriction by avoiding crosscutting or other techniques that would move toward a more unrestricted range of knowledge. Many of the flashback scenes are shot in fairly static long takes, strictly confining us to what participants in the scene could witness. When the youthful Kane confronts Thatcher during the *Inquirer* crusade, Welles could have cut away to the reporter in Cuba sending Kane a telegram or could have shown a montage sequence of a day in the life of the paper. Instead, because this is Thatcher's tale, Welles handles the scene in a long take showing Kane and Thatcher in a face-to-face standoff, which is then capped by a close-up of Kane's cocky response.

We have also seen that Kane's narrative requires us to take each narrator's version as objective within his or her limited knowledge. Welles reinforces this by avoiding shots that suggest optical or mental subjectivity. (Contrast Hitchcock's optical point-of-view angles in *The Birds* and *Rear Window,* pp. 224–225 and 244–245.)

Welles also uses deep-focus cinematography that yields an external perspective on the action. The shot in which Kane's mother signs her son over to Thatcher is a good example. Several shots precede this one, introducing the young Kane. Then there is a cut to what at first seems a simple long shot of the boy **(8.24)**. But the camera tracks back to reveal a window, with Kane's mother appearing at the left and calling to him **(8.25)**. Then the camera continues to track back, following the adults as they walk to another room **(8.26)**. Mrs. Kane and Thatcher sit at a table in the foreground to sign the papers, while Kane's father remains standing farther away at the left, and the boy plays in the distance **(8.27)**.

Welles eliminates cutting here. The shot becomes a complex unit unto itself, like the opening of *Touch of Evil* discussed on pp. 216–217. Most Hollywood directors would have handled this scene in shot/reverse shot, but Welles keeps all of the implications of the action simultaneously before us. The boy, who is the subject of the discussion, remains framed in the distant window through the whole scene; his game leads us to believe that he is unaware of what his mother is doing.

8.24 A progressively deeper shot in *Citizen Kane* begins as a long shot of the young Kane . . .

8.25 . . . becomes an interior view as the camera reveals a window . . .

8.26 . . . and moves backward with Mrs. Kane . . .

8.27 . . . keeping the boy in extreme long shot throughout the rest of the scene.

8.28 Depth and centering in *Citizen Kane*.

8.29 *Citizen Kane:* snow inside and outside the glass ball.

The tensions between the father and the mother are conveyed not only by the fact that she excludes him from the discussion at the table but also by the overlapping sound. His objections to signing his son away to a guardian mix in with the dialogue in the foreground, and even the boy's shouts (ironically, "The Union Forever!") can be heard in the distance. The framing also emphasizes the mother in much of the scene. This is her only appearance in the film. Her severity and clamped-down emotions help motivate the many events that follow from her action here. We have had little introduction to the situation prior to this scene, but the combination of sound, cinematography, and mise-en-scene conveys the complicated action with an overall objectivity.

Every director directs our attention, but Welles does so in unusual ways. *Citizen Kane* offers a good example of how a director can choose between alternatives. In the scenes that give up cutting, Welles cues our attention by using deep-space mise-en-scene (figure behavior, lighting, placement in space) and sound. We can watch expressions because the actors play frontally (8.27). In addition, the framing emphasizes certain figures by putting them in the foreground or in dead center (**8.28**). And, of course, our attention bounces from one character to another as they speak lines. Even if Welles avoids the classical Hollywood shot/reverse shot in such scenes, he still uses film techniques to prompt us to make the correct assumptions and inferences about the story's progression.

Citizen Kane's narration also embeds the narrators' objective but restricted versions within broader contexts. Thompson's investigation links the various tales, so we learn substantially what he learns. Yet he must not become the protagonist of the film, for that would remove Kane from the center of interest. Welles makes a crucial stylistic choice here. By the use of low-key selective lighting and patterns of staging and framing, Thompson is made virtually unidentifiable. His back is to us, he is tucked into the corner of the frame, and he is usually in darkness. The stylistic handling makes him the neutral investigator, less a character than a channel for information.

More broadly still, we have seen that the film encloses Thompson's search and each narrator's recollection within a more omniscient narration. Our discussion of the opening shots of Xanadu is relevant here: film style is used to convey a high degree of non-character-centered knowledge. But when we enter Kane's death chamber, the style also suggests the narration's ability to plumb characters' minds. We see shots of snow covering the frame (for example, **8.29**), which hint at a subjective vision. Later in the film, the camera movements occasionally remind us of the broader range of narrational knowledge, as in the first version of Susan's opera premiere, shown during Leland's story in segment 6. There the camera moves to reveal something neither Leland nor Susan could know about (**8.30–8.32**). The final sequence, which at least partially solves the mystery of "Rosebud," also uses a vast camera movement to give us an omniscient perspective. The camera cranes over objects from Kane's collection, moving forward in space but backward through

8.30 In *Citizen Kane*'s first opera scene, the camera cranes up from the stage . . .

8.31 . . . through the rigging above . . .

8.32 . . . to reveal a stagehand indicating that Susan's singing stinks.

Kane's life to concentrate on his earliest memento, the sled. A salient technique again conforms to pattern by giving us knowledge no character will ever possess.

In looking at the development of the narrative form of *Citizen Kane,* we saw how Kane changes from an idealistic young man to a friendless recluse. The film sets up a contrast between Kane's early life as a newspaper publisher and his later withdrawal from public life after Susan's opera career fails. This contrast is most readily apparent in the mise-en-scene, particularly the settings of the *Inquirer* office and Xanadu. The *Inquirer* office is initially an efficient but cluttered place. When Kane takes over, he creates a casual atmosphere by moving in his furniture and living in his office. The low camera angles tend to emphasize the office's thin pillars and low ceilings, which are white and evenly, brightly lit. Eventually, Kane's collection of crated antiquities clutters his little office. Xanadu, on the other hand, is huge and sparsely furnished. The ceilings are too high to be seen in most shots, and the few furnishings stand far apart. The lighting often strikes figures strongly from the back or side, creating a few patches of hard light in the midst of general darkness. The expanded collection of antiquities and mementoes now is housed in cavernous storerooms.

The contrast between the *Inquirer* office and Xanadu is also created by the sound techniques associated with each locale. Several scenes at the newspaper office (Kane's initial arrival and his return from Europe) involve a dense sound mix with a babble of overlapping voices. Yet the cramped space is suggested by the relative lack of resonance in timbre. In Xanadu, however, the conversations sound very different. Kane and Susan speak their lines to each other slowly, with pauses between. Moreover, their voices have an echo effect that combines with the setting and lighting to convey a sense of huge, empty space.

The transition from Kane's life at the *Inquirer* to his eventual seclusion at Xanadu is suggested by a change in the mise-en-scene at the *Inquirer.* As we have just seen, while Kane is in Europe, the statues he sends back begin to fill up his little office. This hints at Kane's growing ambitions and declining interest in working personally on his newspaper. This change culminates in the last scene in the *Inquirer* office—Leland's confrontation with Kane. The office is being used as a campaign headquarters. With the desks pushed aside and the employees gone, the room looks larger and emptier than it had in earlier scenes. Welles emphasizes this by placing the camera at floor level and shooting from a low angle (5.107). The Chicago *Inquirer* office, with its vast, shadowy spaces, also picks up this pattern **(8.33)**, as do later conversation scenes in the huge rooms of Xanadu (8.28).

Contrast these scenes with one near the end of the film. The reporters invade Kane's museumlike storeroom at Xanadu **(8.34).** Although the echoing inside Xanadu conveys its cavernous quality, the reporters transform the setting briefly by the same sort of dense, overlapping dialogue that characterized the early *Inquirer* scenes and the scene after the newsreel. By bringing together these reporters and Kane's final surroundings, the film creates another contrasting parallel emphasizing the changes in the protagonist.

Parallelism is an important feature throughout *Citizen Kane,* and most of the salient techniques work to create parallels in the ways we've already seen. For example, the use of deep focus and deep space to pack many characters into the frame can create significant similarities and contrasts. Late in Thatcher's account (segment 4), a scene presents Kane's financial losses in the Depression. He is forced to sign over his newspaper to Thatcher's bank. The scene opens with a close-up of Kane's manager, Bernstein, reading the contract **(8.35).** He lowers the paper to reveal Thatcher, now much older, seated opposite him. We hear Kane's voice off-screen, and Bernstein moves his head slightly, the camera reframing a little. Now we see Kane pacing beyond them in a huge office or boardroom **(8.36).** The scene is a single take in which the dramatic situation is created by the arrangement of the figures and the image's depth of field. The lowering of the contract recalls the previous scene, in which we first get a real look at the adult Kane as Thatcher puts

8.33 In *Citizen Kane,* deep-focus photography and rear projection exaggerate the depth of the *Inquirer* office, making the characters seem far apart.

8.34 *Citizen Kane:* deep focus in the final scene.

8.35   The contract scene in *Citizen Kane* . . .

8.36   . . . with Kane in the background of the shot . . .

8.37   . . . echoes this earlier scene's composition . . .

8.38   . . . and revelation of Kane.

8.39   *Citizen Kane:* Susan onstage in her opera debut . . .

8.40   . . . and Kane in the audience.

down the newspaper that has concealed him **(8.37, 8.38).** There Thatcher had been annoyed, but Kane could defy him. Years later in the story, Thatcher has gained control and Kane paces restlessly, still defiant, but stripped of his power over the *Inquirer* chain. The use of a similar device to open these two scenes sets up a contrasting parallel between them.

Editing patterns can also suggest similarities between scenes, as when Welles compares two moments at which Kane seems to win public support. In the first scene, Kane is running for governor and makes a speech at a mammoth rally. This scene is principally organized around an editing pattern that shows one or two shots of Kane speaking, then one or two close shots of small groups of characters in the audience (Emily and their son, Leland, Bernstein, Gettys), then another shot of Kane. The cutting establishes the characters who are important for their views of Kane. Boss Gettys is the last to be shown in the scene, and we expect him to retaliate against Kane's denunciation.

After his defeat, Kane sets out to make Susan an opera star and justify his interest in her to the public. In the scene that parallels Kane's election speech, Susan's debut, the organization of shots is similar to that of the political rally. Again the figure on the stage, Susan, serves as a pivot for the editing. One or two shots of her are followed by a few shots of the various listeners (Kane, Bernstein, Leland, the singing teacher), then back to Susan, and so on **(8.39, 8.40).** General narrative parallels and specific stylistic techniques articulate two stages of Kane's power quest: first his own attempt and then with Susan as his proxy.

As we've seen in Chapter 7, music can bring out parallels as well. For example, Susan's singing is causally central to the narrative. Her elaborate aria in the opera *Salammbo* contrasts sharply with the other main diegetic music, the little song about "Charlie Kane." In spite of the differences between the songs, there is a parallel between them, in that both relate to Kane's ambitions. The "Charlie Kane" ditty seems inconsequential, but its lyrics clearly show that Kane intends it as a political song, and it does turn up later as campaign music. In addition, the chorus girls who sing the song wear costumes with boots and Rough Rider hats, which they place on the heads of the men in the foreground **(8.41).** Thus Kane's desire for war with Spain has shown up even in this apparently simple farewell party for his departure to Europe. When Kane's political ambitions are dashed, he tries to create a public career for his wife instead, but she is incapable of singing grand opera. Again, the songs create narrative parallels between different actions in Kane's career.

As we saw in examining *Citizen Kane*'s narrative, the newsreel is a very important sequence, partly because it provides a map to the upcoming plot events. Because of its importance, Welles sets off the style of this sequence from the rest of the film by distinctive techniques that don't appear elsewhere in *Citizen Kane*. Also, we need to believe that this is a real newsreel in order to motivate Thompson's search for the key to Kane's life. The realistic newsreel sequence also helps establish Kane's power and wealth, which will be the basis of much of the upcoming action.

Welles uses several techniques to achieve the look and sound of a newsreel of the period. Some of these are fairly simple. The music recalls actual newsreels, and the insert titles, outmoded in fictional films, were still a convention in newsreels. But beyond this, Welles employs a number of subtle cinematographic techniques to achieve a documentary quality. Since some of the footage in the newsreel is supposed to have been taken in the silent period, he uses several different film stocks to make it appear that the different shots have been assembled from widely different sources. Some of the footage was printed so as to achieve the jerkiness of silent film run at sound speed. Welles also scratched and faded this footage to give it the look of old, worn film. This, combined with the makeup work, creates a remarkable impression of documentary footage of Kane with Teddy Roosevelt, Adolf Hitler **(8.42),** and other historical figures. In the latter scenes of Kane being wheeled around his estate, the handheld camera, the slats and barriers **(8.43),** and the off-center framing imitate the effects of a newsreel reporter secretly filming Kane. All of these documentary conventions are enhanced by the use of a narrator whose booming voice also mimics the commentary typical in newsreels of the day.

8.41 Costumes create a political reference in *Citizen Kane.*

One of *Citizen Kane*'s outstanding formal features is the way its plot manipulates story time. As we have seen, this process is motivated by Thompson's inquiry and the order in which he interviews Kane's acquaintances. Various techniques assist in the manipulation of order and duration. The shift from a narrator's present recounting to a past event is often reinforced by a *shock cut.* A shock cut creates a jarring juxtaposition, usually by means of a sudden shift to a higher sound volume and a considerable graphic discontinuity. *Citizen Kane* offers several instances: the abrupt beginning of the newsreel after the deathbed shot, the shift from the quiet conversation in the newsreel projection room to the lightning and thunder outside the El Rancho, and the sudden appearance of a screeching cockatoo in the foreground as Raymond's flashback begins **(8.44).** Such transitions create surprise and sharply demarcate one portion of the plot from another.

8.42 In *Citizen Kane,* costume, makeup, and . . .

The transitions that skip over or drastically compress time are less abrupt. Recall, for instance, the languid images of Kane's sled being gradually covered by snow. A more extended example is the breakfast table montage (segment 6) that elliptically traces the decline of Kane's first marriage. Starting with the newlyweds' late supper, rendered in a track-in and a shot/reverse-shot series, the sequence moves through several brief episodes, consisting of shot/reverse-shot exchanges linked by superimpositions of lighted windows whizzing by. (The effect resembles the transitional device of the **whip pan,** a fast panning movement.) In each episode, Kane and Emily become more sharply hostile. The segment ends by tracking away to show the surprising distance between them at the table.

8.43 . . . cinematography simulate newsreel footage.

The music reinforces the sequence's development as well. The initial late supper is accompanied by a lilting waltz. At each transition to a later time, the music changes. A comic variation of the waltz follows its initial statement and then a tense one; then horns and trumpets restate the Kane theme. The final portion of the scene, with a stony silence between the couple, is accompanied by a slow, eerie variation on the initial theme. The dissolution of the marriage is stressed by this theme-and-variations accompaniment. A similar sort of temporal compression and sonic elaboration can be found in the montage of Susan's opera career (segment 7).

Our brief examination of *Citizen Kane*'s style has pointed out only a few of the major patterns in the film. You can find others: the musical motif associated with Kane's power; the "K" motif appearing in Kane's costumes and in Xanadu's settings; the way the decor of Susan's room in Xanadu reveals Kane's attitude toward her; the changes in the acting of individuals as their characters age in the course of the story; and the playful photographic devices, such as the photos that become animated or the many superimpositions during montage sequences. Again and again in *Citizen Kane,* such stylistic patterns sustain and intensify the narrative development and shape the audience's experience in particular ways.

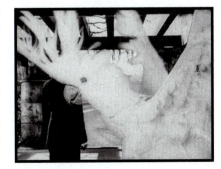

8.44 A shock cut in *Citizen Kane.*

SUMMARY

This concludes our introduction of the basic cinematic techniques. We have suggested ways to analyze stylistic functions in the overall form of individual films. We offer further examples of analyses in Part Five. First, however, there's one more factor that affects our experiences of the films we see.

Often, when we view a film, we think of it as belonging to a type or group of movies. Rather than say, "I'm going to see a film," we may say, "I'm going to see a Western" or "I'm going to see a documentary." Our friends are likely to understand what we mean, because such groupings are widely recognized in our culture. Part Four examines the main ways in which we categorize films.

WHERE TO GO FROM HERE

The Concept of Film Style

Sometimes the concept of style is used evaluatively, to imply that something is inherently good ("Now that's got real style!"). We are using the term descriptively. From our perspective, all films have style, because all films make *some* use of the techniques of the medium, and those techniques will necessarily be organized in some way.

For discussion of the concept of style in various arts, see Monroe C. Beardsley, *Aesthetics: Problems in the Philosophy of Criticism* (New York: Harcourt Brace and World, 1958); J. V. Cunningham, ed., *The Problem of Style* (Greenwich, CT: Fawcett, 1996); and Berel Lang, ed., *The Concept of Style,* rev. ed. (Ithaca, NY: Cornell University Press, 1987).

Pioneering studies of style in the cinema are Erwin Panofsky, "Style and Medium in the Moving Pictures" (originally published in 1937), in Daniel Talbot, ed., *Film: An Anthology* (Berkeley: University of California Press, 1970), pp. 13–32, and Raymond Durgnat, *Films and Feelings* (Cambridge, MA: MIT Press, 1967). Most of the works cited in the "Where to Go from Here" sections of the chapters in Part Three offer concrete studies of aspects of film style.

For essays on a wide variety of styles and films, see Lennard Højbjerg and Peter Schepelern, eds., *Film Style and Story: A Tribute to Torben Grodal* (Copenhagen: Museum Tusculanum Press, 2003). For a survey of the different ways in which critics and historians have approached style, see David Bordwell, *On the History of Film Style* (Cambridge, MA: Harvard University Press, 1997). Bordwell examines film style in the films of many periods, filmmakers, and countries in *Poetics of Cinema* (New York: Routledge, 2008).

An entire book has been written on the production of *Citizen Kane,* shedding much light on how its style was created: Robert L. Carringer's *The Making of Citizen Kane* (Berkeley: University of California Press, 1985). Among other things, Carringer reveals the degree to which Welles and his collaborators used special effects for many of the film's scenes. A tribute to the film, and a reprinting of Gregg Toland's informative article on the film, "Realism for *Citizen Kane,*" is available in *American Cinematographer* 72, 8 (August 1991): 34–42. Graham Bruce illuminates Bernhard Herrmann's musical score for *Citizen Kane* in *Bernard Herrmann: Film Music and Narrative* (Ann Arbor, MI: UMI Research Press, 1985), pp. 42–57. See also Steven C. Smith, *A Heart at Fire's Center: The Life and Music of Bernard Herrmann* (Berkeley: University of California Press, 1991). A detailed analysis of the film's sound is Rick Altman, "Deep-Focus Sound: *Citizen Kane* and the Radio Aesthetic," *Quarterly Review of Film and Video* 15, 3 (December 1994): 1–33.

Recommended DVD Supplements

Supplements for DVDs often discuss individual film techniques and their functions, but they rarely consider how style functions systematically. Here are bonus features that try for a little analysis.

"The Making of *American Graffiti*" deals fairly extensively with the film's style and includes comments by the great sound editor Walter Murch. In "The Leone Style," on the DVD of *The Good, the Bad, and the Ugly,* several apects of the director's approach are discussed: the use of lengthy shots using a slow visual rhythm, juxtapositions of extreme long shots and extreme close-ups, imitations of paintings, and operatic grandeur.

"The Making of *My Own Private Idaho*" deals concretely with style as a formal system, comparing the techniques used at the film's opening and ending, and tracing changes in the style as the story progresses. The featurette covers camera movement and angle, lighting, sets, and acting.

In "Elmer Bernstein and *The Magnificent Seven,*" film music expert Jon Burlingame compares musical and visual rhythm, which are sometimes strikingly in contrast. He also analyzes how the score's themes and orchestrations function in the narrative.

"Anatomy of a Scene" analyzes the style in a sequence from *Far from Heaven.* It covers the production design and costumes, cinematography, acting, editing, and music. At the end, the completed scene is shown.

4

We launched our study of film as art by asking how our experience of a movie is shaped by technology and the process of production, distribution, and exhibition (Chapter 1). Then we considered how that experience is affected by a film's overall form, particularly narrative form (Chapters 2–3). We went on to examine how the techniques of the film medium—mise-en-scene, cinematography, editing, and sound—give the filmmaker a wide range of artistic choices (Chapters 4–8). In the next two chapters, we'll consider how filmmakers and audiences share certain expectations about the kinds of films that can be made and seen.

In most video stores, films are filed under different headings—by star, by period (Silent Movies), occasionally by director (Alfred Hitchcock, Woody Allen), by place of origin (Foreign Films). In order to understand how films work and how we experience them, we need to gain a sense of some significant ways audiences, filmmakers, reviewers, and film scholars sort films into groups.

One popular way of grouping fiction films is by *genre,* such as Westerns, mu-

Types of Films

sicals, war films, science fiction, and so on. These terms are used in everyday writing and talk, yet few of us stop to think how we come to share common assumptions about fitting movies into such categories. In Chapter 9, we'll examine the concept of genres and consider how genre categories affect people's attitudes toward the films they see. We'll look briefly at three widely recognized genres: the Western, the horror film, and the musical.

Another way we group films is based on ideas of how they were made and what effects they attempt to achieve. In Chapter 10, we'll discuss three major types of filmmaking: documentary, experimental, and animation.

Documentary films, as their name implies, document some aspect of the world. They are distinguished from fiction films because they are assumed to assert factual claims about the real world. Another particular kind of filmmaking is termed *experimental.* Such films play with film form and conventions in ways that confound audience expectations and provide unusual emotional appeals or intellectual challenges.

Finally, animated films are defined by the way they are made, using drawings, models, or other subjects photographed frame by frame to create illusory movements that never existed in front of the camera. Although we often think of animated films as being for children,

9
CHAPTER

Film Genres

All moviegoers are familiar with the idea of genre, even if they don't know the term. The word *genre* is originally French, and it simply means "kind" or "type." It's related to another word, *genus,* which is used in the biological sciences to classify groups of plants and animals. When we speak of film genres, we're indicating certain types of movies. The science-fiction film, the action picture, the comedy, the romance, the musical, the Western—these are some genres of fictional storytelling cinema.

Scientists can usually place plants or animals within a single genus with confidence, but film genres lack that sort of scientific precision. Instead, genres are convenient terms that develop informally. Filmmakers, industry decision makers, critics, and viewers all contribute to the formation of a shared sense that certain films seem to resemble one another in significant ways. Genres also change over time, as filmmakers invent new twists on old formulas. Thus defining the precise boundaries between genres can be tricky.

The popular cinema of most countries rests on genre filmmaking. Germany has its *Heimatfilm,* the tale of small-town life. The Hindi cinema of India produces *devotionals,* films centering on the lives of saints and religious figures, as well as *mythologicals* derived from legend and literary classics. Mexican filmmakers developed the *cabaretera,* a type of melodrama centering on prostitutes.

When we think about genre, the examples that come to mind are usually those of fictional live-action films. We'll see in the next chapter that there can be genres of other basic sorts of cinema, too. There are genres of documentary, such as the compilation film and the concert movie. Experimental films and animated films have genres as well.

Understanding Genre

Defining a Genre

Audiences know the genres of their culture very well, and so do filmmakers. The intriguing problem comes in defining just what a genre is. What places a group of films in a genre?

Most scholars now agree that no genre can be defined in a single hard-and-fast way. Some genres stand out by their subjects or themes. A gangster film centers on large-scale urban crime. A science fiction film features a technology beyond the reach of contemporary science. A Western is usually about life on some frontier (not necessarily the American West, as *North to Alaska* and *Drums Along the Mohawk* suggest).

Yet subject matter or theme is not so central to defining other genres. Musicals are recognizable chiefly by their manner of presentation: singing, dancing, or both.

The detective film is partly defined by the plot pattern of an investigation that solves a mystery. And some genres are defined by the distinctive emotional effect they aim for: amusement in comedies, tension in suspense films.

The question is complicated by the fact that genres can be more or less broad. There are large, blanket genre categories that fit many films. We refer commonly to thrillers, yet that term may encompass horror films, detective stories, hostage films such as *Die Hard* or *Speed,* and many others. "Comedy" is a similarly broad term that includes slapstick comedies such as *Liar Liar,* romantic comedies such as *Knocked Up,* parodies such as the *Austin Powers* series, and gross-out comedies such as *There's Something About Mary.* Thus *subgenres* can be devised by critics, viewers, or filmmakers to try to describe more precisely what films are like.

Still, there are limits to the precision with which the concept of genre can be applied. Any category contains both undeniable instances and fuzzy cases. *Singin' in the Rain* is a prime example of a musical, but David Byrne's *True Stories,* with its ironic presentation of musical numbers, is more of a borderline case. And an audience's sense of the core cases can change over history. For modern audiences, a gory film such as *The Silence of the Lambs* probably exemplifies the thriller, whereas for audiences of the 1950s, a prime example would have been an urbane Hitchcock exercise such as *North by Northwest.*

In other cases, films may seem to straddle two genre classifications. Is *Groundhog Day* a romantic comedy or a fantasy? Is *Psycho* a slasher film or a mystery thriller? *War of the Worlds* combines horror, science fiction, and family melodrama. (As we'll see, mixing formulas like this is one important source of innovation and change in genres.) And, further, some films are so distinctive that critics and audiences have trouble assigning them to a category. When *Being John Malkovich* appeared in 1999, TV interviewers joked with the cast and crew about how impossible the film was to describe—hinting that they simply could not place it in a genre.

How are genre categories used? They certainly affect industry officials' decisions about what films to make. While big-budget musicals such as *The Sound of Music* were commonly produced in the 1960s, they are out of fashion now, and more recent musicals such as *Chicago* and *Mamma Mia* were not expensive to produce. On the other hand, horror and action films are currently popular, and executives would be likelier to green-light projects perceived to fit into those genres.

For the vast publicity system that exists around filmmaking, genres are a simple way to characterize a film. In fact, reviewers are often central in gathering and crystallizing notions about genres. In television coverage of entertainment, reporters refer to genres, because they know that most members of the public will easily grasp what they mean.

You may also find that some reviewers tend to dismiss genre films as shallow and trivial, assuming them to be simply formulaic: it's only a Western; it's just a horror film. Undoubtedly, many films in all genres are cheaply and unimaginatively made. Yet some of the greatest films also fall into genres. *Singin' in the Rain* is arguably also one of the best American films. *Grand Illusion* is a war film. *Psycho* is a thriller. *The Godfather* is a gangster film. On the whole, genre is a category best used to describe and analyze films, not to evaluate them.

For viewers, genre often provides a way of finding a film they want to see. If a group plans an evening at the movies, members may express their preferences for a science fiction film, or a thriller, or a romance and then negotiate from there. Some filmgoers are fans of a specific genre and may seek out and exchange information via magazines, Internet sites, or conventions. Science fiction aficionados are one example of such a group, with subgroups pledging allegiance to the *Star Wars* or the *Star Trek* series.

At all levels of the filmmaking and film-viewing processes, then, genres help assure that most members of a culture share at least some general notions about the types of films that compete for our attention.

Analyzing a Genre

As we have seen, genres are based on a tacit agreement among filmmakers, reviewers, and audiences. What gives the films some common identity are shared *genre conventions.*

Certain plot elements may be conventional. We anticipate an investigation in a mystery film; revenge plotlines are common in Westerns; a musical will find ways to provide song-and-dance situations. The gangster film usually centers on the gangster's rise and fall as he struggles against police and rival gangs. We expect a biographical film ("biopic") to trace major episodes in the main character's life. In a cop thriller, certain characters are conventional: the shifty informer, the comic sidekick, the exasperated captain who despairs of getting the squad to follow procedure.

Other genre conventions are more thematic, involving general meanings that are summoned again and again. The Hong Kong martial-arts film commonly celebrates loyalty and obedience to one's teacher. A standard theme of the gangster film has been the price of criminal success, with the gangster's rise to power portrayed as a hardening into egotism and brutality. The screwball comedy traditionally sets up a thematic opposition between a stiff, unyielding social milieu and characters' urges for freedom and innocent zaniness.

Still other genre conventions involve characteristic film techniques. Somber lighting is standard in the horror film and the thriller **(9.1).** The action picture often relies on rapid cutting and slow-motion violence. In the melodrama, an emotional twist may be underscored by a sudden burst of poignant music.

As a visual medium, cinema can also define genres through conventional *iconography.* A genre's iconography consists of recurring symbolic images that carry meaning from film to film.

Objects and settings often furnish iconography for a genre. A close-up of a tommy gun lifted out of a 1920s Ford would probably be enough to identify a film as a gangster movie, while a shot of a long, curved sword hanging from a kimono would place us in the world of the samurai. The war film takes place in battle-scarred landscapes, the backstage musical in theaters and nightclubs, the space-travel film in starships and on distant planets. Even stars can become iconographic—Judy Garland for the musical, John Wayne for the Western, Arnold Schwarzenegger for the action picture, Jim Carrey for comedy.

By knowing conventions, the viewer has a pathway into the film. Such landmarks allow the genre movie to communicate information quickly and economically. When we see the weak sheriff, we strongly suspect that he will not stand up to the outlaw gang. We can then focus attention on the cowboy hero as he is slowly drawn into helping the townspeople defend themselves.

Alternatively, a film can revise or reject the conventions associated with its genre. *Bugsy Malone* is a gangster musical in which children play all the traditional

9.1   In *The Exorcist,* a single streetlight picks out the priest as he arrives at night, while light streams from the room where the possessed girl is confined.

adult roles. *2001: A Space Odyssey* violated several conventions of the science-fiction genre: beginning with a lengthy sequence set in prehistoric times, synchronizing classical music to outer-space action, and ending with an enigmatically symbolic fetus drifting through space. Filmmakers may seek to surprise or shock viewers by breaking their expectations that a certain convention will be followed. (See "A Closer Look.")

Audiences expect the genre film to offer something familiar, but they also demand fresh variations on it. The filmmaker may devise something mildly or radically different, but it will still be based on tradition. The interplay of convention and innovation, familiarity and novelty, is central to the genre film.

"Fixed forms can yield infinite, ingenious variations."

— Joyce Carroll Oates, novelist

Genre History

Because filmmakers frequently play with conventions and iconography, genres seldom remain unchanged for very long. The broader, blanket genres such as thrillers, romances, and comedies may stay popular for decades, but a comedy from the 1920s is likely to be very different from one in the 1960s. Genres change over history. Their conventions get recast, and by mixing conventions from different genres, filmmakers create new possibilities surprisingly often.

Many film genres become established by borrowing existing conventions from other media. The melodrama has clear antecedents in stage plays and novels such as *Uncle Tom's Cabin*. Types of comedy can be traced back to stage farces or comic novels. Musicals draw on both musical comedies and variety reviews.

Yet the film medium always imposes its own distinctive qualities and circumstances on an adopted genre. For example, Western novels were already popular in the 19th century. Yet, although the cinema became commercially successful in 1895, Westerns did not become a film genre until after 1908. Why the delay? It may well have been that the greater length of films around that era (up to roughly 15 minutes), plus the rise of film studios with companies of actors under contract, encouraged more shooting on location. Using rural American landscapes in turn fostered stories involving the frontier, and the Western quickly became a tremendously popular genre. It was also a uniquely American genre, giving U.S. films a way to compete in the growing international market. Thus film genres have their own history, combining borrowings from other arts and distinctive innovations.

One important pressure on genres is technology. The musical film crystallized with the arrival of synchronized sound, and the development of color processes favored genres of spectacle, like Westerns, musicals, and historical dramas. Most recently, computer-generated imagery has made it easy to conjure up unreal creatures and imaginary landscapes. Digital special effects have encouraged the expansion of the fantasy and science-fiction genres, as well as films based on animated cartoons (such as *Speed Racer*) and on comic-book superheroes (**9.2**).

9.2 The emergence of CGI special effects encouraged filmmakers to adapt more comic books for the screen. Now films like *Iron Man* could realistically show superheroes' unearthly powers.

A CONTEMPORARY GENRE: The Crime Thriller

The thriller, like the comedy, is a very broad category, virtually an umbrella genre. There are supernatural thrillers (*The Sixth Sense*), political thrillers (*Munich*), and spy thrillers (*The Bourne Ultimatum*), but many revolve around crime—planned, committed, or thwarted.

During the 1990s and 2000s, many filmmaking countries turned to making crime thrillers. Using few special effects and set in contemporary urban locations, they are comparatively cheap to produce. They offer showy roles to actors, and they allow writers and directors to display their ingenuity in playing with the audience's expectations. Although the genre has fuzzy edges, we can chart some core cases by considering the narrative conventions and the effects that filmmakers try to arouse.

A crime is at the center of the thriller plot, and usually three sorts of characters are involved. There are the lawbreakers, the forces of law, and the innocent victims or bystanders. Typically, the narration concentrates on one of these characters or groups.

In *Double Jeopardy*, a husband fakes his own death in order to run off with his mistress. His wife is found guilty of his murder, but in prison, she discovers that her husband is alive under a new identity. Released on parole, she flees to find her son, but she is pursued by her hard-bitten parole officer. Suspense arises from the double chase and the cat-and-mouse game played by the desperate husband and his embittered "widow," who can now murder him with impunity. The plot action and narration are organized around the wife: her pursuit propels the action forward, and the narration favors her, restricting us largely to what she believes and eventually learns.

Double Jeopardy concentrates on an innocent person who is the target of the crime, and this is one common pattern in the genre. At some point, the victim will usually realize that he or she cannot react passively and must fight the criminal, as in *Duel, The Fugitive, The Net, Breakdown,* and *Panic Room* **(9.3).** In *Ransom,* the father of a kidnapped boy spurns police advice and refuses to pay the ransom, offering it as a bounty on the criminals.

Alternatively, the plot may center on an innocent bystander dropped unexpectedly into a struggle between the criminal and the police. Most of Alfred Hitchcock's films are built around an ordinary person who stumbles into a dangerous situation (*The 39 Steps, North by Northwest, Rear Window*). In *Die Hard,* an off-duty detective is accidentally trapped in a hostage crisis, so he must fight both police and thieves to rescue the other innocents. *Collateral* centers on a taxi driver forced to chauffeur a paid killer from target to target. Thematically, this innocent-centered plot pattern often emphasizes characters discovering resources within themselves—courage, cleverness, even a capacity for violence.

Instead of spotlighting the innocents, the plot may concentrate on the forces of justice. The action then typically becomes an investigation, in which police or private detectives seek to capture the criminal or prevent a crime. A classic example is *The Big Heat,* in which a rogue cop seeks to avenge the death of his family by capturing the mobsters responsible. *Nick of Time, The Bodyguard,* and *In the Line of Fire* present protagonists seeking to forestall a threatened murder. The contemporary serial-killer plot may emphasize police pursuit, offering only glimpses of the criminal. *Se7en* follows two policemen in their efforts to untangle a string of murders emblematic of the seven deadly sins. When a plot highlights the investigators, themes of the fallibility of justice tend to come to the fore.

9.3 Innocents in jeopardy: an unusual camera position for a classic thriller situation in *Panic Room*.

In *L.A. Confidential,* three ill-matched detectives join forces to reveal how official corruption has led to the murders of prostitutes.

Or the crime thriller can put the criminal center stage, as in *The Talented Mr. Ripley.* The plot may center on the adventures of a paid killer; Jean-Pierre Melville's *Le Samourai* is a classic example. There's also the heist or caper film, showcasing a tightly orchestrated robbery. This subgenre became a mainstay in the 1950s, with *The Asphalt Jungle, Bob Le Flambeur,* and *Rififi,* and it's made a comeback in recent years with *Heist, Ronin,* and the *Ocean's 11* series. There's also what we might call the dishonor-among-thieves variant, in which criminals betray one another. *A Simple Plan* portrays nervous and clumsy thieves, whereas *Jackie Brown* traces an expanding web of double-crosses.

Sometimes the thriller will balance its plot and narration between the police and the criminal. Often this tactic draws thematic parallels between the two. In John Woo's *The Killer,* the plot alternates between showing the efforts of a hit man to quit the business, aided by his weak mentor, and showing his cop adversary, who is also under the sway of an older colleague. Michael Mann's *Heat* creates strong parallels between cop and robber, each having problems with the women in their lives. In both *The Killer* and *Heat,* the characters themselves recognize their affinities. In contrast, *Fargo* plays on the sharp differences between the sunny common sense of the policewoman and an almost pitiably blundering kidnapper.

Thrillers obviously aim to thrill us—that is, to startle, shock, and scare. How do we distinguish them from horror films, which seek similar effects? Horror aims to disgust as well as frighten, but the thriller need not involve disgust. The central character of a horror film is a monster who is both fearsome and repellent, but a thriller villain may be quite attractive (the deceptively kind men in *The Minus Man* and *Primal Fear,* the treacherous women in *Red Rock West* and *The Last Seduction*). While suspense and surprise are important in all cinematic storytelling, these responses dominate the crime thriller. The plots highlight clever plans, still more clever blocking moves, and sudden coincidences that upset carefully timed schemes. Tracing out a plan or following an investigation can yield suspense (Will the criminal succeed? How?), while unexpected twists trigger surprise, forcing us to reconsider the odds of the criminal's success.

More specifically, the thriller's effects depend on which characters are highlighted by the plot and narration. If the protagonist is an innocent, the suspense we feel comes from the prospect that the crime will harm him or her. If the hero is a figure of justice, we become concerned that she or he will not be able to protect the innocents.

When the protagonist is the criminal, one way to achieve some sympathy is to rank the lawbreakers on a scale of immorality. The most sympathetic criminals will be ones who are trying to get out of the business (*The Killer*) or those who oppose even more immoral figures. The heroes of *Out of Sight* are easygoing, good-humored thieves ripping off a white-collar embezzler and a band of sociopathic killers. Sometimes criminal protagonists can stretch our sympathies in complicated ways. In *A Simple Plan,* basically good people turn crooked after a momentary weakness, and even though they have done wrong, we may find ourselves hoping that they succeed in their crime. *A History of Violence* provokes us to speculate on the mysterious forces that can make someone a killer **(9.4).**

Like any genre, the crime thriller can mix with others. It blends with the horror film in *From Dusk Till Dawn* and with science fiction in *Blade Runner* and *Minority Report. Rush Hour* pushes the police investigation toward farce, while *Lock, Stock, and Two Smoking Barrels* piles up absurd coincidences around a quartet of petty crooks who steal ganja and money from a gang (who stole the goods from another gang).

9.4 In *A History of Violence,* Tom Stall, quiet owner of a small-town diner, is revealed to have a killer's instincts.

The thriller's emphasis on suspense and surprise encourages filmmakers to mislead the audience, and this can lead to experiments with narrative form. Hitchcock pioneered this tendency by suddenly switching protagonists in *Psycho* and by letting two couples' lives intertwine in *Family Plot*. Many films whose plots play with story time (see pp. 00–00) are crime thrillers. A crime in the story may be replayed in the plot, showing different clues each time (*Snake Eyes*) or presenting different points of view (*The Killing, Jackie Brown*). *Memento* tells its investigation story in reverse order. *The Usual Suspects* creates an unreliable flashback narration, at the end turning a minor character into a major player **(9.5)**. *Bound* consists largely of flashbacks launched from a cryptic present-time situation—a woman tied and gagged in a closet. As the crime story is revealed, we have reason to suspect that at some phase the robbery scheme she and her partner have devised will fail.

Independent filmmakers have found that general audiences will accept narrational experiments when packaged in this genre. For other independents, the genre offers a structure on which they can hang their personal concerns. David Mamet's interest in how people conceal their true motives surfaces in *House of Games* and *The Spanish Prisoner*. Joel and Ethan Coen set *Blood Simple* and *The Man Who Wasn't There* in bleak, small-town locales populated with losers lusting for one big chance. David Lynch uses the genre's tactics of suspense and surprise to summon up a dread-filled atmosphere that may never receive rational explanation. In *Blue Velvet, Lost Highway,* and *Mulholland Drive,* the crimes are ominous but obscure, the criminals nightmarish grotesques, and the innocents not wholly innocent.

Because crime thrillers can be shot fairly cheaply, the genre has offered Hollywood's rivals a path to international distribution. Hong Kong has exported many such films, as has France (*La Femme Nikita*), Britain (*Snatch, Sexy Beast*), Japan (*Fireworks, Cure*), Korea (*Tell Me Something, Nowhere to Hide*), and Thailand (*Bangkok Dangerous*). Audiences worldwide share similar expectations about crime thrillers, and filmmakers can innovate by injecting local cultural traditions into the genre's conventions of plot, character, and theme. Two of our sample analyses, of *Breathless* (pp. 410–411) and of *Chungking Express* (pp. 445–446), focus on non-Hollywood films that imaginatively shift the expectations we bring to the crime thriller.

9.5   The aftermath of the mysterious dockyard explosion that triggers the investigation in *The Usual Suspects*.

Most cinema genres and subgenres become established when one film achieves success and is widely imitated. After several films that resemble one another appear, people begin to compare them. For example, in the late 1990s, the term *gross-out* came to be commonly applied to a group of films, including *Ace Ventura, Pet Detective; There's Something About Mary;* and *American Pie*. But critics then traced this "new" subgenre back to such influential comedies as *Animal House* (1978) and *Porky's* (1981).

Similarly, when the television-related fantasy *Pleasantville* appeared in 1998, some critics linked it to comparable films: *Big* (1988), *Splash* (1984), *Peggy Sue Got Married* (1986), *Groundhog Day* (1993), *The Truman Show* (1998), and *Sliding Doors* (1998). Reviewer Richard Corliss suggested a new term for the subgenre, *fantasies of displacement*. Lisa Schwartzbaum called such films *magical comedies*. Whether these or other phrases ever become common parlance, many viewers might recognize that these films share traits that set them apart. Such comments by reviewers are one way in which new subgenres come to be recognized.

Once a genre is launched, there seems to be no fixed pattern of development. We might expect that the earliest films in the genre are the purest, with genre mixing coming at a late stage. But genre mixing can take place very soon. *Whoopee!*

(1930), a musical from the beginning of talking pictures, is also a Western. *Just Imagine* (1930), one of the first sound science-fiction films, contains a comic song. Some historians have also speculated that a genre inevitably passes from a phase of maturity to one of parody, when it begins to mock its own conventions. Yet an early Western, *The Great K & A Train Robbery* (1926), is an all-out parody of its own genre. Early slapstick comedies often take moviemaking as their subject and ruthlessly poke fun at themselves, as in Charlie Chaplin's farcical *His New Job* (1915).

Typically, genres do not remain constantly successful. Rather, they rise and fall in popularity. The result is the phenomenon known as *cycles*.

A cycle is a batch of genre films that enjoy intense popularity and influence over a distinct period. Cycles can occur when a successful film produces a burst of imitations. *The Godfather* triggered a brief spate of gangster movies. During the 1970s, there was a cycle of disaster movies (*Earthquake, The Poseidon Adventure*). There have been cycles of comedies centering on spaced-out teenagers (*Wayne's World, Bill and Ted's Excellent Adventure, Dude, Where's My Car?*), buddy-cop movies (*Lethal Weapon* and its successors), movies adapted from comic books (*Batman Begins, Spider-Man, Hellboy*), romantic thrillers aimed at a female audience (*Dead Again, Double Jeopardy*), and dramas describing coming of age in African-American neighborhoods (*Boyz N the Hood, Menace II Society*). Few observers would have predicted that science-fiction movies would return in the 1970s, but *Star Wars* created a long-lasting cycle. A cycle of fantasy adventures including the *Lord of the Rings* trilogy, the *Harry Potter* series, and the *Chronicles of Narnia* franchise, emerged in the early 2000s.

It seems likely that a genre never dies. It may pass out of fashion for a time, only to return in updated garb. The sword-and-sandal epic set in ancient times was popular in the 1950s and 1960s, then virtually disappeared until Ridley Scott revived it to considerable acclaim in 2000 with *Gladiator*—inspiring other filmmakers to undertake *Troy, Alexander,* and *300*.

A genre may also change by mixing its conventions with those of another genre. In 1979, *Alien* proved innovative because it blended science-fiction conventions with those of the contemporary horror film, centering on a monster stalking its victims one by one. The rusting spaceship became the futuristic equivalent of the old dark house full of unseen dangers. By the early 2000s, the science-fiction/horror blend was itself quite conventional, as in *Pitch Black* and *Doom*.

The musical and the comedy blend easily with other genres. During the 1930s and 1940s, singing cowboys such as Gene Autry were popular, and the Western musical was revived in the 1960s with *Cat Ballou*. There have been musical melodramas, such as *Yentl* and two versions of *A Star Is Born*. *The Rocky Horror Picture Show* created the musical horror movie.

Comedy as well can blend with any other genre. The dramatic issue at the core of *Barbershop*—whether a son should sustain his father's business for the good of the community—is lightened by sight gags, inventive insults, and scabrous monologues (**9.6**). Mel Brooks and Woody Allen have created comedies out of the conventions of science fiction (*Spaceballs, Sleeper*), Westerns (*Blazing Saddles*), outlaw films (*Take the Money and Run*), thrillers and detective stories (*High Anxiety, Manhattan Murder Mystery*), even historical epics (*History of the World Part I, Love and Death*). The combinations seem almost limitless. In *O Brother, Where Art Thou?* bumbling prison escapees accidentally become country singing stars, and the result is at once an outlaw movie, a social protest film, a slapstick comedy, and a musical.

In some cases, genres influence and mix with one another across cultures. The Japanese swordplay genre, with its conventions of swordplay and revenge, has blended well with a parallel genre, the Western. Sergio Leone based his Italian Western *For a Fistful of Dollars* loosely on the plot of Akira Kurosawa's

"So it's kind of a psychic political thriller comedy with a heart."

"With a heart. And not unlike Ghost *meets* Manchurian Candidate.*"*

— Producer and screenwriter in the opening scene of Robert Altman's *The Player*

9.6 *Barbershop:* Eddie's rants offer a comically skeptical attitude toward Rosa Parks and other African-American icons.

Yojimbo, and the same Japanese director's *Seven Samurai* provided the basis for the Hollywood Western *The Magnificent Seven.* Similarly, widespread fan interest in Hong Kong movies during the 1980s and 1990s led the Wachowski brothers to mix high-tech science-fiction effects with Hong Kong martial-arts choreography in *The Matrix.*

Such mixtures are often consciously recognized by filmmakers and audiences alike. Filmmakers may take elements of two or more successful films, blend them, and spin off an entirely new concept. Similarly, spectators are used to comparing new films with existing ones. If someone who has not seen *Pleasantville* asks a friend what it is like, the reply might be "It's sort of a combination of *The Truman Show* and *Back to the Future.*" That is, it's a fantasy film dealing with television, but it also has a science-fiction element of a time machine.

The fact that genres can intermingle does not, however, mean that there are no distinctions among them. *The Matrix* does not prevent us from differentiating standard Hong Kong martial-arts films from standard Hollywood science-fiction tales. Although we cannot pin down a single description of a genre that will apply for all time, we can recognize that at a given period of film history, filmmakers, reviewers, and audiences manage to distinguish one sort of movie from another.

The Social Functions of Genres

The fact that every genre has fluctuated in popularity reminds us that genres are tightly bound to cultural factors. Why do audiences enjoy seeing the same conventions over and over? Many film scholars believe that genres are ritualized dramas resembling holiday celebrations—ceremonies that are satisfying because they reaffirm cultural values with little variation. At the end of *Saving Private Ryan* or *You've Got Mail,* who can resist a surge of reassuring satisfaction that cherished values—self-sacrificing heroism, the desirability of romantic love—have been validated? And just as one can see these ceremonies as helping us forget the more disturbing aspects of the world, the familiar characterizations and plots of genres may also serve to distract the audience from real social problems.

Some scholars would argue that genres go further and actually exploit ambivalent social values and attitudes. The gangster film, for instance, makes it possible for audiences to relish the mobster's swagger while still feeling satisfied when he receives his punishment. Seen from this standpoint, genre conventions arouse emotion by touching on deep social uncertainties but then channel those emotions into approved attitudes.

Because of the contract between filmmaker and audience, the promise of something new based on something familiar, genres may also respond quickly to broad social trends. During the economic depression of the 1930s, for instance, the Warner Bros.'s musical films introduced social commentary into stage numbers; in *Gold Diggers of 1933,* a singer asks the Depression-era audience to remember "my forgotten man," the unemployed war veteran. More recently, Hollywood producers have tried to tailor romantic comedies to the tastes of twenty-somethings, as in *50 First Dates, Along Came Polly,* and *The Wedding Crashers.* In Chapter 11, we'll consider how another musical, *Meet Me in St. Louis,* bears traces of concerns of the U.S. home front during World War II.

It is common to suggest that at different points in history, the stories, themes, values, or imagery of the genre harmonize with public attitudes. For instance, don't the science-fiction films of the 1950s, with hydrogen bombs creating Godzilla and other monsters, reveal fears of technology run amok? The hypothesis is that genre conventions, repeated from film to film, reflect the audience's pervasive doubts or anxieties. Many film scholars would argue that this reflectionist approach helps explain why genres vary in popularity.

Social processes can also be reflected in genre innovations. Ripley, the female protagonist of *Aliens,* is a courageous, even aggressive, warrior who also has a warm, maternal side **(9.7, 9.8).** This is something of a novelty in the science-fiction genre. Many commentators saw Ripley as a product of attitudes derived from the Women's Movement of the 1970s. Feminist groups argued that women could be seen as active and competent without losing positive qualities associated with feminine behavior, such as gentleness and sympathy. As these ideas spread through mainstream media and social opinion, films such as *Aliens* could turn traditionally masculine roles over to female characters.

Such ways of looking at genre are usually called *reflectionist,* because they assume that genres reflect social attitudes, as if in a mirror. But some critics would object that reflectionist readings can become oversimplified. If we look closely at a genre film, we usually discover complexities that nuance a reflectionist account. For instance, if we look beyond Ripley, the protagonist of *Aliens,* we find that all the characters lie along a continuum running between "masculine" and "feminine" values, and the survivors of the adventure, male or female, seem to blend the best of both gender identities. Moreover, often what seems to be social reflection is simply the film industry's effort to exploit the day's headlines. A genre film may reflect not the audience's hopes and fears but the filmmakers' guess about what will sell.

Whether we study a genre's history, its cultural functions, or its representations of social trends, conventions remain our best point of departure. As examples, we look briefly at three significant genres of American fictional filmmaking.

9.7 In *Aliens,* Ripley learns how to use a weapon . . .

9.8 . . . but can also comfort the orphaned girl the group of soldiers find.

Three Genres

The Western

The Western emerged early in the history of cinema, becoming well established by the early 1910s. It is partly based on historical reality, since in the American West there were cowboys, outlaws, settlers, and tribes of Native Americans. Films also based their portrayal of the frontier on songs, popular fiction, and Wild West shows. Early actors sometimes mirrored this blend of realism and myth: cowboy star Tom Mix had been a Texas Ranger, a Wild West performer, and a champion rodeo rider.

Quite early, the central theme of the genre became the conflict between civilized order and the lawless frontier. From the East and the city come the settlers who want to raise families, the schoolteachers who aim to spread learning, and the bankers and government officials. In the vast natural spaces, by contrast, thrive those outside civilization—not only the American Indians but also outlaws, trappers and traders, and greedy cattle barons.

Iconography reinforces this basic duality. The covered wagon and the railroad are set against the horse and canoe; the schoolhouse and church contrast with the lonely campfire in the hills. As in most genres, costume is iconographically significant, too. The settlers' starched dresses and Sunday suits stand out against Indians' tribal garb and the cowboys' jeans and Stetsons.

Interestingly, the typical Western hero stands between the two thematic poles. At home in the wilderness but naturally inclined toward justice and kindness, the cowboy is often poised between savagery and civilization. William S. Hart, one of the most popular early Western stars, crystallized the character of the "good bad man" as a common protagonist. In *Hell's Hinges* (1916), a minister's sister tries to reform him; one shot represents the pull between two ways of life (**9.9**).

The in-between position of the hero affects common Western plots. He may start out on the side of the lawless, or he may simply stand apart from the conflict. In either case, he becomes uneasily attracted to the life offered by the newcomers to the frontier. Eventually, the hero decides to join the forces of order, helping them fight hired gunmen, bandits, or whatever the film presents as a threat to stability and progress.

As the genre developed, it adhered to a social ideology implicit in its conventions. White populations' progress westward was considered a historic mission, while the conquered indigenous cultures were usually treated as primitive and savage. Western films are full of racist stereotypes of Native Americans and Hispanics. Yet on a few occasions, filmmakers treated Native American characters as tragic figures, ennobled by their closeness to nature but facing the extinction of their way of life. The best early example is probably *The Last of the Mohicans* (1920).

Moreover, the genre was not wholly optimistic about taming the wilderness. The hero's eventual commitment to civilization's values was often tinged with regret for his loss of freedom. In John Ford's *Straight Shooting* (1917), Cheyenne Harry (played by Harry Carey) is hired by a villainous rancher to evict a farmer, but he falls in love with the farmer's daughter and vows to reform. Rallying the farmers, Harry helps defeat the rancher. Still, he is reluctant to settle down with Molly (**9.10**).

Within this set of values, a great many conventional scenes became standardized—the Indians' attack on forts or wagon trains, the shy courting of a woman by the rough-hewn hero, the hero's discovery of a burned settler's shack, the outlaws' robbery of a bank or stagecoach, the climactic gunfight on dusty town streets. Writers and directors could distinguish their films by novel handlings of these elements. In Sergio Leone's flamboyant Italian Westerns, every convention is stretched out in minute detail or amplified to a huge scale, as when the climactic shootout in *The Good, the Bad, and the Ugly* (1966) is filmed to resemble a bullfight (**9.11**).

9.9   The "good bad" hero of *Hell's Hinges* reads the Bible, a bottle of whiskey at his elbow.

9.10   In *Straight Shooting,* the hero stands framed in the farmhouse doorway, halfway between the lure of civilization and the call of the wilderness.

9.11   A low wall creates an arena in which the three-way shoot-out occurs at the end of *For a Few Dollars More*.

There were narrative and thematic innovations as well. After such liberal Westerns of the 1950s as *Broken Arrow* (1950), native cultures began to be treated with more respect. In *Little Big Man* (1970) and *Soldier Blue* (1970), the conventional thematic values were reversed, depicting Indian life as civilized and white society as marauding. Some films played up the hero's uncivilized side, showing him perilously out of control (*Winchester 73,* 1950), or even psychopathic (*The Left-Handed Gun,* 1958). The heroes of *The Wild Bunch* (1969) would have been considered unvarnished villains in early Westerns.

The new complexity of the protagonist is evident in John Ford's *The Searchers* (1956). After a Comanche raid on his brother's homestead, Ethan Edwards sets out to find his kidnapped niece Debbie. He is driven primarily by family loyalty but also by his secret love for his brother's wife, who has been raped and killed by the raiders. Ethan's sidekick, a young man who is part Cherokee, realizes that Ethan plans not to rescue Debbie but to kill her for becoming a Comanche wife. Ethan's fierce racism and raging vengeance culminate in a raid on the Comanche village. At the film's close, Ethan returns to civilization but pauses on the cabin's threshold (**9.12**) before turning back to the desert.

The shot eerily recalls Ford's *Straight Shooting* (9.10); John Wayne even repeats Harry Carey's characteristic gripping of his forearm (**9.13**). Now, however, it seems that the drifting cowboy is condemned to live outside civilization because he cannot tame his grief and hatred. More savage than citizen, he seems condemned, as he says of the souls of dead Comanches, "to wander forever between the winds." This bitter treatment of a perennial theme illustrates how drastically a genre's conventions can change across history.

"I knew Wyatt Earp. In the very early silent days, a couple of times a year he would come up to visit pals, cowboys he knew in Tombstone; a lot of them were in my company. I think I was an assistant prop boy then and I used to give him a chair and a cup of coffee, and he told me about the fight at the O.K. Corral. So in My Darling Clementine, *we did it exactly the way it had been. They didn't just walk up the street and start banging away at each other; it was a clever military manoeuvre."*

— John Ford, director, *Stagecoach*

9.12   The closing shot of *The Searchers*.

9.13   Harry Carey's gesture in *Straight Shooting*.

The Horror Film

While the Western is most clearly defined by subject, theme, and iconography, the horror genre is most recognizable by the emotional effect it tries to arouse. The horror film aims to shock, disgust, repel—in short, to horrify. This impulse is what shapes the genre's other conventions.

What can horrify us? Typically, a monster. In the horror film, the monster is a dangerous breach of nature, a violation of our normal sense of what is possible. The monster might be unnaturally large, as King Kong is. The monster might violate the boundary between the dead and the living, as vampires and zombies do. The monster might be an ordinary human who is transformed, as when Dr. Jekyll drinks his potion and becomes the evil Mr. Hyde. Or the monster might be something wholly unknown to science, as with the creature in the *Alien* films. The genre's horrifying emotional effect, then, is usually created by a character convention: a threatening, unnatural monster.

Other conventions follow from this one. Our reaction to the monster may be guided by other characters who react to it in the properly horrified way. In *Cat People* (1942), a mysterious woman can, apparently, turn into a panther. Our revulsion and fear are confirmed by the reaction of the woman's husband and his coworker (**9.14**). In contrast, we know that *E.T.* is not a horror film because, although the alien is unnatural, he is not threatening, and the children do not react to him as if he is.

The horror plot will often start with the monster's attack on normal life. In response, the other characters must discover that the monster is at large and try to destroy it. (In some cases, as when a character is possessed by demons, others may seek to rescue him or her.) This plot can be developed in various ways—by having the monster launch a series of attacks, by having people in authority resist believing that the monster exists, or by blocking the characters' efforts to destroy it. In *The Exorcist,* for example, the characters only gradually discover that Regan is possessed; after they realize this, they still must struggle to drive the demon out.

The genre's characteristic themes also stem from the intended response. If the monster horrifies us because it violates the laws of nature we know, the genre is well suited to suggest the limits of human knowledge. It is probably significant that the skeptical authorities who must be convinced of the monster's existence are often scientists. In other cases, the scientists themselves unintentionally unleash monsters through their risky experiments. A common convention of this type of plot has the characters concluding that there are some things that humans are not meant to know. Another common thematic pattern of the horror film plays on fears about the environment, as when nuclear accidents and other human-made disasters create mutant monsters like the giant ants in *Them!*

Not surprisingly, the iconography of the horror film includes settings where monsters might be expected to lurk. The old dark house where a group of potential victims gather was popularized by *The Cat and the Canary* in 1927 and has been used recently for *The Haunting* (1999) and *The Others* (2001; **9.15**). Cemeteries can yield the walking dead; scientists' laboratories, the artificial human (as in *Frankenstein*). Filmmakers have played off these conventions cleverly, as when Hitchcock juxtaposed a mundane motel with a sinister, decaying mansion in *Psycho,* or when George Romero had humans battle zombies in a shopping mall in *Dawn of the Dead.* The slasher subgenre has made superhuman killers invade everyday settings such as summer camps and suburban neighborhoods.

Heavy makeup is unusually prominent in the iconography of horror. A furry face and hands can signal transformation into a werewolf, while shriveled skin indicates a mummy. Some actors have specialized in transforming themselves into many frightening figures. Lon Chaney, who played the original Phantom in *The Phantom of the Opera* (1925), was known as "the man of a thousand faces." Boris Karloff's makeup as Frankenstein's monster in *Frankenstein* (1930) rendered him so unrecognizable that the credits of his next film informed viewers that it featured

9.14   A shadow and a character's reaction suggest an offscreen menace in *Cat People.*

An ominous high-angle framing in *The Others,* as the heroine hears a mysterious sound in the room above.

9.16   In *Nosferatu,* Max Schreck's makeup and acting make his Count Orlock eerily like a rat or a bat.

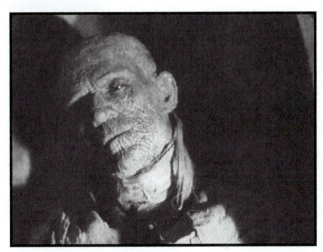

9.17   A tiny gleam reflected in Boris Karloff's eye signals the moment when the monster revives in *The Mummy*.

the same actor. More recently, computer special effects have supplemented makeup in transforming actors into monsters.

Like the Western, the horror film emerged in the era of silent moviemaking. Some of the most important early works in the genre were German—notably, *The Cabinet of Dr. Caligari* (1920) and *Nosferatu* (1922), the first adaptation of the novel *Dracula*. The angular performances, heavy makeup, and distorted settings characteristic of German Expressionist cinema conveyed an ominous, supernatural atmosphere **(9.16).**

Because a horror film can create its emotional impact with makeup and other low-technology special effects, the horror genre has long been favored by low-budget filmmakers. During the 1930s, a secondary Hollywood studio, Universal, launched a cycle of horror films. *Dracula* (1931), *Frankenstein* (1931), and *The Mummy* (1932; **9.17**) proved enormously popular and helped the studio become a major company. A decade later, RKO's B-picture unit under Val Lewton produced a cycle of literate, somber films on minuscule budgets. Lewton's directors proceeded by hints, keeping the monster offscreen and cloaking the sets in darkness. In *Cat People,* for instance, we never see the heroine transform herself into a panther, and we only glimpse the creature in certain scenes. The film achieves its effects through shadows, offscreen sound, and character reaction (9.14).

In later decades, other low-budget filmmakers were drawn to the genre. Horror became a staple of 1960s U.S. independent production, with many films targeted at the teenage market. Similarly, George Romero's *Night of the Living Dead* (1968) was budgeted at only $114,000, but its success on college campuses made it hugely profitable. *The Blair Witch Project* (1999), shot for a reputed $35,000, found an even bigger audience internationally. Low-budget horror remains a profitable genre, with *Cabin Fever* and the *Saw* and *Hostel* franchises drawing large audiences in theaters and on DVD.

During the 1970s, the genre acquired a new respectability, chiefly because of the prestige of *Rosemary's Baby* (1968) and *The Exorcist* (1973). These films innovated by presenting violent and disgusting actions with unprecedented explicitness. When the possessed Regan vomited in the face of the priest bending over her, a new standard for horrific imagery was set.

The big-budget horror film entered into a period of popularity that has not yet ended. Many major Hollywood directors have worked in the genre, and several horror films—from *Jaws* (1975) and *Carrie* (1976) to *The Sixth Sense* (1999) and *The Mummy* (1999)—have become huge hits. The genre's iconography pervades contemporary culture, decorating lunch boxes and theme park rides. Horror classics have been remade (*Cat People, Dracula*), and the genre conventions have been parodied (*Young Frankenstein, Beetlejuice*).

The horror film has sustained an audience for over 30 years, and its longevity has set scholars looking for cultural explanations. Many critics suggest that the 1970s subgenre of family horror films, such as *The Exorcist* and *Poltergeist*, reflects social concerns about the breakup of American families. Others suggest that the genre's questioning of normality and traditional categories is in tune with both the post-Vietnam and the post–Cold War eras: viewers may be uncertain of their fundamental beliefs about the world and their place in it. The continuing popularity of the teen-oriented slasher films from the 1980s to the present might reflect young people's fascination with and simultaneous anxieties about sexuality and violence. Fans are also drawn by the sophisticated special effects and makeup, so filmmakers compete to show ever gorier and more grotesque imagery. For all these reasons, horror-film conventions grew so pervasive that parodies such as the *Scary Movie* franchise and *Shaun of the Dead* became as popular as the films they mocked. Through genre mixing and the give-and-take between audience tastes and filmmakers' ambitions, the horror film has displayed that balance of convention and innovation basic to any genre.

The Musical

If the Western was largely based on the subject matter of the American frontier, and the horror film on the emotional effect on the spectator, the musical came into being in response to a technical innovation. Though there had been occasional attempts to synchronize live vocal and musical accompaniment to scenes of singing and dancing during the silent era, the notion of basing a film on a series of musical numbers did not emerge until the late 1920s with the successful introduction of recorded sound tracks. One of the earliest features to include the human voice extensively was *The Jazz Singer* (1927), which contained almost no recorded dialogue but had several songs.

At first, many musicals were *revues*, programs of numbers with little or no narrative linkage between them. Such revue musicals aided in selling these early sound films in foreign-language markets, where spectators could enjoy the performances even if they could not understand the dialogue and lyrics. As subtitles and dubbing solved the problem of the language barrier, musicals featured more complicated story lines. Filmmakers devised plots that could motivate the introduction of musical numbers.

Two typical plot patterns of the musical emerged during the 1930s. One of these was the *backstage musical,* with the action centering on singers and dancers who perform for an audience within the story world. Warner Bros.'s successful early musical, *42nd Street* (1933), set the classic pattern for backstage musicals by casting dancer Ruby Keeler as the understudy for a big musical star who breaks her leg just before the big opening. The director tells Keeler, "You're going out a youngster, but you've *got* to come back a star!" and indeed she wins the audience's cheers **(9.18).** During the decade, Warner's elaborately choreographed Busby Berkeley musicals, MGM's pairing of the youthful Judy Garland and Mickey Rooney in a series of "Let's put on a show!" plots, and RKO's elegant cycle of films starring the dance team of Fred Astaire and Ginger Rogers all established the conventions of the backstage musical. Later examples included musicals where the characters are film performers, as in *Singin' in the Rain* (1952). More recent backstage musicals are *The Commitments, That Thing You Do!, What's Love Got to Do with It,* and *Dreamgirls.*

Not all musicals take place in a show business situation, however. There is also the *straight musical,* where people may sing and dance in situations of everyday life. Even in backstage musicals, the characters occasionally break into song in an everyday setting. Straight musicals are often romantic comedies, in which characters typically trace the progress of their courtship by breaking into song to express their fears, longings, and joys. We analyze one such film, *Meet Me in St. Louis,* in Chapter 11. In 1968, a French director took the romantic musical to extremes by having his characters in *The Young Girls of Rochefort* sing most of the dialogue in the film, with dozens of passersby joining in dance numbers staged in the town's streets **(9.19).** More recently, Julie Taymor blends romance and social history in *Across the Universe* **(9.20).**

9.18 Ruby Keeler hoofs her way to stardom in *42nd Street*'s title number.

9.19 The citizens of a whole town are drawn into the dance in *The Young Girls of Rochefort.*

9.20 In *Across the Universe,* a young man taking his army draft physical is greeted by the Beatles song "I Want You."

9.21   A flamboyant onstage musical number in *Moulin Rouge!* centers on the rapturous lovers.

In both backstage and straight musicals, the numbers are often associated with romance. Often the hero and heroine realize that they form the perfect romantic couple because they perform beautifully together. This happens in *Top Hat* when the Ginger Rogers character sheds her original annoyance with Fred Astaire during the "Isn't It a Wonderful Day" number, and by the end, they have clearly fallen in love. This plot device has remained a staple of the genre. Astaire again charms his reluctant partner, this time Cyd Charisse, in the "Dancing in the Dark" number in *The Band Wagon* (1953), and John Travolta meets his romantic match on the disco dance floor in *Saturday Night Fever* (1977). In *Moulin Rouge!* the lovers serenade each other, both onstage and off, with classic pop and rock songs **(9.21),** and the dance interludes in the *House Party* series often become courtship rituals.

Musicals have long been associated with children's stories, from *The Wizard of Oz* to recent films such as *Lilo and Stitch*. Many animated features contain musical numbers, a practice going back to Disney's *Snow White and the Seven Dwarfs*. But adult-oriented musicals have taken on somber, even tragic, material. *West Side Story* portrays a romance that tragically crosses ethnic lines, and *Pennies from Heaven* evokes the bleak atmosphere of the Depression through characters who lip-synch to recordings from that era. Biopics of performers, such as *Lady Sings the Blues, Ray,* and *Walk the Line,* become somber backstage musicals.

Still, while the Western and the horror film may explore the darker side of human nature, Hollywood musicals tend to accentuate the positive. High ambitions are rewarded when the show is a hit, and lovers are united in song and dance. In *The Pajama Game,* a strike is averted when the leaders of the union and management become a romantic couple. Some of these conventions persist today. *School of Rock* reconfirms the backstage musical's theme that talent and hard work will eventually win out. Even the grittier *8 Mile* follows the traditional plot pattern showing a gifted young performer overcoming disadvantages and finding success.

The range of subject matter in musicals is so broad that it may be hard to pin down specific iconography associated with the genre. Yet the backstage musical at least had its characteristic settings: the dressing rooms and wings of a theater, the flats and backdrops of the stage (as in 9.18), and the nightclub with orchestra and dance floor. Similarly, performers in these musicals are often recognizable by their distinctive stage costumes. During the 1930s, Fred Astaire wore the most famous top hat in the cinema, a hat so closely associated with his musicals that the beginning of *The Band Wagon*—where Astaire plays a washed-up movie actor—could make a joke about it. Similarly, Travolta's white suit in *Saturday Night Fever* became an icon of the disco era. Opportunities for novelty have always been present in the musical, however, as the musical numbers set in a factory (*The Pajama Game*) or in the prairie (*Oklahoma*) indicate.

The characteristic techniques of the musical are similarly diverse. Musicals tend to be brightly lit, to set off the cheerful costumes and sets and to keep the choreography of the dance numbers clearly visible. For similar reasons, color film stock was applied quite early to musicals, including Eddie Cantor's *Whoopee!* and, as we saw in Chapter 2, *The Wizard of Oz*. In order to show off the patterns formed by the dancers in musical numbers, crane shots and high angles are common. One technique widely used in the musical is not usually evident to viewers: lip-synching to prerecorded songs. On the set, they move their lips in synchronization to a playback of the recording. This technique allows the singers to move about freely and to concentrate on their acting.

The 1935 RKO Astaire–Rogers musical *Swing Time* is one of the exemplary backstage musicals. Early in the film, the hero, a gambler and tap dancer nicknamed Lucky, is trying to quit his stage act and get married. At once, we sense that his fiancée is not right for him; she is not a dancer (and is not even seen during the early scenes in which his colleagues try to trick him into missing the wedding). The opening scenes take place in the conventional settings of the stage, wings, and dressing room of a theater. Later, when Lucky goes to the city and meets the heroine, Penny (a name that echoes Lucky's precious lucky quarter), she quickly takes a strong dislike to him. An amusing scene in the dance school where she works has Lucky pretending to be hopelessly clumsy. Yet when the school's owner fires Penny, Lucky saves her job by suddenly launching into a graceful, virtuoso, and unrehearsed dance with her. By the end, her animosity has disappeared, and the school owner sets the two up to audition at a fashionable club.

Obstacles ensue, primarily in the form of a romantic rivalry between Lucky and the orchestra leader at the club. Further complications result when Penny believes mistakenly that Lucky intends to return to his fiancée. Near the end, Penny seems about to abandon Lucky to marry the conductor. She and Lucky meet, apparently for the last time, and their talk at cross-purposes reveals the link between performance and romance:

PENNY: "Does she dance very beautifully?"

LUCKY: "Who?"

PENNY: "The girl you're in love with?"

LUCKY: "Yes—very."

PENNY: "The girl you're going to marry."

LUCKY: "Oh, I don't know. I've danced with you. I'm never going to dance again."

That Fred Astaire will never dance again is the ultimate threat, and his song "Never Gonna Dance" leads into a duet that reconfirms that they are meant for each other. In the end, Lucky and Penny reconcile.

The film calls on the newly established conventions of the genre. Lucky wears Astaire's classic top hat and formal clothes **(9.22)**. Astaire and Rogers dance in the art deco–style sets that were typical of musical design in the 1930s **(9.23)**. The film departs from convention, however, in a remarkable number, "Bojangles of Harlem," where Astaire pays tribute to the great African-American dancers who had influenced him during his New York stage career in the 1920s. When he appears in blackface here, it is not to exploit a demeaning stereotype but to impersonate Bill "Bojangles" Robinson, the most famous black tap dancer of the era. (The tribute is all the more unusual because Robinson was then costarring in Shirley Temple musicals for a rival studio, Twentieth Century Fox.)

Despite its backstage settings and show business plot, *Swing Time* sets some numbers in an everyday environment. When Lucky visits Penny's apartment, he sings "The Way You Look Tonight" as she shampoos her hair—using a convenient piano in her apartment to accompany himself (though a nondiegetic orchestra plays

CONNECT TO THE BLOG
We discuss other genres on our blog. For the relationship between fantasy and sci-fi films in recent years, see "Swords vs. lightsabers," at www.davidbordwell.net/blog/?p=788. For movies based on superhero comic books, see "Superheroes for sale," at www.davidbordwell.net/blog/?p=2713.

9.22 After losing his suit in a card game, Lucky still wears his top hat in *Swing Time*.

9.23 Astaire and Rogers dance in the art deco nightclub set.

along as well). When the couple visits the snowy countryside, however, there is no diegetic accompaniment at all within the locale as they sing "A Fine Romance"—only an unseen orchestra. As we are reminded over and over in musicals, this world makes it possible for people, at any time and in any place, to express themselves through song and dance.

In studying film, we often need to make explicit some things we ordinarily take for granted—those assumptions so fundamental that we no longer even notice them. Genres, along with more basic types of film such as fiction and documentary, animation and live action, on mainstream and experimental film, are such taken-for-granted categories. At the back of our minds whenever we watch a film, these categories shape what we expect to see and hear. They guide our reactions. They press us to make sense of a movie in certain ways. Shared by filmmakers and viewers alike, these categories are a condition for film art as we most often experience it.

Yet there are other kinds of films than live-action fictional features. There are other modes of filmmaking, that, as we saw in Chapter 1, depend on ways in which the films are made and the intentions of the filmmakers. The most common are documentary, experimental, and animated cinema, and we'll examine these in the next chapter.

SUMMARY

One of the most common ways in which we approach films is by type, or genre. Genres are ways of classifying films that are largely shared across society, by filmmakers, critics, and viewers. Films are most commonly grouped into genres by virtue of similar plot patterns, similar thematic implications, characteristic filmic techniques, and recognizable iconography.

When trying to characterize a film genre, you can ask such questions as these:

1. Before you saw the film, did you know what genre it belonged to? What factors in advance or publicity conversation gave you hints?

2. What conventions in the film signal its genre? How do those conventions function? Do they allow storytelling to be more rapid and economical? Do they aim to arouse strong emotional responses?

3. What genre innovations, if any, can you find in the film? A good way to determine these is to ask if your expectations were thrown off by some developments in the film.

4. Does this film seem to be combining conventions from more than one genre? If so, how does it make the genre elements compatible? Do innovative aspects of the film depend on the genre mixing?

WHERE TO GO FROM HERE

Genres and Society

The conception of a genre's social function as ritual (p. 336) derives from the anthropological theory of Claude Lévi-Strauss. One version of the ritual model is Thomas Schatz, *Hollywood Genres* (New York: Random House, 1981). See also Jane Feuer, *The Hollywood Musical* (London: British Film Institute, 1982), and Rick Altman, *The American Film Musical* (Bloomington: Indiana University Press, 1987). Altman refined and elaborated on his views in his *Film/Genre* (London: British Film Institute, 1999), which examines many issues relating to genre theory.

Another conception of a genre's social function holds that genre films are centrally concerned with social groups—particularly women and racial minorities—that are oppressed and feared by many in a society. The genre's stories and iconography portray those groups as threatening the majority's way of life. The film's action will then work to contain and defeat these elements. One argument for this approach can be found in Robin Wood, "An Introduction to the American Horror Film," in Bill Nichols, ed., *Movies and Methods,* vol. II (Berkeley: University of California Press, 1985), pp. 195–220. For a criticism of this otherness theory, see Noël Carroll's *The Philosophy of Horror;*

or, Paradoxes of the Heart (New York: Routledge, 1990), pp. 168–206.

For a survey of approaches to genre, as well as an analysis of several Hollywood genres, see Steve Neale, *Genre and Hollywood* (London: Routledge, 2000). A variety of approaches is represented in Wheeler Winston Dixon, ed., *Film Genre 2000: New Critical Essays* (Albany: State University of New York Press, 2000).

Specific Genres

The vast array of conventions in the Western genre have been codified, along with major films and figures, in two useful reference books: Phil Hardy, ed., *The Western* (London: Aurum, 1991), and Edward Buscombe, ed., *The BFI Companion to the Western* (New York: Atheneum, 1988). Our discussion of the conventions of the Western has been shaped by John Cawelti's *The Six-Gun Mystique* (Bowling Green, OH: Bowling Green Popular Press, 1975). Howard Hughes summarizes one subgenre of the Western in *Spaghetti Westerns* (Harpenden, England: Pocket Essentials, 2001.)

Noël Carroll explores the affective aesthetics of the horror film in *The Philosophy of Horror,* cited above. Carroll's analysis, which has guided our discussion of the genre, is complemented by Cynthia A. Freeland's *The Naked and the Undead: Evil and the Appeal of Horror* (Boulder, CO: Westview Press, 2000) and by the social account offered by Andrew Tudor's *Monsters and Mad Scientists: A Cultural History of the Horror Movie* (Oxford: Blackwell, 1989). Phil Hardy, ed., *Horror* (London: Aurum, 1985), is a comprehensive reference book.

For a general history of the American musical, see Ethan Mordden, *The Hollywood Musical* (New York: St. Martin's Press, 1981). Essays on specific topics are included in Rick Altman, ed., *Genre: The Musical* (London: Routledge & Kegan Paul, 1981).

A survey of early Hollywood musicals that deals with the revue musicals and the more narratively oriented films of the 1930s is Richard Barrios's *A Song in the Dark: The Birth of the Musical Film* (New York: Oxford University Press, 1995). One of the most important production units concentrating on musicals, run by Arthur Freed, is discussed in Hugh Fordin, *The World of Entertainment: The Freed Unit at MGM* (New York: Doubleday, 1975). *Swing Time* is among the films discussed in Hannah Hyam's *Fred and Ginger: The Astaire–Rogers Partnership 1934–1938* (Brighton: Pen Press, 2007).

Websites

www.filmsite.org/genres.html A wide-ranging discussion of a great many genres, including historical summaries and key examples.

www.lewestern.com/US/1PresentationUS.htm A database devoted to the Western, with information in both French and English.

www.carfax-abbey.com A database of classic and contemporary horror films, with over 150 links to other sites.

www.musicals101.com/index.html A reference site for musical theater and cinema.

Recommended DVD Supplements

Westerns

"The Making of *Silverado*" is in some ways a conventional "making-of" documentary, with sections on rehearsal, storyboards, editing, cinematography, set design, and so on. Yet the overall emphasis is on the film as a Western. Director Lawrence Kasdan tried to revive the classic Western and to pay homage to it at the same time. Interviews with cast and crew reveal the film's techniques, but they often discuss how film form and style worked in service of the old-fashioned Western's conventions. "The Making of *Butch Cassidy and the Sundance Kid*" contains an amount of footage unusual for a late 1960s promotional documentary. It also avoids the mutually congratulatory tone of many supplement interviews, with director George Roy Hill giving a warts-and-all account of the production of this classic Western.

"A Turning of the Earth: John Ford, John Wayne, and *The Searchers*" combines accounts by the participants, contemporary footage of the production, and expert analysis of the film. A biographical overview of one of the major directors of Westerns is "Budd Boetticher—an American Original," on the DVD of one of his classic films, *Seven Men from Now.* Other interesting discussions of Westerns include "Sir Christopher Frayling on *The Magnificent Seven*" and "Leone's West" (*The Good, the Bad, and the Ugly*).

In "An Epic Explored," director James Mangold talks about making *3:10 to Yuma* in an era when Westerns are rare. The same disc has a short but information-packed documentary on the film's production, including rarely discussed topics like a gun that fires dust pellets to simulate bullet strikes. The three documentaries about *Once upon a Time in the West* actually add up to one making-of of just over an hour. Other directors analyze Leone's style, and there is much discussion of the film's place in the Western genre.

Horror Films

"Inside the Labyrinth," though primarily a making-of for *The Silence of the Lambs,* includes considerable discussion of it as a horror or thriller film. Similarly, the making-of "Behind the Scream," on *Scream,* discusses horror-film conventions.

A brief making-of featurette on *Rosemary's Baby* discusses it as "the great horror film without any horror in it," stressing its lack of special effects and its dependence on suggestion rather than explicit displays of the film's monstrous elements.

Quite possibly the most extensive DVD supplement dealing with a horror film is "The Making of *The Frighteners*," a 4½-hour documentary directed by Peter Jackson that deals with every aspect of the production—including a tour of the tiny Weta Digital facility that would later expand exponentially for *The Lord of the Rings*.

Both *Hellboy* and *Hellboy II: The Golden Army* have making-of documentaries that emphasize the monsters used in each. The second movie famously featured 32 types of monsters, created through a wide range of means, from elaborate puppets and costumes to computer-generated creatures.

Musicals

"Musicals Great Musicals: The Arthur Freed Unit at MGM," included on the *Singin' in the Rain* DVD, chronicles the golden era of musical production at the studio that also made *The Wizard of Oz, The Band Wagon, Meet Me in St. Louis,* and other classics. Excerpts from MGM musicals made in the early years of sound make this an exemplary historical survey. The DVD also includes a charming supplement, "What a Glorious Feeling," on the making of *Singin' in the Rain*.

"More Loverly Than Ever: *My Fair Lady* Then and Now," a 1994 documentary dealing not only with the film's history but with its restoration, points out that the film came at the end of a cycle of big-budget adaptations of Broadway musicals.

The "Behind the Music" supplement for *Saturday Night Fever* discusses that enormously popular film's innovations, including central characters who dance but don't sing. It traces how a musical subgenre, in this case arising from the short-lived disco fad of the 1970s, can experience a cycle of sudden success and equally sudden decline.

In "The Nightclub of Your Dreams: The Making of *Moulin Rouge!*" Nicole Kidman talks about singing live during filming rather than the usual lip-synching to a song's playback. There is also a segment on the choreography.

Documentary, Experimental, and Animated Films

Some of the most basic types of films line up as distinct alternatives. We commonly distinguish documentary from fiction, experimental films from mainstream fare, and animation from live-action filmmaking. In all these cases, we make assumptions about how the material to be filmed was chosen or arranged, how the filming was done, and how the filmmakers intended the finished work to affect the spectator. Chapter 3, on narrative form, drew its examples principally from fictional, live-action cinema. Now we'll explore these other important types of films.

Documentary

Before we see a film, we nearly always have some sense whether it is a documentary or a piece of fiction. Moviegoers entering theaters to view *March of the Penguins* expected to see real birds in nature, not wisecracking caricatures like the penguins in *Madagascar*.

What Is a Documentary?

What justifies our assumption that a film is a documentary? For one thing, a documentary typically comes to us identified as such—by its title, publicity, press coverage, word of mouth, and subject matter. This labeling leads us to expect that the persons, places, and events shown to us exist and that the information presented about them will be trustworthy.

Every documentary claims to present factual information about the world, but the ways in which this can be done are just as varied as for fiction films. In some cases, the filmmakers are able to record events as they actually occur. For example, in making *Primary,* an account of John Kennedy and Hubert Humphrey campaigning for the 1960 Democratic presidential nomination, the camera operator and sound recordist were able to closely follow the candidates through crowds at rallies (5.134). But a documentary may convey information in other ways as well. The filmmaker might supply charts, maps, or other visual aids. In addition, the documentary filmmaker may stage certain events for the camera to record.

It's worth pausing on this last point. Some viewers tend to suspect that a documentary is unreliable if it manipulates the events that are filmed. It is true that, very often, the documentary filmmaker records an event without scripting or staging it. For example, in interviewing an eyewitness, the documentarist typically controls where the camera is placed, what is in focus, and so on; the filmmaker likewise controls the final editing of the images. But the filmmaker doesn't tell the witness what to say or how to act. The filmmaker may also have no choice about setting or lighting.

Still, both viewers and filmmakers regard some staging as legitimate in a documentary if the staging serves the larger purpose of presenting information. Suppose you are filming a farmer's daily routines. You might ask him or her to walk toward a field in order to frame a shot showing the whole farm. Similarly, the cameraman who is the central figure in Dziga Vertov's documentary *Man with a Movie Camera* is clearly performing for Vertov's camera (**10.1**).

In some cases, staging may intensify the documentary value of the film. Humphrey Jennings made *Fires Were Started* during the German bombardment of London in World War II. Unable to film during the air raids, Jennings found a group of bombed-out buildings and set them afire. He then filmed the fire patrol battling the blaze (**10.2**). Although the event was staged, the actual firefighters who took part judged it an authentic depiction of the challenges they faced under real bombing. Similarly, after Allied troops liberated the Auschwitz concentration camp near the end of World War II, a newsreel cameraman assembled a group of children and had them roll up their sleeves to display the prisoner numbers tattooed on their arms. This staging of an action arguably enhanced the film's reliability.

Staging events for the camera, then, need not consign the film to the realm of fiction. Regardless of the details of its production, the documentary film asks us to assume that it presents trustworthy information about its subject. Even if the filmmaker asks the farmer to wait a moment while the camera operator frames the shot, the film suggests that the farmer's morning visit to the field is part of the day's routine, and it's this suggestion that is set forth as reliable.

As a type of film, documentaries present themselves as factually trustworthy. Still, any one documentary may not prove reliable. Throughout film history, many documentaries have been challenged as inaccurate. One controversy involved Michael Moore's *Roger and Me*. The film presents, in sequences ranging from the heartrending to the absurd, the response of the people of Flint, Michigan, to a series of layoffs at General Motors plants during the 1980s. Much of the film shows inept efforts of the local government to revive the town's economy. Ronald Reagan visits, a television evangelist holds a mass rally, and city officials launch expensive new building campaigns, including AutoWorld, an indoor theme park intended to lure tourists to Flint.

No one disputes that all these events took place. The controversy arose when critics claimed that *Roger and Me* leads the audience to believe that the events occurred in the *order* in which they are shown. Ronald Reagan came to Flint in 1980, the TV evangelist in 1982; AutoWorld opened in 1985. These events could not have been responses to the plant closings shown early in the film because the plant closings started in 1986. Moore altered the actual chronology, critics charged, in order to make the city government look foolish.

Moore's defense is discussed in "Where to Go from Here" at the end of this chapter. The point for our purposes is that his critics accused his film of presenting unreliable information. Even if this charge were true, however, *Roger and Me* would not therefore turn into a fiction film. An unreliable documentary is still a documentary. Just as there are inaccurate and misleading news stories, so there are inaccurate and misleading documentaries.

A documentary may take a stand, state an opinion, or advocate a solution to a problem. As we'll see shortly, documentaries often use rhetoric to persuade an audience. But, again, simply taking a stance does not turn the documentary into fiction. In order to persuade us, the filmmaker marshals evidence, and this evidence is put forth as being factual and reliable. A documentary may be strongly partisan, but as a documentary, it nonetheless presents itself as providing trustworthy information about its subject.

"There are lots of in-between stages from shooting to public projection—developing, printing, editing, commentary, sound effects, music. At each stage the effect of the shot can be changed but the basic content must be in the shot to begin with."

— Joris Ivens, documentary filmmaker

10.1 Although the central figure of *Man with a Movie Camera* is a real cinematographer, his actions were staged.

10.2 A staged blaze in *Fires Were Started*.

Types of Documentary

Like fiction films, documentaries fall into genres. One common documentary genre is the *compilation* film, produced by assembling images from archival sources. *The Atomic Cafe* compiles newsreel footage and instructional films to suggest how 1950s American culture reacted to the proliferation of nuclear weapons **(10.3)**. The *interview,* or *talking-heads,* documentary records testimony about events or social movements. *Word Is Out* consists largely of interviews with lesbians and gay men discussing their lives.

10.3 Older documentary footage of protective gear incorporated into *The Atomic Cafe.*

The *direct-cinema* documentary characteristically records an ongoing event as it happens, with minimal interference by the filmmaker. Direct cinema emerged in the 1950s and 1960s, when portable camera and sound equipment became available and allowed films such as *Primary* to follow an event as it unfolds. For this reason, such documentaries are also known as *cinéma-vérité,* French for "cinema-truth." An example is *Hoop Dreams,* which traces two aspiring basketball players through high school and into college.

Another common type is the *nature* documentary, such as *Microcosmos,* which used magnifying lenses to explore the world of insects. The Imax format has spawned numerous nature documentaries, such as *Everest* and *Galapagos.* With increasingly unobtrusive, lightweight equipment becoming available, the *portrait* documentary has also become prominent in recent years. This type of film centers on scenes from the life of a compelling person. Terry Zwigoff recorded the eccentricities of underground cartoonist Robert Crumb and his family in *Crumb.* In *American Movie,* Chris Smith followed the difficulties of a Milwaukee filmmaker struggling with budgetary problems and amateur actors to make a horror film **(10.4).**

Very often a documentary pursues several of these options at once. A film may mix archival footage, interviews, and material shot on the fly, as do *Fahrenheit 9/11, The Fog of War,* and *In the Year of the Pig.* This *synthetic* documentary format is also common in television journalism.

The Boundaries Between Documentary and Fiction

In contrast to a documentary, with a fictional film, we assume that it presents imaginary beings, places, or events. We take it for granted that Don Vito Corleone and his family never existed, and that their activities, as depicted in *The Godfather,* never took place. Bambi's mother did not really get shot by a hunter because Bambi, his mother, and their forest companions are imaginary.

10.4   Filmmaker Mark Borchardt and his friend Mike (on left) freely discussed their lives and projects with Chris Smith for *American Movie.*

If a film is fictional, that doesn't mean that it's completely unrelated to actuality. For one thing, not everything shown or implied by a fiction film need be imaginary. *The Godfather* alludes to World War II and the building of Las Vegas, both historical events; it takes place in New York City and in Sicily, both real locales. Nonetheless, the characters and their activities remain fictional, with history and geography providing a context for the made-up elements.

Fictional films are tied to actuality in another way: they often comment on the real world. *Dave,* about an imaginary U.S. president and his corrupt administration, criticizes contemporary political conduct. In 1943, some viewers took Carl Dreyer's *Day of Wrath,* a film about witch-hunts and prejudice in 17th-century Denmark, as a covert protest against the Nazis currently occupying the country. Through theme, subject, characterization, and other means, a fictional film can directly or obliquely present ideas about the world outside the film.

Sometimes our response to a fictional film is shaped by our assumptions about how it was made. The typical fictional film stages all or nearly all its events; they are designed, planned, rehearsed, filmed, and refilmed. The studio mode of production is well suited to creating fiction films, since it allows stories to be scripted and action to be staged until what is captured on film satisfies the decision makers. Similarly, in a fictional film, the characters are portrayed by actors, not photographed directly (as in a documentary). The camera films not Vito Corleone but Marlon Brando portraying the Don.

This assumption about how the film was made typically comes into play when we consider historical films or biographies. *Apollo 13* and *Schindler's List* base themselves on actual events, while *Malcolm X, Walk the Line, W.,* and other *biopics* trace episodes in the lives of people who really existed. Are these documentaries or fictional films? In practice, most such films add purely make-believe characters, speeches, or actions. But even if the films did not tamper with the record in this way, they would remain fictional according to our assumptions about how they were produced. Their events are wholly staged, and the historical agents are portrayed through actors' performances. Just as important, the films don't purport to be documentaries. They are presented as historical re-creations. Like plays or novels based on real-life events, historical and biographical movies convey ideas about history by means of fictional portrayal.

As you might expect, filmmakers have sometimes sought to blur the lines separating documentary and fiction. A notorious example is Mitchell Block's *No Lies,* which purports to present an interview with a woman who has been raped. Audiences are typically disturbed by the woman's emotional account and by the callousness of the offscreen filmmaker questioning her. A final title, however, reveals that the film was scripted and that the woman was an actor. Part of Block's purpose was to show how the look and sound of *cinéma-vérité* documentary can elicit viewers' uncritical belief in what they are shown.

Most fake documentaries—a genre sometimes referred to as *mockumentaries*—are not this serious. Often mock documentaries imitate the conventions of documentaries but do not try to fool audiences into thinking that they portray actual people or events. A classic case is Rob Reiner's *This Is Spinal Tap,* which takes the form of a behind-the-scenes documentary about a completely fictional rock band.

A film may fuse documentary and fiction in other ways. For *JFK,* Oliver Stone inserted compilation footage into scenes in which actors played historical figures such as Lee Harvey Oswald. Stone also staged and filmed the assassination of Kennedy in a pseudo-documentary manner. This material was then intercut with genuine archival footage, creating constant uncertainty about what was staged and what was filmed spontaneously.

Errol Morris's *The Thin Blue Line,* a documentary investigation into a murder, mixes interviews and archival material with episodes performed by actors. The sequences, far from being the jittery reenactments of television true-crime shows, are shot with smooth camera work, dramatic lighting, and vibrant color (**10.5**). Several

CONNECT TO THE BLOG

For a discussion of how animation can be used in documentaries, see "Showing what can't be filmed," at

www.davidbordwell.net/blog/?p=3837.

10.5   Carefully composed shots such as this from *The Thin Blue Line* emphasize that some events have been reenacted.

of these staged sequences dramatize witnesses' alternative versions of how the crime took place. The result is a film that not only seeks to identify the real killer but also raises questions about how fact and fiction may intermingle. (See pp. 425–431.)

Types of Form in Documentary Films

Many, perhaps most, documentaries are organized as narratives, just as fiction films are. William Wyler's World War II–era *Memphis Belle* follows the course of a single raid over Germany, seen largely from inside a B-17 bomber. There are, however, other, nonnarrative types of documentary form.

A film might be intended to convey information in an analytical fashion and draw on what we can term **categorical form.** Or the filmmaker may want to make an argument that will convince the spectator of something. In this case the film draws upon **rhetorical form.** Let's look at each of these types. As we consider each type, we'll analyze one film as a prime example. To get a sense of each film's form, we'll break it into segments, as we did with *Citizen Kane* in Chapter 3. Along the way, we'll discuss how particular stylistic choices support the film's large-scale development.

Categorical Form

Categories are groupings that individuals or societies create to organize their knowledge of the world. Some categories are based on scientific research, and these will often attempt to account exhaustively for all the data in question. For example, scientists have developed an elaborate system to classify every known animal and plant into genus and species.

Most of the categories we use in our daily life are less strict, less neat, and less exhaustive. We tend to group the things around us based on a commonsense, practical approach or on an ideological view of the world. Ordinarily, for example, we do not sort animals we see by genus and species. We use rough categories such as "pets," "wild animals," "farm animals," and "zoo animals." Such groupings are not logically exclusive or exhaustive (at one time or another, some animals might fit into most or all of these categories), yet they suffice for our usual purposes. Ideologically based categories are also seldom strictly logical. Societies do not naturally fall into such categories as "primitive" or "advanced," for example. These are groupings that have been developed out of complex sets of beliefs, and they may not stand up to scrutiny.

If a documentary filmmaker wants to convey some information about the world to audiences, categories may provide a basis for organizing the film's form. A documentary film about butterflies might use scientific classification, showing one type of butterfly and giving information about its habits, then showing another, with more information, and so on. Similarly, a travelogue about Switzerland might offer a sampling of local sights and customs. Often the categories chosen will be loose, commonsense ones that audiences can easily recognize.

One classic documentary organized categorically is Leni Riefenstahl's *Olympia,* Part 2, made in 1936 as a record of the Berlin Olympics. Its basic category is the Olympic Games as an event, which Riefenstahl had to condense and arrange into two feature-length films. Within these films, the games are broken down into subcategories—sailing events, sprinting events, and so on. Beyond this, Riefenstahl creates an overall tone, stressing the games' grandeur and the international cooperation implicit in the gathering.

The categorical film often begins by identifying its subject. Our clichéd travelogue might start with a map of Switzerland. Riefenstahl begins *Olympia*'s second part with athletes jogging and then fraternizing in their clubhouse. Thus they are not differentiated by what sports each specializes in but are only seen as participants in the Olympics. Later the individual sequences will assign the athletes to various events.

10.6   Filmed against the sky, the divers at the end of *Olympia,* Part 2, became soaring shapes rather than individual competitors.

"The whole history of movie making has been to portray extraordinary things, and no one has felt that much confidence in looking at life itself and finding the extraordinary in the ordinary."

— Albert Maysles, documentary filmmaker

In categorical form, patterns of development will usually be simple. The film might move from small to large, local to national, personal to public, and so on. The film on butterflies, for example, might begin with smaller species and work up to large ones, or it might go from drab to colorful types. Riefenstahl organizes *Olympia* according to a large-scale ABA pattern. The early part of the film concentrates on the games as such, rather than on the competition among athletes and countries. Later she shifts to setting up more dramatic tension by focusing on some of the individual athletes and asking whether they will be successful in their events. Finally, in the diving sequence at the end, there is again no differentiation among participants, and the sheer beauty of the event dominates. Thus Riefenstahl achieves her thematic goal of stressing the international cooperation inherent in the Olympics.

Because categorical form tends to develop in fairly simple ways, it risks boring the spectator. If the progression from segment to segment depends too much on repetition ("And here's another example . . ."), our expectations will be easily satisfied. The challenge to the filmmaker using categorical form is to introduce variations and thereby to make us adjust our expectations.

For example, the filmmaker may choose a category that is exciting or broad or unusual enough to present many possibilities for stimulating interest. The Olympics have an innate drama because they involve competition and a potential for beauty through the way the athletes' performances are filmed. For the film that will provide our main example, *Gap-Toothed Women,* Les Blank chose a very odd category that will provoke interest, and one broad enough that many different sorts of women could fit into it. Thus the film's talking-head interviews cover a range of varying viewpoints.

Another way in which the filmmaker can maintain our interest across the segments is through patterned use of film techniques. Our film about butterflies might concentrate on conveying information about types of insects, but it could also exploit the colors and shapes of the various examples to add abstract visual interest. The diving sequence at the end of *Olympia* is famous for its dazzling succession of images of divers filmed from all angles **(10.6).**

Finally, the categorical film can maintain interest by mixing in other kinds of form. While overall the film is organized around its category, it can include small-scale narratives. At one point, *Olympia* singles out one athlete, Glen Morris, and follows him through the stages of his event, because he was an unknown athlete who unexpectedly won the decathlon. Similarly, a filmmaker might take a stance on his or her subject and try to make an ideological point about it, thus injecting a bit of rhetorical form into the film. We'll see that Les Blank hints that treating gap-teeth as a flaw reflects a society's bias about what constitutes beauty.

Categorical form is simple in principle, but filmmakers can use it to create complex and interesting films, as *Gap-Toothed Women* demonstrates.

An Example of Categorical Form: *Gap-Toothed Women*   Les Blank has been making modest, personal documentary films since the 1960s. These are often observations of a single unusual subject as seen by a variety of people, as with his *Garlic Is as Good as Ten Mothers.* Several of Blank's films use categorical organization in original ways that demonstrate how entertaining and thought-provoking this simple approach to form can be.

Gap-Toothed Women was conceived, directed, and filmed by Blank, in collaboration with Maureen Gosling (editor), Chris Simon (associate producer), and Susan Kell (assistant director). The film consists largely of brief interviews with women who have spaces between their front teeth. Why make a film on this unusual, maybe trivial subject? As the film develops, its organization suggests a larger theme: sometimes society has rather narrow notions of what counts as beauty. After introducing the category, the film examines social attitudes, both positive and negative, toward gap-toothed women. If gapped teeth seem to be flaws at the beginning of the film, by the end, being gap-toothed is associated with attractiveness, energy, and creativity.

We can break *Gap-Toothed Women* into these segments:

1. A pretitle sequence introducing a few gap-toothed women
2. A title segment with a quotation from Chaucer
3. Some genetic and cultural explanations for gaps
4. Ways American culture stigmatizes gap-teeth, and efforts to correct or adjust to them
5. Careers and creativity
6. An epilogue: gaps and life

C. Credits

10.7 In *Gap-Toothed Women,* a close view of a woman's mouth with a large gap leads to . . .

These segments are punctuated with songs, as well as with still images from magazine covers and photographs that comment on the subject matter of the interviews.

Over the opening title previously quoted, we hear the sound of someone biting into an apple—an odd sound soon explained in the first interview. The opening image is a startlingly close view of a woman's mouth (**10.7**) as she recalls baby-sitting for her brothers and being baffled when her parents knew when she had stolen bites from forbidden sweets. She has a wide gap between her teeth, and a cut to a close view of an apple shows a bite taken out (**10.8**). The woman's voice refers to her parents' clue: "My signature, which was my teeth marks."

10.8 . . . her "signature" bite on an apple.

Blank sets up the film's category humorously, making the tooth gap a mark of wry individuality, a woman's signature. A quick series of closer views of six smiling mouths follows, culminating in a shot of a woman's entire head. All show gaps and are accompanied by folksy harp music that enhances the cheerful tone.

While quickly establishing the category governing the film, this sequence also sets up a recurring stylistic choice. Usually, documentary talking heads are framed in medium shots or medium close-ups, but Blank also includes many extreme close-ups centering on the subjects' mouths, as in the opening view of gapped teeth (10.7). The emphasis is particularly strong here because Blank zooms in on the mouth, as he will occasionally do later, and the background is neutral, as it will often be. Once we've learned to notice tooth gaps, we'll concentrate on the speaker's mouth even in the more normally composed head shots (**10.9**). Later Blank (in one of his few offscreen comments retained) will coax an elderly woman to grin more broadly to show off her gap (**10.10**). As we start to notice the gaps, we register their differences. Some are wide, some narrow, and we're invited to compare them. By a certain point, the speakers no longer mention them, and the filmmakers seem confident that by then we'll pay attention to them as a visual motif.

10.9 *Gap-Toothed Women:* "My father has a gap, about as wide as mine is; my mom has a gap that's a little smaller.

The next segment switches to slower shots of a woman playing a harp in a garden. The light, pleasant tone of this opening will be echoed at the end by another, even more buoyant, musical performance. In between, the film explores its subjects' attitudes toward being gap-toothed.

During the harpist's performance, the film's title appears in white longhand (**10.11**). This writing recalls the initial woman's reference to her gap-teeth as "my signature." The title leads to a superimposed epigraph: "'The Wife of Bath knew much about wandering by the way. She was gap-toothed, to tell the truth.'—Geoffrey Chaucer, The Canterbury Tales, 1386 A.D." This epigraph suggests that the film's central category originated long ago. Moreover, Chaucer's Wife of Bath is traditionally associated with erotic playfulness, and this element will become a motif in the film as a whole.

The film's third segment deals with where gaps come from and what they are thought to mean. In a cluster of brief interviews, three women mention that other members of their family had gap-teeth as well, so we infer that this is a natural, if unusual, feature that runs in families. All three women speak in a neutral way about

10.10 *Gap-Toothed Women:* We strain to see this woman's gap as she smiles at the camera.

10.11   The film's title is superimposed on a garden scene.

10.12   In *Gap-Toothed Women,* the image of the Wife of Bath stands out incongruously from the dignified group, with her low-cut dress and broad grin.

10.13   *Gap-Toothed Women:* An image from a culture in which gaps are praised.

10.14   *Gap-Toothed Women* integrates images from popular culture to examine social attitudes.

gapped teeth, but the first, mentioning that her mother had worn braces, drops the hint that some people take gapped teeth to be undesirable.

This segment then shifts its focus to how various cultures—specifically, non-white societies—have interpreted gap-teeth. A young Asian woman with a gap speculates on a "stupid" myth that gap-toothed women "are supposed to be sexier." Blank then cuts to a brief clip from the fiction film *Swann in Love,* with the protagonist making love to a beautiful gap-toothed woman in a carriage. Does this confirm the myth? Or only suggest that the myth has been applied to gap-toothed women in general—since the actress is not Asian? This clip from another film introduces a tactic of intercutting images from art and popular culture with the interview footage, as if to suggest how pervasive ideas about gapped teeth are.

The erotic motif brings back the Wife of Bath, now in an engraving showing her riding at the head of a group of pilgrims (**10.12**). A scholarly male voice-over explains that in medieval times being gap-toothed was associated with a love of travel and an amorous nature. There follows a string of interviews developing the motif. A gap-toothed woman tells, in sign language, that she dreamed of kissing her instructor and having their gaps interlock. An African-American woman describes how, in places like Senegal, gaps are seen as lucky or beautiful (**10.13**). An Indian woman asserts that in her culture gaps are so normal as not to require comment. Abruptly, Blank cuts to a modern copy of a sphinx, and we hear a woman's voice claiming that ancient Egyptian women believed that gaps were associated with beautiful singing. Overall, the segment shows that cultures have interpreted gap-teeth very differently, but most don't consider them flaws and many treat them as signs of beauty.

Segment 4 tries to show that, in contrast to these cultures, modern Western society stigmatizes gaps. Several more interviews, intercut with other material, show that women have felt that their own teeth were unattractive. One tells of a dentist who tried to convince her to fix her gap (mocked in a song about "filling your mouth with wires, your head with lies"). But the idea that gapped teeth are ugly is immediately counterbalanced by vigorous editing. Two magazine images of models without gaps are followed by a pretty little African-American girl with a gap; then a photo of Madonna, perhaps the ultimate gap-toothed glamour icon in modern society; and then a *Vogue* cover showing Lauren Hutton, the first major gap-toothed fashion model (**10.14**). As if in reply to these images, a woman says she's worried about her height and weight, as well as her teeth, although she herself is conventionally quite attractive (**10.15**). Her comment is then countered by other opinions, as one woman talks about how in magazines "you never see a person with gapped teeth," and a mother with a gap-toothed toddler recalls that she had hated her own teeth until Lauren Hutton became a successful model. By intercutting the woman's comments with illustrations of what she mentions, Blank achieves an intellectual comparison somewhat akin to Sergei Eisenstein's intellectual montage (**10.16–10.19**). Overall, the editing drives home conflicting attitudes toward what is beautiful.

These interviews are less playful and funny than the opening sequence, but the film becomes light again. Lauren Hutton herself roams through city streets in a vain attempt to find gap-toothed people to interview. The scene turns the usual show business interview upside-down by having celebrity pursue and address ordinary people, a point underlined by Blank's use of a TV-style handheld camera (**10.20**). Hutton is then interviewed in her home, saying that if a person finds herself attractive on the inside, she can be satisfied with her appearance.

The same playfulness is sustained in another musical interlude, folk singer Claudia Schmidt's "I'm a Little Cookie," a song accompanied by 10 photos of gap-toothed girls and teenagers, all smiling. This segues into a series of testimonies about how women have tried to correct their teeth with homemade devices, followed by a mock commercial for an actual device designed to fill in gaps (**10.21**). This segment of the film ends with the interview with the elderly woman who is proud to still have her own teeth, gap and all (10.10).

10.15 A beautiful woman concerned about her physical imperfections.

10.16 A young woman recalls being teased and compared to Howdy Doody . . .

10.17 . . . and a photograph of the gap-toothed puppet appears, followed by . . .

10.18 . . . shot of the woman praising Lauren Hutton which leads to . . .

10.19 . . . a glamorous cover photo of Hutton revealing her gap.

10.20 A handheld camera in *Gap-Toothed Women*.

10.21 *Gap-Toothed Women:* a demonstration of a device designed to invisibly fill in gaps.

10.22 In *Gap-Toothed Women*, cartoonist Dori Seda discusses active women.

10.23 *Gap-Toothed Women* links gaps with creativity.

Segment 5, which we've labeled "Careers and Creativity," begins with another Schmidt song about gaps. As we see images of more gap-toothed women, including Whoopi Goldberg, the song reintroduces the Wife of Bath motif ("old Chaucer knew where the score was at") and leads into an interview with Schmidt herself. She recalls that she used to be defiant about having a gap and extolled "gap power." There follows an interview with the cartoonist Dori Seda, standing beside a poster for the film we're watching and explaining that recognizing her gap helped her link herself to a tradition of unusual women **(10.22).** The film is moving toward associating gapped teeth with pride, comradeship, and creativity.

The next string of interviews reinforces this theme—oddly, by not mentioning gapped teeth at all. The emphasis now falls on women's activities. A sculptor talks of how her work helps communities **(10.23);** the Indian woman seen earlier draws rice-paint patterns on her threshold; a Hispanic woman trucker describes a long, difficult trip through a storm. The editing contrasts these stories with one, told by Catherine de Santis, about Arab women who remove body hair with a hot-wax

10.24   Reportage-style footage of a speech in *Gap-Toothed Women*.

10.25   *Gap-Toothed Women* freezes the frame after the line "You've got a gap between your teeth, hey, no problem."

10.26   *Gap-Toothed Women*'s leukemia survivor leaps and spins to the applause of musicians and onlookers.

concoction—recalling the theme that it can be dangerous to conform to external standards of beauty. More positive instances follow, as a heavy-metal singer explains that she quit her band because of its violent messages, and a gap-toothed woman displays the words "woman" and "peace" painted on her face. A sudden sound bridge plays a dual role here. Over the woman's face, we hear a chorus singing, "They'll be marching, marching, marching when the Army comes to town," as if referring to her antiwar slogans. A cut to a new sequence reveals the music to be diegetic, played by a Salvation Army band before a public speech.

The speech is given by Supreme Court Justice Sandra Day O'Connor (**10.24**). Why is she in the movie? For one thing, she's gap-toothed. For another, her speech emphasizes "creativity, work, and love" as things that make life worthwhile. Since we've just seen several working and creative women, the thematic connection becomes stronger.

O'Connor also says that when creativity is gone, "the will to live seems to go with it." Her remark leads to the final summarizing segment of the film. In a tight shot, a woman's stomach gyrates in a belly dance. We glimpse other costumed women looking on and musicians accompanying the dancer. The dancer's voice-over commentary explains that she is in remission from acute cancer. A cut moves us to a quiet interview with her, identified as Sharyn Sawyer, in everyday clothes against a simple board fence. After facing death, she explains, physical flaws no longer bother her. "You get stepped on by a horse, fine, you know, you've got a scar on your leg. Oh, well, you know, you've got a gap between your teeth, hey, no problem!" To underscore the comment, the film freezes on her cheerful face (**10.25**). Sawyer's spontaneity and commonsense acceptance of physical flaws and aging help put the anxieties of some of the earlier women in perspective.

Another sound bridge—this time, applause that seems to approve of what Sawyer has said—takes us back to the Middle Eastern dance class, where Sawyer performs another lively dance (**10.26**). The credits begin to roll, revealing a very close photo of a smiling gap-toothed mouth, an image that echoes the first shot. A final acknowledgment maintains the film's exuberant tone: "Many thanks to all the wonderful Gap-Toothed women who made this film possible!"

Gap-Toothed Women shows that category-based form need not be a dry recitation of conceptual similarities and differences. A documentary using this organization can take a stance on its subject, play among contrasting attitudes, and entertain an audience. Blank and his collaborators have created a light, often humorous, film in part by choosing an unusual category and in part by the way they use film technique to present it.

Such a film can also create the four levels of meaning that we described in Chapter 2 (pp. 62–65). On the referential level, *Gap-Toothed Women* simply presents a series of gap-toothed women from different races and different cultural and class backgrounds. We may know some of their faces and names from previous experience (Madonna and Whoopi Goldberg most obviously, Claudia Schmidt and Dori Seda to fans of folk music and underground comics). We also know that *Vogue* is a fashion magazine and assume that the magazines with Russian or other foreign writing are those countries' equivalents of *Vogue*.

Moving to the level of explicit meaning, the interviewees display a range of reactions to gap-teeth. Some are obviously proud, some embarrassed, others more ambivalent. Some express quite directly the idea that magazines and other people often stigmatize people with gaps, while others reveal that gaps are admired in some cultures. At one point, the sculptor compares the lack of gap-toothed models in magazines to the notion of black people seeing only white faces in media images. This explicitly links stereotyped attitudes about feminine beauty to racism. In most cases, the filmmakers' voices are not heard; they let their interviewees make these points.

The film's form is not organized as an argument in favor of gap-teeth being a natural, even attractive, trait; yet on the level of implicit meaning, the music and photographs of smiling, gap-toothed women tend to suggest just that. The choice of some very beautiful women who are worried about their gaps cues us to interpret their fears as unnecessary. Certain women's comments are clearly privileged as reflecting the ideas that the filmmakers wish to convey. Dori Seda's discussion of how important it is for women to do things helps define the film's segment on careers and creativity, and the cancer survivor's speech at the end makes anxieties about gapped teeth trivial in relation to the potential joys of life.

Beyond these three levels of meaning, we can also discern symptomatic meanings. Blank began making films in the 1960s, a period when a counterculture based upon protest and distrust of authority emerged. More specifically, it was the era of women's liberation, with its demands for gender equality and the breaking down of feminine stereotypes. By 1987, when the film appeared, the counterculture of the 1960s and 1970s had died down, but many people preserved its ideals. Several of the women interviewed in Blank's film are clearly of this generation and sensibility. Moreover, one legacy of the counterculture has been widespread attention paid to society's pressures on women to conform to limiting ideals of beauty. *Gap-Toothed Women* could be interpreted as reflecting the shift of some radical attitudes of the 1960s into the mainstream—a situation that persists and makes Blank's 1987 film still relevant today.

Rhetorical Form

Another type of documentary film uses *rhetorical* form, in which the filmmaker presents a persuasive argument. The goal in such a film is to persuade the audience to adopt an opinion about the subject matter and perhaps to act on that opinion. This type of film goes beyond the categorical type in that it tries to make an explicit argument.

Rhetorical form is common in all the media. We encounter it frequently in daily life, not just in formal speeches but also in conversation. People often try to persuade each other by argument. Salespeople use persuasion in their jobs, and friends may argue politics over lunch. Television bombards us with one of the most pervasive uses of rhetorical form in film—commercials, which try to induce viewers to buy products or vote for candidates.

We can define rhetorical form in film by four basic attributes. First, it addresses the viewer openly, trying to move him or her to a new intellectual conviction, to a new emotional attitude, or to action. (In the latter case, we may already believe something but need to be persuaded that the belief is important enough to act upon.)

Second, the subject of the film is usually not an issue of scientific truth but a matter of opinion, toward which a person may take a number of equally plausible attitudes. The filmmaker tries to make his or her position seem the most plausible by presenting different types of arguments and evidence. Yet, because the issue cannot be absolutely proved, we may accept the position simply because the filmmaker has made a convincing case for it. Because rhetorical films deal with beliefs and arguments, they involve the expression of ideology; indeed, perhaps no type of film form centers so consistently on explicit meaning and ideological implications.

A third aspect of rhetorical form follows from this. If the conclusion cannot be proved beyond question, the filmmaker often appeals to our emotions, rather than presenting only factual evidence. And fourth, the film often attempts to persuade the viewer to make a choice that will have an effect on his or her everyday life. This may be as simple as what shampoo to use, or it may involve decisions about which political candidate to support or even whether a young person will fight in a war.

Types of Rhetorical Argument   Films can use all sorts of arguments to persuade us to make such choices. Often, however, these arguments are not presented to us *as* arguments. The film frequently presents arguments as if they were simply observations or factual conclusions. Nor does the film tend to point out other opinions. There are three main types of arguments the film may use: relating to the source, to the subject, and to the viewer.

Arguments from source   Some of the film's arguments will rely on what are taken to be reliable sources of information. The film may present firsthand accounts of events, expert testimony at a hearing, or interviews with people assumed to be knowledgeable on the subject. Most political documentaries include talking-head footage of investigators, scholars, or insiders. At the same time, the filmmakers will try to show that they themselves are well informed and trustworthy. They may insert themselves into the interview situation, as Michael Moore does in his documentaries, or they may use a voice-over narrator speaking in tones of crisp conviction.

Subject-centered arguments   The film also employs arguments about its subject matter. Sometimes the film appeals to beliefs common at the time in a given culture. For example, in contemporary America, a large segment of the population is said to believe that most politicians are cynical and corrupt. This may or may not be true of any one politician, but someone running for public office may appeal to that belief and tell potential voters that he or she will bring a new honesty to government.

A second approach the film may take is to use *examples* that support its point. Such evidence may be more or less strong. A taste-test commercial that shows one person choosing the advertiser's product seems to imply that the product really tastes better; yet there is no mention of the other people—perhaps a majority—who prefer other brands.

Further, filmmakers can back up an argument by exploiting familiar, easily accepted argumentative patterns. Students of rhetoric call such patterns *enthymemes,* arguments that rely on widespread opinion and usually conceal some crucial premises.

For example, we might make a film to persuade you that a problem has been solved. We would show that the problem had existed and then show that some action was taken that solved it. The movement from problem to solution is such a familiar pattern of inference that you might assume that we had proved reasonably that the right thing was done. On closer analysis, however, you might discover that the film had a hidden premise, such as "On the assumption that *this* was the best solution, a particular course of action was taken." Perhaps other solutions would have been better, but the film doesn't examine them. The solution presented is not as well justified as the problem–solution pattern would seem to suggest. Shortly, we'll see such enthymematic patterns at work in *The River.*

Viewer-centered arguments   The film may make an argument that appeals to the emotions of the viewer. We are all familiar with politicians who pose with flag, family, and pets. Appeals to patriotism, romantic sentimentality, and other emotions are common in rhetorical films. Filmmakers often draw on conventions from other films to provoke the desired reaction. Sometimes such appeals can disguise the weakness of other arguments of the film and persuade the more susceptible audience members to accept the film's outlook.

A documentary's rhetorical form can organize these arguments and appeals in a variety of ways. Some filmmakers present their basic arguments first, then go on to show evidence and the problem, and explain how they would be addressed by the solution argued for in the film. Other films start with the problem, describe it in detail, and then let the viewer know late in the film what change is being advocated. This second approach may create more curiosity and suspense, leading the viewer to reflect on and anticipate possible solutions.

One common version of rhetorical form suggests that it begins with an introduction of the situation, goes on to a discussion of the relevant facts, then presents proofs that a given solution fits those facts, and ends with an epilogue that summarizes what has come before. *The River,* a documentary made in 1937 by Pare Lorentz, will be our example of rhetorical form. In its overall form, the film adheres to the four-part structure just outlined.

An Example of Rhetorical Form: *The River*   Lorentz made *The River* for the U.S. government's Farm Security Administration. In 1937, the country was making progress toward pulling out of the Depression. Under the administration of Franklin Delano Roosevelt, the federal government used its powers to create public works programs. These programs sought to provide jobs for the large numbers of unemployed workers, as well as to correct various social problems. Although many people tend now to think of Roosevelt's policies as the right ones and to credit him with bringing America out of the Depression, he faced strong political opposition at the time. *The River* hails the Tennessee Valley Authority (TVA) as the solution to the region's problems of flooding, agricultural depletion, and non-electrification. The film had a definite ideological slant: promoting Roosevelt's policies. Thus the film's argument was controversial at the time. It might be considered equally controversial today, given the movement toward getting rid of dams and restoring rivers to their original ecological states.

Let's look at how this film sets out to persuade its audience that the TVA is a good program. *The River* has eleven segments:

C. Credits

1. A prologue title setting forth the subject of the film

2. A description of the rivers that flow into the Mississippi and then into the Gulf of Mexico

3. A history of the early agricultural use of the river

4. The problems caused in the South by the Civil War

5. A section on lumbering and steel mills in the North, and the building of urban areas

6. The floods caused by careless exploitation of the land

7. The current effects of these cumulative problems on people: poverty and ignorance

8. A map and description of the TVA project

9. The dams of the TVA and the benefits they bring

E. An end title

The film seems at first just to be giving us information about the Mississippi. It proceeds for quite a while before its argument becomes apparent. But, by the careful use of repetition, variation, and development, Lorentz builds up a case that really depends on all the segments working together.

The opening credits of the film are shown over an old-fashioned picture of steamboats on the Mississippi and then over a map of the United States (**10.27**). The film immediately suggests to the audience that its makers are reliable and knowledgeable, and that it is an account based on both historical and geographical facts. The same map returns under the prologue in the brief opening segment, which states, "This is the story of a river." Such a statement disguises the rhetorical purpose of the film, implying that the film will be an objectively told story, drawing on narrative form.

Segment 2 continues the introduction with shots of the sky, mountains, and rivers. This motif of the majestic beauty of the Mississippi valley is repeated at the start of later sections and then contrasted with the bleak landscapes that dominate the middle parts of the film. As we see the beauty of the river (**10.28**), a resonant male voice tells us how water flows into the Mississippi from as far away as Idaho and Pennsylvania. The narrator's rich voice accords with conventional notions of a trustworthy person. The narrator was Thomas Chalmers, an opera baritone chosen for just these qualities.

10.27   *The River* begins with a map with the Mississippi River and its tributaries exaggerated in size.

10.28   An idyllic image of nature in *The River*.

Lorentz pays close attention to how the sound track can arouse emotion. While we see rivers swelling as they join, the narrator's commentary is far from the dry, factual tone of most documentaries. The sentences have an urgent rhythm: "Down the Yellowstone, the Milk, the White, and Cheyenne . . . the Cannonball, the Musselshell, the James, and the Sioux." This famous roll call of the rivers, recalling the teeming catalogues of Walt Whitman's poetry, evokes the power and the grandeur of the land. Emotion is also aroused by the spacious folk-song score composed by Virgil Thompson. Thus the film adopts an American tone throughout, appealing to the viewer's patriotic sentiments and implying that the whole country should face up to a particular regional problem.

Segment 2 has established an idyllic situation, with its beautiful images of mountain and river landscapes. The overall development of the film is toward a restoration of this beauty, but with a difference. With segment 3, we move into the section of the film devoted to facts of American history relating to the Mississippi and the problems it causes. Segment 3 begins much as segment 2 did, with a view of clouds. But now things begin to change. Instead of the mountains we saw earlier, we see mule teams and drivers. Again the narrator's voice begins a list: "New Orleans to Baton Rouge . . . Baton Rouge to Natchez . . . Natchez to Vicksburg." This list is part of the brief recounting of the history of the dikes built along the Mississippi to control flooding in pre–Civil War days. The narrator is confirmed as trustworthy and knowledgeable, giving us facts and dates in the nation's history. We see cotton bales loaded onto steamboats, giving a sense of the country's early strength as an exporter of goods. The brisk cutting here, as elsewhere in the film, evokes American enterprise and energy. Graphic discontinuity suggests both change and continuity when Lorentz cuts from a mud-filled sledge (**10.29**) to a plow thrusting in the opposite direction (**10.30**). The different movements suggest a shift in technology, but their similarities suggest the connection between building a dike and farming cotton. Dynamic compositions perform a similar service, as when a canted framing shows workers loading cotton bales onto a steamboat (**10.31**). The off-balance composition, accompanied by sprightly banjo music, makes the bales seem to roll downhill almost effortlessly.

So far the film has seemed to follow its initial purpose of telling a story of the river. But in segment 4, it begins to introduce the problems that the TVA will eventually solve. The film shows the results of the Civil War: destroyed houses and dispossessed landowners, the land worn out by the cultivation of cotton, and people forced to move west. The moral tone of the film becomes apparent, and it is an appealing one. Over images of impoverished people, somber music plays. It is based on a familiar folk tune, "Go Tell Aunt Rhody," which, with its line "The old gray goose is dead" underscores the losses of the farmers. The narrator's voice expresses compassion as he speaks of the South's "tragedy of land impoverished." This at-

10.29 *The River* creates graphic contrast between a sledge . . .

10.30 . . . and a plow.

10.31 A canted framing in *The River*.

titude of sympathy may incline us to accept as true other things that the film tells us. The narrator also refers to the people of the period as "we": "We mined the soil for cotton until it would yield no more." Here the film's persuasive intent becomes evident. It was not literally *we*—you and I and the narrator—who grew this cotton. The use of *we* is a rhetorical strategy to make us feel that all Americans share a responsibility for this problem and for finding a solution.

Later segments repeat the strategies of these earlier ones. In segment 5, the film again uses poetically repetitious narration to describe the lumber industry's growth after the Civil War, listing "black spruce and Norway pine" and other trees. In the images, we see evergreens against the sky, echoing the cloud motif that opened segments 2 and 3 (**10.32**). This creates a parallel between the riches of the agricultural and the industrial areas. A sprightly sequence of logging, accompanied by music based on the tune "Hot Time in the Old Town Tonight," again gives us a sense of America's vigor. A section on coal mining and steel mills follows, enhancing this impression. This segment ends with references to the growing urban centers: "We built a hundred cities and a thousand towns," and we hear a list of some of their names.

Up to this point, we have seen the strengths of America associated with the river valley, with just a hint of problems that growth has sparked. But segment 6 switches tracks and creates a lengthy series of contrasts to the earlier parts. It begins with the same list of trees—"black spruce and Norway pine"—but now we see stumps against fog instead of trees against clouds (**10.33**). Another line returns, but with a new phrase added: "We built a hundred cities and a thousand towns . . . but at what a cost." Beginning with the barren hilltops, we are shown how melting ice runs off, and how the runoff gradually erodes hillsides and swells rivers into flooding torrents. Once more we hear the list of rivers from segment 2, but now the music is somber and the rivers are no longer idyllic. Again there is a parallel presented between the soil erosion here and the soil depletion in the South after the Civil War.

It's worth pausing to comment on Lorentz's use of film style here, for he reinforces the film's argument through techniques that arouse the audience's emotions. The contrast of segment 6 with the lively logging segment that precedes it could hardly be stronger. The sequence begins with lingering shots of the fog-shrouded stumps (10.33). There is little movement. The music consists of threatening, pulsing chords. The narrator speaks more deliberately. Dissolves, rather than straight cuts, connect the shots. The segment slowly builds up tension. One shot shows a stump draped with icicles, and an abrupt cut-in emphasizes the steady drip from them (**10.34**). A sudden, highly dissonant chord signals us to expect danger.

Then, in a series of close-ups of the earth, water gathers, first in trickles (**10.35**), then in streams washing the soil away. By now the music is very rhythmic, with soft, tom-tom-like beats punctuating a plaintive and rising orchestral melody. The narrator begins supplying dates, each time more urgently insistent: "Nineteen-seven" (**10.36**), "Nineteen-thirteen" (**10.37**), "Nineteen-sixteen" (**10.38**), and on up to 1937. With each date, we see streams turning into creeks, and creeks into waterfalls, and eventually rivers overflowing their banks.

As the flooding intensifies, brief shots of lightning bolts are intercut with shots of raging water. The dramatic music is overwhelmed by sirens and whistles. From a situation of natural beauty, the film has taken us to a disaster for which humans were responsible. Lorentz's stylistic choices have blended to convey a sense of rising tension, convincing us of the flood's threat. Were we not to grasp that threat emotionally as well as factually, the film's overall argument would be less compelling. Throughout *The River,* voice, music, editing, and movement within the shot combine to create a rhythm for such rhetorical purposes.

By this point, we understand the information the film is presenting about flooding and erosion. Still, the film witholds the solution and presents the effects of the floods on people's lives in contemporary America. Segment 7 describes government aid to flood victims in 1937 but points out that the basic problem still exists.

10.32 Motifs of pines and clouds in *The River.*

10.33 The pines now transformed into stumps, the clouds into fog.

10.34 In *The River,* shots of icicles dripping lead to a segment on erosion.

10.35   *The River.*

10.36   *The River.*

10.37   *The River.*

10.38   *The River.*

10.39   *The River.*

The narrator employs a striking enthymeme here: "And poor land makes poor people—poor people make poor land." This sounds reasonable on the surface, but upon examination, its meaning becomes unclear. Didn't the rich southern plantation owners whose ruined mansions we saw in segment 4 have a lot to do with the impoverishment of the soil? Such statements are employed more for their poetic neatness and emotional appeal than for any rigorous reasoning they may contain. Scenes of tenant farmer families **(10.39)** appeal directly to our emotional response to such poverty. This segment picks up on motifs introduced in segment 4, on the Civil War. Now, the film tells us, these people cannot go west, because there is no more open land there.

Now the problem has been introduced and discussed, and emotional appeals have prepared the audience to accept a solution. Segment 8 presents that solution and begins the part of the film devoted to the proofs that this solution is an effective one. In segment 8, the map of the opening titles returns, and the narrator says, "There is no such thing as an ideal river in nature, but the Mississippi River is out of joint." Here we have another example of an enthymeme—an inference assumed to be logically valid and factually accurate. The Mississippi may be "out of joint" for certain uses, but would it present a problem to the animals and plants in its ecosystem? This statement assumes that an "ideal" river would be one perfectly suited to *our* needs and purposes. The narrator goes on to give the film's most clear-cut statement of its argument: "The old River *can* be controlled. We had the power to take the Valley apart. We have the power to put it together again."

Now we can see why the film's form has been organized as it has. In early segments, especially 3 and 5, we saw how America developed great agricultural and industrial strength. At the time, we might have taken these events as simple facts of history. But now they turn out to be crucial to the film's argument. That argument might be summarized this way: We have seen that the American people have the power to build and to destroy; therefore, they have the power to build again.

The narrator continues, "In 1933 we started . . . ," going on to describe how Congress formed the TVA. This segment presents the TVA as an already settled solution to the problem and offers no other possible solutions. Thus something that was actually controversial seems to be a matter of straightforward implementation. Here is a case where one solution, because it has so far been effective in dealing with a problem, is taken to be *the* solution. Yet, in retrospect, it is not certain that the massive series of dams built by the TVA was the single best solution to flooding. Perhaps a less radical plan combining reforesting with conservation-oriented farming would have created fewer new problems (such as the displacement of people from the land flooded by the dams). Perhaps local governments rather than the federal government would have been more efficient problem solvers. *The River* does not bother to rebut these alternatives, relying instead on our habitual inference from problem to solution.

10.40 A beautiful lake in *The River.*

10.41 In *The River,* men going to work are framed in low angle against the sky.

10.42 Soon after this, one shot begins on a hillside, also against the sky, then tilts down . . .

Segment 9 contains similarities to and differences from several earlier parts. It begins with a list of dams, which we see in progress or finished. This echoes the lists of rivers, trees, towns, and so on that we have heard at intervals. The serene shots of the artificial lakes that follow link the ending to the beginning, recalling the lyrical river shots of segment 2 (**10.40**). The displaced, flooded-out, and unemployed people from segment 6 seem now to be happily at work, building planned model towns on government loans. Electricity generated by the dams links these rural communities to those "hundred cities and thousand towns" we heard about earlier, bringing to the countryside "the advantages of urban life." Many motifs planted in a simple fashion are now picked up and woven together to act as proofs of the TVA's benefits. The ending shows life as being parallel to the way it was in the beginning—beautiful nature, productive people—but enhanced by modern government planning. The film's middle segments have denied us the picturesque views of mountains and sky we saw at the beginning. But after the introduction of the TVA, such shots return (**10.41–10.43**). Tying the ending back to the beginning, the imagery shows a return to idyllic nature, under the auspices of government planning.

10.43 . . . to reveal the model town.

An upswell of music and a series of images of the dams and rushing water create a brief epilogue summarizing the factors that have brought about the change—the TVA dams. Under the ending titles and credits, we see the map again. A list tells us the names of the various government agencies that sponsored the film or assisted in its making. These again seem to lend authority to the source of the arguments in the film.

The River achieved its purpose. Favorable initial response led a major American studio, Paramount, to agree to distribute the film, a rare opportunity for a government-sponsored short documentary at that time. Reviewers and public alike greeted the film enthusiastically. A contemporary critic's review testifies to the power of the film's rhetorical form. After describing the early portions, Gilbert Seldes wrote, "And so, without your knowing it, you arrive at the Tennessee Valley—and if this is propaganda, make the most of it, because it is masterly. It is as if the pictures which Mr. Lorentz took arranged themselves in such an order that they supplied their own argument, not as if an argument conceived in advance dictated the order of the pictures."

President Roosevelt himself saw *The River* and liked it. He helped get congressional support to start a separate government agency, the U.S. Film Service, to make other documentaries like it. But not everyone was in favor of Roosevelt's policies or believed that the government should set itself up to make films that essentially espoused the views of the administration currently in office. By 1940, the Congress had taken away the U.S. Film Service's funding, and documentary films were once again made only within the separate sections of the government. In such ways, rhetorical form can lead both to direct action and to controversy.

10.44 Maya Deren's *Choreography for Camera* frames and cuts a dancer's movements . . .

10.45 . . . to suggest graceful passage across different times and places.

"One of the things that goes on in Critical Mass (this is also true of much of the rest of my work and of the work by others I admire) is a process of training the spectator to watch the film."

— Hollis Frampton, experimental filmmaker

Experimental Film

Another basic type of filmmaking is willfully nonconformist. In opposition to dominant, or mainstream, cinema, some filmmakers set out to create films that challenge orthodox notions of what a movie can show and how it can show it. These filmmakers work independently of the studio system, and often they work alone. Their films are hard to classify, but usually they are called *experimental* or *avant-garde.*

Experimental films are made for many reasons. The filmmaker may wish to express personal experiences or viewpoints in ways that would seem eccentric in a mainstream context. In *Mass for the Dakota Sioux,* Bruce Baillie suggests a despair at the failure of America's optimistic vision of history. Su Friedrich's *Damned If You Don't,* a story of a nun who discovers her sexuality, presents the theme of release from religious commitment. Alternatively, the filmmaker may seek to convey a mood or a physical quality (**10.44, 10.45**).

The filmmaker may also wish to explore some possibilities of the medium itself. Experimental filmmakers have tinkered with cinema in myriad ways. They have presented cosmic allegories, such as Stan Brakhage's *Dog Star Man,* and highly private japes, as in Ken Jacobs's *Little Stabs at Happiness.* Robert Breer's *Fist Fight* experiments with shots only one or two frames long (6.127); by contrast, the shots in Andy Warhol's *Eat* last until the camera runs out of film. An experimental film might be improvised or built according to mathematical plan. For *Eiga-zuke (Pickled Film),* Japanese American Sean Morijiro Sunada O'Gara applied pickling agents to negative film and then handprinted the blotchy abstractions onto positive stock.

The experimental filmmaker may tell no story, creating poetic reveries such as Willard Maas's *Geography of the Body* (**10.46**) or pulsating visual collages such as *Ballet mécanique,* which serves as one of our main examples here. Alternatively, the filmmaker may create a fictional story, but it usually challenges the viewer. Yvonne Rainer's *Film About a Woman Who . . .* presents its narrative partly through a series of slides that a group of men and women are watching. At the same time, on the sound track, we hear anonymous voices carrying on a dialogue, but we cannot confidently assign any voice to a particular character. Rainer thus forces us to weigh everything we see and hear on its own terms, apart from any involvement with characters (**10.47**).

Any sort of footage may be used for an avant-garde film. Images that a documentarist might take as fragments of actuality can be mobilized for quite different purposes (**10.48**). Bruce Conner pulls footage from travelogues and newsreels to create a sweeping image of the destruction of civilization in *A Movie* (pp. 376–381). Within the experimental mode, such scavenged works are often called *found-footage films.*

Experimentalists have also used staging to express distinct feelings or ideas (**10.49**). By superimposing different portions of a kitchen scene from a fiction film, Ivan Galeta's *Two Times in One Space* creates cycles of people splitting or drifting like phantoms. There is avant-garde animation as well, as in Breer's *Fuji* (pp. 388–390) and Red Grooms's *Tappy Toes* (**10.50**).

The freedom available to experimental film is on flamboyant display in Kenneth Anger's *Scorpio Rising.* Anger takes as his subject the motorcycle culture of the 1960s, and he includes scenes of bikers working on their machines, dressing, reveling, and racing. Alongside footage of bikers glimpsed on the streets or in parties, there are many staged incidents—chiefly around Scorpio, a James Dean–like figure. Anger also cuts in still photos, comic strips, old movies, and Nazi posters. In addition, each segment is accompanied by a rock-and-roll song that adds an ironic or ominous tone to the images. For example, as one young man fetishistically tunes up his bike, Anger shows the figure of death looming over him (**10.51**), and on the sound track we hear, "My boyfriend's back . . . and he's coming after you." This sequence links biking to a death wish, an idea that returns in cartoons and other im-

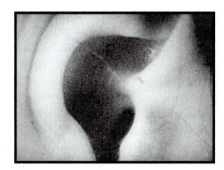

10.46 In *Geography of the Body,* an ear creates an abstract, lyrical composition.

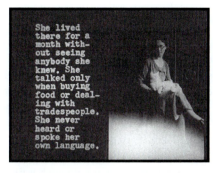

10.47 Thanks to Rainer's combination of images, sounds, and captions in *Film About a Woman Who . . .* , the viewer is left free to imagine several possible stories.

10.49 James Broughton's *Mother's Day* offers static pictures of adults playing children's games.

10.50 Pop-art painter Red Grooms animates cut-out figures to create the cheerful experimental film *Tappy Toes.*

10.51 Death imagery in *Scorpio Rising.*

10.48 Gianfranco Baruchello's *La Verifica inserta* scavenges frames from old features to create a flicker film, here juxtaposing shots including telephones.

agery. In such ways, *Scorpio Rising* creates elusive but powerful associations, suggesting the homoerotic dimensions of bike culture, comparing its rituals to fascism and Christianity, and evoking the possibility that people often model their behavior on images supplied by mass media.

Impossible to define in a capsule formula, avant-garde cinema is recognizable by its efforts at self-expression or experimentation outside mainstream cinema. Yet the boundary lines can be breached. Techniques associated with the avant-garde have been deployed in music videos by Michel Gondry and Chris Cunningham. In fact, Conner, Anger, Derek Jarman, and other experimentalists were early pioneers of music video. And mainstream features have been continually drawing on the avant-garde for ideas and techniques. Over the history of film, the basic modes have cross-fertilized each other constantly.

CONNECT TO THE BLOG

We have written on some recent experimental films in "Lewis Klahr X 3, X 4," at
www.davidbordwell.net/blog/?p=157;
"3 notions about CREMASTER 2," at
www.davidbordwell.net/blog/?p=418;
"Manhattan: Symphony of a great city," at
www.davidbordwell.net/blog/?p=1709;
and "Lines of sight and light," at
www.davidbordwell.net/blog/?p=2198.

10.52   The slowly changing background obliges the viewer to notice the symmetrical geometry of the bridge's design in *Railroad Turnbridge.*

"Thematic interpretation comes from literature: it's been carried over to conventional narrative films, but it shouldn't be grafted onto experimental films, which are often a reaction against such conventions."

— J. J. Murphy, experimental filmmaker

Types of Form in Experimental Films

Like documentaries, experimental films sometimes use narrative form. James Sibley Watson, Jr., and Melville Webber's 1928 film *The Fall of the House of Usher* evokes the atmosphere of the Edgar Allan Poe story through expressionistic sets and lighting. Occasionally, we find an experimental film organized by categories, as in Peter Greenaway's *The Falls,* a mockumentary tracing, in alphabetical order, information about a disparate group of people named Fall. Still other types of form are characteristic of experimental films: abstract form and associational form.

Abstract Form   When we watch a film that tells a story, or surveys categories, or makes an argument, we usually pay little attention to the sheer pictorial qualities of the shots. Yet it's possible to organize an entire film around colors, shapes, sizes, and movements in the images.

How? Consider *Railroad Turnbridge,* by the sculptor Richard Serra. A turnbridge allows a section of railroad tracks to swivel on a central column, clearing space for tall boats passing along the river. Serra set up a camera at the center of a turnbridge and filmed the bridge's movement. The result onscreen is surprising. The bridge is swiveling, but because the camera is anchored to it, the crossed girders and powerful uprights seem monumentally static, and the landscape rotates majestically (**10.52**). There is no argument, no survey of categories. A narrative film might have used the bridge for an exciting chase or fight, but Serra invites us to contemplate the bridge as a geometrical sculpture, all grids and angles, in relation to the curves and sweeps of nature beyond. Serra asks us to notice and enjoy the slowly changing pictorial qualities of line, shape, tonalities, and movement.

Of course, all films contain these qualities. We have seen how the lyrical beauty of the river and lake shots in *The River* functions to create parallels, and the rhythm of its musical score enhances our emotional involvement in the argument being made. But in *The River,* an abstract pattern becomes a means to an end, always subordinate to the rhetorical purposes of the film. It is not organized around abstract qualities but rather emphasizes such qualities only occasionally. In **abstract form,** the *whole* film's system will be determined by such qualities.

Abstract films are often organized in a way that we might call *theme and variations.* This term usually applies to music, where a melody or other type of motif is introduced, and then a series of different versions of that same melody follows—often with such extreme differences of key and rhythm that the original melody becomes difficult to recognize. An abstract film's form may work in a similar fashion. An introductory section will typically show us the kinds of relationships the film will use as its basic material. Then other segments will go on to present similar kinds of relationships but with changes. The changes may be slight, depending on our noticing that the similarities are still greater than the differences. But abstract films also usually depend on building up greater and greater differences from the introductory material. Thus we may find considerable contrast coming into the film, and sudden differences can help us to sense when a new segment has started. If the film's formal organization has been created with care, the similarities and differences will not be random. There will be some underlying principle that runs through the film.

The theme-and-variations principle is clearly evident in J. J. Murphy's *Print Generation.* Murphy selected 60 shots from home movies, then rephotographed them over and over on a contact printer. Each succeeding duplication lost photographic quality, until the final images became unrecognizable. *Print Generation* repeats the footage 25 times, starting with the most abstract images and moving to the most recognizable ones. Then the process is reversed, and the images gradually move back toward abstraction (**10.53, 10.54**). On the sound track, the progression is exactly the opposite. Murphy rerecorded the sound 25 times, but the film begins with the most clearly audible version. As the image clarifies, the sound deteriorates; as the image slips back into abstraction, the sound clarifies. Part of the fascination of this experimental film derives from seeing blobs and sparkles of abstract color become slowly defined as people and landscapes before passing back into abstraction. The film also teases us to discover its overall formal pattern.

As *Railroad Turnbridge* and *Print Generation* indicate, by calling a film's form abstract, we do not mean that the film has no recognizable objects in it. It is true that many abstract films use pure shapes and colors, created by the filmmaker by drawing, cutting out pieces of colored paper, animating clay shapes, and the like. An alternative approach involves using real objects and isolating them from their everyday context in such a way that their abstract qualities come forward. After all, shapes, colors, rhythmic movements, and every abstract quality that the filmmaker uses exist both in nature and in human-made objects. Markings on animals, bird songs, cloud formations, and other such natural phenomena often attract us because they seem beautiful or striking—qualities similar to those that we look for in artworks. Moreover, even those objects that we create for very practical and mundane uses may have pleasing contours or textures. Chairs are made to sit on, but we will usually try to furnish our home with chairs that also look attractive to us.

Because abstract qualities are common, experimental filmmakers often start by photographing real objects. But, since the filmmakers then juxtapose the images to create relations of shape, color, and so on, the film is still using abstract organization in spite of the fact that we can recognize the object as a bird, a face, or a spoon. And, because the abstract qualities in films are shared with real objects, such films call on skills we use in everyday life. Normally, we use our ability to recognize shapes and colors in practical ways, as when we drive and have to interpret traffic signs and lights quickly. But, in watching an abstract film, we don't need to use the shapes, colors, or repetitions that we see and hear for practical purposes. Consequently, we can notice them more fully and see relationships that we would seldom bother to look for during the practical activities of everyday life. In a film, these abstract qualities become interesting for their own sake.

This impractical interest has led some critics and viewers to think of abstract films as frivolous. Critics may call them "art for art's sake," since all they seem to do is present us with a series of interesting patterns. Yet in doing so, such films often make us more aware of such patterns, and we may be better able to notice them in the everyday world as well. No one who has watched *Railroad Turnbridge* can see bridges in quite the same way afterward. In talking about abstract films, we might amend the phrase to "art for life's sake"—for such films enhance our lives as much as do the films of other formal types.

An Example of Abstract Form: *Ballet mécanique* *Ballet mécanique* ("Mechanical Ballet"), one of the earliest abstract films, was also one of the most influential. It remains a highly enjoyable avant-garde film and a classic example of how mundane objects can be transformed when their abstract qualities are used as the basis for a film's form.

Two filmmakers collaborated on *Ballet mécanique* during 1923–1924. They were Dudley Murphy, a young American journalist and aspiring film producer, and Fernand Léger, a major French painter. Léger had developed his own distinctive version of Cubism in his paintings, often using stylized machine parts. His interest in machines transferred well into the cinema, and it contributed to the central formal principles of *Ballet mécanique*.

This title suggests the paradox the filmmakers employ in creating their film's thematic material and variations. We expect a ballet to be flowing, with human dancers performing it. A classical ballet seems the opposite of a machine's movements, yet the film creates a mechanical dance. Relatively few of the many objects we see in the film are actually machines; it mostly uses hats, faces, bottles, kitchen utensils, and the like. But through juxtaposition with machines and through visual and temporal rhythms, we are cued to see even a woman's moving eyes and mouth as being like machine parts.

10.53 Theme and variations in *Print Generation*: in earlier portions of the film, each one-second shot is more or less identifiable.

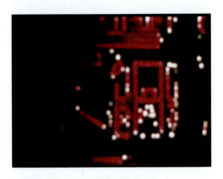

10.54 After many generations of reprinting, the same image becomes abstract, with hot highlights remaining. The color is biased toward red because that is the last layer of the emulsion to fade in rephotography.

10.55   A horse collar in *Ballet mécanique.*

10.56   In *Ballet mécanique,* the figure of Chaplin is highly abstract—recognizably human but also made up of simple shapes that move in a jerky fashion.

Film style plays a crucial role in most films using abstract form. In keeping with its overall formal design, *Ballet mécanique* uses film techniques to stress the geometric qualities of ordinary things. Close framing, masks, unusual camera angles, and neutral backgrounds isolate objects and emphasize their shapes and textures (**10.55**). The film reverses our normal expectations about the nature of movement, making objects dance and turning human action into mechanical gestures.

We cannot segment *Ballet mécanique* by tracing its arguments or dividing it into scenes of narrative action. Rather, we must look for changes in abstract qualities being used at different points in the film. Going by this principle, we can find nine segments in *Ballet mécanique:*

C. A credits sequence with a stylized, animated figure of Charlie Chaplin ("Charlot" in France) introducing the film's title

1. The introduction of the film's rhythmic elements

2. A treatment of objects viewed through prisms

3. Rhythmic movements

4. A comparison of people and machines

5. Rhythmic movements of intertitles and pictures

6. More rhythmic movements, mostly of circular objects

7. Quick dances of objects

8. A return to Charlot and the opening elements

Ballet mécanique uses the theme-and-variations approach in a complex way, introducing many individual motifs in rapid succession, then bringing them back at intervals and in different combinations. Each new segment picks up on a limited number of the abstract qualities from the previous one and plays with these for a while. The final segments use precise elements from early in the film once again, and the ending strongly echoes the opening. The film throws a great deal of material at us in a short time, and we must actively seek to make connections among motifs.

As suggested previously, the introductory portion of an abstract film usually gives us strong cues as to what we can expect to see developed later. *Ballet mécanique*'s animated Chaplin begins this process (**10.56**). Already the human figure is also an object.

Segment 1 surprises us by beginning with a woman swinging in a garden (**10.57**). Yet the film's title may lead us to notice the regular rhythm of the swinging and the puppetlike gestures as the woman repeatedly lifts her eyes and head, then lowers them, a fixed smile on her face. Certain abstract qualities already have become prominent. Suddenly, a rapid succession of images appears, passing too quickly for us to do any more than glimpse a hat, bottles, an abstract white triangle, and other objects. Next a woman's mouth appears, smiling, then not smiling, then smiling again. The hat returns, then the smiling mouth again, then some spinning gears; then a shiny ball circles close to the camera. The woman in the swing returns but now upside down (**10.58**). This segment ends with the shiny ball, now swinging back and forth directly toward the camera, and we are invited to compare its movement with that of the woman in the swing. We are thus confirmed in our expectation that she is not a character but an object, like the bottle or the shiny ball. The same is true of that smiling mouth, which does not suggest an emotion as much as a regularly changing shape. Shapes of objects (a round hat, vertical bottles), direction of movement (the swing, the shiny ball), textures (the shininess of both the ball and the bottles), and the rhythms of the objects' movements will be qualities that draw our attention.

With these expectations set up in the short introductory section, the film goes on to vary its elements. Segment 2 sticks fairly closely to the elements just introduced by beginning with another view of the shiny ball, now seen through a prism. There follow other shots of household objects, similar to the ball in that they are

10.57 The opening shot of *Ballet méca-nique*'s first segment.

10.58 *Ballet mécanique.*

10.59 In *Ballet mécanique,* a prism shot is recognizable as a pot lid, its round shape picking up that of both the ball and the hat of the previous segment.

10.60 A masked shot in *Ballet mécanique.*

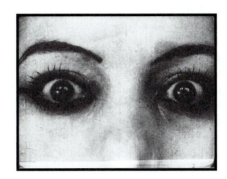

10.61 *Ballet mécanique:* a shot of a woman with open eyes.

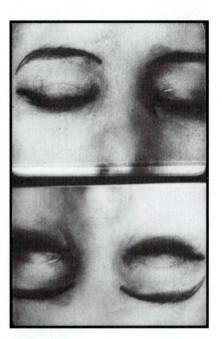

10.62 By the last frame of the same shot, her eyes are closed, and the first frame of the next shows her upside down.

also shiny and are seen through a prism **(10.59)**. Here is a good example of how a mundane object can be taken out of its everyday context and made abstract.

In the middle of the series of prism shots, we see a rapid burst of shots, alternating a white circle and a white triangle. This is yet another motif that will return at intervals, with variations. These shapes invite us to make comparisons: the pot lid is also round whereas the prismatic facets are somewhat triangular. During the rest of segment 2, we see more prism shots, interspersed with another rapid series of circles and triangles, followed by views of a woman's eyes opening and closing, a woman's eyes partially masked off by dark shapes **(10.60),** and finally the smiling/unsmiling mouth from segment 1.

Segment 2 has further confirmed our expectations that the film will compare shapes, rhythms, or textures. We also begin to see a pattern of surprising interruptions of the segments with bursts of brief shots. In segment 1, interruptions were created by shots alternating objects and a single triangle. Now we have twice seen a circle and triangle alternate. The rhythm of editing is as important as the rhythm of movement within individual shots for creating abstract relationships.

Ballet mécanique provides a good example of how filmmakers may work outside the continuity editing system and create dynamic patterns of shots. One of the film's funniest moments comes in segment 2 and depends on a precise graphic match. We see an extreme close-up of a woman's wide-open eyes **(10.61)**. She closes them, leaving her eyeliner and brows as dark crescents against her white skin **(10.62)**. A cut presents us with the same composition, now upside down (10.62). The eyes and brows are in nearly identical positions, but reversed. When the eyes pop open **(10.63)**, we're surprised to find their positions switched; quick cutting makes the match nearly indiscernible. Amusing touches like this make *Ballet mécanique* as enjoyable to watch today as it must have been when it was first shown 80 years ago.

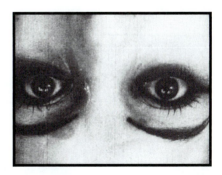

10.63 Later in the second shot, she opens her eyes.

10.64   In *Ballet mécanique,* a strongly horizontal composition is contrasted with . . .

10.65   . . . a strongly vertical one.

10.66   *Ballet mécanique* cuts from a machine part . . .

10.67   . . . to mechanical repetitions of a woman's movements.

Now that its basic patterns are well established, the film begins to introduce greater variations in order to play with our expectations. Segment 3 begins with shots of rows of platelike discs, alternating with spinning shapes reminiscent of a fairground game wheel. Will round shapes and movements provide the main principle of development in this segment? Suddenly, the camera plunges down a twisting fairground slide. We see elements such as marching feet, cars going over the camera, and rapid shots of a carnival ride's cars spinning past. Here different rhythms succeed one another, and common shape seems less important. Many of the objects are new ones, seen out of doors. Yet, after the carnival cars, we see a relatively lengthy shot of a spinning, shiny object—not in a prism view but at least recalling the image of the kitchen utensils seen earlier. The segment ends with the familiar rapid alternation of circle and triangle.

Segment 4 gives us the film's most explicit comparison of humans and machines. We first see a carnival slide from above, picking up on an element from segment 3. The slide stretches horizontally across the screen, and in quick succession, a man's silhouette whizzes down it four times (**10.64**). This may seem a continuation of segment 3's concentration on rhythm, but next we see a machine part, strongly vertical on the screen (**10.65**), with a piston moving up and down rhythmically. Again we see similarities—a tubelike object with another object moving along it—and differences—the compositions use opposing directions, and the four movements of the man are shown in different shots, while the camera holds as the piston moves up and down within one shot. More shots compare the slide and machine parts, ending with one machine seen through a prism.

The familiar alternating circle and triangle return, but with differences: now the triangle is sometimes upside down, and each shape remains on the screen slightly longer. The segment continues with more spinning shiny objects and machine parts; then it reintroduces the motif of the woman's masked eye (similar to 10.60). Now the motions of this eye are compared to machine parts.

Segment 4 closes with one of *Ballet mécanique*'s most famous and daring moments. After a shot of a rotating machine part (**10.66**), we see 7 identically repeated shots of a laundry woman climbing a stair and gesturing (**10.67**). The segment returns to the smiling mouth, then gives us 11 more repetitions of the same shot of the laundry woman, a shot of a large piston, and 5 more repetitions of the laundry woman shot. This insistent repetition makes the woman's movements as precise as those of the machine. Even though she is seen in a real place, we cannot see her as a character but must concentrate on her movements' rhythms. Segment 4 is quite different from earlier ones, but it does bring back motifs: The prism recurs briefly (from segment 2), spinning shiny objects recall those of segment 3, and the woman's eyes and mouth (segments 1 and 2) return, having been absent from segment 3.

Segment 4 has been the culmination of the film's comparison of mechanical objects with people. Now segment 5 introduces a strong contrast by concentrating on printed intertitles. Unlike other segments, this one begins with a black screen, which is gradually revealed to be a dark card on which a white zero is painted.

Unexpectedly, an intertitle appears: "ON A VOLÉ UN COLLIER DE PERLES DE 5 MILLIONS" ("A pearl necklace worth 5 million has been stolen"). In a narrative film, this might give us story information, but the filmmakers use the printed language as one more visual motif for rhythmic variation. There follows a series of quick shots, with large zeros, sometimes one, sometimes three, appearing and disappearing, shrinking and growing. Parts of the intertitle appear in isolation ("on a volé"), participating in this dance of letters. The film plays with an ambiguity: Is the zero really an "0," the first letter of the sentence? Or is it part of the number 5,000,000? Or is it a stylized representation of the pearl necklace itself? Beyond this sort of play with a visual pun, the zero recalls and varies the circle motif that has been so prominent in the film.

More punning occurs as the zero gives way to a picture of a horse collar—which resembles the zero visually but also refers to the word *collier* (which in French can mean either "necklace" or "collar"). Editing makes the collar bob about in its

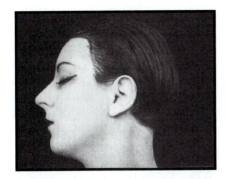

10.68 *Ballet mécanique*'s series of circular shapes begins with a woman's head, eyes closed, turning . . .

10.69 . . . after which we see a statue swing toward and away from the camera.

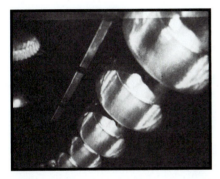

10.70 *Ballet mécanique:* a brief shot of kitchen utensils.

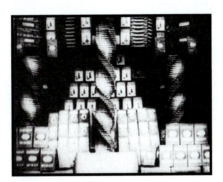

10.71 In *Ballet mécanique,* spiral shapes seem to freeze the gyrating motions that have made up so much of the film.

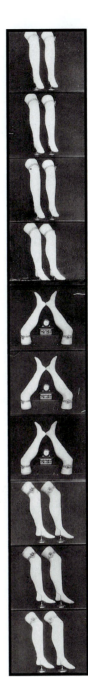

10.72 In *Ballet mécanique,* very short shots make mannequin legs "dance."

own little dance (10.55) and alternate with moving zeros and parts of the intertitle sentence, sometimes printed backward—to emphasize their graphic, rather than informative, function. This segment has been very different from earlier ones, but even here a couple of motifs are repeated. Just before the horse collar is introduced, we see the masked woman's eye briefly, and, in the course of the rapid flashes of intertitles, one tiny shot of a machine part is inserted.

After this point, the film moves toward variations that are closer to the elements of the opening segments. Segment 6 shows us rhythmic movements involving mostly circular shapes **(10.68, 10.69).** Once again the comparison of person and object comes forward. An abstract circular shape grows, cueing us to watch for the recurrence of this shape. A woman's face appears in a prismed view; she passes a piece of cardboard with holes cut in it before her face, with her expression continually changing in a mechanical fashion. We see the circles and triangles alternate again, but this time in four different sizes. A quick series of shots of rows of shiny kitchen utensils follows **(10.70),** with short bursts of black film interspersed. This blackness picks up and varies the dark backgrounds of the intertitles in segment 5, and the shiny pots and other utensils reintroduce a motif that has appeared in every segment *except* 5. The motif of rows of objects had come in segment 3, while the swinging motion of the utensils in many of these shots echoes the swinging of the woman and the shiny ball from way back in segment 1.

Segment 7 continues the turn back to the beginning. It begins with a shot of a display window **(10.71).** The circle motif returns, leading into a set of dances that vary key motifs. Very rapid editing makes a pair of mannequin legs dance **(10.72);** then the legs start to spin within the shots. The shiny ball motif returns, but now two balls spin

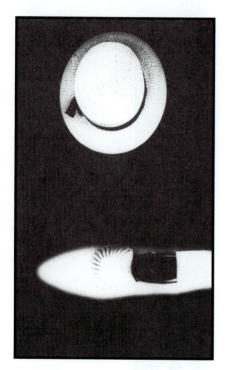

10.73   Shapes create graphic contrast in *Ballet mécanique.*

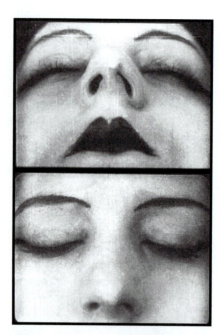

10.74   In *Ballet mécanique,* slight changes of composition make a face "nod."

10.75   The final shot of *Ballet mécanique.*

in opposite directions. Then a hat and a shoe alternate quickly **(10.73),** and the editing creates a startlingly abstract effect. At first, we see the different shapes distinctly, but as the brief shots continue to alternate, we notice variations. The hat changes position, and sometimes the shoe points in one direction, sometimes the other. The cutting rhythm accelerates, and the shots become so short that we see only a single white object pulsating, morphing from circle to lozenge and back again. The filmmakers use the graphic contrasts they've created to make us aware of apparent motion, our tendency to see movement in a series of slightly different still pictures. This is one process that makes cinema itself possible. (See Chapter 1.)

After the shoe-and-hat duet, more shots of the woman follow, again cut to make her face execute a series of artificial shifts. Two slightly different views of a woman's face quickly alternate, inducing us to see the head as nodding **(10.74).** Finally, quick shots of bottles make them seem to change position in a dancelike rhythm. Here, where the mechanical ballet becomes most explicit, the film draws together elements from its beginning, and from the previous segment, where the recapitulation of the earlier segments had begun. Segment 7 avoids motifs from the center of the film—segments 3–5—and thus gives us a sense both that the film is continuing to develop and that it is coming full circle.

The final segment makes this return more obvious by showing us the Chaplin figure again. Now its movements are even less human, and at the end, most of its parts seem to fall away, leaving the head alone on the screen. The spinning head may remind us of the woman's profile (10.68) seen earlier. But the film is not quite over. Its last shot brings back the woman from the swing in segment 1, now standing in the same garden smelling a flower and looking around. Seen in another context, her gestures might seem ordinary to us **(10.75).** But by now, as Hollis Frampton puts it (p. 366), the film has trained us sufficiently for us to make the connection between this shot and what has preceded it. Our expectations have been so strongly geared to seeing rhythmic, mechanical movement that we will probably see her smiles and head gestures as *un*natural, like other motifs we have seen in the film. Léger and Murphy end their abstract film by emphasizing how much they have altered our perception of ordinary objects and people.

Associational Form   Many experimental films draw on a poetic series of transitions that create what we may term **associational form.** Associational formal systems suggest ideas and expressive qualities by grouping images that may not have any immediate logical connection. But the very fact that the images and sounds are juxtaposed prods us to look for some connection—an *association* that binds them together.

Godfrey Reggio's *Koyaanisqatsi* is a clear example of associational form. The film is built out of shots of widely different things—airplanes and buttes, subways and clouds, rockets and pedestrians. At one point, rows of frankfurters are pumped out of a machine and fed onto an assembly line. Reggio then cuts to fast-motion shots of commuters riding escalators. The juxtaposition has no narrative connection, and the pictorial qualities are not as strongly stressed as they would be in *Ballet mécanique.* Instead, the shots evoke the idea of impersonal, routine sameness, perhaps suggesting that modern life makes people into standardized units. The filmmaker has created an association among unlike things.

Koyaanisqatsi illustrates the unique qualities of associational form. The film surely presents a process, but it does not tell a story in the manner of narrative filmmaking. It offers no continuing characters, no specific causal connections, and no temporal order among the scenes. The film has a point, perhaps several, but it doesn't attempt to persuade us of it through an argument, giving reasons and offering evidence to lead us to a conclusion. There is no voice-over narrator as in *The River* to define problems and marshall evidence. Nor does the film explore a clear-cut set of categories. It centers on majestic nature and destructive technology, very loose and open-ended ideas. But *Koyaanisqatsi* is not purely a pictorial exercise either, in the manner of abstract form. The connections we make among its images sometimes involve visual qualities, but these qualities are associated with broader concepts and emotions.

This process is somewhat comparable to the techniques of metaphor and simile used in lyric poetry. When the poet Robert Burns says, "My love is like a red, red rose," we do not leap to the conclusion that his love is prickly to the touch, bright red, or vulnerable to aphids. Rather, we look for the possible conceptual links: her beauty is the most likely reason for the comparison.

A similar process goes on in associational films. Here the imagery and the metaphorical connections that poetry conveys through language are presented in a more direct fashion. A filmmaker could film a woman he loved in a garden and suggest by visual juxtaposition that she is like the flowers that surround her. (Indeed, this might be an implicit meaning that viewers could assign to *Ballet mécanique*'s last shot, if it were taken out of context.) Some critics would consider associational form the closest that cinema can come to lyric poetry.

The imagery used in associational form may range from the conventional to the strikingly original, and the conceptual connections can be readily apparent or downright mystifying. These possibilities are not necessarily linked: a highly original juxtaposition might have an obvious emotional or conceptual implication. Again, poetry offers examples. Many religious, patriotic, romantic, and laudatory poems use strings of images to create an expressive tone. In "America the Beautiful," the images of "spacious skies," "purple mountains' majesty," and "fruited plain" add up to suggest the patriotic fervor expressed in the chorus, "God shed his grace on thee."

Another poem might be more elusive in its effect, giving us less explicit statements of the associative qualities of its imagery. The Japanese poetic form called *haiku* usually juxtaposes two images in a brief three-line form, in order to create an immediate emotion in the reader. Here, for example, is a haiku by the Japanese poet Kakei:

The eleventh moon—
Storks listlessly
Standing in a row

Kakei's images are somewhat cryptic, and the purpose for connecting them is somewhat mysterious. Yet, if we are willing to fill in with our imaginations, as one is supposed to do with haiku, the effect should be a mood, evoking autumnal stillness with perhaps a trace of melancholy. This tone isn't present in either the moon or the storks but results from the juxtaposition of the two images.

So far we have looked at associational form working at a fairly small-scale level: the side-by-side juxtaposition of images. Associational form also creates larger-scale patterns that can organize an entire film. Yet because associational formal systems are unlimited in their subjects and means of organization, it's impossible to define a conventional set of parts into which an associational film will fall. Some films will show us a series of amusing images, while others may offer us frightening ones. Still, we can make a start at understanding associational form by noticing that it usually accords with a few general principles.

First, the filmmaker typically groups images together in larger sets, each of which creates a distinct, unified part of the film. Each group of images can then contrast with other groups of images. This principle of grouping is also seen in abstract form, as our *Ballet mécanique* analysis shows. Second, as in other types of form, the film uses repeated motifs to reinforce associational connections. Third, associational form strongly invites interpretation, the assigning of general meanings to the film, as in the environmentalist implications of *Koyaanisqatsi*.

The associational small-scale connections, the distinct large-scale parts, the repeated motifs, the cues for interpretation—all these factors indicate that associational organization puts demands on the viewer. This is why so many filmmakers seeking to push the boundaries of form use associational patterns. Although associational form may use striking, original, even puzzling, juxtapositions, it may still elicit a fairly familiar emotion or idea. The explicit point of *Koyaanisqatsi* is not particularly subtle or novel. Here, as in many associational films, the purpose is to make a familiar emotion or concept vivid by means of new imagery and fresh juxtapositions.

Other associational films are more complex and evocative. The filmmaker will not necessarily give us obvious cues to the appropriate expressive qualities or concepts. He or she may simply create a series of unusual and striking combinations and leave it up to us to tease out their relations. Kenneth Anger's *Scorpio Rising*, for instance, explicitly associates motorcycle gangs with traditional religious groups and with Nazi violence, but it also suggests, more elusively, that gang regalia and rituals have homoerotic aspects. Like other sorts of film form, associational form can offer implicit as well as more explicit meanings.

An Example of Associational Form: A Movie Bruce Conner's film *A Movie* illustrates how associational form can confront us with evocative and mysterious juxtapositions, yet can at the same time create a coherent film that has an intense impact on the viewer.

Conner made *A Movie,* his first film, in 1958. Like Léger, he worked in the visual and plastic arts and was noted for his *assemblage* pieces—collages built up of miscellaneous found objects. Conner took a comparable approach to filmmaking. He typically used footage from old newsreels, Hollywood movies, soft-core pornography, and the like. By working in the found-footage genre, Conner juxtaposed two shots from widely different sources. When we see the two shots together, we strive to find some connection between them. From a series of juxtapositions, our activity can create an overall emotion or concept.

A Movie uses a musical accompaniment that helps establish these emotions and ideas. As with the images, Conner chose music that already existed: three portions of Respighi's well-known tone poem *The Pines of Rome*. The music is important to the film's form, since it has distinct sections. Moreover, the atmosphere of each segment is different, corresponding to the music. The beginning of what we'll identify as segment 3, showing women carrying totems, the crash of the Hindenburg dirigible, and some daring acrobats, gains its ominous effect largely from the eerie score. Likewise, the driving music accompanying segment 4 sweeps a string of horrendous disasters into one plunging apocalyptic rush. Conner's use of *The Pines of Rome* shows vividly how associational form can create both general ideas and strong emotional effects.

We can break *A Movie* into four large-scale segments. Each segment consists of related images, marked off from other segments by a shared expressive idea and by a distinct musical accompaniment.

1. An introductory portion with the film's title and director's name and projectionists' markings

2. Quick, dynamic music with images of moving animals and vehicles on land

3. A more mysterious, tense section stressing precariously balanced objects in air and water

4. Frightening images of disaster and war interspersed with more lyrical, mysterious scenes

In only 12 minutes, *A Movie* leads us through a range of emotionally charged ideas and qualities. It also creates a distinct developmental thread. In segments 2–4, many shots emphasize accidents or aggressive actions, and while some of these seem funny or trivial at first, they gradually accumulate and become more serious. By segment 4, a series of war scenes and natural disasters presents practically an apocalyptic vision. *A Movie*'s tone finally eases in its closing underwater scenes.

Segment 1   This segment does far more than give us the title and the filmmaker's name, and for that reason, we have numbered it as the first segment rather than separating it off as a credits sequence. At first, we see blank black leader, over which the brisk opening of *The Pines of Rome* begins. This stresses the importance of the music in the film, since we hear it before seeing any images. Then the words "Bruce Conner" appear, remaining on the screen for many seconds. Because we do not need that much time to read the name, we may begin to sense that the film will playfully thwart our expectations.

After the name, we see more black leader, then white leader, then a quick flicker effect rapidly alternating two frames of the word "A" with a blank white leader, and finally the word "Movie." The word "By" appears, with more white frames, then "Bruce Conner," as before. Now a black leader appears, with markings that usually appear on the first portion of the film strip but that are seldom projected on the screen for the audience to see: splice cues, dots, and other signs. Then, suddenly, "End of Part Four" flashes on the screen.

We might think that Conner is simply playing with the graphic qualities of titles and leader marks, as Léger and Murphy did in segment 5 of *Ballet mécanique* with its dance of intertitles and zeros. But here Conner uses graphics with conventional meanings: leaders and credits usually signal the beginning, while "End of Part Four" implies we have already seen a considerable part of the film. Once again *A Movie* signals us that it will not be an ordinary film—not one in which the parts follow in logical order. We must expect odd juxtapositions. Moreover, the flicker and leader markings stress the physical qualities of the film medium itself. The title *A Movie* reinforces this reference to the medium, cueing us to watch this assemblage of shots *as* bits of film.

The opening continues with a countdown leader, beginning with "12" and flashing other numbers at one-second intervals—again, more signals to the projectionist, but seldom seen by the audience. Is *this* the beginning, then? But after "4," we are startled to see the film's first moving image: a "nudie" shot of a woman taking off her stockings. The shot is very worn, with lines and scratches, and we surmise that Conner scavenged it from an old stag film. Here *A Movie* helps us to focus our expectations by suggesting that it will involve more found footage of this

"Part of the creation of the sequence you're thinking about happened during the process of collecting film. I snip out small parts of films and collect them on a larger reel. Sometimes when I tail-end one bit of the film onto another, I'll find a relationship that I would have never thought about consciously—because it doesn't create a logical continuity, or it doesn't fit my concept of how to edit a film."

— Bruce Conner, experimental filmmaker

10.76   In *A Movie,* from a shot of galloping horses pulling a wagon, Conner cuts to . . .

10.77   . . . similar horses, but now pulling a fire engine on a city street.

10.78   A graphic match in *A Movie* links wagon . . .

10.79   . . . and tank.

type. After the nude shot, the countdown leader continues to "1," then the words "The End" appear. Another joke: this is the end of the leader, not of the film. Yet even this is untrue, since more leader appears, with "Movie" backward, more projectionists' signals, and a repeating number "1" that flickers in time to the music's quick tempo, then goes to black.

Segment 2   Although the music runs continuously over the transition, in segment 2, we begin to see a very different kind of image. A series of 12 shots shows us mounted Indians sitting on a hill, then chasing a fleeing wagon train, with Hopalong Cassidy recognizable as one of the cowboys. More old film footage follows, this time a clip suggesting a story situation that will continue from shot to shot: a fight between Indians and settlers. But Conner shows us this scene only to refer briefly to the conventional kind of movie he is *not* making **(10.76, 10.77)**. The association here seems clear enough; we move from horses to more horses, all in rapid motion. The next change, moving toward imagery of cavalry, confirms this association among horse-drawn vehicles.

There follows a shaky shot of a charging elephant. Now we must stretch our associations to account for this: maybe the link is through a series of rapidly moving animals? This seems safe enough to assume, as we see two more shots of horses' running legs. But the next shot shows a speeding locomotive's wheels. We must generalize the terms of the association still further—the rapid motion of animals and vehicles on land. (The "on land" idea may not seem important at this point, but it will become significant in contrast to the later segments, which often emphasize air and water.) The next series of shots, repeating these motifs and introducing a military tank, seems to confirm this overall idea of rushing movement.

Conner's editing creates the effect of one rushing mass of activity by a simple convention: common screen direction. The animals and vehicles move from left to right, or come directly at the camera, creating shots that cut together in traditional continuity (10.76, 10.77). The effect is to suggest a colossal rush toward a single target. The impossibility of this juxtaposition is amusing, but it also suggests that humans, animals, and machines are caught up in an energetic planetary race—but toward what? The urgency of this sequence is heightened by graphic matches on objects hurtling out at the viewer **(10.78, 10.79)**.

This sense of frantic activity continues into the later part of segment 2, which moves from the tank to a series of shots of race cars speeding around tracks. Since these shots initially confirm our expectations about moving animals and vehicles, they are less challenging to us—at first. Then one race car crashes, followed by two other similar crashes; and the segment ends with the long, spectacular fall of an old-fashioned car off a cliff. The sense of movement has become less funny and exhilarating, more uncontrolled and frightening. The tone of amusement has shifted toward one based on shock and horror in the face of so much devastation. Again, this effect is created by tight coordination of cutting, music, and movement in the frame. For instance, the frenzied buildup in the musical score accompanies the string of race car crashes. Blaring, dissonant phrases begin to punctuate the music at regular intervals, and Conner's editing times each one to coincide with a car crash. The manic energy of the tumultuous race has turned reckless and self-destructive.

During the crashes, the music has built up to a frenzied climax, and it cuts off abruptly as a "The End" title flashes on the screen. This parody of the ending of a conventional film suggests that the crashes have resulted from all that rushing motion earlier in the segment. At this point, we might begin to sense that there has been an underlying tone of aggression and danger from the start: the attacking Indians, the cavalry, the charging elephant, the tank, and so on. This element will be intensified in segments 3 and 4.

Segment 3   More black leader continues the transition set up by the "The End" title, and there is a pause before the music of segment 3 begins. (As at the film's opening, it plays at first over the darkness.) But this time the music is slow, bleak, and slightly ominous. The "Movie" title and more black leader move us into a series of shots very different from those of segment 2. Two Polynesian women carry large, totemlike objects on their heads. Leader and a title interrupt once more, introducing a short series of shots of a large dirigible in flight **(10.80)** and of an acrobat couple performing on a small platform and tightrope high above a street **(10.81).** If the women and the dirigible are associated through balancing, the dirigible is linked to the acrobats not only by that but also by an emphasis on heights and danger. This portion of the segment ends with a shot of a small plane plunging downward through fleecy clouds, as if, having lost its balance, it is falling. Slow, sinister music has cued us how to react to these floating and falling objects; without the music, we might take them to be lyrical, but in context, they suggest a vague threat. This passage ends with more titles: "A," "Movie," "By," and "Bruce Conner," followed by black leader.

10.80   *A Movie:* images of heights . . .

The next part of the segment begins with an apparent incongruity between music and image. A series of shots shows parts of a submarine, including an officer looking through a periscope (6.36). The next shot seems to suggest that he sees a bikini-clad woman (6.37). This shot picks up the stag film motif from segment 1 and points out the paradox of this juxtaposition. We know the shots of the officer and the woman come from different films—yet, at the same time, we cannot help but interpret the shots as showing him looking at her, and thus we find the moment comic. As earlier parts of the film reminded us of endless credit sequences, perhaps this makes fun of point-of-view editing and the Kuleshov effect.

10.81   . . . and danger.

The same principle underlies the next shots, as the officer orders a torpedo fired, and we see it seeming to race toward the woman, creating a sexual pun. This, too, is funny, as is the atomic-bomb orgasm that seems to result. But, as in the first segment, there is an overtone of threat and aggression—now specifically sexual aggression—in these images. They move quickly from humor to disaster as additional mushroom cloud shots undercut the joke. Moreover, the music that plays through the submarine–woman series is slow, quiet, and ethereal—*not* appropriate to the erotic joke, but more suited to the images of the bomb blasts.

This music carries us into a series of shots of waves and wavelike movements that seem to result from the bomb: a ship engulfed by fog or smoke, surfers and rowing teams battered by heavy waves, water-skiers and motorboaters falling during stunts. During this, the music's ethereal quality gives way to a slow melody with a dynamic tempo, played on low stringed instruments; this creates a more ominous tone. The first accidents seem trivial, as when water-skiers fall over. But gradually, things become more disturbing. A motorboat driver plows into a pile of debris and is hurled out.

10.82   An inexplicably grotesque image from *A Movie*.

Abruptly, people are seen riding odd bicycles **(10.82).** The move from the boat to the bikes takes us briefly away from the accident series to a string of shots showing people deliberately doing things that look grotesque. Additional shots show motorcyclists riding through mud and water, and a plane trying to land on a lake and flipping over.

The whole segment has developed steadily, introducing tension at the beginning and then juxtaposing the humorous (the submarine–woman scene) with the disastrous (the bomb) and trivial accidents with grotesque actions. The sequence ends in an odd way: black leader appears after the plane crash, with the music building up toward a climax. This is followed by a close view of Theodore Roosevelt speaking vigorously, seemingly angry, with bared teeth **(10.83).** Immediately, there follows a shot of a collapsing suspension bridge, with the music swelling up as the pieces fall **(10.84)** and then fading down. Although these shots are difficult to interpret, the association of human-caused disasters with one of America's most belligerent presidents would seem to link even the toppling bridge to human, especially political, aggression.

10.83   In this puzzling shot from *A Movie,* Roosevelt speaks vigorously, seemingly angry, with bared teeth.

Segment 4   Once more *A Movie* marks off its segments clearly, with black leader again accompanying the opening of the third portion of *The Pines of Rome.* An

10.84   A collapsing bridge in *A Movie.*

10.85   *A Movie.*

10.86   A brief moment of peace in *A Movie.*

10.87   *A Movie:* a frightening image of a buckling bridge.

10.88   *A Movie:* more disasters as a ship sinks.

10.89   *A Movie:* the diver in the final scene.

eerie gong and low, slow chords create a distinctly ominous mood. Segments 2 and 3 both built up toward accidents and disasters. Now segment 4 begins with a series of images of military planes being shot out of the sky and firing on the ground, followed by a series of explosions against a dark sky.

Yet the next passage juxtaposes shots of disasters with some shots that are inexplicable in this context. All the images of planes and explosions seem associated with war and disaster. Now we see two planes flying past an Egyptian pyramid **(10.85)**. As with so many of the earlier juxtapositions, we must abruptly switch our assumptions about how these shots relate to one another, since now we see nonmilitary planes. But immediately, two shots of an erupting volcano appear. Clearly, the connection between them and the previous shot is mainly created by the pictorial similarity of mountains and pyramids. Are we back to disasters again? Seemingly not, for we next see an elaborate church ceremony, and all our expectations are thwarted. But the disaster motif returns as strongly as ever: the burning dirigible *Hindenburg,* tanks, more race car crashes, and tumbling bodies.

All these images create tension, but the next shots we see are of people parachuting from a plane. Interestingly, this action is not threatening, and the people here are not hurt. Yet in the context of the earlier accidents, and because of the ominous music, we have begun to expect some sort of disaster as the likeliest subject of each shot. Now even these innocent actions seem threatening and again may be seen as linked to military and political aggression.

The next series of shots is equally innocent in itself but takes on mysterious and ominous overtones as part of the overall segment. We see a burning balloon floating to earth, reminding us of the floating dirigible and *Hindenburg* footage. Shots of palm trees, cattle, and other images follow, suggesting some idyllic Middle Eastern or African setting **(10.86)**. This brief respite, however, leads into one of the film's eeriest and most striking moments: three shots of a suspension bridge writhing and buckling as if shaken by a giant hand **(10.87)**. This is followed by the most intense disaster images in the whole film, including the burning *Hindenburg:* a sinking ship **(10.88)**, a firing-squad execution, bodies hanging on a scaffold, dead soldiers, and a mushroom cloud. A shot of a dead elephant and hunters introduces a brief series of shots of suffering Africans. The music has built up during this, becoming steadily less ominous and more triumphant with fanfares of brass instruments.

After the climactic series of disaster shots, the tone shifts one more time. A relatively lengthy series of underwater shots follows a scuba diver. He explores a sunken wreck encrusted with barnacles **(10.89)**. It recalls the disasters just witnessed, especially the sinking ship (10.88). The music builds to a triumphant climax as the diver swims into the ship's interior. The film ends on a long-held musical chord over more black leader and a final shot looking up toward the surface of the sea. Ironically, there is no "The End" title at this point.

A Movie has taken us through its disparate footage almost entirely by means of association. There is no argument about why we should find these images disturbing or why we should link volcanoes and earthquakes to sexual or military aggression. There are no categorical similarities between many of the things juxtaposed and no story told about them. Occasionally, Conner does use abstract qualities to compare objects, but this is only a small-scale strategy, not one that organizes the whole film.

In building its associations, *A Movie* uses the familiar formal principles of repetition and variation. Even though the images come from different films, certain elements are repeated, as with the series of horse shots in segment 1 or the different airplanes. These repetitions form motifs that help unify the whole film.

Moreover, these motifs return in a distinct pattern. We have seen how the titles and leader of the opening come back in some way in all the segments and how the "nudie" shot of segment 1 is similar to the one used with the submarine footage in segment 3. Interestingly, not a single motif that appears in segment 2 returns in segment 3, creating a strong contrast between the two. But then segment 4 picks up and varies many of the motifs of both 2 and 3. As in so many films, the ending thus seems to develop and return to earlier portions. The dead elephant, the tanks, and the race cars all hark back to the frantic race of segment 2, while the tribal people, the *Hindenburg* disaster, the planes, the ships, and the bridge collapse all continue motifs begun in 3. The juxtapositions that have obvious links play on repetition, while startling and obscure ones create contrast. Thus Conner has created a unified work from what would seem to be a disunified mass of footage.

The pattern of development is also strikingly unified. Segment 1 is primarily amusing, and a sense of hurtling exhilaration also carries through most of segment 2, up to the car crashes. But we have seen that the subjects of all the shots in segment 2 could also suggest aggression and violence, and they all relate in some way to the disasters to come. Segment 3 makes this more explicit but uses some humor and playfulness as well. By segment 4, the mixture of tones has largely disappeared, and an intensifying sense of doom replaces it. Now even odd or neutral events seem ominous.

Unlike the more clear-cut *Koyaanisqatsi*, *A Movie* withholds explicit meanings. Still, *A Movie*'s constantly shifting associations invite us to reflect on a range of implicit meanings. From one standpoint, the film can be interpreted as presenting the devastating consequences of unbridled aggressive energy. The horrors of the modern world—warfare and the hydrogen bomb—are linked with more trivial pastimes, such as sports and risky stunts. We are asked to reflect on whether both may spring from the same impulse, perhaps a kind of death wish. This impulse may, in turn, be tied to sexual drives (the pornographic motif) and political repression (the recurring images of people in developing countries).

Another interpretation might see the film as commenting on how cinema itself stirs our emotions through sex, violence, and exotic spectacle. In this sense, *A Movie* is "a movie" like any other, with the important difference that its thrills and disasters are actual parts of our world.

What of the ending? The scuba diver epilogue also offers a wide range of implicit meanings. It returns to the beginning in a formal sense: along with the Hopalong Cassidy segment, it is the longest continuous action we get. It might offer a kind of hope, perhaps an escape from the world's horrors. Or the images may suggest humankind's final death. After despoiling the planet, the human can only return to the primeval sea.

Like much of *A Movie,* the ending is ambiguous, saying little but suggesting much. Certainly, we can say that it serves to relax the tension aroused by the mounting disasters. In this respect, it demonstrates the power of an associational formal system: its ability to guide our emotions and to arouse our thinking simply by juxtaposing different images and sounds.

The Animated Film

Most fiction and documentary films photograph people and objects in full-sized, three-dimensional spaces. As we have seen, the standard shooting speed for such *live-action* filmmaking is typically 24 frames per second.

Animated films are distinguished from live-action ones by the unusual kinds of work done at the production stage. Instead of continuously filming an ongoing action in real time, animators create a series of images by shooting one frame at a time. Between the exposure of each frame, the animator changes the subject being photographed. Daffy Duck does not exist to be filmed, but a carefully planned and executed series of slightly different drawings of Daffy can be filmed as single frames. When projected, the images create illusory motion comparable to that of live-action filmmaking. Anything in the world—or indeed the universe—that the filmmaker can manipulate can be animated by means of two-dimensional drawings, three-dimensional objects, or digital information stored in a computer.

Because animation is the counterpart to live action, any sort of film that can be filmed live can be made using animation. There are animated fiction films, both short and feature-length. There can also be animated documentaries, usually instructional ones. Animation provides a convenient way of showing things that are normally not visible, such as the internal workings of machines or the extremely slow changes of geological formations. Ari Folman took this idea further in his documentary *Waltz with Bashir*. After interviewing Israeli army veterans, he sought to represent their dreams and recollections in hallucinatory animated imagery (**10.90**).

With its potential for distortion and pure design, animation lends itself readily to experimental filmmaking as well. Many classic experimental animated films employ either abstract or associational form. For example, both Oskar Fischinger and Norman McLaren made films by choosing a piece of music and arranging abstract shapes to move in rhythm to the sound track. Later in this chapter, we'll examine an example of abstract animation in Robert Breer's *Fuji*.

There are several distinct types of animation. The most familiar is *drawn* animation. From almost the start of cinema, animators drew and photographed long series of cartoon images. At first, they drew on paper, but copying the entire image, including the setting, over and over proved too time-consuming. During the 1910s, studio animators introduced clear rectangular sheets of celluloid, nicknamed **cels.** Characters and objects could be drawn on different cels, and these could then be layered like a sandwich on top of an opaque painted setting. The whole stack of cels would then be photographed. New cels showing the characters and objects in slightly different positions could then be placed over the same background, creating the illusion of movement (**10.91**).

10.90   A recurring memory image in *Waltz with Bashir* shows soldiers wading toward an eerily beautiful bombardment.

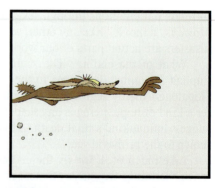

10.91   Two layered cels from a Road Runner cartoon, with Wile E. Coyote on one cel and the patches of flying dust on another.

10.92 Limited animation in *Silent Möbius.*

10.93 A nearly abstract but recognizable bird etched directly into the black emulsion in *Blinkety Blank.*

10.94 *The Adventures of Prince Achmed* (1926), the first feature-length animated film.

The cel process allowed animators to save time and to split up the labor among assembly lines of people doing drawing, coloring, photography, and other jobs. The most famous cartoon shorts made during the 1930s to the 1950s were made with cels. Warner Bros. created characters such as Bugs Bunny, Daffy Duck, and Tweety Bird; Paramount had Betty Boop and Popeye; Disney made both shorts (Mickey Mouse, Pluto, Goofy) and, beginning with *Snow White and the Seven Dwarfs* in 1937, feature-length cartoons.

Cel animation continued well into the 1990s, with big-budget studio cartoons employing *full* animation. This approach renders figures in fine detail and supplies them with tiny, nonrepetitive movements. (See 4.133, as well as 5.137–5.139.) Cheaper productions use *limited* animation, with only small sections of the image moving from frame to frame. Limited animation is mainly used on television, although Japanese theatrical features (**10.92**) exploited it to create flat, posterlike images.

Some independent animators have continued to draw on paper. Robert Breer, for example, uses ordinary white index cards for his witty, quasi-abstract animated films. We will examine his *Fuji* shortly.

Cels and drawings are photographed, but an animator can work without a camera as well. He or she can draw directly on the film, scratch on it, and attach flat objects to it. Stan Brakhage taped moths' wings to film stock in order to create *Mothlight*. The innovative animator Norman McLaren made *Blinkety Blank* by engraving the images frame by frame, using knives, needles, and razor blades (**10.93**).

Another type of animation that works with two-dimensional images involves *cut-outs*. Sometimes filmmakers make flat puppets with movable joints. Lotte Reiniger specialized in lighting her cut-outs in silhouette to create delicate, intricate fairy tales, as in **10.94**. Animators can also manipulate cut-out images frame by frame to create moving collages; Frank Mouris's exuberant *Frank Film* presents a flickering dance of popular-culture imagery (**10.95**). A very simple form of cut-out animation involves combining flat shapes of paper or other materials to create pictures or patterns. The rudimentary shapes and unshaded colors of *South Park: Bigger, Longer & Uncut* (as well as the television series from which it derives) flaunt deliberately crude cut-out animation.

Three-dimensional objects can also be shifted and twisted frame by frame to create apparent movement. Animation of objects falls into three closely related categories: clay, model, and pixillation. *Clay animation*, often termed *claymation*, sometimes actually does involve modeling clay. But more often, Plasticine is used, since it is less messy and is available in a wider range of colors. Sculptors create objects and characters of Plasticine, and the animator then presses the flexible material to change it slightly between exposures.

Although clay animation has been used occasionally since the early years of the 20th century, it has grown enormously in popularity since the mid-1970s. Nick

10.95 Household objects perform comic dances in *Frank Film.*

"You don't very often see model animation which is well lit, do you? For me, that's part of the comedy of it; I love the idea that you're making a thriller and it all looks authentic, but the lead character is in fact a Plasticine penguin."

— Nick Park, animator, *The Wrong Trousers*

10.101 In *Princess Mononoke,* five portions of the image (the grass and forest, the path and motion lines, the body of the Demon God, the shading of the Demon God, and Ashitaka riding away) were joined by computer, giving smoother, more complex motions than regular cel animation could achieve.

10.102 Early in *Duck Amuck,* the background tapers off into white blankness.

10.103 An inappropriate background for a swashbuckler appears in the blank space.

An Example of Narrative Animation: *Duck Amuck*   During the golden age of Hollywood short cartoons, from the 1930s to the 1950s, Disney and Warner Bros. were rivals. Disney animators had far greater resources at their disposal, and their animation was more elaborate and detailed than the simpler style of the Warner product. Warner cartoonists, despite their limited budgets, fought back by exploiting the comic fantasy possible in animated films and playing with the medium in imaginative ways.

In Warner Bros. cartoons, characters often spoke to the audience or referred to the animators and studio executives. For example, the Warner unit's producer Leon Schlesinger appeared in *You Ought to Be in Pictures,* letting Porky Pig out of his contract so that he could try to move up to live-action features. The tone of the Warner cartoons distinguished them sharply from the Disney product. The action was faster and more violent. The main characters, such as Bugs Bunny and Daffy Duck, were wisecracking cynics rather than innocent altruists like Mickey Mouse.

The Warner animators tried many experiments over the years, but perhaps none was so extreme as *Duck Amuck,* directed by Charles M. (Chuck) Jones in 1953. It is now recognized as one of the masterpieces of American animation. Although it was made within the Hollywood system and uses narrative form, it has an experimental feel because it asks the audience to take part in an exploration of techniques of cel animation.

As the film begins, it seems to be a swashbuckler of the sort Daffy Duck had appeared in before, such as *The Scarlet Pumpernickel* (1950)—itself a parody of one of Errol Flynn's most famous Warner Bros. films. The credits are written on a scroll fastened to a wooden door with a dagger, and when Daffy is first seen, he appears to be a dueling musketeer. But almost immediately he moves to the left and passes the edge of the painted background (**10.102**). Daffy is baffled, calls for scenery, and exits. A giant animated brush appears from outside the frame and paints in a barnyard (**10.103**). When Daffy enters, still in musketeer costume, he is annoyed but changes into a farmer's outfit. Such quick switches continue throughout the film, with the paintbrush and a pencil eraser adding and removing scenery, costumes, props, and even Daffy himself, with dizzying illogic. At times the sound cuts out, or the film seems to slip in the projector, so that we see the frame line in the middle of the screen (**10.104**).

All these tricks result in a peculiar narrative. Daffy repeatedly tries to get a plot, any plot, going, and the unseen animator constantly thwarts him. As a result, the film's principles of narrative progression are unusual. First, it gradually becomes apparent to us that the film is exploring various conventions and techniques of animation: painted backgrounds, sound effects, framing, music, and so on. Second, the outrages perpetrated against Daffy become more extreme, and his frustration mounts steadily. Third, a mystery quickly surfaces, as we and Daffy wonder who this perverse animator is and why he is tormenting Daffy.

10.104 In *Duck Amuck,* as the image apparently slips in the projector, Daffy's feet appear at the top and his head at the bottom.

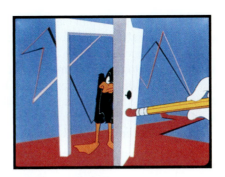

10.105 A pencil protruding into the frame finally begins to reveal *Duck Amuck*'s fiendish animator.

10.106 As in many other Warner Bros. cartoons, Bugs turns and speaks to the audience after he triumphs over Daffy.

10.107 In *Duck Amuck,* Daffy is trapped without background or sound track.

At the end, the mystery is solved when the animator blasts Daffy with a bomb and then closes a door in his face **(10.105).** The next shot moves us to the animation desk itself, where we see Bugs Bunny, who has been the animator playing all the tricks on Daffy. He grins at us: "Ain't I a stinker?" **(10.106).** To a spectator who has never seen a Warner Bros. cartoon before, this ending would be puzzling. The narrative logic of *Duck Amuck* depends largely on knowing the character traits of the two stars. Bugs and Daffy often costarred in other Jones cartoons, and invariably the calm, ruthless Bugs would get the better of the manic Daffy.

Duck Amuck's use of animation techniques is just as unconventional as its narrative form. Because the action moves so quickly, we might fail on first viewing to note that aside from the credits title and the familiar "That's All, Folks!" logo, the film contains only four separate shots—three of which come in quick succession at the end. The bulk of the cartoon consists of a single lengthy and continuous shot—animation's equivalent of a long take. Yet the settings and situations change quickly as the paintbrush and pencil transform the image and Daffy moves in and out of the frame. Often he appears against a stark white background **(10.107).** Such moments emphasize the fact that in cel animation, the figures and background are layers that could easily be photographed separately. In *Duck Amuck,* the only certain space is that of the frame itself—a quality quite different from the clearly established locales provided in more conventional cartoons.

Similarly, the temporal flow becomes warped as Daffy moves into and out of diegetic situations, launching into one possible plotline only to find it cut short by the mystery animator. Daffy keeps assuming that he is at the beginning of the cartoon, but time is flowing inexorably by in the outer cartoon, *Duck Amuck* itself. (Traditionally, cartoons were around seven minutes long to fit into the shorts section of movie theater programs.) At one point more than halfway through, Daffy shouts, "All right! Let's get this picture started!" Immediately a "The End" title appears, but Daffy pushes it aside and tries to take charge: "Ladies and gentlemen, there will be no further delays, so I shall attempt to entertain you in my own inimitable fashion," going into a soft-shoe routine against the blank background.

Duck Amuck also plays with onscreen and offscreen space. Many of the startling transformations we witness come from outside the limits of the frame. Most important, the unknown animator occupies the space from which the camera photographs the scene, with the brush and pencil coming in from under the camera. Daffy enters and exits frequently, and the frame often moves to reveal or conceal new portions of the scenery. When the sound cuts out entirely, Daffy asks to get it back (10.107), and then we hear a scratchy sound, as if from a phonograph somewhere outside the frame playing a worn record. This unseen phonograph provides inappropriate noises—a machine gun when Daffy strums the guitar, a donkey's

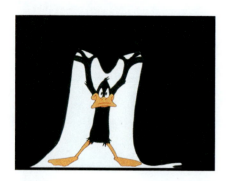

10.108 In *Duck Amuck,* Daffy struggles to preserve a bit of space for himself as the frame collapses on him.

bray when he breaks it—an elaborate joke on the fact that in animated films, the sound is never really produced by the characters and objects we see on the screen.

The most spectacular gag involving the space outside the edges of the image comes when the top of the frame seems to collapse, dripping down onto Daffy like black syrup **(10.108).** For a moment, we have the contradictory situation of having the space that we know should be invisible outside the frame suddenly become visible on the screen.

The inventiveness of *Duck Amuck* sets it apart from more conventional Hollywood animated films. Yet it also motivates its play with the medium through its adherence to narrative form, the genre of comedy, and familiar characters (Bugs mistreating Daffy, as usual). It is possible to go even further in exploring the medium of animation and to depart from narrative altogether, as our second example shows.

An Example of Experimental Animation: *Fuji*   In contrast to smooth Hollywood narrative animation, Robert Breer's 1974 film *Fuji* looks disjointed and crudely drawn. It doesn't involve a narrative but instead, like *Ballet mécanique,* develops according to principles of abstract form.

Fuji begins without a title or credits, as a bell rings three times over blackness. A cut leads not to animated footage but to a shaky, fuzzy shot through a train window, with someone's face and eyeglasses partially visible at the side in the extreme foreground. In the distance, what might be rice paddies slide by. This shot and most of the rest of the film are accompanied by the clacking, rhythmic sound of a train.

More black leader creates a transition to a very different image. Against a white background, two flat shapes, like keystones with rounded corners, alternate frame by frame, one red, the other green. The effect is a rapid flicker as the two colored shapes drift about the frame in a seemingly random pattern. Another stretch of black introduces a brief, fuzzy shot of a man in a dark suit running across the shot in a strange corridor.

More black leader follows. Then, against a white background, a jagged line moves and changes shape, briefly coming together to form a crude tracing of the running man's movement, then collapsing quickly into an abstract line and reforming into a running man. During this shot, colors shift and change rapidly.

Within this spurt of images, Breer has aroused our curiosity about what kind of film we are watching. He has also introduced most of the motifs that will be varied across the film to create its principles of abstract form. For one thing, the regular clack and hum of the train sets up a rhythm that will govern the movement on the screen. A flicker effect in which images change every one or two frames will recur through much of the film. Even when the same shape remains on the screen for a longer stretch, its color and outline often jitter in a rough rhythm.

Such attempts to avoid smooth movement and to explore the possibilities offered by different types of abstract drawings are common in experimental animation. *Fuji* is distinctive, however, in part because of its juxtaposition of live-action footage and animated images that are obviously sketchily traced from the live-action frames. Here Breer is manipulating a technique commonly used in Hollywood cartoons (and, more recently, Japanese anime): **rotoscoping.** The rotoscope is a machine used to project live-action footage, frame by frame, onto a drawing board, so that an animator can trace the outlines of the figures. The original purpose of rotoscoping was not to make the characters in the cartoon look exactly like those in the live-action film, for in fact their appearances are often quite different. Rather, a character's movement is usually smoother and more lifelike if traced from a live model. Disney's animated features, such as *Snow White and the Seven Dwarfs* and *Cinderella,* used extensive rotoscoping for their human characters. (Computer animation works with a similar principle but uses three-dimensional tracing and mapping.)

Breer takes rotoscoping, a technique intended to create smooth motion, and uses it in quite a different way. For one thing, he often traces only part of a figure,

10.109 Early in *Fuji,* we see flickering images that include single frames of blurry live-action footage of the train's interior . . .

10.110 . . . alternating with single frames of parts of that same view in crude tracings of the conductor's body.

10.111 A simply sketched view of a mountain and passing bridge in *Fuji.*

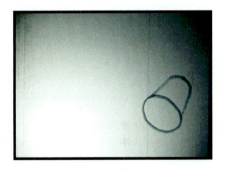

10.112 *Fuji*'s most conventional animation: a paper-cup shape rolling in an arc against a white background.

leaving it against a blank white background instead of tracing it onto a cel and combining it with painted scenery. In other cases, he traces the background itself rather than the moving figures, as with the train interior that appears in various colors. He also photographs his rough pencil drawings, rather than tracing them neatly onto cels in ink, as a Hollywood animator would do. By changing the color so often and by moving from image to image so quickly, Breer's animation avoids all sense of smoothness. (Breer uses blank index cards for his drawings, deliberately avoiding the illusion of depth that cel animation can achieve.)

Most of the flickering images in *Fuji* are two frames long, and here Breer may be playing off the fact that in Hollywood cartoons of the studio era, each set of cels was actually photographed for two frames in a row, to save time and labor. In the Hollywood films, the movement still appears smooth and continuous on the screen, while Breer creates such noticeable differences between each pair of frames that the effect looks jerky.

Perhaps most daringly, Breer includes bits of the original live-action footage from which he made his tracings. As a result, we are led to see many of the images in the film *as* tracings **(10.109, 10.110).** In effect, Breer has taken one of the most realistic animation techniques, the rotoscope, and used it to create a dazzling, abstract exploration of movement and perception in cinema.

The opening section of *Fuji* is based chiefly on shapes derived from train interiors. The second, lengthier section, which forms the rest of the film, begins with a stylized series of views of a mountain that we assume from the title is Mount Fuji. Again we see shifting colors and shapes, but as before, some of the footage seems to have been traced from live-action frames. The train sound continues, and as sparsely sketched buildings, bridges, poles, and fields move jerkily past in the foreground, we are likely to take this view to be one seen from a moving train—though in this case Breer does not alternate live-action and traced footages **(10.111).**

The mountain footage creates planes in depth: fields and buildings in the middle ground pass by, while the distant mountain remains in the same spot. At times colors or abstract shapes appear for a frame or two, and we are likely to perceive them as being in the extreme foreground, near the train and thus visible only as a blurred flash. Yet, even though the mountain remains in the same spot, its simple black outline frequently shifts slightly, and the color changes constantly, making the sky now red, now blue. The smooth sense of motion that rotoscoped footage could create is undermined, and the stable mountain actually shimmers constantly. In this way, Breer simultaneously suggests realistic depth and flat, abstract shapes in the images.

To underline this contrast between conventional animation and the abstract techniques of *Fuji,* Breer includes one ordinary rotoscoped motion **(10.112).** This paper cup shape, drawn with the simplest of perspective cues, is the only object

"What attracted me to the footage was the mountain in the background and the possibility for motion perspective in the foreground. The film plays with deep space and the picture plane on the screen."

— Robert Breer, animator

CONNECT TO THE BLOG
We profile another great
experimental animator in "Len Lye,
Renaissance Kiwi."

See http://www.davidbordwell.net/
blog/?p=1086.

in the film to move so smoothly. We also, however, see the cup changing color or superimposed over the more abstract, flickering images of the mountain. At other times, the cup shape is seen as just a flat blob of color. Indeed, the rounded keystone shapes near the beginning are flat, nonperspectival versions of this cup.

At other points, the neat perspective renderings of the cup suddenly twist into skewed trapezoids or fold up into straight lines. Thus even the most conventional of animated movements can collapse in this pulsating, unstable space. With this and dozens of other devices, Breer explores and displays many of the perceptual tricks on which drawn animation is based. While *Duck Amuck* flaunts the unique powers of animation in order to create comedy and deflate our narrative expectations, *Fuji*, an experimental film, takes animation techniques as its very subject. The result is a film that asks the viewer to enjoy its abstract design and reflect as well on the possibilities of animated filmmaking.

SUMMARY

In most situations, when we watch a film, we have some idea of what type it will be. If we are seeing a documentary, we expect to learn something, perhaps in a way that will entertain or move us in the process. An experimental film, however, will probably challenge us, rather like a game, to figure out its patterns and strategies. Animated films that we encounter in theaters will most likely amuse and entertain us.

In watching a documentary film, we can ask ourselves just what it is trying to tell us. Does it present one or more categories of things? If so, how are these organized? Is the filmmaker trying to convey an attitude about the topic? Are there abstract or narrative portions that lend interest to its subject? Or is the topic organized as an argument? Does the filmmaker present convincing evidence or rely more on emotional appeal cloaked as logic?

As we have seen, experimental films often employ abstract or associational formal patterns. From moment to

moment, try to understand the connections among shots or small-scale segments. Is there a similarity in shapes on the screen, in directions of movement, or in colors? If so, the film probably uses abstract form. But if you detect some similarities in subject matter that shift in odd but evocative ways as the film progresses, associational form is probably at work.

Animated films can present narratives, convey documentary information, or experiment with the medium. In most cases, however, you should be able to detect generally what techniques were used in making the film. Is the movement on the screen based on drawings or on moving puppets, clay figures, flat cut-outs, or computer-generated images? Keeping in mind that most animated films are made by shooting only one or two frames at a time, you should be able to imagine the amount of work that goes into this mode of filmmaking.

WHERE TO GO FROM HERE

Documentary Films

Bill Nichols provides an overview of types of documentaries and issues relating to them in his *Introduction to Documentary* (Bloomington: Indiana University Press, 2001). For histories of documentary, see Richard Meran Barsam, *Non-Fiction Film: A Critical History,* rev. ed. (Bloomington: Indiana University Press, 1992), and Erik Barnouw, *Documentary: A History of the Non-Fiction Film,* 2nd ed. (New York: Oxford University Press, 1993).

Much contemporary work on documentary has centered on how this mode of filmmaking can be differentiated from fiction. Bill Nichols's *Representing Reality* (Bloomington: Indiana University Press, 1991) explores this ques-

tion. See also Michael Renov, ed., *Theorizing Documentary* (New York: Routledge, 1993); the essays by Noël Carroll and Carl R. Plantinga in Carroll and David Bordwell, eds., *Post-Theory: Reconstructing Film Studies* (Madison: University of Wisconsin Press, 1996); Plantinga's *Rhetoric and Representation in Nonfiction Film* (Cambridge: Cambridge University Press, 1997); and Michael Tobias, ed., *The Search for Reality: The Art of Documentary Filmmaking* (Studio City, CA: Wiese, 1997).

For studies of some of the most historically important documentary filmmakers, see Kevin Jackson, ed., *The Humphrey Jennings Reader* (Manchester, England: Carcanet, 1993); Thomas W. Benson and Carolyn Anderson, *Reality Fictions: The Films of Frederick Wiseman* (Carbondale: Southern Illinois University Press, 1989); Gary Evans, *John Grierson and the National Film Board: The Politics of Wartime Propaganda* (Toronto: University of Toronto Press, 1984); Paul Rotha, *Robert J. Flaherty: A Biography* (Philadelphia: University of Pennsylvania Press, 1983); Randolph Lewis, *Emile de Antonio: Radical Filmmaker in Cold War America* (Madison: University of Wisconsin Press, 2000); and Douglas Kellner and Dan Streible, eds., *Emile de Antonio: A Reader* (Minneapolis: University of Minnesota Press, 2000).

Alan Rosenthal presents case studies of several important film and television documentaries, including Barbara Koppel's *Harlan County, U.S.A.,* in *The Documentary Conscience: A Casebook in Film Making* (Berkeley: University of California Press, 1980).

On *Roger and Me*

On its release, *Roger and Me* was hailed as one of the best films of 1989, winning large audiences in the United States and abroad. It seemed a likely contender for an Academy Award until a series of articles pointed out that the film diverged from the actual chronology of events. The major revelations appeared in Harlan Jacobson's interview with director Michael Moore ("Michael and Me," *Film Comment* 25, 6 [November–December 1989]: 16–30). This often heated conversation explores different conceptions of documentary accuracy.

When challenged by Jacobson about the order of events, Moore granted that "the chronology skips around a bit. That's why I don't use dates in the film" (p. 111). He claimed that he had sought to portray the entire 1980s and that the chronology of the film was not intended to be exact. Moore also said that rearranging events made the film more entertaining and allowed him to condense a decade down to a manageable viewing length.

The controversy is discussed in Carley Cohan and Gary Crowdus, "Reflections on *Roger and Me,* Michael Moore, and His Critics," *Cinéaste* 17, 4 (1990): 25–30. Carl Plantinga finds *Roger and Me* an example of an expressive documentary, a trend that also includes the work of Errol Morris ("The Mirror Framed: A Case for Expression in Documentary," *Wide Angle* 13, 2 [April 1991]: 40–53).

Experimental Films

Good general studies of experimental cinema are P. Adams Sitney, *Visionary Film: The American Avant-Garde 1943–1978,* 3rd ed. (New York: Oxford University Press, 2002); Scott MacDonald, *Avant-Garde Film: Motion Studies* (Cambridge: Cambridge University Press, 1993); and Paul Arthur, *A Line of Sight: American Avant-Garde Film Since 1965* (Minneapolis: University of Minnesota Press, 2005). Jan-Christopher Horak's anthology *Lovers of Cinema: The First American Film Avant-Garde, 1919–1945* (Madison: University of Wisconsin Press, 1995) deals with

an earlier, often neglected, period. It contains an essay by William Moritz, "Americans in Paris: Man Ray and Dudley Murphy," that examines the background of *Ballet mécanique.* Scott MacDonald has published his interviews with many recent and current avant-garde filmmakers in his five-volume series *A Critical Cinema: Interviews with Independent Filmmakers* (Berkeley: University of California Press, 1988–2006).

There are many works dealing with more specific aspects of experimental cinema. Found-footage film is discussed in William C. Wees, *Recycled Images* (New York: Anthology Film Archives, 1993), and Cecilia Hausheer and Christoph Settele, eds., *Found Footage Film* (Luzern: VIPER/zyklop, 1992). A major trend in American avant-garde cinema is covered by Jack Sargeant, ed., *Naked Lens: Beat Cinema* (London: Creating Books, 1997). Lauren Rabinovitz discusses female experimental filmmakers in *Points of Resistance: Women, Power & Politics in the New York Avant-Garde Cinema, 1943–71* (Chicago: University of Chicago Press, 1991), including material on Maya Deren. For essays spanning the history of computer-generated experimental films by one of its early practitioners, see Malcolm Le Grice, *Experimental Cinema in the Digital Age* (London: British Film Institute, 2001).

Several of the experimental filmmakers mentioned in this book have been the subject of studies. On Maya Deren, see Bruce R. McPherson, ed., *Essential Deren* (Kingston, NY: Docutext, 2005). See also Peter Boswell, Joan Rothfuss, and Bruce Jenkins, *2000 BC: The Bruce Conner Story Part II* (New York: Distributed Art Publishers, 1999). (In keeping with Conner's sense of humor, there is no Part I.) The work of Andy Warhol in various media has received extensive coverage, but the books most directly focused on his films include Michael O'Pray, ed., *Andy Warhol: Film Factory* (London: British Film Institute, 1989), and Ann Abrahams, *Warhol Films* (Amsterdam: Rongwrong, 1989). See also Bill Landis, *Anger: The Unauthorized Biography of Kenneth Anger* (New York: HarperCollins, 1995); Regina Cornwell, *Snow Seen: The Films and Photographs of Michael Snow* (Toronto: Peter Martin, 1980); and Philip Monk, "Around Wavelength: The Sculpture, Film and Photo Work of Michael Snow," in *The Michael Snow Project: Visual Art 1951–1993* (Toronto: Art Gallery of Ontario, 1994).

A shot-by-shot analysis of *Ballet mécanique* may be found in Standish Lawder, *The Cubist Cinema* (Berkeley: University of California Press, 1975).

Animated Films

The most comprehensive history of animation to date is Giannalberto Bendazzi's *Cartoons: One Hundred Years of Cinema Animation* (London: John Libbey, 1994), which is truly international in its scope. Donald Crafton concentrates on the silent era in his *Before Mickey: The Animated Film 1898–1928* (1982; 2nd ed., Chicago: University of Chicago Press, 1993). John Grant's *Masters of Animation* (New

York: Watson-Guptill, 2001) provides brief introductions to major international animators.

Many histories concentrate on Hollywood animation, particularly in the era of studio-made shorts. See Leonard Maltin, *Of Mice and Magic: A History of American Animated Cartoons* (New York: New American Library, 1980), and Michael Barrier, *Hollywood Cartoons: American Animation in Its Golden Age* (New York: Oxford University Press, 1999). Allan Neuwirth offers behind-the-scenes accounts in *Makin' Toons: Inside the Most Popular Animated TV Shows and Movies* (New York: Allworth Press, 2003), which deals with the era since *Who Framed Roger Rabbit?* (1988).

Good general introductions to the various techniques of animation are Roger Noake's *Animation: A Guide to Animated Film Techniques* (London: MacDonald Orbis, 1988) and Kit Laybourne's *The Animation Book* (New York: Three Rivers, 1998).

An in-depth consideration of the artistic properties of animation is Maureen Furniss's *Art in Motion: Animation Aesthetics* (Sydney: John Libbey, 2007).

Specific types of animation are dealt with in Robert Russett and Cecile Starr, ed., *Experimental Animation: An Illustrated Anthology* (New York: Van Nostrand Reinhold, 1976), which contains an interview with Roger Breer; Lotte Reiniger's *Shadow Puppets, Shadow Theatres and Shadow Films* (Boston: Publishers Plays, 1970), dealing with silhouette animation; and Michael Frearson's *Clay Animation: American Highlights 1908 to the Present* (New York: Twayne, 1994). Peter Lord and Brian Sibley's *Cracking Animation: The Aardman Book of 3-D Animation* (London: Thames & Hudson, 2004) deals with clay animation, drawing entirely on the work of the British firm Aardman, whose productions include the Wallace and Gromit films of Nick Park.

Most books on computer animation aim at teaching the techniques to aspiring practitioners. Isaac V. Kerlow's *The Art of 3D Computer Animation and Effects,* 4th ed. (Hoboken, NJ: Wiley, 2009) contains a historical introduction and explains how the techniques we discussed in Part Three, such as lighting and camera movement, are simulated using computer programs. The most widely used CGI animating program, Maya, is explained (including an instructional CD-ROM) in *The Art of Maya,* 4th ed. (Sybex, 2007). Andrew Chong's *Digital Animation* (Lausanne: AVA Publishing, 2008) presents a history of computer techniques in films and games, with many excellent illustrations.

Works about individual animators include Valliere T. Richard's *Norman McLaren: Manipulator of Movement* (Newark: University of Delaware Press, 1982); Donald Crafton's *Emile Cohl, Caricature, and Film* (Princeton, NJ: Princeton University Press, 1990); Peter Hames, ed., *Dark Alchemy: The Films of Jan Švankmajer* (Trowbridge, Wiltshire, England: Flicks Books, 1995); John Canemaker's *Tex Avery: The MGM Years, 1942–1955* (Atlanta: Turner, 1996); Leslie Cabarga's *The Fleischer Story* (New York:

Nostalgia Press, 1976), which deals with Dave and Max Fleischer (Betty Boop and Popeye); Maureen Furniss, ed., *Chuck Jones: Conversations* (Jackson: University Press of Mississippi, 2005); Mike Barrier, *The Animated Man: A Life of Walt Disney* (Berkeley: University of California Press, 2007); and Ray Harryhausen and Tony Dalton, *Ray Harryhausen: An Animated Life* (London: Aurum Press, 2003).

We frequently blog about animation on "Observations on film art and *Film Art.*" For animation's place in the film industry, see "Too many toons? Then why are they making so much money?" at www.davidbordwell.net/blog/?p=338. We speculate on why modern animated features often seem better than their live-action competitors in "By Annie standards," at www.davidbordwell.net/blog/?p=178.

On the humor in the Warner Bros. films of one of the great animators of the studios' golden age, see "Pausing and chortling: A tribute to Bob Clampett," at www.davidbordwell.net/blog/?p=1991. We offer an extensive list of the films created by the Aardman studio (of "Wallace and Gromit" fame) in "Tracking down Aardman creatures." See www.davidbordwell.net/blog/?p=1795.

The Pixar animation studio has several times furnished us with blog topics. On editing in computer animation, see "Reflections on *Cars,*" at www.davidbordwell.net/blog/?p=16; "Rat rapture," at www.davidbordwell.net/blog/?p=1207; and "A glimpse into the Pixar kitchen," at www.davidbordwell.net/blog/?p=2205. On Disney, see "Uncle Walt the artist," at www.davidbordwell.net/blog/?p=247.

Japanese Anime

Although many countries have made animated films, the worldwide commercial market has long been dominated by American cartoons, particularly those from the Disney studio. Until quite recently, theatrical animation was so expensive that only large companies could support it. In the 1970s, however, small Japanese companies emerged as rivals to Hollywood firms. They began producing hundreds of what came to be known as *anime* (pronounced AH-nee-may), which quickly became part of the world's film culture.

The films came in many genres. Science-fiction efforts such as *Macross, Gundam,* and *Fist of the North Star* proved particularly popular, as did postapocalyptic cyberpunk sagas, most notably *Bubblegum Crisis* and *Akira.* There were also fantasy comedies (*Urusei Yatsura, Ranma ½*), serious dramas (*Grave of the Fireflies*), and children's films of a quiet charm rarely achieved by the brash Disneys (notably Hayao Miyazaki's *Kiki's Delivery Service* and *My Neighbor Totoro*). Some anime defies description, including the nutty *Project A-Ko* and the erotic-mythical *Urotsukidoji: Legend of the Overfiend.*

Lacking the funding of the big U.S. companies, Japanese animators learned to do more with less. They couldn't duplicate the incessant bustle and flashy depth effects that Disney preferred, so they worked with static shots enhanced by slight motions: winds rustling a dress, a tear rolling down a cheek, even just the shimmer in a character's eyes. Directors also concentrated on *mecha* figures—robots and giant machines, which with their chunky outlines and stiff movements are easier to animate than the flexible human body. When required to animate humans, the Japanese often encased them in hard-body space suits (in effect turning them into robots) or rendered them as fairly flat shapes, as in comic strips. And many works of anime explore subtle changes in color produced by light, liquid, mist, and reflections—all easier to depict than a landscape teeming with figures.

Some TV anime made their way to television in Europe and North America, and *Akira, Ghost in the Shell,* and *Pokémon: The First Movie* had successful English-language releases. Still, video has been the source of anime for Western *otaku* (obsessive fans), who hold conventions and spend hours online discussing their favorites. For historical background, see Helen McCarthy's *Anime! A Beginner's Guide to Japanese Animation* (London: Titan, 1993) and *The Anime Movie Guide* (London: Titan, 1996). McCarthy has also written a detailed study of the creator of Kiki, Totoro, Princess Mononoke and the fantastic creators of *Spirited Away, Hayao Miyazaki: Master of Japanese Animation* (Berkeley, CA: Stone Bridge, 1999). Two reference books are Gilles Poitras, *The Anime Companion: What's Japanese in Japanese Animation?* (Berkeley, CA: Stone Bridge, 1999), and Jonathan Clements and Helen McCarthy, *The Anime Encyclopedia: A Guide to Japanese Animeation Since 1917* (Berkeley, CA: Stone Bridge, 2001). John A. Lent, ed., *Animation in Asia and the Pacific* (London: John Libbey, 2001), contains several essays on anime, as well as related Asian animation.

Websites

www.documentary.org The site of *International Documentary* magazine. A clearinghouse of information about professional documentary filmmaking, with announcements, festival news, and reviews.

dmoz.org/Arts/Movies/Filmmaking/Experimental A portal to various websites on experimental cinema.

www.hi-beam.net/cgi-bin/flicker.pl The Flicker website is a clearinghouse for information about experimental cinema: artists, films, and upcoming programs around the world. Filmmakers also post short films here. The companion site, Frameworks, **www.hi-beam.net/fw.html,** hosts lengthy and ongoing discussions of experimental film.

www.keyframeonline.com Provides information on various aspects of the current animation industry.

www.public.iastate.edu/~rllew/animelinks.html Animation directing you to many specific sites.

www.awn.com/?int_check=yes Animated World Network, a site with directories, current news, and feature articles.

www.bcdb.com The Big Cartoon Database, with information on American animation. A comparable site, **www.toonopedia.com**, includes data on comic strips and comic books as well as films.

Recommended DVD Supplements

DVDs of documentaries and experimental films seldom include supplements, so for these two types of films, we'll list some major films that are available.

Documentary

Feature-length documentary films on DVD include *4 Little Girls* (HBO Home Video), *The Wild Parrots of Telegraph Hill* (New Video Group), *The Story of the Weeping Camel* (New Line Home Video), *Enron—The Smartest Guys in the Room* (Magnolia; this disc includes a making-of supplement), *The Cruise* (Live/Artisan), *Grizzly Man* (Lions Gate), *Control Room* (Lions Gate), *Winged Migration* (Sony), *The War Room* (MCA Home Video), *Born into Brothels* (Thinkfilm), *The Gleaners and I* (Zeitgeist), *The UP Series* (1964 onward, First Run Features), *Super Size Me* (Hart Sharp Video), *Burden of Dreams* (Criterion), and *Sans soleil* (Criterion). Short films are collected in *Full Frame Documentary Shorts,* vols. 1–5 (New Video Group).

Classic documentaries on DVD include *Why We Fight* (1943, Edi Video), *Memphis Belle* (1944, Aircraft Films), *Triumph of the Will* (1934, Synapse), *Kon-Tiki* (1951, Image Entertainment), *In the Year of the Pig* (1969, Homevision), *Point of Order!* (1964, New Yorker Video), and *Salesman* (1969, Criterion). Pioneering documentary maker Robert Flaherty is represented by *Nanook of the North* (Criterion) and *Man of Aran* (Homevision). *Listen to Britain and Other Films by Humphrey Jennings* (Image) collects works by the great British filmmaker.

Experimental

An extensive, seven-disc, 155-film survey of experimental cinema is *Unseen Cinema: Early American Avant-Garde Film 1894–1941* (Image Entertainment; a book of the same name, published by the Anthology Film Archives, was printed separately). There is some overlap in contents between this and *Avant Garde–Experimental Cinema of the 1920s & 1930s* and *Avant-Garde 2: Experimental Cinema 1928–1954* (Kino Video), but the latter concentrates largely on European films. *American Treasures IV: Avant-garde Film 1947–1986* (Image) contains many classic experimental films from the postwar era. Luis Buñuel's *Un Chien andalou* (1928, Transflux Films) and *L'Age d'or* (1930, Kino video) are Surrealist classics.

Individual full-length experimental films available include *Koyaanisqatsi* (MGM), *Berlin: Symphony of a Great City* (Image Entertainment), and *Man with a Movie Camera* (Image Entertainment).

Collections of individual experimentalists' work include *By Brakhage: An Anthology,* with 26 films by Stan

Brakhage (Criterion; this collection also includes interviews with the filmmaker), *Maya Deren: Experimental Films* (Mystic Fire Video), *The Guy Maddin Collection* (Zeitgeist), *The Brothers Quay Collection* (Zeitgeist), and *The Films of Kenneth Anger,* vols. 1 and 2 (Fantoma). Documentaries about experimental filmmakers include *In the Mirror of Maya Deren* (Zeitgeist Films) and *Brakhage* (Zeitgeist Films).

Animation

"The Making of *Bambi:* A Prince Is Born" discusses the technique and style of the design. The "Art Design: Impressions of the Forest" section includes an excellent explanation of the multiplane camera that was used to create depth effects in this and other Disney films. The "Tricks of the Trade" excerpt has more on the multiplane camera, discussing depth cues and demonstrating the use of the technique in the opening of *Bambi.* "Inside the Disney Archive" shows examples of both cels and backgrounds, including lengthy backgrounds used to simulate camera movement. "*Bambi:* Inside Walt's Story Meetings" has actors reading transcriptions of meetings from the period of the film's production, discussing a wide variety of narrative and stylistic possibilities as scenes from the film itself play.

"No Strings Attached: The Making of *Pinocchio*" is another excellent documentary on a Disney classic.

"The Hatching of *Chicken Run*" has a little background information on Aardman animation, also responsible for the "Wallace and Gromit" and "Creature Comforts" series. It deals with the specifics of animation, including how three-point lighting works on a very small scale. (The "Poultry in Motion" supplement, aimed at children, is far less informative.) The DVD of *Wallace & Gromit: The Curse of the Were-rabbit* includes several informative and entertaining pieces: "How Wallace and Gromit Went to Hollywood," a history of director Nick Park's career with Aardman; "Behind the Scenes of 'Wallace & Gromit: The Curse of the Were-rabbit'"; "A Day in the Life of Aardman: Studio Tour"; and "How to Make a Bunny," a demonstration of how Plasticine figures are created.

The DVD of *The Incredibles* contains two making-of supplements. The first, "Making of *The Incredibles,*" is only mildly informative, focusing mainly on how wacky and eccentric the Pixar team is. The second, "More Making of *The Incredibles,*" is an excellent overview of the basic techniques for making a complex CGI film, from character design, to three-point lighting, to sound effects.

Some major animators have been profiled in DVD supplements. "Jiří Trnka: Puppet Animation Master" *(The Puppet Films of Jiří Trnka)* offers a sketch of the great Czech animator's career. The DVD set *Norman McLaren: The Collector's Edition* contains a feature-length biography, "Creative Process: Norman McLaren," including many clips. McLaren used so many imaginative filmmaking methods that "Creative Process" suggests the vast range of animation possibilities.

5

Criticism isn't an activity limited to those people who write articles or books about films. If you seek to understand a film, you're engaged in a process of criticism. You may be unsure, for example, why one scene was included in a film; your search for the function of that scene in the context of the whole is a first step in a critical examination. People who discuss a film they have seen are participating in criticism.

Up to this point, we've looked at concepts and definitions that should enable a filmgoer to analyze a film systematically. The critic approaches a film already knowing that formal patterns, such as repetitions and variations, will probably be important and should be examined. The critic will also be alert for principles of narrative and non-narrative form, and she or he will watch for salient uses of the various film techniques. The critic will also ground his or her claims in specific evidence from the film.

Critical Analysis of Films

So far, we've looked at all the techniques that constitute a film; we have also laid out basic principles that govern a film's narrative or non-narrative form. Our examples and analyses have shown how elements of a film function in an overall system. But the only way to gain an ability to analyze films is through practice—in viewing, reading criticism, and writing about films yourself. Today thousands of young people are writing about films on the Internet, so you have no excuse for waiting! To guide you in the sort of writing that constitutes film analysis, we conclude our look at films as formal systems with a series of brief sample essays on individual films.

An analyst usually scrutinizes a film with some sort of purpose in mind. You may want to understand a film's perplexing aspects, reveal the process that created a pleasurable response, or convince someone that the film is worth seeing. Our sample analyses have two primary purposes. First, we want to illustrate how film form and film style work together in a variety of films. Second, we seek to provide models of short critical analyses, exemplars of how an essay might illuminate some aspects of a film's workings.

Because an analyst is limited by his or her purposes, there is little chance of getting everything, of accounting for each facet of a film. As a result, these analyses don't exhaust the films. You might study any one of them and find many more points of interest than we have been able to present here. Indeed, whole books can be and have been written about single films without exhausting them.

11 CHAPTER

Film Criticism:
Sample Analyses

Each of the four major sections of this chapter emphasizes different aspects of various films. We begin by discussing three classical narrative films: *His Girl Friday, North by Northwest,* and *Do The Right Thing.* Since classically constructed films are familiar to most viewers, it is important to study closely how they work.

We move to three films that represent alternatives to classical norms. *Breathless* relies on ambiguity of character motivation and on stretches of rambling action, all presented through loose, casual techniques. In contrast, *Tokyo Story* uses selective deviations from classical norms to create a highly rigorous style. In *Chungking Express,* the viewer's expectation that two groups of characters will converge is rechanneled to focus interest on narrative parallels.

Documentary films can go beyond direct recording and suggest a wide range of meanings. This section considers two examples of how formal and stylistic processes can expand a documentary's implications. The first, *Man with a Movie Camera,* documents a day in the life of the Soviet Union, but it also celebrates the power of cinema to transform reality. *The Thin Blue Line* tells the story of a miscarriage of justice; at the same time, it invites us to reflect on the difficulties of responsibly investigating any crime.

Finally, we move to analyses that emphasize social ideology. Our first example, *Meet Me in St. Louis,* is a film that accepts a dominant ideology and reinforces the audience's belief in that ideology. In contrast, *Raging Bull* shows how a film can display ambiguity in its ideological implications.

We could have emphasized different aspects of any of these films. *Meet Me in St. Louis,* for example, is a classical narrative film and could be considered from that perspective. Similarly, *Man with a Movie Camera* could be seen as offering an alternative to classical continuity editing. And any of the films represents an ideological position that could be analyzed. Our choices suggest only certain angles of approach; your own critical activities will discover many more.

Those activities are the focus of the Appendix to this chapter. There we suggest some ways in which you can prepare, organize, and write a critical analysis of a film. We draw on the following sample analyses for examples of various strategies that you can apply in your own writing.

The Classical Narrative Cinema

His Girl Friday

1940. Columbia. Directed by Howard Hawks. Script by Charles Lederer from the play *The Front Page* by Ben Hecht and Charles MacArthur. Photographed by Joseph

CONNECT TO THE BLOG
For a consideration of what film critics do, including evaluation, and what part the Internet now plays, see "In critical condition," at

www.davidbordwell.net/blog/?p=2315.

CONNECT TO THE BLOG
For thoughts on the history and purposes of film criticism, see "Love isn't all you need," at

www.davidbordwell.net/blog/?p=4102.

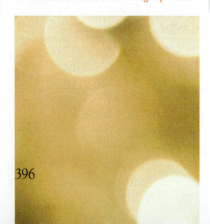

Walker. Edited by Gene Harlick. Music by Morris W. Stoloff. With Cary Grant, Rosalind Russell, Ralph Bellamy, Gene Lockhart, Porter Hall.

The dominant impression left by *His Girl Friday* is that of speed: it is often said
to be the fastest sound comedy ever made. So let's slow it down analytically. By
breaking the film into parts and seeing how the parts relate to one another causally,
temporally, and spatially, we can suggest how classical narrative form and specific
film techniques are used to create this whirlwind experience.

His Girl Friday can be segmented into 13 scenes, set in the following locales:
(1) the *Morning Post* offices, (2) the restaurant, (3) the Criminal Courts pressroom,
(4) Walter's office, (5) Earl Williams's cell, (6) the pressroom, (7) a precinct jail,
(8) the pressroom, (9) the sheriff's office, (10) the street outside the prison, (11) the
pressroom, (12) the sheriff's office, and (13) the pressroom. All of these scenes are
marked off by dissolves except for the transition between 8 and 9, which is simply
a cut.

Within these scenes, smaller units of action occur. Scene 1, occupying almost
14 minutes of screen time, introduces almost all of the major characters and sets
two plotlines in motion. Or consider scene 13: almost every major character appears
in it, and it runs for about 33 minutes.

We could break the longer scenes into smaller parts on the basis of changing
character interactions. Thus scene 1 comprises (a) our introduction to the newspaper office, (b) the first conversation between Hildy and Bruce, (c) Walter's discussion of the past with Hildy, (d) Walter's conference with Duffy about the Earl
Williams case, (e) Hildy's telling Walter that she's remarrying, and (f) Walter's introduction to Bruce. To grasp the construction of other lengthy scenes, you may divide them into similar segments. It may be, in fact, that the somewhat theatrical feel
of the film comes from its practice of segmenting its scenes by character entrances
and exits (rather than, say, by frequent shifts of place). In any event, the developing
patterns of character interaction contribute a great deal to the hubbub and speed of
the film.

The scenes function, as we would expect, to advance the action. As we saw
in Chapter 3 (pp. 82–84), classical Hollywood cinema often constructs a narrative around characters with definite traits who want to achieve specific goals. The
clash of these characters' contrasting traits and conflicting goals propels the story
forward in a step-by-step process of cause and effect. *His Girl Friday* has two such
cause–effect chains:

1. *The romance.* Hildy Johnson wants to quit newspaper reporting and settle
   down with Bruce Baldwin. This is her initial goal. But Hildy's editor and ex-
   husband, Walter Burns, has a different goal: he wants her to continue as his
   reporter and to remarry him. Given these two goals, the characters enter into a
   conflict in several stages. First, Walter lures Hildy by promising a nest egg for
   the couple in exchange for her writing one last story. But Walter also plots to
   have Bruce robbed. Learning of this, Hildy tears up her story. Walter continues to delay Bruce, however, and eventually wins Hildy through her renewed
   interest in reporting. She changes her mind about marrying Bruce and stays
   with Walter.

2. *Crime and politics.* Earl Williams is to be hanged for shooting a policeman.
   The city's political bosses are relying on the execution to ensure their reelec-
   tion. This is the goal shared by the mayor and the sheriff. But Walter's goal
   is to induce the governor to reprieve Williams and thus unseat the mayor's
   party at the polls. Through the sheriff's stupidity, Williams escapes and is
   concealed by Hildy and Walter. In the meantime, a reprieve does arrive from
   the governor; the mayor bribes the messenger into leaving. Williams is discovered, but the messenger returns with the reprieve in time to save Williams
   from death and Walter and Hildy from jail. Presumably, the mayor's machine
   will be defeated at the election.

CONNECT TO THE BLOG
How did *His Girl Friday* go from
obscurity to being hailed as a
masterpiece? See "Creating a classic,
with a little help from your pirate
friends," at
www.davidbordwell.net/blog/?p=1809.

The crime-and-politics line of action is made to depend on events in the romance line at several points. Walter uses the Williams case to lure Hildy back to him, Hildy chases the Williams story instead of returning to Bruce, Bruce's mother reveals to the police that Walter has concealed Williams, and so on. More specifically, the interplay of the two lines of action alters the goals of various characters. In Walter's case, inducing Hildy to write the story fulfills his goals of embarrassing the politicos and of tempting Hildy back. Hildy's goals are more greatly changed. After she destroys her article, her decision to report on Earl Williams's jailbreak marks her acceptance of Walter's goal. Her subsequent willingness to hide Williams and her indifference to Bruce's pleas firmly establish her goals as linked to Walter's. In this way, the interaction of the two plotlines advances Walter's goals but radically alters Hildy's.

Within this general framework, the cause–effect sequencing is complex and deserves a closer analysis than space permits here. But consider, for example, the various ways in which Walter's delaying tactics (involving his confederates Duffy, Louie, and Angie) set up short-term chains of cause and effect in themselves. Also interesting is the way Bruce is steadily shouldered out of the romance plot, becoming more and more passive as he is shuttled in and out of precinct jails. In this regard, Earl Williams undergoes a parallel experience as he is manipulated by Hildy, the sheriff, the psychologist, and Walter. We could also consider the function of the minor characters, such as Molly Malloy (Williams's platonic sweetheart), Bruce's mother, the other reporters, and especially Pettibone, the delightful emissary from the governor.

We could also note how the scenes hook into one another: an event at the end of one scene becomes a cause leading to an effect—the event that begins the next scene. For example, at the end of the first scene, Walter offers to take Bruce and Hildy to lunch; scene 2 starts with the three of them arriving at the restaurant. This exemplifies the linearity of classical narrative: almost every scene ends with a dangling cause, the effect of which is shown at the beginning of the next scene. In *His Girl Friday*, this linear pattern helps keep the plot action moving rapidly forward, setting up each new scene quickly at the end of the previous one.

The cause–effect logic of the film illustrates yet another principle of classical narrative structure: closure. No event is uncaused. (Even Pettibone's arrival is no lucky accident, for we know that the governor is under pressure to decide about the case.) More important, both lines of action are clearly resolved at the end: Williams is saved and the politicians are disgraced. Bruce, having gone home with mother, leaves Walter and Hildy preparing for a second honeymoon no less hectic than their first.

So much for causality. What of narrative time? Classical Hollywood cinema typically subordinates time to the narrative's cause–effect relations, and one common way is to set a deadline for the action. Thus a temporal goal is wedded to a causal one, and the time becomes charged with cause–effect significance. The deadline is also a convention of the newspaper genre, adding a built-in time and suspense factor. But in *His Girl Friday*, each of the two plots has its own deadlines as well. The mayor and the sheriff face an obvious deadline: Earl Williams must be hanged before next Tuesday's election and before the governor can reprieve him. In his political strategizing, Walter Burns faces the other side of the same deadline: he wants Williams reprieved. What we might not expect is that the romance plot has deadlines as well.

Bruce and Hildy are set to leave on a train bound for Albany and for marriage at four o'clock that very day. Walter's machinations keep forcing the couple to postpone their departure. Add to this the fact that when Bruce comes to confront Hildy and Walter, he exits with the defiant ultimatum "I'm leaving on the nine o'clock train!" (Hildy misses that train as well.) The temporal structure of the film, then, depends on the cause–effect sequence. If Earl Williams were to be hanged next month, or if the election were two years off, or if Bruce and Hildy were plan-

"If you'll ever listen to some people who are talking, especially in a scene of any excitement, they all talk at the same time. All it needs is a little extra work on the dialogue. You put a few words in front of somebody's speech and put a few words at the end, and they can overlap it. It gives you a sense of speed that actually doesn't exist. And you can make the people talk a little faster."

— Howard Hawks, director

ning a marriage at some distant future date, the sense of dramatic pressure would be lacking. The numerous overlapping deadlines under which all of the characters labor have the effect of squeezing together all the lines of action and sustaining the breathless pace of the film.

Another aspect of *His Girl Friday*'s patterning of time reinforces this pace. Though the plot presents events in straightforward chronological order, it takes remarkable liberties with story duration. Of course, since the primary story action consumes about nine hours (from around 12:30 P.M. to around 9:30 P.M.), we expect that certain portions of time *between* scenes will be eliminated. And so they have been. What is unusual is that the time *within* scenes has been accelerated.

At the start of the very first scene, for example, the clock in the *Post* office reads 12:36; after 12 minutes of screen time have passed, the same clock reads 12:57. It's important to note that there have been no editing ellipses in the scene; the story duration has simply been compressed. If you time scene 13, you will find even more remarkable acceleration. People leave on long trips and return less than 10 minutes later. Again, the editing presents continuity of duration: it is story time that goes faster than screen time. This temporal compression combines with frenetically rushed dialogue and occasionally accelerated rhythmic editing (for example, the reporters' cries just before Williams's capture) to create the film's breakneck pace.

Space, like time, is here subordinate to narrative cause and effect. Hawks's camera moves unobtrusively to reframe the characters symmetrically in the shot. (Watch any scene silent to observe the subtle balancing act that goes on during the dialogue scenes. An example is shown in 5.144–5.146.) Straight-on camera angles predominate, varied by an occasional high-angle shot down on the prison courtyard or on Williams's cell bars. Why, we might ask in passing, does the prison receive this visual emphasis in the camera angle and the lighting?

The restriction of the action to very few locales might seem a handicap, but the patterns of character placement are remarkably varied and functional. Walter's persuading Hildy to write the story is interesting from this standpoint (**11.1, 11.2**; note the gestures). And spatial continuity in the editing anticipates each dramatic point by judiciously cutting to a closer shot or smoothly matching on action so that we watch the movements and not the cuts (**11.3, 11.4**). The change in the position of Walter's arms, so apparent in our illustrations, goes unnoticed because of Hildy's broader and more emphatic gestures. Virtually every scene, especially the restaurant episode and the final scene, offers many fine examples of classical continuity editing. In all, space is used to delineate the flow of the cause–effect sequence.

We might highlight for special attention one specific item of both sound and mise-en-scene. It is plausible that newspapermen in 1939 use telephones, but *His Girl Friday* makes the phone integral to the narrative. Walter's duplicity demands phones. At the restaurant, he pretends to be summoned away to a call; he makes and breaks promises to Hildy via phones; he directs Duffy and other minions by phone. More generally, the pressroom is equipped with a veritable flotilla of phones, enabling the reporters to contact their editors. And, of course, Bruce keeps calling Hildy from the various police stations in which he continually finds himself. The telephones thus constitute a communications network that permits the narrative to be relayed from point to point.

But Hawks also visually and sonically orchestrates the characters' use of the phones. There are many variations. One person may be talking on the phone, or several may be talking in turn on different phones, or several may be talking at once on different phones, or a phone conversation may be juxtaposed with a conversation elsewhere in the room. In scene 11, there is a polyphonic effect of reporters coming in to phone their editors, each conversation overlapping with the preceding one. Later, in scene 13, while Hildy frantically phones hospitals, Walter screams into another phone (**11.5**). And when Bruce returns for Hildy, a helter-skelter din arises that eventually sorts itself into three sonic lines: Bruce begging Hildy to

11.1 In *His Girl Friday,* as Walter and Hildy pace in a complete circuit around the desk . . .

11.2 . . . Walter assumes dynamic and comic postures.

11.3 In the opening scene of *His Girl Friday,* Hildy's action of throwing her purse at Walter . . .

11.4 . . . is matched at the cut to a more distant framing.

11.5   *His Girl Friday.*

listen, Hildy obsessively typing her story, and Walter yelling into the phone for Duffy to clear page one ("No, no, leave the rooster story—that's human interest!"). Like much in *His Girl Friday,* the telephones warrant close study for the complex and various ways in which they are integrated into the narrative, and for their contribution to the rapid tempo of the film.

North by Northwest

1959. MGM. Directed by Alfred Hitchcock. Script by Ernest Lehman. Photographed by Robert Burks. Edited by George Tomasini. Music composed by Bernard Herrmann. With Cary Grant, Eva Marie Saint, James Mason, Leo G. Carroll, Jesse Royce Landis.

Hitchcock long insisted that he made thrillers, not mystery films. For him, creating a puzzle was less important than generating suspense and surprise. While there are important mystery elements in films such as *Notorious* (1946), *Stage Fright* (1950), and *Psycho* (1960), *North by Northwest* stands as almost a pure example of Hitchcock's belief that the mystery element can serve as merely a pretext for intriguing the audience. The film's tight causal unity enables Hitchcock to create an engrossing plot that fulfills the norms of classical filmmaking. This plot is presented through a narration that continually emphasizes suspense and surprise. (For more on thrillers, see pp. 332–334.)

Like most spy films, *North by Northwest* has a complex plot, involving two major lines of action. In one line, a gang of spies mistakes advertising agency executive Roger Thornhill for an American agent, George Kaplan. Although the spies fail to kill him, he becomes the chief suspect in a murder that the gang commits. He must flee the police while trying to track down the real George Kaplan. Unfortunately, Kaplan does not exist; he is only a decoy invented by the United States Intelligence Agency (USIA). Thornhill's pursuit of Kaplan leads to the second line of action: his meeting and falling in love with Eve Kendall, who is really the mistress of Philip Van Damm, the spies' leader. The spy-chase line and the romance line further connect when Thornhill learns that Eve is actually a double agent, secretly working for the USIA. He must then rescue her from Van Damm, who has discovered her identity and has resolved to kill her. In the course of all this, Thornhill also discovers that the spies are smuggling government secrets out of the country in pieces of sculpture.

From even so bare an outline, it should be evident that the film's plot presents many conventional patterns to the viewer. There's the search pattern, seen when Thornhill sets out to find Kaplan. There's also a journey pattern: Thornhill and his pursuers travel from New York to Chicago and then to Rapid City, South Dakota, with side excursions as well. In addition, the last two-thirds of the plot is organized around the romance between Thornhill and Eve. Moreover, each pattern develops markedly in the course of the film. In the course of his search, Thornhill must often assume the identity of the man he is trailing. The journey pattern gets varied by all the vehicles Thornhill uses—cabs, train, pickup truck, police car, bus, ambulance, and airplane.

Most subtly, the romance line of action is constantly modified by Thornhill's changing awareness of the situation. Believing that Eve wants to help him, he falls in love with her. But then he learns that she sent him to the murderous appointment at Prairie Stop, and he becomes cold and suspicious. When he discovers her at the auction with Van Damm, his anger and bitterness impel him to humiliate her and make Van Damm doubt her loyalty. Only after the USIA chief, the "Professor," tells him that she is really an agent does Thornhill realize that he has misjudged and endangered her. Each step in his growing awareness alters his romantic relation to Eve.

This intricate plot is unified and made comprehensible by other familiar strategies. *North by Northwest* has a strict time scheme, comprising four days and nights (followed by a brief epilogue on a later night). The first day and a half take place

11.6 On the train, when Thornhill and Eve kiss, his hands close tenderly around her hair, but . . .

11.7 . . . later in her hotel room, when she tries to embrace him after his narrow escape from death, his hands freeze in place, as if he fears touching her.

11.8 Early in *North by Northwest*, a shot of two spies looking off left is followed by . . .

11.9 . . . a shot of Thornhill from their POV.

11.10 An advancing truck as seen by Thornhill.

11.11 A trooper's fist coming toward the camera, again from Thornhill's POV.

in New York; the second night on the train to Chicago; the third day in Chicago and at Prairie Stop; and the fourth day at Mount Rushmore. The timetable is neatly established early in the film. Van Damm, having abducted Roger as Kaplan, announces, "In two days you're due at the Ambassador East in Chicago, and then at the Sheraton Johnson Hotel in Rapid City, South Dakota." This itinerary prepares the spectator for the shifts in action that will occur in the rest of the film. Apart from the time scheme, the film also unifies itself through the characterization of Thornhill. He is initially presented as a resourceful liar when he steals a cab from another pedestrian. Later, he will have to lie in many circumstances to evade capture. Similarly, Roger is established as a heavy drinker, and his ability to hold his liquor will enable him to survive Van Damm's attempt to force him to kill himself when driving while drunk.

A great many motifs are repeated and help make the film cohere. Roger is constantly in danger from heights: his car hangs over a cliff; he must sneak out on the ledge of a hospital; he has to clamber up Van Damm's modernistic clifftop house; and he and Eve wind up dangling from the faces on Mount Rushmore. Thornhill's constant changing of vehicles also constitutes a motif that Hitchcock varies. A subtler example is the motif that conveys Thornhill's growing suspicion of Eve (**11.6, 11.7**).

Still, narrative unity alone cannot explain the film's strong emotional appeal. In Chapter 3's discussion of narration, we used *North by Northwest* as an example of a hierarchy of knowledge (p. 95). We suggested that as the film progresses, sometimes we are restricted to what Roger knows, but at other times, we know significantly more than he does. At still other moments, our range of knowledge, while greater than Roger's, is not as great as that of other characters. Now we are in a position to see how this constantly changing process helps create suspense and surprise across the whole film.

The most straightforward way in which the film's narration controls our knowledge is through the numerous optical point-of-view (POV) shots Hitchcock employs. This device yields a degree of subjective depth: we see what a character sees more or less as she or he sees it. More important here, the optical POV shot restricts us only to what that character learns at that moment. Hitchcock gives almost every major character a shot of this sort. The very first optical POV we see in the film is taken from the position of the two spies who are watching Roger apparently respond to the paging of George Kaplan (**11.8, 11.9**). Later, we view events through the eyes of Eve, of Van Damm, of his henchman Leonard, and even of a clerk at a ticket counter.

Nevertheless, by far the greatest number of POV shots are attached to Thornhill. Through his eyes, we see his approach to the Townsend mansion, the mail he finds in the library, his drunken drive along the cliff, and the airplane that is "crop dusting where there ain't no crops." Some of the most extreme uses of optical POV give us Roger's experience directly (**11.10, 11.11**).

Thornhill's optical POV shots function within a narration that is often restricted not only to what he *sees* but also to what he *knows*. The plane attack at Prairie Stop, for example, is confined wholly to Roger's range of knowledge. Hitchcock could have cut away from Roger waiting by the road in order to show us the villains plotting in their plane, but he does not. Similarly, when Roger is searching for George Kaplan's room and gets a phone call from the two henchmen, Hitchcock could have used crosscutting to show the villains phoning from the lobby. Instead, we learn that they are in the hotel no sooner than Roger does. And when Thornhill and his mother hurry out of the room, Hitchcock does not use crosscutting to show the villains in pursuit. This makes it more startling when Roger and his mother get on the elevator and discover the two men there already. In scenes like these, confining us to Thornhill's range of knowledge sharpens the effect of surprise.

Sometimes the same effect comes from the film's restricting us to Roger's range of knowledge and then giving us information that he does not at the moment have. On p. 89, we suggested that this sort of surprise occurs when the plot shifts us from Roger's escape from the United Nations murder to the scene at the USIA office, where the staff discuss the case. At this point, we learn that there is no George Kaplan—something that Roger does not discover for many more scenes to come.

The abrupt shifts from Roger's range of knowledge yield a similar effect during the train trip from New York to Chicago. During several scenes, Eve Kendall helps Thornhill evade the police. Finally, they are alone and relatively safe in her compartment. At this point, the narration shifts the range of knowledge. A message is delivered to another compartment. Hands unfold a note: "What do I do with him in the morning?" The camera then moves back to show us Leonard and Van Damm reading the message. Now we know that Eve is not merely a sympathetic stranger but someone working for the spy ring. Again, Roger will learn this much later. In such cases, the move to a less restricted range of information lets the narration put us a notch higher than Thornhill in the hierarchy of knowledge.

Such moments evoke surprise, but we have already noted that Hitchcock claimed in general to prefer to generate suspense (p. 90). Suspense is created by giving the spectator more information than the character has. In the scenes we have just mentioned, once the effect of surprise has been achieved, the narration can use our superior knowledge to build suspense across several sequences. After the audience learns that there is no George Kaplan, every attempt by Thornhill to find him builds up suspense about whether he will discover the truth. Once we learn that Eve is working for Van Damm, her message to Roger on behalf of Kaplan will make us uncertain as to whether Roger will fall into the trap.

In these examples, suspense arises across a series of scenes. Hitchcock also uses unrestricted narration to build up suspense within a single scene. His handling of the UN murder differs markedly from his treatment of the scene showing Roger and his mother in Kaplan's hotel room. In the hotel scene, Hitchcock refused to employ crosscutting to show the spies' pursuit. At the United Nations, however, he crosscuts between Roger, who is searching for Townsend, and Valerian, one of the thugs following him. Just before the murder, a rightward tracking shot establishes Valerian's position in the doorway (something of which Roger is wholly unaware). Here crosscutting and camera movement widen our frame of knowledge and create suspense as to the scene's outcome.

The sequence in Chicago's Union Station is handled similarly. Here crosscutting moves us from Roger shaving in the men's room to Eve talking on the phone. Then another lateral tracking shot reveals that she is talking to Leonard, who is giving her orders from another phone booth. We now are certain that the message she will give Roger will endanger him, and the suspense is increased accordingly. (Note, however, that the narration does not reveal the conversation itself. As often happens, Hitchcock conceals certain information for the sake of further surprises.)

Thornhill's knowledge expands as the lines of action develop. On the third day, he discovers that Eve is Van Damm's mistress, that she is a double agent, and that Kaplan doesn't exist. He agrees to help the Professor in a scheme to clear Eve of any suspicion in Van Damm's eyes. When the scheme (a faked shooting in the Mount Rushmore restaurant) succeeds, Roger believes that Eve will leave Van Damm. Once more, however, he has been duped (as we have). The Professor insists that she must go off to Europe that night on Van Damm's private flight. Roger resists, but he is knocked out and held captive in a hospital. His escape leads to the final major sequence of the film.

Here the plot resolves all its lines of action, and the narration continues to expand and contract our knowledge for the sake of suspense and surprise. This climactic sequence comprises almost 300 shots and runs for several minutes, but we can conveniently divide the sequence into three sections.

In the first section, Roger arrives at Van Damm's house and reconnoiters. He clambers up to the window and learns from a conversation between Leonard and Van Damm that the piece of sculpture they bought at the auction contains microfilm. More important, he watches Leonard inform Van Damm that Eve is an American agent. This action is conveyed largely through optical POV (**11.12, 11.13**; also 3.15–3.17). At two moments, as Leonard and Van Damm face each other, the narration gives us optical POV shots from each man's standpoint (**11.14, 11.15**), but these are enclosed, so to speak, within Roger's ongoing witnessing of the situation. For the first time in the film, Roger has more knowledge of the situation than any other character. He knows how the smuggling has been done, and he discovers that the villains intend to murder Eve.

The second phase of the sequence can be said to begin when Roger enters Eve's bedroom. She has gone back downstairs and is sitting on a couch. Again, Hitchcock emphasizes the restriction to Thornhill's knowledge by means of optical POV shots (**11.16, 11.17**). In order to warn Eve, he uses his ROT monogrammed matchbook (a motif set up on the train as a joke). He tosses the matchbook down toward Eve. This initiates still more suspense when Leonard sees it, but he unconcernedly puts it in an ashtray on the coffee table. When Eve notices the matchbook, Hitchcock varies his handling of optical POV from the first subsegment. There he was willing to show us the face-off between Van Damm and Leonard (11.14, 11.15). Now

11.12   In *North by Northwest,* Thornhill watches in dismay . . .

11.13   . . . as Leonard betrays Eve to Van Damm.

11.14   When Van Damm reacts by punching Leonard, he is seen from Leonard's POV . . .

11.15   . . . and then Leonard is seen from his POV.

11.16   Later, Thornhill's glance down at the living room is followed by . . .

11.17   . . . a high-angle POV framing appropriate to his position on the balcony upstairs.

11.18   When Eve notices the matchbook, she is seen from Thornhill's viewpoint upstairs.

"In North by Northwest during the scene on Mount Rushmore I wanted Cary Grant to hide in Lincoln's nostril and have a fit of sneezing. The Parks Commission of the Department of Interior was rather upset at this thought. I argued until one of their number asked me how I would like it if they had Lincoln play the scene in Cary Grant's nose. I saw their point at once."

— Alfred Hitchcock, director

he does not show us Eve's eyes at all. Instead, through Roger's eyes, we see her back stiffen; we *infer* that she is looking at the matchbook **(11.18).** Again, though, Roger's range of knowledge is the broadest, and his optical POV encloses another character's experience. On a pretext, Eve returns to her room, and Roger warns her not to get on the plane.

As the spies make their way to the landing field outside, Roger starts to follow. Now Hitchcock's narration shifts again to show Van Damm's housekeeper spotting Roger's reflection in a television set. As earlier in the film, we know more than Roger does, and this generates suspense when she walks out . . . and returns with a pistol aimed at him.

The third section of the climax takes place outdoors. Eve is about to get in the plane when a pistol shot distracts the spies' attention long enough for her to grab the statuette and race to the car Roger has stolen. This portion of the sequence confines us to Eve's range of knowledge, accentuating it with shots from her optical POV. The pattern of surprise interrupting a period of suspense—here, Roger's escape from the house interrupting Eve's tense walk to the plane—will dominate the rest of the sequence.

There follows a chase across the presidents' faces on Mount Rushmore. Some crosscutting informs us of the spies' progress in following the couple, but on the whole, the narration restricts us to what Eve and Thornhill know. As usual, some moments are heightened by optical POV shots, as when Eve watches Roger and Valerian roll down what seems to be a sheer drop. At the climax, Eve is dangling over the edge while Roger is clutching one of her hands and Leonard grinds his foot into Roger's other hand. It is a classic, not to say clichéd, situation of suspense. Again, however, the narration reveals the limits of our knowledge. A rifle shot cracks out and Leonard falls to the ground. The Professor has arrived and captured Van Damm, and a marksman has shot Leonard. Once more, a restricted range of knowledge has enabled the narration to spring a surprise on the audience.

The same effect gets magnified at the very end. In a series of optical POV shots, Roger pulls Eve up from the brink. But this gesture is made continuous, in both sound and image, with that of him pulling her up to a train bunk. The narration ignores the details of their rescue in order to cut short the suspense of Eve's plight. Such a self-conscious transition is not completely out of place in a film that has taken time for offhand jokes. (During the opening credits, Hitchcock himself is shown being shut out of a bus. As Roger strides into the Plaza Hotel, about to be plunged into his adventure, the Muzak is playing "It's a Most Unusual Day.") This concluding twist shows once again that Hitchcock's moment-by-moment manipulation of our knowledge yields a constantly shifting play between the probable and the unexpected, between suspense and surprise.

Do The Right Thing

1989. Forty Acres and a Mule Filmworks (distributed by Universal). Directed and scripted by Spike Lee. Photographed by Ernest Dickerson. Edited by Barry Alexander Brown. Music by Bill Lee et al. With Danny Aiello, Ossie Davis, Ruby Dee, Giancarlo Esposito, Spike Lee, Bill Nunn, John Turturro, Rosie Perez.

At first viewing, Spike Lee's *Do The Right Thing,* with its many brief, disconnected scenes, restlessly wandering camera, and large number of characters without goals might not seem a classical narrative film. And, indeed, in some ways, it does depart from classical usage. Yet it has the redundantly clear action and strong forward impetus that we associate with classical filmmaking. It also fits into a familiar genre of American cinema—the social problem film. Moreover, closer analysis reveals that Lee has also drawn on many traits of classicism to give an underlying unity to this apparently loosely constructed plot.

Do The Right Thing takes place in the predominantly African-American Bedford–Stuyvesant section of Brooklyn during a heat wave. Sexual and racial tensions rise as Mookie, an irresponsible pizza delivery man, tries to get along with his Puerto Rican girlfriend, Tina, and with his Italian American boss, Sal. An elderly drunk, Da Mayor, sets out to ingratiate himself with his sharp-tongued neighbor, Mother Sister. An escalating quarrel between Sal and two customers, Buggin' Out and Radio Raheem, leads to a fight in which Radio Raheem is killed by police. A riot ensues, and Sal's pizzeria is burned.

Do The Right Thing has many more individual sequences than, say, *His Girl Friday,* with its neatly delineated 13 scenes (pp. 397–398). Even lumping together some of the very briefest scenes, there are at least 42 segments. Laying out a detailed segmentation of *Do The Right Thing* might be useful for another analysis, but here we want to concentrate on how Lee weaves his many scenes into a whole.

One important means of unifying the film is its setting. The entire narrative is played out on one block in Bedford–Stuyvesant. Sal's Famous Pizzeria and the Korean market opposite create a spatial anchor at one end of the block, and much of the action takes place there. Other scenes are played out in or in front of the brownstone buildings that line most of the rest of the street. Encounters among members of this neighborhood provide the causality for the narrative.

To match the limited setting, the action takes place in a restricted time frame—from one morning to the next. Structuring a film around a brief slice of the life of a group of characters is rare but not unknown in American filmmaking, as with *Street Scene, Dead End, American Graffiti, Nashville,* and *Magnolia.*

The radio DJ Mister Señor Love Daddy provides a running motif that also binds the film's events together. He appears in close-up in the first shot of the opening scene, and this initial broadcast provides important information about the setting and the weather—a heat wave that intensifies the characters' tensions and contributes to the final violent outbreak. As the DJ speaks, the camera tracks slowly out and cranes up to reveal the street, still empty in the early morning. At intervals throughout the film, Mister Señor Love Daddy also provides commentary on the action, as when he tells a group of characters spewing racist diatribes to "chill out." The music he plays creates sound bridges between otherwise unconnected scenes, since the radios in different locations are often tuned to his station. The end of the film echoes the beginning, as the camera tracks with Mookie in the street and we hear the DJ's voice giving a similar spiel to the one on the previous morning, then dedicating the final song to the dead Radio Raheem.

As the setting and the use of the neighborhood radio station suggest, *Do The Right Thing* centers more on the community as a whole than on a few central characters. On the one hand, there are older traditions that are worth preserving, represented by the elderly characters: the moral strength of the matriarch Mother Sister, the decency and courage of Da Mayor, the wit and common sense of the three chatting men—ML, Sweet Dick Willie, and Coconut Sid. On the other hand, the younger people need to create a new community spirit by overcoming sexual and racial conflict. The women are portrayed as trying to make the angry young African-American men more responsible. Tina pressures Mookie to pay more attention to her and to their son; Jade lectures both her brother Mookie and the excitable Buggin' Out, telling the latter he should direct his energies toward doing "something positive in the community." The emphasis on community is underscored by the fact that most of the characters address one another by their nicknames.

One of the main conflicts in the film arises when Sal refuses to add some pictures of African-American heroes to his "Hall of Fame" photo gallery of Italian Americans. Sal might have become a sort of elder statesman in the community, where he has run his pizzeria for 25 years. He seems to like the kids who eat his pizza, but he also views the restaurant as entirely his domain, emphatically declaring that he's the boss. Thus he reveals his lack of real integration into the community and ends by goading the more hot-headed elements into attacking him.

In creating its community, *Do The Right Thing* includes an unusually large number of characters for a classical film. Again, however, a closer examination shows that only eight of them provide the main causal action: Mookie, Tina, Sal, Sal's son Pino, Mother Sister, Da Mayor, Buggin' Out, and Radio Raheem. The others, intriguing or amusing as they may be, are more peripheral, mainly reacting to the action set in motion by these characters' conflicts and goals. (Some modern American screenwriting manuals recommend seven to eight important characters as the maximum for a clearly comprehensible film, so Lee is not departing from tradition as much as it might seem.) Moreover, the main causal action falls into two related lines, as in traditional Hollywood films: one involves the community's relations to Sal and his sons; the other deals with Mookie's personal life. Mookie becomes the pivotal figure, linking the two lines of action.

Do The Right Thing also departs from classical narrative conventions in some ways. Consider the characters' goals. Usually, the main characters of a film formulate clear-cut, long-range goals that bring them into conflict with one another. In *Do The Right Thing,* most of the eight main characters create goals only sporadically; the goals are sometimes introduced fairly late in the film, and some are vague.

Buggin' Out, for example, demands that Sal put up pictures of some black heroes on the pizzeria wall. When Sal refuses and throws him out, Buggin' Out shouts to the customers to boycott Sal's. Yet a little while later, when he tries to persuade his neighbors to participate in the boycott, they all refuse, and his project seems to sputter out. Then, later in the film, Radio Raheem and the mentally retarded Smiley agree to join him. Their visit to the pizzeria to threaten Sal then precipitates the climactic action. Ironically, Buggin' Out's goal is briefly achieved when Smiley puts a photograph of Malcolm X and Martin Luther King Jr. on the wall of the burning pizzeria—but by that point, Buggin' Out is on his way to jail.

Mookie's goal is hinted at when we first see him. He is counting money, and he constantly emphasizes that he just wants to work and get paid. His repeated reference to the fact that he is due to be paid in the evening creates the film's only appointment, helping to emphasize the compressed time scheme. Yet his purpose remains unclear. Does he simply want the money so that he can move out of his sister's apartment, as she demands? Or does he also plan to help Tina care for their son?

Sal's goal is similarly vague—to keep operating his pizzeria in the face of rising tensions. Da Mayor articulates one of the few really clear-cut goals in the film when he tells Mother Sister that someday she will be nice to him. After he persistently acts courteously and bravely, she does in fact relent and become his friend. Sal's virulently racist son Pino has a goal—trying to convince his father that they should sell the pizzeria and get out of the black neighborhood. Perhaps he will get his desire at the end, although the narrative leaves open the question of whether Sal will rebuild.

In traditional classical films, clear-cut goals generate conflict, since the characters' desires often clash. Lee neatly reverses this pattern by playing down goals but creating a community that is full of conflict from the very beginning of the film. Racial and sexual arguments break out frequently, and insults fly. Such conflict is tied to the fact that *Do The Right Thing* is a social-problem film. Its didactic message gives it much of its overall unity. Everything that happens relates to a central question: With the community riven with such tensions, what can be done to heal it?

The characters' goals and actions suggest some of the possible ways of reacting to the situation. Some of the characters desire simply to avoid or escape this tense atmosphere—Pino by leaving the neighborhood, Da Mayor by overcoming Mother Sister's animosity. Mookie attempts to stay out of trouble by not siding with either Sal or his black friends in their escalating quarrel; only the death of Radio Raheem drives him to join in, and indeed initiate, the attack on Sal's pizzeria.

Other characters attempt to solve their problems. One central goal is Tina's desire to get Mookie to behave more responsibly and spend time with her and with their child. There is a suggestion at the end that she may be succeeding to some extent. Mookie gets his pay from Sal and says that he will get another job and that he's going to see his son. The last shot shows him walking down the now-quiet street, hinting that he may really visit his son more regularly in the future.

The central question in the film, however, is not whether any one character will achieve his or her goals. It is whether the pervasive conflicts can be resolved peacefully or violently. As the DJ says on the morning after the riot, "Are we gonna live together—together are we gonna live?"

Do The Right Thing leaves unanswered questions at the end. Will Sal rebuild? Is Mookie really going back to see his son? Most important, though the conflict that flared up has died down, the tension is still present in the community, waiting to resurface. The old problem of how to tame it remains, and so the film does not achieve complete closure. Indeed, such an ending is typical of the social-problem genre. While the immediate conflict may be resolved, the underlying dilemma that caused it remains.

That is also why there is a deliberate ambiguity at the end. Just as we are left at the end of *Citizen Kane* to wonder whether the revelation of the meaning of "Rosebud" explains Kane's character, in *Do The Right Thing* we are left to ponder what "the right thing" is. The film continues after the final story action, with two nondiegetic quotations from Martin Luther King Jr. and Malcolm X. The King passage advocates a nonviolent approach to the struggle for civil rights, while Malcolm X condones violence in self-defense.

Do The Right Thing refuses to suggest which leader is right—although the narrative action and use of the phrase "by any means necessary" at the end of the credits seem to weight the film's position in favor of Malcolm X. Still, the juxtaposition of the two quotations, in combination with the open-ended narrative, also seems calculated to spur debate. Perhaps the implication is that each position is viable under certain circumstances. The line of action involving Sal's pizzeria ends in violence; yet at the same time, Da Mayor is able to win Mother Sister's friendship gently.

As in its narrative structure, the style of *Do The Right Thing* stretches the traditional techniques of classical filmmaking. It begins with a credits sequence during which Rosie Perez performs a vigorous and aggressive dance to the rap song "Fight the Power." The editing here is strongly discontinuous, as she wears sometimes a red dress, sometimes a boxer's outfit, and sometimes a jacket and pants. One moment she is on the street; then she suddenly appears in an alley. This brief sequence, which is not part of the narrative, employs the flashy style made familiar by MTV and by television commercials. Lee himself has made both music videos and commercials.

11.19 In *Do The Right Thing,* this shot/reverse-shot conversation between Jade and . . .

Nothing in the rest of *Do The Right Thing* is quite as discontinuous or extreme as the credits sequence, but Lee uses a loose version of the traditional continuity system. He draws on a broad range of techniques, handling some scenes in virtuosic long takes, others with shot/reverse shot, and still others with extensive camera movements. In two cases, he even cuts together two takes of the same action, so that the plot presents a single important story event twice: when Mookie first kisses Tina and when the garbage can hits Sal's window. One result of this varied style is a suggestion of the vigor and variety of the community itself.

Despite the many quick changes of locale, Lee uses continuity devices to establish space clearly. As we saw in Chapter 6, he is adept at using shot/reverse shot without breaking the axis of action (6.79–6.84, from *She's Gotta Have It,* pp. 243–244). *Do The Right Thing* similarly contains many shot/reverse-shot conversations where the eyelines are consistent **(11.19, 11.20).** Yet Lee opts to handle other conversations without any editing. The lengthy conversation in which Pino asks Sal to sell the pizzeria is handled in one long take **(11.21–11.23).**

11.20 . . . Buggin' Out uses correct eyeline directions.

Cinematic technique frequently emphasizes the community as a whole. Indeed, one reason the film has so many segments is that there are frequent cuts from one action to another. The narration is largely unrestricted, flitting from one group of characters to another, seldom lingering with any individual. Similarly, complex

11.21   This long take in *Do The Right Thing* begins with a track-in . . .

11.22   . . . toward Sal and Pino and lasts until Smiley appears outside . . .

11.23   . . . and Pino chases him away.

11.24   Da Mayor and Mother Sister talk and then move out into her front room, the camera tracking with them and . . .

11.25   . . . passing through the window as they reach it, craning down . . .

11.26   . . . to a close view of Mookie, on the way to the pizzeria.

11.27   Radio Raheem orders a slice of pizza from Sal, who has ordered him to turn his radio off.

11.28   One shot from a motif of Mookie walking across a chalk drawing.

camera movements follow characters through the street, catching glimpses of other activities going on in the background. Other camera movements slide away from one line of action to another. On the morning after the riot, Da Mayor wakes up in Mother Sister's apartment and the camera shifts to Mookie (**11.24–11.26**).

The dense sound track helps characterize the community. As Mookie walks past a row of houses, the sounds of radios tuned to different stations fade up and down, hinting at the offscreen presence of the inhabitants. The music broadcast by the DJ plays a large role in drawing the many brief scenes together, with the same song carrying over various exchanges of dialogue. The different ethnic groups are characterized by the types of music they listen to.

Style also stresses the underlying problems in the community. Radio Raheem's threatening demeanor is emphasized in some scenes by his direct address into a wide-angle lens (**11.27**). Mookie's self-absorption and lack of interest in the neighborhood is suggested in a visual motif of high-angle views showing him stepping unheedingly on a cheerful chalk picture of a house that a little girl is drawing on the pavement (**11.28**). Sound contributes to the racial tensions, as in the scenes where Radio Raheem annoys people by playing his rap song at high volume.

Do The Right Thing, despite its stretching of traditional Hollywood conventions, remains a good example of a contemporary approach to classical filmmaking. Its style reflects the looser techniques that became conventions of post-1960s cinema—an era when the impact of television and European art films inspired filmmakers to incorporate somewhat more variety into the Hollywood system. Even the plot's departures from tradition are somewhat motivated because Lee adopts the basic purpose of the social problem film—to make us think and to stir debate.

Narrative Alternatives to Classical Filmmaking

Breathless (À Bout de souffle)

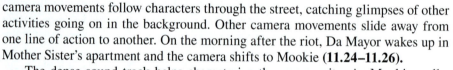

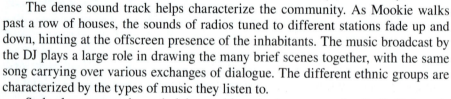

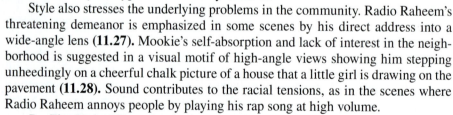

1960. Les Films Georges de Beauregard, Impéria Films and Société Nouvelle de Cinéma. Directed by Jean-Luc Godard. Story outline by François Truffaut, dialogue by Godard. Photographed by Raoul Coutard. Edited by Cécile Decugis. Music by

Martial Solal. With Jean-Paul Belmondo, Jean Seberg, Daniel Boulanger, Henri-Jacques Huet, Van Doude, Jean-Pierre Melville.

In some ways, *Breathless* imitates a 1940s Hollywood staple, the **film noir,** or "dark film." Such films dealt with hard-boiled detectives, gangsters, or ordinary people tempted into crime. Often a seductive femme fatale lured the protagonist into a dangerous scheme for hidden purposes of her own (for example, *The Maltese Falcon* and *Double Indemnity*). *Breathless*'s plot links it to a common noir vehicle—the outlaw movie involving young criminals on the run (such as *They Live by Night* and *Gun Crazy*).

The bare-bones story could serve as the basis of a Hollywood script. A car thief, Michel, kills a motorcycle cop and flees to Paris in order to get money to escape to Italy. He also tries to convince Patricia, an American art student and aspiring writer with whom he had a brief affair, to go with him. After equivocating for nearly two days, she agrees. Just as Michel is about to receive the cash he needs, Patricia calls the police, and they kill him.

Yet Godard's presentation of this story could never pass for a polished studio product. For one thing, Michel's behavior is presented as driven *by* the very movies that *Breathless* imitates. He rubs his thumb across his lips in imitation of his idol Humphrey Bogart. Yet he is a petty thief whose life spins out of control. He can only fantasize himself as a romantic Hollywood tough guy.

The film's ambivalent attitude toward classical Hollywood cinema also pervades form and technique. As we've seen, the norms of classical style and storytelling promote narrative clarity and unity. In contrast, *Breathless* appears awkward and casual, almost amateurish. It makes character motivations ambiguous and lingers over incidental dialogue. Its editing jumps about frenetically. And, whereas films noirs were made largely in the studio, where selective lighting could swathe the characters in a brooding atmosphere, *Breathless* utilizes location shooting with available lighting.

These strategies make Michel's story quirky, uncertain, and deglamorized. They also ask the audience to enjoy the film's rough-edged reworking of Hollywood formulas. An opening title dedicates the film to Monogram Pictures, a Poverty Row studio that churned out B-movies. The title seems to announce a film that is indebted to Hollywood but not wholly bound by its norms.

Like many protagonists in classical Hollywood films, Michel has two main goals. In order to leave France, he must search for his friend Antonio, the only one who can cash a check for him. He also hopes to persuade Patricia to go with him, and it becomes apparent as the action progresses that, despite his flippant attitude, his love for her outweighs his desire to escape.

In a classical film, these goals would drive the action along fairly steadily. Yet in *Breathless,* the plot moves in fits and starts. Brief scenes—some largely unconnected to the goals—alternate with long stretches of seemingly irrelevant dialogue. Most of *Breathless*'s 22 separate segments run four minutes or less. One 43-second scene consists simply of Michel pausing in front of a theater and looking at a picture of Bogart.

Scenes containing crucial action are sometimes brief and confusing. The murder of the traffic cop, an event that triggers much of what follows, is handled in a very elliptical fashion. In long shot, we see the officer approaching Michel's car, parked in a side road. In medium long shot, Michel reaches into the car for the gun. A close shot of his head follows, as the cop's voice is heard saying, "Don't move or I'll drill you" (**11.29**). Two very brief close-ups pan along Michel's arm and along the gun (**11.30, 11.31**), with the sound of a gunshot. We then get a glimpse of the cop falling into some underbrush (**11.32**), followed by an extreme long shot of Michel, running far across a field. So much action has been left out that we can barely comprehend what is happening, let alone judge whether Michel shot deliberately or by accident.

11.29 In *Breathless*'s murder scene, brief shots . . .

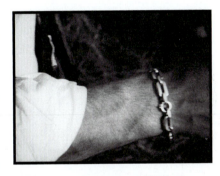

11.30 . . . give glimpses of Michel's actions . . .

11.31 . . . in pointing a gun . . .

11.32 . . . and the death of the cop, without showing anything clearly.

In contrast to the whirlwind presentation of this key action, a lengthy conversation in the middle of the film brings the narrative progression almost to a standstill. For nearly 25 minutes, Michel and Patricia chat in her bedroom. At some points, Michel attempts to further his goals, trying vainly to phone Antonio and to persuade Patricia to come to Rome. Most of the conversation, however, is trivial, as when Michel criticizes the way Patricia puts on lipstick or when she asks whether he prefers records or the radio. The pair try to outstare each other, and they discuss Patricia's new poster. So rambling is their exchange that some critics have assumed that the dialogue was improvised (although Godard attests that it was all scripted).

At one point, Patricia suggests that she will not run off with him because she does not know if she loves him. Michel: "When will you know?" Patricia: "Soon." Michel: "What does that mean—soon? In a month, in a year?" Patricia: "Soon means soon." So although the pair make love, by the end of the long scene (which occupies nearly a third of this 89-minute film), we still do not have a definite step forward or backward in Michel's courting of Patricia, and he has made no progress toward escaping. Such scenes make him seem more like a wandering, easily distracted delinquent than the desperate, driven hero of a film noir.

It is not until the scene outside the *Tribune* office that another decisive causal action occurs. A passerby (played by Godard) recognizes Michel from a newspaper photograph and tells the police. This triggers a chain of events that will lead to Michel's death. Yet now the plot meanders once more. In the next scene, Patricia participates in a news conference with a famous novelist, a character unrelated to the main action. Most of the questions asked by the reporters deal with the differences between men and women, but the novelist's responses seem more playful than meaningful. Finally, Patricia asks him his greatest ambition, and he replies enigmatically, "To become immortal and then to die." Patricia's puzzled glance into the camera that ends the scene hints at the ambiguity that will linger at the film's end.

After Detective Vital questions Patricia at the *Tribune* office, she and Michel realize that the police are on his trail. Now *Breathless* begins to progress in a somewhat more conventional way. In the next scene, Patricia says that she loves Michel "enormously," and they steal a car. Here Michel seems to reach his romantic goal, as Patricia commits herself to fleeing with him. When Antonio agrees to bring the cash the next morning, Michel moves toward his second goal. We might anticipate possible outcomes: the pair will escape, or one or both will be killed in the attempt. The next morning, however, Patricia confounds our expectations by betraying Michel to Vital. Even then Michel has a last chance. Antonio arrives just before the police, with money and a getaway car—yet Michel cannot bring himself to leave Patricia.

The ending is particularly enigmatic. As Michel lies bleeding to death, Patricia looks down at him. He slowly makes the same playful faces at her that he had made during their bedroom conversation. Muttering, "That's really disgusting" ("C'est vraiment dégueulasse"), he dies. Patricia asks Detective Vital what he said, and Vital misreports Michel's last words: "He said, 'You are really a bitch'" ("Il a dit, 'Vous êtes vraiment une dégueulasse'"). We are left to ponder what Michel thought was disgusting—Patricia's betrayal, his own last-minute failure to flee, or simply his death. In the final shot, Patricia looks out at the camera, asks what "dégueulasse" means, rubs her lips with the Bogart-inspired gesture that Michel has used throughout the film (**11.33**), and abruptly turns her back on us as the image fades out.

Breathless achieves a degree of closure: Michel fails to achieve his goals. But we are left with many questions. Although Michel and Patricia talk constantly about themselves, we learn remarkably little about why they act as they do. Unlike characters in classical films, they do not have a set of clearly defined traits. The film begins with Michel saying, "All in all, I'm a dumb bastard," and in a way, his actions bear this out. Yet we never learn background information that would explain his decisions. Why did he become a car thief? Since he casually leaves his female accomplice early in the film, what makes him willing to risk death to stay with Pa-

11.33 Patricia's enigmatic gesture at the end of *Breathless.*

tricia, a woman whom he has known only briefly? Because dying for the love of an unworthy woman is what a would-be Hollywood hero is supposed to do?

Patricia's traits and goals are even more amorphous and ambiguous. When Michel first finds her selling newspapers on the Champs Elysées, she is far from welcoming. Yet at the scene's end, she runs back to give him a kiss. She keeps saying she wants to get a job as a *Tribune* reporter and to write a novel, yet she seems to throw these ambitions away when she thinks she loves Michel. Patricia also tells Michel she is pregnant by him, but she has not received the final test results, and she never raises this as a reason she should stay in Paris. She often says that she is scared, yet after she and Michel steal a car, she remarks, "It's too late now to be scared." This hints that she has resolved her own doubts and has thrown in her lot with Michel. When she suddenly betrays him, she does not intend that he should be killed but simply wants to force him to leave her. Still, her speech about why she informed on Michel seems not really to explain her abrupt change of heart. Just as Michel is ill-suited to be a tough guy, Patricia is too naive and indecisive to play the role of the classic femme fatale.

In the outlaw film noir, the characters are intensely committed to each other; here Michel and Patricia seem to have few strong feelings about what they do. When the treacherous woman deceives the noir hero, he often becomes bitterly disillusioned; but Michel apparently does not blame Patricia for betraying him. It is as if these ambivalent, diffident, confused characters are unable to play out the desperately passionate roles that the Hollywood tradition has assigned to them.

Breathless's elliptical, occasionally opaque, narrative is presented through techniques that are equally unconventional. As we have seen, Hollywood films use a three-point system of key light, fill light, and backlight, carefully controlled in a film studio (pp. 128–129). *Breathless* was shot entirely on location, even for interiors. Godard and cinematographer Raoul Coutard opted not to add any artificial light in the settings. As a result, the characters' faces sometimes fall into shadow **(11.34).**

Filming on location, especially in small apartments, would ordinarily make it difficult to obtain a variety of camera angles and movements. But taking advantage of new portable equipment, Coutard was able to film while hand-holding the camera. Several lengthy tracking shots follow the characters **(11.35).** Coutard apparently sat in a wheelchair to film this shot, as well as more elaborate movements that follow the characters in interiors **(11.36).** Such shots recall the location shooting of many films noirs, such as the final airport scenes of Stanley Kubrick's *The Killing*, but the low camera position and the passersby who turn to look at the actors (as with the man at the right in 11.35) call attention to the technique in a way that departs from Hollywood usage.

11.34 When Patricia sits against a window and lights a cigarette, the natural light of the scene illuminates her only from behind.

11.35 Michel's first meeting with Patricia as she strolls along the Champs Elysées selling papers occurs in a three-minute take.

11.36 When Michel visits a travel agent trying to claim his check, the framing glides and turns with ease as he moves around the desks and through the corridors.

11.37   When Michel pauses in front of a movie theater and looks at a photo on display . . .

11.38   . . . Bogart seems to look back at him in reverse shot.

11.39   The last frame of one shot during Michel's visit to an old girlfriend . . .

11.40   . . . and the first of the next shot, creating a jump cut.

11.41   In the first shot, Patricia moves from left to right . . .

11.42   . . . and in the next, she is walking right to left, a flagrant violation of conventional screen direction.

Even more striking than the mise-en-scene is Godard's editing. Again he sometimes follows tradition, but at other points, he breaks away. Standard shot/reverse-shot cutting organizes several scenes **(11.37, 11.38)**. Similarly, when Michel spots the man examining the telltale photo in the newspaper, Godard supplies correctly matched glances. Since this is a turning point in the plot, the adherence to the 180° rule makes it evident that the man has spotted Michel and may inform on him.

Yet what makes the film still quite jolting today are its violations of continuity editing. In Hollywood films made before the 1960s, the jump cut, in which a segment of time is eliminated without the camera being moved to a new vantage point (pp. 254–257), was deplored. Yet *Breathless* employs jump cuts throughout. In an early scene, when Michel visits an old girlfriend, jump cuts shift their positions abruptly **(11.39, 11.40)**. We have seen another example, when Godard presents a series of jump cuts of Patricia during a conversation in a car (6.137, 6.138, again showing the last and first frames of contiguous shots).

Even when Godard shifts the camera position between cuts, he may drop out a bit of time or mismatch the actors' positions. At many cuts, the action seems to jerk forward. One effect of this jumpy editing is to enliven the rhythm. At times, as during the murder of the police officer, we have to be very alert to follow the action. The elliptical editing also makes certain scenes stand out by contrast: the lengthy single-take scenes with moving camera and the rambling 25-minute conversation in Patricia's apartment.

Aside from avoiding matches on action, Godard often flaunts the moments when he does not adhere to the 180° rule, as when Patricia walks along reading a paper **(11.41, 11.42)**. In the opening scene, as Michel's accomplice points out a car he wants to steal, the eyelines are quite unclear, and we get little sense of where the two are in relation to each other.

"On À Bout de souffle, he'd [Godard] ask the script-girl what kind of shot was required next to fulfill the requirements of traditional continuity. She'd tell him, and then he'd do the exact opposite."

— Raoul Coutard, cinematographer

The film's sound often reinforces these editing discontinuities. When the characters' dialogue and other diegetic sounds continue over the jump cuts, we are forced to notice the contradiction: time is apparently omitted from the visual track but not from the sound track. The location shooting also created situations in which ambient noises intrude on the dialogue. A passing siren outside Patricia's apartment nearly overwhelms her conversation with Michel during the long central scene. Later the press conference with Parvulesco inexplicably takes place on an airport observation platform, where the loud whines of nearby planes drown out conversation. Such scenes lack the balance of volumes of the well-mixed Hollywood sound track.

Godard's avoidance of the rules of smooth sound and picture steers *Breathless* away from the glamorous portrayals seen in the Hollywood crime film. The stylistic awkwardness suits the pseudo-documentary roughness of filming in an actual, hectic Paris. The discontinuities are also consistent with other nontraditional techniques, like the motif of the characters' mysterious glances into the camera. In addition, the jolts in picture and sound create a self-conscious narration that makes the viewer aware of its stylistic choices. In making the director's hand more apparent, the film presents itself as a deliberately unpolished revision of tradition.

Godard did not set out to criticize Hollywood films. Instead, he took genre conventions identified with 1940s America and gave them a contemporary Parisian setting and a modern, self-conscious treatment. He thereby created a new type of hero and heroine. Aimless, somewhat banal, lovers on the run became central to later outlaw movies such as *Bonnie and Clyde, Badlands,* and *True Romance.* More broadly, Godard's film became a model for directors who wished to create exuberantly offhand homages to, and reworkings of, Hollywood tradition. This attitude would be central to the stylistic movement that *Breathless* helped launch, the French New Wave. (See Chapter 12, pp. 475–477.)

Tokyo Story (Tokyo Monogatari)

1953. Shochiku/Ofuna, Japan. Directed by Yasujiro Ozu. Script by Ozu and Kogo Noda. Photographed by Yuharu Atsuta. With Chishu Ryu, Chieko Higashiyama, So Yamamura, Haruko Sugimura, Setsuko Hara.

We have seen how the classical Hollywood approach to filmmaking created a stylistic system (continuity) in order to establish and maintain a clear narrative space and time. The continuity system is a specific set of guidelines that a filmmaker may follow. But some filmmakers do not use the continuity system. They may flaunt the guidelines by violating them, as Godard does in *Breathless,* creating a casual yet lively film. Or they may develop a set of alternative guidelines—at least as strict as Hollywood's—that allows them to make films that are quite distinct from classical films.

Yasujiro Ozu is one such filmmaker. His approach to the creation of a narrative differs from that used in more classical films like *His Girl Friday* or *North by Northwest.* Instead of making narrative events the central organizing principle, Ozu tends to decenter narrative somewhat. As a result, spatial and temporal structures come forward and create their own interest. *Tokyo Story,* the first Ozu film to make a considerable impression in the West, offers an enlightening introduction to some of Ozu's characteristic filmmaking strategies.

Tokyo Story presents a simple narrative of an elderly provincial couple who visit their grown children in Tokyo, only to find themselves treated as inconvenient nuisances. The narrative is quiet and contemplative, yet Ozu's style does not simply conform to some characteristically spiritual Japanese system of filmmaking. Indeed, Japanese filmmakers and critics found his nonclassical approach as puzzling as did Western audiences. By creating a systematic alternative method of shaping spatial and temporal relations, Ozu sought to engage the spectator's attention more deeply. In Hollywood, style is subservient to narrative, but Ozu makes it an equal partner. We watch the narrative action, the spatial relations, and the temporal relations unfold

11.43   In *Tokyo Story,* a shot of Noriko at her desk . . .

11.44   . . . leads to a shot of a building . . .

11.45   . . . and then another of construction . . .

11.46   . . . before shifting to the locale for the next scene.

simultaneously, and all are equally dramatic and engaging. As a result, even a simple narrative like that of *Tokyo Story* becomes fresh and fascinating.

Tokyo Story's narration is, by classical standards, rather oblique. Sometimes we learn of important narrative events only after they have occurred. The last portion of *Tokyo Story,* for example, involves a series of events surrounding the sudden illness and death of the grandmother of the family. Although the grandparents are the film's two central characters, we do not see the grandmother falling ill. We hear about it only when her son and daughter receive telegrams with the news. Similarly, the grandmother's death occurs between scenes. In one scene, her children are gathered by her bedside; in the next scene, they are mourning her.

Yet these ellipses are not evidence of a fast-paced film such as *His Girl Friday,* which must cover a lot of narrative ground in a hurry. On the contrary, the sequences of *Tokyo Story* often linger over details: the melancholy conversation between the grandfather and his friends in a bar as they discuss their disappointment in their children or the grandmother's walk on a Sunday with her grandchild. The result is a shift in the narrative balance. Key narrative events are deemphasized by means of ellipses, whereas narrative events that we do see in the plot are simple and understated.

Accompanying this shift away from a presentation of the most highly dramatic events of the narrative is a sliding away from narratively significant space. Scenes do not begin and end with shots that frame the most important narrative elements in the mise-en-scene. Instead of the usual transitional devices, such as dissolves and fades, Ozu typically employs a series of separate transitional shots linked by cuts. And these transitional shots often show spaces not directly connected with the action of the scene; the spaces are usually *near* where that action will take place. The opening of the film, for example, has five shots of the port town of Onomichi—the bay, schoolchildren, a passing train—before the sixth shot reveals the grandparents packing for their trip to Tokyo. Although a couple of important motifs make their first appearances in these first five shots, no narrative causes occur to get the action underway. (Compare the openings of *His Girl Friday* and *North by Northwest.*) Nor do these transitional shots appear only at the beginning. Several sequences in Tokyo start with shots of factory smokestacks, even though no action ever occurs in these locales.

These transitions have only a minimal function as establishing shots. Sometimes the transitions don't establish space at all but tend to confuse the space of the upcoming scene. After the daughter-in-law, Noriko, gets a phone call at work telling her of the grandmother's illness, the scene ends in a medium shot of her sitting pensively at her desk; the only diegetic sound is the loud clack of typewriters **(11.43).** A nondiegetic musical transition comes up in this shot. Then there is a cut to a low-angle long shot of a building under construction **(11.44).** Riveting noises replace the typewriters, with the music continuing. The next shot is another low angle of the construction site **(11.45).**

A cut changes the locale to the clinic belonging to the eldest son, Dr. Hirayama. The sister, Shige, is present. The music ends and the new scene begins **(11.46).** In this segment, the two shots of the construction site are not necessary to the action.

The film does not give us any indication of where the building under construction is. We might assume that it is outside Noriko's office, but the riveting sound is not audible in the interior shots.

As usual, we should look for the functions of such stylistic devices. It is hard to assign such transitional shots either explicit or implicit meanings. For example, someone might propose that the transitional shots symbolize the new Tokyo that is alien to the visiting grandparents from a village reminiscent of the old Japan. But often the transitional spaces do not involve outdoor locales, and some shots are within the characters' homes. A more systematic function, we suggest, is narrational, having to do with the flow of story information.

Ozu's narration alternates between scenes of story action and inserted portions that lead us to or away from them. As we watch the film, we start to form expectations about these wedged-in shots. Ozu emphasizes stylistic patterning by creating anticipation about when a transition will come and what it will show. The patterning may delay our expectations and even create some surprise.

For example, early in the film, Mrs. Hirayama, the doctor's wife, argues with her son, Minoru, over where to move his desk to make room for the grandparents. This issue is dropped, and there follows a scene of the grandparents' arrival. This ends on a conversation in an upstairs room. Transitional music again comes up over the end of the scene. The next shot frames an empty hallway downstairs that contains Minoru's school desk, but no one is in the shot. There follows an exterior long shot of children running along a ridge near the house; these children are not characters in the action. Finally, a cut back inside reveals Minoru at his father's desk in the clinic portion of the house, studying. Here the editing creates a very indirect route between two scenes, going first to a place where we expect a character to be (at his own desk) but is not; then the scene moves completely away from the action, outdoors. Only then, in the third shot, does a character reappear and the action continue. In these transitional passages, a kind of game emerges, one that asks us to form expectations not only about story action but about the editing and mise-en-scene.

Within scenes, Ozu's editing patterns are as systematic as those of Hollywood, but they tend to be sharply opposed to continuity rules. For example, Ozu does not observe the 180° line, the axis of action. Nor is his violation of these rules occasional, as John Ford's is in *Stagecoach* (p. 244). Ozu frequently cuts 180° across the line to frame the scene's space from the opposite direction. This, of course, violates rules of screen direction, since characters or objects on the right in the first shot will appear on the left in the second, and vice versa. At the beginning of a scene in Shige's beauty salon, the initial interior medium shot frames Shige from opposite the front door **(11.47)**. Then a 180° cut reveals a medium long shot of a woman under a hair dryer; the camera now faces the rear of the salon **(11.48)**. Another 180° cut presents a new long shot of the room, again oriented toward the door, and the grandparents come into the salon **(11.49)**. Rather than being an isolated violation of continuity rules, this is Ozu's typical way of framing and editing a scene.

"I don't think the film has a grammar. I don't think film has but one form. If a good film results, then that film has created its own grammar."

— Yasujiro Ozu, director

11.47 In the beauty salon, systematic cutting moves from one side of the axis of action . . .

11.48 . . . to the other side . . .

11.49 . . . and back again.

11.50   From this head-on view of Noriko and the grandmother . . .

11.51   . . . there is a cut to a tails-on view of them.

11.52   *Tokyo Story.*

11.53   *Tokyo Story.*

11.54   *Tokyo Story.*

11.55   *Tokyo Story.*

11.56   *Tokyo Story.*

11.57   *Tokyo Story.*

Ozu is a master of matching on action, but he often does so in unusual ways. For example, as Noriko and the grandmother walk toward the door of Noriko's apartment, there is a 180° cut (**11.50, 11.51**). The women's movements are closely matched, but because the consistent camera height and distance create such similar framings, the effect at the cut is to make it seem momentarily that the pair bump into themselves. Their screen positions, left to right, are also abruptly reversed, something that is usually considered an error in continuity. A classical filmmaker would most likely avoid such an unusual cut, but Ozu uses it here and in other films as part of his distinctive style.

As these examples illustrate, Ozu does not restrict his camera and editing patterns to the semicircular space on one side of the axis of action. He cuts in a full circle around the action, usually in segments of 90° or 180°. This means that backgrounds change drastically, as in both previous examples. In a Hollywood film, the camera rarely crosses the axis of action to look at the fourth wall. Because surroundings change more frequently in *Tokyo Story,* they become more prominent in relation to the action; the viewer must pay attention to setting or become confused.

The transitional shots that prolong or thwart the viewer's expectations and the 360° space that asks us to notice surroundings can work together. When the grandparents visit a spa at Atami, the scene begins with a long shot along a hallway (**11.52**). Latin-style dance music plays offscreen, and several people walk through the hall. The next shot (**11.53**) is a long shot of another hallway upstairs, with a maid carrying a tray; two pairs of slippers are just visible by a doorway at the lower left. Next comes a medium long shot of a hallway by a courtyard (**11.54**). More people bustle through. A medium shot of a mah-jongg game follows (**11.55**); there is the sound of talking and pieces moving about. Then Ozu cuts 180° across the axis, framing another mah-jongg table (**11.56**). The first table is now in the background, viewed from the opposite side. The next cut returns to the medium long shot along the courtyard hallway (**11.57**). In all of these shots, we have not yet seen the grandparents, who are the only major characters present at the spa. Finally, there is a medium shot of the two pairs of slippers by the door in the upper hallway **(11.58),** suggesting that this is the grandparents' room. The panes of glass in the wall reflect the lively movement of the offscreen party, and the loud music and talk are still audible. A medium shot of the Hirayamas in bed, trying to sleep through the noise, finally reveals the narrative situation, and a conversation begins between the couple **(11.59).** For seven shots, the film slowly explores the space of the scene, gradually letting us discover the situation. The presence of the slippers in the second shot (11.53) is almost unnoticeable. It hints that the grandparents are there, but the revelation of their whereabouts is then put off for several more shots.

In these ways, Ozu draws our attention away from the strictly causal functions of space and makes space important in its own right. He does the same with the flat space of the screen. (Examples of graphic matches from Ozu films are found in 6.128–6.131.) The stylistic device is characteristic of Ozu, who seldom uses the graphic match for any narrative purpose. In *Tokyo Story,* a conversation situation leads to a shot/reverse-shot pattern but again with cuts 180° across the axis of action. The two men speaking are framed so that each looks off right. (In Hollywood, upholders of the continuity system would claim that this implies that both are looking off toward the same thing.) Because they are positioned similarly in the frame, the result is a strong graphic match from one shot to another **(11.60, 11.61).** In this respect, Ozu's style owes something to abstract form (see Chapter 10, pp. 368–374). It is as if he sought to make a narrative film that would still make graphic similarities as evident as they are in an abstract film like *Ballet mécanique.*

The use of space and time in *Tokyo Story* is not willfully obscure, nor does it have a symbolic function in the narrative. Rather, it suggests a different relationship among setting, duration, and story action than exists in the classical film. Space and time no longer simply function unobtrusively to create a clear narrative line. Ozu brings them forward and makes them into prominent aesthetic elements in their own right. A large part of the film's appeal lies in its strict but playful treatment of figures, settings, and movement. Ozu does not eliminate narrative, but he opens it out. *Tokyo Story* and his other films allow other stylistic devices to exist independently alongside narrative. The result is that the viewer is invited to participate in his films in a new way.

Chungking Express (Chung Hing sam lam)

1994. Jet Tone, Hong Kong. Directed by Wong Kar-wai. Script by Wong Kar-wai. Photographed by Andrew Lau Wai-keung and Christopher Doyle. With Brigitte Lin Ching-hsia, Takeshi Kaneshiro, Tony Leung Chiu-wai, Faye Wong Jingwen.

Contemporary Hollywood filmmakers have sometimes explored what has been called the *web-of-life plot.* Instead of two primary lines of action, as in *His Girl Friday* or *North by Northwest,* some recent films weave together a large number of plotlines, often involving many characters. Precedents for this can be found in *Grand Hotel* (1932) and *Nashville* (1976), but in the 1990s, such films as *Short Cuts, Pulp Fiction, Magnolia, Traffic,* and *Love Actually* made this sort of plotting more common. The plotlines may at first seem completely isolated from one another, but usually they converge, revealing unexpected causal connections. In *Magnolia,* the characters are linked through television (all are connected in one way or another to the television producer Earl Partridge) and through chance encounters (as when the police patrolman meets Partridge's unhappy daughter).

The audience expects a web-of-life plot to reveal unforeseen relations among the disparate characters. Seen from this standpoint, *Chungking Express* constitutes an intriguing experiment in nonclassical form. It is broken into two distinct stories, each organized around a different batch of characters, and the two stories aren't crosscut but simply set side by side. One question viewers commonly ask is, What has director Wong Kar-wai accomplished by putting these two stories in the same film?

11.58 *Tokyo Story.*

11.59 *Tokyo Story.*

11.60 A graphic match created by cutting across the line from the grandfather . . .

11.61 . . . to his friend as they converse.

"[Financiers in Asia] always ask, 'Is it a cop story or a gangster story?' So you have to choose. One or the other. . . . So with Chungking Express, *I said it is a cop* and *a gangster story. We have gangsters, and we have cops. But it is not a gangster/cop story. It's just about their lives, and that's it."*

— Wong Kar-wai, director

In the first tale, Officer 223 (for ease of recall, we'll call him Officer 1) has just broken up with his girlfriend and lives in hope that she'll take him back before May 1, his 25th birthday. Wandering the city at night, he runs into a mysterious woman in dark glasses and a blonde wig. He doesn't know that she runs a drug-smuggling outfit. She has hired some Indian down-and-outs to swallow bags of cocaine and fly out of the country, but they have defected with the drugs. She must recover the shipment or face the wrath of her boss, a Westerner who runs a bar. Officer 1 meets her in a bar and takes her to a cheap hotel, where she sleeps off her drinking and he eats snacks. In the morning, he leaves her; she posts an affectionate message on his pager before returning to the bar and shooting her boss dead.

The second and longer tale introduces Officer 633 (Officer 2), who is happy with his girlfriend, a flight attendant. But one day she leaves him. He is still trying to get over their affair when Faye, a counterwoman at his favorite fast-food spot, the Midnight Express, takes an interest in him. The flight attendant leaves Officer 2's keys at the Midnight Express for him to pick up, and Faye uses them to explore his apartment while he's out. She tidies it up and redecorates it to try to cheer him up, leaving fresh soap and towels and filling his aquarium with fish. After catching her in the apartment, he realizes she's flirting with him, so he packs up his girlfriend's things and sets off to meet Faye for a date. But she stands him up, leaving for California—the place she had always hoped to visit. A year later, Officer 2 has bought the Midnight Express and is renovating it when she returns. Now *she's* a flight attendant, and there is a hint that their romance might finally begin.

What links the two parts? Both employ handheld camera work, moody music, and voice-over commentaries drifting in and out. But a common style is normally not enough to justify putting two stories together. Since both protagonists are policemen, we might expect them to encounter one another, but they never do; the first is a plainclothes detective, while the second pounds a beat. Nor does the mysterious blonde's drug smuggling ever impinge on the cops' activities; Officer 1 is ignorant of her racket, and Officer 2 doesn't, for instance, investigate the murder of the bar owner, as he might in another kind of plot. The two strands do share one locale: both Officer 1 and Officer 2 hang out at the Midnight Express. Nonetheless, this doesn't connect the parts causally, since Officer 1 meets Faye only once, and he never becomes a rival for her affections. As if to tease sharp-eyed repeat viewers, Wong inserts into the first part a brief, distant shot of each main character who will appear in the second part—Officer 2, the flight attendant, and Faye (**11.62**). But they are unknown to us on the initial viewing, and they aren't presented as shaping the story action in the first part.

It is as if Wong has juxtaposed the two stories in such a way to demand that we find our own connections between them. By analyzing narrative form and style, we can bring to light some intriguing similarities and differences, which in turn point to a set of themes that unify the film.

In broad narrative terms, the two parts stand in sharp contrast. The first takes place on the Kowloon peninsula of Hong Kong, in and around Chungking Man-

11.62 In *Chungking Express,* while the mysterious blonde woman lounges outside a shop, Faye (whom we do not meet until part two) leaves with a stuffed toy (perhaps destined for Officer 2's apartment).

sions, a decaying block of cheap guest quarters, shops, and Indian restaurants. (The Cantonese title of the film translates as "Chungking Jungle," and it may tease the local viewer into believing that eventually the second story will return to this neighborhood.) The second part takes place on Hong Kong Island, across the bay from Kowloon, in the vicinity of the Midnight Express. The Kowloon of part one teems with crime; Officer 1 chases suspects down at gunpoint, while the blonde works for a drug cartel. Part two presents a far less threatening world, where romance can blossom and the cop on the beat drops in for snacks. The English-language title of the film fuses the basic locales of each part, balancing Chungking Mansions with Midnight Express in a single phrase.

The two parts offer very different time schemes as well. The first part takes place over a short span, about four days, and the action labors under deadlines. Officer 1 has given May, his ex-girlfriend, the month of April to come back to him. The blonde's deadline for the smuggling operation has been set by her boss, and she meets it by shooting him and flying out of Hong Kong on May 1. The second part has a much looser time frame and no strong deadlines. Over a period of weeks, Officer 2's girlfriend leaves him, Faye invades his apartment, he transfers his beat, and after a series of casual encounters they finally make a date . . . that Faye ignores, suddenly departing. The action concludes a year later when she flies back to Hong Kong.

Yet within these broad contrasts, some echoes do emerge. Each man is coming out of a love affair; each meets a woman by chance; quickly or slowly, each becomes attached to her; the woman abruptly departs. The characters' goals are also revealing. Officer 1 seeks a new woman to love, and although Officer 2 is content to drift, Faye seems to try to ease his broken heart. These goals are presented more vaguely and pursued more erratically than in a Hollywood film, but the parallels suggest that *Chungking Express* revolves around romance. The more closely we look at cause–effect chains, motifs, and visual style, the more evidence we find that the film is comparing ways in which people try to find love.

The two policemen's romantic problems shape their attitudes toward time. Neither man is sensitive to the fact that love affairs must adjust to change. In part one, ruled by fast pace and deadlines, Officer 1 has been pining for a month and now wants to find a new girlfriend immediately. Officer 2, suddenly dumped by his girlfriend, can't summon up the energy to restart his love life. Both men fill their stretches of waiting with cycles of repetitive behavior. Officer 1 badgers May's family and then calls old girlfriends to ask for a date. Officer 2 repeatedly visits the Midnight Express, first to pick up snacks for himself and his girlfriend, then simply to brood; after he switches his shift, he frequents a food stall on another street. Although one wants a sudden adventure and the other falls back on routine, both are caught in spirals of inactivity. Wong emphasizes this through parallel images of each man moping in his apartment (**11.63, 11.64**).

11.63   Officer 1 at home, disconsolate.

11.64   Officer 2 broods about his lost love.

11.65   After his morning run, Officer 1 gets the pager message wishing him a happy birthday.

11.66   Officer 2 had discarded the mock boarding pass Faye left him; now he waits for it to dry so he can read it.

They need a change—or, according to the film's most pervasive motif, a change of menu. Food is central to both stories, announced at the start in the headlong tracking shots through Chungking Mansions, the cafés filled with eaters. Officer 1 measures the time he waits for May (who loved pineapple) in pineapple cans, each day buying one with a May 1 expiration date. On the last day, he gorges himself, emptying the 30 cans he has saved. When he meets the blonde, he asks if she likes pineapple. Similarly, Officer 2 always orders chef's salads at the Midnight Express. In contrast, women are presented as craving varied menus. As the blonde studies Officer 1 in the bar, her voice-over commentary remarks, "Knowing someone doesn't mean keeping them. People change. A person may like pineapple today and something else tomorrow." When Officer 2 brings home pizza and fish and chips, his girlfriend leaves him. He muses that she realized that she had a choice of lovers as well as dinners.

The food motif goes on to define the men's attitudes toward change. While the blonde sleeps in a Chungking Mansions hotel room, Officer 1 stuffs himself with hamburgers, salads, and fries. Once outside, he thinks that she has forgotten him, but her pager message ("Happy birthday") leads him to wish that the expiration date on his memory of her will last forever. No longer treating a girlfriend as a fast-food snack, Officer 1's sense of time has expanded; instead of seeking a new future, he treasures a moment in the past **(11.65)**.

As the countergirl Faye invades Officer 2's life, she replaces his cheap tinned fish with another brand, spikes his water jug to help him sleep, and pushes him out of his self-pity (in which he imagines his towel crying and his soap wasting away). When she skips their date, she leaves him a fake boarding pass she inks onto a napkin; at first he discards it, but then, in a composition paralleling that of Officer 1's meditation on his pager message, he dries it in a snack-shop rotisserie **(11.66)**. A year later, Officer 2 has embraced a varied menu. He has bought the Midnight Express, and when Faye returns, he persuades her to write him a new pass. Before he had been reluctant to travel with her, but now, when she asks where he wants to fly, he replies, "Wherever you want to take me." He has broken out of routine and is willing to accept change.

This last scene sums up another motif, airplane flight, that runs through both parts and marks parallels. Both are associated with women's desire for change. In the first part, the blonde prepares her drug mules for a flight, and she flees her crime by taking an early plane out. In the second part, Officer 2's air hostess is replaced by Faye, who, when she first meets her rival, measures herself against her **(11.67)**. Musical motifs also signal the importance of change. The repeated reggae song in the first part states, "It's not every day that's gonna be the same way, there must be a change somehow." The second part highlights the song "What a Difference a Day Makes" and repeats the Mamas and Papas' "California Dreamin'," which expresses

11.67 Faye, who will become a flight attendant, measures herself against the woman who dumped Officer 2.

11.68 The blonde woman of part one muses . . .

11.69 . . . in a posture similar to that of Faye in part two.

a wish to leave for sunnier surroundings. Several pictorial motifs link the two main women, including their shoes, their dark glasses, and their habit of slipping into reverie **(11.68, 11.69).**

If the film's primary theme is indeed the acceptance of change as part of love, then the two parts are cunningly designed to lead the audience toward it indirectly. The first part begins with the blonde hurrying through Chungking Mansions, then shows Officer 1 racing after a criminal and colliding with her before moving on. Her femme fatale disguise and the drug deal suggest that this is the start of a crime thriller (see pp. 322–324). But soon the smuggling situation is overwhelmed by Officer 1's romantic yearnings, and the blonde woman's abrupt shooting of her boss ends the crime line of action. The second tale begins, and Officer 2's placid routine and personal problems take over. The thriller elements have served largely as bait, luring us to study the characters before the plot switches genres and becomes an open-ended romantic comedy.

Wong signals the genre shift through a stylistic parallel. As Officer 1 collides with the blonde, the frame freezes, and in voice-over he says, "Fifty-seven hours later I fell in love with this woman." When at the end of the first part Officer 1 revisits the Midnight Express, he bumps into Faye **(11.70).** His commentary remarks, "Six hours later . . ." The image fades out and fades in on Officer 2 approaching the snack bar **(11.71),** and we hear Officer 1 continue, ". . . She fell in love with another man." We will never see Officer 1 again. These voice-over remarks (highly implausible on grounds of realism—how could Officer 1 know that Faye falls in love with Officer 2?) mark the film's romantic parallels explicitly.

Since the lines of action in the two parts aren't linked causally, the film may at first disappoint the viewer's expectations. But Wong's strategy invites the audience to seek other connections. The parallel situations point to the idea that change is as necessary to love as variety is to diet. The thematic implications are reinforced by

11.70 Part one of *Chungking Express* ends with Officer 1 bumping into Faye at the Midnight Express.

11.71 Part two begins with Officer 2 approaching the Midnight Express; he will replace Officer 1 as the film's male protagonist.

mise-en-scene, cinematography, music, and voice-over commentary. Yet *Chungking Express* isn't heavy-handed, partly because it slides cleverly from crime movie to stop-and-start romance and partly because it invites us to appreciate its playful artifice.

Documentary Form and Style

Man with a Movie Camera (Chelovek s kinoapparatom)

Made 1928, released 1929. VUFKU, Union of Soviet Socialist Republics. Directed by Dziga Vertov. Photographed by Mikhail Kaufman. Edited by Elizaveta Svilova.

In some ways, *Man with a Movie Camera* might seem to be a straight reportorial documentary, yet it does not try to give the impression that the reality it presents is unaffected by the medium of film. Instead, Dziga Vertov proclaims the manipulative power of editing and cinematography to shape a multitude of tiny scenes from everyday reality into a highly idiosyncratic, even somewhat experimental, documentary.

11.72 Vertov's regular cinematographer, Mikhail Kaufman, as the cameraman in *Man with a Movie Camera.*

Vertov's name is usually linked to the technique of editing; in Chapter 6 (p. 277), we quoted a passage in which he equated the filmmaker with an eye, gathering shots from many places and linking them creatively for the spectator. Vertov's theoretical writings also compare the eye to the lens of the camera, in a concept he termed the "kino eye." (*Kino* is the Russian word for "cinema," and one of his earlier films is called *Kino-Glaz,* or *Cinema-Eye.*)

Man with a Movie Camera takes this idea—the equation of the filmmaker's eye with the lens of the camera—as the basis for the entire film's associational form. The film becomes a celebration of the documentary filmmaker's power to control our perception of reality by means of editing and special effects. The opening image shows a camera in close-up. Through a double-exposure effect, we see the cameraman of the film's title suddenly climb, in extreme long shot, onto the top of the giant camera (**11.72**). He sets up his own camera on a tripod and films for a bit, then climbs down again. This play on shot scale within a single image emphasizes at once the power the cinema has to alter reality in a seemingly magical way.

11.73 Vertov alters an ordinary street scene by exposing each side of the image separately, with the camera canted in opposite directions.

Cinematographic special effects of this sort appear as a motif throughout the film. These are not intended to be unnoticeable, as in a science-fiction film. Instead, they flaunt the fact that the camera can alter everyday reality. A typical example is shown in **11.73**. Later Vertov uses pixillation to animate objects (**11.74**). In another scene, he conveys the sound of a radio by superimposing images of a dancer and of a hand playing a piano against a single black background **(11.75).** This motif of virtuosic special effects culminates in the famous final shot **(11.76).**

At several points in the film, the camera is also personified, associated by editing with the actions of human beings. One brief segment shows the camera lens focusing and then a blurry shot of flowers coming into sharp focus. This is followed immediately by a comic juxtaposition rapidly intercutting two elements: a woman's fluttering eyelids as she dries her face with a towel, and a set of venetian blinds opening and closing. Finally, another shot shows the camera lens with a diaphragm closing and opening. A human eye is like venetian blinds, the lens is like an eye— all can open and close, admitting or keeping out light. Later, pixillation allows the camera to move by itself **(11.77)** and finally then to walk off on three legs.

Man with a Movie Camera belongs to a genre of documentaries that first became important during the 1920s: the *city symphony.* There are many ways of making a film about a city, of course. One might use categorical form to lay out its geography or scenic attractions, as in a travelogue. Rhetorical form could make arguments about aspects of city planning or government policies that need changing. A narrative might stress a city as the backdrop for many characters' actions, as in Rossellini's *Rome Open City* or Jules Dassin's semidocumentary crime drama *The Naked City.* Early city symphonies, however, established the convention of taking candid (or occasionally staged) scenes of city life and linking them, usually without commentary, through associations to suggest emotions or concepts. Associational form is evident in such early examples of the genre as Alberto Cavalcanti's *Rien que les heures* (1926) and Walter Ruttmann's *Berlin, Symphony of a Great City* (1927). More recent films like Godfrey Reggio's *Koyaanisqatsi* (1983) and *Powaqqatsi* (1988) use similar techniques, avoiding voice-over narration in favor of a musical accompaniment that along with juxtapositions of images creates particular moods and evokes certain concepts. (See pp. 172–175.)

In *Man with a Movie Camera*'s opening, we see a camera operator filming, then passing between the curtains of an empty movie theater and moving toward the screen. Then we see the theater opening, the spectators filing in, the orchestra preparing to play, and the film commencing. The film that we and the audience watch seems at first to be a city symphony laying out a typical day in the life of a town (as Ruttmann's *Berlin* does). We see a woman asleep, mannequins in closed shops, and empty streets. Soon a few people appear, and the city wakes up. Indeed, much of *Man with a Movie Camera* follows a rough principle of development that progresses from waking up through work time to leisure time. But early in the waking-up portion, we also see the cameraman again, setting out with his equipment, as if starting his workday. This action creates the first of many deliberate inconsistencies. The cameraman now appears in his own film, and Vertov emphasizes this by cutting back immediately to the sleeping woman who had been the first thing we saw in the film-within-a-film.

Throughout *Man with a Movie Camera,* we see the same actions and shots being filmed, edited, and viewed, in scrambled order, by the onscreen audience. Toward the end of the film, in fact, we see the audience in the theater watching the cameraman on the screen, filming from a moving motorcycle. Moreover, in this late portion of the film, many motifs from all the earlier parts of the day return, many now in fast motion; the simple order of the ordinary city symphony is broken and jumbled. Vertov creates an impossible time scheme, once more emphasizing the extraordinary manipulative powers of the cinema. The film also refuses to show only one city, instead mixing footage filmed in Moscow, Kiev, and Odessa, as if the cameraman hero can move effortlessly across the USSR during this "day" of filming. Vertov's view of the cinema's relation to the cityscape is well conveyed in one shot that uses an extraordinary deep-focus composition to place the camera in the foreground, looming over the distant buildings **(11.78).** In sum, *Man with a Movie Camera* is a city symphony, but it goes beyond the genre as well.

11.74 A crayfish executes a little dance in the course of this shot.

11.75 Superimposition to suggest sound.

11.76 *Man with a Movie Camera* ends with an eye superimposed over the camera lens, staring straight out at us.

11.77 The animated camera comes out of its box, climbs onto the tripod, and demonstrates how its various parts work.

11.78 The camera pans madly about to capture various views of the city.

11.79 Framing and lighting enhance the dynamism of throbbing, gleaming machine parts.

Apart from its exuberant celebration of the powers of cinema, Vertov's film contains many explicit and implicit meanings, some of which may be missed by viewers who do not read Russian. Explicitly, the film seeks both to praise and to criticize aspects of Soviet society a decade after the Revolution. Many of the film's juxtapositions involve machines and human labor. Under Stalin, the USSR was beginning a major push toward industrialization, and the mechanized factories are portrayed as fascinating places full of bustling movement **(11.79)**. The camera operator scales a huge factory smokestack or swings suspended over a dam to capture all this activity. Workers are seen not as oppressed but as participating cheerfully in the country's growth, as when one young woman laughs and chats as she folds cigarette boxes on an assembly line.

Vertov also points out weak spots in contemporary life, such as lingering class inequalities. Shots in a beauty shop suggest that some bourgeois values have survived the Revolution, and the leisure-time sequence near the end contrasts workers involved in outdoors sports with chubby women exercising in a weight-loss gym. Vertov also takes pains to criticize drunkenness, a major social problem in the USSR. One of the first shots within the inner film shows a derelict sleeping outdoors, juxtaposed with a huge bottle advertising a café. A shop front that we repeatedly see advertises wine and vodka, and later there is a scene where the cameraman visits this bar. When he leaves, we see shots of workers' clubs, converted from former churches. The contrast between these two places where workers can spend their leisure time is made clear through associational crosscutting: A woman shooting at targets in one of the clubs seems to be shooting away bottles of beer that disappear (through stop-motion) from a crate in the bar. During the 1920s, government officials instituted an explicit policy whose goal was to use the cinema and workers' clubs to replace both the tavern and the church in the lives of Soviet citizens. (Since the government's biggest source of income came from its monopoly on vodka sales, the policy also aimed at making cinema a major alternative source of revenue.) Thus *Man with a Movie Camera* seems to be subtly promoting this policy by using playful camera techniques to make both the cinema and the clubs seem attractive.

Implicitly, *Man with a Movie Camera* can be seen as an argument for Vertov's approach to filmmaking. He opposed narrative form and the use of professional actors, preferring that films use the techniques of the camera and the editing table to create their effects on the audience. He was not, however, entirely against controlling the mise-en-scene, and several scenes of this film—particularly the woman waking up and washing—clearly would have had to be staged. Throughout *Man with a Movie Camera,* associational juxtapositions compare the work of making a film with the other sorts of work depicted. The camera operator awakes and goes to work in the morning, like other workers. Like them, he uses a machine in his craft; the camera's crank is at various points compared with the crank on a cash register or with moving parts on factory equipment. The moving parts of the projector in the theater also resemble parts of the factory machines we see in various sequences.

Vertov further demonstrates how the film that we and the audience within the film are watching is a product of specific labor. We see the editor at work (Elizaveta Svilova, Vertov's wife and the actual editor of *Man with a Movie Camera*). Her gestures of scraping the film and putting cement on it with a brush to make a splice are cut in with shots in a beauty parlor, where a manicurist wields a nail file and a similar brush. At various times in the film, we see many of the same shots in different contexts: on our screen, on the screen within the movie theater, in freeze frame, being filmed, being cut apart or spliced by the editor, in fast-motion, and so on. We must therefore view them not only as moments of recorded reality but also as pieces of a whole that is put together through much effort on the part of these film workers. Finally, the camera operator has to resort to various means, sometimes dangerous, to obtain his shots; he not only climbs a huge smokestack but also crouches across the tracks to film an oncoming train and rides a motorcycle one-handed as he cranks the camera to capture the action of a race.

Filmmaking is thus presented as a job or craft, rather than an elite-oriented art. Judging from the delighted reactions of the audience we see in the theater, Vertov hoped that the Soviet public would find his celebration of filmmaking educational and entertaining.

This implicit meaning relates to a symptomatic meaning we can also see in the film. During the late 1920s, Soviet authorities wanted films that would be easily understandable and would convey propagandistic messages to a far-flung, often illiterate, populace. They were increasingly critical of filmmakers such as Sergei Eisenstein and Vertov, whose films, though celebrating revolutionary ideology, were extremely complex. In Chapter 6, we saw how Eisenstein adopted a dense, discontinuous style of editing. While Vertov disagreed in many ways with Eisenstein, particularly over the latter's use of narrative form, both belonged to a larger stylistic movement called Soviet Montage, whose history we'll examine in Chapter 12 (pp. 467–469). Both used very complex editing that they hoped would create predictable reactions in their audiences. With its contradictory time scheme and rapid editing (it contains over 1700 shots, more than twice what most Hollywood films of the same period had), *Man with a Movie Camera* is unquestionably a difficult film, especially for an audience unaccustomed to the conventions of Montage filmmaking. Perhaps more Soviet spectators would have learned over time to enjoy such films as *October* and *Man with a Movie Camera* and to react to them with the delight evident in the audience in Vertov's film. Over the next few years, however, authorities increasingly criticized Vertov and his colleagues, limiting their ability to experiment with concepts like the kino eye. Vertov was constrained in his later projects, but *Man with a Movie Camera* eventually came to be recognized, in the Soviet Union and abroad, as a classic experiment in using associational form within documentary.

The Thin Blue Line

1988. An American Playhouse production (PBS). Directed by Errol Morris. Photographed by Stefan Czapsky, Robert Chappell. Edited by Paul Barnes. Music by Philip Glass.

On a west Dallas highway one night in 1976, a police officer named Robert Wood was fatally shot by a driver he had pulled over. His partner, Teresa Turko, saw the killer drive off, but it took months of investigation for the police to discover that the car had been stolen by David Harris. Harris, a 16-year-old from the small town of Vidor, admitted to being in the car but said that the killer was Randall Adams, a man with whom he had hung around that day. Adams was tried for murder, found guilty, and sentenced to death. Eventually, through an appeal process, his sentence was commuted to life imprisonment. Harris, because of his age and his cooperation with the police, was given a suspended sentence.

In 1985, documentary filmmaker Errol Morris met Randall Adams while he was researching a film on a prominent Dallas psychiatrist known as "Dr. Death" because of his record of submitting evidence that sent defendants to the electric chair. Morris became convinced that Adams had been unjustly convicted, and over the next three years, he prepared a film on the case.

The Thin Blue Line illustrates how a documentary can use narrative form, for at root it tells the story of events leading up to and following the murder of Officer Wood. Yet the film's narration enriches that basic story. By juggling time, inserting many details, developing the reenactments of the killing into a powerful pattern, and subtly engaging our sympathy for Randall Adams, Morris not only takes us through a criminal case but also suggests how difficult the search for truth can be.

The overall plot guides us through the story events, but not in a wholly linear way. The film breaks fairly clearly into 31 sequences, although many contain brief flashbacks to the interrogation and the crime, and some contain fairly lengthy reenactments. (The longer reenactments are signaled by italics.)

C. Opening credits.

1. Dallas, Randall Adams, and David Harris are introduced.

2. Officer Wood is shot. *First shooting reenactment*

3. Adams is arrested and interrogated. *First interrogation reenactment*

4. Police describe the interrogation and the beginning of the investigation. *Second interrogation reenactment*

5. Police describe the two officers' states of mind. *Second shooting reenactment*

6. Police search for the car, even using hypnotism. *Third shooting reenactment*

7. Big break: David Harris is discovered in Vidor, Texas.

8. Harris accuses Randall Adams of the shooting.

9. Adams responds to Harris's charge.

10. Adams is interrogated. *Third interrogation reenactment*

11. Police explain the mistaken auto identification.

12. Adams's two lawyers are introduced and describe their inquiry into Harris's hometown.

13. Adams's lawyers discuss Harris as a criminal; the judge describes his attitude toward police.

14. Adams recounts Harris's version of events. *Fourth shooting reenactment*

15. Adams explains his alibi.

16. Trial: Officer Turko testifies, implicating Adams. *Fifth shooting reenactment*

17. Trial: New witnesses emerge. Mr. and Mrs. Miller claim to have seen Adams shoot Wood. *Sixth shooting reenactment*

18. Adams's lawyers and Mrs. Carr rebut the Miller couple's testimony.

19. Trial: Third new witness, Michael Randell, claims to have seen Adams shoot Wood. *Seventh shooting reenactment*

20. Trial: Jury declares Adams guilty.

21. Trial: Judge sentences Adams to death.

22. Adams reacts to the death sentence.

23. Adams's lawyers petition for a retrial and lose.

24. Adams's appeal is supported by the U.S. Supreme Court; his sentence is commuted to life in prison.

25. Vidor detective explains: Harris is arrested again.

26. Rethinking the case: Witnesses reflect, and Harris hints that he has lied. *Eighth shooting reenactment*

27. Vidor detective explains: Harris has committed a murder in town.

28. Adams: "The kid scares me"; he reflects on the mistake of letting Harris go free.

29. Harris, now on death row, reflects on his childhood.

30. Final interview on audiotape: Harris calls Adams a "scapegoat" and virtually confesses.

31. Title: Current situation of the two men.

E. Closing credits.

Segments 1–3 form a prologue, introducing the essential information and arousing our curiosity and concern. The opening sequence presents the city of Dallas; the two main characters, Randall Adams and David Harris; and their current situation: both men are in jail. What has brought them there? They tell of meeting each other and spending the day drinking, smoking marijuana, and going to a drive-in movie. Segment 2 is the first of many shocking reenactments of the shooting of Officer Wood at the dark roadside. Here, as in all the others, actors play the participants, and the framing often conceals their faces, concentrating instead on details of action or setting. The third sequence depicts Adams's arrest and interrogation, which he describes as intimidating and which is shown in a reenactment **(11.80)**.

Then the film's plot flashes back to explain events leading up to Adams's arrest, concentrating on the police investigation (segments 4–11). In the course of this, David Harris names Randall Adams as the killer (8), and Adams is arrested and interrogated (10). Eventually, the confusion about the make of the car is cleared up, though Morris hints that the police investigation was muddled (11). These sequences are interrupted by two more reenactments of Adams's questioning and two reenactments of the death of Officer Woods.

The longest stretch of the film (segments 12–24) centers on Randall Adams's confrontation with the courts. After his lawyers and the judge are introduced (12–13), we're given two conflicting versions of events—Adams's and Harris's (14–15). Three surprise witnesses identify Adams as the shooter (16–19), although some of the testimony is undercut by a woman who claims that two witnesses bragged to her about trying to earn a reward (18). Once more, at certain moments, the crime is reenacted. The jury finds Adams guilty (20), and he's sentenced to death (21–22). The legal maneuvers that follow put Adams in prison for life without parole (23–24).

The film has answered one question posed at the outset: now we know how Randall Adams got to prison. But what of David Harris, who is also serving time? The final large section of the film continues the story after the trial, concentrating on Harris's criminal career. Harris is arrested for other crimes (25), and then Morris inserts a sequence (26) designed to suggest his guilt in the Woods case. The surprise eyewitnesses are shown to be unreliable and confused, and as having things to hide. Most tellingly, Harris explains, "Of course I picked out Randall Adams." In the next sequence, a detective in Harris's hometown of Vidor explains how Harris invaded a man's home, violently abducted his girlfriend, and fatally shot the man (27). Harris, now revealed as a polite, easygoing sociopath, reflects on his childhood, when his brother drowned and his father seemed to become more distant (29). But whatever sympathy he might arouse is undercut by his final acknowledgment, captured by Morris on audiotape, that Randall Adams is innocent (30). A title explains that Adams is still serving his life sentence, while Harris is on death row (31).

In outline, then, this is a straightforward tale of crime and injustice. The film's explicit meaning was compelling enough to trigger a new inquiry into the case, and Adams was freed in 1989. But Morris's film is more than a brief for the defense. It demands a great deal of the viewer; it does not spell out its message in the manner of most documentaries. We tend to side with Randall Adams and to distrust the police, prosecutors, and "eyewitnesses" aligned against him, but Morris does not explicitly favor Adams and criticize the others. The film's form and style shape our sympathies rather subtly. At another level, the film denies the viewer many of the usual aids for determining what happened on that night in 1976. Instead, it asks us to heighten our attention, to concentrate on details, and to weigh the incompatible information we are given. Morris's detective story asks us to reflect on the obstacles to arriving at the truth about any crime.

The film's materials are for the most part the stuff of any true-crime report. Morris uses talking-head interviews, newspaper headlines, maps, archival photos, and other documents to present information about the crime. He also includes reenactments of key events, signaled as such. Nonetheless, other documentary conventions are missing. There is no voice-over narrator explaining the situation, and

11.80 The questioning of Randall Adams, staged so that its status as a reenactment is unmistakable.

"I wanted to make a film about how truth was difficult to know, not impossible to know."

— Errol Morris, director

11.81   A police detective gives his version of Adams's interrogation.

11.82   The motel where Adams stayed; in light of Adams's fate, the billboard in the background becomes ironic.

11.83   The popcorn machine at the drive-in, filmed ominously in the foreground while the clock serves as the basis for David Harris's testimony.

11.84   While Harris the teenager is associated with popcorn, Adams the panicked victim is associated with an ashtray full of cigarettes.

no captions identify the speakers or provide dates. The reenactments don't carry the "Dramatization" caption seen in television documentaries. As a result, we're forced to evaluate what we see and hear without help. This extra responsibility is intensified by a framing that is rare in most documentary interviews: several of the speakers look straight out at the camera (**11.81**). This somewhat unnerving direct address (which is even more prominent in other films by Morris) puts us in the position of detectives, forcing us to judge each person's testimony. Moreover, the use of paper documents is fairly cryptic: the film doesn't always specify their source, and the extreme close-ups often show only fragments of text. (One shot of a news article frames these partial phrases: ". . . ved to be a 1973 . . . earing Texas licens . . . with the letters H . . .") And Philip Glass's repetitive score is hardly conventional documentary music, especially for a true-crime story. With its mournful, unresolved harmonies and nervously oscillating figures, the music arouses tension, but it also creates an eerie distance from the action: it throbs on, unchanged whether it accompanies an empty city landscape or a violent murder.

Other formal and stylistic qualities complicate the plot. For example, when an interviewee mentions a particular place, Morris tends to insert a quick shot of that locale (**11.82**). Such abrupt interruptions wouldn't be used in a normal documentary, since they don't really give us much extra information. It's as if Morris wants to suggest the vast number of tiny pieces of information that an investigator must process. Similarly, during most reenactments, the participants' faces aren't shown. Instead, the scenes are built out of many close-ups: fingers resting on a steering wheel, a milkshake flying through the air in slow motion, the popcorn machine at a drive-in (**11.83**). Again, Morris stresses the apparently trivial details that can affect our sense of what really happened on the highway. Yet, carefully composed and lit in high-key, the details also become evocative motifs. Some inserts comment ironically on the situation (11.82). Others, such as the ever-present clocks and watches, indicate the ominous passing of time; even the slowly shattering flashlight and the milkshake dribbling onto the pavement suggest the life pumping out of the fatally wounded officer. Morris's systematic withholding of information invites us to fill in parts of the story, and by amplifying apparently minor details he also invites us to build up implicit meanings.

Central to those meanings are our attitudes toward the people presented in the film. By and large, the plot is shaped to create sympathy for Randall Adams. He is the first person we see, and Morris immediately makes him appealing by letting him explain that he was grateful to find a good job immediately after coming to Dallas. "It's as if I was meant to be here." Morris presents him as a decent, hardworking man railroaded by the justice system. The interrogation of Adams is associated with filled ashtrays, making him seem nervous and vulnerable (**11.84**), as do the repeated close-ups of newspaper photos of his frightened eyes. When the accusers state their case, Morris keeps us on Adams's side by letting him rebut them. In segment 9, Adams replies to Harris's charge that he was the shooter; in segment 15, Adams presents his alibi in reply to Harris's claims about the time frame of events. By the end, Adams becomes the authoritative commentator. In segment 28, after Harris has committed another murder, Adams reminds us that a life could have been saved if the Dallas police hadn't released Harris. At this point, our sympathies for Adams are strong, and we understand why he reverses his initial judgment on Dallas: it's now "hell on earth."

Our acceptance of Adams's account is subtly reinforced by the many reenactments of the murder. They are clearly set off as reconstructions by their use of techniques more closely associated with the fiction film, particularly film noir (**11.85**; also 10.6). They also distinguish themselves from the restagings shown on true-crime television shows, which tend to include the faces of actors and which are usually shot in a loose, hand-held style suggesting that we are witnessing the real event.

The reenactments present different versions of the crime in accord with different witnesses' recollections. By presenting contradictory versions of what happened that night, Morris may seem to be suggesting that everyone involved saw things from his or her own perspective, and so there is no final fact of the matter. But the overall progression of the film leads us to a likely conclusion: that David Harris, on his own, killed Wood. Rather than suggesting that truth is relative, the incompatible reconstructions dramatize the conflicting testimony. Like jurors or courtroom spectators, we have to decide on the most plausible version, and the plot develops the reenactments in a strongly suggestive pattern.

In the segments devoted to the police investigation, the restagings emphasize matters of procedure. Did Officer Turko identify the car correctly? No, the police detectives eventually decide; but both before and after they arrive at this conclusion, Morris shows us two different cars, making the options visually concrete. Another question is just as important: Did Turko back up Officer Wood according to procedure, or did she remain in the car? Morris dramatizes both possibilities, but he leads us to infer that she probably was inside the car drinking her milkshake, since in the crime scene sketch, spilled chocolate liquid was found near the car. It is a matter of probabilities, and we can never be certain; but on the evidence we are given, we infer that she probably did not back up Wood.

The reenactments of Officer Wood's murder in the investigation section have concentrated on police procedure, but during the trial section, the reenactments suggest different versions of what was happening in the killer's car. Was David Harris ducking down in the front seat? Was Adams's bushy silhouette confused with a fur-lined coat collar? When the surprise witnesses are introduced, Morris shows reenactments that present their cars passing the murder scene. Again, the reconstructions present the alternatives neutrally, but some become more plausible than others, especially once the eyewitnesses are rebutted by other testimony or betrayed by their own evasive answers.

The last reenactment, presented in the section devoted to David Harris, shows how Harris could have committed the murder, and significantly, it is accompanied by his voice-over commentary virtually confessing to it. Now, after many other reenactments, this one is presented as most worthy of our belief. Morris carefully refrains from saying explicitly that Harris was the killer. But the development of the reconstructions, eliminating the most questionable versions and focusing more and more on the identity of the driver, pushes us toward accepting this as the likeliest account.

As in any narrative film, then, the manner of storytelling, the play with narration and knowledge, shapes our attitudes toward the characters. By letting Adams comment on other characters, and by arranging the reenactments so as to point eventually toward David Harris's guilt, the film aligns us with Randall Adams, the innocent victim. Correspondingly, Morris uses other stylistic devices to make us mistrust the forces set against Adams. The film doesn't present the Dallas law officers as brutal villains; all are soft-spoken and articulate, and Judge Metcalfe comes across as calm and patient. But the editing gives Adams's account prominence and allows him to answer their charges, so we are inclined to appraise their words cautiously.

Most overtly critical of the authorities are two nearly comic digressions close to the sort of associational form exploited by Bruce Conner in *A Movie* (pp. 365–370). Judge Metcalfe recalls that he grew up with a great respect for law and order because his father was present when FBI agents shot the gangster John Dillinger (**11.86**). Morris cuts to a scene from a Hollywood crime movie that presents Dillinger's death (**11.87**). Metcalfe also supplies background trivia about the woman who betrayed Dillinger, and when he says she was sent back to her native Romania, Morris cuts to a map of Bucharest (a moment of self-parody, since he has used maps many times in the course of the film). A parallel montage appears during the remarks of one eyewitness, who says she always imagined herself as a girl detective, as in

11.85   An echo of film noir: in a reenactment, Officer Wood is shown approaching the car.

11.86   Judge Metcalfe recalls the death of Dillinger . . .

11.87   . . . and Morris cuts to a B-movie scene showing the outlaw's death, as if to recall an earlier attempt at the sort of reenactments in *The Thin Blue Line*.

11.88   Dallas cityscapes with blinking red lights.

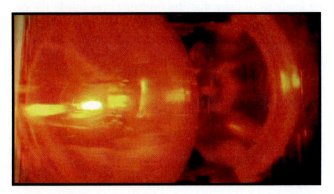

11.89   The motif is reiterated in frequent shots of rotating police-car lights.

11.90   The film's opening title announces the red motif.

1950s TV shows. Morris lets her voice-over commentary run during a clip from a B-film in which a young woman helps a detective capture a crook. These sequences encourage us to see Adams's adversaries as holding a conception of crimefighting derived from popular movies.

The color motifs that evoke police authority and duplicity are subtler. The first few shots of the film show skyscrapers and other structures, each with a single blinking red light **(11.88).** After a cut to Randall Adams beginning his tale, the screen goes dark, and we see the rotating red light of a police car, an image that will recur elsewhere in the film **(11.89),** before cutting to David Harris's account of how he came to Dallas. The motif of redness links Dallas and the police as forces aligned against Adams, and it suggests an explanation for why in the opening title credit, the word *Blue* is lettered in red **(11.90).** The film's title is taken from Judge Metcalfe's reference to the prosecutor's summation, in which he called the police the "thin blue line" between civilization and anarchy. By coloring the line red, Morris not only evokes bloodshed, but he links the police blue to the ominous blinking red lights of the opening.

The motif expands further into Judge Metcalfe's account of the death of Dillinger, who was betrayed by the notorious "woman in red." Metcalfe claims that in fact she wasn't actually wearing red; her orange dress merely looked red in a certain light. David Harris, throughout his interviews in the film, is shown wearing an orange prison uniform, suggesting that he is another figure of betrayal and perhaps hinting at his relationship to the red of the police-car light. As a documentarist, Morris probably didn't dictate what outfit Harris wore, but he did create other images that emphasize the color motif, and he did decide to retain Metcalfe's (fairly irrelevant) remarks about the woman in red. Like many documentarists, Morris highlighted certain aspects of existing footage to bring out thematic implications.

The story of Randall Adams's unjust imprisonment is presented as an intersection of several people's lives. Instead of simplifying the case for the sake of clarity, Morris treats it as a point where many stories crisscross—the private lives of the eyewitnesses, the professional rivalries among lawyers, the Dillinger tale, TV crime dramas, scenes from the drive-in movie Adams and Harris attended. Any crime, the film suggests, will consist of this tangle of threads. Any crime will seem buried in an avalanche of details (license numbers, car makes, spilled milkshakes, TV schedules), and it will engender many alternative scenarios about what really happened. *The Thin Blue Line* builds these aspects of an investigation into its very structure and style. The narration grants each version of the shooting its time onscreen, but it finally guides us to eliminate the implausible ones. It dwells on trivial details, but finally discards certain ones as less important. And it shows that a crime's complex mass of testimony and evidence can be sorted out. The film presents itself as both an account of what really happened on that Texas highway and a meditation on how persistent inquirers can eventually arrive at truth.

Form, Style, and Ideology

Meet Me in St. Louis

1944. MGM. Directed by Vincente Minnelli. Script by Irving Brecher and Fred F. Finklehoffe, from the book by Sally Benson. Photographed by George Folsey. Edited by Albert Akst. Music by Hugh Martin and Ralph Blane. With Judy Garland, Margaret O'Brien, Mary Astor, Lucille Bremer, Leon Ames, Tom Drake.

Just over halfway through *Meet Me in St. Louis,* Alonzo Smith announces to his assembled family that he has been transferred to a new job in New York City. "I've got the future to think about—the future for all of us. I've got to worry about where the money's coming from," he tells the dismayed group. These ideas of family and future, central to the form and style of the film, also create an ideological framework within which the film gains meaning and impact.

All of the films we have analyzed could be examined for their ideological standpoints. Any film combines formal and stylistic elements in such a way as to create an ideological stance, whether overtly stated or tacit. We've chosen to stress the ideology of *Meet Me in St. Louis* because it provides a clear example of a film that doesn't seek to change people's ways of thinking. Instead, it tends to reinforce certain aspects of a dominant social ideology. In this case, *Meet Me in St. Louis,* like most Hollywood films, seeks to uphold what are conceived as characteristically American values of family unity and home life.

Meet Me in St. Louis is set during the preparations for the Louisiana Purchase Exposition in St. Louis, with the fair itself becoming the culmination of the action. The film displays its form in a straightforward way, with a title card announcing each of its four sections with a different season **(11.91).** In this way, the film

"I don't shoot elegant pictures. Mr. Vincente Minnelli, he shot elegant pictures."

— Billy Wilder, director

11.91   The opening title card, "Summer 1903," in *Meet Me in St. Louis.*

11.92   The transition into the world of 1903 St. Louis.

simultaneously suggests the passage of time (equated with a movement toward the spring 1904 fair, which will bring the fruits of progress to St. Louis) and the unchanging cycle of the seasons.

The Smiths, living in a big Victorian house, form a large but close-knit family. The seasonal structure allows the film to show the Smiths at the traditional times of family unity, the holidays; we see them celebrating Halloween and Christmas. At the end, the fair becomes a new sort of holiday, the celebration of the Smiths' decision to remain in St. Louis.

The opening of the film quickly introduces the idea of St. Louis as a city on the boundary between tradition and progress. The fancy candy-box title card for summer forms a vignette of white and red flowers around an old-fashioned black-and-white photo of the Smiths' house. As the camera moves in, color fades into the photo, and it comes to life **(11.92)**. Slow, subdued chords over the title card give way to a bouncy tune more in keeping with the onscreen movement. Horse-drawn beer wagons and carriages move along the road, but an early-model automobile (a bright red, which draws our eye) passes them. Already the motif of progress and inventions becomes prominent; it will develop quickly into the emphasis on the upcoming fair.

As Lon Smith, the son, arrives home by bicycle, a dissolve inside to the kitchen launches the exposition. One by one we meet the family members as they go about their daily activities through the house. The camera follows the second youngest daughter, Agnes, as she goes upstairs singing "Meet Me in St. Louis" **(11.93).** She encounters Grandpa, who takes up the song as the camera follows him briefly. By means of close matches on action on the characters' passing the song along, the image track yields a flow of movement that presents the house as full of bustle and music. Grandpa hears offscreen voices singing the same song. He moves to a window, and a high-angle shot from over his shoulder shows the second oldest sister, Esther, stepping out of a buggy **(11.94).** Her arrival brings the sequence full circle back to the front of the house.

The house remains the main image of family unity throughout most of the film. Aside from the expedition of the young people on the trolley to see the construction of the fair, the Christmas dance, and the final fairground sequence, the entire action of the film takes place in or near the Smith house. Although Mr. Smith's job provides the reason to move to New York, we never see him at his office. In the opening sequence, the family members return home one by one, until they all gather around the dinner table. Every seasonal section of the film begins with a

11.93 The song "Meet Me in St. Louis" introduces us to the characters and locations.

11.94 The importance of the family house: A window frames our first view of the heroine . . .

similar candy-box title card and a move in toward the house. In the film's ideology, the home appears to be a self-sufficient place; other social institutions become peripheral, even threatening.

This vision of the unified family within an idealized household places the women at the center. The narration does not restrict our knowledge to a single character's range, but it tends to concentrate on what the Smith women know. Mrs. Smith, the oldest daughter Rose, the youngest daughter Tootie, and in particular Esther are the characters around which the narration is organized. Moreover, women are portrayed as the agents of stability. The action in the story constantly returns to the kitchen, where Mrs. Smith and the maid, Katie, work calmly in the midst of small crises. The men present the threat to the family's unity. Mr. Smith wants to take the family to New York, thereby destroying its ties with the past. Lon goes away to the East, to college at Princeton. Only Grandpa, as representative of the older generation, sides with the women in their desire to stay in St. Louis. In general, the narrative's causality makes any departure from the home problematic—an example of how a narrative's principles of development can generate an ideological premise.

Within the family, there are minor disagreements, but the members cooperate. The two older sisters, Rose and Esther, help each other in their flirtations. Esther is in love with the boy next door, John Truitt, and marriage to him poses no threat to the family unity. Several times in the film, she gazes across at his house without having to leave her own home. First, she and Rose go out onto the porch to try to attract his attention; then she sits in the window to sing "The Boy Next Door" **(11.95).** Finally, much later, she sits in a darkened bedroom upstairs and sees John pull his shade just after they have become engaged. That the girls might want to travel, or to educate themselves beyond high school, is never considered. By concentrating on the round of small incidents in the household and neighborhood, the film blocks consideration of any alternative way of living—except the dreaded move to New York.

Many stylistic devices build up a picture of a happy family life. The Technicolor design contributes greatly to the lushness of the mise-en-scene, making the costumes, the surroundings, and the characters' hair color stand out richly (5.5). The characters wear bright clothes, with Esther often in blue. She and Rose wear red and green, to the Christmas dance **(11.96).** This strengthens the association of the family unity with holidays and incidentally makes the sisters easy to pick out in the swirling crowd of pastel-clad dancers. In 5.5, the shot from the trolley scene, Esther is conspicuous because she is the only woman in black amidst the generally bright-colored dresses.

11.95   . . . and later her song, "The Boy Next Door."

11.96   Christmas party gowns form part of the film's holidays motif.

Meet Me in St. Louis is a musical, and music plays a large part in the family's life. Songs come at moments of romance or gathering. Rose and Esther sing "Meet Me in St. Louis" in the parlor before dinner. When Mr. Smith interrupts them on returning from work—"For heaven's sake, stop that screeching!"—he is immediately characterized as opposed to the singing and to the fair. Esther's other songs show that her romance with John Truitt is a safe and reasonable one. A woman does not have to leave home to find a husband: she can find him right in her own neighborhood ("The Boy Next Door") or by riding the trolley ("The Trolley Song"). Other songs accompany the two parties, and Esther sings "Have Yourself a Merry Little Christmas" to Tootie, the youngest sister, after the Christmas dance. Here she tries to reassure Tootie that life in New York will be all right if the family can remain together.

But already there is a sense that such unity is in danger. Esther sings, "Someday soon we all will be together, if the Fates allow / Until then we'll have to muddle through somehow." We know already that Esther has achieved her romantic goal and become engaged to John Truitt. If the Smiths do move to New York, she will have to decide between him and her family. By this point, the plot has reached an impasse; whichever way she decides, the old way of life will be destroyed. The narrative needs a resolution, and Tootie's hysterical crying in reaction to the song leads Mr. Smith to reconsider his decision.

Tootie's destruction of the snow people after Esther's song is a striking image of the threat to family unity posed by the move to New York. As the winter season section opened, the children were building the snow people (and a dog) in the yard. In effect, they had created a parallel to their own family **(11.97)**. At first these snow people were part of the comic scene in which Esther and Katie persuade Lon and Rose to go to the Christmas dance together. But when Tootie becomes hysterical at the prospect of leaving St. Louis, she runs down in her nightgown to smash the snow people. The scene is almost shocking, since Tootie seems to be killing the doubles of her own family **(11.98)**. This moment has to be emotional because it must motivate the father's change of mind. He realizes that his desire to move to New York threatens the family's harmony. This realization leads to his decision to stay in St. Louis.

Two other elements of the mise-en-scene create motifs that stress the family's comfortable life. The Smiths live surrounded by food. In the initial scene, the women are making ketchup, which is shortly served at the family dinner. After the scene in which Rose's boyfriend fails to propose to her by phone, the tensions are reconciled, and the maid serves large slices of corned beef.

11.97 Snow people of various sexes and sizes parallel the family.

11.98 Tootie's attack on the snow people.

11.99 A framing in depth stresses the family as a group, with a plate of cake prominent on the piano in the foreground.

11.100 At each pause in the long-take camera movement, the chandelier is framed in the upper portion of the screen.

In the Halloween scene, the connection between plentiful food and family unity becomes even more explicit. At first, the children gather around to eat cake and ice cream, but the father arrives home and makes his announcement about moving to New York. The family members depart without touching their food. Only when they hear the mother and father singing at the piano do they gradually drift back to eat **(11.99).** The words of the song—"Time may pass, but we'll be together"—accompany their actions. The use of food as a motif associates the family's life in the house with plenty and with the individual's place as part of a group. At the fair in the last sequence, they decide to visit a restaurant together. Thus the food motif returns at the moment of their reaffirmation of their life together in St. Louis.

Another motif of family unity involves light. The house is ablaze much of the time. As the family sits together at dinner, the low evening sun sends bright yellow rays through the white curtains. Later, one of the loveliest scenes involves Esther's request that John accompany her through the downstairs to help her turn out the lights. This action is primarily accomplished in one long take, with a crane shot following the characters from room to room **(11.100).** As the rooms darken and the couple moves out to the hall, the camera cranes down to a height level with their faces. The shot contains a remarkable shift of tone. It begins with Esther's comically contrived excuse ("I'm afraid of mice") to keep John with her and develops gradually toward a genuinely romantic mood.

The Halloween sequence takes place entirely at night and makes light a central motif. The camera initially moves in toward the house's glowing yellow windows. Tense, slightly eerie music makes the house seem an island of safety in the darkness. As Tootie and Agnes go out to join the other children in playing tricks, they are silhouetted against the flames of the bonfire the group has gathered around. At first the fire seems threatening, contradicting the earlier associations of light with safety and unity, but this scene actually harmonizes with the previous uses of light. Tootie is excluded from the group activities because she is "too little." After she proves herself worthy, she is allowed to help feed the flames along with the others. Note particularly the long track-back as Tootie leaves the fire to play her trick; the fire remains in the background of the shot, appearing as a haven she has left behind **(11.101).** Indeed, the first sequence of the Halloween section of the film becomes a sort of miniature working out of the entire narrative structure. Tootie's position as a part of the group is abandoned as she moves away from the fire, then triumphantly affirmed as she returns to it.

Similarly, light plays an important part in the resolution of the threat to the family's unity. Late on Christmas Eve, Esther finds Tootie awake. They look out the window at the snow people standing in the yard below. A strip of yellow light falls across the snow, suggesting the warmth and safety of the house they plan to leave (11.98). Tootie's hysterical crying, however, leads Mr. Smith to reconsider his decision. As he sits thinking, he holds the match, with which he was about to light his cigar, unnoticed in his hand until it burns his fingers. Combined with the slow playing of the "Meet Me in St. Louis" theme, the flame serves to emphasize his distraction and his gradual change of mind.

As he calls his family down to announce his decision not to move, he turns up all the lights. The dim, bleak halls full of packing boxes become again the scene of busy activity as the family gathers. The lamps' glass shades are red and green, identifying the house with the appropriate Christmas colors and recalling Esther's and Rose's party dresses. The announcement of the decision leads directly to the opening of the presents, as if to emphasize that staying in St. Louis will not create any financial hardship for the family.

As night falls in the final fair sequence, the many lights of the buildings come on, dazzlingly reflected in lakes and canals **(11.102).** Here the film ends, with the family gazing in awe at the view. Once more light signifies safety and family enjoyment. These lights also bring the other motifs of the film together. The father had originally wanted to move to New York as a provision for his family's future. In deciding to stay in St. Louis, he had told them: "New York hasn't got a copyright on opportunity. Why, St. Louis is headed for a boom that'll make your head swim. This is a great town." The fair confirms this. St. Louis allows the family to retain its unity, comfort, and safety and yet have all the benefits of progress. The film ends with this dialogue:

MOTHER: There's never been anything like it in the whole world.

ROSE: We don't have to come here in a train or stay in a hotel. It's right in our own hometown.

TOOTIE: Grandpa, they'll never tear it down, will they?

GRANDPA: Well, they'd better not.

ESTHER: I can't believe it. Right here where we live. Right here in St. Louis **(11.103).**

These lines do not *create* the film's ideology, which has been present in the narrative and stylistic devices throughout. The dialogue simply makes explicit what has been implicit all along. (Compare this with the line "There's no place like home" in *The Wizard of Oz*—another MGM musical, made five years earlier.)

11.101   A terrified Tootie moves into the darkness to play her trick.

11.102   The motif of light culminates in the revelation of the fairgrounds.

11.103   The film's final shot, with Esther's dazzled reaction to the fair.

The fair solves the problems of the future and family unity. The family is able to go to a French restaurant without going away from home. The ending also restores the father's position as at least the titular head of the family. Only he is able to remember how to get to the restaurant and prepares to guide the group there.

Understanding a film's ideology typically involves analyzing how form and style create meaning. As Chapter 2 suggested, meaning can be of four general types: referential, explicit, implicit, and symptomatic. Our analysis of *Meet Me in St. Louis* has shown how all four types work to reinforce a social ideology—in this case, the values of tradition, home life, and family unity. The referential aspects of the film presuppose that the audience can grasp the difference between St. Louis and New York, and that it knows about international expositions, American family customs, national holidays, and so on. These address the film to a specifically American audience. The explicit meaning of the film is formulated by the final exchange we have just considered, in which the small city is discussed as the perfect fusion of progress and tradition.

We have also traced out how formal construction and stylistic motifs contribute to one major implicit meaning: the family and home as creating a "haven in a heartless world," the central reference point for the individual's life. What, then, of symptomatic meanings?

Generally, the film expresses one tendency of many social ideologies in its attempt to naturalize social behavior. Chapter 2 mentioned that systems of values and beliefs may seem unquestionable to the social groups that hold them. One way that groups maintain such systems is to assume that certain things are beyond human choice or control, that they are simply natural. Historically, this habit of thought has often been used to justify oppression and injustice, as when women, minority groups, or the poor are thought to be naturally inferior. *Meet Me in St. Louis* participates in this general tendency, not only in its characterization of the Smith women (Esther and Rose are simply presumed to want husbands) but in the very choice of a white, upper-middle-class household as an emblem of American life. A more subtle naturalization is evident in the film's overall formal organization. The natural cycle of the seasons is harmonized with the family's life, and the conclusion of the plot takes place in the spring, the time of renewal.

We can also focus on more historically specific symptomatic meanings. The film was released in November 1944 (just in time for Christmas). World War II was still raging. The audience for this film would have consisted largely of women and children whose male relatives had been absent for extended periods, often overseas. Families were often forced apart, and the people who remained behind had to make considerable sacrifices for the war effort. In a time when women were required to work in defense plants, factories, and offices (and many were enjoying the experience), there appeared a film that restricted the range of women's experiences to home and family, and yearned for a simpler time when family unity was paramount.

Meet Me in St. Louis can thus be seen as a symptom of a nostalgia for prewar, pre-Depression America. In a 1944 audience, parents of young fighting men would remember the 1903–1904 period as part of their own childhoods. All of the formal devices—narrative construction, seasonal segmentation, songs, color, and motifs—can thus be seen as reassuring the viewers. If the women and others left at home can be strong and hold their families together against threats of disunity, domestic harmony will eventually return. From this perspective, *Meet Me in St. Louis* upholds dominant conceptions of American family life and may even propose an ideal of family unity for the postwar future.

Raging Bull

1980. United Artists. Directed by Martin Scorsese. Script by Paul Schrader and Mardik Martin. From the book *Raging Bull* by Jake La Motta, with Joseph Carter and Peter Savage. Photographed by Michael Chapman. Edited by Thelma Schoonmaker. With Robert De Niro, Cathy Moriarty, Joe Pesci, Frank Vincent, Nicholas Colasanto, Theresa Saldana.

In analyzing *Meet Me in St. Louis,* we argued that the film upholds a characteristically American ideology. It's also possible for a film made in Hollywood to take a more ambivalent attitude toward ideological issues. Martin Scorsese's *Raging Bull* does so by taking violence as its central theme.

Violence is widespread in American cinema, often serving as the basis for entertainment. Extreme violence has become central to several genres, such as science-fiction and horror films. Such genres often rely in part on making their violence very stylized, usually thanks to special effects, and hence minimally disturbing. *Raging Bull* uses a different tactic, drawing on conventions of cinematic realism to make violence visceral and disturbing. Thus, even though it's in some ways less savage than many other films of its era—not a single death occurs, for instance—it contains several scenes that are hard to bear. Not only the brutal boxing matches but also the equally harsh quarrels in everyday life bring violence to the fore.

Scorsese's film is loosely based on the career of boxer Jake La Motta, who became the world middleweight champion in 1949. *Raging Bull* uses the boxing scenes (based on real fights) as emblematic of the violence that pervades Jake's life.

Indeed, he seems incapable of dealing with people without picking quarrels, making threats, or becoming violent. His two marriages, especially that with his second wife, Vickie, are full of bickering and domestic abuse. Although his closest relationship is apparently with his brother Joey, who initially manages his career, Jake eventually thrashes Joey in a jealous rage and permanently alienates him. Moreover, while Jake's actions hurt others, he also wreaks havoc on himself, driving away everyone he loves and leading him to a pathetic career as an overweight stand-up comic and then as an actor reciting speeches from famous plays and films.

How are we to understand the ideology of a film that makes such a vicious bully its hero? We might be tempted to posit either/or interpretations. Either the film celebrates Jake's murderous rage, or it condemns him as a pathological case. Yet in settling on one of these simple notions, we would fail to confront the film's uneasy balance of sympathy for and revulsion toward its central character. We suggest that *Raging Bull* uses a variety of strategies, both of narrative and style, to make Jake a case study in the role of violence in American life. Scorsese thus creates a complex context within which Jake's actions must be judged.

This context can be best approached by examining the formal structure of *Raging Bull*'s narrative. If we were to segment the film into its individual scenes, we would come up with a long list. Although there are some lengthy sequences, most are quite short. In all we arrive at 46, including the opening credits and the closing quotation title, but these can be usefully grouped into 12 major parts:

1. The opening credits, shown over a lengthy shot of Jake warming up alone in a boxing ring.

2. Backstage in a nightclub, 1964. Jake practices a poem he will recite.

   Flashback begins:

3. 1941. Expository scenes of Jake losing a match, fighting with his wife, seeing Vickie, and having his first date with her.

4. 1943. Two matches with Sugar Ray Robinson, separated by a love scene between Jake and Vickie.

5. A montage sequence alternating a series of fights, 1944 to 1947, and home movies of Jake's private life.

6. A lengthy series of scenes in 1947, including three in the Copacabana nightclub, establishing Jake's jealousy over Vickie and hatred of the mob. He ends by throwing a fight for them.

7. 1949. An argument with Vickie, followed by Jake's winning the middleweight champion bout.

8. 1950. Jake beats up Vickie and his brother Joey in an unjustified jealous rage. He defends his title and fights Robinson again.

9. 1956. Jake retires and buys a nightclub in which he does comedy routines. Vickie leaves him, and he is arrested on a morals charge.

10. 1958. Jake does his comedy act in a cheap strip joint; he fails to persuade Joey to reconcile with him.

    Flashback ends.

11. 1964. Jake prepares to go onstage to perform his recital.

12. A black title with a biblical quotation and the film's dedication.

The beginning and ending of the film are vital in shaping our attitude toward Jake's career. The first image shows him warming up in the ring before an unspecified fight **(11.104)**. Several filmic devices create our initial impressions of the protagonist. He bounces up and down in place, in slow motion. This slow tempo is accompanied by languid classical music, suggesting that his boxing warm-up is like a dance. The deep-space staging places the ring's ropes prominently in the

11.104   The slow-motion opening shot of *Raging Bull.*

foreground and makes the ring seem huge, emphasizing Jake's solitude. This long take continues through the main credits, establishing boxing as both a beautiful and a lonely sport. The image remains abstract and remote: it is the only scene in the narrative that does not take place in a year specified by a superimposed title.

A straight cut to segment 2 shows Jake, suddenly fat and old, again practicing. He is going over his lines for a one-man show that consists of readings from famous literature and of a poem he has written about himself: "So give me a stage / Where this bull here can rage / And though I can fight / I'd much rather recite—That's entertainment!" This episode takes place quite late in the story, after the long struggles of his boxing career. Not until segment 11 will the plot return to this moment in the story, with Jake continuing to rehearse his lines. In segment 11, as the manager summons him onstage, he does some boxer-style warm-up punches to build his confidence, muttering rapidly over and over, "I'm the boss, I'm the boss."

By framing most of the story as a flashback, Scorsese links violence with entertainment. Jake's gesture of spreading his arms as he says, "That's entertainment!" in segment 2 resembles the triumphant raising of his glove-clad hands whenever he wins a fight in the lengthy central flashback. Correspondingly, *Raging Bull* ignores Jake's early life and concentrates on two periods: his boxing career and his turn to stand-up comedy and literary recitations. Both periods present him as trying to control his life and the people around him. "I'm the boss," the last line spoken in the film, sums up Jake's attitude.

The plot structure we've outlined also traces a rise-and-fall pattern of development. After segment 7, Jake's high point, his life runs downhill and his violence appears more and more savagely self-destructive. In addition, certain motifs highlight the role of violence in his life and the lives of those around him. During a rest period in his very first prizefight (segment 3), a fistfight breaks out in the stands—suggesting at the outset that violence spills beyond the ring. Domestic relations are expressed through aggression, as in the tough-guy shoving between Jake and Joey and in Joey's disciplining his son by threatening to stab him.

Most vividly, violence is turned against women. Both Jake and Joey insult and threaten their wives, and Jake's beating of both his wives forms a grim counterpoint to his battles in the ring. During the first scene at the Copacabana, women emerge as targets of abuse. Jake accuses Vickie of flirting with other men; he insults a boxer and a mob member by suggesting that both are like women; and even the comedian onstage mocks women in the audience. Scene by scene, the organization of incidents and motifs suggests that male aggression pervades American life.

Scorsese puts Jake's violence in context by means of film techniques. In general, by appealing to conventions of realism, the film's style makes the violence in *Raging Bull* disturbing. Many of the fights are filmed with the camera on a Steadicam brace, which yields ominous tracking movements or close shots emphasizing grimaces. Backlighting, motivated by the spotlights around the ring, highlight droplets of sweat or blood that spray off the boxers as they are struck **(11.105)**. Rapid editing, often with ellipses, and loud, stinging cracks intensify the physical force of punches. Special makeup creates effects of blood vessels in the boxers' faces spurting grotesquely. Scorsese treats the violent scenes outside the ring differently, favoring long shots and less vivid sound effects.

He creates a realistic social and historical context by using other conventions. One of these is a series of superimposed titles that identify each boxing match by date, locale, and participants. This narrational ploy yields a quasi-documentary quality.

The most important factor creating realism, however, is probably the acting. Aside from Robert De Niro, the cast was chosen from virtually unknown actors or nonactors. As a result, they did not bring glamorous star associations to the film. De Niro was known mainly for his grittily realistic performances in Scorsese's *Mean Streets* and *Taxi Driver,* as well as Michael Cimino's *The Deer Hunter.* In *Raging*

11.105   Realistic violence in the boxing scenes.

Bull, the actors speak with thick Bronx accents, repeat or mumble many of their lines, and make no attempt to create likable characters. In the publicity surrounding the film, much was also made of the fact that De Niro gained 60 pounds in order to play Jake as an older man. The film emphasizes De Niro's transformation by cutting straight from a medium close-up of Jake at the end of segment 2, in 1964 (**11.106**), to a similar framing of him in the ring in 1941 (**11.107**). Such realism in the acting and other techniques makes it difficult for us to accept the film's violence casually, as we might in a conventional horror or crime film.

Through its narrative structure and its use of the stylistic conventions of realism, the film thus offers a criticism of violence in American life, both in the ring and in the home. Yet the film doesn't permit us to condemn Jake as merely a raging bull. It also presents violence as fascinating and ambiguous. Although the fight scenes favor brutal realism, aspects of them are distorted in mesmerizing ways. The sounds of punches assault our ears with shuddering impact. The sound mix for the fights blended animal cries, airplane motors, whizzing arrows, and even music, but the sources are unrecognizable because they are slowed down or played backward.

More broadly, violence is made disturbingly attractive even in the scenes outside the ring because the narration concentrates far more on the perpetrators of the violence than on the victims. In particular, the three important female characters—Jake's first wife, Joey's wife Lenore, and Vickie—have little to do in the action except take abuse or rail ineffectually against it. We never learn why they are initially attracted to the violent men they marry or why they stay with them so long. At first Vickie seems to admire Jake for his fame and his flashy car, but her willingness to sustain their marriage for so long is not explained. Indeed, her sudden decision to leave him after 11 years has no specific motivation.

Such victims of Jake's violence serve chiefly to provoke him to respond. One portion of the action focuses on his pummeling of a "pretty" fighter to whom he thinks Vickie is attracted. Another deals with Jake's violent reaction to his irrational belief that Joey and Vickie have had an affair. It is notable that after this crisis, when Jake beats Joey up, Joey becomes as peripheral a figure as Vickie. We glimpse him briefly watching Jake's bloody title defeat and then see a short scene of him resisting Jake's offer of reconciliation. The film thus offers no positive counterweight to Jake's excesses.

Another indication of the narration's fascination with Jake's violence is the descent into subjective presentation. Several scenes show events from his point of view, using slow motion to suggest that we are seeing not just what he sees but how he reacts subjectively to it. This technique becomes especially vivid when Jake sees Vickie with other men and becomes jealous. Similarly, in the final fight with Robinson, Jake's vision of his opponent is shown via a point-of-view framing. The POV imagery also incorporates a combined track-forward and zoom-out to make the ring seem to stretch far into the distance, while a decrease in the frontal light makes Robinson appear even more menacing (**11.108**). Other deviations from realism, such as the thunderous throbbing on the sound track during Jake's major victory bout, also suggest that we're entering Jake's mind.

In part Scorsese justifies the film's fascination with violence by emphasizing how self-destructive Jake is. However much he hurts other people, he injures himself at least as much. He also quickly regrets having hurt people, as several parallel scenes show. In segment 3, Jake has a vicious argument with his first wife in which he threatens to kill her but then immediately says, "Come on, honey, let's be—let's be friends. Truce, all right?" Later, after he has beaten Vickie up for her imagined infidelities, he apologizes and persuades her to stay with him. These domestic reconciliations are echoed in the big title fight where he defeats the current champion, Marcel Cerdan, then walks to his opponent's corner and magnanimously embraces him.

Sympathy for Jake is reinforced by other means. *Raging Bull* suggests that he is strongly masochistic, using his aggression to induce others to inflict pain on him.

11.106   A graphic match moves the film from the end of the 1964 opening . . .

11.107   . . . to Jake in 1941.

11.108   Jake's point of view during a fight.

11.109   A close-up links violence and sexuality as Jake asks Vickie to kiss his bruises.

"I was fascinated by the self-destructive side of Jake La Motta's character, by his very basic emotions. What could be more basic than making a living by hitting another person on the head until one of you falls or stops? . . . I put everything I knew and felt into that film, and I thought it would be the end of my career. It was what I call a kamikaze way of making movies: pour every-thing in, then forget about it and go find another way of life."

— Martin Scorsese, director

This notion is emphasized in the love scene in segment 4. There he childishly asks Vickie to caress and kiss the wounds from his triumph over Sugar Ray Robinson **(11.109)**. Soon Jake denies himself sexual gratification by pouring ice water into his shorts. The scene then leads directly into a fight in which Robinson defeats him.

This defeat is paralleled in segment 8, another boxing scene, when Jake simply stands and goads Robinson into beating him to a pulp. The motif of masochism comes to a climax in segment 9, when Jake is thrown into solitary confinement in a Dade County jail. A long, disturbing take has Jake beating his head and fists against the prison wall, as he asserts that he is not an animal and berates himself as stupid.

More implicitly, the film suggests a strain of repressed homosexuality in Jake's aggressiveness. His embrace of the defeated opponent, Cerdan, in his title fight, as well as his urging of Robinson to attack him in his final bout, suggest such an interpretation. In segment 6, when Jake sits down at a nightclub table and jokes about how pretty his upcoming opponent is, he tauntingly offers him as a sex partner to a mobster he suspects of being in love with Vickie. In segment 8, one scene begins with an erotically suggestive slow-motion shot of seconds' hands massaging Jake's torso. In general, there is a hint that Jake's fascination with boxing and his refusal to deal with his domestic life stem from an unacknowledged homosexual urge. Such an implication goes against the usual ideology of Hollywood, which assumes that a heterosexual romance is the basis for most narratives.

Ultimately, the ideological stance that *Raging Bull* offers is far from being as straightforward as that of *Meet Me in St. Louis.* Instead of displaying an idealized image of American society, the film criticizes one pervasive aspect of that society: its penchant for unthinking violence. Yet it also displays a considerable fascination with that violence and with its main embodiment, Jake.

The film's ambiguity intensifies at the end. In segment 12, a biblical quotation appears: "So, for the second time, [the Pharisees] summoned the man who had been blind and said: 'Speak the truth before God. We know this fellow is a sinner.' 'Whether or not he is a sinner, I do not know,' the man replied. 'All I know is this: once I was blind and now I can see.'"

As this quotation emerges line by line, we are cued to relate it to the protagonist. Has Jake achieved some sort of enlightenment through his experiences? Several factors suggest not. Despite being a poor actor, he continues to perform literary recitals, trying to regain his public ("I'm the boss"). Furthermore, the speech he practices at the end is the famous "I could have been a contender" passage from *On the Waterfront.* In that film, a failed boxer blamed his brother for his lack of a chance to succeed. Is Jake now blaming Joey or someone else for his decline? Or is it possible that he has become aware enough of his faults to ironically recall a film in which the hero also comes to realize his mistakes?

After the biblical quotation, there appears Scorsese's dedication of the film: "Remembering Haig R. Manoogian, teacher, May 23, 1916–May 26, 1980, With love and resolution, Marty." Now the biblical quotation may equally apply to Scorsese, himself from the tough Italian neighborhoods of New York. Were it not for people like this teacher, he might have ended up somewhat like Jake. And perhaps the film professor, who helped him "to see," enabled Scorsese to present Jake with a mixture of detachment and sympathy.

As a cinema student, Scorsese was well aware of innovative foreign films such as *Breathless* and *Tokyo Story,* so it's not surprising that his own work invites differing interpretations. The film's ending places *Raging Bull* in a tradition of Hollywood films (such as *Citizen Kane*) that avoid complete closure and opt for a degree of ambiguity, a denial of either/or answers. Such ambiguity can render the film's ideology equivocal, generating contrasting and even conflicting implicit meanings.

Writing a Critical Analysis of a Film

An analytical film essay for a class or publication typically runs 5–15 double-spaced pages. As an analysis, it points out how how various parts of the film fit together systematically. Like a screening report and a review, the analytical essay includes descriptions, but the descriptions are typically more detailed and extensive. Like the review, the analytical essay also puts forth the writer's opinion, but here the opinion doesn't usually address the ultimate worth of the film. When you analyze a film, you're defending your view of the ways parts of the movie work together.

Think about a sad song. You could *describe* the song in various ways ("It's about a woman who wants out of a dead-end relationship"), or you could *evaluate* it ("It's too sentimental"). But you can also *analyze* it, talking about how the lyrics, the melody, and the instrumentation work together to create the feeling of sadness or to make the listener understand the relationship. That's the sort of thing people who study film do when they analyze movies.

The analytical essay is also an argumentative piece. Its goal is to allow you to develop an idea you have about the film by supplying good reasons for taking that idea seriously. The sample analyses in Chapter 11 are argumentative essays. For instance, in analyzing *The Thin Blue Line*, we argue that the film tells a real-life story in a way that suggests how difficult the search for truth can be (pp. 427–430). Likewise, our discussion of *Raging Bull* tries to show that the film is critical of violence as used in mass entertainment while still displaying a fascination with its visceral appeal (pp. 440–441).

Preparing to Write

How do you come up with an argument for your essay? The preparatory work usually consists of three steps:

Step 1: Develop a Thesis That Your Essay Will Explain and Support

Start by asking yourself questions. What do you find intriguing or disturbing about the film? What makes the film noteworthy, in your opinion? Does it illustrate some aspect of filmmaking with special clarity? Does it have an unusual effect on the viewer? Do its implicit or symptomatic meanings (pp. 63–64) seem to have particular importance?

Your answer to such questions will furnish the *thesis* of your analysis. The thesis, in any piece of writing, is the central claim your argument advances. It encapsulates your opinion, but not in the way that a film review states your evaluation of the movie. In an analytical essay, your thesis is one way to help other viewers understand the movie. In our analysis of *His Girl Friday* (pp. 397–398), our thesis is that the film uses classical narrative devices to create an impression of speed. With respect to *Chungking Express* (pp. 445–446), our the thesis is that the film draws us to seek thematic links between two story lines that do not connect causally.

Typically, your thesis will be a claim about the film's functions, its effects, or its meanings (or some mixture of all three). For instance, we argue that by creating a wide variety of characters in *Do The Right Thing,* Spike Lee builds up interconnected plotlines; this allows him to explore the problems of maintaining a community (pp. 404–408). In our discussion of *North by Northwest,* we concentrate more on how the film achieves the effects of suspense and surprise (pp. 400–404). The analysis of *Meet Me in St. Louis* emphasizes how technique carries implicit and symptomatic meanings about the importance of family life in America (pp. 431–438).

Your thesis will need some support, some reasons to believe it. Ask yourself, "What would back up my thesis?" and draw up a list of points. Some of these reasons will occur to you immediately, but others will emerge only as you start to study the film more closely. And the reasons, which are conceptual points, will in turn need backup—typically, evidence and examples. You can sum up the structure of an argumentative essay in the acronym **TREE**: **T**hesis supported by **R**easons which rest upon **E**vidence and **E**xamples.

Step 2: Draw Up a Segmentation of the Entire Film

Analyzing a film is a bit like investigating a building's design. When we walk through a building, we notice various features—the shape of the doorway, the sudden appearance of an immense atrium. We may not, however, have a very strong sense of the building's overall architecture. If we are students of architecture, though, we want to study the design of the whole building, and so we'd examine the blueprints to understand how all the individual parts fit together. Similarly, we experience a film scene by scene, but if we want to understand how the various scenes work together, it's helpful to have a sense of the film's overall shape.

Movies don't come equipped with blueprints, however, so we have to make our own. The best way to grasp the overall shape of the movie is to make a segmentation, as we suggest in earlier chapters. (See in particular pp. 72–73, 105–106, 397, 426, and 439). Breaking the film into sequences gives you a convenient overview, and your segmentation will often suggest things that will support or help you nail down your thesis. For example, in studying *The Thin Blue Line,* we made a separate list of all the flashbacks to the murder. When we saw them lined up on our page, we spotted the pattern of development in them that became part of our analysis (pp. 425–431).

Now that you have a segmentation, you can go on to see how the parts are connected. In examining a non-narrative film, you will need to be especially alert to its use of categorical, rhetorical, abstract, or associational principles. See our analysis of *Gap-Toothed Women* (pp. 354–359) for an example of how you can base an analysis on the overall shape of the film.

If the film presents a narrative, your segmentation can help you answer questions like these: How does each scene set up causes and effects? At what point do we understand the characters' goals, and how do those goals develop in the course of the action? What principles of development connect one scene to another? The pattern of the reenactments of the shooting and the various interrogations in *The Thin Blue Line* would be difficult to discern without writing them out.

Should you include your segmentation in your written analysis? Sometimes it will make your argument clearer and more convincing. We think that a broad scene breakdown helps illustrate some key points in our discussions of *His Girl Friday* (p. 396). Perhaps your argument will gain strength if you bring out a still finer-grained segmentation; we do this in considering the three subsegments of the final chase scene in *North by Northwest* (pp. 400–404).

Whether or not your segmentation finally surfaces in your written analysis, it's good to get in the habit of writing out a fairly detailed segmentation every time you examine a film. It will help you get an overall sense of the film's design. You probably noticed that nearly every one of our analyses includes, early on, a statement about the film's underlying formal organization. This provides a firm basis for more detailed analysis. Writing out a segmentation is also good practice if you want to become a filmmaker yourself: screenwriters, directors, and other creative personnel usually work from a plot outline that is, more or less, a segmentation.

Step 3: Note Outstanding Instances of Film Technique

As you watch the film, you should jot down brief, accurate descriptions of the various film techniques used. You can get ideas for analyzing stylistic patterns from Chapters 8 and 10. Once you have determined the overall organizational structure of the film, you can identify salient techniques, trace out patterns of techniques across the whole film, and propose functions for those techniques. These techniques will often support or refine your thesis.

As a start, be alert for techniques taken one by one: Is this a case of three-point lighting? Is this a continuity cut? Just as important, you should be sensitive to context: What is the function of the technique here? Again a segmentation will help you by drawing attention to patterning. Does the technique repeat or develop across the film?

At any moment in a film, so much is going on that it's easy to be overwhelmed by all the technical elements. Shot composition, performance, lighting, camera movement, color design, dialogue, music—all these things can be changing from second to second. Often, beginning film analysts are uncertain as to what techniques are most relevant to their thesis. Sometimes they try to describe every single costume or cut or pan, and they wind up drowning in data.

This is where planning your paper's thesis in advance helps you. Your thesis will make certain techniques more pertinent than others. For example, we argue that in *North by Northwest* Hitchcock creates suspense and surprise by manipulating our range of knowledge (pp. 400–404). Sometimes he lets us know more than the main character, Roger Thornhill, and this builds up suspense: Will Thornhill walk into the traps that we know are awaiting him? Other times we know only as much as Thornhill does, so that we're as surprised as he is at a new turn of events. Hitchcock devotes particular film techniques to creating these effects. Cross-cutting between lines of action gives us more knowledge than Thornhill has, while POV camera work and cutting restrict us to his understanding of certain situations.

So other techniques, such as lighting or performance style, aren't as relevant to our thesis about *North by Northwest*. (They might, however, be very relevant to some other thesis about it—say, that it treats thriller conventions somewhat comically.) By contrast, we emphasize acting technique more in our discussion of *Raging Bull,* because acting is pertinent to our discussion of the film's use of realistic conventions. Similarly, the editing in *Meet Me in St. Louis* would be interesting from the standpoint of another argument, but it is not central to the one that we are making, so it goes almost completely unmentioned.

Once you have a thesis, an awareness of the overall shape of the film, and a set of notes on the techniques relevant to your thesis, you are ready to organize your analytical essay.

Organizing and Writing

Broadly speaking, an argumentative piece has this underlying structure:

Introduction: Background information or a vivid example, leading up to:

Statement of the thesis

Body: Reasons to believe the thesis

Evidence and examples that support the thesis

Conclusion: Restatement of the thesis and discussion of its broader implications

All of our analyses in Chapter 11 adhere to this basic structure. The opening portion seeks to lead the reader into the argument to come, and the thesis is introduced at the end of this introduction. Where the introduction is brief, as in the *His Girl Friday* analysis, the thesis comes at the end of the first paragraph (p. 396). Where more background material is needed, the introduction is somewhat longer, and the thesis is stated a little later. In the *Thin Blue Line* essay, the thesis comes at the end of the third paragraph (p. 425).

You can sometimes postpone the full statement of a thesis by casting it as a tantalizing question, as we do in our analysis of *Chungking Express* (p. 417). We end the second paragraph by asking what the film accomplishes by following one brief plot with a second one containing a new set of characters. But if you pursue the question-based structure, be sure to provide at least a hint of the answer fairly soon (as we do in the brief sixth paragraph on p. 418, just over one page into the essay) to guide the rest of your argument.

As you know, the building block of any piece of writing is the paragraph. Each slot in the argumentative pattern outlined above will be filled by one or more paragraphs. The introduction is at least one paragraph, the body will be several paragraphs, and the conclusion will be one or two paragraphs.

Typically, the introductory paragraphs of a film analysis don't display much concrete evidence. Instead, this is the place to introduce the thesis you want to advance. Often this involves situating the thesis in relation to some background information. For example, the first paragraph of our analysis of *The Thin Blue Line* summarizes the crime and investigation that are the subject matter of the film. The second paragraph sketches the circumstances that shaped the making of the film, and the third paragraph states the thesis: that finding truth is difficult.

If you're adventurous, you may wish to avoid background information. You can start with one concrete piece of evidence—say, an intriguing scene or detail from the film—before you move quickly to state your thesis. Our *Meet Me in St. Louis* piece uses this sort of opening (p. 431).

Writing a film analysis poses a particular problem of organization. Should the body of the argument follow the film's progress in chronological order, so that each paragraph deals with a scene or major part? In most cases, this can work. We try it with our *Gap-Toothed Women* discussion, which traces out the patterns of development across the film (pp. 354–359). By and large, however, you strengthen your argument by following a more conceptual structure of the sort indicated in our outline.

Recall that the body of your essay offers reasons to believe the thesis. You'll back those points up with evidence and examples. Consider our analysis of *Breathless* (pp. 408–413). Our thesis is that Godard's film both pays homage to film noir outlaw movies and *reworks* their conventions through a rough-edged treatment. This thesis obliges us to use a comparison-and-contrast strategy. But first we start with a paragraph of background (p. 408), sketching the relevant Hollywood outlaw movie traditions. The second paragraph shows how the basic story of *Breathless* resembles the criminal-couple-on-the-run movie. The next three paragraphs make the point that Godard's film also reworks Hollywood conventions: Michel seems to be imitating tough-guy stars, while the film's form and style seem casual, as if aiming to let the audience enjoy a new, more self-conscious version of an American crime movie.

Since the essay relies on comparison and contrast, the body of the piece explores the film's similarities to and differences from Hollywood conventions. The next 11 paragraphs seek to establish these points about the film's narrative form:

1. Michel is like a Hollywood protagonist in certain ways (p. 409).

2. The action is, however, much choppier and more digressive than in a Hollywood film. (p. 409).

3. The death of the policeman is handled more abruptly and disconcertingly than in a normal action movie (pp. 409–410).

4,5. By contrast, the bedroom conversation of Patricia and Michel is untypical of Hollywood genre scenes because it is very static, marking little progress toward Michel's goals (p. 410).

6. Once the plot starts moving again, it stalls again (p. 410).

7,8. Moving toward resolution, the plot again picks up, but the finale remains enigmatic and open-ended (p. 410).

9,10. Overall, Michel and Patricia are puzzling and hard to read as characters (p. 411).

11. The characterization of the couple is thus sharply different from that of the romantic couple in most outlaws-on-the-run plots (p. 411).

Each of these points constitutes a reason to accept the thesis that *Breathless* uses genre conventions but also revises them in unsettling ways.

Supporting reasons may be of many sorts. Several of our analyses distinguish between reasons based on the film's overall narrative form and reasons based on stylistic choices. The portion of the *Breathless* essay we've just reviewed offers evidence to support our claims about the film's reworking of Hollywood narrative conventions. The paragraphs that follow this material (pp. 411–413) discuss Godard's similarly self-conscious use of stylistic strategies. In analyzing *Meet Me in St. Louis,* we concentrate more on reviewing various motifs that create particular thematic effects. In either case, the argument rests on a thesis, supported by reasons, which are in turn supported by evidence and examples.

If you organize the essay conceptually rather than as a blow-by-blow résumé of the action, you may find it useful to acquaint your reader with the plot action at some point. A brief synopsis soon after the introduction may do the trick. (See our *North by Northwest* analysis, pp. 400–404, or our *Chungking Express* discussion, pp. 417–422.) Alternatively, you may wish to cover basic plot material when you discuss segmentation, characterization, causal progression, or other topics. The crucial point is that you aren't obligated to follow the film's order.

Typically, each reason for the thesis becomes the topic sentence of a paragraph, with more detailed evidence displayed in the sentences that follow. In the *Breathless* example, each main point is followed by specific examples of how plot action, dialogue, or film techniques at once refer to Hollywood tradition and loosen up the conventions. Here is where your detailed notes about salient scenes or techniques will be very useful. You can select the strongest and most vivid instances of mise-en-scene, cinematography, editing, and sound to back up the main point that each paragraph explores.

The body of the analysis can be made more persuasive by several other tactics. A paragraph that compares or contrasts this film with another might help you zero in on specific aspects that are central to your argument. You can also include an in-depth analysis of a single scene or sequence that drives your argumentative point home. We use this tactic in discussing several films' endings, chiefly because a concluding section often reveals broad principles of development. For instance, in our *North by Northwest* essay, we examine the film's final twist as typical of the way the narrative manipulates our knowledge to create surprise and suspense (p. 404).

In general, the body of the argument should progress toward stronger or subtler reasons for believing the thesis. In discussing *The Thin Blue Line,* we start by tracing how the film provides a kind of reconstructed investigation, leading to the killer (pp. 425–427). Only then do we ask: is the film more than a neutral report of the case (pp. 427–428)?

This leads us to argue that the filmmaker has subtly aligned our sympathies with Randall Adams (p. 428). Yet the film goes beyond aligning us with Adams. It also bombards us with a great deal of information, some of it fairly minute, even trivial. The purpose, we suggest, is to urge the viewer to sort out conflicting data and notice details (pp. 428–429). This is a fairly complex point that would probably not come across if introduced early on. After the analysis has worked through more clear-cut matters, it's easier to consider such nuances of interpretation.

How to end your argumentative essay? Now is the time to restate the thesis (skillfully, not repeating previous statements word for word) and to remind the reader of the reasons to entertain the thesis. The ending is also an opportunity for you to try for some eloquence, a telling quotation, a bit of historical context, or a concrete motif from the film itself—perhaps a line of dialogue or an image that encapsulates your thesis. We try this tactic in our analysis of sound in *The Prestige* (pp. 302–303). In making preparatory notes, ask yourself constantly: Is there something here that can create a vivid ending?

Just as there is no general recipe for understanding film, there is no formula for writing incisive and enlightening film analyses. But there are principles and rules of thumb that govern good writing of all sorts. Only through writing, and constant rewriting, do these principles and rules some to seem second nature. By analyzing films, we can understand the sources of our pleasure in them and share that understanding with others. If we succeed, the writing itself can give pleasure to ourselves and our readers.

SUMMARY

Key Questions for an Analytical Essay

To help you craft an effective analytical essay, ask yourself these questions:

1. Do I have a thesis? Is it stated clearly early in my essay?

2. Do I have a series of reasons supporting the thesis? Are these arranged in logical and convincing order (with the strongest or most complicated reason coming last)?

3. Are my supporting reasons backed up? Do my segmentation and stylistic analysis provide specific evidence and examples for each reason you offer?

4. Does my beginning orient my reader to the direction of my argument? Does my concluding paragraph reiterate my thesis and provide a vivid ending?

A Sample Analytical Essay

The following paper was written by a sophomore for an introductory film course. The assignment asked for an analytical essay on Martin Scorsese's *King of Comedy,* concentrating on two or three scenes of particular importance to the paper's thesis. A segmentation of the film (not included here) was attached.

Note how the essay begins with some general observations and then focuses its thesis in the second paragraph.

In order to trace the greater blurring of fantasy and reality in the film, the author develops a strategy of comparison and contrast. Each paragraph develops specific evidence of the various techniques Scorsese uses, considering editing, sound, camerawork, and staging. The paper concludes by speculating on how these techniques affect the viewer and reinforce one of the film's themes. A crisp summary line drives home the main thesis: "our final image of Rupert may be an image of the man or it may be an image from the man."

Fantasy and Reality in *The King of Comedy*

by Amanda Robillard

America is obsessed with fame. Television shows and magazines have been created in order to let the masses delve into the personal lives of their favorite stars. Friends gossip about people they have never met, but whom they feel they know because of the mass media. The lives of celebrities may not be perfect, but they definitely are exciting. Learning about your favorite star's life is an entertaining escape from what can seem a mundane existence.

Fame becomes alluring because a fantasy world surrounds it. Martin Scorsese's film *The King of Comedy* focuses on Rupert Pupkin's obsession with fame. Not only is he obsessed with a famous comedian, but he is consumed with becoming a famous comedian himself and comes to believe that his idol is more than willing to help him in his quest. Pupkin's obsession goes beyond a mere interest in fame; it takes over his life to the point that he can no longer distinguish reality from the fantasies he has concocted. Because the viewer is allowed to see these fantasies through Rupert's eyes, one can track his progression further and further into his fantasy world. In *The King of Comedy,* Scorsese uses various aspects of style in order to manipulate the boundaries between fantasy and reality in such a way as to draw a parallel between Rupert's progressive withdrawal into his own fantasies and the viewer's inability to tell the difference between the two.

The first fantasy scene of *The King of Comedy,* segment 3, blurs the line between fantasy and reality, but the line is nonetheless still discernible. Here Scorsese uses aspects of style to create a coherent fantasy that is easily recognizable as such. It is distinctly separate from surrounding scenes of reality while at the same time drawing on them in order to create the fantasy.

A combined use of sound and editing is used to tie the fantasy to reality. This is apparent both in the scenes that surround segment 3 and within the scene itself. Rupert invites Jerry to lunch at the end of segment 2. This invitation leads into a shot of Jerry and Rupert seated in a restaurant in the following scene. This link from actual dialogue to fantasy is a continuing pattern throughout the film, brought out by first mentioning the act in a real conversation and then having it carried out in a fantasy later in the film. Editing the scenes together in such a way is one device used to blur the distinction between fantasy and reality.

Within the scene, juxtaposing Rupert's fantasy with his acting it out in his mother's basement serves to create a distinction between the two. Sometimes reverse-shots of Rupert show him dressed for lunch; at other moments, the reverse-shots show him in his basement, dressed differently. Similarly, while still seeing an image of Jerry and Rupert eating lunch together in a restaurant, we hear Rupert's mother yelling for him to keep quiet or inquiring whom he is talking to. The editing and sound techniques guide the viewer back into reality, where Rupert is actually enacting the fantasy in his basement. Again, however, some elements carry over between fantasy and reality. Photographs behind Jerry in the fantasy are echoed by photographs on the wall behind Rupert in his basement. Jerry also happens to be wearing the same shirt and tie that he had in the previous scene, although with a different jacket. Also, the source of lighting seems to be coming from Rupert's right in both fantasy and reality, although it is softer in the shots in his basement.

Film History

Film Art and Film History

"Not everything is possible at all times." This aphorism of art historian Heinrich Wölffin might serve as a slogan for our final chapter. So far, our survey of film art has examined various formal and stylistic possibilities, and we've drawn our examples from the entire range of film history. But film forms and techniques don't exist in a timeless realm, equally accessible to all filmmakers. In particular historical circumstances, certain possibilities are present while others are not. Griffith could not make films as Godard does, nor could Godard make films as Griffith did. This chapter asks, What are some ways in which film art has been treated in particular historical contexts?

We consider those contexts first by period and then by nation. Although there are other equally good tools for tracing change, it's illuminating to note filmmaking trends in different times and places. In some of our cases, we'll look for what are typically called *film movements*. A film movement consists of two elements:

1. Films that are produced within a particular period and/or nation and that share significant traits of style and form

2. Filmmakers who operate within a common production structure and who share certain assumptions about filmmaking

There are other ways of defining a historical context (for example, biographical study or genre study), but the category of *movement* corresponds most closely to the emphasis of this book. The concepts of formal and stylistic systems permit us to compare films within a movement and to contrast them with films of other movements.

Our range of choice will be narrowed still further. We're concerned with Hollywood and selected alternatives. We'll trace the development of the commercial American narrative cinema while contrasting it to other approaches to style and form.

Because we're exploring historical contexts, we go beyond noting stylistic and formal qualities. For each period and nation, we'll also sketch relevant factors that affect the cinema. These factors include the state of the film industry, artistic theories held by the filmmakers themselves, pertinent technological features, and cultural and economic elements. These factors necessarily help explain how a particular trend began, what shaped its development, and what affected its decline. This material will also provide a context for particular films we've already discussed; for example, the following section on early cinema situates Lumière and Méliès in their period.

Needless to say, what follows is drastically incomplete. The writing of serious film history is in its early stages, and we must often rely on secondary sources that will eventually be superseded. Moreover, there are many unfortunate omissions.

CONNECT TO THE BLOG
Some filmmakers have tried to escape this inevitability by imitating older films. Does it work? On *The Good German,* see "Not back to the future, but ahead to the past," at
www.davidbordwell.net/blog/?p=66;
on *Casino Royale,* see "Can they make up like they used to? continued," at
www.davidbordwell.net/blog/?p=195.

Important filmmakers who don't relate to a trend or movement (for example, Tati, Bresson, and Kurosawa) are absent, as are certain important film movements, such as French populist cinema of the 1930s and Brazil's Cinema Nôvo movement of the early 1960s. What follows simply seeks to show how certain possibilities of film form and style were explored within a few typical and well-known historical periods.

Early Cinema (1893–1903)

In order to create the illusion of movement, still pictures must appear in rapid succession. To prepare them and display them at the right rate, certain technologies are necessary. Most basically, there must be a way of recording a long series of images on some sort of support. In principle, one could simply draw a string of images on a strip of paper or a disc. But photography offered the cheapest and most efficient way to generate the thousands of images needed for a reasonably lengthy display. Thus the invention of photography in 1826 launched a series of discoveries that made cinema possible.

Early photographs required lengthy exposures (initially hours, later minutes) for a single image; this made photographed motion pictures, which need 12 or more frames per second, impossible. Faster exposures, of about $\frac{1}{25}$ second, became possible by the 1870s, but only on glass plates. Glass plates weren't usable for motion pictures since there was no practical way to move them through a camera or projector. In 1878, Eadweard Muybridge, an American photographer, did make a series of photographs of a running horse by using a series of cameras with glass plate film and fast exposure, but he was primarily interested in freezing phases of an action, not re-creating the movement by projecting the images in succession.

In 1882, another scientist interested in analyzing animal movement, the Frenchman Étienne-Jules Marey, invented a camera that recorded 12 separate images on the edge of a revolving disc of film on glass. This constituted a step toward the motion picture camera. In 1888, Marey built the first camera to use a strip of flexible film, this time on paper. Again, the purpose was only to break down movement into a series of stills, and the movements photographed lasted a second or less.

In 1889, George Eastman introduced a crude flexible film base, celluloid. Once this base was improved and camera mechanisms had been devised to draw the film past the lens and expose it to light, the creation of long strips of frames became possible.

Projectors had existed for many years and had been used to show slides and other shadow entertainments. These magic lanterns were modified by the addition of shutters, cranks, and other devices to become early motion picture projectors.

One final device was needed if films were to be projected. Since the film stops briefly while the light shines through each individual frame, there had to be a mechanism to create an *intermittent* motion of the film. Marey used a Maltese cross gear on his 1888 camera, and this became a standard part of early cameras and projectors.

A flexible and transparent film base, a fast exposure time, a mechanism to pull the film through the camera, an intermittent device to stop the film, and a shutter to block off light—all these innovations had been achieved by the early 1890s. After several years, inventors working independently in many countries had developed different film cameras and projection devices. The two most important firms were the Edison Manufacturing Company in America, owned by inventor Thomas A. Edison, and Lumière Frères in France, the family firm of Louis and Auguste Lumière.

By 1893, Thomas A. Edison's assistant, W.K.L. Dickson, had developed a camera that made short 35mm films. Interested in exploiting these films as a novelty, Edison hoped to combine them with his phonograph to show sound movies. He had Dickson develop a peep-show machine, the *Kinetoscope* (**12.1**), to display these films to individual viewers.

CONNECT TO THE BLOG

For a detailed account, see our other textbook, *Film History: An Introduction.* We discuss how we wrote it in "Around the world in 750 pages," at

www.davidbordwell.net/blog/?p=3682.

CONNECT TO THE BLOG

Early cinema was influenced by other media of its day, including narrative painting. We suggest some similarities in "Professor sees more parallels between things, other things."

See www.davidbordwell.net/blog/?p=901.

12.1 The Kinetoscope held film in a continuous loop threaded around a series of bobbins.

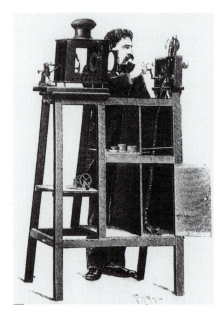

12.2   Placing a magic lantern behind the Lumière camera turned it into a projector.

12.3   The hinged portion of the Black Maria's roof, at the center, swung open for filming.

Since Edison believed that movies were a passing fad, he did not develop a system to project films onto a screen. This task was left to the Lumière brothers. They invented their own camera independently; it exposed a short roll of 35mm film and also served as a projector **(12.2).** On December 28, 1895, the Lumière brothers held one of the first public showings of motion pictures projected on a screen, at the Grand Café in Paris.

There had been several earlier public screenings, including one on November 1 of the same year by the German inventor Max Skladanowsky. But Skladanowsky's bulky machine required two strips of wide-gauge film running simultaneously and hence had less influence on the subsequent technological development of the cinema. Although the Lumières didn't wholly invent cinema, they largely determined the specific form the new medium was to take. Edison himself was soon to abandon Kinetoscopes and form his own production company to make films for theaters.

The first films were simple in form and style. They usually consisted of a single shot framing an action, usually at long-shot distance. In the first film studio, Edison's Black Maria **(12.3),** vaudeville entertainers, famous sports figures, and celebrities like Annie Oakley performed for the camera. A hinged portion of the roof opened to admit a patch of sunlight, and the entire building turned on a circular rail (visible in 12.3) to follow the sun's motion. The Lumières, however, took their cameras out to parks, gardens, beaches, and other public places to film everyday activities or news events, as in their *Arrival of a Train at La Ciotat* (5.61).

Until about 1903, most films showed scenic places or noteworthy events, but narrative form also entered the cinema from the beginning. Edison staged comic scenes, such as one copyrighted 1893 in which a drunken man struggles briefly with a policeman. The Lumières made a popular short *L'Arroseur arrosé* (*The Waterer Watered,* 1895), also a comic scene, in which a boy tricks a gardener into squirting himself with a hose (4.8).

After the initial success of the new medium, filmmakers had to find more complex or interesting formal properties to keep the public's interest. The Lumières sent camera operators all over the world to show films and to photograph important events and exotic locales. But after making a huge number of films in their first few years, the Lumières reduced their output, and they ceased filmmaking altogether in 1905.

12.4 Méliès's glass-sided studio admitted sunlight from a variety of directions.

In 1896, Georges Méliès purchased a projector from the British inventor Robert William Paul and soon built a camera based on the same mechanism. Méliès's first films resembled the Lumières' shots of everyday activities. But as we have seen (pp. 113–115), Méliès was also a magician, and he discovered the possibilities of simple special effects. In 1897, Méliès built his own studio. Unlike Edison's Black Maria, Méliès's studio was glass-sided like a greenhouse, so that the studio did not have to move with the sun **(12.4)**.

Méliès also began to build elaborate settings to create fantasy worlds within which his magical transformations could occur. We have already seen how Méliès thereby became the first master of mise-en-scene technique (4.3–4.6). From the simple filming of a magician performing a trick or two in a traditional stage setting, Méliès progressed to longer narratives with a series of tableaux. Each consisted of one shot, except when the transformations occurred. These were created by cuts designed to be imperceptible on the screen. He also adapted old stories, such as *Cinderella* (1899), or wrote his own. All these factors made Méliès's films extremely popular and widely imitated.

During this early period, films circulated freely from country to country. The French phonograph company Pathé Frères moved into filmmaking from 1901 on, establishing production and distribution branches in many countries. Soon Pathé was the largest film concern in the world, a position it retained until 1914, when the beginning of World War I forced it to cut back production. In England, several entrepreneurs managed to invent or obtain their own filmmaking equipment and made scenics, narratives, and trick films from 1895 into the early years of the 20th century. Members of the Brighton School (primarily G. Albert Smith and James Williamson), as well as others like Cecil Hepworth, shot their films on location or in simple open-air studios (as in **12.5**). Their innovative films circulated abroad and influenced other filmmakers. Pioneers in other countries invented or bought equipment and were soon making their own films of everyday scenes or fantasy transformations.

From about 1904 on, narrative form became the most prominent type of filmmaking in the commercial industry, and the worldwide popularity of cinema continued to grow. French, Italian, and American films dominated world markets. Later, World War I was to restrict the free flow of films from country to country, and Hollywood emerged as the dominant industrial force in world film production,

12.5 G. Albert Smith's *Santa Claus* (1898).

contributing to the creation of distinct differences in the formal traits of individual national cinemas.

The Development of the Classical Hollywood Cinema (1908–1927)

Edison was determined to exploit the money-making potential of his company's invention. He tried to force competing filmmakers out of business by bringing patent-violation suits against them. One other company, American Mutoscope & Biograph, managed to survive by inventing cameras that differed from Edison's patents. Other firms kept operating while Edison fought them in court. In 1908, Edison cooperated with Biograph to bring these other companies under control by forming the Motion Picture Patents Company (MPPC), a group of 10 firms based primarily in Chicago, New York, and New Jersey. Edison and Biograph were the only stockholders and patent owners. They licensed other members to make, distribute, and exhibit films.

The MPPC never succeeded in eliminating its competition. Numerous independent companies were established throughout this period. Biograph's most important director from 1908 on, D. W. Griffith, formed his own company in 1913, as did other filmmakers. The United States government brought suit against the MPPC in 1912; in 1915, it was declared a monopoly.

Around 1910, film companies began to move permanently to California. Some historians claim that the independent companies fled west to avoid the harassment of the MPPC, but some MPPC companies also made the move. Among the advantages of Hollywood were the climate, which permitted shooting year-round, and the great variety of terrains—mountains, ocean, desert, city—available for location shooting. Soon Hollywood and other small towns on the outskirts of Los Angeles played host to film production.

The demand for films was so great that no single studio could meet it. This was one of the factors that had led Edison to accept the existence of a group of other companies, although he tried to control them through his licensing procedure. Before 1920, the American industry assumed the structure that would continue for decades: a few large studios with individual artists under contract and a peripheral group of small, independent producers. In Hollywood, the studios developed a factory system, with each production under the control of the producer, who usually did not work on the actual making of the films. Even an independent director such as Buster Keaton, with his own studio, distributed his films through larger companies, first Metro and then United Artists.

Gradually, through the 1910s and 1920s, the smaller studios merged to form the large firms that still exist today. Famous Players joined with Jesse L. Lasky and then formed a distribution wing, Paramount. By the late 1920s, most of the major companies—MGM (a merger of Metro, Goldwyn, and Mayer), Fox Film Corporation (merged with 20th Century in 1935), Warner Bros., Universal, and Paramount—had been created. Though in competition with one another, these studios tended to cooperate to a degree, realizing that no one firm could satisfy the market.

Within this system of mass-production studios, the American cinema became definitively oriented toward narrative form. Early films had consisted primarily of tableaux or vaudeville skits (12.5). One of Edison's directors, Edwin S. Porter, made some of the first films to use principles of narrative continuity and development. Among these was *The Life of an American Fireman* (1903), which showed the race of the firefighters to rescue a mother and a child from a burning house. Although this film used several important classical narrative elements (a fireman's premonition of the disaster, a series of shots of the horse-drawn engine racing to the house), it still had not worked out the logic of temporal relations in cutting. Thus we see the rescue of a mother and her child twice, from both inside and outside the

CONNECT TO THE BLOG
Hollywood wasn't the only place where film form and style were developing in the 1910s. For an international survey of the important year 1913, see "Lucky '13," at
www.davidbordwell.net/blog/?p=2674.

"The cinema knows so well how to tell a story that perhaps there is an impression that it has always known how."

— André Gaudreault, film historian

house. Porter had not realized the possibility of intercutting the two locales within the action or matching on action to convey narrative information to the audience.

In 1903, Porter made *The Great Train Robbery,* in some ways a prototype for the classical American film. Here the action develops with a clear linearity of time, space, and logic. We follow each stage of the robbery **(12.6),** the pursuit, and the final defeat of the robbers. In 1905, Porter also created a simple parallel narrative in *The Kleptomaniac,* contrasting the fates of a rich woman and a starving woman who are both caught stealing.

British filmmakers were working along similar lines. Indeed, many historians now believe that Porter derived some of his editing techniques from films such as James Williamson's *Fire!* (1901) and G. A. Smith's *Mary Jane's Mishap* (1903). The most famous British film of this era was Lewin Fitzhamon's 1905 film *Rescued by Rover* (produced by a major British firm, Cecil Hepworth), which treated a kidnapping in a linear fashion similar to that of *The Great Train Robbery.* After the kidnapping, we see each stage of Rover's journey to find the child, his return to fetch the child's father, and their retracing of the route to the kidnapper's lair. All the shots along the route maintain consistent screen direction, so that the geography of the action is completely intelligible **(12.7, 12.8).**

In 1908, D. W. Griffith began his directing career. Over the next five years, he would make hundreds of one- and two-reelers (running about 15 and 30 minutes, respectively). These films created relatively complex narratives in short spans. Griffith certainly didn't invent all the devices with which he has been credited, but he did give many techniques strong narrative motivation. For example, a few other filmmakers had used simple last-minute rescues with crosscutting between the rescuers and victims, but Griffith developed and popularized this technique (6.101–6.104). By the time he made *The Birth of a Nation* (1915) and *Intolerance* (1916), Griffith was creating lengthy sequences by cutting among several different locales. During the early teens, he also directed his actors in an unusual way, concentrating on subtle changes in facial expression (4.32). To catch such nuances, he set up his camera closer than did many of his contemporaries, framing his actors in medium long shot or medium shot. Griffith's films were widely influential. In addition, his dynamic, rapid editing in the final chase scenes of *Intolerance* was to have a considerable impact on the Soviet Montage style of the 1920s.

The refinement of narratively motivated cutting occurs in the work of a number of important filmmakers of the period. One of these was Thomas H. Ince, a producer and director responsible for many films between 1910 and the end of World War I. He devised a unit system, whereby a single producer could oversee the making of several films at once. He also called for tight narratives, with no digressions or loose ends. *Civilization* (1915) and *The Italian* (1915) are good examples of films directed or supervised by Ince. He also supervised the popular Westerns of William S. Hart (p. 328), who directed many of his own films.

Another prolific filmmaker of this period (and later years as well) was Cecil B. De Mille. Not yet engaged in the creation of historical epics, De Mille made a series of feature-length dramas and comedies. His *The Cheat* (1915) reflects important changes occurring in the studio style between 1914 and 1917. During that period, the glass-roofed studios of the earlier period began to give way to studios dependent on artificial lighting rather than mixed daylight and electric lighting. *The Cheat* used spectacular effects of chiaroscuro, with only one or two bright sources of light and no fill light. According to legend, De Mille justified this effect to nervous exhibitors as *Rembrandt lighting.* This so-called Rembrandt, or *north,* lighting was to become part of the classical repertoire of lighting techniques. *The Cheat* also greatly impressed the French Impressionist filmmakers, who occasionally used similar stark lighting effects.

Like many American films of the teens, *The Cheat* uses a linear pattern of narrative. The first scene **(12.9)** introduces the hard lighting but also quickly establishes the Japanese businessman as a ruthless collector of objects; we see him

12.6   The robbers in the telegraph office in *The Great Train Robbery,* preparing to board the train seen through the window.

12.7   In *Rescued by Rover,* the heroic dog leads his master along a street from the right rear moving toward the left foreground . . .

12.8   . . . and the pair is moving from right to left as they reach their destination.

CONNECT TO THE BLOG
On two of the most important filmmakers of the early classical period, see our entries on William S. Hart in "Rio Jim, in discreet fragments," at www.davidbordwell.net/blog/?p=2590, and Douglas Fairbanks in "His Majesty the American," at www.davidbordwell.net/blog/?p=3044.

12.9 The opening scene of *The Cheat* introduces the branding motif . . .

12.10 . . . that returns later when the villain brands the heroine.

12.11 In Fred Niblo's *The Three Musketeers* (1921), a long shot of the group leads to . . .

12.12 . . . a cut-in to the central character, played by Douglas Fairbanks.

"That evening I tried to increase my knowledge of motion-picture technique by going to the movies. I sat with a stop watch and notebook and tried to estimate the number of cuts or scenes in a thousand-foot reel, the length of individual scenes, the distance of the subject from the camera, and various other technical details."

— King Vidor, director, recalling the night before he began directing his first film, c. 1912

burning his brand onto a small statue. The initial action motivates a later scene in which the businessman brands the heroine, who has fallen into his power by borrowing money from him **(12.10)**. *The Cheat* was evidence of the growing formal complexity of the Hollywood film.

The period 1909–1917 saw the development of the basic continuity principles. Eyeline matches occur with increasing frequency from 1910 on. The match on action developed at about the same time and was in common use by 1916. It appears in such Douglas Fairbanks films as *The Americano* (1916) and *Wild and Woolly* (1917). Shot/reverse shot was used only occasionally between 1911 and 1915, but it became widespread by 1916–1917; instances occur in such films as De Mille's *The Cheat* (1915), Hart's Western *The Narrow Trail* (1917), and Griffith's *A Romance of Happy Valley* (1919). During this period, films rarely violated the axis-of-action rule in using these techniques.

By the 1920s, the continuity system had become a standardized style that directors in the Hollywood studios used almost automatically to create coherent spatial and temporal relations within narratives. A match on action could provide a cut to a closer view in a scene **(12.11, 12.12)**. A three-way conversation around a table would no longer be handled in a single frontal shot. Note the clear spatial relations in **12.13–12.17**, shots from *Are Parents People?* (Malcolm St. Clair, 1925). At the time, screen direction was usually respected, as in this case. When an awkward match might have resulted from the joining of two shots, the filmmakers could cover it by inserting a dialogue title.

Keaton's *Our Hospitality* (1923), which we examined in Chapter 4, provides another early example of a classical narrative. Keaton's mastery of classical form and style are evident in the carefully motivated recurrences of the various narrative elements and in the straightforward causal development from the death of Willie McKay's father in the feud to Willie's final resolution of the feud.

By the end of the silent era, in the late 1920s, the classical Hollywood cinema had developed into a sophisticated movement, but the Hollywood product was remarkably standardized. All of the major studios used the same production system, with a similar division of labor at each. Independent production was less important. Some independent firms made low-budget films, often Westerns, for small and rural theaters. Even powerful Hollywood stars and producers had trouble remaining independent. Keaton gave up his small studio in 1928 to go to MGM under contract; there his career declined, partly because of the incompatibility of his old working methods with the rigid production patterns of the huge studio. Griffith, Mary Pickford, Fairbanks, and Charles Chaplin were better off. Forming a distributing corporation of their own, United Artists, in 1919, they were able to continue independent production at small companies under their umbrella corporation, though Griffith's company soon failed, and the careers of Fairbanks and Pickford declined soon after the introduction of sound.

12.13 In an establishing shot from *Are Parents People?* the daughter sits down at the table.

12.14 In the medium shot she looks leftward toward her father . . .

12.15 . . . who looks rightward at her in the reverse shot.

12.16 The daughter then turns to look to the right at her mother . . .

12.17 . . . who also returns her gaze in reverse shot.

12.18 *Madame Dubarry:* a crowd scene in the Tribunal of the French Revolution.

There were alternative kinds of films being made during the silent era—most of them in other countries. After examining these alternative movements, we'll return to consider the classical Hollywood cinema after the coming of sound.

German Expressionism (1919–1926)

At the start of World War I, the output of the German film industry was relatively small, though some impressive pictures had been made there. Germany's 2000 movie theaters were playing mostly French, American, Italian, and Danish films. America and France banned German films from their screens immediately, but Germany was not even in a solid enough position to ban French and American films, for then the theaters would have had little to show.

To combat imported competition, as well as to create its own propaganda films, the German government began to support the film industry. In 1916, film imports were banned except from neutral Denmark. Production increased rapidly; from a dozen small companies in 1911, the number grew to 131 by 1918. But government policy encouraged these companies to band together into cartels.

The war was unpopular with many in Germany, and rebellious tendencies increased after the success of the Russian Revolution in 1917. Widespread strikes and antiwar petitions were organized during the winter of 1916–1917. To promote pro-war films, the government, the Deutsche Bank, and large industrial concerns combined several small film firms to create the large company UFA (short for Universum Film Aktiengesellschaft) in late 1917. Backed by these essentially conservative interests, UFA was a move toward control of not only the German market but the postwar international market as well.

With this huge financial backing, UFA was able to gather superb technicians and build the best-equipped studios in Europe. These studios later attracted foreign filmmakers, including the young Alfred Hitchcock. During the 1920s, Germany coproduced many films with companies in other countries, thus helping to spread German stylistic influence abroad.

In late 1918, with the end of the war, the need for overt militarist propaganda disappeared. Although mainstream dramas and comedies continued to be made, the German film industry concentrated on three genres. One was the internationally popular adventure serial, featuring spy rings, clever detectives, or exotic settings. Another was a brief sex exploitation cycle, which dealt "educationally" with such topics as homosexuality and prostitution. Also, UFA set out to copy the popular Italian historical epics of the prewar period.

This last type of film proved financially successful. In spite of continued bans on and prejudice against German films in America, England, and France, UFA finally was able to break into the international market. In September 1919, Ernst Lubitsch's *Madame Dubarry,* an epic of the French Revolution **(12.18),** inaugurated

CONNECT TO THE BLOG

For a discussion of the restoration of another historical epic by Lubitsch, *Das Weib des Pharao,* see "Preserving two masters," at

www.davidbordwell.net/blog/?p=3116.

"Everything is composition; any image whatsoever could be stopped on the screen and would be a marvellously balanced painting of forms and lights. Also, it is one of the films which leaves in our memories the clearest visions—precise and of a slightly static beauty. But even more than painting, it is animated architecture."

— François Berge, French critic, on Fritz Lang's *The Nibelungen*

12.19   The heroine's flamboyantly Expressionistic bedroom in Robert Wiene's *Genuine.* As she leans backwards, she blends with the curved, spiky shapes behind her.

12.20   The insane asylum set of *The Cabinet of Dr. Caligari.*

the magnificent UFA Palast theater in Berlin. This film helped reopen the world film market to Germany. Released as *Passion* in the United States, this film was extremely popular. It was not enthusiastically received in France, where its premiere was considerably delayed by charges that it was anti-French propaganda. But it did well in most markets, and other Lubitsch historical films were soon exported. In 1923, he became the first German director to be hired by Hollywood.

Some small companies briefly remained independent. Among these was Erich Pommer's Decla (later Decla-Bioscop). In 1919, the firm undertook to produce an unconventional script by two unknowns, Carl Mayer and Hans Janowitz. These young writers wanted *The Cabinet of Dr. Caligari* to be made in an unusually stylized way. The three designers assigned to the film—Hermann Warm, Walter Reimann, and Walter Röhrig—suggested that it be done in an Expressionist style. As an avant-garde movement, Expressionism had first been important in painting (starting about 1910) and had been quickly taken up in theater, then in literature and architecture. Now company officials consented to try it in the cinema, apparently believing that this might be a selling point in the international market.

This belief was vindicated in 1920 when Decla's inexpensive film *The Cabinet of Dr. Caligari* (1920) created a sensation in Berlin and then in the United States, France, and other countries. Because of its success, other films in the Expressionist style soon followed. The result was a stylistic movement in cinema that lasted several years.

The success of *Caligari* and other Expressionist films kept Germany's avantgarde directors largely within the industry. A few experimental filmmakers made abstract films, like Viking Eggeling's *Diagonal-symphonie* (1923), or Dada films influenced by the international art movement, like Hans Richter's *Ghosts Before Breakfast* (1928). Big firms such as UFA (which absorbed Decla-Bioscop in 1921), as well as smaller companies, invested in Expressionist films because these films could compete with those of America. Indeed, by the mid-1920s, the most prominent German films were widely regarded as among the best in the world.

The first film of the movement, *Caligari,* is also one of the most typical examples. One of its designers, Warm, claimed, "The film image must become graphic art." *Caligari,* with its extreme stylization, was indeed like a moving Expressionist painting or woodcut print. In contrast to French Impressionism, which bases its style primarily on cinematography and editing, German Expressionism depends heavily on mise-en-scene. Shapes are distorted and exaggerated unrealistically for expressive purposes (4.2). Actors often wear heavy makeup and move in jerky or slow, sinuous patterns. Most important, all of the elements of the mise-en-scene interact graphically to create an overall composition. Characters do not simply exist within a setting but rather form visual elements that merge with the setting **(12.19).** We have already seen an example of this in 4.105, where the character Cesare collapses in a stylized forest, his body and outstretched arms echoing the shapes of the trees' trunks and branches.

In *Caligari,* the Expressionist stylization functions to convey the distorted viewpoint of a madman. We see the world as the hero imagines it to be. This narrative function of the settings becomes explicit at one point, when the hero enters an asylum in his pursuit of Caligari. As he pauses to look around, he stands at the center of a pattern of radiating black-and-white lines that run across the floor and up the walls **(12.20).** The world of the film is literally a projection of the hero's vision.

Later, as Expressionism became an accepted style, filmmakers didn't motivate Expressionist style as the narrative point of view of mad characters. Instead, Expressionism often functioned to create stylized situations for fantasy and horror stories (as with *Waxworks,* 1924, and *Nosferatu,* 1922; see 9.16) or historical epics (as with *The Nibelungen,* 1923–1924). Expressionist films depended greatly on their designers. In the German studios, a film's designer received a relatively high salary and was often mentioned prominently in the advertisements.

12.21 *Metropolis* contained many large, Expressionistic sets, including this garden, with pillars that appear to be made of melting clay.

12.22 In *M,* reflections and a display of knives in a shop window create a semi-abstract composition that mirrors the murderer's obsession.

A combination of circumstances led to the disappearance of the movement. The rampant inflation of the early 1920s in Germany actually favored Expressionist filmmaking, partly by making it easy for German exporters to sell their films cheaply abroad. Inflation discouraged imports, however, for the tumbling exchange rate of the mark made foreign purchases prohibitively expensive. But in 1924, the U.S. Dawes Plan helped to stabilize the German economy, and foreign films came in more frequently, offering a degree of competition unknown in Germany for nearly a decade. Expressionist film budgets, however, were climbing. The last major films of the movement, F. W. Murnau's *Faust* (1926) and Fritz Lang's *Metropolis* (1927), were costly epics that helped drive UFA deeper into financial difficulty, leading Erich Pommer to quit and try his luck briefly in America **(12.21).** Other personnel were lured away to Hollywood as well. Murnau left after finishing *Faust,* his last German film. Major actors (such as Conrad Veidt and Emil Jannings) and cinematographers (such as Karl Freund) went to Hollywood as well. Lang stayed on, but after the criticisms of *Metropolis*'s extravagance on its release, he formed his own production company and turned to other styles in his later German films. At the beginning of the Nazi regime in 1933, he too left the country.

Trying to counter the stiffer competition from imported Hollywood films after 1924, the Germans also began to imitate the American product. The resulting films, though sometimes impressive, diluted the unique qualities of the Expressionist style. Thus, by 1927, Expressionism as a movement had died out. But as Georges Sadoul has pointed out, an expressionist (spelled with a lowercase "e" to distinguish it from the Expressionist movement proper) tendency lingered on in many of the German films of the late 1920s and even into such 1930s films as Lang's *M* (1930; see **12.22**) and *Testament of Dr. Mabuse* (1932). And because many of the German filmmakers came to the United States, Hollywood horror films also displayed film noir's expressionist tendencies in their settings and lighting. Although the German movement lasted only about seven years, expressionism has never entirely died out as a trend in film style.

French Impressionism and Surrealism (1918–1930)

During the silent era, a number of film movements in France posed major alternatives to classical Hollywood narrative form. Some of these alternatives, such as abstract cinema and Dada filmmaking, are not specifically French and constituted instead a part of the growing international avant-garde. But two alternatives to the American mode remained quite localized. Impressionism was an avant-garde style that operated largely within the film industry. Most of the Impressionist filmmakers started out working for major French companies, and some of their avant-garde works proved financially successful. In the mid-1920s, most formed their own independent companies but remained within the mainstream commercial industry by renting studio facilities and releasing their films through established firms. The other alternative movement, Surrealism, lay largely outside the film industry. Allied with the Surrealist movement in other arts, these filmmakers relied on their own means and private patronage. France in the 1920s offers a striking instance of how different film movements may coexist in the same time and place.

Impressionism

World War I struck a serious blow to the French film industry. Personnel were conscripted, many film studios were shifted to wartime uses, and much export was halted. Yet the two major firms, Pathé Frères and Léon Gaumont, also controlled circuits of theaters. They needed to fill vacant screens, and so in 1915, American films began increasingly to flood into France. Represented by De Mille's *The Cheat* and films featuring Pearl White, Douglas Fairbanks, Charlie Chaplin, and William S. Hart, the Hollywood cinema dominated the market by the end of 1917. After the war, French filmmaking never fully recovered: In the 1920s, French audiences saw eight times more Hollywood footage than domestic footage. The film industry tried in several ways to recapture the market, mostly through imitation of Hollywood production methods and genres. Artistically, however, the most significant move was the firms' encouragement of younger French directors: Abel Gance, Louis Delluc, Germaine Dulac, Marcel L'Herbier, and Jean Epstein.

These directors differed from their predecessors. The previous generation had regarded filmmaking as a commercial craft, but the younger filmmakers wrote essays proclaiming cinema to be an art comparable to poetry, painting, and music. Cinema should, they said, be purely itself and should not borrow from the theater or literature. Impressed by the verve and energy of the American cinema, the young theorists compared Chaplin to Nijinsky and the films of Rio Jim to *The Song of Roland*. Cinema should, above all, be (like music) an occasion for the artist to express feelings. Gance, Delluc, Dulac, L'Herbier, Epstein, and other, more tangential members of the movement sought to put this aesthetic into practice as filmmakers.

Between 1918 and 1928, in a series of extraordinary films, the younger directors experimented with cinema in ways that posed an alternative to the dominant Hollywood formal principles. For these directors, cinema was an art of emotion, so the intimate psychological narrative dominated their practice. The interactions of a few characters, usually a love triangle (as in Delluc's *L'Inondation,* 1924; Epstein's *Coeur fidèle,* 1923, and *La Belle nivernaise,* 1923; and Gance's *La Dixième symphonie,* 1918), would serve as the basis for the filmmaker's exploration of fleeting moods and shifting sensations.

As in the Hollywood cinema, psychological causes were paramount, but the school gained the name Impressionist because of its interest in giving narration considerable psychological depth, revealing the play of a character's consciousness. The interest falls not on external physical behavior but on *inner* action. To a degree unprecedented in international filmmaking, Impressionist films manipulate plot time and subjectivity. To depict memories, flashbacks are common; sometimes the bulk of a film will be one flashback or a series of them. Even more striking is the films' insistence on registering characters' dreams, fantasies, and mental states. Dulac's *The Smiling Mme. Beudet* (1923) consists almost entirely of the main character's fantasy life, her imaginary escape from a dull marriage. Despite its epic

"Another period arrived, that of the psychological and impressionist film. It would seem stupid to place a character in a given situation without penetrating into the secret realm of his inner life, and the actor's performance is explained by the play of thoughts and of visualized sensations."

— Germaine Dulac, director

length (over five hours), Gance's *La Roue* (1922) rests essentially on the erotic relations among only four people, and the director seeks to trace the development of each character's feelings in great detail. Impressionism's emphasis on personal emotion gives the films' narratives an intensely psychological focus.

The Impressionist movement earned its name as well for its use of film style. The filmmakers experimented with ways of rendering mental states by means of cinematography and editing. In Impressionist films, irises, masks, and superimpositions function as traces of characters' thoughts and feelings (**12.23**). In *La Roue,* the image of Norma is superimposed over the smoke from a locomotive, representing the fantasy of the engine driver, who is in love with her.

To intensify the subjectivity, the Impressionists' cinematography and editing present characters' perceptual experience, their optical impressions. These films use a great deal of point-of-view cutting, showing a shot of a character looking at something, then a shot of that thing, from an angle and distance replicating the character's vantage point. When a character in an Impressionist film gets drunk or dizzy, the filmmaker renders that experience through distorted or filtered shots or vertiginous camera movements. In **12.24,** from L'Herbier's *El Dorado* (1920), a man is drinking in a cabaret.

The Impressionists also experimented with pronounced rhythmic editing to suggest the pace of an experience as a character feels it, moment by moment. During scenes of violence or emotional turmoil, the rhythm accelerates—the shots get shorter and shorter, building to a climax, sometimes with shots only a few frames long. In *La Roue,* a train crash is presented in accelerating shots ranging from 13 frames down to 2, and a man's last thoughts before he falls from a cliff are rendered in a blur of many single-frame shots (the first known use of such rapid editing). In *Coeur fidèle,* lovers at a fair ride in whirling swings, and Epstein presents their giddiness in a series of shots 4 frames, then 2 frames, long. Several Impressionist films use a dance to motivate a markedly accelerated cutting rhythm. More generally, the comparison of cinema to music encouraged the Impressionists to explore rhythmic editing. In such ways, subjective shooting and editing patterns function within Impressionist films to reinforce the narrative treatment of psychological states.

Impressionist form created certain demands on film technology. Gance, the boldest innovator in this respect, used his epic *Napoléon* (1927) as a chance to try new lenses (even a 275mm telephoto), multiple frame images (called Polyvision), and widescreen ratio (the celebrated triptychs; see 5.63). The most influential Impressionist technological innovation was the development of new means of frame mobility. If the camera was to represent a character's eyes, it should be able to move with the ease of a person. Impressionists strapped their cameras to cars, carousels, and locomotives. For Gance's *Napoléon,* the camera manufacturer Debrie perfected a handheld model that let the operator move on roller skates. Gance lashed the machine to wheels, cables, pendulums, and bobsleds. In *L'Argent* (1928), L'Herbier sent his camera gliding through huge rooms and even plummeting straight down toward the crowd from the dome of the Paris stock exchange (**12.25**).

Such innovations had given French filmmakers the hope that their films could win the popularity granted to Hollywood's product. During the 1920s, the Impressionists operated somewhat independently; they formed their own production companies and leased studio facilities from Pathé and Gaumont in exchange for distribution rights. Some Impressionist films did prove moderately popular with French audiences. But by 1929, most foreign audiences had not taken to Impressionism; its experimentation was attuned to elite tastes. Moreover, although production costs were rising, Impressionists such as Gance and L'Herbier became even more free-spending. As a result, filmmakers' companies either went out of business or were absorbed by the big firms. Two behemoth productions of the decade, *Napoléon* and *L'Argent,* failed and were reedited by the producers; they were among the last Impressionist films released. With the arrival of the sound film, the French film industry tightened its belt and had no money to risk on experiments.

12.23   In *Coeur fidèle,* the heroine looks out a window, and a superimposition of the foul jetsam of the waterfront conveys her dejection at working as a barmaid in a dockside tavern.

12.24   In *El Dorado,* a man's tipsiness is conveyed by means of a curved mirror that stretches his body sideways.

12.25   In *L'Argent,* the camera drops toward the floor of the stock exchange in an effort to convey the traders's frenzied excitement.

CONNECT TO THE BLOG
We review the DVD of *La Roue* in "An old-fashioned, sentimental avant-garde film."

See www.davidbordwell.net/blog/?p=3720.

Impressionism as a distinct movement may be said to have ceased by 1929. But the influences of Impressionist form—the psychological narrative, subjective camera work, and editing—were more long-lived. They continued to operate, for example, in the work of Alfred Hitchcock and Maya Deren, in Hollywood montage sequences, and in certain American genres and styles (the horror film, film noir).

Surrealism

Whereas the French Impressionist filmmakers worked within the commercial film industry, the Surrealist filmmakers relied on private patronage and screened their work in small artists' gatherings. Such isolation is hardly surprising, since Surrealist cinema was a more radical movement, producing films that perplexed and shocked most audiences.

Surrealist cinema was directly linked to Surrealism in literature and painting. According to its spokesperson, André Breton, "Surrealism [was] based on the belief in the superior reality of certain forms of association, heretofore neglected, in the omnipotence of dreams, in the undirected play of thought." Influenced by Freudian psychology, Surrealist art sought to register the hidden currents of the unconscious, "in the absence of any control exercised by reason, and beyond any aesthetic and moral preoccupation."

Automatic writing and painting, the search for bizarre or evocative imagery, the deliberate avoidance of rationally explicable form or style: these became features of Surrealism as it developed in the period 1924–1929. From the start, the Surrealists were attracted to the cinema, especially admiring films that presented untamed desire or the fantastic and marvelous (for example, slapstick comedies, *Nosferatu,* and serials about mysterious supercriminals). In due time, painters such as Man Ray and Salvador Dalí and writers such as Antonin Artaud began dabbling in cinema, while the young Spaniard Luis Buñuel, drawn to Surrealism, became its most famous filmmaker.

Surrealist cinema is antinarrative, attacking causality itself. If rationality is to be fought, causal connections among events must be dissolved, as in *The Seashell and the Clergyman* (1928; scripted by Artaud, filmed by the Impressionist Germaine Dulac; see **(12.26).** In Dalí and Buñuel's *Un Chien andalou* (*An Andalusian Dog,* 1928) the hero drags two pianos, stuffed with dead donkeys, across a parlor. In Buñuel's *L'Age d'or* (1930), a woman begins obsessively sucking the toes of a statue.

Many Surrealist films tease us to find a narrative logic that is simply absent. Causality is as evasive as in a dream. Instead, we find events juxtaposed for their disturbing effect. The hero gratuitously shoots a child (*L'Age d'or*), a woman closes her eyes only to reveal eyes painted on her eyelids (Ray's *Emak Bakia,* 1927), and—most famous of all—a man strops a razor and deliberately slits the eyeball of an unprotesting woman (*Un Chien andalou,* **12.27**). An Impressionist film would motivate such events as a character's dreams or hallucinations, but in these films, character psychology is all but nonexistent. Sexual desire and ecstasy, violence, blasphemy, and bizarre humor furnish events that Surrealist cinema employs with a disregard for conventional narrative principles. The hope was that the free form of the film would arouse the deepest impulses of the viewer. Buñuel called *Un Chien andalou* "a passionate call to murder."

The style of Surrealist cinema is eclectic. Mise-en-scene is often influenced by Surrealist painting. The ants in *Un Chien andalou* come from Dalí's pictures; the pillars and city squares of *The Seashell and the Clergyman* hark back to the Italian painter Giorgio de Chirico. Surrealist editing is an amalgam of some Impressionist devices (many dissolves and superimpositions) and some devices of the dominant cinema. The shocking eyeball slitting at the start of *Un Chien andalou* relies on some principles of continuity editing (and indeed on the Kuleshov effect). However, discontinuous editing is also commonly used to fracture any organized temporal-spatial coherence. In *Un Chien andalou,* the heroine locks the man out of a room

12.26   *The Seashell and the Clergyman:* the clergyman's distorted view of a threatening military officer, inexplicably dressed in baby's clothes.

12.27   The shocking eye-slitting scene in *Un chien andalou.*

only to turn to find him inexplicably behind her. On the whole, Surrealist film style refused to canonize any particular devices, since that would order and rationalize what had to be an "undirected play of thought."

The fortunes of Surrealist cinema shifted with changes in the art movement as a whole. By late 1929, when Breton joined the Communist Party, Surrealists were embroiled in internal dissension about whether communism was a political equivalent of Surrealism. Buñuel left France for a brief stay in Hollywood and then returned to Spain. The chief patron of Surrealist filmmaking, the Vicomte de Noailles, supported Jean Vigo's *Zéro de Conduite* (1933), a film of Surrealist ambitions, but then stopped sponsoring the avant-garde. Thus, as a unified movement, French Surrealism was no longer viable after 1930. Individual Surrealists continued to work, however. The most famous was Buñuel, who continued to work in his own brand of the Surrealist style for 50 years. His later films, such as *Belle de Jour* (1967) and *The Discreet Charm of the Bourgeoisie* (1972), continue the Surrealist tradition.

Soviet Montage (1924–1930)

Following the Russian Revolution in October 1917, the new Soviet government faced the difficult task of controlling all sectors of life. Like other industries, the film production and distribution systems took years to build up a substantial output that could serve the aims of the new government.

During World War I, there were a number of private production companies operating in Moscow and Petersburg. With most imports cut off, these companies did quite well making films for the domestic market. The most distinctive Russian films made during the mid-1910s were slow-paced melodramas that concentrated on bravura performances by actors playing characters caught in extremely emotional situations. Such films showcased the talents of Ivan Mozhukin and other popular stars **(12.28)** and were aimed mainly at the large Russian audience, seldom being seen abroad.

12.28 In Yakov Protazanov's 1916 *The Queen of Spades*, the gambling-addicted hero, played by Mozhukin, imagines himself winning at cards, with his vision superimposed at the right.

These film companies resisted the move made directly after the Revolution to nationalize all private property. They simply refused to supply films to theaters operating under the control of the government. In July 1918, the government's film subsection of the State Commission of Education put strict controls on the existing supplies of raw film stock. As a result, producers began hoarding their stock; the largest firms took all the equipment they could and fled to other countries. Some companies made films commissioned by the government, while hoping that the Reds would lose the Civil War and that things would return to pre-Revolutionary conditions.

In the face of shortages of equipment and difficult living conditions, a few young filmmakers made tentative moves that would result in the development of a national cinema movement. Dziga Vertov began working on documentary footage of the war; at age 20, he was placed in charge of all newsreels. Lev Kuleshov, teaching in the newly founded State School on Cinema Art, performed a series of experiments by editing footage from different sources into a whole that creates an impression of continuity. Kuleshov was perhaps the most conservative of the young Soviet filmmakers, since he was basically trying to systematize principles of editing similar to the continuity practices of the classical Hollywood cinema (pp. 227–228). Thus, even before they were able to make films, Kuleshov and his young pupils were working at the first film school in the world and writing theoretical essays on the new art form. This grounding in theory would be the basis of the Montage style.

In 1920, Sergei Eisenstein worked briefly in a train carrying propaganda to the troops in the Civil War. He returned that year to Moscow to produce plays in a workers' theater. In May 1920, Vsevolod Pudovkin made his acting debut in a play presented by Kuleshov's State Film School. He had been inspired to go into filmmaking by seeing Griffith's *Intolerance,* which was first shown widely in Russia in

12.29 *The Extraordinary Adventures of Mr. West in the Land of the Bolsheviks:* a gang of thieves terrifies the naive American, Mr. West, by presenting him with clichéd caricatures of fierce Soviet revolutionaries.

"Everyone who has had in his hands a piece of film to be edited knows by experience how neutral it remains, even though a part of a planned sequence, until it is joined with another piece, when it suddenly acquires and conveys a sharper and quite different meaning than that planned for it at the time of filming."

— Sergei Eisenstein, director

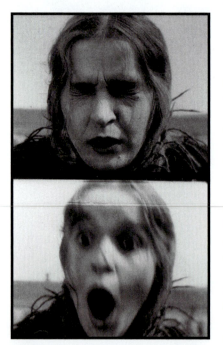

12.30 In *House on Trubnoi Square,* Montage director Boris Barnet uses a jump cut to convey the heroine's sudden realization that a streetcar is headed straight for her.

1919. American films, particularly those of D. W. Griffith, Douglas Fairbanks, and Mary Pickford, which kept circulating to fill the void left by the low output of new Soviet productions, were a tremendous influence on the filmmakers of the emerging Soviet movement.

None of the important filmmakers of the Montage style was a veteran of the pre-Revolutionary industry. All came from other fields (for example, Eisenstein from engineering and Pudovkin from chemistry) and discovered the cinema in the midst of the Revolution's ferment. The Czarist-era filmmakers who remained active in the USSR in the 1920s tended to stick to older traditions. One popular director of the Czarist period, Yakov Protazanov, went abroad briefly after the Revolution but returned to continue making films whose style and form owed almost nothing to the theory and practice of the new filmmakers.

Protazanov's return coincided with a general loosening of government restrictions on private enterprise. In 1921, the country was facing tremendous problems, including a widespread famine. In order to facilitate the production and distribution of goods, Lenin instituted the New Economic Policy (NEP), which for several years permitted private management of business. For film, the NEP meant a sudden reappearance of film stock and equipment belonging to the producers who had not emigrated. Slowly, Soviet production began to grow as private firms made more films. The government attempted, with little success, to control the film industry by creating a central distribution company, Goskino, in 1922.

"Of all the arts, for us the cinema is the most important," Lenin stated in 1922. Since Lenin saw film as a powerful tool for education, the first films encouraged by the government were documentaries and newsreels such as Vertov's newsreel series *Kino-Pravda,* which began in May 1922. Fictional films were also being made from 1917 on, but it was not until 1923 that a Georgian feature, *Red Imps,* became the first Soviet film to compete successfully with the foreign films predominant on Soviet screens. (And not until 1927 did the Soviet industry's income from its own films top that of the films it imported.)

The Soviet Montage style displayed tentative beginnings in 1924, with Kuleshov's class from the State Film School presenting *The Extraordinary Adventures of Mr. West in the Land of the Bolsheviks* **(12.29).** This delightful film, along with Kuleshov's next film, *The Death Ray* (1925), showed that Soviet directors could apply Montage principles and come up with amusing satires or exciting adventures as entertaining as the Hollywood product.

Eisenstein's first feature, *Strike,* was released early in 1925 and initiated the movement proper. His second, *Potemkin,* premiered later in 1925, was successful abroad and drew the attention of other countries to the new movement. In the next few years, Eisenstein, Pudovkin, Vertov, and the Ukrainian Alexander Dovzhenko created a series of films that are classics of the Montage style.

In their writings and films, these directors championed the powers of editing. Until the late 1910s, most Russian fiction films had based their scenes around lengthy, fairly distant shots that captured the actors' performances. Analytical editing was rare. But films from Hollywood and from the French Impressionist filmmakers told their stories through fast cutting, including frequent close framings. Inspired by these imports, the young Soviet directors declared that a film's power arose from the combination of shots. Montage seemed to be the way forward for modern cinema.

Not all of the young theoreticians agreed on exactly what the Montage approach to editing should be. Pudovkin, for example, believed that shots were like bricks, to be joined together to build a sequence. Eisenstein disagreed, saying that the maximum effect would be gained if the shots did not fit together perfectly, if they created a jolt for the spectator. Many filmmakers in the montage movement followed this approach **(12.30).** Eisenstein also favored juxtaposing shots in order to create a concept, as we have already seen with his use of conceptual editing in

12.31 In *Storm over Asia,* after a medium close-up of an elaborate piece of jewelry being lowered over the head of a priest, there is a cut . . .

12.32 . . . to a close-up of a servant placing a necklace around the neck of the officer's wife . . .

12.33 . . . then a cut back to a large headdress being positioned on a priest's head . . .

12.34 . . . juxtaposed with a close-up of a tiara being set on the wife's head.

October (pp. 422–425). Vertov disagreed with both theorists, favoring a cinema-eye approach to recording and shaping documentary reality (pp. 257–260).

Pudovkin's *Storm over Asia* makes use of conceptual editing similar to that of Eisenstein's *October.* Shots of a military officer and his wife being dressed in their accessories are intercut with shots of the preparation at the temple **(12.31–12.34).** Pudovkin's parallel montage points up the absurdity of both rituals.

The Montagists' approach to narrative form set them apart from the cinemas of other countries. Soviet narrative films tended to downplay character psychology as a cause; instead, social forces provided the major causes. Characters were interesting for the way these social causes affected their lives. As a result, films of the Soviet Montage movement did not always have a single protagonist. Social groups could form a collective hero, as in several of Eisenstein's films. In keeping with this downplaying of individual personalities, Soviet filmmakers often avoided well-known actors, preferring to cast parts by searching out nonactors. This practice was called **typage,** since the filmmakers would often choose an individual whose appearance seemed at once to convey the type of character he or she was to play. Except for the hero, Pudovkin used nonactors to play all of the Mongols in *Storm over Asia.*

By the end of the 1920s, each of the major directors of this movement had made about four important films. The decline of the movement was not caused primarily by industrial and economic factors as in Germany and France. Instead, the government strongly discouraged the Montage style. By the late 1920s, Vertov, Eisenstein, and Dovzhenko were being criticized for their excessively formal and esoteric approaches. In 1929, Eisenstein went to Hollywood to study the new technique of sound; by the time he returned in 1932, the attitude of the film industry had changed. While he was away, a few filmmakers carried their Montage experiments into sound cinema in the early 1930s. But the Soviet authorities, under Stalin's direction, encouraged filmmakers to create simple films that would be readily understandable to all audiences. Stylistic experimentation or nonrealistic subject matter was often criticized or censored.

This trend culminated in 1934, when the government instituted a new artistic policy called Socialist Realism. This policy dictated that all artworks must depict revolutionary development while being firmly grounded in realism. The great Soviet directors continued to make films, occasionally masterpieces, but the Montage experiments of the 1920s had to be discarded or modified. Eisenstein managed to continue his work on Montage but occasionally incurred the wrath of the authorities up until his death in 1948. As a movement, the Soviet Montage style can be said to have ended by 1933, with the release of such films as Vertov's *Enthusiasm* (1931) and Pudovkin's *Deserter* (1933).

The Classical Hollywood Cinema After the Coming of Sound

The introduction of sound technology came about through the efforts of Hollywood firms to widen their power. During the mid-1920s, Warner Bros. was expanding its facilities and holdings. One of these expansions was the investment in a sound system using records in synchronization with film images (12.35).

By releasing *Don Juan* (1926) with orchestral accompaniment and sound effects on disc, along with a series of vaudeville shorts with singing and talking, Warner Bros. began to popularize the idea of sound films. In 1927, *The Jazz Singer* (a part-talkie with some scenes accompanied only by music) was a tremendous success, and the Warner Bros. investment began to pay off.

The success of *Don Juan, The Jazz Singer,* and the shorts convinced other studios that sound contributed to profitable filmmaking. Unlike the early period of filmmaking and the Motion Picture Patents Company, there was now no fierce competition within the industry. Instead, firms realized that whatever sound system the studios finally adopted, it would have to be compatible with the projection machinery of any theater. Eventually, a sound-on-film rather than a sound-on-disc system became the standard and continues so to the present. (That is, as we saw in Chapter 1, the sound track is printed on the strip of film alongside the image.) By 1930, most theaters in America were wired for sound.

For a few years, sound created a setback for Hollywood film style. The camera had to be put inside a sound booth so that its motor noise would not be picked up by the microphone. The components of a dialogue scene in a 1928 MGM film can be seen in 12.36. The camera operator could hear only through his earphones, and the camera could not move except for short pans to reframe. The bulky microphone, on the table at the right, also did not move. The actors had to stay within a limited space if their speech was to register on the track. The result of such restrictions was a brief period of static films resembling stage plays.

> *"You know, when talkies first came in they were fascinated by sound—they had frying eggs and they had this and that—and then people became infatuated with the movement of the camera; I believe, the big thing right now is to move a handheld camera. I think the director and his camerawork should not intrude on the story."*
>
> — George Cukor, director

12.35   An early projector with a turntable (lower center) attached.

12.36   A posed publicity still demonstrated the limitations of early sound filming.

Still, from the very beginning of sound filming, solutions were found for these problems. Sometimes several cameras, all in soundproof booths, would record the scene from different angles simultaneously. The resulting footage could be cut together to provide a standard continuity editing pattern in a scene, with all the sound synchronized. The whole camera booth might be mounted on wheels to create camera movements, or a scene might be shot silent and a sound track added later. Early sound films such as Rouben Mamoulian's *Applause* (1929) demonstrate that the camera soon regained a great flexibility of movement. Later, smaller cases, enclosing only the camera body, replaced the cumbersome booths. These *blimps* (**12.37**) permitted cinematographers to place the camera on movable supports. Similarly, microphones mounted on booms and hanging over the heads of the actors could also follow moving action without a loss of recording quality.

Once camera movement and subject movement were restored to sound films, filmmakers continued to use many of the stylistic characteristics developed in Hollywood during the silent period. Diegetic sound provided a powerful addition to the system of continuity editing. A line of dialogue could continue over a cut, creating smooth temporal continuity. (See pp. 248–249.)

Within the overall tradition of continuity style and classical narrative form, each of the large studios developed a distinctive approach of its own. Thus MGM, for example, became the prestige studio, with a huge number of stars and technicians under long-term contract. MGM lavished money on settings, costumes, and special effects, as in *The Good Earth* (1937), with its locust attack, and *San Francisco* (1936), in which the great earthquake of 1906 is spectacularly re-created. Warner Bros., in spite of its success with sound, was still a relatively small studio and specialized in less expensive genre pictures. Its series of gangster films (*Little Caesar, Public Enemy*) and musicals (*42nd Street, Gold Diggers of 1933, Dames*) were among the studio's most successful products. Even lower on the ladder of prestige was Universal, which depended on imaginative filmmaking rather than established stars or expensive sets in its atmospheric horror films, such as *Frankenstein* (1931) and *The Old Dark House* (1932; **12.38**).

CONNECT TO THE BLOG
Some of these early sound and color films can be hard to find, but we look at some DVD collections that provide lots of information and clips in "All singing! All dancing! All teaching!"
See www.davidbordwell.net/blog/?p=1783.

12.37   A blimped camera during the early 1930s allowed the camera tripod to be placed on a rolling dolly.

12.38   Heavy shadows, spiky shapes, and eccentric performances mixed a menacing atmosphere with a touch of humor in *The Old Dark Horse.*

12.39   *Under a Texas Moon* (1930): typical two-strip Technicolor, with mostly orange and green hues.

CONNECT TO THE BLOG
B-movies were a major part of 1930s film production. Our colleagues join us in discussing just what constituted a B-movie in Hollywood in "Bs in their bonnets: A three-day conversation well worth the reading."
See www.davidbordwell.net/blog/?p=438.
More specifically, we consider the Charlie Chan and Mr. Moto series in "Charlie, meet Kentaro";
See www.davidbordwell.net/blog/?p=484.

One major genre, the musical, became possible only with the introduction of sound. Indeed, the original intention of the Warners when they began their investment in sound equipment was to circulate vaudeville acts on film. The form of most musicals involved separate numbers inserted into a linear narrative, although a few revue musicals simply strung together a series of numbers with little or no connecting narrative. One of the major studios, RKO, made a series of musicals starring Fred Astaire and Ginger Rogers: *Swing Time* (George Stevens, 1936) illustrates how a musical can be a classically constructed narrative (see pp. 281–282).

During the 1930s, color film stocks became widely used for the first time. In the 1920s, a small number of films had Technicolor sequences, but the process was crude, using only two colors in combination to create all other hues. The result tended to emphasize greenish-blue and pink tones; it was also too costly to use extensively **(12.39)**. By the early 1930s, however, Technicolor had been improved. It now used three primary colors and thus could reproduce a large range of hues. Though still expensive, it was soon proved to add hugely to the appeal of many films. After *Becky Sharp* (1935), the first feature-length film to use the new Technicolor, and *The Trail of the Lonesome Pine* (1936), studios began using Technicolor extensively. The Technicolor process was used until the early 1970s. (For a variety of examples of Technicolor, running from the 1940s to the 1960s, see 4.1, 4.11, 4.41–4.43, 5.5, and 5.47.)

Technicolor needed a great deal of light on the set, and the light had to favor certain hues. Thus brighter lights specifically designed for color filmmaking were introduced. Some cinematographers began to use the new lights for black-and-white filming. These brighter lights, combined with faster film stocks, made it easier to achieve greater depth of field with more light and a smaller aperture. Many cinematographers stuck to the standard soft-focus style of the 1920s and 1930s, but others began to experiment. By the late 1930s, there was a definite trend toward a deep-focus style.

Mervyn Leroy's *Anthony Adverse* (1936), Alfred L. Werker's *The Adventures of Sherlock Holmes* (1939), and the Sam Wood–William Cameron Menzies *Our Town* (1940) all used deep focus to a considerable degree. But it was *Citizen Kane* that in 1941 brought deep focus strongly to the attention of spectators and filmmakers alike. Orson Welles's compositions placed the foreground figures close to the camera and the background figures deep in the space of the shot (5.39). In some cases, the apparently deep-focus image was achieved through matte work and rear projection. Overall, *Citizen Kane* helped make the tendency toward deep focus a major part of classical Hollywood style in the next decade. Many films using the technique soon appeared. *Citizen Kane*'s cinematographer, Gregg Toland, worked on some of them, such as *The Little Foxes* (12.40).

The light necessary for deep focus also tended to lend a hard-edged appearance to objects. Gauzy effects were largely eliminated, and much 1940s cinema became visually quite distinct from that of the 1930s. But the insistence on the clear narrative functioning of all these techniques remained strong. The classical Hollywood narrative modified itself over the years but did not change radically.

12.40   William Wyler stages in depth in *The Little Foxes.*

Italian Neorealism (1942–1951)

There is no definitive source for the term *Neorealism,* but it first appeared in the early 1940s in the writings of Italian critics. From one perspective, the term represented a younger generation's desire to break free of the conventions of ordinary Italian cinema. Under Mussolini, the motion picture industry had created colossal historical epics and sentimental upper-class melodramas (nicknamed *white-telephone films*), and many critics felt these to be artificial and decadent. A new realism was needed. Some critics found it in French films of the 1930s, especially works by Jean Renoir. Other critics turned closer to home to praise films like Luchino Visconti's *Ossessione* (1942).

Today most historians believe that Neorealist filmmaking was not a complete break with Italian cinema under Mussolini. Pseudo-documentaries such as Roberto Rossellini's *White Ship* (1941), even though propagandistic, prepared the way for more forthright handling of contemporary events. Other current trends, such as regional dialect comedy and urban melodrama, encouraged directors and scriptwriters to turn toward realism. Overall, spurred by both foreign influences and indigenous traditions, the postwar period saw several filmmakers beginning to work with the goal of revealing contemporary social conditions. This trend became known as the Neorealist movement.

Economic, political, and cultural factors helped Neorealism survive. Nearly all the major Neorealists—Rossellini, Vittorio De Sica, Visconti, and others—came to the movement as experienced filmmakers. They knew one another, frequently shared scriptwriters and personnel, and gained public attention in the journals *Cinema* and *Bianco e Nero.* Before 1948, the Neorealist movement had enough friends in the government to be relatively free of censorship. There was even a correspondence between Neorealism and an Italian literary movement of the same period modeled on the *verismo* of the previous century. The result was an array of Italian films that gained worldwide recognition: Visconti's *La Terra Trema* (1947); Rossellini's *Rome Open City* (1945), *Paisan* (1946), and *Germany Year Zero* (1947); and De Sica's *Shoeshine* (1946) and *Bicycle Thieves* (1948).

Neorealism created a somewhat distinctive approach to film style. By 1945, the fighting had destroyed most of Cinecittà, the large Roman studio complex, so sets were in short supply and sound equipment was rare. As a result, Neorealist mise-en-scene relied on actual locales, and its photographic work tended toward the raw roughness of documentaries. Rossellini has told of buying bits of negative stock from street photographers, so that much of *Rome Open City* was shot on film with varying photographic qualities.

Shooting on the streets and in private buildings made Italian camera operators adept at cinematography that often avoided the three-point lighting system of Hollywood (4.36). Although Neorealist films often featured famous stage or film actors, nonactors were also recruited for their realistic looks and behavior. For the adult "star" of *Bicycle Thieves,* De Sica chose a factory worker: "The way he moved, the way he sat down, his gestures with those hands of a working man and not of an actor . . . everything about him was perfect." The Italian cinema had a long tradition of dubbing, and the ability to postsynchronize dialogue permitted the filmmakers to work on location with smaller crews and to move the camera freely. With a degree

12.41   Shooting in the streets for the death of Pina in *Rome Open City*: Francesco is thrown into a truck by Nazi soldiers . . .

12.42   . . . Pina breaks through the guards . . .

12.43   . . . and a rough, bumpy shot taken from the truck shows her running after it.

12.44   One of the magnificent landscapes in depth in *La Terra Trema*.

12.45   In *Bicycle Thieves*, the hero takes shelter along with a group of priests during a rain shower. The incident doesn't affect the plot and seems as casual as any moment in daily life.

"The sentiment of [Bicycle Thieves] is expressed overtly. The feelings invoked are a natural consequence of the themes of the story and the point of view it is told from. It is a politically committed film, fueled by a quiet but burning passion. But it never lectures. It observes rather than explains."

— Sally Potter, director, *Orlando*

of improvisational freedom in the acting and setting went a certain flexibility of framing, well displayed in the death of Pina in *Rome Open City* (**12.41–12.43**), the final sequence of *Germany Year Zero*, and *La Terra Trema* (**12.44**). The tracking shots through the open-air bicycle market in *Bicycle Thieves* illustrate the possibilities that the Neorealist director found in returning to location filming.

Perhaps even more influential was the Neorealist sense of narrative form. Reacting against the intricately plotted white-telephone dramas, the Neorealists tended to loosen up narrative relations. The earliest major films of the movement, such as *Ossessione, Rome Open City,* and *Shoeshine,* contain relatively conventionally organized plots (albeit with unhappy endings). But the most formally innovative Neorealist films allow the intrusion of noncausally motivated details (**12.45**). Although the causes of characters' actions are usually seen as concretely economic and political (poverty, unemployment, exploitation), the effects are often fragmentary and inconclusive. Rossellini's *Paisan* is frankly episodic, presenting six anecdotes of life in Italy during the Allied invasion; often we are not told the outcome of an event, the consequence of a cause.

The ambiguity of Neorealist films is also a product of narration that refuses to yield an omniscient knowledge of events. The film seems to admit that the totality of reality is simply unknowable. This is especially evident in the films' endings. *Bicycle Thieves* concludes with the worker and his son wandering down the street, their stolen bicycle still missing, their future uncertain. Although ending with the suppression of the Sicilian fishermen's revolt against the merchants, *La Terra Trema* does not cancel the possibility that a later revolt will succeed. Neorealism's tendency toward slice-of-life plot construction gave many films of the movement an open-ended quality quite opposed to the narrative closure of the Hollywood cinema.

As economic and cultural forces had sustained the Neorealist movement, so they helped bring it to an end. When Italy began to prosper after the war, the government looked askance at films so critical of contemporary society. After 1949, censorship and state pressures began to constrain the movement. Large-scale Italian film production began to reappear, and Neorealism no longer had the freedom of the small production company. In addition, the Neorealist directors, now famous, began to pursue more individualized concerns: Rossellini's investigation of Christian humanism and Western history, De Sica's sentimental romances, and Visconti's examination of upper-class milieus. Most historians date the end of the Neorealist movement with the public attacks on De Sica's *Umberto D* (1951). Nevertheless, Neorealist elements are still quite visible in the early works of Federico Fellini (*I. Vitelloni,* 1954, is a good example) and Michelangelo Antonioni (*Cronaca di un amore,* 1951); both directors had worked on Neorealist films. The movement exercised a strong influence on individual filmmakers such as Ermanno Olmi and Satyajit Ray and on groups such as the French New Wave.

The French New Wave (1959–1964)

The late 1950s and early 1960s saw the rise of a new generation of filmmakers around the world. In country after country, there emerged directors born before World War II but grown to adulthood in the postwar era of reconstruction and rising prosperity. Japan, Canada, England, Italy, Spain, Brazil, and the United States all had their new waves or young cinema groups—some trained in film schools, many allied with specialized film magazines, most in revolt against their elders in the industry. The most influential of these groups appeared in France.

In the mid-1950s, a group of young men who wrote for the Paris film journal *Cahiers du cinéma* made a habit of attacking the most artistically respected French filmmakers of the day. "I consider an adaptation of value," wrote François Truffaut, "only when written by a *man of the cinema.* Aurenche and Bost [the leading script-writers of the time] are essentially literary men and I reproach them here for being contemptuous of the cinema by underestimating it." Addressing 21 major directors, Jean-Luc Godard asserted, "Your camera movements are ugly because your subjects are bad, your casts act badly because your dialogue is worthless; in a word, you don't know how to create cinema because you no longer even know what it is." Truffaut and Godard, along with Claude Chabrol, Eric Rohmer, and Jacques Rivette, also praised directors considered somewhat outdated (Jean Renoir, Max Ophuls) or eccentric (Robert Bresson, Jacques Tati).

More important, the young men saw no contradiction in rejecting the French filmmaking establishment while loving blatantly commercial Hollywood. The young rebels of *Cahiers* claimed that in the works of certain directors—certain *auteurs* (authors)—artistry existed in the American cinema. An **auteur** usually did not literally write scripts but managed nonetheless to stamp his or her personality on studio products, transcending the constraints of Hollywood's standardized system. Howard Hawks, Otto Preminger, Samuel Fuller, Vincente Minnelli, Nicholas Ray, Alfred Hitchcock—these were more than craftsmen. Each person's total output constituted a coherent world. Truffaut quoted Giraudoux: "There are no works, there are only auteurs." Godard remarked later, "We won the day in having it acknowledged in principle that a film by Hitchcock, for example, is as important as a book by Aragon. Film auteurs, thanks to us, have finally entered the history of art." And indeed, many of the Hollywood directors these critics and filmmakers championed have become recognized as great artists.

Writing criticism didn't satisfy these young men. They itched to make movies. Borrowing money from friends and filming on location, each started to shoot short films. By 1959, they had become a force to be reckoned with. In that year, Rivette filmed *Paris nous appartient* (*Paris Belongs to Us*); Godard made *À Bout de souffle* (*Breathless*); Chabrol made his second feature, *Les Cousins;* and in April, Truffaut's *Les Quatre cent coups* (*The 400 Blows*) won the Grand Prize at the Cannes Festival.

The novelty and youthful vigor of these directors led journalists to nickname them *la nouvelle vague*—the *New Wave.* Their output was staggering. All told, the five central directors made 32 feature films between 1959 and 1966; Godard and Chabrol made 11 apiece. So many films must of course be highly disparate, but there are enough similarities for us to identify a broadly distinctive New Wave approach to style and form.

The most obviously revolutionary quality of the New Wave films was their casual look. To proponents of the carefully polished French *cinema of quality,* the young directors must have seemed hopelessly sloppy. The New Wave directors had admired the Neorealists (especially Rossellini) and, in opposition to studio filmmaking, took as their mise-en-scene actual locales in and around Paris. Shooting on location became the norm **(12.46).** Similarly, glossy studio lighting was replaced by available light and simple supplemental sources. Few postwar French films would have shown the dim, grimy apartments and corridors featured in *Paris Belongs to Us.*

> "We were all critics before beginning to make films, and I loved all kinds of cinema—the Russians, the Americans, the neorealists. It was the cinema that made us—or me, at least—want to make films. I knew nothing of life except through the cinema."
>
> — Jean-Luc Godard, director

12.46 *Les Bonnes femmes:* while a serial killer stalks them, two of the heroines sit idly at work. Like many New Wave directors, Claude Chabrol followed the Neorealists in shooting on locations like this drab appliance shop.

12.47 In *Vivre sa vie,* a clip from Dreyer's *The Passion of Joan of Arc . . .*

12.48 *. . . helps dramatize the heroine's feelings as she watches it.*

Cinematography changed, too. The New Wave camera moves a great deal, panning and tracking to follow characters or trace out relations within a locale. Furthermore, shooting cheaply on location demanded flexible, portable equipment. Fortunately, Eclair had recently developed a lightweight camera that could be hand-held. (That the Eclair had been used primarily for documentary work accorded perfectly with the realistic mise-en-scene of the New Wave.) New Wave filmmakers were intoxicated with the new freedom offered by the handheld camera. In *The 400 Blows,* the camera explores a cramped apartment and rides a carnival centrifuge. In *Breathless,* the cinematographer held the camera while seated in a wheelchair to follow the hero along a complex path in a travel agency's office (11.36).

One of the most salient features of New Wave films is their casual humor. These young men deliberately played with the medium. In Godard's *Band of Outsiders,* the three main characters resolve to be silent for a minute, and Godard dutifully shuts off *all* the sound. In Truffaut's *Shoot the Piano Player,* a character swears that he's not lying: "May my mother drop dead if I'm not telling the truth." Cut to a shot of an old lady keeling over.

Along with humor came esoteric references to other films, Hollywood or European. There are homages to admired auteurs: Godard characters allude to *Johnny Guitar* (Ray), *Some Came Running* (Minnelli), and "Arizona Jim" (from Renoir's *Crime of M. Lange*). In *Les Carabiniers,* Godard parodies Lumière, and in *Vivre sa vie,* he visually quotes *La Passion de Jeanne d'Arc* (**12.47, 12.48**). Hitchcock is frequently cited in Chabrol's films, and Truffaut's *Les Mistons* re-creates a shot from a Lumière short. Such citations, the New Wave directors felt, acknowledged that cinema, like literature and painting, had lofty traditions that could be honored.

New Wave films also pushed further the Neorealist experimentation with plot construction. In general, causal connections became quite loose. Is there actually a political conspiracy going on in *Paris Belongs to Us?* Why is Nana shot at the end of *Vivre sa vie?* In *Shoot the Piano Player,* the first sequence consists mainly of a conversation between the hero's brother and a man he accidentally meets on the street; the latter tells of his marital problems at some length, even though he has nothing to do with the film's narrative.

Moreover, the films often lack goal-oriented protagonists. The heroes may drift aimlessly, engage in actions on the spur of the moment, or spend their time talking and drinking in a café or going to movies. New Wave narratives often introduce startling shifts in tone, jolting our expectations. When two gangsters kidnap the hero and his girlfriend in *Shoot the Piano Player,* the whole group begins a comic discussion of sex. Discontinuous editing further disturbs narrative continuity; this tendency reaches its limit in Godard's jump cuts (6.137, 6.138, 11.39, 11.40).

Perhaps most important, the New Wave film typically ends ambiguously. We have seen this already in *Breathless* (pp. 410–411). Antoine in *The 400 Blows* reaches the sea in the last shot, but as he moves forward, Truffaut zooms in and freezes the frame, ending the film with the question of where Antoine will go from there (3.8). In Chabrol's *Les Bonnes Femmes* and *Ophelia*, in Rivette's *Paris Belongs to Us*, and in nearly all the work of Godard and Truffaut in this period, the looseness of the causal chain leads to endings that remain defiantly open and uncertain.

Despite the demands that the films placed on the viewer and despite the critical rampages of the filmmakers, the French film industry wasn't hostile to the New Wave. The decade 1947–1957 had been good to film production: the government supported the industry through enforced quotas, banks had invested heavily, and there was a flourishing business of international coproductions. But in 1957, cinema attendance fell off drastically, chiefly because television became more widespread. By 1959, the industry was in a crisis. The independent financing of low-budget films seemed to offer a good solution. New Wave directors shot films much more quickly and cheaply than did reigning directors. Moreover, the young directors helped one another out and thus reduced the financial risk of the established companies. Thus the French industry supported the New Wave through distribution, exhibition, and eventually production.

Indeed, it is possible to argue that by 1964, although each New Wave director had his or her own production company, the group had become absorbed into the film industry. Godard made *Le Mépris* (*Contempt*, 1963) for a major commercial producer, Carlo Ponti; Truffaut made *Fahrenheit 451* (1966) in England for Universal; and Chabrol began turning out parodies of James Bond thrillers.

Dating the exact end of the movement is difficult, but most historians select 1964, when the characteristic New Wave form and style had already become diffused and imitated (by, for instance, Tony Richardson in his 1963 English film *Tom Jones*). Certainly, after 1968, the political upheavals in France drastically altered the personal relations among the directors. Chabrol, Truffaut, and Rohmer became firmly entrenched in the French film industry, whereas Godard set up an experimental film and video studio in Switzerland, and Rivette began to create narratives of staggering complexity and length (such as *Out One*, originally about 12 hours long). By the mid-1980s, Truffaut had died, Chabrol's films were often unseen outside France, and Rivette's output had become esoteric. Rohmer retained international attention with his ironic tales of love and self-deception among the upper-middle class (*Pauline at the Beach* [1982] and *Full Moon over Paris* [1984]). Godard continued to attract notoriety with such films as *Passion* (1981) and his controversial retelling of the Old and New Testaments, *Hail Mary* (1983). In 1990, he released an elegant, enigmatic film ironically entitled *Nouvelle vague*, one that bears little relationship to the original tendency. In retrospect, the New Wave not only offered several original and valuable films but also demonstrated that renewal in the film industry could come from talented, aggressive young people inspired in large part by the sheer love of cinema.

The New Hollywood and Independent Filmmaking

Midway through the 1960s, the Hollywood industry seemed very healthy, with blockbusters such as *The Sound of Music* (1965) and *Dr. Zhivago* (1965) yielding huge profits. But soon problems arose. Expensive studio projects failed miserably. Television networks, which had paid high prices to broadcast films after theatrical release, stopped bidding for pictures. American movie attendance flattened out at around 1 billion tickets per year (a figure that, despite home video, remained constant until the early 1990s). By 1969, Hollywood companies were losing over $200 million annually.

Producers fought back. One strategy was to produce counterculture-flavored films aimed at young people. The most popular and influential were Dennis Hopper's low-budget *Easy Rider* (1969) and Robert Altman's *M*A*S*H* (1970). By and large, however, other "youthpix" about campus revolution and unorthodox lifestyles proved disappointing at the box office. What did help lift the industry's fortunes were films aimed squarely at broader audiences. The most successful were Francis Ford Coppola's *The Godfather* (1972); William Friedkin's *The Exorcist* (1973); Steven Spielberg's *Jaws* (1975) and *Close Encounters of the Third Kind* (1977); John Carpenter's *Halloween* (1978); and George Lucas's *American Graffiti* (1973), *Star Wars* (1977), and *The Empire Strikes Back* (1980). In addition, films by Brian De Palma (*Obsession,* 1976) and Martin Scorsese (*Taxi Driver,* 1976; *Raging Bull,* 1980) attracted critical praise.

These and other directors came to be known as the movie brats. Instead of coming up through the ranks of the studio system, most had gone to film schools. At New York University, the University of Southern California, and the University of California at Los Angeles, they had not only mastered the mechanics of production but also learned about film aesthetics and history. Unlike earlier Hollywood directors, the movie brats often had an encyclopedic knowledge of great movies and directors. Even those who did not attend film school were admirers of the classical Hollywood tradition.

As had been the case with the French New Wave, these film-buff directors produced some personal, highly self-conscious films. The movie brats worked in traditional genres, but they also tried to give them an autobiographical coloring. Thus *American Graffiti* was not only a teenage musical but also Lucas's reflection on growing up in central California in the 1960s. Martin Scorsese drew on his youth in New York's Little Italy for his crime drama *Mean Streets* (1973; **12.49**). Coppola imbued both *Godfather* films with a vivacious and melancholy sense of the intense bonds within the Italian American family. Paul Schrader poured his own obsessions with violence and sexuality into his scripts for *Taxi Driver* and *Raging Bull* and the films he directed, such as *Hard Core* (1979).

Since movies had been a major part of the young directors' lives, many films of the New Hollywood were based on the old Hollywood. De Palma's films borrowed heavily from Hitchcock, with *Dressed to Kill* (1980) an overt redoing of *Psycho.* Peter Bogdanovich's *What's Up, Doc?* (1972) was an updating of screwball comedy, with particular reference to Howard Hawks's *Bringing Up Baby.* Carpenter's *Assault on Precinct 13* (1976) derived partly from Hawks's *Rio Bravo;* the editing is credited to "John T. Chance," the character played by John Wayne in Hawks's Western.

12.49 *Mean Streets*: Scorsese uses depth staging and deep focus for the famous "Mook" confrontation.

At the same time, many directors admired the European tradition, with Scorsese drawn to the visual splendor of Luchino Visconti and British director Michael Powell. Some directors dreamed of making complex art films in the European mold. The best-known effort is probably Coppola's *The Conversation* (1974), a mystery-story reworking of Antonioni's *Blow-Up* (1966) that plays ambiguously between reality and hallucination (p. 177).

Robert Altman and Woody Allen, in quite different ways, displayed creative attitudes fed by European cinema. Altman's *Three Women* (1977) and Allen's *Interiors* (1978), for example, owed a good deal to Ingmar Bergman's work. More influential were their innovations on other fronts. Allen revived the American comedy of manners in *Annie Hall* (1977), *Manhattan* (1979), and *Hannah and Her Sisters* (1985). Altman's *McCabe and Mrs. Miller* (1971) and *The Long Goodbye* (1973) displayed rough-edged performances, dense soundtracks, and a disrespectful approach to genre. His *Nashville* (1975) built its plot out of the casual encounters among two dozen characters, none of whom is singled out as the protagonist. Altman explored this narrative form throughout his career, notably in *A Wedding* (1978), *Short Cuts* (1993), and *A Prairie Home Companion* (2006). Such network-based plotting became a common option for independent films such as *Magnolia* (1999), *Crash* (2005), and *Me and You and Everyone We Know* (2005).

Altman and Allen were of a slightly older generation, but many movie brats proved to be the most continuously successful directors of the era. Lucas and Spielberg became powerful producers, working together on the Indiana Jones series and personifying Hollywood's new generation. Coppola failed to sustain his own studio, but he remained an important director. Scorsese's reputation rose steadily: By the end of the 1980s, he was the most critically acclaimed living American filmmaker.

During the 1980s, fresh talents won recognition, creating a New New Hollywood. Many of the biggest hits of the decade continued to come from Lucas and Spielberg, but other, somewhat younger directors were successful too: James Cameron (*The Terminator*, 1984; *Terminator 2: Judgment Day*, 1991), Tim Burton (*Beetlejuice*, 1988; *Batman*, 1989), and Robert Zemeckis (*Back to the Future*, 1985; *Who Framed Roger Rabbit*, 1988). Many of the successful films of the 1990s came from directors from both these successive waves of the Hollywood renaissance: Spielberg's *Jurassic Park* (1993), De Palma's *Mission: Impossible* (1996), and Lucas's *The Phantom Empire* (1999), as well as Zemeckis's *Forrest Gump* (1994), Cameron's *Titanic* (1997), and Burton's *Sleepy Hollow* (1999).

The resurgence of mainstream film was also fed by filmmakers from outside Hollywood. Many directors came from abroad—from Britain (Tony and Ridley Scott), Australia (Peter Weir, Fred Schepisi), Germany (Wolfgang Peterson), the Netherlands (Paul Verhoeven), and Finland (Rennie Harlin). During the 1980s and 1990s, more women filmmakers also became commercially successful, such as Amy Heckerling (*Fast Times at Ridgemont High*, 1982; *Look Who's Talking*, 1990), Martha Coolidge (*Valley Girl*, 1983; *Rambling Rose*, 1991), and Penelope Spheeris (*Wayne's World*, 1992).

Several directors from independent film managed to shift into the mainstream, making medium-budget pictures with widely known stars. David Lynch moved from the midnight movie *Eraserhead* (1978) to the cult classic *Blue Velvet* (1986), while Canadian David Cronenberg, a specialist in low-budget horror films such as *Shivers* (1975), won wider recognition with *The Dead Zone* (1983; **12.50**) and *The Fly* (1986). The New New Hollywood also absorbed some minority directors from independent film. Wayne Wang was the most successful Asian American filmmaker (*Chan Is Missing*, 1982; *Smoke*, 1995). Spike Lee (*She's Gotta Have It*, 1986; *Malcolm X*, 1992) led the way for young African-American directors such as Reginald Hudlin (*House Party*, 1990), John Singleton (*Boyz N the Hood*, 1991), Mario van Peebles (*New Jack City*, 1991), and Allen and Albert Hughes (*Menace II Society*, 1993).

Still other directors remained independent and more or less marginal to the studios. In *Stranger Than Paradise* (1984) and *Down by Law* (1986), Jim Jarmusch

"I love the idea of not being an independent filmmaker. I've liked working within the system. And I've admired a lot of the older directors who were sort of 'directors for hire.' Like Victor Fleming was in a contract all those years to Metro and Selznick and Mayer . . . he made Captains Courageous. *And you know, his most famous films:* Wizard of Oz *and* Gone with the Wind."

— Steven Spielberg, producer/director

12.50   *The Dead Zone*: the hero, a psychic possessed by visions of future events, imagines a fire.

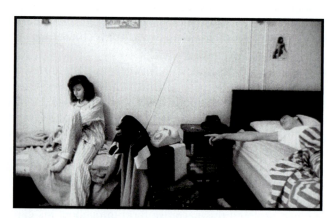

12.51   Eva and Willie, the listless protagonists of *Stranger Than Paradise*. "These characters," Jarmusch explains, "move through the world of the film in a kind of random, aimless way, like looking for the next card game or something."

12.52   In *Jurassic Park* Spielberg harks back to Orson Welles's use of depth compositions.

CONNECT TO THE BLOG
We take a look back at the fall 1994 season and ask whether Hollywood filmmaking has really changed all that much since in "Fantasy franchises, or franchise fantasies?"

See www.davidbordwell.net/blog/?p=1043.

presented quirky, decentered narratives peopled by drifting losers **(12.51)**. Allison Anders treated the contemporary experiences of disaffected young women, either in small towns (*Gas Food Lodging*, 1992) or city centers (*Mi Vida Loca*, 1994). Leslie Harris's *Just Another Girl on the IRT* (1994; 1.34) likewise focused on the problems of urban women of color.

Stylistically, no single coherent film movement emerged during the 1970s and 1980s. The most mainstream of the young directors continued the tradition of classical American cinema. Continuity editing remained the norm, with clear signals for time shifts and new plot developments. Some directors embellished Hollywood's traditional storytelling strategies with new or revived visual techniques. In films from *Jaws* onward, Spielberg used deep-focus techniques reminiscent of *Citizen Kane* (5.39, **12.52**). Lucas developed motion-control techniques for filming miniatures for *Star Wars,* and his firm Industrial Light and Magic (ILM) became the leader in new special-effects technology. Spielberg and Lucas also led the move toward digital sound and high-quality theater reproduction technology.

Less well funded Hollywood filmmaking cultivated more flamboyant styles. Scorsese's *Taxi Driver, Raging Bull* (pp. 438–442), and *The Age of Innocence* (1993) use camera movement and slow motion to extend the emotional impact of a scene.

De Palma has been an even more outrageous stylist; his films flaunt long takes, startling overhead compositions, and split-screen devices. Coppola experimented with fast-motion black-and-white in *Rumble Fish* (1983), phone conversations handled in the foreground and background of a single shot (*Tucker,* 1988), and old-fashioned special effects to lend a period mood to *Bram Stoker's Dracula* (1993).

Several of the newer entrants into Hollywood enriched mainstream conventions of genre, narrative, and style. We have already seen one example of this strategy in our discussion of Spike Lee's *Do The Right Thing* (pp. 404–408). Another intriguing example is Wayne Wang's *The Joy Luck Club* (1993; 12.53). Set among Chinese American families, the film concentrates on four emigrant mothers and their four assimilated daughters. In presenting the women's lives, the film adheres to narrative principles that recall *Citizen Kane.* At a party, the three surviving mothers recall their lives before coming to America, and a lengthy flashback is devoted to each one. Alongside each mother's flashback, however, the plot sets flashbacks tracing the experiences of each woman's daughter in the United States. The result is a rich set of dramatic and thematic parallels. Sometimes the mother–daughter juxtapositions create sharp contrasts; at other times, they blend together to emphasize commonalities across generations. The women's voice-over commentaries always orient the viewer to the shifts in narration while still enabling Wang and his screenwriters to treat the flashback convention in ways that intensify the emotional effect.

A similar effort to revise conventions pervades the work of other independent directors. The brothers Joel and Ethan Coen treat each film as a pretext for exploring cinema's expressive resources. In *Raising Arizona* (1987), high-speed tracking shots combine with distorting wide-angle close-ups to create comic-book exaggerations (12.54). A somewhat similar approach is taken in Gregg Araki's gay road picture *The Living End* (1992). In films such as *Trust* (1991), Hal Hartley mutes a melodramatic plot through slow pacing, brooding close-ups, and dynamic foreground/background compositions (12.55).

Independent directors of the 1980s and 1990s have also experimented with narrative construction. The Coens' *Barton Fink* (1991) passes unnoticeably from a satiric portrait of 1930s Hollywood into a hallucinatory fantasy. Quentin Tarantino's *Reservoir Dogs* (1993) and *Pulp Fiction* (1994) juggle story and plot time in ways that recall the complex flashbacks of the 1940s. Unlike the flashbacks in *The Joy Luck Club,* moreover, the switches are not motivated as characters' memories; the audience is forced to puzzle out the purposes served by the time shifts. In *Daughters of the Dust* (1991), Julie Dash incorporates the rich Gullah dialect and explores a complex time scheme that seeks to fuse present and future. In one scene, optical effects give the characters a glimpse of a child who is as yet unborn.

In the 1980s and 1990s, while younger studio directors adapted classical conventions to modern tastes, an energetic independent film tradition began pushing the envelope. By the 2000s, the two trends were merging in surprising ways. As independent films began to win larger audiences, major studios eagerly acquired distribution companies such as Miramax and October Films. Much media journalism fostered the impression that Hollywood was becoming subverted by independent filmmaking, but in fact, more and more, the major studios controlled audiences' access to formerly independent productions. The Sundance Film Festival, founded as a forum for the off-Hollywood scene, came to be treated as a talent market by the studios, which often bought films in order to line up the filmmaker for more mainstream projects. Thus after Kevin Smith found success with *Clerks* (1994), he directed *Mallrats* (1995), a tame twenty-something comedy for Universal. Robert Rodriguez's similarly microbudgeted *El Mariachi* (1992) proved a hit, so he was hired to remake it as an all-out action picture starring Antonio Banderas (*Desperado,* 1995).

Yet sometimes the big-budget films of independent filmmakers conveyed a distinctly experimental attitude. Kevin Smith used the star-filled *Dogma* (1999) to

12.53 *The Joy Luck Club.*

12.54 Wide-angle tracking shots follow crawling babies along the floor and under furniture in *Raising Arizona.*

12.55 In *Trust,* a melodramatic scene between mother and daughter is intensified through deep-space staging and a tight close-up.

CONNECT TO THE BLOG
Some independent filmmakers use sensationalism to call attention to their work. See "Visionary Outlaw Mavericks on the dark edge; or, Indie Guignol," at
www.davidbordwell.net/blog/?p=339.

12.56 An ambiguous image that recurs throughout *The Limey:* it may be construed either as a flashback to the protagonist's trip to the United States or as a flash-forward to his trip back to Britain, presented in the final scene.

CONNECT TO THE BLOG

For a discussion of director James Mangold and his relationship to the traditions of classical Hollywood filmmaking, see "Legacies," at

www.davidbordwell.net/blog/?p=1261.

CONNECT TO THE BLOG

Why do some filmmakers take such a long time between movies? We explore some possible reasons in "Running on almost empty."

See www.davidbordwell.net/blog/?p=367.

question Catholic doctrine. David O. Russell, who had worked his way into the system with off-kilter comedies (*Spanking the Monkey,* 1994; *Flirting with Disaster,* 1996), made *Three Kings* (1999), an action picture that criticized Gulf War policies and that reveled in a flamboyant, digital-era style. Following in the path of *Pulp Fiction,* studio pictures began to play more boldly with narrative form. A genre thriller such as *The Sixth Sense* (1999) encouraged viewers to see it twice in order to detect how the narration had misled them. Stories might be told through complicated flashbacks, as in Steven Soderbergh's *The Limey* (**12.56**). (See also box, pp. 87–89.) A film might reveal that one character was the imaginary creation of another (*Fight Club,* 1999), or that a person could crawl into another's brain (*Being John Malkovich,* 1999), or that the external world was merely an illusion produced by sophisticated software (*The Matrix,* 1999) or a novelist (*Stranger than Fiction*). In their willingness to experiment with ambiguous and teasing modes of narration, many American studio films began rivaling their overseas counterparts such as *Breaking the Waves* (1996), *Sliding Doors* (1998), and *Run Lola Run* (1998).

At the start of the new century, many of the most thrilling Hollywood films were being created by a robust new generation, born in the 1960s and 1970s and brought up on videotape, video games, and the Internet. Like their predecessors, these directors were reshaping the formal and stylistic conventions of the classical cinema while also making their innovations accessible to a broad audience.

Hong Kong Cinema: 1980s–1990s

While the New Hollywood directors were revamping American films, a young generation of directors in Hong Kong found footing in their industry and recast its traditional genres and creative methods. The result was not a unified film movement, but a local cinema with a robust identity. Hong Kong's innovations in cinematic style and storytelling vigorously influenced world filmmaking well into the twenty-first century.

Hong Kong produced films in the silent era and during the 1930s, although World War II halted production. When the industry revived in the 1950s, the most powerful studio was Shaw Brothers. Shaws owned theaters throughout East Asia and used Hong Kong as a production base for films in several languages, chiefly Mandarin Chinese. Shaws made films in many genres, but among its biggest successes were dynamic, gory swordfighting films (*wuxia pian,* or "tales of martial chivalry"). In the 1970s, another studio, Golden Harvest, triumphed with kung-fu films starring Bruce Lee. Although Lee completed only four martial-arts films before his death in 1973, he brought Hong Kong cinema to worldwide attention and forever identified it with films of acrobatic and violent action.

Several major directors worked in this period. Most famous is King Hu, who started as a Shaws director. In films like *Dragon Gate Inn* (1967) and *The Valiant Ones* (1975; 5.69), Hu reinvigorated the *wuxia pian* through graceful airborne swordplay and inventive cutting. Chang Cheh, another Shaws director, turned the swordplay film toward violent male melodrama (such as *The One-Armed Swordsman,* 1967) before specializing in flamboyant kung-fu films such as *Crippled Avengers* (also called *Mortal Combat,* 1978). Neither King Hu nor Chang Cheh was a practitioner of martial arts, but Lau Kar-leung was a fight choreographer before becoming a full-fledged director. Lau created a string of inventive films (such as *36th Chamber of Shaolin,* 1978, and *The Eight-Diagram Pole Fighter,* 1983) that showcased a range of dazzling marital-arts techniques.

By the early 1980s, traditional kung-fu was fading in popularity, and Shaws turned from moviemaking to its lucrative television business. At the same time, a new generation of directors came forward. One group had little formal education but had grown up in the film industry, working as stuntmen and martial artists. Among those who became directors were choreographers Yuen Wo-ping and Yuen

12.57 Rapid movements into and out of the frame are characteristic of Hong Kong film style. In this shot from *Peking Opera Blues,* the sheriff and his captive rise into the foreground as the three heroines watch from the rear.

12.58 John Woo's debt to the Western: a striking long shot as a hero walks to meet his fate in *A Better Tomorrow.*

Kuei (*Yes, Madam!,* 1985). Sammo Hung choreographed, directed, and starred in many lively action films (such as *Eastern Condors,* 1987).

The most famous graduate of the studio system was Jackie Chan, who labored as a copy of Bruce Lee before finding his feet in comic kung-fu. With *Drunken Master* (1978, directed by Yuen Wo-ping), he became a star throughout Asia and gained the power to direct his own films. In the early 1980s, Chan and his colleagues realized that kung-fu could be incorporated into Hollywoodish action-adventure movies. Chan made the historical adventure *Project A* (1983, also starring Hung) and the contemporary cop drama *Police Story* (1985). These and others were huge hits across Asia, partly because of Chan's lovably goofy star persona, and partly because of his ingenious and dangerous action scenes (6.47–6.49).

Another group of directors had more formal training, with many attending film schools in the United States or Britain. When Ann Hui, Allen Fong, and others returned to Hong Kong, they found work in television before moving on to feature filmmaking. For a time, they constituted a local art cinema, attracting attention at festivals with such films as Hui's *Boat People* (1982). But most of this group gravitated toward independent companies turning out comedies, dramas, and action films. Tsui Hark was the leader of this trend. As both director and producer, Tsui revived and reworked a range of genres: swordplay fantasy (*Zu: Warriors of the Magic Mountain,* 1979), romantic comedy (*Shanghai Blues,* 1984), historical adventure (*Peking Opera Blues,* 1986; **12.57**), supernatural romance (*A Chinese Ghost Story,* 1987, directed by Ching Siu-tung), and classic kung-fu (*Once upon a Time in China,* 1990).

Seeing the success that modern cops-and-crooks films were then enjoying, Tsui partnered with John Woo on *A Better Tomorrow* (1986), a remake of a 1960s movie (**12.58**). Woo was something of an in-between figure, having been a successful studio comedy director during the 1970s. With Tsui as producer, *A Better Tomorrow* became Woo's comeback effort, one of the most successful Hong Kong films of the 1980s and a star-making vehicle for the charismatic Chow Yun-fat. Tsui, Woo, and Chow teamed again for a sequel and for the film that made Woo famous in the West, *The Killer* (1989), a lush and baroque story of the unexpected alliance between a hitman and a detective (**12.59**).

Hong Kong cinema of the 1980s and early 1990s simmered with almost reckless energy. The rushed production schedules didn't allow much time to prepare scripts, so the plots, borrowing freely from Chinese legend and Hollywood genres, tended to be less tightly unified than those in U.S. films. They avoided tight linkage of cause and effect in favor of a more casual, episodic construction—not, as in Italian Neorealism, to suggest the randomness of everyday life but rather to permit chases and fights to be inserted easily. While action sequences were meticulously

12.59   Cop and hitman as blood brothers in *The Killer*.

12.60   Stylized blocks of light for *The Longest Nite* (1998).

CONNECT TO THE BLOG

Since one of David's specialties is Hong Kong cinema, he often blogs on the subject. For a discussion of Edward Yang and Charles Wang in "Two Chinese men of the cinema," see

www.davidbordwell.net/blog/?p=1097.

On *Ashes of Time*, see "Ashes to Ashes (Redux)," at

www.davidbordwell.net/blog/?p=3133.

For stylistic analysis of *City of Violence*, see "A glance at blows," at

www.davidbordwell.net/blog/?p=3208.

On director Tsui Hark and his production work, see "Happy Birthday, Film Workshop," at

www.davidbordwell.net/blog/?p=4210.

choreographed, connecting scenes were often improvised and shot quickly. Similarly, the kung-fu films had often bounced between pathos and almost silly comedy, and this tendency to mix tones continued through the 1980s. In *A Better Tomorrow*, for example, Tsui appears in a slapstick interlude involving a cello. Again, because of rushed shooting, the plots often end abruptly, with a big action set-piece but little in the nature of a mood-setting epilogue. One of Tsui's innovations was to provide more satisfying conclusions, as in the lilting railroad station finale of *Shanghai Blues*.

At the level of visual style, Hong Kong directors brought the action film to a new pitch of excitement. Gunmen (and gunwomen) leaped and fired in slow motion, hovering in midair like 1970s swordfighters and kung-fu warriors. John Woo, who had been an assistant director for Chang Cheh, pushed such shots to extravagant limits. Directors also developed florid color designs, with rich reds, blues, and yellows glowing out of smoky nightclubs or narrow alleyways. Well into the 1990s, unrealistically tinted mood lighting was a trademark of Hong Kong cinema **(12.60)**. Above all, everything was sacrificed to constant motion; even in dialogue scenes, the camera and the characters seldom stood still.

Aiming to energize the viewer, the new action directors built on the innovations of King Hu and his contemporaries. They developed a staccato cutting technique based on the tempo of martial-arts routines and Peking Opera displays, alternating rapid movement with sudden pauses. If shot composition was kept simple, an action could be cut to flow across shots very rapidly, while another cut could accentuate a moment of stillness **(12.61–12.63)**. Most Hong Kong directors were unaware of the Soviet Montage movement, but in their efforts to arouse viewers kinesthetically

12.61   Crisp editing in *Yes, Madam!* In a shot only 7 frames long, Michele Yeoh swings swiftly . . .

12.62   . . . to knock the villain spinning (15 frames) . . .

12.63   . . . before she drops smoothly into a relaxed posture on the rail (17 frames).

through expressive movement and editing, they were reviving ideas of concern to 1920s filmmakers.

The 1990s brought the golden age of Hong Kong action cinema to a close. Jackie Chan, John Woo, Chow Yun-fat, Sammo Hung, and action star Jet Li began working in Hollywood, with Yuen Wo-ping designing the action choreography for *The Matrix* (1999) and *Crouching Tiger, Hidden Dragon* (2000). A recession after Hong Kong's 1997 handover to China depressed the local film industry. As Hollywood began imitating Hong Kong movies (as in *The Replacement Killers,* 1998), local audiences developed a taste for U.S. films. At the same time, the art-cinema wing became more ambitious, and festivals rewarded the offbeat works of Wong Kar-wai (see the analysis of *Chungking Express,* pp. 417–422). The action tradition was maintained by only a few directors such as Johnnie To, whose laconic film noir *The Mission* (1999) brought a leanness and pictorial abstraction to the gangster genre.

WHERE TO GO FROM HERE

General

Allen, Robert C., and Douglas Gomery. *Film History: Theory and Practice.* New York: Random House, 1985.

Bordwell, David. *On the History of Film Style.* Cambridge, MA: Harvard University Press, 1997.

Gomery, Douglas. *The Hollywood Studio System: A History.* London: BFI Publishing, 2005.

Lanzoni, Rémi Fournier. *French Cinema: From Its Beginnings to the Present.* New York: Continuum, 2002.

Luhr, William, ed. *World Cinema Since 1945.* New York: Ungar, 1987.

Salt, Barry. *Film Style and Technology: History and Analysis,* 2nd ed. London: Starword, 1992.

Thompson, Kristin, and David Bordwell. *Film History: An Introduction,* 3rd ed. New York: McGraw-Hill, 2010.

Silent Cinema

Abel, Richard, *The Ciné Goes to Town: French Cinema 1896–1914.* Berkeley: University of California Press, 1994.

Allen, Robert C. *Vaudeville and Film, 1895–1915: A Study in Media Interaction.* New York: Arno, 1980.

Brewster, Ben, and Lea Jacobs. *Theatre to Cinema: Stage Pictorialism and the Early Feature Film.* Oxford: Oxford University Press, 1997.

Cherchi Usai, Paolo. *Silent Cinema: An Introduction.* London: British Film Institute, 2000.

Cherchi Usai, Paolo, and Lorenzo Codelli, eds. *Before Caligari: German Cinema, 1895–1920.* Pordenone: Edizioni Biblioteca dell' Immagine, 1990.

Dibbets, Karl, and Bert Hogenkamp, eds. *Film and the First World War.* Amsterdam: Amsterdam University Press, 1995.

Elsaesser, Thomas, ed. *Early Cinema: Space, Frame, Narrative.* London: British Film Institute, 1990.

Fell, John L., ed. *Film Before Griffith.* Berkeley: University of California Press, 1983.

Fullerton, John, ed. *Celebrating 1895: The Centenary of Cinema.* Sydney: John Libbey, 1998.

Grieveson, Lee, and Peter Krämer, eds. *The Silent Cinema Reader.* London: Routledge, 2004.

Gunning, Tom. *D. W. Griffith and the Origins of American Narrative Film: The Early Years at Biograph.* Urbana and Chicago: University of Illinois Press, 1991.

Hammond, Paul. *Marvelous Méliès.* New York: St. Martin's Press, 1975.

Hendricks, Gordon. *The Edison Motion Picture Myth.* Berkeley: University of California Press, 1961.

Leyda, Jay, and Charles Musser, eds. *Before Hollywood: Turn-of-the-Century Film from American Archives.* New York: American Federation of the Arts, 1986.

Musser, Charles. *Before the Nickelodeon: Edwin S. Porter and the Edison Manufacturing Company.* Berkeley: University of California Press, 1991.

———. *The Emergence of Cinema: The American Screen to 1907.* New York: Scribner, 1991.

Pratt, George, ed. *Spellbound in Darkness.* Greenwich, CT: New York Graphic Society, 1973.

Rossell, Deac. *Living Pictures: The Origins of the Movies.* Albany: State University of New York Press, 1998.

Tsivian, Yuri, ed. *Testimoni silenziosi: Film russi 1908–1919.* Pordenone: Edizioni Biblioteca dell'Immagine, 1989. (Bilingual in Italian and English.)

Youngblood, Denise. *The Magic Mirror: Moviemaking in Russia, 1908–1918.* Madison: University of Wisconsin Press, 1999.

Classical Hollywood Cinema

Balio, Tino, ed. *The American Film Industry,* rev. ed. Madison: University of Wisconsin Press, 1985.

Bordwell, David, Janet Staiger, and Kristin Thompson. *The Classical Hollywood Cinema: Film Style and Mode of Production to 1960.* New York: Columbia University Press, 1985.

Bowser, Eileen. *The Transformation of Cinema, 1907–1915.* New York: Scribner, 1990.

Brownlow, Kevin. *The Parade's Gone By.* New York: Knopf, 1968.

DeBauche, Leslie Midkiff. *Reel Patriotism: The Movies and World War I.* Madison: University of Wisconsin Press, 1997.

Gomery, Douglas. *Shared Pleasures: A History of American Moviegoing.* Madison: University of Wisconsin Press, 1992.

Hampton, Benjamin B. *History of the American Film Industry.* 1931. Reprinted. New York: Dover, 1970.

Keil, Charlie. *Early American Cinema in Transition: Story, Style, and Filmmaking, 1907–1918.* Madison: University of Wisconsin Press, 2001.

Keil, Charlie, and Shelley Stamp, eds. *American Cinema's Transitional Era: Audiences, Institutions, Practices.* Berkeley: University of California Press, 2004.

Koszarski, Richard. *An Evening's Entertainment: The Age of the Silent Feature Picture, 1915–1928.* New York: Scribner, 1990.

Staiger, Janet. *Interpreting Films: Studies in the Historical Reception of American Cinema.* Princeton, NJ: Princeton University Press, 1992.

Vasey, Ruth. *The World According to Hollywood, 1928–1939.* Madison: University of Wisconsin Press, 1997.

German Expressionism

Barlow, John D. *German Expressionist Film.* Boston: Twayne, 1982.

Budd, Mike, ed. *The Cabinet of Dr. Caligari: Texts, Contexts, Histories.* New Brunswick, NJ: Rutgers University Press, 1990.

Eisner, Lotte. *The Haunted Screen.* Berkeley: University of California Press, 1969.

———. *Fritz Lang.* New York: Oxford University Press, 1977.

———. *F. W. Murnau.* Berkeley: University of California Press, 1983.

Kracauer, Siegfried. *From Caligari to Hitler.* Princeton, NJ: Princeton University Press, 1947.

Kreimeier, Klaus. *The UFA Story: A History of Germany's Greatest Film Company 1918–1945.* Trans. Robert and Rita Kimber. New York: Hill & Wang, 1996.

Myers, Bernard S. *The German Expressionists.* New York: Praeger, 1963.

Robinson, David. *Das Cabinet des Dr. Caligari.* London: British Film Institute, 1997. (In English.)

Scheunemann, Dietrich, ed. *Expressionist Film: New Perspectives.* Rochester, NY: Camden House, 2003.

Selz, Peter. *German Expressionist Painting.* Berkeley: University of California Press, 1957.

Thompson, Kristin. *Herr Lubitsch Goes to Hollywood: German and American Film After World War I.* Amsterdam: Amsterdam University Press, 2005.

Willett, John. *Expressionism.* New York: McGraw-Hill, 1970.

———. *The New Sobriety: Art and Politics in the Weimar Republic, 1917–1933.* London: Thames & Hudson, 1978.

French Impressionism

Abel, Richard. *French Cinema: The First Wave, 1915–1929.* Princeton, NJ: Princeton University Press, 1984.

———. *French Film Theory and Criticism, 1907–1939,* vol. 1. Princeton, NJ: Princeton University Press, 1988.

Brownlow, Kevin. *"Napoleon": Abel Gance's Classic Film.* New York: Knopf, 1983.

Clair, René. *Cinema Yesterday and Today.* New York: Dover, 1972.

King, Norman. *Abel Gance: A Politics of Spectacle.* London: British Film Institute, 1984.

Soviet Montage

Bordwell, David. *The Cinema of Eisenstein.* Cambridge, MA: Harvard University Press, 1993.

Bowlt, John, ed. *Russian Art of the Avant-Garde.* New York: Viking Press, 1973.

Carynnyk, Marco, ed. *Alexander Dovzhenko: Poet as Filmmaker.* Cambridge, MA: MIT Press, 1973.

Eisenstein, S. M. *S. M. Eisenstein: Writings 1922–1934,* Richard Taylor, ed. London: British Film Institute, 1988; *Eisenstein, Volume 2, Towards a Theory of Montage,* Michael Glenny and Richard Taylor, eds. London: British Film Institute, 1991; *Eisenstein Writings 1934–1947,* Richard Taylor, ed. London: British Film Institute, 1996. *Beyond the Stars: The Memoirs of Sergei Eisenstein,* vol. 4, Richard Taylor, ed., William Powell, trans. London: British Film Institute, 1995.

Kepley, Jr., Vance. *In the Service of the State: The Cinema of Alexander Dovzhenko.* Madison: University of Wisconsin Press, 1986.

———. *The End of St. Petersburg.* London: I. B. Tauris, 2003.

Kuleshov, Lev. *Kuleshov on Film.* Ed. and trans. Ronald Levaco. Berkeley: University of California Press, 1974.

Leyda, Jay. *Kino,* 3rd ed. Princeton, NJ: Princeton University Press, 1983.

Lodder, Christina. *Russian Constructivism.* New Haven, CT: Yale University Press, 1983.

Michelson, Annette, ed. *Kino-Eye: The Writings of Dziga Vertov.* Berkeley: University of California Press, 1984.

Nilsen, Vladimir. *The Cinema as a Graphic Art.* New York: Hill & Wang, 1959.

Petric, Vlada. *Constructivism in Film: The Man with a Movie Camera—A Cinematic Analysis.* London: Cambridge University Press, 1987.

Pudovkin, V. I. *Film Technique and Film Acting.* New York: Grove Press, 1960.

Schnitzer, Luda, Jean Schnitzer, and Marcel Martin, eds. *Cinema and Revolution.* New York: Hill & Wang, 1973.

Taylor, Richard. *The Politics of the Soviet Cinema, 1917–1929.* Cambridge: Cambridge University Press, 1979.

Taylor, Richard, and Ian Christie, eds. *The Film Factory: Russian and Soviet Cinema in Documents, 1896–1939.* Cambridge, Mass.: Harvard University Press, 1988.

———. *Inside the Film Factory: New Approaches to Russian and Soviet Cinema.* London: Routledge, 1991.

Youngblood, Denise. *Soviet Cinema in the Silent Era, 1918–1933.* Ann Arbor, MI: UMI Research Press, 1985.

The Classical Hollywood Cinema After the Coming of Sound

Balio, Tino. *Grand Design: Hollywood as a Modern Business Enterprise, 1930–1939.* New York: Scribner, 1993.

Balio, Tino, ed. *The American Film Industry,* rev. ed. Madison: University of Wisconsin Press, 1985.

———. *Hollywood in the Age of Television.* Boston: Unwin Hyman, 1990.

Bordwell, David, Janet Staiger, and Kristin Thompson. *The Classical Hollywood Cinema: Film Style and Mode of Production to 1960.* New York: Columbia University Press, 1985.

Crafton, Donald. *The Talkies: American Cinema's Transition to Sound 1926–1931.* New York: Scribner, 1997.

Koszarski, Richard, ed. *Hollywood Directors, 1914–1940.* New York: Oxford University Press, 1976.

Maltby, Richard. *Harmless Entertainment: Hollywood and the Ideology of Consensus.* Metuchen, NJ: Scarecrow, 1983.

———. *Hollywood Cinema,* 2nd ed. Oxford: Blackwell, 2003.

Schatz, Thomas. *Boom and Bust: American Cinema in the 1940s.* Berkeley: University of California Press, 1997.

Silver, Alain, and Elizabeth Ward. *Film Noir: An Encyclopedic Reference to the American Style.* Woodstock, NY: Overlook Press, 1979.

Walker, Alexander. *The Shattered Silents: How the Talkies Came to Stay.* New York: Morrow, 1979.

"Widescreen." Issue of *Velvet Light Trap* 21 (Summer 1985).

Italian Neorealism

Armes, Roy. *Patterns of Realism.* New York: A. S. Barnes, 1970.

Bazin, André. "Cinema and Television." *Sight and Sound* 28, 1 (Winter 1958–59): 26–30.

———. *What Is Cinema?* vol. 2. Berkeley: University of California Press, 1971.

Bondanella, Peter. *Italian Cinema from Neorealism to the Present.* New York: Ungar, 1983.

Brunette, Peter. *Roberto Rossellini.* New York: Oxford University Press, 1987.

Leprohon, Pierre. *The Italian Cinema.* New York: Praeger, 1984.

Liehm, Mira. *Passion and Defiance: Film in Italy from 1942 to the Present.* Berkeley: University of California Press, 1984.

Marcus, Millicent. *Italian Film in the Light of Neorealism.* Princeton, NJ: Princeton University Press, 1986.

Overbey, David, ed. *Springtime in Italy: A Reader on Neo-Realism.* London: Talisman, 1978.

Sitney, P. Adams. *Vital Crises in Italian Cinema: Iconography, Stylistics, Politics.* Austin: University of Texas Press, 1995.

The French New Wave

Crisp, Colin. *The Classic French Cinema, 1930–1960.* Bloomington: Indiana University Press, 1994.

Godard, Jean-Luc. *Godard on Godard.* New York: Viking Press, 1972.

Hillier, Jim, ed. *Cahiers du Cinéma: The 1950s: Neo-Realism, Hollywood, New Wave.* Cambridge, MA: Harvard University Press, 1985.

———. *Cahiers du Cinéma: The 1960s: New Wave, New Cinema, Reevaluating Hollywood.* Cambridge, MA: Harvard University Press, 1986.

Insdorf, Annette. *François Truffaut.* New York: William Morrow, 1979.

McCabe, Colin. *Godard: A Portrait of the Artist at Seventy.* New York: Farrar, Straus & Giroux, 2003.

Mussman, Toby, ed. *Jean-Luc Godard.* New York: Dutton, 1968.

Neupert, Richard. *A History of the French New Wave Cinema,* 2nd ed. Madison: University of Wisconsin Press, 2007.

Sterritt, David. *The Films of Jean-Luc Godard: Seeing the Invisible.* Cambridge: Cambridge University Press, 1999.

Truffaut, François. *The Films in My Life.* Trans. Leonard Mayhew. New York: Simon & Schuster, 1978.

The New Hollywood and Independent Filmmaking

Andrew, Geoff. *Stranger Than Paradise: Maverick Film-Makers in Recent American Cinema.* London: Prion, 1998.

Bordwell, David. *The Way Hollywood Tells It: Story and Style in Modern Movies.* Berkeley: University of California Press, 2006.

Diawara, Manthia, ed. *Black American Cinema.* New York: Routledge, 1993.

Donahue, Suzanne Mary. *American Film Distribution: The Changing Marketplace.* Ann Arbor, MI: UMI Research Press, 1987.

Fuchs, Cynthia, ed. *Spike Lee Interviews.* Jackson: University Press of Mississippi, 2002.

Goodwin, Michael, and Naomi Wise. *On the Edge: The Life and Times of Francis Coppola.* New York: Morrow, 1989.

King, Geoff. *American Independent Cinema.* Bloomington: Indiana University Press, 2005.

Levy, Emmanuel. *Cinema of Outsiders: The Rise of American Independent Film.* New York: New York University Press, 1999.

Lewis, Jon, ed. *The New American Cinema.* Durham, NC: Duke University Press, 1998.

McBride, Joseph. *Steven Spielberg: A Biography.* New York: Simon & Schuster, 1997.

McGilligan, Patrick. *Robert Altman: Jumping off the Cliff.* New York: St. Martin's Press, 1989.

Neale, Steve, and Murray Smith, eds. *Contemporary Hollywood Cinema.* New York: Routledge, 1998.

Noriega, Chon A. *Chicanos and Film: Representation and Resistance.* Minneapolis: University of Minnesota Press, 1992.

Pye, Michael, and Lynda Myles. *The Movie Brats: How the Film Generation Took Over Hollywood.* New York: Holt, Rinehart & Winston, 1979.

Reid, Mark A. *Redefining Black Film.* Berkeley: University of California Press, 1993.

Thompson, Kristin. *The Frodo Franchise: The Lord of the Rings and Modern Hollywood.* Berkeley: University of California Press, 2007.

———. *Storytelling in the New Hollywood: Understanding Classical Narrative Technique.* Cambridge, MA: Harvard University Press, 1999.

Welbon, Yvonne. "Calling the Shots: Black Women Directors Take the Helm." *Independent* 15, 2 (March 1992): 18–22.

Contemporary Hong Kong Cinema

Bordwell, David. *Planet Hong Kong: Popular Cinema and the Art of Entertainment.* Cambridge, MA: Harvard University Press, 2000.

Charles, John. *The Hong Kong Filmography, 1977–1997.* Jefferson, NC: McFarland, 2000.

Fu, Poshek, and Desser, David, eds. *The Cinema of Hong Kong: History, Arts, Identity.* Cambridge: Cambridge University Press, 2000.

Logan, Bey. *Hong Kong Action Cinema.* London: Titan Books, 1995.

Teo, Stephen. *Hong Kong Cinema: The Extra Dimensions.* London: British Film Institute, 1997.

Yau, Esther C. M., ed. *At Full Speed: Hong Kong Cinema in a Borderless World.* Minneapolis: University of Minnesota Press, 2001.

Recommended DVDs

Most of the films mentioned in this chapter are available on DVD. (*Rome Open City* was issued under its original American release title, *Open City.*) Kino Video (www.kino .com) and Image Entertainment (www.image-entertainment .com) have brought out many older classics.

Some collections of early films offer an easy way to get a quick overview of a period, filmmaker, or genre. For a brief introduction to the period up to 1913, *Landmarks of Early Film* (1 disc, Image Entertainment) offers 40 shorts. *Edison: The Invention of the Movies* (4 discs, Kino Video and the Museum of Modern Art) collects 140 films from the Thomas A. Edison Company, including *The Great Train Robbery.* It contains interviews with film historians and archivists, as well as program notes and documents. *The Movies Begin: A Treasury of Early Cinema 1894–1913* (5 discs, Kino Video) gathers 133 films arranged thematically: Volume 1, "*The Great Train Robbery* and Other Primary works"; Volume 2, "The European Pioneers" (including films by the Lumières and early British filmmakers); Volume 3, "Experimentation and Discovery" (mostly early Brit-

ish and French films); Volume 4, "The Magic of Méliès"; and Volume 5, "Comedy, Spectacle and New Horizons."

Slapstick Encyclopedia (5 discs, Image Entertainment) surveys the golden age of comedy shorts—the 1910s and early 1920s. *The Harold Lloyd Comedy Collection* (7 discs, New Line) provides an extensive program of films with one of the masters of silent comedy, as well as a disc of bonus material.

A broad range of types of films is collected in *Treasures from American Film Archives: 50 Preserved Films* (4 discs), *More Treasures from American Film Archives, 1894–1931* (3 discs, Image Entertainment), and *Treasures III: Social Issues in American Film 1900–1934* (4 discs, Image Entertainment). These include documentaries, home movies, animation, experimental cinema, and fiction films such as D. W. Griffith's 1911 one-reeler *The Lonedale Operator* (illustrating his command of early intercutting), Cecil B. De Mille's The *Godless Girl* (1928), and Ernst Lubitsch's masterpiece of classical continuity filmmaking, *Lady Windermere's Fan* (1925). Each boxed set includes a book of detailed program notes.

Recommended Blog Entries on "Observations on film art and *Film Art*"

We have written several entries on film archives and the restoration and exhibition of older movies. See "American (movie) madness," at www.davidbordwell.net/blog/?p=2326, on the commercial value of those movies to DVD release, on what restoration involves, and on Sony/Columbia's restoration program—specifically, its rejuvenation of Frank Capra's early 1930s classic, *American Madness.* Turner Classic Movies has been a major force for the restoration and exhibition of older films, and we salute it in "From Hollywood to Atlanta to us," at www.davidbordwell.net/blog/?p=335.

We sum up trends in moviemaking during 2006 in "An appetite for artifice," at www.davidbordwell.net/blog/?p=237.

We also occasionally write about historically important films. On a British wartime tale, see "Cavalcanti + Ealing = a little-known gem," at www.davidbordwell.net/blog/?p=2303. On Béla Tarr's *Satan's Tango,* see "TANGO marathon," at www.davidbordwell.net/blog/?p=31.

When we attend film festivals, we often comment on a wide range of modern films from all over the world. You can find information on films we've seen at festivals in Vancouver, Hong Kong, Bologna, and other places by going to the "Festivals" tag on our blog: www.davidbordwell.net/blog/?cat=9.

GLOSSARY

abstract form   A type of filmic organization in which the parts relate to one another through repetition and variation of such visual qualities as shape, color, rhythm, and direction of movement.

Academy ratio   The standardized shape of the film frame established by the Academy of Motion Picture Arts and Sciences. In the original ratio, the frame was 1⅓ times as wide as it was high (1.33:1); later the width was normalized at 1.85 times the height (1.85:1).

aerial perspective   A cue for suggesting depth in the image by presenting objects in the distance less distinctly than those in the foreground.

anamorphic lens   A lens for making widescreen films using regular *Academy ratio* frame size. The camera lens takes in a wide field of view and squeezes it onto the frame, and a similar projector lens unsqueezes the image onto a wide theater screen.

angle of framing   The position of the frame in relation to the subject it shows: above it, looking down (a high angle); horizontal, on the same level (a straight-on angle); below it, looking up (a low angle). Also called camera angle.

animation   Any process whereby artificial movement is created by photographing a series of drawings (see also *cel animation*), objects, or computer images one by one. Small changes in position, recorded frame by frame, create the illusion of movement.

aspect ratio   The relationship of the frame's width to its height. The standard *Academy ratio* is currently 1.85:1.

associational form   A type of organization in which the film's parts are juxtaposed to suggest similarities, contrasts, concepts, emotions, and expressive qualities.

asynchronous sound   Sound that is not matched temporally with the movements occurring in the image, as when dialogue is out of synchronization with lip movements.

auteur   The presumed or actual author of a film, usually identified as the director. Also sometimes used in an evaluative sense to distinguish good filmmakers (*auteurs*) from bad ones.

axis of action   In the *continuity editing* system, the imaginary line that passes from side to side through the main actors, defining the spatial relations of all the elements of the scene as being to the right or left. The camera is not supposed to cross the axis at a cut and thus reverse those spatial relations. Also called the 180° line. (See also *180° system.*)

backlighting   Illumination cast onto the figures in the scene from the side opposite the camera, usually creating a thin outline of highlighting on those figures.

boom   A pole upon which a microphone can be suspended above the scene being filmed and that is used to change the microphone's position as the action shifts.

camera angle   See *angle of framing.*

canted framing   A view in which the frame is not level; either the right or the left side is lower than the other, causing objects in the scene to appear slanted out of an upright position.

categorical form   A type of filmic organization in which the parts treat distinct subsets of a topic. For example, a film about the United States might be organized into 50 parts, each devoted to a state.

cel animation   Animation that uses a series of drawings on pieces of celluloid, called *cels* for short. Slight changes between the drawings combine to create an illusion of movement.

CGI   Computer-generated imagery: using digital software systems to create figures, settings, or other material in the frame.

cheat cut   In the *continuity editing* system, a cut that presents continuous time from shot to shot but that mismatches the positions of figures or objects.

cinematography   A general term for all the manipulations of the film strip by the camera in the shooting phase and by the laboratory in the developing phase.

close-up   A framing in which the scale of the object shown is relatively large; most commonly, a person's head seen from the neck up, or an object of a comparable size that fills most of the screen.

closure   The degree to which the ending of a narrative film reveals the effects of all the causal events and resolves (or "closes off") all lines of action.

continuity editing   A system of cutting to maintain continuous and clear narrative action. Continuity editing relies on matching screen direction, position, and temporal relations from shot to shot. For specific techniques of continuity editing, see *axis of action, crosscutting, cut-in, establishing shot, eyeline match, match on action, reestablishing shot, screen direction, shot/reverse shot.*

contrast   In cinematography, the difference between the brightest and darkest areas within the frame.

crane shot   A shot with a change in framing accomplished by placing the camera above the subject and moving through the air in any direction.

crosscutting   Editing that alternates shots of two or more lines of action occurring in different places, usually simultaneously.

cut   (1) In filmmaking, the joining of two strips of film together with a splice. (2) In the finished film, an instantaneous change from one framing to another. See also *jump cut.*

cut-in   An instantaneous shift from a distant framing to a closer view of some portion of the same space.

deep focus   A use of the camera lens and lighting that keeps objects in both close and distant planes in sharp focus.

deep space   An arrangement of mise-en-scene elements so that there is a considerable distance between the plane closest to the camera and the one farthest away. Any or all of these planes may be in focus. See also *shallow space.*

depth of field   The measurements of the closest and farthest planes in front of the camera lens between which everything will be in sharp focus. A depth of field from 5 to 16 feet, for example, would mean everything closer than 5 feet and farther than 16 feet would be out of focus.

dialogue overlap   In editing a scene, arranging the cut so that a bit of dialogue coming from shot A is heard under a shot that shows another character or another element in the scene.

diegesis   In a narrative film, the world of the film's story. The diegesis includes events that are presumed to have occurred and actions and spaces not shown onscreen. See also *diegetic sound, nondiegetic insert, nondiegetic sound.*

diegetic sound   Any voice, musical passage, or sound effect presented as originating from a source within the film's world. See also *nondiegetic sound.*

digital intermediate   A strip of film is developed and scanned, frame by frame, to create a digital copy of sequence or a whole movie. The digital copy is manipulated with computers. When finished, it is scanned frame by frame onto a strip of negative film, which will be used to make prints to send to theaters.

direct sound   Music, noise, and speech recorded from the event at the moment of filming; opposite of *postsynchronization.*

discontinuity editing   Any alternative system of joining shots together using techniques unacceptable within *continuity editing* principles. Possibilities include mismatching of temporal and spatial relations, violations of the *axis of action,* and concentration on graphic relationships. See also *elliptical editing, graphic match, intellectual montage, jump cut, nondiegetic insert, overlapping editing.*

dissolve   A transition between two shots during which the first image gradually disappears while the second image gradually appears; for a moment the two images blend in *superimposition.*

distance of framing   The apparent distance of the frame from the mise-en-scene elements. Also called camera distance and shot scale. See also *close-up, extreme close-up, extreme long shot, medium close-up, medium shot, plan américain.*

distribution   One of the three branches of the film industry; the process of marketing the film and supplying copies to exhibition venues. See also *exhibition, production.*

dolly   A camera support with wheels, used in making *tracking shots.*

dubbing   The process of replacing part or all of the voices on the sound track in order to correct mistakes or rerecord dialogue. See also *postsynchronization.*

duration   In a narrative film, the aspect of temporal manipulation that involves the time span presented in the *plot* and assumed to operate in the *story.* See also *frequency, order.*

editing   (1) In filmmaking, the task of selecting and joining camera takes. (2) In the finished film, the set of techniques that governs the relations among shots.

ellipsis   In a narrative film, the shortening of *plot* duration achieved by omitting some *story* duration. See also *elliptical editing, viewing time.*

elliptical editing   Shot transitions that omit parts of an event, causing an *ellipsis* in plot duration.

establishing shot   A shot, usually involving a distant framing, that shows the spatial relations among the important figures, objects, and setting in a scene.

exhibition   One of the three branches of the film industry; the process of showing the finished film to audiences. See also *distribution, production.*

exposure   The adjustment of the camera mechanism in order to control how much light strikes each frame of film passing through the aperture.

external diegetic sound   Sound represented as coming from a physical source within the story space that we assume characters in the scene also hear. See also *internal diegetic sound.*

extreme close-up   A framing in which the scale of the object shown is very large; most commonly, a small object or a part of the body.

extreme long shot   A framing in which the scale of the object shown is very small; a building, landscape, or crowd of people will fill the screen.

eyeline match   A cut obeying the *axis of action* principle, in which the first shot shows a person looking off in one direction and the second shows a nearby space containing what he or she sees. If the person looks left, the following shot should imply that the looker is offscreen right.

fade   (1) *Fade-in:* a dark screen that gradually brightens as a shot appears. (2) *Fade-out:* a shot that gradually disappears as the screen darkens. Occasionally, fade-outs brighten to pure white or to a color.

fill light   Illumination from a source less bright than the *key light,* used to soften deep shadows in a scene. See also *three-point lighting.*

film noir   "Dark film," a term applied by French critics to a type of American film, usually in the detective or thriller genres, with low-key lighting and a somber mood.

film stock   The strip of material upon which a series of still photographs is registered; it consists of a clear base coated on one side with a light-sensitive emulsion.

filter   A piece of glass or gelatin placed in front of the camera or printer lens to alter the quality or quantity of light striking the film in the aperture.

flashback   An alteration of story order in which the plot moves back to show events that have taken place earlier than ones already shown.

flash-forward   An alteration of story order in which the plot presentation moves forward to future events and then returns to the present.

focal length   The distance from the center of the lens to the point at which the light rays meet in sharp focus. The focal length determines the perspective relations of the space represented on the flat screen. See also *normal lens, telephoto lens, wide-angle lens.*

focus   The degree to which light rays coming from the same part of an object through different parts of the lens reconverge at the same point on the film frame, creating sharp outlines and distinct textures.

following shot   A shot with framing that shifts to keep a moving figure onscreen.

form   The overall system of relationships among the parts of a film.

frame   A single image on the strip of film. When a series of frames is projected onto a screen in quick succession, an illusion of movement is created.

framing   The use of the edges of the film frame to select and to compose what will be visible onscreen.

frequency In a narrative film, the aspect of temporal manipulation that involves the number of times any *story* event is shown in the *plot*. See also *duration, order.*

front projection A composite process whereby footage meant to appear as the background of a shot is projected from the front onto a screen; figures in the foreground are filmed in front of the screen as well. This is the opposite of *rear projection.*

frontal lighting Illumination directed into the scene from a position near the camera.

frontality In staging, the positioning of figures so that they face the viewer.

function The role or effect of any element within the film's form.

gauge The width of the film strip, measured in millimeters.

genres Various types of films that audiences and filmmakers recognize by their familiar narrative conventions. Common genres are musical, gangster, and science fiction films.

graphic match Two successive shots joined so as to create a strong similarity of compositional elements (e.g., color, shape).

handheld camera The use of the camera operator's body as a camera support, either holding it by hand or using a harness.

hard lighting Illumination that creates sharp-edged shadows.

height of framing The distance of the camera above the ground, regardless of the *angle of framing.*

high-key lighting Illumination that creates comparatively little contrast between the light and dark areas of the shot. Shadows are fairly transparent and brightened by *fill light.*

ideology A relatively coherent system of values, beliefs, or ideas shared by some social group and often taken for granted as natural or inherently true.

intellectual montage The juxtaposition of a series of images to create an abstract idea not present in any one image.

internal diegetic sound Sound represented as coming from the mind of a character within the story space. Although we and the character can hear it, we assume that the other characters cannot. See also *external diegetic sound.*

interpretation The viewer's activity of analyzing the implicit and symptomatic meanings suggested in a film. See also *meaning.*

iris A round, moving *mask* that can close down to end a scene (iris-out) or emphasize a detail, or that can open to begin a scene (iris-in) or to reveal more space around a detail.

jump cut An elliptical cut that appears to be an interruption of a single shot. Either the figures seem to change instantly against a constant background, or the background changes instantly while the figures remain constant. See also *ellipsis.*

key light In the three-point lighting system, the brightest illumination coming into the scene. See also *backlighting, fill light, three-point lighting.*

lens A shaped piece of transparent material (usually glass) with either or both sides curved to gather and focus light rays. Most camera and projector lenses place a series of lenses within a metal tube to form a compound lens.

linearity In a narrative, the clear motivation of a series of causes and effects that progress without significant digressions, delays, or irrelevant actions.

long shot A framing in which the scale of the object shown is small; a standing human figure would appear nearly the height of the screen.

long take A shot that continues for an unusually lengthy time before the transition to the next shot.

low-key lighting Illumination that creates strong contrast between light and dark areas of the shot, with deep shadows and little *fill light.*

mask An opaque screen placed in the camera or printer that blocks part of the frame off and changes the shape of the photographed image, leaving part of the frame a solid color. As seen on the screen, most masks are black, although they can be white or colored.

masking In exhibition, stretches of black fabric that frame the theater scene. Masking can be adjusted according to the *aspect ratio* of the film to be projected.

match on action A continuity cut that splices two different views of the same action together at the same moment in the movement, making it seem to continue uninterrupted.

matte shot A type of *process shot* in which different areas of the image (usually actors and setting) are photographed separately and combined in laboratory work.

meaning (1) *Referential meaning*: allusion to particular items of knowledge outside the film that the viewer is expected to recognize. (2) *Explicit meaning*: significance presented overtly, usually in language and often near the film's beginning or end. (3) *Implicit meaning*: significance left tacit, for the viewer to discover upon analysis or reflection. (4) *Symptomatic meaning*: significance that the film divulges, often against its will, by virtue of its historical or social context.

medium close-up A framing in which the scale of the object shown is fairly large; a human figure seen from the chest up would fill most of the screen.

medium long shot A framing at a distance that makes an object about four or five feet high appear to fill most of the screen vertically. See also *plan américain,* the special term for a medium long shot depicting human figures.

medium shot A framing in which the scale of the object shown is of moderate size; a human figure seen from the waist up would fill most of the screen.

mise-en-scene All of the elements placed in front of the camera to be photographed: the settings and props, lighting, costumes and makeup, and figure behavior.

mixing Combining two or more sound tracks by recording them onto a single one.

mobile frame The effect on the screen of the moving camera, a *zoom lens,* or certain *special effects*; the framing shifts in relation to the scene being photographed. See also *crane shot, pan, tilt, tracking shot.*

monochromatic color design Color design that emphasizes a narrow set of shades of a single color.

montage (1) A synonym for *editing.* (2) An approach to editing developed by the Soviet filmmakers of the 1920s; it emphasizes dynamic, often discontinuous, relationships between shots and the juxtaposition of images to create ideas not present in either shot by itself. See also *discontinuity editing, intellectual montage.*

montage sequence   A segment of a film that summarizes a topic or compresses a passage of time into brief symbolic or typical images. Frequently, *dissolves, fades, superimpositions,* and *wipes* are used to link the images in a montage sequence.

motif   An element in a film that is repeated in a significant way.

motion control   A computerized method of planning and repeating camera movements on miniatures, models, and process work.

motivation   The justification given in the film for the presence of an element. This may be an appeal to the viewer's knowledge of the real world, to genre conventions, to narrative causality, or to a stylistic pattern within the film.

narration   The process through which the *plot* conveys or withholds *story* information. The narration can be more or less restricted to character knowledge and more or less deep in presenting characters' mental perceptions and thoughts.

narrative form   A type of filmic organization in which the parts relate to one another through a series of causally related events taking place in time and space.

nondiegetic insert   A shot or series of shots cut into a sequence, showing objects that are represented as being outside the world of the narrative.

nondiegetic sound   Sound, such as mood music or a narrator's commentary, represented as coming from a source outside the space of the narrative.

nonsimultaneous sound   Diegetic sound that comes from a source in time either earlier or later than the images it accompanies.

normal lens   A lens that shows objects without severely exaggerating or reducing the depth of the scene's planes. In 35mm filming, a normal lens is 35 to 50mm. See also *telephoto lens, wide-angle lens.*

offscreen sound   Simultaneous sound from a source assumed to be in the space of the scene but outside what is visible onscreen.

offscreen space   The six areas blocked from being visible on the screen but still part of the space of the scene: to each side and above and below the frame, behind the set, and behind the camera. See also *space.*

180° system   The continuity approach to editing dictates that the camera should stay on one side of the action to ensure consistent left-right spatial relations between elements from shot to shot. The 180° line is the same as the *axis of action.* See also *continuity editing, screen direction.*

order   In a narrative film, the aspect of temporal manipulation that involves the sequence in which the chronological events of the *story* are arranged in the *plot.* See also *duration, frequency.*

overlap   A cue for suggesting represented depth in the film image by placing objects partly in front of more distant ones.

overlapping editing   Cuts that repeat part or all of an action, thus expanding its viewing time and plot duration.

pan   A camera movement with the camera body turning to the right or left. On the screen, it produces a mobile framing that scans the space horizontally.

pixillation   A form of single-frame animation in which three-dimensional objects, often people, are made to move in staccato bursts through the use of stop-action cinematography.

plan américain   A framing in which the scale of the object shown is moderately small; the human figure seen from the shins to the head would fill most of the screen. This is sometimes referred to as a *medium long shot,* especially when human figures are not shown.

plan-séquence   A French term for a scene handled in a single shot, usually a *long take.*

plot   In a narrative film, all the events that are directly presented to us, including their causal relations, chronological order, duration, frequency, and spatial locations. Opposed to *story,* which is the viewer's imaginary construction of all the events in the narrative. See also *duration, ellipsis, frequency, order, viewing time.*

point-of-view shot (POV shot)   A shot taken with the camera placed approximately where the character's eyes would be, showing what the character would see; usually cut in before or after a shot of the character looking.

postsynchronization   The process of adding sound to images after they have been shot and assembled. This can include *dubbing* of voices, as well as inserting diegetic music or sound effects. It is the opposite of *direct sound.*

process shot   Any shot involving rephotography to combine two or more images into one or to create a special effect; also called composite shot. See also *matte shot, rear projection, special effects.*

production   One of the three branches of the film industry; the process of creating the film. See also *distribution, exhibition.*

racking focus   Shifting the area of sharp focus from one plane to another during a shot; the effect on the screen is called rack-focus.

rate   In shooting, the number of frames exposed per second; in projection, the number of frames thrown on the screen per second. If the two are the same, the speed of the action will appear normal, whereas a disparity will create slow or fast motion. The standard rate in sound cinema is 24 frames per second for both shooting and projection.

rear projection   A technique for combining a foreground action with a background action filmed earlier. The foreground is filmed in a studio, against a screen; the background imagery is projected from behind the screen. The opposite of *front projection.*

reestablishing shot   A return to a view of an entire space after a series of closer shots following the *establishing shot.*

reframing   Short panning or tilting movements to adjust for the figures' movements, keeping them onscreen or centered.

rhetorical form   A type of filmic organization in which the parts create and support an argument.

rhythm   The perceived rate and regularity of sounds, series of shots, and movements within the shots. Rhythmic factors include beat (or pulse), accent (or stress), and tempo (or pace).

rotoscope   A machine that projects live-action motion picture frames one by one onto a drawing pad so that an animator can trace the figures in each frame. The aim is to achieve more realistic movement in an animated film.

scene   A segment in a narrative film that takes place in one time and space or that uses crosscutting to show two or more simultaneous actions.

screen direction The right-left relationships in a scene, set up in an establishing shot and determined by the position of characters and objects in the frame, by the directions of movement, and by the characters' eyelines. *Continuity editing* will attempt to keep screen direction consistent between shots. See also *axis of action, eyeline match, 180° system.*

segmentation The process of dividing a film into parts for analysis.

sequence Term commonly used for a moderately large segment of film, involving one complete stretch of action. In a narrative film, often equivalent to a *scene.*

shallow focus A restricted *depth of field,* which keeps only one plane in sharp focus; the opposite of *deep focus.*

shallow space Staging the action in relatively few planes of depth; the opposite of *deep space.*

shot (1) In shooting, one uninterrupted run of the camera to expose a series of frames. Also called a *take.* (2) In the finished film, one uninterrupted image, whether or not there is mobile framing.

shot/reverse shot Two or more shots edited together that alternate characters, typically in a conversation situation. In *continuity editing,* characters in one framing usually look left; in the other framing, right. Over-the-shoulder framings are common in shot/reverse-shot editing.

side lighting Lighting coming from one side of a person or an object, usually in order to create a sense of volume, to bring out surface tensions, or to fill in areas left shadowed by light from another source.

simultaneous sound Diegetic sound that is represented as occurring at the same time in the story as the image it accompanies.

size diminution A cue for suggesting represented depth in the image by showing objects that are farther away as smaller than foreground objects.

soft lighting Illumination that avoids harsh bright and dark areas, creating a gradual transition from highlights to shadows.

sound bridge (1) At the beginning of one scene, the sound from the previous scene carries over briefly before the sound from the new scene begins. (2) At the end of one scene, the sound from the next scene is heard, leading into that scene.

sound over Any sound that is not represented as coming from the space and time of the images on the screen. This includes both nondiegetic sounds and nonsimultaneous diegetic sound. See also *nondiegetic sound, nonsimultaneous sound.*

sound perspective The sense of a sound's position in space, yielded by volume, timbre, pitch, and, in stereophonic reproduction systems, binaural information.

space Most minimally, any film displays a two-dimensional graphic space, the flat composition of the image. In films that depict recognizable objects, figures, and locales, a three-dimensional space is represented as well. At any moment, three-dimensional space may be directly depicted, as onscreen space, or suggested, as *offscreen space.* In narrative film, we can also distinguish among story space—the locale of the totality of the action (whether shown or not)—and plot space—the locales visibly and audibly represented in the scenes.

special effects A general term for various photographic manipulations that create fictitious spatial relations in the shot, such as *superimposition, matte shots,* and *rear projection.*

story In a narrative film, all the events that we see and hear, plus all those that we infer or assume to have occurred, arranged in their presumed causal relations, chronological order, duration, frequency, and spatial locations. Opposed to *plot,* which is the film's actual presentation of events in the story. See also *duration, ellipsis, frequency, order, space, viewing time.*

storyboard A tool used in planning film production, consisting of comic-strip-like drawings of individual shots or phases of shots with descriptions written below each drawing.

style The repeated and salient uses of film techniques characteristic of a single film or a group of films (for example, a filmmaker's work or a national movement).

superimposition The exposure of more than one image on the same film strip or in the same shot.

synchronous sound Sound that is matched temporally with the movements occurring in the images, as when dialogue corresponds to lip movements.

take In filmmaking, the shot produced by one uninterrupted run of the camera. One shot in the final film may be chosen from among several takes of the same action.

technique Any aspect of the film medium that can be chosen and manipulated in making a film.

telephoto lens A lens of long focal length that affects a scene's perspective by enlarging distant planes and making them seem close to the foreground planes. In 35mm filming, a lens of 75mm length or more. See also *normal lens, wide-angle lens.*

three-point lighting A common arrangement using three directions of light on a scene: from behind the subjects (*backlighting*), from one bright source (*key light*), and from a less bright source balancing the key light (*fill light*).

tilt A camera movement with the camera body swiveling upward or downward on a stationary support. It produces a mobile framing that scans the space vertically.

top lighting Lighting coming from above a person or an object, usually in order to outline the upper areas of the figure or to separate it more clearly from the background.

tracking shot A mobile framing that travels through space forward, backward, or laterally. See also *crane shot, pan,* and *tilt.*

typage A performance technique of Soviet Montage cinema. The actor's appearance and behavior are presented as typical of a social class or other group.

underlighting Illumination from a point below the figures in the scene.

unity The degree to which a film's parts relate systematically to each other and provide motivations for all the elements included.

variation In film form, the return of an element with notable changes.

viewing time The length of time it takes to watch a film when it is projected at the appropriate speed.

whip pan   An extremely fast movement of the camera from side to side, which briefly causes the image to blur into a set of indistinct horizontal streaks. Often an imperceptible cut will join two whip pans to create a trick transition between scenes.

wide-angle lens   A lens of short focal length that affects a scene's perspective by distorting straight lines near the edges of the frame and by exaggerating the distance between foreground and background planes. In 35mm filming, a wide-angle lens is 35mm or less. See also *normal lens, telephoto lens.*

wipe   A transition between shots in which a line passes across the screen, eliminating one shot as it goes and replacing it with the next one.

zoom lens   A lens with a focal length that can be changed during a shot. A shift toward the *telephoto* range enlarges the image and flattens its planes together, giving an impression of magnifying the scene's space, while a shift toward the *wide-angle* range does the opposite.

CREDITS

Grateful acknowledgment is made for use of the following:

Figure 1.10–1.11 Wisconsin Center for Film and Theater Research; 1.14 Courtesy Scott Sklenar, Rocky Gersbach, and Matt Rockwell of Star Cinema, Fitchburg, Wisconsin; 1.26–1.27 The Museum of Modern Art Film Stills Archive; 1.33 Wisconsin Center for Film and Theater Research; 1.41 Courtesy Keith Stern, McKellan.com; 1.44 Wisconsin Center for Film and Theater Research; 4.131 Courtesy of Norman McLaren with permission of the National Film Board of Canada; 5.35 Courtesy Ernie Gehr; 5.192–5.194 Courtesy Michael Snow; 6.36–6.37 Courtesy of Bruce Conner; 10.53–10.54 Courtesy J. J. Murphy; 10.72 The Museum of Modern Art Film Stills Archive; 10.76–10.89 Courtesy Bruce Conner; 10.93 Courtesy Norman McLaren with permission of the National Film Board of Canada; 11.43–11.61 *Tokyo Story* directed by Yasujiro Ozu, 1953 © 1953 Shochiku, Co., Ltd.; 12.1 George Eastman House; 12.35 The Museum of Modern Art Film Stills Archive; 12.36–12.37 Wisconsin Center for Film and Theater Research.

RECOMMENDED DVD SUPPLEMENTS

Alien (20th Century Fox Home Entertainment), "Collector's Edition," 2 discs

Amadeus: Director's Cut (Warner Bros.), "Two-Disc Special Edition"

American Graffiti (Universal), "Collector's Edition," 1 disc

Armageddon (The Criterion Collection), 2 discs

Bambi (Disney), "Platinum Edition," 2 discs

Black Narcissus (The Criterion Collection), 1 disc

Butch Cassidy and the Sundance Kid (20th Century Fox), "Special Edition," 1 disc

Charlie and the Chocolate Factory (Warner Bros.), "Two-Disc Deluxe Edition"

Chicken Run (Dreamworks Home Entertainment), "Special Edition," 1 disc

Contempt (The Criterion Collection), 2 discs

Dancer in the Dark (New Line Home Video), 1 disc

Darby O'Gill and the Little People (Disney)

The Da Vinci Code (Sony) (supplements appear on all editions)

The Dark Knight (Warner Home Video), "Two-Disc Special Edition + Digital Copy"

Far from Heaven (Universal)

The Frighteners (Universal), "Peter Jackson's Director's Cut," 1 disc

The Godfather (Paramount), "The Godfather DVD Collection," 5 discs

The Golden Compass (New Line Home Entertainment), "New Line Two-Disc Platinum Series"

The Good, the Bad, and the Ugly (MGM), "Special Edition," 2 discs

A Hard Day's Night (Miramax), 2 discs

Hellboy (Columbia Tristar Home Entertainment), "Two-Disc Special Edition"

Hellboy II: The Golden Army (Universal Studios Home Entertainment), "Three-Disc Special Edition"

The Incredibles (Disney), "Two-Disc Collector's Edition"

Iron Man (Paramount) "Two-Disc Special Collectors' Edition"

Jaws (Universal), "Anniversary Collector's Edition," 1 disc

Jurassic Park (Universal), "Collector's Edition," 1 disc

King Kong (Warner Bros.), "Two-Disc Special Edition"

King Kong: Peter Jackson's Production Diaries (Universal), 2 discs

The Lord of the Rings 3 volumes (New Line Home Entertainment), "Special Extended DVD Edition," 4 discs each

The Magnificent Seven (Metro-Goldwyn-Mayer), "Collector's Edition," 2 discs

Magnolia (New Line Home Video), 2 discs

Master and Commander (20th Century Fox Home Entertainment), "Collector's Edition," 2 discs

Moulin Rouge! (20th Century Fox Home Entertainment), 2 discs

My Fair Lady (Warner Bros.), "Two-Disc Special Edition"

My Own Private Idaho (The Criterion Collection), 2 discs

Norman McLaren: The Collector's Edition (Milestone), 2 discs

North by Northwest (Warner Bros.), 1 disc

Oklahoma! (20th Century Fox Home Entertainment), "50th Anniversary Edition," 2 discs

Once upon a Time in the West (Paramount), "Special Collector's Edition," 2 discs

Pickpocket (The Criterion Collection), 1 disc

Pinocchio (Walt Disney Studios Home Entertainment), Platinum Edition

Pirates of the Caribbean: Dead Man's Chest (Disney), "Two-disc Special Edition"

Pulp Fiction (Miramax Home Entertainment), "Collector's Edition," 2 discs

Rosemary's Baby (Paramount), 1 disc

Russian Ark (Wellspring), 1 disc

Saturday Night Fever (Paramount), "25th Anniversary DVD Edition," 1 disc

Scream (Dimension Home Video), "The Ultimate Scream Collection," 4 discs

The Searchers (Warner Home Video), "Ultimate Collector's Edition," 2 discs

Seven Men from Now (Paramount), "Special Collector's Edition," 1 disc

The Silence of the Lambs (Metro-Goldwyn-Mayer), "Special Edition," 1 disc

Silverado (Sony Pictures Home Entertainment), 2 discs

Sin City (Dimension), 2 discs

Singin' in the Rain (Warner Bros.), "Two-Disc Special Edition"

Speed (20th Century Fox Home Entertainment), "Five Star Collection," 2 discs

Terminator 2: Judgment Day (Artisan), "Extreme DVD," 2 discs

3:10 to Yuma (Lionsgate), 1 disc

Titus (20th Century Fox Home Entertinment), 2 discs

Toy Story/Toy Story 2 (Disney/Pixar), "Collector's Edition: The Ultimate Toy Box," 3 discs

20,000 Leagues Under the Sea (Disney), "Special Edition," 2 discs

Wallace & Gromit: The Curse of the Were-Rabbit (DreamWorks), 1 disc

War of the Worlds (2005) (DreamWorks Home Entertainment), "Two-Disc Limited Edition"

The Wizard of Oz (Warner Home Video), "Two-Disc Special Edition"

Zodiac (Paramount), "Two-Disc Special Collector's Edition" (Director's Cut)

INDEX

Scorcese, Martin, 33, 442. *See also King of Comedy; Raging Bull*
  film style of, 480
  King of Comedy, 447–449
  on lenses, 175
  Mean Streets, 440, 478, *478*
  Raging Bull, 18, *189, 201*, 396, 444, 478
  Taxi Driver, 440, 478
scores. *See* musical score
Scorpio Rising, 284, 366–367, *367*
Scott, Ridley
  Alien, 197, 335
  Blade Runner, 333
  Gladiator, 22, 335
  Matchstick Men, 259
screen direction, **237–238**
screen size
  Bogdanovich on, 45
  exhibition and, 43, 45–47
screen space
  color contrast and, 149–150
  composition and, 148–151
  in *His Girl Friday*, 399
  movement and, 151
  in *Tokyo Story*, 416–417
screenplays
  Collateral, 4–5
  stages of, 17
screenwriter, 17
script supervisor, 19
scriptwriting. *See also* dialogue; screenplays
  documentaries, 17
  in film production, 16–17
Se7en, 194, 332
The Searchers, 171, 339, *339*
The Seashell and the Clergyman, 466, *466*
Seberg, Jean, 145, *145*, 151
second assistant director, 19
second unit, 24
second unit director, 19
The Secret Adventures of Tom Thumb, 384
Seda, Dori, 357, 359
segmentation. *See* plot segmentation
selective focus, 178
Serene Velocity, 177, *177*
Serra, Richard, *Railroad Turnbridge*, 368, *368*
set decorator, 18
set dresser, 18
set unit, 18
setting
  color and, 123
  digital effects for, 123
  of *Do The Right Thing*, 405
  film style and, 4–5
  of *Meet Me in St. Louis*, 431–432
  in mise-en-scene, 121, 123–124
  in *Our Hospitality*, 160
setup, 90
The Seven Samurai, 138–139, *139*, 224, 292, 336
  graphic match in, 226, *226*

sound in, 278–279
70mm (film), 11, *12*
Shadow of a Doubt
  film style in, 316–319, *317–319*
  screenplay for, 4, 16
Shahani, Kumar, *Kasba*, 170, *171*
shallow-space composition, **154**
Shanghai Express, *133*
Shanley, John Patrick, *Doubt*, 203
Shaun of the Dead, 342
Shaw Brothers, 482
Shayamalan, M. Night
  Signs, 212
  The Sixth Sense, 78–79, 97, *97, 133*, 296, 342, 482
She Wore a Yellow Ribbon, 118, *119*, 282
Sher, Stacy, 33
She's Gotta Have It, 479
  continuity editing in, 243, *244*
The Shining, 46, 83
  patterns in, 69–70, *70*
Shivers, 479
shock cuts, 325
Shoe Shine, 473–474
Shoot the Piano Player, 476
shooting phase
  director's crew during, 19–20
  filming scene during, 21–22
  photography unit in, 20
  producer's crew in, 21
  sound unit in, 20–21
  visual-effects unit in, 21
shooting script, 17
Short Cuts, 479
shot/reverse shot, **239**
  in *Do The Right Thing*, 407, *407*
  in early cinema, 460
  in *The Maltese Falcon*, 242
Shrek 2, 38
sidelight, **136**
Signs, 212
Sijan, Slobodan, 243
The Silence of the Lambs, 118, 223, 285, *296*, 329
  film style in, 315, *315*
  sound bridge in, 296
silent film. *See* early cinema
Silent Möbius, *383*
similarity, 68
Simon, Chris, 354
Simple Men, 178, *178*
A Simple Plan, 333
simultaneous sound, **295**
Sin City, 15
Singer, Bryan
  Superman Returns, *14*
  The Usual Suspects, 86, 90, 334, *334*
Singin' in the Rain, 27, 205, 294, 329, 343
single-frame films, 256
Singleton, John, 479

Sisters, 191, *192*
Sisters of Gion, 215–216, *216*
Siu-tung, Ching, 483
16mm (film), 11, *12*
The Sixth Sense, 78–79, 97, *97, 133*, 296, 342, 482
size diminution, **153**
Sjöström, Victor, *Ingeborg Holm*, 223
slates, 21, *21*
Sleep, 223
Sleepy Hollow, 479
Sliding Doors, 87–88, *89*, 334, 482
slow-motion effect, 172
Slumdog Millionaire, 30, 35, 99, *99*
  subjectivity and, 95, *96*
Smalley, Philips, *Suspense*, *192*
small-scale film production, 30–32
The Smiling Mme. Beudet, 464
Smith, Chris, *American Movie*, 351, *351*
Smith, G. Albert
  Mary Jane's Mishap, 459
  Santa Claus, 457, *457*
Smith, Kevin
  Clerks, 30, 481
  Dogma, 481–482
  Mallrats, 481
Smith, Lee, 231
Smoke, 479
Snow, Michael. *See also Wavelength*
  La Région centrale, 223
  Wavelength, 177
Snow White and the Seven Dwarfs, 344, 383, 388
Sobocinski, Piotr, 312–313
social ideology, **65**
  film form and, 431
  in *Meet Me in St. Louis*, 431–438
  in New Hollywood cinema, 478
  in *Raging Bull*, 438–442
Soderbergh, Steven
  Che, 14
  The Limey, 482, *482*
  Ocean's 11, 333
  Out of Sight, 87, 333
Sokurov, Aleksandr
  Alexandra, 278
  Russian Ark, 214–215, *215*
Soldier Blue, 339
Solondz, Todd, *Palindromes*, 82
Something Different, 79
Sonatine, 99, *99*, 205
The Song of Roland, 464
sound. *See also* diegetic sound; musical score; nondiegetic sound; sound bridge; sound effects; sound mixing; sound tracks
  anticipation and, 270
  Apocalypse Now, localization of, 294
  asynchronous, 294
  audience expectations with, 269
  in *Breathless*, 413
  in *Citizen Kane*, 274